Unfinished Histories
Empire and Postcolonial Resonance in Central Africa and Belgium

Unfinished Histories

Empire and Postcolonial Resonance
in Central Africa and Belgium

Edited by

Pierre-Philippe Fraiture

Leuven University Press

Published with the support of the KU Leuven Fund for Fair Open Access and the European Research Council (# 818343, 'Philosophy and Genre: Creating a Textual Basis for African Philosophy')

Published in 2022 by Leuven University Press / Presses Universitaires de Louvain / Universitaire Pers Leuven. Minderbroedersstraat 4, B-3000 Leuven (Belgium).

Selection and editorial matter © Pierre-Philippe Fraiture, 2022
Individual chapters @ The respective authors, 2022

This book is published under a Creative Commons Attribution Non-Commercial Non-Derivative 4.0 Licence.

Attribution should include the following information: Pierre-Philippe Fraiture (ed.), *Unfinished Histories: Empire and Postcolonial Resonance in Central Africa and Belgium*. Leuven: Leuven University Press, 2022. (CC BY-NC-ND 4.0)

Unless otherwise indicated all images are reproduced with the permission of the rights-holders acknowledged in captions and are expressly excluded from the CC BY-NC-ND 4.0 license covering the rest of this publication. Permission for reuse should be sought from the rights-holders.

ISBN 978 94 6270 357 5
ISBN 978 94 6166 491 4
ISBN 978 94 6166 492 1
https://doi.org/10.11116/9789461664914
D/2022/1869/55
NUR: 612

Layout: Crius Group
Cover design: Daniel Benneworth-Gray
Cover illustration: *Mémoire*, Sammy Baloji

Contents

9 Acknowledgements

11 Thinking, Performing, and Overcoming Belgium's 'Colonial Power Matrix'? An Introduction
Pierre-Philippe Fraiture

Part 1 – Regimes of Knowledge and Decolonisation

43 Must Leopold Fall? The Renovation of the AfricaMuseum and Belgium's Place in International Debates on the Decolonisation of Public Heritage
Dónal Hassett

63 Imperial Fictions: Belgian Novels about Rwanda
Nicki Hitchcott

81 Confronting the Colonial Past? Genocide Education in Francophone Belgian Schools
Catherine Gilbert

Part 2 – International Resonances

103 Imperial Entanglements of the Congo/African Institute, Colwyn Bay, Wales (1889–1911)
Robert Burroughs

121 Performative Challenges to Belgium's Colonial Amnesia: Mobilising Archives and Resonant Spaces
Yvette Hutchison

143 Writing in Ciluba: From Colonial Extirpation to the Challenge of Globalisation
Albert Kasanda

Part 3 — Imperial Practices and Their Afterlives

167 Media Representations of Burundi's 2020 Elections in Belgium and Burundi
Caroline Williamson Sinalo

189 Living with Ruination: Rural Neglect and the Persistence of 'Grey' Colonial Architecture in Kongolo, Tanganyika, DRC
Reuben A. Loffman

211 Cash Crops and Clichés: Agriculture, Contact Zones, and Afterlives of Belgian Colonialism
Sarah Arens

231 The Legacy of Alexis Kagame: Responses to Conceptions of Colonisation and Evangelisation in Rwanda
Chantal Gishoma

Part 4 — Trans-African Entanglements

253 'Depuis la Flamandchourie': Legacies of Belgian Colonialism in Sony Labou Tansi's Kinshasa
Sky Herington

271 Landscaping and Escaping the Colony in Mudimbe's, Ruti's, and Nayigiziki's Works'
Maëline Le Lay

293 Récit d'enfance, récit de distance: Gaby as implicated subject in Gaël Faye's Petit Pays
Hannah Grayson

Part 5 – The Emergence of Diasporic Agents

315 'Without Art Congo Is Just a Mine': Art as the Restoration of Shattered Bodies
Bambi Ceuppens

337 From Leopold III's Masters of the Congo Jungle to Contemporary Congolese Eco-Cinema: Postcolonial Resonance
Matthias De Groof

359 Tracking the Potholes of Colonial History: Sinzo Aanza's *Généalogie d'une banalité* and Fiston Mwanza Mujila's *Tram 83*
Pierre-Philippe Fraiture

381 Bibliography

411 About the authors

417 Index

Acknowledgements

I am dedicating this book to my good friend Éric Damanet. Thank you for the precious archives!

As ever, thanks to Alison and to our two daughters, Manon and Ella, for their love and unflinching support. I would also like to express my deepest gratitude to my colleagues on the European Research Council Project 'African Philosophy and Genre' – Michelle Clarke, Chantal Gishoma, Albert Kasanda, Benedetta Lanfranchi, Emiliano Minerba, and Alena Rettová – for discussing this project online and at the University of Bayreuth. Thank you to Matthew Allen for producing the index and to Orane Onyekpe-Touzet for administering the two research workshops (September 2020 and February 2021) that led to the publication of this edited volume. My gratitude goes as well to Mirjam Truwant, the Acquisitions Editor at Leuven University Press. I am very grateful for her immensely valuable advice throughout this process; to Annemie Vandezande, the Leuven UP Marketing Manager, to Danielle Carter, the freelance Editor, to Beatrice Van Eeghem, the Managing Editor, and the two anonymous readers for their useful comments on the original manuscript. I would also like to thank the University of Warwick and the School of Modern Languages & Cultures for their continuous support, and the Institute of Advanced Studies at Warwick for financing the two above-mentioned workshops ('Central Africa and Belgium: Empire and Postcolonial Resonance'). Thank you to Sammy Baloji for taking part in the first workshop and for allowing me to use one of his photomontages for the front cover of *Unfinished Histories*, and, of course, to all the contributors of this collective volume. The Open Access publication of this book benefitted from the generous support of the European Research Council and the KU Leuven Fund for Fair Open Access.

A special thought for Gérard Houbion.

Pierre-Philippe Fraiture

Thinking, Performing, and Overcoming Belgium's 'Colonial Power Matrix'?

An Introduction

Pierre-Philippe Fraiture

Belgium once had an empire in Central Africa. The historical processes informing this imperial presence – the foundation of the Congo Free State (CFS) in 1885, its demise, the emergence of the Belgian Congo in 1908, and the subsequent absorption of 'Ruanda-Urundi' by Belgium under the aegis of the League of Nations in 1922 – are well documented and have generated a voluminous collection of responses in all fields of knowledge and human activities. This edited book will reflect on this colonial past but, more crucially, appraise the many post-colonial traces and legacies of this past in Belgium, the Democratic Republic of the Congo (DRC), Rwanda, and Burundi.[1] The post-colonial period and the independence of the Congo (1960) and that of Burundi and Rwanda in 1962 did not herald a completely new era but marked, more prosaically, the beginning of decolonisation. This process, which is unarguably still unfolding *now*, cannot be univocally defined. One of the chief aims of this volume will be to explore how this contested notion has shaped cultural debates and responses in the geographical areas under scrutiny. It would be an understatement to say that this post-colonial period has been marked by violence. Real violence, as tragically exemplified by the continuous string of civil wars, pogroms, ethnic cleansing, and genocides, but also cultural and epistemological violence as political emancipation did not elicit the expected cultural autonomy.

This period has witnessed the rise and often the fall of extraordinary and larger-than-life political figures, such as Mobutu Sese Seko, Patrice Lumumba,[2] Pierre Mulélé, Prince Louis Rwagasore,[3] Laurent and Joseph Kabila, Jean-Baptiste Bagaza, Juvénal Habyarimana, and Paul Kagame. It has also coincided with cultural experiments in the field of literature, thought, music, and the arts and the emergence, in Central Africa and in the diaspora, of formidably creative individuals and (public) intellectuals like Sony Labou Tansi, V. Y. Mudimbe, Papa Wendo, Clémentine Faïk-Nzuji, and Tshibumba Kanda Matulu. At the same time, Central African cultures have continued to attract the attention of scholars and have, in fact, often been mobilised to develop original empirical and theoretical research, as illustrated by the works by Jan Vansina, Johannes Fabian, Colette Braeckman, Luc de Heusch, Bogumil Jewsiewicki, Filip De Boeck, Mathieu Zana Aziza Etambala, Sammy Baloji, David Van Reybrouck, Thierry Michel, Isidore Ndaywel è Nziem, Didier Gondola, and Nancy Rose Hunt. In the wake of the Rwandan genocide of 1994, other important statements have appeared, not only to account for this unfathomable tragedy, as exemplified by the vast corpus of novels, films, and testimonies on this event, but also to reappraise more distant events such as Leopold's anti-slavery campaign, the Red Rubber Scandal, the publication of *Tintin au Congo*,[4] and the assassination of Lumumba, in addition to the role and significance of the AfricaMuseum in a post-colonial Belgium.

Written sixty years after the independence of most sub-Saharan African former colonies, this book aims to explore the enduring influence of this Belgian colonial past in Belgium, its former colonial domains, and beyond. We will privilege here cultural and epistemological issues pertaining to the emergence of critical voices, whether intellectuals in the human sciences (e.g. history and anthropology), novelists, playwrights, musicians, artists, filmmakers, art critics, journalists, art curators, urban planners, and geographers, and, as already indicated above, we will favour particular past and contemporary events through which the many intertwinements between Central Africa and Belgium can be examined.

In this title, *Unfinished Histories: Empire and Postcolonial Resonance in Central Africa and Belgium*, every word is equally significant. The ambition is to explore the long-term legacies and the material and immaterial traces of Belgian colonialism in Central Africa, and, as importantly, to measure the effects and consequences of colonial and postcolonial encounters, and clashes, on Belgium itself. How this short-lived empire has continued to shape African-ness and Belgian-ness is a question that is worth investigating and which has unarguably remained underinvestigated. 'Central Africa' as a geographical entity is understood here to comprise the DRC, Rwanda, and Burundi.

The DRC did not exist as a geographical reality before 1885, when it became the Congo Free State, and later the Belgian Congo, from 1908 to 1960. Therefore, the unification of this huge and disparate territory is an *invention*, and my own use of this word is a reference to the formidably relevant work conducted by V. Y. Mudimbe on colonial Africa in the aptly named *The Invention of Africa*, a book mapping the discourses and concepts that facilitated Africa's entry into a Western order of knowledge.[5] It was an invention because it regarded itself as the beginning of a new temporality that was supposed to benefit the locals and paved the way for their incorporation into a *progressive* historicity. However, in this process of homogenisation, the African 'space of experience' was utterly denied at the expense of a *modern* 'horizon of expectation', to refer to the two cardinal notions developed by Reinhart Koselleck in his examination of modernity and historical time.[6] The Congolese territory was divided into provinces – again at the expense of other precolonial subdivisions – when the Congo was made up of the semi-nomadic (Luba, Kuba, Lunda, and Kongo) states whose influences were felt well beyond the current boundaries of the DRC.[7] In this process of territorial dismembering, time itself was spatialised and divided into precolonial and *modern* provinces.[8]

The context in which the colonisation of Ruanda and Burundi took place was very different but equally demeaning. Ruanda-Urundi, as it was then referred to, had first been colonised by Germany in the wake of the Berlin Conference. After the Treaty of Versailles, it became not a Belgian colony but a mandate under the terms defined by the newly created League of Nations. In actual fact, Ruanda-Urundi was managed in the same way as a colony. The Belgian colonisers, following a trend initiated by their German predecessors, were keen to emphasise, in fact overstate, the innate order presiding over the social and ethnic structure of Ruanda-Urundi. This other *invention* (of the Nilotic Tutsi) had catastrophic consequences for post-colonial Rwanda. And it continues to have catastrophic consequences in eastern Congo and in Burundi in particular.[9]

The history of Belgian colonialism is complex. It involved many stakeholders from a religiously and linguistically divided country. But also international actors who, from the beginning, were attracted by Leopold's project and the many resources – natural, mineral, and human – offered by the new colony. The word 'resource' is important because when the Congo Free State was set up, the Congolese were not regarded as agents but as resources to facilitate the profit-driven objectives of this enterprise, that is, what commentators have rightly called *Raubwirtschaft*, in other words, a type of economic model based on plunder and loot.[10] Leopold II was a modern-day entrepreneur, and the irony is that he never set foot in *his* Congo. Despite some improvements from the early days of the Congo Free State until 1960, and 1962 in the case of Ruanda-Urundi, it must be said that Belgian colonial rule largely remained predicated on issues of economic profitability. Until the end of the Second World War, forced labour was part and parcel of the legislative apparatus set in place by Leopold, then briefly cancelled when the Congo became Belgian on 18 October 1908, but swiftly reinstated in 1909 in the 'Colonial Charter'[11] when the colonisers realised that they would continue to be faced with labour shortages in large infrastructural projects, particularly those involving the construction of roads and railways, the farming of cash crops, and the launching of military operations.[12] Until the bitter end, then, Belgian colonialism, in the Congo and in Ruanda-Urundi, remained a violent, discriminatory, and coercive system.

Violence and coercion were also at the roots of the epistemological invention to which these colonies were submitted. The colonial library, another richly evocative phrase coined by Mudimbe to account for the West's epistemic takeover of Africa,[13] was a site of violence and a zone where knowledge itself was necessarily constrained. Central Africa became an object of knowledge, and in the process of this objectification, it was turned into a commodity. By 1895, a mere ten years after the official birth of the Congo Free State, Alphonse-Jules Wauters, the Belgian geographer who would act as the editor-in-chief of the *Mouvement géographique* until 1922,[14] listed 3800 scientific works on the Congo alone.[15] By parenthesis, this journal, the *Mouvement géographique*, aptly illustrates the paradoxical nature of imperial knowledge production and its deliberate reluctance to separate science from propaganda. Indeed, it was created in 1884 to inform the general public on the geographical expeditions – in fact, military operations – conducted by colonial *heroes* such as H. M. Stanley and Francis Dhanis under the aegis of the Association Internationale Africaine, the organisation that paved the way for the creation of the Congo Free State.[16] Interestingly, the *Movement géographique* was taken over by the Compagnie du Congo pour le Commerce et l'Industrie (CCCI),[17] the all-powerful trade and industry private conglomerate headed by Albert Thys, the Belgian tycoon who would oversee major infrastructural projects in the colony.[18] The CCCI survived several regime changes and was only liquidated in 1971 under Mobutu.[19] It had financial ties with very company that mattered in the colony and in Belgium: the Forminière, the Union Minière du Haut-Katanga (UMHK), the Compagnie du Chemin de fer du Bas-Congo au Katanga, and the Société Générale de Belgique.[20] As such, the CCCI can be regarded as a crucial Belgo-Congolese *lieu de mémoire.*

This knowledge-mapping operation would accelerate and, gradually, affect all areas of human activities, be they practical, intellectual, or spiritual. It would be implemented by the Congo Museum (in Tervuren), the Royal Colonial Institute, the Colonial University in Antwerp,[21] and by an army of semi-private researchers who would often work in conjunction with (and with the partial support of) these public institutions. The problem, however, with colonial knowledge is that it remained largely instrumental and at the service of the extractive and exploitative logic of Belgian colonialism. The irony is that this knowledge did not disappear after decolonisation and that, while it has continued to contaminate contemporary perceptions of Africa, it has also critically fed the reflection of many scholars, artists, critics, and writers in Central Africa and in the former metropole.[22]

In the last sixty years, two major attitudes have prevailed. First, one of oblivion and indifference. For the majority of Belgians, the colonial past, when it was not couched in dubious nostalgia, was simply eschewed, although many families had an aunt, an uncle, a grandfather,[23] or more distant relatives and acquaintances with some degree of colonial credentials.[24] This state of affairs was compounded by the quasi absence of any critical references to the Congo, Rwanda, and Burundi and their respective histories in school curricula, even though some rare criticisms of Leopold II and the Belgian royal family started appearing in isolated Flemish textbooks by the end of the 1970s.[25] As someone who was educated in Belgium (Wallonia) many years after the political demise of Belgian colonialism, I can attest to this glaring deficiency. Apart from one passing allusion to Leopold's 'œuvre' when I was ten years old, I cannot recall any single reference to this long chapter of the national history in my own schooling.[26] By parenthesis, this word – 'œuvre' – is anything but neutral. As it is normally employed to account for exceptional undertakings and selfless achievements, its use in this specific context smacks of ignorance and (neocolonial) paternalism. Well after political decolonisation, it certainly bore witness to the survival of the grandiloquently jingoistic terminology that had characterised Belgian school textbooks during the colonial era.[27]

In Central Africa, the relationship to this colonial past in the immediate years after political decolonisation was even more complicated, as the 1960s were marred by political coups, interethnic violence, and human rights violations. In Burundi, decolonisation maintained the political hegemony of the Tutsi and the 'institutionalized ethnic pathology' bequeathed by the Belgians.[28] Well after 1993, the country experiences mass killings of Twa and Hutu and counter-reprisals against the Tutsi.[29] In Rwanda, on the other hand, the years leading to independence witnessed the rise of the Parmhutu,[30] a political organisation that persecuted the Tutsi minority and fomented the 1994 Rwandan genocide against the Tutsi. In the Congo, the early years of independence were marked by the assassination of Lumumba, the Katangese and South-Kasai secessions, Maoism-inspired armed rebellions,[31] and the rise of Mobutu, who eventually seized power in 1965 against the backdrop of the Cold War.[32] In Burundi, Rwanda, and (by then) Zaire, the next two decades coincided with the consolidation of neocolonialism, particularly after the 1973–75 world economic recession, an event that increased Africa's dependence on foreign aid and the econometric logic of the International Monetary Fund.[33] In this new context in which the old colonial order, albeit officially disbanded, was still surreptitiously operating, there was little appetite among Central African intellectuals to reassess the aftermath of Belgian rule. This said, the period was marked by an attempt on the part of the Mobutu regime to reconfigure the country's national identity through a process of Zairianisation. Also known as the politics of authenticity, this initiative, which was defended by official spokespersons such as Kutumbagana Kangafu,[34] advocated not a return to precolonial world views but the promotion of intrinsically Congolese values, languages, and cultural production. This vast programme, which combined ideas previously developed by early supporters of an African philosophy,[35] successfully launched Congolese – *Zairian* – culture in Africa and beyond. Rumba musicians but also visual artists, writers, and theologians were able to benefit from this politics of authenticity and to contribute to the cultural vibrancy of Kinshasa.[36] After the economic crises of the 1970s, however, the tenets underpinning authenticity were increasingly used to formulate chauvinistic views and foment ethnic division.

The second attitude to have emerged from this post-colonial period is altogether less dependent on the strictures of an enduring coloniality as it was, in fact, adopted to challenge the very basis of this coloniality. Its main proponents are to be found in cultural spheres, grassroots collectives, investigative journalism, and academia. If Belgium went through a period of amnesia in the first two decades or so after decolonisation,[37] the mid-1980s, notably in the wake of the centenary of the Congo Free State in 1985, witnessed the emergence of a more dialogical environment, which elicited not only the beginning of a (at first limited) critical self-examination among Belgian intellectuals but also more productive encounters between Belgians and Africans.

The exhibition *Zaïre 1885–1985. Cent ans de regards belges* was held at the Botanique cultural centre in Brussels in 1985 and focused on Belgian colonial propaganda and on a wide range of objects, including literature, news items, postcards, photographs, advertisements, art pieces, and everyday objects. The aim of this display was to showcase how the *regards belges* [Belgian perceptions] of the Congo and Congolese had developed in the previous hundred years and how these images, in turn, had created disparaging and racially abusive stereotypes that were still prevalent at the time of this exhibition,[38] curated by the Brussels-based NGO Coopération par l'Éducation et la Culture (CEC).[39] This event was critically important and has since generated other imagology-inspired exhibits, colloquia, and publications,[40] which, over the years, have increasingly generated dialogues between Belgian and African figures. While focusing on the memory of the Belgian Congo and, later, on that of the 1994 Rwandan genocide,[41] the activities conducted by the CEC have predominantly been driven by an ambition to combat racism and equip the Belgian public and Belgium-based African (and Global South) diasporas with (pedagogical) tools to forge better intercultural links and cohabit in a more equitable society. Albeit not strictly speaking historical in its approach – indeed, it primarily conceives of itself as 'observatoire des stéréotypes'[42] – the CEC, through its many interventions in the last four decades, has contributed to a better understanding of the deep-seated historical roots of Eurocentrism and post-colonial racism.

In this silence-breaking operation, the interventions of individual authors have been equally effective. In addition to benefitting from the critical insights of imagology and some of its most dynamic proponents – from Martine Loutfi[43] to Edward Said[44] – this new appraisal of Belgian colonialism also prioritised the idea that African experiences had to be mediated by Africans themselves. *Tango Ya Ba Noko*, a collection of Zairian testimonies on the colonial era,[45] exemplifies this new focus on first-hand witnesses as a means to produce more reliable accounts of a past that until the beginning of the 1980s had remained largely obfuscated and shaped by the colonial doxa. This collection was a collaborative venture between a group of researchers based in Brussels and Kinshasa and published under the aegis of the Centre d'Étude et de Documentation Africaines (CEDAF)/Afrika Studie- en Documentatiecentrum (ASDOC), a group that included the most influential specialists of the period.[46] This collection presents itself as a series of interviews of Zairians who had worked – as nurses, soldiers, priests, and clerical staff – and lived alongside their Belgian supervisors. The responses given by the interviewees offer a nuanced picture of colonial life in the Congo and Ruanda-Urundi and provide a wealth of fascinating information on racial segregation, the *évolué* status,[47] the role of missionary education and Western medicine, and the significance of the French language in daily life. Although some of these witnesses look back nostalgically at the colonial period, it must be said that, overall, their personal stories offer grim and chilling accounts of the conditions in which the colonised were forced to live under Belgian rule. The first interviewee of this volume is none other than Paul Lomami Tshibamba, the pioneer of Congolese literature in French and feted author of *Ngando*, the magic realist novel exploring colonial Kinshasa through the prism of Kongo mythology.[48] In his answers to the interviewer's candid questions, Lomami Tshibamba also paints a damning picture of life under Belgian imperialism:

> We realised that by utilising blacks, whom they called indigènes [natives], the missionaries and the representatives of Bula Matari worked hands in hands towards the exploitation of the country. For this enterprise to be successful, blacks had to be morally and psychologically forced into submission. For the other category of whites working in private firms, it was imperative to use coercion to control their black workers. Whenever native workers made a mistake, missionaries would be immediately informed, approach the offenders, and remind them that their negative and hostile behaviour would lead them to Hell and make God unhappy. As they knew that natives were profoundly religious, they exploited this argument to the full and almost all Sunday sermons revolved around it.[49]

Thirty-five years after the publication of *Ngando*, a book that had been awarded the literary prize of the 1948 Brussels Colonial Fair,[50] this statement would reiterate, in plain words, what the novel had poeticised.

The return of memory in the 1980s coincided with the rise of the witness and the proliferation of declarations – like that of Lomami Tshibamba – in which colonial times took centre stage. And this act of witnessing in the first person would increasingly pervade academic writing, shape researchers' interventions, and inflect 'their emotions, their investments in their life's work, and their values', as suggested by Aleida Assmann.[51] V.Y. Mudimbe's trajectory as a scholar is a point in case. Until the publication of *The Invention of Africa* in 1988, he was an *African* intellectual, that is, a scholar who had dedicated his research to the examination of the factors informing Africa's discursive alienation. Although a groundbreaking book, *The Invention*, as acknowledged by Mudimbe himself in the introduction, was built on 'presuppositions and hypotheses' already developed before and on which he had been working for the previous 'fifteen years'[52] from *L'Autre face du royaume* (1973) to *L'Odeur du père* (1982).

For all their pessimism and painstaking dissections of Africa's 'gnostic malady',[53] these three essays are nonetheless underpinned by a utopian project, an ambition to contribute to a better future and the creation of the Fanon-inspired 'new man'. This oft-quoted passage, situated at the very end of *The Invention*, attests to Mudimbe's adherence to a logic of progress:

> I believe that the geography of African gnosis also points out the passion of a subject-object who refuses to vanish. He or she has gone from the situation in which he or she was perceived as a simple functional object to the freedom of thinking of himself or herself as the starting point of an absolute discourse. It has also become obvious, even for this subject, that the space interrogated by the series of explorations in African indigenous systems of thought is not a void.[54]

Here, Mudimbe plainly says that his archaeology of African discourses is transformative and emancipatory and provides a clear rupture from the colonial matrix. For this reason, *The Invention of Africa*, like his previous essays, is informed by the future-oriented – progressive – logic of the 'modern time regime', as this phrase is explored by Aleida Assmann, and specifically by this regime's ability of 'dramatizing and accelerating the break from the past'.[55]

In his later essays, however, Mudimbe, the *modern* African scholar, became a *Congolese* witness. Indeed, subsequent publications are marked by a clear engagement with the Congo's colonial past through personal memories, recurrently summoned to reflect on his own experiences as a former colonised and *évolué*. This memorial exercise is extensive and touches on many aspects of his youth,[56] his assimilation of the Benedictine world view,[57] his retreat as a novice monk at the monastery of Gihindamuyaga in Rwanda, and his return to secular life in 1961 after disapproving of the 'scandalous' role played by the Catholic Church in the ethnic conflicts between Hutu and Tutsi in a soon-to-be independent Rwanda.[58]

These memories of imperial violence, but also of cultural, religious, and linguistic acculturation during Belgian colonial rule, constitute a significant phenomenological archive, and, beyond the examples of Lomami Tshibamba and Mudimbe, it is interesting to note that since the 1990s there has been increased interest in this past, whether as lived and witnessed experience or as fictionalisation and artistic reappropriations. This process of amplified memorialisation has taken place at the expense of the modern project and its attendant delivery of a better future.[59] Here the present is no longer absorbed by the future, and the management of the latter's progressive potential but is marked by a reinvestment in the Belgian imperial past understood as a cluster of unfinished stories. Progress, as a force for change, has been superseded by a focus on present inequalities, that is, on *present past* traces that the idea of progress itself had not been able to eradicate. As argued by Mike Savage in *The Return of Inequality*, the 'importance of *duration*' needs to be reasserted:

> This involves resisting the blandishment of an epochalism that sees the past as 'left behind'. History is not a skating rink, around which we can swoop to pick up attractive bouquets of flowers hither and thither. Instead, history has a force and a direction that cannot be reversed. Understanding our now-time means that we have to go beyond modernity's mundane differentiation of time into linear and separable blocks of past, present, and future. Recognizing the logic of capital accumulation and the build up of wealth in recent decades impresses on us that the force of the past is increasing.[60]

This memorialisation has invariably been triggered by the crises faced by Central Africa in the 1990s: the disintegration and then the fall of the Mobutu regime, the Rwandan genocide, the subsequent armed conflicts generated by these two events until today, and the new scramble for Central Africa. These catastrophes, and their devastating effects in neighbouring countries such as Angola, Uganda, and Tanzania, have revealed the lingering presence of Belgian imperialism, not only in Central Africa but also in post-colonial Belgium, among Flemish- and French-speaking Belgians and Afro-Belgians from the African diaspora.[61]

In the last three decades, the exploration of this past has generated a large volume of responses. In the wake of the federalisation of Belgium, a process that started in the early 1960s and is ongoing,[62] the country's literary heritage has been submitted to renewed analyses and has been scrutinised to evaluate how literature, including colonial literature, has contributed to the construction of a specifically Belgian imaginary. It soon appeared that beyond erudition, and knowledge for knowledge's sake, the reassessment of this imaginary would form the basis for more ethical reflections and formulations on colonial repentance, historical agency, and the role of the (imperial) archive both understood as 'excision', 'as that which limits' because 'based on a set of exclusions' *and* 'excess, as *unlimited*, in the sense of the endless readings to which it gives rise'.[63] If Belgian colonialism inspired many authors, it must be pointed out that this literary activity – swept under the carpet ['sous le boisseau'[64]] by critics and readers – was above all conducted in French rather than in Dutch. For this reason, the available literary criticism on the francophone corpus[65] significantly outweighs the existing scholarship on the Flemish one.[66]

In a recently published anthology dedicated to *The Congo in Flemish Literature*, Luc Renders and Jeroen Dewulf remind us that 'despite the fact that most Belgians who lived in the Congo came from Flanders, the de facto official language in the colony was French'.[67] This colonial literature in French and in Dutch, albeit not a monolith in terms of content and quality, said more about Belgium than its 'putative object' – the Congo and Ruanda-Urundi – to use Said's words in his own description of the orientalist tradition.[68] The instrumentalisation of the Congo by Flemish nationalists is exemplary of this tendency to tropicalise[69] Belgian conflicts. Although they would compare their own inferior status to that of the Congolese suffering under the yoke of a colonial francophone ruling class, Flemish authors, as Renders and Dewulf argued, rarely challenged the legitimacy of the Belgian civilising mission and frequently adopted a derogatory terminology 'to establish a hierarchy vis-à-vis the Congolese'. The comparison served another purpose and was used as a means to 'distinguish themselves from the nation's French-speaking bourgeoisie. By portraying themselves as the "blacks of Belgium", Flemish nationalists primarily dissociated themselves from the patriotic rhetoric of Belgium's francophone elite'.[70] By and large, then, this colonial corpus, whether by francophone or Flemish authors, proves to be a fascinating resource to identify the main colonial and missionary discourses informing Belgian rule in Ruanda-Urundi and the Congo,[71] examine the interaction of White and Black characters against colonial segregation,[72] delve into Central African precolonial history,[73] and register, more rarely it must be said, anticolonial sentiments expressed by these writers and their narrators and protagonists.[74]

This increased interest in all things colonial was further intensified by the publication of journalistic blockbusters such as Adam Hochschild's *King Leopold's Ghost* (1998),[75] Ludo De Witte's *The Assassination of Lumumba* (1999),[76] and, later, David Van Reybrouck's *Congo: the Epic History of a People* (2010).[77] The popularity of the first two was aided by the large-scale mediatisation of the 1994 Rwandan genocide against the Tutsi.[78] Adam Hochshild's bestseller popularised the idea of an African Holocaust at a time when the Shoah itself was submitted to systematic memorialisation in academia and beyond and across a wide range of cultural artefacts.[79] Like the Rwandan genocide, Ludo De Witte's book triggered a parliamentary inquiry into Belgium's involvement in the elimination of the Congo's first premier. As it was published in 2010, Van Reybrouck's *Congo*, for its part, significantly benefitted from the publicity surrounding the fiftieth anniversary of Congo's independence.[80] While based on verifiable facts, these three books are all characterised by their authors' literary posture. De Witte's narrative reads like a whodunnit; Hochschild's exploration of Leopoldian abuses is presented as a 'story', and Van Reybrouck's book – even though the epithet 'epic' was added to the English-language title – has all the features of an *epic* history in which a first-person narrator, Van Reybrouck himself, is also involved in the historical account.

This tendency to blur the lines between story and history – to engage with experienced (lived and witnessed) histories to weave stories – is one of the main features of this period. The Rwandan genocide has elicited the publication of numerous narratives told from the perspective of first- and second-hand witnesses.[81] The same tendency has been observed across the other countries considered in our book, where a glut of fictional works has emerged to reflect on this colonial past, its main figures, episodes, and enduring echoes in our here and now. It would be impossible to list them all, but what is striking is that, in addition to the publication of fictional accounts by acknowledged international authors such as Barbara Kingsolver,[82] Éric Vuillard,[83] and Mario Vargas Llosa,[84] this surge of material on Central Africa – recent books by Lieve Joris,[85] David Van Reybrouck,[86] Jean Leroy,[87] Jean-Pierre Orban[88] and Marcel-Sylvain Godefroid[89] spring to mind – has been driven by a new generation of post-colonial Flemish and francophone writers from Belgium.

Equally interesting are the responses produced by Central African writers, scholars, and artists, whether based in their countries of origin, in Belgium, or in the wider diaspora. Here, too, it would be impossible to be exhaustive. The indirect, direct, and often sublimated exploration of the region's imperial past and its present resonances features highly in this production. Pie Tshibanda's humorous but also devastatingly poignant account of his trajectory as a Congolese asylum seeker in *Un Fou noir au pays des blancs* revealed to large audiences the ravages of ordinary racism at the hands of officious Belgian bureaucrats.[90] While adopting the stand-up comedy format, Pie Tshibanda reminds his spectators that Belgians, too, were once unwanted intruders in his native land. His candid account brings home the complexities of Belgo-Congolese history. Pie Tshibanda was born and bred in Kolwezi, Katanga, but his parents were originally from Kasai. In a desperate move to cling to power and avoid further political dissidence in Katanga, Mobutu, from the early 1990s onwards, manipulated public opinion and persuaded ethnic Katangese – "'Katangais authentiques'"[91] – to turn against Katanga-based Luba-Kasai. This campaign led to the persecution, massacres, and forced expulsions of Luba-Kasai like Pie Tshibanda, who arrived in Belgium in 1995 to claim asylum. However, this ethnic conflict, as often in the former Belgian empire, has its roots in colonial Congo, where Baluba were enticed by the Belgian administration to migrate to Katanga to work in the province's thriving industries. Before being forced into exile, Pie Tshibanda worked as a psychologist for the Gécamines, the company that took over the operations of the UMHK after Mobutu's nationalisations of the mining sector in 1967.[92]

Fiction writers from Rwanda, Congo, and, to a lesser extent, Burundi[93] – where, however, Roland Rugero has emerged as a leading voice in this discussion[94] – have also participated in this search for imperial traces. The Rwandan genocide, as already argued in this introduction, has been one of the major triggers of this literary explosion. A plethora of authors – Yolande Mukagasana's, Scholastique Mukasonga's, and Camille Karangwa's autobiographical novels come to mind – have unearthed the colonial origins of racial hatred.[95] In Congo, this search has gradually grown in significance. In early post-colonial fictions by writers such as Georges Ngal and V. Y. Mudimbe, there was little direct focus on the colonial period. In *Giambatista Viko ou le viol du discours africain*[96] [Giambatista Viko or the Violation of the African Discourse] and *L'Errance*[97] [Wandering], the discussion remained abstract and driven by the scholarly arguments that circulated among Congolese and African academics during a period – from the 1960s to the 1980s – overwhelmingly dominated by a quest for cultural authenticity and an ambition to dissect intellectual alienation and its effects on African scholars. V. Y. Mudimbe's novels follow a similar pattern, and although they are studded with explicit references to Congo's first and second Republics, they are largely concerned with epistemological questions in which Africa and the West, rather than Zaire and Belgium, are pitted against one another. Interestingly, the few real-life Belgian figures appearing in his novels are employed to castigate Western anthropology and the methodological deficiencies and approximations of its practitioners.[98] In *L'Écart*[99] [*The Rift*[100]], Jan Vansina is mentioned as a barely disguised 'J. Dansine', but this reference is less about the former colonial power as it is about lampooning the West, the abstract entity continuing to wreak havoc in neocolonial Africa.

In recent narratives by Congolese authors, this Belgo-Congolese history has resurfaced more prominently. In *Kin-la-joie, Kin-la-folie* [Kin-the-Joy, Kin-the-Folly], Achille Ngoye explores the cultural, legal, and economic pitfalls associated with migrancy from Zaire to Belgium,[101] an issue also broached by Clémentine Faïk-Nzuji in 'Frisson de la mémoire' [Memory Shiver].[102] In *La Dette coloniale* [The Colonial Debt], Maguy Kabamba reopens old wounds – colonial extractivism and Lumumba's assassination – while denouncing Zairian masculinist culture and Belgium's cynical support of Mobutu's regime.[103] With *Tu le leur diras* [You Will Tell Them], Clémentine Faïk-Nzuji taps into her own family history to offer a bottom-up account of Belgo-Congolese history from the early years of the CFS until the beginning of the twenty-first century.[104]

Recently, we have witnessed the emergence of a new generation of Congolese writers living 'between continents and languages while being rooted in their own imaginary' and producing a type of 'literature that is neither singularly linguistic, disciplinary, or territorial'.[105] In the past decade, the memory of Belgian extractivism has generated further literary responses, as in the case of novels by In Koli Jean Bofane,[106] Fiston Mwanza Mujila,[107] and Sinzo Aanza.[108] One of the many interesting aspects of these recent novels is that they are part of a wider cultural phenomenon involving Congolese artists such as Sammy Baloji whose work as a photographer and filmmaker has overwhelmingly focused on the legacies of Belgian mining in the DRC.[109] By recycling and creatively doctoring colonial archives – photographs of human subjects (colonisers and colonised), (post)colonial urban spaces, and industrial sites – Baloji intimates that the spectres from the past are still roaming Congo's dilapidated mining infrastructures and shaping Congolese imaginaries. In its directness and propensity to engage with Congo's socio-economic history and the many images thereof, Baloji's work echoes other experiments in DRC and Africa – artists such as Tshibumba Kanda Matulu, Michèle Magema, Freddy Tsimba, and Romuald Hazoumé come to mind – in which the distant past is a present past. Baloji's art possesses a documentary dimension. It provides a reflection on the spaces, objects, and objectifying processes responsible for the birth of modern Congo under the Belgians and after. In this exploration – his collaboration with Filip De Boeck in *Suturing the City*[110] comes to mind – the visual is often put into dialogue with anthropological research. His work also draws its inspirational drive from archives held at the AfricaMuseum in Tervuren, a place that has contributed to Baloji's trajectory as an artist[111] and curator.[112] The reappropriations of archives has been at the heart of the most daring artistic experiments of these last ten years.[113] By curating *Congo as Fiction*,[114] the Rietberg Museum of Zurich set out to establish a dialogue between colonial archives – photos, texts, artefacts, and sound documents – collected by the German anthropologist Hans

Himmelheber during his travels in the Congo in 1938/39 and a group of Congolese artists: 'The exhibition shows how artists – past as well as present – critically deal with and assess the repercussions of colonialism, Christian proselytization, and global trade'.[115] To make this encounter possible, the curators

> [...] invited six contemporary artists from the Congo and the diaspora to engage critically with Himmelheber's archives from their own perspective. Sinzo Aanza, Fiona Bobo, Michèle Magema, Yves Sambu, and David Shongo, along with Sammy Baloji (and indirectly Fiston Mwanza Mujila), participated in a dialogic process in the form of brief artistic residencies. They created artworks in reaction to the historical objects, photographs, and texts from Himmelheber; works that focus, comment on, and thereby update the older art and its acquisition as well as the archive and its origins in the context of colonization. Added to that were further works by Angali, Steve Bandoma, Hilaire Kuyangiko Balu, Aimé Mpane, Chéri Samba, Monsengo Shula and Pathy Tshindele. The artists all refer formally and in terms of content to historical art and thereby to their own cultural heritage and firmly, but in entirely different ways, confront the colonial past and the social practice of remembering as well as the exploitation and inequality persisting until today in the Congo.[116]

With 'Mabele Eleki Lola!' [The Earth, Brighter than Paradise], a temporary exhibition held at the AfricaMuseum in 2021, Freddy Tsimba, the Congolese sculptor who was trained by traditional blacksmiths and master casters, also experimented with the archival resources from the colonial period.[117] This exhibition, curated by the Congolese novelist Jean Bofane, showcased some of Tsimba's most iconic pieces, such as his *Maison Machettes* [Machete House] and human bodies made of empty bullet cases, chains, and surgical scissors. Accompanied by extracts of Bofane's forthcoming novel (*Nation cannibale*[118]), in which Tsimba himself is the main character, the bulk of this exhibition focused on contemporary DRC and explored the way in which Tsimba recycles objects of death, repression, and bodily mutilation to transcend Afro-pessimism and advocate, through the transmutation operated by his metal sculptures, the life-giving power of artistic creativity. Tsimba's repurposing of metal scraps and debris is also aimed at Christianity, this imported religion that promised paradise when, to paraphrase the ironic title of this exhibition, the earth is brighter. This onslaught on Christianity, and its attendant subjugation,[119] is captured by an assemblage of soldered mousetraps in the shape of a crucifix but also by a sculpture made of plastic wastes and representing a decapitated pregnant woman tearing her belly open with a gigantic crucifix. These artefacts speak to colonial and post-colonial oppression, and presented alongside photographs of colonial and present-day Pentecostal churches, they also testify to the enduring influence of the missionary enterprise in contemporary DRC: 'Religion has always played an essential role in the Congo to control people's minds. It erases ancestral memory and influences imaginaries'.[120]

The exploration of Congo's ancestral (Kuba) rights and cultures is also at the core of Blaise Ndala's novel *Dans le Ventre du Congo* [In Congo's Belly].[121] Published in the wake of the 2020 Black Lives Matter movement, which in turn reignited the 'Leopold Must Fall' controversy in Belgium and beyond,[122] this narrative examines in detail the present pastness of colonial Congo for contemporary Belgians and Congolese. The novel establishes a dialogue between different temporal strata of Belgo-Congolese history from the establishment of the CFS to the beginning of the twenty-first century. It takes the readers to precolonial Kasai, when the region was still ruled by an independent Kuba monarchy. It explores the way in which CFS agents coerced Congolese dignitaries into accepting the terms of unconscionable treaties against the backdrop of the Red Rubber scandal. It follows the trajectory of Tshala, a Kuba princess, who, after experiencing a short but passionate romantic interlude with a colonial administrator in the late 1950s, is raped by a Belgian African art dealer in Leopoldville, abducted to Belgium, and forced to impersonate the role of a primitive in the 'native village' of the 1958 Brussels World's Fair.[123] Described by Matthew Stanard as 'the last such show in a long line of "human zoos" in Europe and in the U.S.',[124] this village, set at the foot of the Atomium, was erected – and *staged* – by the Belgians to satisfy the visitors' quest for exoticism and to show off Belgium's technological superiority.[125] While reluctantly performing her role, Tshala is hit by another performer and dies of her injuries. Her whereabouts and her death remain a mystery for her family in Kasai. Forty-five years after these events, Nyota Kwete, Tshala's niece, arrives in Belgium, officially to study but also to investigate the circumstances that had led to Tshala's disappearance. Although improbable and somewhat far-fetched, Nyota Kwete's inquiry reconstructs the events that had for four decades been silenced and kept away from public consciousness. This inquiry is conceived as a 'machine à remonter le temps' [time machine].[126] It revisits a little-known episode of late colonialism, but it also reveals that contemporary Belgium – and some of its most prominent institutions such as its universities, museums, and football clubs – is still struggling to overcome structural racism and incorporate the truth of this past in the national narrative. In this investigation, the AfricaMuseum plays a central role and is presented as the very locus where the commodification and the spectacularisation of racial difference became routinised. Indeed, Nyota Kwete discovers that the town of Tervuren and, more specifically the church of Saint-Jean-l'Évangéliste, hosts, in the form of seven tombs, 'the biggest African memorial in this country'.[127] This unofficial memorial takes Nyota Kwete back to 1897, the year when the CFS organised an international exhibition on the Congo in what would later become the Museum of the Belgian Congo in 1910 before being renamed, after decolonisation, the Royal Museum for Central Africa, or the AfricaMuseum.[128] While showcasing the achievements of the CFS, this event also involved the erection of a Congolese village and the forced recruitment of Congolese natives ['indigènes'] 'of the best possible quality' by a team of Belgian physicians.[129] Of the nearly 270 Congolese mobilised for this performance, seven did not survive the harsh conditions under which they were put by the exhibition curators. Their bodies were first disposed of in a mass grave, and a decade later they were transferred to the cemetery of Saint-Jean-l'Évangéliste, where they were buried – religiously – for a second time.[130] Interestingly, when on 8 December 2018 a refurbished AfricaMuseum was officially reopened, another unofficial ceremony was organised in this church cemetery to pay tribute to these seven victims of the 'barbarie des Belges' [Belgian barbarism].[131]

Despite a somewhat contrived tendency to amass improbable coincidences and accumulate reality effects – often in the form of real historical figures such as Lumumba, Mobutu, Marcel Ntsoni (aka Sony Labou Tansi), and Antoine Wendo Kolosoy crossing paths with the novel's protagonists – *Dans le Ventre du Congo* provides a compelling examination of the way in which this colonial past has been swept under the carpet, ideologised, fabricated, reinvented, and memorialised since 1885. The novel also spatialises this colonial question and its legacies by focusing on Brussels and other locations in Flanders, Wallonia, Belgian Congo/DRC, Rwanda, and Burundi. This comprehensive spatialisation reflects the shape of the investigation conducted by Nyota Kwete, who in her quest for the truth is aided by DRC-based Congolese, Belgians, and Congolese from the diaspora. This ambition to reconcile actors who would have stood on the opposite sides of the colour bar is a fundamental element of this novel, which also alludes to the various attempts on part of the Belgian government to set up Truth and Reconciliation-style parliamentary inquiry commissions to determine the role of Belgium in the Rwandan genocide against the Tutsi, in Lumumba's assassination,[132] and, in the wake of George Floyd's murder, to investigate the part played by Belgium during the colonial period.[133] Blaise Ndala, who is also a human rights lawyer, reopens, by means of a fictional theatre play provocatively entitled *Les Testicules de Tintin* [Tintin's Testicles] and written by one of the novel's characters, the contentious question of mixed-race children fathered and invariably abandoned by the colonisers.[134] These children – the so-called *enfants métis* – 'were often held in suspicion by the [colonial] Administration' because it was thought that they would foment 'indigenous revolts'.[135] Via this play (in the novel), Ndala, then, reminds his readers of an obvious but still neglected fact: that truth and reconciliation cannot be achieved in the absence of equality. While capturing the zeitgeist of the early 2020s, this novel also demands moral and material reparations from the former colonial power.

This issue of the *enfants métis* is yet another example of the present pastness of the colonial period. Between 1945 and 1960, it was legally acceptable, in the Belgian Congo and in Ruanda-Urundi, to forcefully remove mixed-raced children from their families and send them to religious orphanages where they would be fostered and kept away from their biological parents. Nowadays, this coercive framework would be regarded as a gross violation of one's human rights. In 2021, five women who were submitted to this treatment and abused by their carers between 1948 and 1961 sued the Belgian state for committing a crime against humanity. The Belgian government officially apologised in 2019 for taking more than fifteen thousand infants from their African mothers but the five plaintiffs lost their case. Although recognising that the situation in which they were put is 'unacceptable' from today's perspective, the court ruled that it would be legally impossible to prosecute the Belgian state for acts that were not regarded as illegal during the colonial period.[136] This issue of the *enfants métis*, then, is a useful reminder that while the colonial past continues to shape our post-colonial present, this present is rarely equipped to hold the past to account.

As argued in this introduction, the past three decades have provided countless examples of symbolic acts and performances to come to terms with the colonial past and its legacies. The latest episodes of this unfinished history include the visit of the Belgian royal couple, King Philippe I and Queen Mathilde of Belgium, to the DRC in June 2022 but also the return of Lumumba's tooth to his relatives and the welcoming of Congolese authorities at the Palais d'Egmont on 20 June 2022. At this official ceremony, the current Belgian prime minister, Alexander De Croo, apologised for the colonial crimes committed under Belgian rule and said that 'colonialism – in Congo, Burundi and Rwanda – has shamefully tarnished the history of our country'.[137] One needs to point out that this important act of restitution was held in the very building where the Belgo-Congolese 'Table ronde' conference took place in the run-up to Congolese independence in 1960.[138] It remains to be seen whether these apologies will herald a new era between Central Africa and Belgium. Although the memorial process examined in this book has released a much-needed catharsis, it has offered little in the way of actual reparations. This partial failure to compensate the victims and their descendants is, as will be shown now, one of the running threads of this edited volume.

Structure and Objectives

This book assesses the resonance of the colonial library (as this notion was understood by Mudimbe in *The Invention of Africa*). Sixty years after political decolonisation, this archive still haunts our post-colonial present. In fact, this post-colonial present is a *present past* or, better, a 'hot past' (to use the expression coined by Aleida Assmann): a past, as she argues, that 'does not automatically vanish by virtue of the sheer passing of time but stays present in the "bloodlands" of Europe and in other places all over the world'.[139]

This edited volume deals with grave issues but refrains from drawing mournful conclusions. It will also provide the opportunity to delve into the way in which artists, scholars and scientists, writers, and activists have challenged the primacy of the colonial library to develop new perspectives, produce new knowledge, and critically reappropriate cultures that were once silenced, stereotyped, or misrepresented by the advocates of the colonial library. Of course, this process of reappropriation has not happened as dualistically, but it is interesting to observe that colonialism and its major sites (of memory) and actors often provide the basis for novel historiographical perspectives on the countries examined in this book.

As illustrated by existing archives such as Æquatoria[140] and Mukanda,[141] the available bibliography on 'Belgian' Central Africa is immense. This book will draw on these archives and, as suggested in this introduction, engage with some of the major publications on the subject, not only by Belgian scholars but also by key (established and emerging) international figures from Central Africa and beyond. Of course, it would be impossible to name them all, but the important point here is that the cohort of scholars referred to in this short introduction testifies to the good health, and sheer multidisciplinarity, of a field that, for want of a better appellation, I would call 'Central African Studies'.

There are many books on the Congo, Rwanda, and Burundi and their development before and after Belgian imperialism. There are, however, very few books (and none in English to my knowledge) on the memory and memorialisation of this historical process across a whole region including the Congo, Rwanda, Burundi, *and* Belgium. There is a plethora of recent (and sometimes exacting) publications on the Belgian Congo. This book partly coincides with the brief pursued by the editors (Bambi Ceuppens, Vincent Viaene, and David Van Reybroeck) of *Congo in België: koloniale Cultuur in de metropool* (2009), as I am also of the view that Belgium and its former colonies have become what they are because of reciprocal influences that can be traced in politics, architecture, popular culture, art, museal practices, missionary proselytism, and consumption habits. Their respective histories have been shaped by a bidirectional process ('tweericthingsverkeer'[142]) whose evolving manifestations are pervasive. Our edited volume also overlaps with Matthew Stanard's *The Leopard, the Lion and the Cock* (2019) in that it is our intention here to identify colonial *lieux de mémoire*. However, Stanard focuses overwhelmingly on colonial monuments in Belgian public spaces, whereas this volume's contributors are interested in examining not only the tangible but also the more elusive traces of this past in Belgium and beyond. Our book reflects some of the objectives and scholarly pursuits of *Koloniaal Congo: een geschiedenis in vragen/Le Congo Colonial: une histoire en questions*, edited by Idesbald Goddeeris, Amandine Lauro, and Guy Vanthemsche (2020). Indeed, we also aim to approach this imperial past from a multidisciplinary perspective and read this history through a wide range of *objects* pertaining to politics, science, development, and education. However, there is in *Unfinished Histories: Empire and Postcolonial Resonance in Central Africa and Belgium* a more sustained focus on culture (architecture, literature, performance, cinema, photography, and art) and an ambition to approach these cultural domains not only in Congo but also in the other countries included in our brief. The scholarship on Rwanda and Burundi is equally vast, but our book is predicated on the belief that the examination of these two countries offers fresh insights into the strategies adopted by educators, novelists, the media, and the Catholic Church to appraise their past accountability and develop a set of more ethical responses to undermine a still pervasive 'colonial power matrix'.[143] This book, finally, endeavours to situate these debates within a trans-African and transnational context, and it is hoped that this focus on Belgium and its former colonies will also provide the opportunity to reflect on the multifaceted ramifications of decolonisation for a variety of fields and actors.

Focusing on Belgian colonialism as a lived but also remembered experience, this book will be divided into five thematic parts.

Part one explores 'The Decolonisation of Belgian Public Institutions and Regimes of Knowledge' and pays particular attention to the way in which Belgium's colonial past is presented and narrated by public bodies and institutions such as schools, museums, and state-funded publishers. In his chapter, Dónal Hassett offers an analysis of the recent overhaul of the AfricaMuseum. Although inspired by the methodologies of the 'New Museology', it is argued here that the museum leadership only paid lip service to the decolonial possibilities of this curatorial school of thought and did not quite yield its former – colonial – authority. The new exhibit denounces colonial violence but does not address its deep-seated epistemic structure. The AfricaMuseum leadership also failed to empower the experts from the African diaspora called upon to participate in the renovation project and to initiate a credible programme of restitution of African artefacts.[144] Nicki Hitchcott's contribution focuses on the representation of post-1994 Rwanda in three novels by francophone Belgian writers: Huguette de Broqueville' s *Uraho? Es-tu toujours vivant* (1997), Bernard Dan's *Le Garçon du Rwanda* (2014), and Joseph Ndwaniye's *La Promesse faite à ma sœur* (2018 [2006]). Belgium's inability to acknowledge its historic responsibility for the

1994 genocide against the Tutsi is investigated through these authors' narrative choices and tropes. By providing an analysis of the strategies of denial, obfuscation, and avoidance adopted by these novelists, it is demonstrated that Belgium's imperial gaze has survived well into the twenty-first century. Next, Catherine Gilbert's chapter examines the space dedicated to colonial history in Belgium's school curricula. While establishing key differences between Flemish and French-speaking regions, Gilbert argues that the shortage of educational materials is particularly acute with regards to the 1994 Rwandan genocide. Although valuable teaching initiatives have been developed, notably with the support of the Fédération Wallonie-Bruxelles, it is argued here that recent attempts at decolonising knowledge and pedagogical practices often lack cohesion, as they invariably depend on the goodwill and energy of isolated individuals or memory networks like Ibuka and RCN Justice & Démocratie.

Part two examines the 'International Ramifications of Belgian Colonialism and Its Aftermath'. Robert Burroughs's focus on Britain's little-documented support of the Congo Free State runs counter to many facile accounts in which Britain is invariably presented as the unbiased champion of the humanitarian campaign that precipitated Leopold's demise. By delving into the development of the Congo Institute in Colwyn Bay (Wales), a school that set out from 1889 to 1911 to evangelise young Africans freshly arrived from Africa, this chapter shows that this institute, while complicit in the violence and abuse that had brought Leopold into international disrepute, also became a hotbed for early pan-Africanists. Yvette Hutchinson's chapter focuses on the notion of disavowed memory. She shows here that political activists and playwrights have increasingly interrogated colonial monuments and histories to combat amnesia and critically engage with the most contested aspects of European and Belgian imperialism. Colonial archives – whether the equestrian statue of Leopold II in Ostend or the 1913 Ghent world exhibition – have been seized upon to performatively re-engage with past *and* present violence. In this discussion, Hutchinson brings into dialogue the Flemish-Moroccan theatre maker Chokri Ben Chikha and Brett Bailey, the South African performance artist and enfant terrible. Albert Kasanda, for his part, analyses the emergence of Ciluba as a written language under Belgian rule. While serving a logic of imperial domination, the transcription of Ciluba accelerated the entry of Luba culture into modernity. After independence, French retained its position as official language, but the four main national languages – Lingala, Swahili, Kikongo, *and* Ciluba – were accorded an increasing role in culture and education. By focusing on *Ndi muluba* (2004) by François Kabasele, Kasanda identifies the strategies adopted by Luba intellectuals to reconcile their traditional culture with the demands of a globalised world.

Part three is dedicated to the persistence of 'Imperial Practices and Power Dynamics' in the regions explored in this book. Caroline Williamson Sinalo's contribution focuses on the 2020 presidential elections in Burundi and analyses the narrative and discursive strategies adopted by four media outlets: Radio Télévision Nationale du Burundi, SOS Médias Burundi, *La Libre Belgique*, and *Le Soir*, the two major francophone Belgian broadsheets. These elections, which took place against the backdrop of the Covid-19 pandemic and the resurgence of ethnic tensions, offer an ideal terrain to identify how Belgian (neo)colonialism and the main religious, racial, and medical prejudices underpinning this enterprise are remembered but also obfuscated now by Burundian and Belgian journalists. Next, Reuben Loffman's chapter explores colonial architecture in present-day Kongolo (south-eastern DRC), a town that played a crucial role when the colony's railway network was developed in the early twentieth century. Via the notion of 'imperial ruination' (Laura A. Stoler), it is shown here that Kongolo's former colonial administrative and ecclesiastical buildings are in a state of utter dilapidation and have continued to dynamically shape economic and social hierarchies. These architectural traces are a living archive enabling us now to assess the enduring influence of the Catholic Church and the DRC government's inability to invest in its hinterland. Sarah Arens focuses on the long-term impact of Belgian colonial land management in Central Africa and the enduring stereotypes generated by this process. She demonstrates here that Belgium was prompt at developing agrarian and agronomical sciences to exploit its overseas territories in Congo and Ruanda-Urundi. Two main scientific figures – Edmond Leplae and Emile de Wildeman – are favoured in this analysis to investigate how Belgian agrarian sciences imposed new paradigms and disrupted local epistemologies and farming practices. In a context dominated by evolutionist theses, African farming was pitted against the project of agricultural modernisation implemented by the Belgian colonisers. In her chapter, Chantal Gishoma examines the legacy of Alexis Kagame. She shows that he was, throughout his career as a Catholic priest, scholar, and poet, tirelessly devoted to the celebration of the poetic and conceptual resources of Kinyarwanda, Rwandan dynastic history, and culture. In this exercise, he advocated modern progress *and* combat the most Eurocentric aspects of modernity. Although a contested figure, notably for his explicit support of the Hamitic hypothesis, Gishoma shows here that Kagame is a crucial character to understand Belgo-Rwandan politico-cultural entanglements from the colonial period until now.

Part four will develop further the literary threads woven by Hitchcott, Gilbert, and Hutchison in the previous sections but focus more specifically on the 'Trans-African Entanglements' elicited by literary activity in DRC, Rwanda, and Burundi. Sky Herington examines the shadowy presence of Belgian colonialism in Sony Labou Tansi's writing. The selected texts, a short story and two unpublished plays written between 1970 and 1984, offer insights into the continuing racial, architectural, and spatial legacies of Belgian imperialism in Leopoldville/Kinshasa. By delving into Sony's ability to summon significant figures (Lumumba) and historical episodes (the Katangese secession) and blur the divide between past, present, and future, this piece demonstrates that Sony's representations of urban spaces, while revealing the enduring influence of neocolonial violence, are also means to assert Congo's cultural creativity. In her contribution, Maëline Le Lay focuses on the landscapes of the Great Lakes Region. Through narratives by V. Y. Mudimbe, Antoine Ruti, and Saverio Naigiziki, Le Lay demonstrates that the representation of natural and domesticated landscapes is highly significant from a political perspective. The landscape, whether walked, experienced, or imagined, is an active entity that is summoned to re-enact the past and decipher the toponymic territorialisation that underpinned the imperial conquest in Congo and Ruanda-Urundi. Some iconic loci – the garden, the mission, and the road or railroad – are also used by these authors to critique colonial violence and misappropriations. Hannah Grayson, for her part, focuses on Gaël Faye's bestselling *Petit pays* [Small Country] (2016) and analyses how this text explores systemic injustice in Burundi in the period leading to the 1994 Rwandan genocide. Via the notion of 'implicated subject' (Michael Rothberg), Grayson demonstrates that this novel blurs the divide between the ontologically fixed notions of guilt and innocence. By focusing on the main character's dual-narrative perspective – as a child and as an adult – this chapter offers a complex picture of the genocide and shows that actors only indirectly implicated in acts of violence can also be viewed as culpable.

Part five examines the 'Emergence of Diasporic Agents' in the realm of culture and in a context dominated by a dynamic of antagonistic exchanges between the West and the Global South. In her chapter, Bambi Ceuppens highlights a paradox. She explores the enduring influence of 'Congoisms', the demeaning stereotypes whereby the Congo is reduced to the 'heart of darkness'. But she also reveals the formidable creativity of its artists and Rumba musicians. She opposes the ahistorical 'authentic' art developed under Mobutu to the performative open-endedness of pieces produced by self-taught artists such as Cheri Samba. By exploring post-Mobutu era art in a global context, this analysis underscores the rise of a new breed of artists such as Kiri Katembo and Gosette Lubondo who, while engaging with the country's (post)colonial reality, often eschew realism. Matthias De Groof brings out the parallels between two documentaries shot in the Virunga Park: *The Masters of the Congo Jungle* (1958), a high-budget film produced under the patronage of Leopold III, and *Mother Nature* (2020), a short directed by Maisha Maene under the aegis of Yole!Africa, a Goma-based

NGO and cultural collective. Although critical of colonialism, which is seen as environmentally detrimental, *The Masters* remained tethered to the tropes that had been used to promote progress. *Mother Earth*, on the other hand, engages more directly with the social, cultural, and ecological ravages caused by (post)colonial extractivism in this part of DRC. Finally, in my own contribution, I focus on two novels: Sinzo Aanza's *Généalogie d'une banalité* (2015) and Fiston Mwanza Mujila's *Tram 83* (2014). I will ascertain how these two texts explore the memorial aftermath of former colonial sites such as the 'cordon sanitaire', Stanley's Congolese railway projects, extractivism, and, specifically, contemporary 'creusage' (artisanal ore mining). In this chapter I will also argue that these sites are employed by these two Congolese polymaths to conduct a reflection on the novel as a genre, assess its limits, and probe its intermedial possibilities and ability to build connections with music and the visual arts.

Notes

1. 'Post-colonial' is used in a chronological meaning here and refers to the period after the political independence and the official demise of Belgian colonial rule in the region. 'Postcolonial', on the other hand, is not strictly linked to chronology. One can argue, for example, that Aimé Césaire's *Cahier d'un retour au pays natal* [Notebook of a Return to My Native Land], albeit first published in 1939, i.e. in the heyday of French imperialism, was 'postcolonial' because its author was able to envisage a future after colonialism.
2. To this date, Lumumba remains the most researched Congolese, a figure blurring the divide between the historical and the mythical. On this hybrid status, see, among many publications: Pierre Halen and and János Riesz (eds.), *Patrice Lumumba entre dieu et diable: un héros africain dans ses images* (Paris: L'Harmattan, 1997); Jean Tshonda Omasombo, 'Lumumba. Drame sans fin et deuil inachevé de la colonisation', *Cahiers d'Études Africaines*, 173-74 (2004), 221-61; Karen Bouwer, *Gender and Decolonization in the Congo: the Legacy of Patrice Lumumba* (New York: Palgrave Macmillan, 2010); Julien Bobineau, *Koloniale Diskurse im Vergleich. Die Repräsentation von Patrice Lumumba in der kongolesischen Lyrik und im Belgischen Drama* (Berlin: Lit Verlag, 2019)' Matthias De Groof (ed.), *Lumumba in the Arts* (Leuven: Leuven University Press, 2020).
3. On this figure who was, like Lumumba, assassinated in mysterious circumstances and with the logistical support of Belgium, see Ludo de Witte, *Moord in Burundi: België en de liquidatie van premier Louis Rwagasore* (Antwerp: EPO, 2021).
4. For a postcolonial reading of Hergé's classic comic, see Nancy Rose Hunt, 'Tintin and the Interruptions of Congolese Comics', in Paul S. Landau and Deborah D. Kaspin (eds.), *Images and Empires: Visuality in Colonial and Postcolonial Africa* (Berkley; Los Angeles; London: University of California Press, 2002), pp. 90-123. For an analysis of recent Congolese comic strips, see Véronique Bragard and Christophe Dony, 'Congostrip: la bande dessinée congolaise', *La Revue Nouvelle* (July-August 2010), 92-98; and V. Bragard, 'Melancholia and Memorial Work: Representing the Congolese Past in Comics', in Binita Mehta and Pia Mukherji (eds.), *Postcolonial Comics: Text, Event, Identities* (New York: Routledge, 2015), pp. 92-110.
5. V. Y. Mudimbe, *The Invention of Africa: Gnosis, Philosophy, and the Order of Knowledge* (Bloomington; Indianapolis: Indiana University Press; London: James Currey, 1988).
6. See R. Koselleck, *Futures Past: on the Semantics of Historical Time*, trans. by and with an Introduction by Keith Tribe (New York: Columbia University Press, 2004 [1983]).
7. See Isidore Ndaywel è Nziem, 'The political system of the Luba and Lunda: its emergence and expansion', in Bethwell A. Ogot (ed.), *General History of Africa, V: Africa from the Sixteenth to the Eighteenth Century* (Oxford: Heinemann International; Berkeley: University of California Press; Paris: UNESCO, 1992), pp. 290-99; Edouard Bustin, *Lunda under Belgian Rule: The Politics of Ethnicity* (Cambridge, MA; London: Harvard University Press, 1975); Koen Bostoen and Inge Brinkman (eds.), *The Kongo Kingdom: The Origins, Dynamics and Cosmopolitan Culture of an African Polity* (Cambridge: Cambridge University Press, 2018);
8. For an analysis of the racial consequences of this spatialisation of time, see my book: P.-P. Fraiture, *Past Imperfect. Time and African Decolonization, 1945-1960* (Liverpool: Liverpool University Press, 2021).
9. See René Lemarchand, *Burundi: Ethnic Conflict and Genocide* (Washington, DC: Woodrow Wilson Center Press; Cambridge; New York: Cambridge University Press, 1996), pp. 34-41.
10. See Yves Segers and Leen Van Molle, 'L'Agriculture dans le Congo colonial. Un succès aux dépens de la population rurale?', in Idesbald Goddeeris, Amandine Lauro, and Guy Vanthemsche (eds.), *Le Congo colonial: une histoire en questions* (Waterloo: Renaissance du Livre, 2020), pp. 167-81 (p. 171).
11. Julia Seibert, 'Travail forcé', in Goddeeris, Lauro, and Vanthemsche (eds.), *Le Congo colonial*, pp. 141-54 (p. 143).
12. On this over-exploitative dimension of the Belgian colony, see Enika Ngongo, 'The Forgotten African Soldiers and Porters of the Belgian Colonial Forces in the First World War', *Journal of Belgian History*, XLVIII, 1-2 (2018), 14-33.
13. Mudimbe, *The Invention of Africa*, p. 175.
14. Élise Henry, 'Le *Mouvement géographique*, entre géographie et propagande coloniale', *Belgeo*, 1 (2008), 27-46 (27).
15. A.-J. Wauters, *Bibliographie du Congo 1880-1895. Catalogue méthodique de 3.800 ouvrages, brochures, notices et cartes relatifs à l'histoire, à la géographie et à la colonisation du Congo* (Brussels: Administration du Mouvement Géographique, 1895).
16. V. Y. Mudimbe, *The Idea of Africa* (Bloomington; Indianapolis: Indiana University Press; London: James Currey, 1994), pp. 105-06.

17. Henry, 'Le *Mouvement géographique…*', p. 41.
18. Pierre-Luc Plasman, *Léopold II, potentat congolais. L'Action royale face à la violence coloniale*, preface by Michel Dumoulin (Brussels: Racine, 2017), p. 74.
19. Compagnie du Congo pour le Commerce et l'Industrie. CCCI | AfricaMuseum – Archives [accessed 17 September 2021].
20. René Lemarchand, *Political Awakening in the Congo: the Politics of Fragmentation* (Berkeley; Los Angeles: University of California Press, 1964), p. 115.
21. For a decolonial reassessment of this oft-forgotten institution, see Pieter Boons and Sandrine Collard (eds.), *Contemporay Artists Tracing Colonial Tracks: Congoville/Hedendaagse Kunstenaars Bewandelen Koloniale Sporen* (Leuven: Leuven University Press, 2021). This book is the catalogue of an exhibition held at the Middelheim Museum in Antwerp in 2021.
22. Luc Tuymans's artistic reexamination of Belgium's colonial past is perhaps one of the most powerful examples from the post-colonial generation. On his work, see Alisson Bisschop, 'L'Histoire coloniale de la Belgique exposée à Venise: Luc Tuymans et la série Mwana Kitoko (Beautiful White Man)', *Histoire de l'Art*, 80.1 (2017), 141–52.
23. This reflects my own experience: in the 1920s, my grandparents moved to Tshikapa where my own father was born just before the Second World War.
24. See Jean-Luc Vellut, 'Ressources scientifiques, culturelles et humaines de l'africanisme en Belgique. Perspectives sur un patrimoine d'outre-mer et sa mise en valeur', *Cahiers africains*, 9–11 (1994), 115–44.
25. Matthew G. Stanard, *The Leopard, the Lion and the Cock: Colonial Memories and Monuments in Belgium* (Leuven: Leuven University Press, 2019), p. 113. This assessment is partly based on Benoît Verhaegen's 'La colonisation et la décolonisation dans les manuels d'histoire en Belgique', in Marc Quaghebeur and Émile Van Balberghe (eds.), with Nadine Fettweis and Annick Vilain, *Papier blanc, encre noire. Cent ans de culture francophone en Afrique centrale (Zaïre, Rwanda et Burundi)*, 2 vols (Brussels: Éditions Labor, 1992), pp. 333–79.
26. This absence is well documented. See also: Herman Van Goethem, 'Foreword by Herman Van Goethem, Rector University of Antwerp', in Boons and Collard (eds.), *Congoville*, pp. 8–10 (p. 8).
27. Valérie Rosoux, 'The Two Faces of Belgium in the Congo: Perpetrator and Rescuer', *European Review of International Studies*, 1.3 (2014), 16–38 (19–20).
28. L. A. Ndimurwimo and M. L. M. Mbao, 'Rethinking Violence, Reconciliation and Reconstruction in Burundi', *Potchefstroom Elektroniese Regsblad*, 18.4 (2015), 847–900 (854), <https://doi.org/10.4314/pelj.v18i4.04>.
29. Ibid., p. 852.
30. Léon Saur, 'La frontière ethnique comme outil de conquête du pouvoir: le cas du Parmehutu', *Journal of Eastern African Studies*, 3.2 (2009), 303–16.
31. See Benoît Verhaegen, *Rébellions au Congo*, 2 vols (Brussels: CRISP, 1966).
32. On the decolonial features of this period in the Congo, see Pedro Monaville, *Students of the World: Global 1968 and Decolonization in the Congo* (Durham, NC: Duke University Press, 2022). See also: Frank Gerits, '"Défendre l'œuvre que nous réalisons en Afrique": Belgian Public Diplomacy and the Global Cold War (1945-1966)', *Dutch Crossing: Journal of Low Countries Studies* ('The Cold War in the Benelux (1945-1991): Current Trends, New Perspectives'), 40.1 (2016), 68-80.
33. Frederick Cooper, *Africa since 1940: The Past of the Present* (Cambridge: Cambridge University Press, 2002), pp. 159–60.
34. Kutumbagana Kangafu, *Discours sur l'authenticité: Essai sur la problématique idéologique du 'recours à l'authenticité'* (Kinshasa: Presses africaines, 1973).
35. See Léopold Sédar Senghor, 'Ce que le noir apporte', in Jean Verdier et al. (eds.), *L'Homme de couleur* (Paris: plon, 1939), pp. 292–314; Placide Tempels, *La Philosophie bantoue*, with a preface, 'Niam M'Paya ou de la fin que dévorent les moyens', by Aloune Diop, trans. by A. Rubbens (Paris: Présence africaine, 1949); Cheikh Anta Diop, *Nations nègres et culture: De l'antiquité nègre égyptienne aux problèmes culturels de l'Afrique noire d'aujourd'hui* (Paris: Présence africaine, 1955).
36. See Bob W. White, *Rumba Rules: The Politics of Dance Music in Mobutu's Zaïre* (Durham, NC: Duke University Press, 2008).
37. See Antoon van den Braembussche, 'The Silence of Belgium: Taboo and Trauma in Belgian Memory', *Yale French Studies*, 102 (2002), 34–52.
38. See the catalogue of this exhibition: Jean-Pierre Jacquemin (ed.), *Zaïre 1885–1985. Cent ans de regards belges* (Brussels: Coopération par l'Éducation et la Culture, 1985).
39. See 'A propos' (cec-ong.org) [accessed 22 September 2021].
40. See, among other titles: Jean-Pierre Jacquemin et al. (eds.), *Racisme. Continent obscur. Clichés, stéréotypes, phantasmes à propos des Noirs dans le Royaume de Belgique* (Brussels: C.E.C. – Le Noir du Blanc/Wit over Zwart, 1991) and Jean-Pierre Jacquemin and Françoise De Moor (eds.), *Notre Congo. Onze Kongo. La propagande coloniale belge: fragments pour une étude critique* (Brussels: C.E.C., 2000).

41. See the special issue – 'Ecrire pour le Rwanda' – edited by the CEC – in *Intersections*, 2 (2014) and published to commemorate the twentieth anniversary of the Rwandan genocide.
42. Observatoire des stéréotypes (cec-ong.org) [accessed 22 September 2021].
43. M. Loutfi, *Littérature et colonialisme: l'expansion coloniale vue dans la littérature romanesque française (1871–1914)* (Paris; La Haye: Mouton, 1971).
44. E. W. Said, *Orientalism: Western Conceptions of the Orient*, with a new afterword (London: Penguin, 1995 [1978]).
45. Didier de Lannoy, Mabiala Seda Diangwala, and Bongeli Yeikelo Ya Ato (eds.), 'Tango Ya Ba Noko, "le temps des oncles": recueil de témoignages zaïrois', in *Les Cahiers du CEDAF/ASDOC-Studies*, 5-6 (1986).
46. Such as Clémentine Faïk-Nzuji, Benoît Verhaegen, Catherine Coquery-Vidrovitch, V. Y. Mudimbe, Jean-Luc Vellut, Jean Stengers, Crawford Young, Buaka Tulu Kia Mpansu, Ilunga Kabongo, Laurent Monnier, and Jean Van Lierde, among many others.
47. For a recent analysis of this sociocultural category, see Daniel Tödt, *The Lumumba Generation: African Bourgeoisie and Colonial Distinction in the Belgian Congo*, trans. by Alex Skinner (Berlin; Boston: De Gruyter, 2021).
48. P. Lomami Tshibamba, *Ngando*, preface by Gaston-Denys Périer (Brussels: Éditions Georges A. Deny, 1949)
49. P. Lomami Tshibamba, 'Témoignage de Lomami Tshibamba recueilli par Emongo Lomomba', in *Les Cahiers du CEDAF/ASDOC-Studies*, 5-6 (1986), 49-69 (53-54). My translation. All translations are mine unless otherwise stated.
50. Mukala Kadima-Nzuji, *La Littérature zaïroise de langue française (1945-1960)* (Paris: ACCT/Karthala, 1984), pp. 229-330.
51. A. Assmann, *Is Time Out of Joint?: On the Rise and Fall of the Modern Time Regime* (Ithaca, NY: Cornell University Press, 2020), p. 6.
52. Mudimbe, *The Invention of Africa*, p. xi.
53. A phrase coined by D. A. Masolo in a chapter dedicated to Mudimbe's work in *African Philosophy in Search of Identity* (Bloomington: Indiana University Press; Edinburgh: Edinburgh University Press, 1994), p. 188.
54. Mudimbe, *The Invention of Africa*, p. 200.
55. Assmann, *Is Time Out of Joint?*, p. 99.
56. Mudimbe, *Parables and Fables: Exegesis, Textuality and Politics in Central Africa* (Madison: University of Wisconsin Press, 1991), pp. 94-95 and 102-103.
57. Ibid., p. 94.
58. Mubimbe, *Les Corps glorieux des mots et des êtres: esquisse d'un jardin africain à la bénédictine* (Paris: Présence Africaine; Montreal: Humanitas, 1994). p. 75. On these events, see Friedrich Stenger, *White Fathers in Colonial Central Africa: a Critical Examination of V.Y. Mudimbe's Theories on Missionary Discourse in Africa* (Münster; Hamburg; London: LIT Verlag, 2001), p. 14.
59. Assmann, *Is Time Out of Joint?*, pp. 9-10.
60. M. Savage, *The Return of Inequality: Social Change and the Weight of the Past* (Cambridge, MA; London: Harvard University Press, 2021), p. 103. On this text but also Thomas Piketty's *A Brief History of Equality*, trans. by Steven Rendall (Cambridge, MA: The Belknap Press of Harvard University Press, 2022) and Gurminder K. Bhambra and John Holmwood, *Colonialism and Modern Social Theory* (Cambridge; Medford, MA: Polity, 2021), see William Davies, 'Destination Unknown', *London Review of Books*, 9 June 2022, pp. 15-18. In this fascinating article, Davies argues, via these three books, that modernity and its focus on the delivery of more equality through progress 'lasted barely a hundred years' (p. 15) (from 1870 to 1970). The subsequent period was marked by the emergence of a new 'inequality paradigm' and the realisation that most wealth was '"unearned"', i.e. 'inherited' (p. 15). And for Savage, in particular, 'there is a link between an "inequality paradigm" (focused especially on wealth, rather than income) and movements such as Black Lives Matter and Rhodes Must Fall, which seek to address the economic legacy of historical injustice' (pp. 15–16).
61. See Idesbald Goddeeris, 'Postcolonial Belgium: The Memory of the Congo', *Interventions*, 17.3 (2015), 434–51. On the Central African diaspora in Belgium, see Adam Ilke, Sarah Demart, Marie Godin, and Bruno Schoumaker, *Des Citoyens aux racines africaines. Un portrait des Belgo-Congolais, Belgo-Rwandais et Belgo-Burundais* (Brussels: Fondation Roi Baudouin, 2017).
62. See Els Witte, Jan Craeybeckx, and Alain Meynen, *Political History of Belgium: From 1830 Onwards* (Brussels: ASP, 2009), pp. 361–91.
63. Sarah Nutall, 'Literature and the Archive: the Biography of Texts', in Carolyn Hamilton et al. (eds.), *Refiguring the Archive* (Dordrecht; Boston; London: Kluwer Academic Publishers, 2002), pp. 283–300 (p. 295).
64. Marc Quaghebeur, 'Des textes sous le boisseau', in Marc Quaghebeur et al. (eds.), *Papier blanc, encre noire*, pp. vii–xciv.
65. In addition to the many publications initiated by Marc Quaghebeur and his collaborators at the Archives et Musée de la Littérature (AML) in Brussels, see also Pierre Halen's numerous publications on the subject and notably: *Le Petit Belge avait vu grand. Une littérature coloniale* (Brussels: Éditions Labor, 1993); and P. Halen and János Riesz (eds.), 'Images de l'Afrique et du

Congo/Zaïre dans les lettres françaises de Belgique et alentour', *Textyles* [Hors Série, 1] (1993) https://doi.org/10.4000/textyles.2184; Antoine Tshitungu Kongolo (ed.), *Aux pays du fleuve et des grands lacs. Chocs et rencontres des cultures (de 1885 à nos jours)*, preface by Marc Quaghebeur (Brussels: AML Editions, 2000); see also my own *Le Congo belge et son récit à la veille des indépendances. Sous l'empire du royaume* (Paris: Éditions L'Harmattan, 2003). See also the two following books in which fascinating links are established between colonial and post-colonial literatures from the DRC: Maëline Le Lay, '*La Parole construit le pays': théâtre, langues et didactisme au Katanga (République Démocratique du Congo)* (Paris: Honoré Champion, 2014) and Silvia Riva, *Nouvelle histoire de la littérature du Congo-Kinshasa*, prefaces by V.Y. Mudimbe and Marc Quahgebeur, trans. Collin Fort (Paris: L'Harmattan, 2000).
66. See Koen Bogers and Patrick Wymeersch, *De Kongo in de Vlaamse fiktie- en reisverhalen*, accompanied by a summary in French: 'Le Congo dans la fiction et les récits de voyages flamands' (pp. 141–55) (Brussels: CEDAF/ASDOC., 1987); Luc Renders, 'In Black and White: a Bird's Eye Overview of Flemish Prose on the Congo, *Tydskrif vir Letterkunde* [special issue on 'The Congo in Literature', ed. by L. Renders and Henriette Roos], 46.1 (2009), 109–22. In this article, Renders focuses on colonial but also post-colonial authors. This special issue was published to mark the centenary of the takeover of the Congo by Belgium in 1908. See also, for a focus on post-colonial Flemish fiction: Thomas Hendriks, 'Queer Complicity in the Belgian Congo: Autobiography and Racial Fetishism in Jef Geeraerts' (Post)Colonial Novels', *Research in African Literatures*, 45.1 (2014), 63–84.
67. L. Renders and J. Dewulf (eds.), *The Congo in Flemish Literature: an Anthology of Flemish Prose on the Congo, 1870s-1990s* (Leuven: Leuven University Press, 2020), pp. 11–12.
68. Edward Said, *Orientalism: Western Conceptions of the Orient*, with a new Afterword (London: Penguin Books, 1995 [1978]), p. 22.
69. Isidore Ndaywel è Nziem, *Histoire générale du Congo. De l'héritage ancien à la République Démocratique* (Paris; Brussels: Duculot, 1998), pp. 500–04.
70. Renders and Dewulf (eds.), *The Congo in Flemish Literature*, p. 17.
71. Pierre Ryckmans, *Barabara* (Brussels: Larcier, 1947) and Adolf Verreet, *Het zwarte leven van Mabumba* (Leuven: Davidsfonds, 1935).
72. See Henri Cornélus, *Kufa* (Brussels: Renaissance du Livre, 1954).
73. See Henri Drum, *Luéji ya Kondé* (Brussels: Éditions de Belgique, 1932).

74. See two significant examples of this: Geo Duncan, *Blancs et Noirs* (Rixensart: Éditions de Belgique, 1949) and Gerard Walschap, *Oproer in Congo* (Amsterdam: Elsevier, 1953).
75. A. Hochschild, *King Leopold's Ghost: a Story of Greed, Terror and Heroism in Colonial Africa* (Boston: Houghton Mifflin, 1998).
76. L. De Witte, *The Assassination of Lumumba*, trans. Ann Wright and Renée Fenby (London: Verso, 2001). First published in Dutch: *De moord op Lumumba* (Kessel-Lo: Van Halewyck, 1999).
77. D. van Reybrouck, *Congo: the Epic History of a People*, trans. Sam Garrett (London: Fourth Estate, 2014).
78. On this mediatisation, see Virginie Brinker, *La Transmission littéraire et cinématographique du génocide des Tutsi au Rwanda* (Paris: Classiques Garnier, 2014).
79. See Michael Rothberg, *Multidirectional Memory: Remembering the Holocaust in the Age of Decolonization* (Stanford: Stanford University Press, 2009).
80. A date that 'witnessed a plethora of publications on the Congo' as argued by Idesbald Goddeeris in 'Postcolonial Belgium, *Interventions: International Journal of Postcolonial Studies*, 17.3 (2018), 434–51 (437).
81. See Nicki Hitchcott, *Rwanda Genocide Stories: Fiction After 1994* (Liverpool: Liverpool University Press, 2017).
82. B. Kingsolver, *The Poisonwood Bible* (New York: Harper Flamingo, 1998).
83. É. Vuillard, *Congo* (Arles: Actes Sud, 2012).
84. Mario Vargas Llosa, *El sueño del celta* (Buenos Aires: Alfaguara, 2010). English translation: *The Dream of the Celt*, trans. Edith Grossman (London: Faber & Faber, 2013).
85. See, among many other publications based on the Congo: L. Joris, *Terug naar Kongo* (Leuven: Kritak; Amsterdam: Meulenhoff, 1987) and *Het uur van de rebellen* (Amsterdam: Augustus, 2006). Both books appeared in English as: *Back to Congo*, trans. Stacey Knecht (London: Macmillan, 1992) and *The Rebel's Hour*, trans. Liz Waters (London: Atlantic, 2008).
86. David Van Reybrouck, *Missie* (Brussels: Koninklijke Vlaamse Schouwburg, 2007).
87. J. Leroy, *Les Funérailles de Monsieur Lumumba*, preface by Antoine Tshitungu Kongolo (Cuesmes: Éditions du Cerisier, 2007).
88. J.-P. Orban, *Toutes les îles de l'océan* (Paris: Mercure de France, 2014).
89. M.-S. Godfroid, *Le Bureau des reptiles* (Neufchâteau: Weyrich, 2013).
90. This spectacle is based on the novel by P. Tshibanda: *Un Fou noir au pays des blancs* (Brussels: Pré aux sources, 1999).
91. Isidore Ndaywel è Nziem, *Histoire générale du Congo*, p. 776.

92. Benjamin Rubbers and Emma Lochery, 'Labour Regimes: a Comparative History', in B. Rubbers (ed.), *Inside Mining Capitalism: the Micropolitics of Work on the Congolese and Zambian Copperbelts* (Rochester, NY: Boydell & Brewer/James Currey, 2021), pp. 27–54 (p. 37).
93. See Juvénal Ngorwanubusa, *La Littérature de langue française au Burundi*, preface by Marc Quaghebeur (Brussels: Archives & Musée de la Littérature, 2013).
94. See R. Rugero, *Baho!* (Paris: Vents d'ailleurs, 2012).
95. See Y. Mukagasana, with Patrick May, *La Mort ne veut pas de moi* (Paris: Fixot, 1997); S. Mukasonga, *Notre-Dame du Nil* (Paris: Gallimard, 2012) and C. Karangwa, *Le Chapelet et la machette: sur les traces du génocide rwandais* (Pretoria: Éditions du jour, 2003) which focus on the complicity of the Catholic Church in the genocide.
96. G. Ngal, *Giambatista Viko ou le viol du discours africain* (Lubumbashi: Alpha-Omega, 1975).
97. G. Ngal, *L'Errance* (Yaoundé: CLÉ, 1979).
98. I have explored this question in *V. Y. Mudimbe: Undisciplined Africanism* (Liverpool: Liverpool University Press, 2013), pp. 83–106.
99. V. Y. Mudimbe, *L'Écart* (Paris: Présence Africaine, 1979).
100. V. Y. Mudimbe, *The Rift*, trans. Marjolijn de Jager (Minneapolis; London: University of Minnesota Press, 1993).
101. Achille-Flor Ngoye, *Kin-la-joie, Kin-la-folie* (Paris: L'Harmattan, 1993).
102. C. M. Faïk-Nzuji, 'Frisson de la mémoire', one of the short stories from her collection *La Fiancée à vendre et treize autres nouvelles* (Saint-Maur-des-Fossés: Sépia/RFI/ACCT, 1993), pp. 203–29).
103. Maguy Kabamba, *La Dette coloniale* (Montreal: Éditions Humanitas, 1994).
104. C. M. Faïk-Nzuji, *Tu le leur diras. Le récit véridique d'une famille congolaise au cœur de l'histoire de son pays, 1890–2000* (Braine-l'Alleud: Alice Éditions, 2005).
105. Silvia Riva, 'Congolese Literature as Part of Planetary Literature' *Journal of World Literature*, 6 (2021), special issue 'Contemporary Congolese Literature as World Literature', ed. by Silvia Riva and Julien Jeusette, 216–44 (232).
106. In Koli Jean Bofane, *Congo Inc. Le testament de Bismarck* (Arles: Actes Sud, 2014).
107. F.M. Mujila, *Tram 83* (Paris: Éditions Métailié, 2014) and *La Danse du vilain* (Paris: Éditions Métailié, 2020).
108. S. Aanza, *Généalogie d'une banalité* (La Roque d'Anthéron: Vents d'Ailleurs, 2015).
109. See Sammy Baloji, *Mémoire/Kolwezi* (Brussels: Africalia & Stichting Kunstboek, 2014).
110. Filip De Boeck and Sammy Baloji, *Suturing the City: Living Together in Congo's Urban Worlds* (London: Autograph, 2016).
111. See Johan Lagae and Sabine Cornélis (eds.), *Congo Far West. Sammy Baloji et Patrick Mudekereza en résidence au Musée Royal de l'Afrique centrale. Arts, sciences et collections* (Milan: Silvana Editoriale; Tervuren: Musée royal de l'Afrique centrale, 2011).
112. S. Baloji, 'About *Congo Art Works*', in Bambi Ceuppens and Sammy Baloji (eds.), *Congo Art Works: Popular Painting* (Brussels: Éditions Racine/Royal Museum for Central Africa, 2016), pp. 63–86.
113. On these artistic reappropriations, see Gabriella Nugent, *Colonial Legacies: Contemporary Lens-Based Art and the Democratic Republic of Congo* (Leuven: Leuven University Press, 2021).
114. 'Congo as Fiction: Art Worlds between Past and Present', 22 November 2020 to 15 March 2021.
115. CONGO AS FICTION – Museum Rietberg [accessed 3 December 2021].
116. Michaela Oberhofer and Nanina Guyer, 'Introduction: Fictions and Art Worlds of the Congo Between Past and Present', in Nanina Guyer and Michaela Oberhofer (eds.), *Congo as Fiction: Art Worlds Between Past and Present* (Zurich: Museum Rietberg/Verlag Sheidegger & Spiess, 2020), pp. 10–29 (p. 13).
117. See the catalogue of this exhibition: In Koli Jean Bofane, with Pascal Blanchard, Henry Bunjoko and Bogumil Jewsiewicki, *Freddy Tsimba: Mabele Eleki Lola! La Terre Plus Belle Que Le Paradis!* (Brussels: Kate'Art Éditions, 2020).
118. Bofane, *Nation cannibale* (Arles: Actes Sud, forthcoming, 2022).
119. Bofane, *Freddy Tsimba: Mabele Eleki Lola!*, p. 33.
120. Ibid.
121. B. Ndala, *Dans le ventre du Congo* (Paris: Seuil, 2021).
122. See University removes link to colonialist | News | The Times [accessed 6 December 2021].
123. On this event, see Sarah Van Beurden, '"Un Panorama de nos valeurs africaines": Belgisch Congo op Expo 58', in Bambi Ceuppens, Vincent Viaene and David Van Reybroeck (eds.), *Congo in België: koloniale Cultuur in de metropool* (Leuven: Leuven University Press, 2009), pp. 299–311.
124. Stanard, *The Leopard, the Lion and the Cock*, p. 63.
125. See, Guy Vanthemsche, *Belgium and the Congo, 1885–1980*, trans. Alice Cameron and Stephen Windross (Cambridge: Cambridge University Press, 2012), p. 70.
126. Ndala, *Dans le ventre du Congo*, p. 185.
127. Ibid., p. 294.
128. I have examined the genesis of this institution in the following book: *La Mesure de l'autre. Afrique subsaharienne et roman ethnographique de Belgique et de France (1918–1940)* (Paris: Éditions Honoré Champion, 2007); see chapter I, 'Savoirs Ethnographiques et fictions d'empire'. See also Maarten Couttenier, *Congo tentoongesteld: een*

geschiedenis van de Belgische antropologie en het museum van Tervuren (1882–1925) (Leuven: Acco, 2005).
129. Ndala, *Dans le ventre du Congo*, p. 293.
130. Ibid., p. 294.
131. Commémoration des Congolais morts à Tervuren, en marge de l'ouverture de l'AfricaMuseum – Le Soir [accessed 7 December 2021].
132. See Colette Braeckman, *Lumumba, un crime d'État. Une lecture critique de la Commission parlementaire belge* (Brussels: Les Éditions Aden, 2009).
133. Martine Dubuisson, 'Une Commission parlementaire sur le passé colonial belge dès la rentrée', *Le Soir*, 18 June 2020, Une commission parlementaire sur le passé colonial belge dès la rentrée – Le Soir [accessed 3 February 2021].
134. On this question, see: Lissia Jeurissen, *Quand le métis s'appelait mulâtre. Société, droit et pouvoir coloniaux face à la descendance des couples Eurafricains dans l'ancien Congo Belge* (Louvain-La-Neuve: Academia Bruylant, 2003) and Assumani Budagwa, *Noirs, Blancs, métis: la Belgique et la ségrégation des métis du Congo Belge et du Ruanda-Urundi. 1908-1960*, preface by Colette Braeckman (Céroux-Mousty: Budagwa éditeur, 2014). This issue, as pointed out in an email (25 October 2021) sent to me and the *New York Times* journalist Elian Peltier by Pierre Halen was already hotly debated during the colonial period. See: Fr. Alphonse Cruyen, 'Le problème des enfants mulâtres au Congo', in *Congrès international pour l'Étude des Problèmes résultant du Mélange des Races (11–12 octobre 1935)* (Brussels, Belgium), pp. 29–44. Cruyen, a Scheut missionary, was an advocate of the 'system of racialisation' and was of the view that since these children were rejected by African and European milieux, they needed to be ascribed to a 'third [métis] category', as argued by Emma Van Hooste, in 'Metis in the Belgian Congo: an Archival Research on the Racial Categorisation and Colonial Treatment of Metis', unpublished MA dissertation, Ghent University (2020), p. 23. See also Elian Peltier's article: 'Torn from Parents in the Belgian Congo, Women seek Reparations', *New York Times*, 3 November 2021, Torn From Parents in the Belgian Congo, Women Seek Reparations – The New York Times (nytimes.com) [accessed 3 November 2021].
135. Ndala, *Dans le ventre du Congo*, pp. 270–71.
136. 'RD Congo: 5 femmes métisses déboutées par un tribunal belge après avoir porté plainte pour crime contre l'humanité', *Le Soir*, 8 December 2021, RD Congo: 5 femmes métisses déboutées par un tribunal belge après avoir porté plainte pour crime contre l'humanité – Le Soir [accessed 8 December 2021].
137. Ceremonie teruggave stoffelijke resten Lumumba – Cérémonie de restitution de la dépouille de Lumumba – YouTube [accessed 22 June 2022].
138. Ndaywel è Nziem, *Histoire générale du Congo*, pp. 545–48.
139. Aleida Assmann, 'Transformations of the Modern Time Regime', in Berber Bevernage and Chris Lorenz (eds.), *Breaking Up Time: Negotiating the Borders Between Present, Past, and Future* (Göttingen: Vandenhoeck & Ruprecht, 2013), pp. 39–56 (53).
140. http://www.aequatoria.be/04engels/04oarchives_en/04oarchives_en.htm [accessed 14 December 2021].
141. https://mukanda.univ-lorraine.fr/s/mukanda/page/welcome [accessed 14 December 2021].
142. Ceuppens et al., *Congo in België*, pp. 14–21.
143. Ramón Grosfoguel, 'Decolonizing Post-Colonial Studies and Paradigms of Political-Economy: Transmodernity, Decolonial Thinking, and Global Coloniality', *Transmodernity: Journal of Peripheral Cultural Production of the Luso-Hispanic World*, 1.1 (2011), https://doi.org/10.5070/T411000004
144. A plan of restitution is, however, now being mooted by the Belgian Government and Congolese partners such as André Yoka, the general director of Congo's 'Institut National des Arts'. See Véronique Kiesel, https://www.lesoir.be/408568/article/2021-11-25/kinshasa-applaudit-la-volonte-belge-de-rendre-au-congo-des-objets-traditionnels, 25 November 2021 [accessed 25 November 2021].

PART 1
Regimes of Knowledge and Decolonisation

Must Leopold Fall?
The Renovation of the AfricaMuseum and Belgium's Place in International Debates on the Decolonisation of Public Heritage

Dónal Hassett

> 'None of us starts with a clean slate but the historicity of the human condition also requires that practices of power and domination be renewed'.
> Michel-Rolph Trouillot.[1]

In December 2018, the Royal Museum for Central Africa (RMCA) in the Brussels suburb of Tervuren reopened its doors to the public after five years of extensive renovations. Guido Gryseels, the director who oversaw the transformation of what had often been described as 'Europe's last unreconstructed museum of the colonial era',[2] vaunted 'the work of decolonisation' realised through the renovation and expressed hope that it would 'become a real space of contact and dialogue for all people truly interested in Africa'.[3] No one, including the museum's leadership, would claim that the RMCA was starting with anything like a 'clean slate'. Indeed, the renovation had been premised in part on the idea that the RMCA needed to 'shed its colonial image'.[4] But the extent to which the process and outcomes of the renovation represented a renewal, a reshaping, or a rejection of the 'practices of power and domination' that had long defined this most colonial of museums remains highly contested. The story of the RMCA's transformation is illustrative not just of shifting and competing understandings of colonial pasts and presents in Belgium but also of broader international trends in the way institutions and societies grapple with empire and its legacies.

The institutional history of the RMCA and the ways in which it has always been both reflective and constitutive of broader attitudes to colonial pasts and presents in Belgium is the subject of a rich historiography.[5] It has also been incorporated into broader comparative histories of the colonial museum within Europe.[6] I do not intend to revisit that ground here. Instead, this chapter seeks to place the renovation and the critiques that followed into the context of broader evolution of international heritage practices by examining the chronologies of change at the RMCA, considering how change was conceptualised by those leading the renovation and its critics, and finally, asking what future lies in store for the institution. In doing so, it seeks to move past longstanding narratives of exceptionality that have surrounded both Belgian attitudes to colonialism generally and the RMCA specifically to ask what lessons they can offer to heritage professionals, activists, historians, and engaged citizens in other parts of the world.

Contested Chronologies of Change

The reopening of the RMCA was by no means the only major event on the international heritage scene to mark the final weeks of 2018. On 21 November, the Senegalese essayist and scholar Felwine Sarr and the French art historian Bénédicte Savoy launched their Report on the Restitution of African Cultural Heritage, calling for the widescale return of expropriated artefacts to Africa as a means to open a 'pathway toward establishing new cultural relations based on a newly reflected upon ethical relation'.[7] Two weeks later, on 6 December, the newly constructed Museum of Black Civilisations was inaugurated in Dakar, Senegal. Its director, the archaeologist Hamady Bocoum, promised that this avowedly transnational and Pan-African institution would 'introduce a radical paradigm shift towards a new era of museum practice', that would, he affirmed, 'no longer content itself with the inherited institutions of colonialism'.[8] These two interventions offered a bold decolonising vision of how the heritage of Africans and Afro-descendant peoples should be preserved, collected, curated, and interpreted. In contrast, the new and shiny RMCA that once aspired to be a leading exemplar of the post-colonial multicultural museum came under sustained criticism from scholars and activists as outdated and regressive as soon as it reopened its doors. What happened between 2005, when the museum's leadership felt comfortable claiming that it was 'a forerunner internationally'[9] and 2020, when its operational director acknowledged that 'when societal demands change at a speed higher than the slow museum setup allows, the museum is always behind'?[10] The story of the eclipsing of the RMCA's renovation is one not just of an institutional incapacity to deliver profound change but also of the shifting definitions of change within the colonial museum over the last two decades.

The long overdue reforms at the RMCA that began at the turn of the millennium coincided with the high point of the influence of the so-called New Museology within colonial museums. The incorporation of theoretical insights into museum practice from the 1970s on led to a greater stress on institutional reflexivity within museums, as critical scholars and practitioners sought to deconstruct and move past old visions of the museum as an elite, authoritative, and monolithic cultural institution.[11] Although the New Museology embraced a range of sometimes contradictory, sometimes complementary perspectives, it was defined by a broad commitment to transform the museum from a 'site of determined edification', reflecting the narratives of ruling elites, into a space of 'educational engagement' with diverse publics and histories.[12] The social responsibility of museums to represent and reflect the lives of all in the communities they served became central to the rhetoric, if not always the practice, that emerged from the New Museology.[13] This found concrete expression in the participatory methodologies that sought to engage with those sections of society from which museum collections originated, so-called 'source communities'.[14] While the New Museology presented challenges for all types of cultural institutions, it was particularly disruptive and potentially transformative for museums whose origins lay in the display of collections amassed through the exploitation of colonised populations.

By the time the RMCA was starting down the long path towards renovation, colonial museums across the Global North had already begun to deploy methodologies drawn from the New Museology to transform their exhibitions.[15] One concept in particular came to embody this new vision for the old colonial museum: the 'contact zone'. Originally articulated by the literary scholar Mary Louise Pratt, the term was popularised in the museum sector by the cultural historian James Clifford.[16] Clifford argued that engagement with what are often called 'source communities' can transform museums into 'places of hybrid possibility and political negotiation, sites of exclusion and struggle'.[17] In the Cliffordian vision, the kind of mutual if uneven forms of reciprocity that arose from contact between institutions and 'source communities' opens a space in which the 'aspirations of subaltern and dominant populations can be articulated' alongside, intertwined with, and in conflict with one another.[18] This concept became prominent in the rhetoric, if not always the praxis, surrounding the reinvention of colonial museums throughout the 1990s and early 2000s.

The influence of the New Museology was clear to see in the language deployed and some of the structures created in the renovation plans for the RMCA. In their public presentation of the initial outlines of the renovation, leading members of the museum's team asserted their belief that the application of 'research and museological expertise' could 'transform the RMCA without compromising any of the institution's attributes'.[19] The fairly vague commitment outlined in the document to the RMCA 'shedding its colonial identity,[20] evolved over time to become a recognition that the new RMCA would have to engage in reflection about its 'own history as a colonial institution'.[21] The museum was, according to its leadership, to be reimagined as 'a place of contact between peoples and cultures' in which 'African communities' would be empowered 'to voice themselves'.[22]

This iteration of the museum as 'contact zone' would find expression in specific structures set up to formalise relationships with African diasporic communities in Belgium. Initially invited to participate in a work group, representatives of the diaspora were subsequently formally integrated into the museum's structures in the COMRAF (Comité de concertation Musée Royal de l'Afrique Centrale-Associations Africaines), a consultative body bringing them together with RMCA staff members.[23] The COMRAF helped organise a number of temporary exhibitions and events at the RMCA or with the institution's support in the lead-up to the renovation.[24] It also featured prominently in the museum's promotion of the renovation process at national and international levels, solidifying the impression that the RMCA was transforming, through the application of practices integral to the New Museology, into a leading post-colonial museum.

Prior to the closure for renovation, the RMCA hosted a range of significant temporary exhibitions that each deployed elements of the New Museology to reinterpret the museum's overtly colonial displays. These exhibitions hinted at the potential, the limits, and the contradictions at the heart of efforts to mobilise the New Museology to remake the colonial museum. In October 2000, the RMCA opened its first openly self-critical exhibition, entitled 'Exit Congo Museum'. Ethnologist and curator Boris Wastiau focused on exposing the ways in which the provenance, cultural and geographical origins, symbolic and practical functions, and authorship of artefacts had been misrepresented in the museum's displays and challenging the public to think through the broader power dynamics and colonial logics underpinning them.[25] Interspersed among these new critical displays was a selection of contemporary art pieces, curated by Congolese artist Toma Muteba Luntumbue, that sought to 'break the codes of hegemonic' forms of representation within the museum.[26] While this new departure was limited in scope and met with resistance among some of the RMCA staff, it did seem to offer a vision of how the museum could, through co-productive forms of curation, begin to deconstruct its own role in propagating racist and colonial ideas about Africa, past and present.[27]

A subsequent exhibition in 2005, entitled 'Memory of the Congo: The Colonial Era' and curated by historian Jean-Luc Vellut, was much less radical in its narrative but found a much wider audience. While the greater focus on the lived experience of Congolese under colonial rule was commended, some academics critiqued its 'defensive' narrative of atrocities that insisted on the importance of contextualisation and the distinction it drew between the Leopoldian regime and the subsequent Belgian administration.[28] Here the museum struggled to reconcile what it saw as its mission to engage and educate, without alienating the broader Belgian public, with its commitment to a critical vision of the museum past, exposing the tensions between the different priorities encoded within New Museology approaches. The controversies it generated reflected and fuelled a broader, activist-led interrogation of Belgium's attitudes towards its colonial past that would have significant repercussions for the conception and reception of the renovation.[29]

Finally, to mark the fiftieth anniversary of Congolese independence, the RMCA hosted an exhibition entitled 'Indépendance: Congolese Tell Stories of Fifty Years of Independence', curated by the Afro-Belgian anthropologist Bambi Ceuppens. This exhibition was radical in its centring of Congolese perspectives and in its focus on interviews and popular cultural material produced by and for Congolese rather than the older types of 'ethnographic' objects traditionally valorised by the museum.[30] Its curator has argued that, rather than fixating primarily on a denunciatory narrative of past colonial violence, the museum should dedicate itself to the promotion of African narratives as the best of form of restorative justice, 'highlighting their artistic mastery, creativity, humanity, ingenuity, and resilience as actors in their own history and creators of their own cultures'.[31] In doing so, she advocated a critical vision of the museum as 'contact zone', in line with Clifford's original conception, that seeks to remake the museum by empowering those it once excluded and belittled to tell their own stories.[32]

The hegemony of references to New Museology practices in conceptions of reform within the RMCA in this period is clear. The RMCA was variously reinvented in these exhibitions as a space for the interrogation of institutional complicity in colonial violence and the propagation of racism, a site for the education of the broader public on African pasts and presents, and a venue for the articulation of African visions of their own history. The museum leadership's presentations of the renovation to scholarly audiences stressed each of these aspects, arguing that the combination of new museological approaches with the institution's scientific expertise would transform a relic of pro-colonial museology into a model for the post-colonial museum. At no point in this initial period before the doors of the museum shut for the definitive renovation did the intellectual framework of decolonisation feature in the public discourse of the RMCA.[33] The renovation was not conceived of as a 'decolonisation' of the institution but rather as a modernisation effort, one that would strip the displays of their overt racism; diversify the museum's publics, staff, and collaborators; and ensure the institution was relevant to contemporary Belgian and African societies.

In his 2020 account of the renovation of the RMCA, the museum's director of operations, Bruno Verbergt, rebuffed criticism of the minimal impact of decolonising perspectives on the new exhibition by arguing that such ideas were marginal at the time the renovation process had begun. There is, perhaps, a kernel of truth to his claim that the museum 'had developed all its intentions and concepts well before the terminology of, and academic, activist, and public pressure for, decolonization became as widespread as it is now'.[34] And yet, critiques calling for the decolonisation of museums and the epistemologies underpinning them had been around for decades. Writing in his famous *Discourse on Colonialism*, Aimé Césaire argues that Europe's pride in its museums and their colonial objects was misplaced. It would have been 'better if they had let those civilisations develop and flourish rather than offering up random limbs, dead limbs, duly labelled, for us to admire'.[35] Césaire's insistence that the history of colonialism is not one of 'kilometres of roads, canals, and railways', or indeed of museum collections amassed, but rather one of 'societies emptied of themselves, cultures trampled underfoot […] extraordinary possibilities eviscerated' would echo through broader appeals for cultural and intellectual decolonisation over the decades that followed.[36]

These 'extraordinary possibilities' were of great interest to the scholars of the new field of decolonial studies that emerged, primarily from Latin America, in the 1990s and 2000s. They developed an analysis of the 'coloniality of power' in the contemporary world that challenged the universalism of Western modes of thought,[37] highlighted the eradication of indigenous epistemes,[38] and celebrated the potential of forms of living and thinking that exist, as far as possible, outside of, and often against, a Western modernity that is inextricably bound to colonial logics.[39] Decolonial studies' focus on the way in which colonialism was and is intrinsic to European modernity and its highlighting of the marginalisation of alternative systems of interpreting the world and the objects within it have clear resonances in debates around the decolonisation of the museum. Of course, decolonial approaches coexist, sometimes uneasily, with a whole range of pre-existing and evolving postcolonial critiques that also seek to challenge and undo colonial logics, whether in the museum or in society more broadly. These have all contributed to the growing calls for radical change to cultural institutions, especially colonial museums.

Finally, strands of both intellectual thought and praxis that have come into prominence in Africa itself in recent years, from the Rhodes Must Fall movement in South Africa and beyond to Cameroonian philosopher Achille Mbembe's critiques of the necropolitics of the museum, have fuelled calls for a deeper interrogation of the coloniality of cultural institutions in the Global North and Global South.[40] The fusion of these different strands of critique led to an increasing contestation within the heritage sector of the authority of Western epistemologies and of the potential of old participatory models of reform.

By the time the doors of the museum closed for the wholescale renovation, the approaches that had initially informed the planning stage of the renovation were increasingly questioned by heritage professionals. In particular, the distinction between the limited recalibration within institutions provided by New Museological concepts such as the museum as 'contact zone' and a more radical change delivered by a form of cultural 'decolonisation' became key. In her 2009 account of her participation in co-curation at the new National Museum of the American Indian in the United States, the Indigenous scholar Amy Lonetree welcomed the 'important collaborative methodologies' advanced by the museum but balked at the use of the language of 'decolonisation' to describe displays that 'failed to tell the hard truths of colonisation and the genocidal acts that have been committed against Indigenous people'.[41] Real change could not be effected without honesty about the pervasive violence of colonialism and its enduring legacies within the museum and society more broadly. Robin Boast's 2011 article drew the attention of curators in Europe, including at least one staff member at the RMCA,[42] to a range of critical perspectives on the co-option of the 'contact zone' concept by museums and their inattention to the 'fundamental asymmetries' inherent to the relationship between institutions and the communities whose heritage they detained and displayed.[43] He argued that, for museums to transcend their coloniality, they would have to go beyond the 'engagement' advocated by the New Museology and recognise that the institutional conceptualisation, structures, and practices of the museum would have to be 'completely redrafted'. Museums must 'learn to let go of their resources, even at times of the objects, for the benefit and use of communities and agendas far beyond its knowledge and control'.[44] Well before the definitive closure of the RMCA for the renovation, prominent voices within the international heritage community were arguing that yielding authority was key to delivering radical change to the colonial museum. But would the leadership of the museum listen?

Conceptualising Change at the RMCA

At the heart of the dispute over both the processes and the results of the renovation is a fundamental disagreement over what change should look like, not just within the RMCA but within the colonial museum more broadly. While there was broad agreement that the RMCA's openly pro-colonial displays would have to go, there was no consensus as to what would replace them and who would shape the new exhibition. The new displays and the discourse they generated would crystallise many of the tensions around the persistence of colonial pasts that were not necessarily specific to the RMCA or to the Belgian context. Here multiple competing visions of how the colonial museum should be remade were pitted against each other in arguments that resonate far beyond the palatial halls of the RMCA.

When presenting the plans for the new RMCA at an international academic conference in 2014, the museum's director, Gryseels, outlined for his audience the key distinction between what he suggested was the 'colonial' museology that defined the museum pre-renovation and the 'post-colonial' model that it hoped to embody post-renovation.[45] The principles he elaborated did advocate a real break with the museum's openly colonialist museological practices, but for those who were unconvinced by the renovation, they were insufficiently radical to undo the colonial logics underpinning the institution. Firstly, the director committed to abandoning the 'contrast between European "civilization" and African "primitiveness"' and instead being guided by 'a principled insistence on African cultures and an age-long history of cultural influence'. This did mark a significant rupture with past practice but, in the eyes of the critics of the renovation, fell short of the necessary challenge to the universality of Western epistemologies and interrogation of their use to represent African experiences, past and present.[46] His commitment to ending the 'juxtaposition of timeless nature and culture' in the representation of Africa and Africans and insisting on Africa's 'long and dynamic history' was notable, but again, critics felt the renovation process insufficiently acknowledged Africans' long history of studying, analysing, and representing their own societies.[47] For Gryseels, the museum's gaze would have to turn from 'specimens and objects' to African men and women. For the critics, the gaze itself was limiting and problematic; African men and women should be represented within the complexities of African societies.[48] While the new RMCA would shift from presenting ethnographic objects 'on the basis of aesthetic and material criteria' to telling 'the story of their history, origin, use and meaning', the director made no mention in his presentation of the question of future restitution, seen by many critics of the colonial museum as fundamental to establishing a new ethical relationship in international heritage.[49] Finally, the new museum was to move away from 'European representing Africans' and instead prioritise 'Africans representing themselves'. This, as we shall see, was one of the most criticised aspects of the renovation, as activists insisted that real change would mean Africans and members of the diaspora shaping the terms of their own representation.[50] The tensions between these competing ideas about whether and how the museum could break free from the colonial logics that had long defined it would be reflected within the new exhibition spaces and the reaction they provoked.

The museum's new 'Ritual and Ceremonies' display is emblematic of the broader conflict between rival visions of change within the colonial museum. Using the lens of anthropology, this room narrates the life journeys of the inhabitants of Central Africa by focusing on key rites of passage. The unabashedly racist language and openly exoticising imagery that had once been the staple of the RMCA's anthropological was now banished. The room includes direct testimonies from residents of region about their experiences of and relationships with culturally specific rituals and ceremonies. It also features popular cultural and artistic representations of the role these rites occupy in contemporary Congolese society. Thus, the display seems to tick most of the boxes in the 'post-colonial' museum column suggested by the director.

However, this same display has been the subject of extensive critique from the advocates of a radical decolonisation of the museum. The RMCA's insistence on viewing the inhabitants of Central Africa through the 'prism of rituals and ceremonies' is, as Congolese historian Elikia M'Bokolo puts it, 'the product of a colonial gaze', perpetuating a long tradition of anthropological fetishisation of African cultural practices.[51] Moreover, the fact that the displays combine testimonies and cultural production from contemporary Central Africa, a welcome addition to the museum, with artefacts from the collection accumulated during the colonial period, leads to a dangerous flattening of chronologies in the exhibition.[52] The old chronopolitics that openly asserted African backwardness may be gone, but the new displays, in their focus on rituals, imply a timelessness to African lives, presenting them as bound to ancient (albeit evolving) traditions but unmoored from contemporary political, social, and economic realities. Central Africans remain the subject of the anthropological gaze.

Similar tensions are also evident in the reactions the new exhibition's historical narrative has provoked. The museum now openly acknowledges the violence underpinning the colonial project, displaying objects of torture and including accounts of the exploitation and brutality that defined experiences of Belgian colonial rule. Its 'Representations' corner interrogates the way Africans have been portrayed in European narratives, showing a degree of institutional reflexivity and awareness of the links between contemporary racism and colonialism. The museum's new display includes some information on Central Africa's precolonial past and the history of Congo, Burundi, and Rwanda after the formal end of colonialism, pointing the public to African histories prior to and after colonisation. Prominent African experts offer critical assessments of the colonial period and its longer legacies in African societies, an example of what the museum director would likely dub 'Africans representing themselves'. Here again we see how the key categories identified by Gryseels have shaped the new exhibition.

However, both the historical narrative promoted within the displays and the way the museum yields its authority to legitimise it remain deeply controversial. In a break with the institutional reflexivity advocated by the New Museology, one of the exhibit panels in the history section confidently asserts that 'historians share fundamentally the same reconstruction and narrative of the colonial past'.[53] This is contrasted with the 'very controversial' debate around the colonial period in Belgian society more broadly, underlining of the museum's self-conception as a 'positivist' institution telling a 'truth that ought to be neutral'.[54] Here we can see how even the attenuated authority conferred on the museum by New Museology approaches proves too restrictive and the RMCA reverts to type by affirming its academic authority over Central African pasts and presents. Indeed, the analysis offered by critical African voices within the exhibition itself, accessible only to the dedicated visitor who is willing to watch all the media presentations, contradict the claim in the display, yet their expertise does not win them a place among the 'historians' described in the panel. This is one of a number of examples throughout the exhibition where the commitment of the RMCA leadership to what they considered to be 'scientific views' over 'personal opinions' limited their capacity to engage in the sort of critical analysis necessary for the delivery of the post-colonial museum they themselves claimed to envision, let alone the decolonised museum their critics advocate.[55]

The exhibition may highlight a range of gross acts of violence perpetrated by the Leopoldian and, to a lesser extent, Belgian administration in Congo, but it eschews a structural analysis that explains how they relate to the social and cultural project of colonialism, in which the museum itself is enmeshed. The positive presentation of colonial healthcare within the displays reinforces the idea that different elements of the colonial project can be disaggregated from each other, a logic that is both heavily contested among historians and seems to underpin the broader renovation project of the museum. Whereas the museum is conscious of the need to acknowledge some of the violence perpetrated during the colonial period, it is largely silent on the continued interference of the Belgian state and international corporations in the region after formal decolonisation. Instead, we are told that 'the post-colonial history of Burundi, Congo, and Rwanda is dominated by complex, tragic, and controversial conflicts' whose sole relationship to Belgium seems to be that they occasionally feature in 'the Belgian Press'. The need for 'balance', seen as a marker of positivist, fact-based narratives of the colonial past, seems not to apply to the post-colonial period.

The same persistence of colonial practices would be central to critiques of the museum's collaboration with the Afro-Belgian diaspora. When the RMCA reopened its doors to the public in December 2018, the otherwise celebratory press release acknowledged the ongoing tensions with the representatives of the diaspora community. The euphemistic claim that 'despite our best intentions, cooperation has not always been easy' offered little insight into how and why the RMCA's much-vaunted collaborative model had failed.[56] The museum's reliance on and public trumpeting of participatory methods seems to have been completely impervious to the increasing body of scholarship and praxis that questioned the limitations of a 'contact zone' model of collaboration for the colonial museum. In 2014, six expert representatives were nominated by the COMRAF to take a more active (though still not clearly delineated) role in the renovation. The informality of this procedure, done without a public call, coupled with remuneration packages below typical rates for experts, called into question the value the RMCA would assign to their input.[57] That this new subgroup had no official title – variously called the Group of 6, the Diaspora Group, or the Diaspora – was indicative of the ambiguity surrounding its role.[58] The Group's initial plans to launch a consultative process involving international experts co-selected with the museum's administration were scotched by the leadership, who had already laid down the parameters of the renovation themselves.[59] The diasporic experts were to serve as consultants, passive actors in the renovation who could offer opinions but not make decisions. Collaboration would take place on the RMCA's terms.

The status of curatorial consultants, and the oft precarious conditions of employment and limited powers of decision-making that came with it, had been central to the way institutions conceived of community co-curation in the wake of the New Museology. However, by the time the RMCA's renovation was under way, this model was increasingly contested by experts from source communities. In her November 2017 article, 'The Museum Will Not Be Decolonised', the independent scholar Sumaya Kassim recounted her experience as a curator brought in to address the colonial history of the Birmingham Museum and Art Gallery.[60] The stress she placed on the emotional labour, the precarity of employment, and the limited agency of the team of co-curators chimes directly with the accounts of some of the COMRAF's experts. Indeed, in her scathing assessment of the consultation process for the renovation of the RMCA, the COMRAF expert and art historian Anne Wetsi Mpoma approvingly quoted Kassim's assertion that 'decolonising is deeper than just being represented'.[61] In her critical assessment of the renovated museum, the Afro-Belgian anthropologist and fellow Group of Six member Gratia Pungu went as far as to suggest that the opacity of the operation of the renovation and its marginalisation of the consultants to 'might even recall the way the "native" subjects were treated in the colonial era'.[62] When the representatives asked the RMCA to formalise the position of experts from the diaspora into the future by providing an office and an official status in the museum once it was reopened, they were rebuffed by the director, who informed the Group that if the conditions under which they were working were unsatisfactory, he could always find other African partners.[63] This assertion of power led to a definitive rupture and saw the withdrawal of the Group from the process, meaning that the participative methodologies were abandoned in the final stages of the renovation. The museum's vision of an ill-defined 'consultative and to a certain extent also co-creative' role, couched in the language if not the practice of the New Museology, proved incompatible with the Group's call for a fundamental redistribution of power and resources rooted in a radical vision of the decolonising museum.[64]

The museum's insistence on maintaining its monopoly on decision-making was reflective of its commitment to its own epistemic authority. The leadership's resistance to yielding control to and embracing the suggestions of the Group was, in part, due to a narrow and exclusionary understanding of the concept of 'expertise'. Although the highly qualified members of the Group had specialist expertise accredited by Western institutions, they were understood to be providing only 'sensitivity expertise' within the renovation process.[65] The curatorial authority of the RMCA's in-house experts was left completely intact, and the Groups' critiques of the enduring coloniality of the displays were largely ignored.[66] Their role, it seemed, was to adjudicate whether displays were openly racist or not, not to expose and undo enduring colonial logics within the exhibit. Here we can see the sharp contrast between 'contact zone' models of collaboration, which 'appropriate resources that are necessary for the academy' and ignore those 'that were not necessary', and a more radical form of change, 'decolonising the museum', which grapples with the broader coloniality of the museum as an institution.[67] Ultimately, activists outside the museum and many of those working within the COMRAF and the Group of Six came to see the process as an 'instrumentalisation of black bodies' to obscure the enduring 'coloniality of the institution'.[68]

The RMCA's commitment to asserting its institutional authority was perhaps most evident in its attitude towards its ownership of and control over the items in the collection acquired through acts of violence and exploitation in the former colonies. A central axis of the project had been to transform the institution's collection from the booty of colonial conquest and exploitation into what the new displays called the 'heritage of humanity' by using the frameworks of the New Museology to recontextualise and revalorise the collection. The museum was to move away from the ahistorical colonial models of display that grouped items by their aesthetic qualities and instead focus on the cultural contexts in which they were produced; their cultural, social, and economic significance; and their use within their society of origin. The end result, like many other applications of New Museology principles to the new exhibit, is inconsistent and incoherent. The new 'Unrivalled Art' exhibit celebrates the ingenuity of African cultural production but relies on an 'old-fashioned display of objects as masterpieces' that elevates their aesthetic significance over their cultural, social, or spiritual meanings.[69] Likewise, the museum's narrative of the origins of its collection is uneven throughout the renovated displays. While in some places, the expropriation that defined the acquisition of artefacts is openly acknowledged, elsewhere euphemisms such as 'collected by', 'originating from', or 'acquired in' obscure the true nature of collection processes. This is true even in cases, such as that of the *nkisi nkondi* associated with Alexandre Delcommune, where staff at the RMCA have done extensive research on the particular history of plunder that led to the artefact's incorporation into the collection.[70] Here, the imperative to recast the collection as a part of a universal and global culture that the museum had every right to showcase to a Belgian public won out over its supposed commitment to institutional reflexivity and interrogation of the museum's colonial past.

The final stages of the renovation coincided with a resurgence in claims for the restitution of artefacts acquired in the coercive context of the colonial system both within Belgian society and across the Global North more broadly. Congolese nationalists had called for the return of cultural heritage in the dying days of Belgian rule in Congo while the Mobutu regime had successfully secured the return of a limited number of artefacts from the RMCA's collections to bolster its claim to embody Zairian *authenticité*.[71] As Sarah Van Beurden has shown, the museum (and the Belgian state) agreed to the return of these artefacts, the majority of which had only recently arrived in Belgium from the collections of museums in the colony itself, only because their transfer was deemed a 'gift', not an act of restitution.[72] The museum's insistence on its authority over its collections would persist during the renovation and after the reopening, even in the face of increasing contestation. The publication of an open letter by Mireille-Tsheusi Robert, president of the anti-racist activist organisation BAMKO-CRAN, denouncing the exploitative forms of collaboration proposed by the RMCA and calling for a new restitution programme opened a heated debate in Belgian society.[73] Critical voices within the museum expressed support for the idea that the legal frameworks of ownership should not trump the 'undeniable moral argument in favour of restitution'.[74] The museum leadership was less committal, placing itself in the camp of the restitution sceptics, alongside figures like Tristam Hunt of the Victoria and Albert Museum and Wiebke Ahrndt of the German Overseas Museum, who defended a supposedly universal model of heritage.[75] Gryseels rejected the idea 'of the return of the totality' of the museum's collections, citing the lack of demand from African countries and the 'catastrophic' political situation of states like Congo where 'nothing works'.[76] He evoked a previous 'bad experience' of restitution when artefacts were returned to Mobutu's Zaire and ended up on the black market. Here, the museum director deployed what Achille Mbembe has described as 'the strategies of obfuscation used by those who are convinced [...] that the conqueror is always right and that the pillaged booty is his just reward'.[77] While he did concede that he would consider the return of 'certain masterpieces of symbolic value' to an institution 'with good conditions of security and conservation', Gryseels, it seemed, believed that the collection rightfully belonged in Brussels and any future restitution, however minor, should be in the gift of the administrators of the RMCA.[78]

Ultimately, the assertion of institutional authority – authority of episteme, of decision-making, and of ownership – became the focal point for critiques of the renovation of the RMCA. The (often uneven) application of methodologies from the New Museology did change both the displays and the narrative presented to the public in the RMCA, but the extent to which this change represented a real rupture with the institution's colonial past is very much disputed. While the renovation had been designed to help the museum 'shed its colonial image', significant sections of Belgian society and the broader international heritage sector had come to embrace a much more profound vision of transformation within the colonial museum by the time the RMCA's doors reopened. The enduring coloniality of the discourses of knowledge it deployed to interpret its collections, the structures it used to govern the participation of diaspora communities in the renovation, and its attitudes towards the ownership of the artefacts it displayed meant that the RMCA's renovation did not rise to this new challenge. The whole process had represented a renewal and not a rejection of the 'practices of power and domination' that had always defined the institution.

Conclusion

The story of the RMCA's renovation shines a light on the shifting norms within both Belgian society and the international heritage sector when it comes to grappling with the legacies of colonialism. In a context where statues of King Leopold II were being toppled by crowds or removed by municipalities across Belgium and European governments and cultural institutions were gradually adopting restitution policies, the new RMCA increasingly looked out of date. The renovation seemed to have implemented yesterday's changes for tomorrow's museum. The leadership's efforts to recast the renovation as the beginning of a long process of 'decolonisation' showed an awareness of this broader cultural shift and an attempt to respond to it rhetorically, if not in praxis.[79] However, ascribing the shortcomings of the renovation to the inability of the 'slow museum' to adapt to shifts in museological practice and societal attitudes obscures the broader structural and methodological pitfalls that dogged the process.[80] The fact that the museum leadership was not cognisant of the rise of radical conceptions of decolonisation was not the cause of the RMCA's difficulties but rather a symptom of the broader and enduring coloniality that defined the institution and would hamper efforts to effect radical change. As long as the renovation was designed, in the words of its director and senior staff members, to 'transform the RMCA without compromising any of the institution's attributes', its capacity to transcend the institution's long and deep-seated entanglement with the colonial project was limited.[81] Where the rhetoric and, to a lesser extent the practices, of the New Museology promised to rid the museum of its openly pro-colonial and racist discourses, they could not, and did not, deliver the fundamental change the museum's critics desired.

The RMCA's renovation thus serves as a cautionary tale of the limits of the types of change that can be realised within the colonial museum by embracing the language and praxis of the New Museology. The imperative towards institutional reflexivity, the diversification of voices and narratives within the displays, and forms of co-production, however limited, did leave a positive mark on the new RMCA. The critical commentary on colonial violence and its legacies, the integration of popular cultural production from Central Africa, the presence of African expert and lay voices in multimedia displays, and the interventions from African and diasporic artists in parts of the new exhibition captured some of the transformative potential that had been shown in the preceding temporary exhibitions. The uneven application of these museological interventions throughout the new displays gave rise to what even the museum's director recognised was a disjointed narrative.[82] However, the main problem with the renovation was not the inconsistent implementation of New Museological practices but rather the belief, whether sincere or cynical, among the RMCA leadership that a combination of the insights of the New Museology with the institution's scientific expertise was sufficient to free the museum from the shackles of its coloniality. While many of the concepts and practices associated with the New Museology, including the crucial notion of the 'contact zone', are grounded in drawing attention to and seeking to mitigate the unequal power dynamics within the museum, they have increasingly been 'used instrumentally as a means of masking far more fundamental asymmetries, appropriations, and biases'.[83] This seems to hold true in the case of the RMCA, where, for all the leadership's trumpeting of its embrace of New Museological practices, there was no real reckoning with the enduring coloniality of the epistemologies, the structures, and the power dynamics that defined the museum in the past and the present.

Since the RMCA reopened, the leadership has embraced the language of decolonisation, insisting that the renovation marked the beginning of a 'transition process' of indeterminate length that will eventually transform the museum.[84] For this rhetorical shift to have any practical meaning, the institution must show itself willing to yield some of its authority and engage in a more-than-superficial interrogation of its complicities, past and present, in perpetuating the logics of colonialism in the narrative of its displays, in its collaborative practices, and in its governance of its collections. On this final point, pressure within Belgian society and the broader international heritage community has already led to change within the RMCA. The publication of a report in June 2021 by an independent group of experts, including some professionals who work at the RMCA and members of the COMRAF, advocating for a proactive policy of restitution of heritage acquired in the coercive context of colonial rule fuelled calls for a shift in policy.[85] The announcement in early July 2021 that the Belgian state was committing to the principle of restitution of artefacts acquired 'by force and by violence in illegitimate conditions' met with reactions ranging from enthusiasm to hostility within the museum.[86] Director Gryseels underlined his openness to future restitution, and while he highlighted the practical obstacles that might postpone the process, his acknowledgement that the destiny of these objects post-restitution is a matter for the Congolese alone is an important step towards the kind of renunciation of authority required to decolonise the museum.[87] We have yet, however, to see the kind of critical engagement with decolonising activists and methodologies that has characterised recent practice across Belgium's northern border in the former Dutch colonial Tropenmuseum, where the exhibition's critics were empowered to reimagine the displays.[88] Nor have we seen the RMCA leadership embrace 'the idea of decolonizing', in the words of Wayne Modest, head of the Tropenmuseum's Research Centre for Material Culture, 'as a commitment to the labour to undo [...] an unravelling, or reorganization, or rethinking, a disintegration' of the museum as a colonial institution.[89] As long as its institutional authority remains intact, the museum cannot be said to have begun the process of decolonisation.

The key lesson to be drawn from the story of the RMCA's renovation is that the end goal of processes of grappling with the impact of colonialism across cultural institutions can no longer be the preservation of the institution in the face of shifting societal and museological norms. Instead, the priority must be given to building a new and ethical relationship to the representation, interpretation, and narration of African pasts and presents. This requires a willingness to relinquish control over the systems of knowledge through which African and diasporic experiences are refracted, as well as the authority, institutional and epistemic, to shape their narration, and the collections of objects used to represent them. This type of open-ended and radical programme of change is disruptive, potentially even destructive, to institutions wedded to old structures of governmentality rooted in the colonial past and to neoliberal goal-oriented forms of management embedded in neocolonial presents. Yet the prospect of forging a new and truly universal cultural heritage through a profound rupture with the coloniality of the past and present is surely worth exploring for the RMCA and other institutions in the Global North.

Notes

1. Michel-Rolph Trouillot, *Silencing the Past: Power and the Production of History* (Boston: Beacon, 1995), p. 151.
2. Alex Marshall, 'Belgium's Africa Museum Had a Racist Image. Can It Change That?' *New York Times*, 4 December 2018: https://www.nytimes.com/2018/12/08/arts/design/africa-museum-belgium.html [accessed 15 April 2020]
3. Royal Museum for Central Africa, 'Dossier de Presse, Ouverture de l'AfricaMuseum', 8 December 2018, p. 6, p. 33, p. 35. https://press.africamuseum.be/sites/default/files/media/Persdossier-FR%20web.pdf [Accessed 23 April 2020].
4. Guido Gryseels, Gabrielle Landry and Koeki Claessens, 'Integrating the Past: Transformation and Renovation of the Royal Museum for Central Africa, Tervuren, Belgium', *European Review*, 13.4 (2005), 637–47 (639).
5. Matthew Stanard, *Selling the Congo: A History of European Pro-Empire Propaganda and the Making of Belgian Imperialism* (London: University of Nebraska Press, 2011) and Debora L. Silverman, 'Diasporas of Art: History, the Tervuren Royal Museum for Central Africa, and the Politics of Memory in Belgium, 1885–2014', *The Journal of Modern History*, 87. 3 (2015), 615–67, (622–26).
6. Robert Aldrich, 'Colonial museums in a postcolonial Europe', *African and Black Diaspora: An International Journal*, 2.2 (2009), 137–56 and Dominique Taffin (ed.), *Du Musée colonial au musée des Cultures du monde* (Paris: Maisonneuve et Larose, 2000).
7. Felwine Sarr and Bénédicte Savoy, 'The Restitution of African Cultural Heritage: Towards a New Relational Ethics', Report for President Macron (Paris: November 2018), p. 29.
8. 'Le musée des civilisations noires: une vision d'avenir, Interview de Hamady Bocoum', *Présence Africaine*, 197.1 (2018), 183–94, (186).
9. Gryseels, Landry and Claessens, 'Integrating the Past', p. 646.
10. Bruno Verbergt, 'Transitioning the Museum: Managing Decolonization at the Royal Museum for Central Africa (2000–2020)', *Journal of Cultural Management and Cultural Policy*, 2 (2020), 141–69, (160).
11. Max Ross, 'Interpreting the New Museology', *Museum and Society*, 2.2 (2004), 84–103 (84–85).
12. Robin Boast, 'Neocolonial Collaboration: Museum as Contact Zone Revisited', *Museum Anthropology*, 34.1, 56–70, (67).
13. Vikki McCall and Clive Gray, 'Museums and the 'new museology': theory, practice and organisational change', *Museum Management and Curatorship*, 29.1 (2014), 19–35, (20–21).
14. Laura Peers and Alison K. Brown, 'Introduction', in L. Peers and A. K. Brown (eds.), *Museums and Sources Communities* (London: Routledge, 2003), pp. 1–16.
15. Boast, 'Neocolonial Collaboration', p. 56.
16. Mary Louise Pratt, 'Arts of the Contact Zone', *Profession*, (1991), 33–40, and James Clifford, 'Museums as Contact Zones', in James Clifford (ed.), *Routes: Travel and Translation in the Late Twentieth Century* (Cambridge MA: Harvard University Press, 1997), pp. 188–219.
17. Clifford, 'Museums as Contact Zones', p. 194.
18. Ibid., p. 218.
19. Gryseels, Landry, and Claessens, 'Integrating the Past', p. 639.
20. Ibid., p. 645.
21. Guido Gryseels, 'Towards the Renewal and the Renovation of the Royal Museum for Central Africa', Paper Presented at the Africa-Atlanta 2014 Conference, p. 9. https://leading-edge.iac.gatech.edu/aaproceedings/towards-the-renewal-and-the-renovation-of-the-royal-museum-for-central-africa/ [accessed 20/04/2021]
22. Gryseels, Landry, and Claessens, 'Integrating the Past', p. 643.
23. Hein Vanhee, 'On Shared Heritage and Its (False) Promises', *African Arts*, 49.3 (2016), 1–7 (7).
24. Ibid.
25. Aurélie Roger, 'D'une mémoire coloniale à une mémoire du colonial. La reconversion chaotique du Musée Royal de l'Afrique Centrale, ancien musée du Congo Belge', *Cadernos de Estudos Africanos*, 9.10 (2006), 43–75, (49–50).
26. Toma Muteba Luntumbue, 'Finding Means to Cannibalise the Anthropological Museum', in Margareta von Oswald and Jonas Tinius (eds.), *Across Anthropology: Troubling Colonial Legacies, Museums, and the Curatorial* (Leuven: Leuven University Press, 2020), pp. 174–85, (p. 179).
27. Roger, 'D'une mémoire coloniale', p. 6.
28. For positive assessments of the exhibition see: Jean-Pierre Chrétien, 'Le passé colonial: le devoir d'histoire', *Politique africaine*, 98.2 (2005), 141–48 and Matthew G. Standard, *The Leopard, the Lion, and the Cock Colonial Memories and Monuments in Belgium* (Leuven: Leuven University Press, 2019), pp. 196–97. For critical assessments see: Jan-Bart Gewald, 'More than Red Rubber and Figures Alone: A Critical Appraisal of the Memory of the Congo Exhibition at the Royal Museum for Central Africa, Tervuren, Belgium', *The International Journal of African Historical Studies*, 39.3 (2006), 471–86 and Antoine Tshitungu Kongolo, 'La mémoire du Congo: les manqués d'une expo', *La Libre Belqique*, 27 April 2005.

29. Silverman, 'Diasporas of Art', p. 631.
30. Véronique Bragard, '"Indépendance!": The Belgo-Congolese Dispute in the Tervuren Museum', *Human Architecture: Journal of the Sociology of Self-Knowledge*, 9.4 (2011), 93–104, (98).
31. Bambi Ceuppens, 'From Colonial Subjects/Objects to Citizens: The Royal Museum for Central Africa as Contact-Zone', in Francesca Lanz and Elena Montanari (eds.), *Advancing Museum Practices* (Turin: Umberto Allemandi & C., 2014), pp. 83–99 (p. 96).
32. Ibid., p. 94.
33. The concept of 'decolonisation' as a cultural process or museological strategy does not appear in the museum's annual reports until 2016. Reports are available from 2002 onwards on the museum's website: https://www.africamuseum.be/en/about_us/annual_reports [accessed 01/06/2021].
34. Verbergt, 'Transitioning the Museum', p. 148.
35. Aimé Césaire, *Discours sur le colonialisme* (Paris: Présence Africaine, 1955), p. 35.
36. Ibid., p,13.
37. Aníbal Quijano, 'Coloniality of Power, Eurocentrism, and Latin America', *Nepantla*, 1 (2000), 533–80.
38. Boaventura de Sousa Santos, *Epistemologies of the South: Justice Against Epistemicide* (London: Routledge, 2014).
39. Walter D. Mignolo, 'DELINKING: The rhetoric of modernity, the logic of coloniality and the grammar of decoloniality', *Cultural Studies*, 21.2–3 (2007), 449–514.
40. For an exploration of the connection between Rhodes Must Fall and decolonial thought see Sabelo J. Ndlovu-Gatsheni, *Epistemic Freedom in Africa: Deprovincialization and Decolonization* (New York: Routledge, 2018), pp. 221–42. For Mbembe on the colonial museum see *Necropolitics*, trans. S. Corcoran (Durham, NC: Duke University Press, 2019), pp. 170–72.
41. Amy Lonetree, 'Museums as Sites of Decolonization; Truth Telling in National and Tribal Museums', in Susan Sleeper-Smith (ed.), *Contesting Knowledge: Museums and Indigenous Perspectives* (London: University of Nebraska Press, 2009), pp. 322–38 (323).
42. The article is mentioned in Ceuppens, 'From Colonial Subjects/Objects', p. 95.
43. Boast, 'Neocolonial Collaboration', p. 62.
44. Ibid., p. 67.
45. Gryseels, 'Towards the Renewal and the Renovation', pp. 11–12.
46. Arnaud Limond-Mertes, 'Tervuren rénové, une lecture critique', *Ensemble!*, 99 (2019), 63–72 (67).
47. Arnaud Limond-Mertes,'Un espace de démonstration du "génie du colonialisme": Interview avec Elikia M'Bokolo', *Ensemble!*, 99 (2019), 49–55 (52).
48. Lismond-Mertes, '"Une renovation ratée"', p. 35.
49. Achille Mbembe, 'La vérité est que l'Europe nous a pris des choses qu'elle ne pourra jamais restituer', *Le Monde*, 01 December 2018.
50. Mireille-Tshuesi Robert, 'Lettre ouverte au musée colonial du Congo à tervuren. Comment osez-vous ?!', https://6274c06d-5149-4618-88b2-ac2fdc6ef62d.filesusr.com/ugd/3d95e3_61db44196fa84233852196b4aa4552c5.pdf [accessed 04 June 2021].
51. Limond-Mertes,'Un espace de démonstration du "génie du colonialisme"', p. 52.
52. Limond-Mertes, 'Tervuren rénové, une lecture critique', p. 69.
53. Ibid., pp. 66–67.
54. Verbergt, 'Transitioning the Museum', p. 160.
55. Arnaud Lismond-Mertes, '"Nous connaissons un succès spectaculaire": Interview avec Guido Gryseels', *Ensemble!*, 99 (2019), 24–31 (26).
56. RMCA, 'Dossier de Presse, Ouverture de l'AfricaMuseum', p. 9.
57. Nouria Ouali, 'Muséologie et colonialité du pouvoir. L'exemple de la « participation » des diasporas africaines au processus de rénovation du Musée royal de l'Afrique centrale de Tervuren', *Migrations Société*, 182.4 (2020), 77–95 (86).
58. Gratia Pungu, 'N'est pas post-colonial qui veut… La postcolonie, une alternative muséale utopique', https://6274c06d-5149-4618-88b2-ac2fdc6ef62d.filesusr.com/ugd/3d95e3_e5ff44323157448283e04058bc9cf6ee.pdf [accessed 04 May 2021].
59. Arnaud Lismond-Mertes, '"Comprenez notre déception": Interview avec Billy Kalonji', *Ensemble!*, 99 (2019), 37–38.
60. Sumaya Kassim, 'The Museum Will Not Be Decolonised', *Media Diversified*, 15 November 2017, https://mediadiversified.org/2017/11/15/the-museum-will-not-be-decolonised/ [accessed 04 May 2019].
61. Anne Wetsi Mpoma, 'Quand le temple dédié à la colonisation belge fait peau neuve', https://docs.wixstatic.com/ugd/3d95e3_86cdb150e1844154bc756110001487f6.pdf [accessed 04 May 2019].
62. Lismond-Mertes, '"Une renovation ratée"', p. 36.
63. Lismond-Mertes, '"Comprenez notre déception"', p. 38.
64. Verbergt, 'Transitioning the Museum', p. 163.
65. Cédric Vallet, 'Musée de Tervuren: Décolonisation Impossible?' *Médor*, 10 December 2018, https://medor.coop/fr/articles/reportage-musee-tervuren-Congo-MRAC-colonialisme/ [accessed 04 May 2019].
66. Lismond-Mertes, '"Une rénovation ratée"', p. 36.
67. Boast, Neocolonial Collaboration', pp. 66–67.
68. Sarah Demart, 'Resisting Extraction Politics: Afro-Belgian Claims, Women's Activism, and the Royal Museum for Central Africa', in *Across*

69. *Anthropology*, ed. by van Oswald and Tinius, pp. 143–72, p. 149.
70. Sarah van Beurden, 'Museum renovation and the politics of collection and possession', https://africasacountry.com/2019/04/renovating-the-africamuseum, [accessed 03 May 2021].
71. Ibid.
72. Sarah Van Beurden, 'The Art of (Re)Possession: Heritage and The Cultural Politics of Congo's Decolonization', *The Journal of African History*, 56.1 (2015), 143–64.
73. Ibid., p. 158.
74. Robert, 'Lettre ouverte'.
75. 'Carte blanche: Le dialogue sur les trésors coloniaux doit l'emporter sur le paternalisme', *Le Soir*, 17 October 2018, https://www.lesoir.be/185112/article/2018-10-17/carte-blanche-le-dialogue-sur-les-tresors-coloniaux-doit-lemporter-sur-le [accessed 05 May 2019].
76. See Dónal Hassett, 'Acknowledging or Occluding "The System of Violence"? The Representation of Colonial Pasts and Presents in Belgium's AfricaMuseum', *Journal of Genocide Research*, 22.1 (2020), 26–45 (41).
77. Michel Bouffioux, 'Guido Gryseels, directeur du Musée de l'Afrique centrale: « C'est le moment du débat »', http://www.lusingatabwa.com/2018/03/guido-gryseels-directeur-du-musee-de-l-afrique-centrale-c-est-le-moment-du-debat.html [accessed 06 May 2019].
78. Achille Mbembe, 'À propos de la restitution des artefacts africains conservés dans les musées d'Occident', *Analyse Opinion Critique*, 5 October 2018, https://aoc.media/analyse/2018/10/05/a-propos-de-restitution-artefacts-africains-conserves-musees-doccident/ [accessed 05 May 2019].
79. Bouffioux, 'Guido Gryseels, directeur du Musée'.
80. Lismond-Mertes, '"Nous connaissons un succès spectaculaire"', p. 29.
81. Verbergt, 'Transitioning the Museum', pp. 158–60.
82. Gryseels, Landry, and Claessens, 'Integrating the Past', p. 639.
83. Lismond-Mertes, '"Nous connaissons un succès spectaculaire"', p. 29.
84. Boast, 'Neocolonial Collaboration', p. 67.
85. Verbergt, 'Transitioning the Museum', pp. 158–60.
86. Restitution Belgium, 'Ethical Principles for the Management and Restitution of Colonial Collections in Belgium', (Restitution Belgium, 2021), https://restitutionbelgium.be/en/report [accessed 07 July 2021]
87. Ghizlane Kounda, 'La Belgique présente sa politique de restitution des œuvres: « Une approche systémique qui permet d'éviter de restituer au cas par cas »', *RTBF Info*, 07 July 2021, https://www.rtbf.be/info/monde/detail_la-belgique-presente-sa-politique-de-restitution-des-uvres-une-approche-systemique-qui-permet-d-eviter-de-restituer-au-cas-par-cas?id=10798431 [accessed 08 July 2021].
88. Ibid.
89. Iris Van Huis, 'Contesting Cultural Heritage: Decolonizing the Tropenmuseum as an Intervention in the Dutch/European Memory Complex', in Tuuli Lähdesmäki, Luisa Passerini, Sigrid Kaasik-Krogerus and Iris van Huis (eds.), *Dissonant Heritages and Memories in Contemporary Europe* (London: Palgrave Macmillan, 2019), pp. 215–48, (pp. 226–42).
90. Wayne Modest, 'Decolonizing Museums in Practice Part 3', *American Anthropologist*, https://www.americananthropologist.org/podcast/decolonizing-museums-in-practice-part-3 [accessed 30 June 2021].

Imperial Fictions

Belgian Novels about Rwanda

Nicki Hitchcott

On 7 April 1994, the day after the shooting down of the Rwandan presidential plane, which triggered the genocide against the Tutsi, fifteen UN peacekeepers were stationed outside Prime Minister Agathe Uwiligiyimana's home when the house came under attack from the Rwandan Armed Forces. The prime minister and her husband were both killed trying to escape, and all the blue helmets were captured. Five of the peacekeepers were from Ghana, ten from Belgium. While the Ghanaians were released almost immediately, the ten Belgian paratroopers were taken to the Kigali Military Camp where they were brutally murdered in ways that mirrored the killings of the Tutsi in the genocide.[1] Belgium responded by withdrawing all its troops, leaving the UN peacekeeping forces in Rwanda (UNAMIR) seriously undermined. According to Danielle de Lame, the assassination of the blue helmets forced Belgium into a difficult confrontation with its colonial past:

> The killing of the ten Belgian paratroopers on the very day the genocide started, and under gruesome circumstances akin to those of the other killings of the day, made Belgians suddenly discover the hatred felt for them by a people whose love they had taken for granted and from whom they expected gratitude.[2]

Two years later, the Belgian Senate's Foreign Affairs Commission launched a parliamentary inquiry into Belgium's role in the events in Rwanda in 1994 and into who was responsible for the deaths of the UN peacekeepers.[3]

Prepared by then Senate Vice Presidents Guy Verhofstadt and Philippe Mahoux, the report from the 1996–97 parliamentary inquiry points out that both the murder of the ten Belgian paratroopers and the genocide itself were perpetrated by Rwandans.[4] According to the report, the motive for killing the soldiers was to destabilise the UN peacekeeping force, but it also acknowledges that the killings could have been a reaction to rumours that Belgium had been responsible for shooting down the presidential plane. While the report does conclude that 'with hindsight, the international community, and some of its components, including Belgium, failed in April 1994', it presents Belgians as the victims, evidenced not only by the murder of the UN soldiers but also by the murder of Belgian citizens and what is described as the 'anti-Belgian climate' in Rwanda at the time. The 'anti-Belgian climate' is explained in the report as Rwanda's reaction to Belgium's refusal to deliver arms that Rwanda had paid for at the start of the 1990 Civil War, and the withdrawal of all Belgian troops in April 1994. The impact of Belgian's colonial past is examined only in relation to the failure of the peacekeeping forces to abide by the unwritten rule that, for reasons of neutrality, UN troops should not be deployed from former colonial powers.

Belgium's deep entanglement with Rwanda dates to World War I, when Germany lost control of the territory of Ruanda-Urundi in 1916. Formalised in 1922 by the League of Nations, Belgium's mandate to govern lasted forty years, ending in 1962 when Rwanda became independent. Yet reflections on the Belgian empire almost always overlook Rwanda, particularly in public discourse. While Belgium as a colonial power has increasingly been the subject of postcolonial scholarship, particularly in the last thirty years, this work has focused on King Leopold II and the former Belgian Congo.[5] Indeed, Belgium's forty-year long colonial rule of both Rwanda and Burundi seems to have been, for the most part, conveniently forgotten. This is confirmed by Idesbald Goddeeris, for whom 'a decolonisation of the [Belgian] mind has yet to occur' because Belgium lacks the 'dynamic memory policy' and 'vivid postcolonial debate' of its European neighbours.[6]

Writing specifically about the Congo, Goddeeris explains Belgium's postcolonial exceptionalism partly by the fact that migration to the country from the former empire is much lower than in, for example, France or the United Kingdom.[7] Yet, despite the small size of its migrant population, Belgium has become what Camilla Orjuela calls 'a center for Rwandan diaspora activism' over the past twenty-six years.[8] In 2010, there were forty thousand Rwandans in Belgium, mostly in Brussels, many of whom had migrated there after 1994.[9] Today, the Rwandan community in Belgium includes survivors, bystanders, opponents, and perpetrators of the genocide as well as children from each of these groups. This diversity, as Orjuela explains, generates contrasting, often highly conflictual versions of how the shared past is remembered.[10] Most recently, in July 2020, following the rise of the Black Lives Movement in Belgium, the Belgian government announced its decision to set up a truth and reconciliation commission to investigate its colonial past. The only Rwandan member of the commission is Brussels-based lawyer Laure Uwase, whose father, Anastase Nkundakozera, was convicted of crimes of genocide in a Rwandan Gacaca court. Uwase is the former secretary general of Jambo ASBL, a Rwandan youth movement based in

Belgium and, according to Tutsi survivors, a platform for negationists. The very different versions of Rwanda's story in the Belgian diaspora are further complicated by the memory narrative constructed by the former colonial power and reproduced in different Belgian media. In this essay, I focus on how the Belgian colonial master narrative of colonial complacency and post-colonial silence has been translated into three fictional texts about Rwanda, all written by authors from Belgium and published between 1997 and 2018.[11]

Since 1994, there has been a significant number of creative responses to the genocide from authors inside and outside Rwanda. The best-known novels are those produced by the team of writers who took part in the 1998 'Writing with a Duty to Memory' literary mission, but there are also twelve writers born in Rwanda who have produced important works of fiction about the genocide.[12] While much has been written about the texts produced by that project, and my own research has focused on fictional works by authors born in Rwanda, little attention has been given to creative writing about the genocide from inside the former colonial power.[13] This essay makes a first attempt to address that critical gap by focusing on literary production by authors from Belgium, beginning with a discussion of the new edition of Joseph Ndwaniye's novel *La Promesse à ma sœur*.[14] While Ndwaniye's novel is in a slightly different category of Belgian novel in that its author is originally from Rwanda, the new edition includes extensive paratextual apparatus by a Belgium-born writer and is accompanied by an online pedagogical dossier also compiled by a Belgian.[15] The other two texts are both by Belgian writers born in Belgium: Huguette de Broqueville's *Uraho? Es-tu toujours vivant*, published in 1997, just three years after the genocide against the Tutsi, and Bernard Dan's more recent 2014 novel, *Le Garçon du Rwanda*.[16] The conclusion will draw together what these rather different works of fiction tell us about Belgium's past and present relationship with Rwanda and reflect on the ethical implications of these fictional representations of Rwanda's postcolonial history. Underpinning the discussion is Madelaine Hron's important point that the key function of fiction about Rwanda in 1994 is an ethical one, which she defines as,

> not only to represent genocide, but also to resist the exterminationist ideology which engendered it. In the case of Rwanda, this genocidal ideology, founded on ethnic divisionism between Hutu and Tutsi, again derives from a complex causality – be it the ethnographic Hamitic myth, Belgian colonial nepotism, the post-independence pogroms and exile of the Tutsi, or Anglophone and Francophone neocolonial interventions – which writers of *itsembabwoko* must somehow address, simplify and resist in their works.[17]

Joseph Ndwaniye, *La Promesse faite à ma sœur*

Ndwaniye's debut novel, *La Promesse faite à ma sœur*, in which the protagonist returns to Rwanda in 2003 to find out what happened to his family during the genocide, was first published in 2006 by Brussels-based publisher Les Impressions Nouvelles.[18] In 2018, the publisher reprinted the novel as part of its 'Espace Nord' collection, defined as 'the Belgian heritage collection'.[19] A link from the publisher's website takes you the Espace Nord pages, where the collection is described as 'entirely devoted to the francophone literature of Belgium' and 'a useful tool for discovering and promoting Belgian authors'.[20]

Among a list of over one hundred authors in this collection, Ndwaniye is one of only two writers of African origin.[21] Yet, despite his Rwandan roots, the website presents him as a Belgian author, incorporated into the literary canon of the former colonial power.[22] The decision to move Ndwaniye's novel into the Espace Nord collection suggests that the francophone administration has finally recognised the need for Belgian people, particularly secondary school children, to acknowledge and understand what happened in Rwanda, using fiction as an entry point for discussion.[23] Books in the collection are primarily aimed at Belgian schoolteachers and their students. In this case, the reprinted text of *La Promesse faite à ma sœur* is followed by a thirty-page dossier by Belgian poet and librarian Rony Demaeseneer. This includes an essay with a glossary of Kinyarwanda words, an interview with Joseph Ndwaniye, and a bibliography of French-language works consulted.[24] In addition to the materials provided in the published book, each title in the collection has its own pedagogical dossier that can be freely downloaded from the Espace Nord website.[25] The online dossier to accompany Ndwaniye's novel was published one year later than the new printed edition and coincided with the twenty-fifth anniversary of the genocide against the Tutsi.

Although there is little academic scholarship on *La Promesse faite à ma sœur*, it is an important fictional response to the genocide against the Tutsi.[26] Written by an exiled Hutu author, it carefully illustrates the complex nature of Rwandan subject positions in relation to the genocide. While there is no autobiographical pact as such, there are many similarities between Ndwaniye's own story and that of his narrator-protagonist Jean Seneza. Rather than describe the horror of what happened in 1994, the novel focuses on before and mostly after the genocide, illustrating the difficulties faced by those who were absent witnesses in coming to terms with what happened.[27] When he returns to Rwanda, Jean finds out that his sister and her children have all been killed, but his twin brother, Thomas, is now in prison, accused of crimes of genocide. As a result of his journey home, Jean finds himself in an ambivalent position, associated with an alleged perpetrator who, as his twin brother, is the man who most resembles himself, but Jean is also what some might see as a Hutu survivor by destination, since other members of his family were attacked and killed.[28] After revisiting his birth country, Jean finds himself wondering what he would have done if he had still been living in Rwanda during the genocide.

The ethical ramifications of this grey zone in which many Rwandans found themselves during and after 1994 inform some of the suggested activities in the book's accompanying pedagogical dossier, which tries to find a balance between reflecting on the universal questions raised by the novel (about guilt, forgiveness, and responsibility) and the need to educate secondary school students about the specific nature of the genocide against the Tutsi. While it does a reasonable job of presenting some of the key facts in Rwandan history, what is troubling about the contents of the pedagogical dossier is the way in which it underplays the role of the Belgian colonial administration in the history of the genocide. In this respect, it reflects the content of Ndwaniye's novel, in which the afterlife of colonialism is presented only in terms of the narrator's Belgian childhood friends in his home village and his eventual decision to leave Rwanda to study and later work in Brussels.

In the online dossier, racist ideas about Hutu and Tutsi are traced back to missionaries, explorers, and anthropologists. These racist ideas, the dossier informs us, included the infamous Hamitic hypothesis, which identified Tutsi as Caucasian outsiders who were closer to the Whites than the majority Bantu Hutu and therefore superior to them: 'The basis of the racist Hamitic ideology was quite simply invented by the White Fathers who wrote what became the official version of the History of Rwanda in line with their essentially racist points of view'.[29] While the Hamitic hypothesis does indeed have its roots in the scientific racism of the nineteenth century, and the Catholic missionaries (White Fathers) did play an important part in this, it was the Belgian colonial authorities who institutionalised the imagined ethnic categories that became so important in the genocide against the Tutsi, as René Lemarchand reminds us:

> In its efforts to make more 'legible' the complex ethnic configurations of the [Great Lakes] region, the colonial state contributed significantly to formalizing and legitimizing the Hutu-Tutsi polarity. [...] Time and again historians have drawn attention to the perverse effects of the colonizer's recourse to Hamitic and Bantu labels, as if to impose its own normative construction on Hutu and Tutsi.[30]

From the beginning of its period of colonial rule, and in collaboration with the White Fathers, Belgium began to draw up 'race policies' for Rwanda.[31] Yet the dossier attempts to disculpate the Belgian colonial administration by emphasising that they were simply carrying on a system of division that was already in place: 'The Belgians were so impressed by this natural order of things that a series of administrative measures taken between 1926 and 1932 institutionalised the division between the two races'.[32] To suggest that the implementation of Belgium's colonial reforms, which included the 1933 classification of the whole country's population based on physical characteristics, was simply following the 'natural order of things' is to repeat a colonial lie, as Mahmood Mamdani explains:

> It is Belgian reform of the colonial state in the decade from the mid-1920s to the mid-1930s that constructed Hutu as *indigenous* Bantu and Tutsi as *alien* Hamites. It is also Belgian colonialism that made for a political history in Rwanda different from that in standard indirect rule colonies, like Uganda and Congo, in tropical Africa.[33]

Through their reforms, the Belgian colonial authorities racialised what had previously been a mobile socio-political distinction in Rwanda, thereby pitting Hutu against Tutsi. Later, Belgium's shifting support from the Tutsi minority elite to the dissatisfied Hutu majority played a key role in fomenting the anti-Tutsi ideology that drove the 1994 genocide.[34] Gérard Prunier notes that, from the very beginning of the 'Muyaga' or the so-called 'Social Revolution' of 1959, 'the Belgian authorities showed extreme partiality for Hutu, even letting them burn Tutsi houses without intervening'.[35] As Rwanda hurtled towards independence amid sporadic violence and waves of Tutsi emigration to neighbouring countries, the UN strongly encouraged Brussels to push for reconciliation in Rwanda.[36] Belgium responded by declaring a state of emergency and placing Rwanda under the command of Guy Logiest, a Belgian army colonel who had been working with the Force Publique in the Congo.[37] Alongside Grégoire Kayibanda, the leader of the Party of the Hutu Emancipation Movement (PARMEHUTU), Logiest managed to keep the UN at bay and establish what a UN Trusteeship Commission Report described in March 1961 as 'the racial dictatorship of one party' – the PARMEHUTU or 'Hutu Power'.[38]

While the online dossier includes a sample of the Hutu ten commandments that served as a manifesto for Hutu Power, there is no mention that the 1959 'social revolution' was, as Lemarchand puts it, 'powerfully assisted if not engineered by the Belgian authorities'.[39] Instead, we learn that in 1946 Belgium signed an agreement with the UN for Ruanda-Urundi to become independent; this despite the fact that the 1950s was a time of massive Hutu unrest, encouraged by both Flemish-speaking missionaries and the francophone Belgian colonial authorities. Tutsi chiefs were replaced with Hutu, and many Tutsi were massacred in the run-up to the so-called social revolution. None of this is mentioned. After independence, the pedagogical dossier moves swiftly on to the genocide itself, with no further mention of Belgium at all, not even the much-publicised killing of the ten Belgian peacekeepers that I used to open this essay, and which, according to de Lame, caused a sea change in the way Belgians thought about Rwanda. Suddenly, the 'self-confidence and paternalism', which, de Lame argues, had previously characterised Belgium's view of its colonial past in Rwanda, were shattered when Belgian lives were brutally taken.[40] This sense of betrayal on the part of the coloniser is strongly conveyed in the second novel under discussion: Huguette de Broqueville's novel *Uraho? Es-tu toujours vivant*, published in 1997, just three years after the genocide.

Huguette de Broqueville, *Uraho? Es-tu toujours vivant?*

De Broqueville was born in Rochefort, Belgium, in 1931 and died in 2015. Like Joseph Ndwaniye, she was a member of the francophone PEN club of Belgium, serving as the club's president for several years. She was a prolific and award-winning writer and journalist, with *Uraho? Es-tu toujours vivant* her most successful novel. *Uraho?* has been translated into Hungarian, Romanian, and Finnish and, although de Broqueville was not herself a Christian, won the Prix des Scriptores Christiani (the Belgian association of Christian writers) in 1998 and the Prix Henri Davignon de l'Académie royale de langue et de littérature françaises de Belgique in 2000. *Uraho?* is also the only Belgian novel about the genocide listed in the literary works section of Colette Braeckman's entry on Rwanda in Prem Poddar, Rajeev Patke, and Lars Jensen's 2008 *Historical Companion to Postcolonial Literatures – Continental Europe and Its Empires*.[41] Despite all this recognition, *Uraho?* has received relatively little academic attention outside Belgian literary circles. According to Pierre Halen, the lack of scholarship on de Broqueville's novel can be explained simply by the fact that it was published in Belgium.[42]

Uraho? recounts a woman's relationship with her only brother, an unnamed Belgian priest posted in Rwanda before, during, and after the genocide against the Tutsi. Like Ndwaniye's novel, *Uraho?* can be categorised as auto-fiction.[43] Indeed, the preface by French writer and diplomat Pierre de Boisdeffre removes any ambiguity around the author and narrator as one and the same when he attributes lines from the first-person narration to de Broqueville herself.[44] My own research into de Broqueville's family tree has identified her brother as Ferdinand Drion du Chapois, a White Father who died on 25 November 1994, having spent twenty-eight years as a missionary in Rwanda.[45] Through its first-person narrative, *Uraho?* conveys both the author's grief for her dead brother, but also

Belgium's and the Catholic Church's mourning for the colonial territory of Ruanda-Urundi that, as de Lame implies, was only finally lost in April 1994, despite Rwanda having been independent since 1962.

Catholicism in Rwanda dates to the founding of the first mission in 1900, but Christianity did not really begin to take hold until the interwar period when Belgium took control.[46] The Catholic Church was an important part of the Belgian colonial apparatus, which drew on the White Fathers' knowledge of the country and its language to cultivate a Rwandan elite based on 'ethnic' differences that the churches helped to define. According to Timothy Longman, 'churches helped make genocide possible by making ethnic violence understandable and acceptable to the population'.[47] By 1932, the Catholic Church was the main social institution in Rwanda, and it controlled the education system, which clearly differentiated Tutsi from Hutu.[48] By 1994 around 90 per cent of Rwandans were Christian and 60 per cent Roman Catholic.[49] As the number of Rwandan Catholics grew in the post-war period, the church leaders simultaneously followed the colonial authorities in switching allegiance from Tutsi to Hutu and focusing on developing a new counter-elite (see Chantal Gishoma's chapter in this volume). As Longman notes, churches have always been 'important actors' in Rwanda's political struggles.[50] Much has been written about the roles of individual priests during the genocide, particularly those who colluded with the *génocidaires* in the execution of thousands of people who had fled to the churches for safety only to become victims of large-scale and bloody massacres.[51] Whereas some priests were targeted as opponents of the genocidal government's policies, others were complicit in crimes of genocide. Two thirds of the Catholic priests working in Rwanda in 1994 were either killed or fled. Many of those who remained in the country openly condemned the Rwandan Patriotic Front (RPF) and voiced support for the interim genocidal government.[52]

In his preface to de Broqueville's *Uraho?*, Boisdeffre presents Rwanda as a failed colonial project and, in doing so, points to the strong alliance between church and state in the colonial period. According to the narrator, 'What was astonishing was that these people had for a long time been patiently educated, trained and Christianised by a white coloniser'.[53] While Halen reads the colonialist exoticism of Boisdeffre as completely at odds with de Broqueville's writing, I find that de Broqueville's narrator continues the 'us and them' colonial racism that Halen identifies in Boisdeffre's preface.[54] The narrative switches from the benevolent paternalism towards Rwanda found in earlier imperial fictions, such as Ivan Reisdorff's 1978 pseudo-detective novel, *L'Homme qui demanda du feu*, to rage at what the narrator presents as ingratitude for the civilising mission performed by people like her brother.[55] In the closing pages of *Uraho!*, the narrator describes a photograph of her brother in the classic pose of a 'white saviour':

'An image of my brother surrounded by Rwandan children. And he is smiling. Wearing a sunhat, his eternal sunhat'.[56] Rwandan people are described first in generic, racist terms as 'magnificently brown or black Africans', in harmony with the earth (p. 24), polite and deferential to the White Father's sister, always smiling (p. 30), and then as oversexed, bloodthirsty killers for whom killing and sex have become inextricably linked (p. 96).

Uraho? is a novel filled with violence. Unlike Ndwaniye, de Broqueville does not seem to be prevented by her position as a secondary witness from providing often extremely graphic descriptions of acts of genocide. For example, one scene describes Antoine, a member of the *interahamwe* militia, slicing body parts from Alfred, a Tutsi man who was once his friend, in front of Alfred's wife and children. His fellow militiaman Cyprien then kills Alfred's wife with a blow to her carotid artery, at which point the narrator observes, 'the children see the blood gush out like a fountain in spring, a burst of red from a wild orchid as the mother lets out a scream' (p. 87). The poetic language used to describe this violent act is uncomfortable for the reader, but at the same time, the reference to an exotic flower reminds us of our comfortable distance from the horrific events described.

While de Broqueville makes some attempt to emphasise the universalism of genocide and our collective guilt in the case of Rwanda, the text falls repeatedly back into racialised differentiation. For example, in describing some Rwandan women watching acts of violence, the narrator compares their impotence with that of 'us', the readers, who also did nothing to stop the massacres:

> If we were not able to do anything, if the world has criticised us for doing nothing, we feel guilty because we too are **capable** of those same atrocities. There lies the secret of our guilt. There lies the hypocrisy of those who bombard us with criticism. **Them and us, we are all capable of the worst.** (p. 91)[57]

The suggestion that 'we' could not have done anything to stop the violence absolves Belgium and its people from any responsibility for what happened in Rwanda. Paradoxically, the text's insistence on the fact that there is something inherently human about crimes of genocide ('we are all capable of the worst'), reinforces the *Heart of Darkness* myth that has become a cliché in studies of the Great Lakes region and was the founding myth of the European colonial mission: 'No animal would do that. [...] Not animals, not savages, not monsters, we are human. Plain and simple' (p. 91). Ironically, the apparent dismissal of the language of colonial racism ('not animals, not savages') serves only to reinforce the distance between 'them' and 'us'. De Broqueville's Rwanda is stained with blood, with a 'black fury that can be described not as bestial but as human'

(p. 91). The reader infers that 'we' could not have done anything to stop the violence because 'we' are different from 'them' – this despite the repeated mention of our common humanity.

De Broqueville's reader sees Rwanda through the first-person narrator's imperial gaze, itself a vision refracted through that of her brother, the White Father. At the end of May 1994, her brother is evacuated to Belgium for his own safety, only to return in October 1994 once the genocide is over. When her brother finally dies of despair in post-genocide Rwanda, de Broqueville surrounds his death with an excess of Christian imagery. Rwanda under the RPF is compared to the garden of Gethsemane, the brother's return to the stations of the cross (p. 127), and his death is presented as a Christlike sacrifice: 'He offered up his suffering and his life for Rwanda' (p. 130). Furthermore, the brother's despair and subsequent death is closely linked in the novel to the victory of the RPF, the exiled Tutsi army who invaded Rwanda in October 1990, thereby launching the Civil War, and who fought the *interahamwe* and the Rwandan Armed Forces to end the genocide in July 1994. After listing a catalogue of RPF crimes against Hutu, which her brother apparently discovers (p. 127), the narrator concludes with a description of the RPF as a group of elegantly dressed liars: 'Immaculately groomed, the RPF categorically denies everything. Keep lying and something of the truth will always remain, as Voltaire said. My brother died because of it' (p. 128). By suggesting a causal effect between the actions of the RPF and the death of the White Father, the text reveals the political allegiances of the Catholic Church in Rwanda, which Mamdani describes as 'both the brains and the hands of the colonial state' (p. 99).

In August 1994, twenty-seven priests exiled in the DRC wrote to the Vatican presenting the genocide as an interethnic conflict and condemning the RPF:

> To speak of genocide and to insinuate that only Hutus killed Tutsis is to be ignorant that Hutus and Tutsis have been each others' [*sic*] executioners. We dare even to confirm that the number of Hutu civilians killed by the army of the RPF exceeds by far the number of Tutsi victims of the ethnic troubles.[58]

Immediately after the genocide, the relationship between the Belgium government and the RPF was, as Rachel Hayman explains, one of 'mutual distrust'.[59] For the RPF leadership, this lack of trust was based on Belgium's past support of Hutu Power and the genocidal regime in Rwanda as well as their withdrawal of UN troops during the genocide. Belgium, on the other hand, lacked confidence in the RPF's ability to stabilise Rwanda, a feeling that was strengthened when Rwanda become involved in massacres in the Democratic Republic of the Congo in the late 1990s.[60] In *Uraho?* Belgian distrust of the RPF is further reflected in the text's descriptions of RPF soldiers as devils and snakes (p. 125). Whereas Halen reads the abundance of diabolical imagery in de Broqueville's novel as a manifestation of the self-proclaimed agnostic author's inability to contemplate tragedy caused by human actions,[61] the association of these images with the RPF also suggests an internalisation of the Hutu Power mythology that the RPF were devils with long tails, cloven hoofs, and big ears, and that all Tutsi were snakes.[62]

Focusing on the Congo, Georgi Verbeeck identifies two central paradigms in Belgian colonial memory narratives: the first he describes as 'the loss of our Congo', characterised by nostalgia, heroisation, and a positioning of the colonial power as undeserved victim of the failure of its civilising mission; the second, the 'innocence thesis', presents Belgium as too small to have played a significant role in decolonisation and presents Belgian people as the targets of violence.[63] Both of these are played out in de Broqueville's novel in relation to Rwanda. Perhaps most problematic is the equivalence suggested in this text between the Tutsi and the Belgians as innocent victims in 1994. We see this in repeated scenes where the narrator's brother is threatened by the *interahamwe* for being *umubiligi* ['Belgian' in Kinyarwanda] and, of course, in his ultimate death, presented as an indirect result of RPF war crimes.

Bernard Dan, Le Garçon du Rwanda

Whereas in both the new edition of *La Promesse faite à ma sœur* and *Uraho? Es-tu toujours vivant*, the damage inflicted on Rwanda through forty years of Belgian control does not receive a mention, Bernard Dan's enigmatic novel *Le Garçon du Rwanda* does make reference to Belgium's role in Rwanda.[64] However, the genocide against the Tutsi is not the main focus of *Le Garçon du Rwanda*, which was published in 2014 by French independent publisher Les Editions de l'Aube. Although the author is Belgian and based in Brussels, where he also works as a paediatric neurologist, the novel is set in Paris, where the first-person narrator, Esther Lyon, spends much of her time in a sleep clinic, hoping to be cured of her extreme insomnia. In the clinic, she meets Camille Boulanger, the eponymous 'garçon du Rwanda', whom she had once met in a hospital waiting room in 1994, and who is now working as a polysomnographic technician, someone who specialises in the diagnosis and treatment of sleep disorders. The narrative unfolds around the friendship between the two characters, who end up spending nights together at the clinic exchanging stories and watching DVDs. Not until two thirds of the way into the novel is any real mention made of the genocide in Rwanda. It is then introduced by the author in a rather heavy-handed manner when Esther randomly picks, as a DVD for them to watch, Sydney Pollack's 1982 feature film, *Tootsie*:

> Quite by chance I pulled out a DVD with a title in the worst possible taste: *Tootsie*. Think about it! Camille hadn't yet told me that staggering Belgian story, the one about the identity cards identifying an individual as Tutsi from one generation to the next: tall, with a small nose, lighter skin or even the owner of at least ten cows. That arbitrary label, permanent and hereditary, was very useful to the colonial power in the collection of taxes and for organising the colonised people's society on its own terms, then reorganising it on a whim. It was also terrifyingly practical in helping the assassins in their selective carnage. As for the film *Tootsie*, it's a gentle comedy about a man hiding his identity. (p. 167)

Like the clumsy pun created by the film's title, the reference here to hiding one's identity is no coincidence: Camille's identity is also concealed, since he has been adopted by a French family and cannot even remember his birth name. He tells Esther very little about Rwanda, which he refers to as 'the land of evil' (p. 221) and 'the kingdom of mindless violence' (p. 182). More significantly, as the narrator notes here, Camille says nothing about Belgium's role in creating imagined identities (so-called ethnicities) in Rwanda – identities that eventually had to be hidden when in 1994 many Tutsi tried to pass as Hutu in an attempt to save their own lives.

This brief, yet significant mention of the history of ethnic identity cards, which allowed Belgium to organise and reorganise Rwandan society at will and then helped the killers identify their targets, is the only instance in the novel in which Belgium is explicitly implicated in the narrative of the genocide. Elsewhere the influence of Belgian colonial rule on Rwanda's history is alluded to only briefly and enigmatically. When Camille eventually returns to Rwanda to discuss possibly setting up a sleep clinic there, the local deputy director of the university hospital tells him he is sorry his country was once a Belgian colony, not because of Belgium's contribution to the genocide but, he says, because the Belgian empire was just too small. He adds that he would have preferred Rwanda to have been a colony of France (p. 230).

In other words, the 'staggering Belgian story' of colonial rule is a story that is couched in ambivalence. Dan's decision to set the novel in France with a French narrator-protagonist implicitly shifts responsibility for the genocide against the Tutsi from Belgium to France. This displacement of responsibility is reinforced in the novel by the metaphorical link between Esther's insomnia and the guilt of the French nation. Camille tells Esther that her illness is 'France's illness […]

It's an illness that she caught because she closed her eyes to people like Kamou et Samembe [...] She can't sleep any more. She's afraid to dream' (pp. 179–80). Having first named him Oscar, Camille's adoptive French parents renamed him Camille when the previously mute child pronounced the word 'Kamou' on sight of a pack of Camel cigarettes (p. 98); Samembe is the name Esther gave Camille before she knew him and which she found in a library book about the *Bami du Rwanda* (p. 32). By accusing Esther and France of having closed their eyes on 'Kamou' and 'Samembe', Camille's words remind us of France's and the rest of the Global North's refusal to acknowledge the genocide against the Tutsi and to see Rwanda as it really was. The emphasis on naming and renaming also implicitly recalls the damaging effects of colonial classification, but not necessarily in relation to the history of Belgian rule. Esther receives Camille's description of her illness as if she is on trial: 'It was the result of a criminal trial. The guilty verdict and the sentence' (p. 180). Her sentence is a lifetime without sleep and a fear of dreams. At this point, Esther's first-person narration directly addresses the reader, wondering why she has become a scapegoat for the sins of France and asks, 'Is the story of Esther and Camille just a sinister "roman à clef" for you too; a painful allegory in which France chats with post-genocide Rwanda?' (p. 180) Here, the status of the text as a 'roman à clef' is explicitly confirmed in the narration. Although the allegorical nature of Dan's novel seems to emphasise France's rather than Belgium's role in the genocide, asking this question directly of the reader implicitly reminds us that France was not the only guilty party in the story of Rwanda.

Of course, France was deeply implicated in the genocide against the Tutsi and stands accused of training and arming the militia, widespread rape, and helping perpetrators escape during Operation Turquoise.[65] Moreover, France had gradually taken Belgium's place as what Prunier calls the 'tutelary power' in Rwanda in the years leading up to 1994.[66] At the start of the 1990 Civil War, then French president François Mitterrand was quick to send in troops and voice his support for Habyarimana's government. Brussels, on the other hand, withdrew its soldiers from Rwanda just one month into the Civil War, mainly for reasons of domestic politics.[67] In fact, it could be argued that it was Belgium more than France that 'closed its eyes' on Rwanda: Prunier writes that, during the genocide, 'among the countries with strong links to Rwanda, Belgium hardly reacted at all since it seemed that the government and the public had both been paralysed by the torture and death of their ten Blue Helmets in early April'.[68] This paralysis seems to have continued into the twenty-first century in the Belgian nation's unstated refusal to confront and acknowledge the impact of its colonial history in Rwanda.

Conclusion

Researchers tend to differentiate Belgium from the other European colonial powers, describing it as both a 'latecomer' to empire and a 'latecomer' to critically reappraising its colonial past.[69] While scholars such as Goddeeris and Verbeeck suggest that a critical re-evaluation of Belgian colonialism in the Congo is finally starting to gain momentum in the twenty-first century, Belgium's role in Rwanda is rarely mentioned. Indeed, the recently redesigned AfricaMuseum in Tervuren makes no mention at all of Belgium's role in the identity politics that culminated in the genocide against the Tutsi and focuses mostly on the Congo.[70] Even Belgian scholars such as de Lame, who recognise that in both Rwanda and Belgium 'dealing with the legacy of colonization remains fundamental to any attempt to determine the future',[71] challenge the connection made by scholars such as Mamdani and Lemarchand between Belgian colonisation and the genocide.[72]

Despite the 1996–97 parliamentary inquiry and Guy Verhofstadt's ensuing public apology, then as prime minister, to the people of Rwanda in April 2000, the silence around the genocide continues. It will be interesting to see the outcome of the 2020 Truth and Reconciliation Commission, since the Belgian cultural response to the country's role in Rwanda seems to be one of avoidance and denial. This was exemplified in the reaction of the Belgian government to the death of the ten UN peacekeepers in April 1994. More recently, we see this in what has become a somewhat controversial memorial to the genocide: Tom Frantzen's sculpture, *Under the same sky*, in the Woluwe-Saint-Pierre district of Brussels. For Orjuela, the sculpture 'invites a recollection of the historical bond between Belgium and Rwanda, highlighting brotherhood and renewal, while avoiding a direct reference to the past of colonialism and Belgium's pivotal role in the identity politics which eventually led to genocide'.[73]

This same strategy of avoidance and denial seems to be reflected in Belgian fictional production. Over a period of almost twenty years, the three very different novels I have discussed reflect the people of Belgium's continued refusal to confront the afterlife of their country's colonial politics in Rwanda. It is surely no coincidence that only one of the novels is (partly) set in Belgium: the narrator-protagonist of *La Promesse faite à ma sœur* lives in Brussels, but most of the action takes place in Rwanda. In the final chapter of the novel, Jean bumps into one of his Belgian colleagues on his metro journey to work. She asks him if he managed to see the gorillas during his time in Rwanda. Jean thinks this is a stupid question but answers her anyway, wishing that she had asked him about people or politics rather than primates, and conceding that 'she probably no longer remembered what had happened less than ten years earlier' (p. 194). This moment exemplifies the different responses between members of the Rwandan diaspora and those of the former colonial power. Whereas Belgians may choose not to remember Rwanda, even in the year of the tenth commemoration of the genocide, Rwandans like Jean cannot ever forget.

The fact that both Ndwaniye's new edition and Dan's novel were published to coincide with important anniversaries of the Genocide against the Tutsi (the twentieth anniversary for *Le Garçon du Rwanda* and the twenty-fifth for *La Promesse faite à ma sœur*) suggests that the genocide is not completely forgotten, even if it is only remembered as part of a publisher's marketing strategy. Yet, both Dan's text and the Ndwaniye paratext do little to challenge the Belgian version of its colonial history of Rwanda that we see in de Broqueville's earlier novel. Of course, the relationship between fiction and truth is a complex one, and as my previous work has shown, there are contesting versions of the 'truth' about the genocide against the Tutsi.[74] However, historical research has identified a strong and irrefutable connection between the Belgian colonial legacy and what happened in Rwanda. These three examples of Belgian imperial fictions serve to reinforce rather than challenge a colonial narrative that had devastating consequences for Rwanda and its people in 1994.

Notes

1. Journalist Scott Peterson, who was in Rwanda during the genocide, writes that the Belgian soldiers' Achilles tendons were cut to prevent them from running. They were then castrated and forced to choke on their own genitals. See Scott Peterson, *Me Against My Brother: At War in Somalia, Sudan, and Rwanda* (New York: Routledge, 2000), p. 292.
2. Danielle de Lame, '(Im)possible Belgian Mourning for Rwanda', *African Studies Review*, 48.2 (2005), 33–43 (38).
3. As part of the investigation, Verhofstadt and Mahoux travelled to Kigali to better understand the circumstances of the paratroopers' murder.
4. Sénat de Belgique 1–611/7: Commission d'enquête parlementaire concernant les événements du Rwanda, rapport au nom de la commission d'enquête par MM. Mahoux et Verfhofstadt, 6 December 1997. https://www.senate.be/www/?MIval=/publications/viewPubDoc&TID=16778570&LANG=fr [accessed 24 July 2020].
5. See, for example, Martin Ewans, 'Belgium and the Colonial Experience', *Journal of Contemporary European Studies*, 11.2 (2003), 167–80; Idesbald Goddeeris, 'Postcolonial Belgium: The Memory of the Congo', *Interventions: International Journal of Postcolonial Studies*, 17.3 (2015), 434–51.
6. Idesbald Goddeeris, 'Colonial Streets and Statues: Postcolonial Belgium in the Public Space', *Postcolonial Studies*, 18.4 (2015), 397–409 (404).
7. Ibid.
8. Camilla Orjuela, 'Remembering Genocide in the Diaspora: Place and Materiality in the Commemoration of Atrocities in Rwanda and Sri Lanka', *International Journal of Heritage Studies* (2019) DOI: https://doi.org/10.1080/13527258.2019.1644529 [accessed 22 July 2020].
9. J. B., 'Bruxelles est la première ville rwandaise hors d'Afrique'. *La Libre.be*, 16 September 2010 https://www.lalibre.be/regions/bruxelles/bruxelles-est-la-premiere-ville-rwandaise-hors-d-afrique-51b8c435e4b0de6db9bd7437 [accessed 22 July 2020].
10. Orjuela, 'Remembering Genocide in the Diaspora'.
11. My thanks to Pierre-Philippe Fraiture, Kate Mackenzie, and Charlotte Wirth for their comments on an earlier draft of this chapter.
12. Nicki Hitchcott, *Rwanda Genocide Stories: Fiction after 1994* (Liverpool: Liverpool University Press, 2015).
13. Madelaine Hron, 'Itsembabwoko "à la française"? – Rwanda, Fiction and the Franco-African Imaginary', *Forum for Modern Language Studies*, 45.2 (2009), 162–75 (164).
14. Joseph Ndwaniye, *La Promesse faite à ma sœur* (Espace Nord, 2018), originally published in 2006 by Les Impressions Nouvelles (note that the new edition wrongly dates the original as 2007).
15. Ndwaniye has been living in Belgium where he works as a nurse since 1986.
16. Huguette de Broqueville, *Uraho? Es-tu toujours vivant* (Grâce-Hollogne: Éditions Mols, 1997); Bernard Dan, *Le Garçon du Rwanda* (La Tour d'Aigues: L'Aube, 2014).
17. Hron, 'Itsembabwoko "à la française"?…', p. 165. 'Itsembabwoko' is a Kinyarwanda word for the extermination of a people (Hron, p. 162) and is a term that did not exist before 1994 (see Oliver Barlet, 'Representing the *Itsembabwoko*', *Black Camera, an International Film Journal*, 4.1 (2012), 234–51 (234).
18. Ndwaniye has published another novel: *Le Muzungu mangeur d'hommes* (Brussels: Aden, 2012), and *Plus fort que la hyène* (Ciboure: La Cheminante, 2018), an illustrated novella for young adults. His short story, 'Le Rêve' was published online by Fédération Wallonie-Bruxelles in 2013: http://www.fureurdelire.cfwb.be/index.php?eID=tx_nawsecuredl&u=0&file=fileadmin/sites/fdl/upload/fdl_super_editor/fdl_editor/documents/publications/Plaquettes_2013/9951_Reve_Ndwaniye.pdf&hash=9c8dc53f5f5fead49672f14cf7117552ec2029b5 [accessed 23 July 2020].
19. 'la collection patrimoniale belge'. All translations are my own.
20. https://www.espacenord.com/a-propos/ [accessed 20 July 2020].
21. The other is Malika Madi, born in Belgium of Algerian origin (https://www.espacenord.com/auteurs/). Titles for the Espace Nord collection are selected by an all-White committee that includes Belgian writers and academics but is mostly composed of people employed by the Fédération Wallonie-Bruxelles, which financially supports Les Impressions Nouvelles.
22. Ndwaniye is also a member of the Association des écrivains belges de langue française https://www.ecrivainsbelges.be/index.php?option=com_content&view=article&id=233&Itemid=154 [accessed 22 July 2020].
23. Les Impressions Nouvelles also organised a public discussion between Ndwaniye and Jacques Roisin, author of *Dans la nuit la plus noire se cache l'humanité. Récits de justes du Rwanda* (Brussels: Les Impressions Nouvelles, 2017) on 20 May 2019 to accompany the exhibition of Bruce Clarke's exhibition, 'Les Hommes de-

bout' at the Bibliothèque de l'Université du Travail de Charleroi https://www.espacenord.com/25-ans-du-genocide-rwandais/ [accessed 28 August 2020).

24. Unfortunately, Demaeseneer's essay on *La Promesse faite à ma sœur* contains a number of factual errors about writing from and about Rwanda: Yolande Mukagasana is wrongly credited with the authorship of the Groupov play *Rwanda 94* and is described as a writer of 'contes'; Pius Ngandu Nkashama's tale *Yolena* is wrongly identified as the first work of fiction about the genocide published in 1995 when it was in fact published in 2006 (in Ndwaniye, *La Promesse*, p. 214).

25. For *La Promesse faite à ma sœur*, the dossier has been compiled by Valériane Wiot, a French and History teacher seconded to the Belgian Service de la Promotion des Lettres. It consists of extracts from documents mostly taken from the Didier-Hatier textbook series, 'Construire l'Histoire' alongside suggestions for classroom activities based on the text and its context. See Claude Allard, Coralie Snyers, Isabelle Van der Borght and Viviane Van Liempt, *Construire l'Histoire. Tome 4: Un monde en mutation (de 1919 à nos jours)* (Namur: Didier-Hatier, 2008).

26. Hron's article discusses *La Promesse* (pp. 169–70). See also Hitchcott, *Rwanda Genocide Stories*, pp. 75–70 and 88–92. Another example of a Rwandan text that articulates the difficult position of the absent witness is Scholastique Mukasonga's short story collection, *L'Iguifou: nouvelles rwandaises* (Paris: Gallimard, 2010).

27. Hitchcott, *Rwanda Genocide Stories*, p. 46.

28. As a Rwandan Hutu, Jean is not, strictly speaking, a survivor of the genocide against the Tutsi.

29. 'Rapport de l'OUA, Rwanda, le génocide qu'on aurait pu stopper' (2000), quoted in Valériane Wiot, *Joseph Ndwaniye, La Promesse à ma sœur, carnet pédagogique* (Brussels: Espace Nord/Fédération Wallonie-Bruxelles, 2019), p. 9.

30. René Lemarchand, *The Dynamics of Violence in Central Africa* (Philadelphia, PA: University of Pennsylvania Press, 2009) p. 9.

31. Mahmood Mamdani, *When Victims Become Killers: Colonialism, Nativism, and the Genocide in Rwanda* (Princeton, NJ: Princeton University Press, 2001), p. 88.

32. Rapport de l'OUA, 'Rwanda, le génocide qu'on aurait pu stopper', 2000, quoted in Wiot, p. 9.

33. Mamdani, *When Victims*, p. 16. Emphasis added.

34. The colonial authorities shifted their allegiance to the growing Hutu counter-elite in the postwar period when their power began to be challenged and the Tutsi started to call for independence. See Gérard Prunier, *The Rwanda Crisis: History of a Genocide* (New York: Columbia University Press, 1995), pp. 43–44.

35. Prunier, *The Rwanda Crisis*, p. 49.

36. Ibid., pp. 51–53.

37. Ibid., p. 49.

38. Quoted in Prunier, *The Rwanda Crisis*, p. 53.

39. Lemarchand, *The Dynamics of Violence*, p. 31.

40. De Lame, '(Im)possible Belgian Mourning…', p. 39. Conversely, as de Lame notes, the positive image of Belgium promoted by the Catholic Church was shattered, not only by the role of priests during the genocide, but also when Belgium quickly withdraw its troops (p. 41).

41. Colette Braeckman, 'The Rwandan Genocide of the 1990s', in Prem Poddar, Rajeev S. Patke and Lars Jensen (eds.), *A Historical Companion to Postcolonial Literatures – Continental Europe and its Empires* (Edinburgh: Edinburgh University Press, 2008), pp. 49–51 (p. 51).

42. Pierre Halen, 'De l'inusable imagerie du Cœur des ténèbres et de sa résurgence dans quelques représentations du génocide au Rwanda', in Isaac Bazié and Hans-Jürgen Lüsebrink (eds.), *Violences postcoloniales: Représentations littéraires et perceptions médiatiques* (Berlin: Lit Verlag, 2011), pp. 65–87 (p. 82).

43. Note that Halen describes it as a 'livre de témoignages' (p. 82); and Boisdeffre as a novel, essay, and testimony all in one (*Uraho?* p. 10)

44. Pierre Boisdeffre, 'Préface', in de Broqueville, *Uraho?*, pp. 9–13 (p. 10).

45. https://gw.geneanet.org/nobily?lang=en&n=drion+du+chapois&oc=0&p=ferdinand [accessed 5 January 2021].

46. Mamdani, *When Victims*, pp. 95–96.

47. Timothy Longman, 'Church Politics, and Genocide in Rwanda', *Journal of Religion in Africa*, 31.2 (2001), 163–86 (166).

48. Prunier, *The Rwanda Crisis*, pp. 32–34; Mamdani, p. 89–90.

49. Julius O. Adekunle, *Culture and Customs of Rwanda* (Westport, CT: Greenwood Press, 2007), p. 35.

50. Longman, 'Church Politics…', p. 168.

51. See, for example, Tharcisse Gatwa, *The Churches and Ethnic Ideology in the Rwandan Crises 1900–1994* (Milton Keynes: Regnum Books, 2005); Timothy Longman, *Christianity and Genocide in Rwanda* (Cambridge University Press, 2010); Carol Rittner, John. K. Roth and Wendy Whitworth (eds.), *Genocide in Rwanda: Complicity of the Churches?* (St Paul, MN: Paragon, 2004).

52. Mamdani, *When Victims*, p. 226.

53. Boisdeffre, 'Préface', in de Broqueville, *Uraho?*, p. 12.

54. Halen, 'De l'inusable imagerie…', p. 83

55. Ivan Reisdorff, *L'Homme qui demanda du feu* (Brussels: Editions Labor, 1995).

56. De Broqueville, p. 141. Hereafter page references will be in parentheses in the text. For a dis-

cussion of the 'white saviour' paradigm, see Teju Cole 'The White Saviour Industrial Complex' https://www.theatlantic.com/international/archive/2012/03/the-white-savior-industrial-complex/254843/ [accessed 5 January 2021].
57. In bold in the original text
58. Quoted in Longman, 'Church Politics', p. 181.
59. Rachel Hayman, 'Abandoned Orphan, Wayward Child: the United Kingdom and Belgium in Rwanda since 1994', *Journal of Eastern African Studies*, 4.3 (2010), 341–60 (343).
60. Ibid.
61. Halen, 'De l'inusable imagerie…', p. 82. The suggestion here is that, because de Broqueville is unable to accept that humans could commit genocide, she can only explain it in supernatural terms. In my reading, the use of such imagery is yet another example of de Broqueville's colonial racism towards the Rwandan people in general and the RPF in particular.
62. Rwandan authors Camille Karangwa and Vénuste Kayimahe both evoke this same myth (See Karangwa, *Le Chapelet et la machette: sur les traces du génocide rwandais* (Pretoria: Éditions du jour, 2003), p. 53, p. 98) and Vénuste Kayimahe, *La Chanson de l'aube* (Toulouse: Izuba, 2014), p. 92)
63. Georgi Verbeeck, 'Legacies of an Imperial Past in a Small Nation. Patterns of Postcolonialism in Belgium', *European Politics and Society*, DOI: 10.1080/23745118.2019.1645422 [accessed 15 July 2020].
64. Rony Demaeseneer mentions Dan's novel in his postscript to Ndwaniye's *La Promesse à ma sœur* where he simply highlights the fact that Dan is also an author who practises medicine (Ndwaniye, *La Promesse*, p. 213).
65. Hron, 'Itsembabwoko "à la française" ? …', p. 163.
66. Prunier, *The Rwanda Crisis*, p. 89 (n. 87).
67. Ibid., pp. 107–08.
68. Ibid., p. 274.
69. Verbeeck, 'Legacies of an Imperial Past…'.
70. Charlotte Wirth, 'Belgiens schweres koloniales Erbe', *Reporter*, 4 January 2019 https://www.reporter.lu/neues-museum-fehlende-debatte-belgiens-schweres-koloniales-erbe/ [accessed 21 July 2020].
71. De Lame, '(Im)possible Belgian Mourning…', p. 35.
72. Ibid., p. 37.
73. Orjuela, 'Remembering Genocide in the Diaspora', p. 3.
74. Nicki Hitchcott, 'The (Un)believable Truth about Rwanda', *Australian Journal of French Studies*, 56.2 (2019), 199–215.

Confronting the Colonial Past?
Genocide Education in Francophone Belgian Schools

Catherine Gilbert

With the seismic social shifts of recent decades – and particularly with the local and global events, such as the Black Lives Matter movement, taking place over the last two years – Belgium has been forced to confront its colonial past in very public ways, whether through attempts to 'decolonise' public institutions such as the Royal Museum for Central Africa,[1] the removal of colonial-era statues,[2] or declarations to incorporate the teaching of Belgian colonial history into secondary education.[3] This chapter will engage with these memory debates from the perspective of teaching about Rwandan history in Belgian schools. Rwanda is in a unique position in terms of Belgian colonial and post-colonial history. As part of the relatively small Belgian territory of Ruanda-Urundi from 1922 to 1962, Rwandan colonial history is often overshadowed by that of Congo in the public domain in Belgium. Nevertheless, Belgium is also deeply implicated in Rwanda's more recent history. The policies of the Belgian colonial administration had a direct impact on increasing ethnic divisionism and violence in post-independence Rwanda,[4] which ultimately culminated in the 1994 genocide against the Tutsi, a period of one hundred days during which more than one million Rwandans were killed. Moreover, it was the execution of ten Belgian peacekeepers on the first day of the genocide, 7 April 1994, that prompted the UN to withdraw the bulk of its UNAMIR forces, a decision that enabled the genocidal slaughter to continue unimpeded.[5]

What is remembered and what is taught in Belgium about Rwanda's colonial past and recent history is therefore of primary importance, both for Belgian youth to learn about their country's difficult past and their own 'implication' in Rwanda's history[6] and for the Rwandan diaspora in Belgium to see their experiences reflected in the education system. Nevertheless, there is still no systematic structure in place for teaching about colonial history in Belgium, especially given the linguistic divides and the federalised education system, and Belgian teachers enjoy a certain amount of freedom to decide what to teach in their own classrooms. This results in students being exposed to different aspects of colonial history to different degrees across Belgium's Flemish- and French-speaking regions.

Two further key issues also restrict the way Rwandan history is taught in Belgian schools. First, much of the focus of Belgian colonial history is still centred on the Congo Free State and the atrocities committed under Leopold II. Moreover, the Congolese diaspora represents by far the largest from Belgium's former colonies (with more than 280,000 Congolese currently living in Belgium), and as a result, questions of Congolese history are more visible in the public domain.[7] Second, memory of the national colonial past frequently takes a back seat in Belgian politics, with the international history of World War I and the Holocaust a priority focus. Most often, teaching about the genocide against the Tutsi is done in the context of Holocaust education, a context in which the colonial relationship between Belgium and Rwanda is sidelined. This chapter addresses some of these shortcomings in Belgian education by examining specific teaching materials recently developed to help teach about Rwandan history, as well as identifying the education-focused memory networks behind these initiatives and the way these networks are invested in broader conceptions of citizenship education in Belgium.

It is first necessary to briefly address the ways in which Belgian colonial history has come to the fore in recent years. In February 2019, a UN report underlined the link between the legacies of colonialism and the endemic nature of present-day racism faced by people of African descent in Belgium.[8] The report stressed the need for a critical reinterrogation of the past in order to overcome their historical 'social invisibility' and ensure their recognition in Belgian society. This issue garnered significant attention in spring 2020 with the Black Lives Matter movement, which saw the largest racial protests in Belgium's history. This was followed, on 30 June 2020, by a historic expression of regret from the Belgian king to Congo's President Tshisekedi on the sixtieth anniversary of Congolese independence. The king's letter expressed 'the deepest regrets for the wounds of the past', for the violence and cruelty inflicted in the Congo Free State and the suffering and humiliation of the colonial period that followed.[9] This was an important admission that Belgium's role as colonial oppressor continued long after the death of Leopold II, although this stopped short of an official apology.

According to Romain Landmeters, 'teaching colonial history in schools remains by far the most important demand from Afro-descendants in Belgium'.[10] Moreover, there is a growing insistence on the incorporation of African voices into the teaching of this history. According to a 2017 survey conducted among Afro-descendants in Belgium, 'the miserable and essentialising view of Africa plagued by war, corruption and poverty constituted a form of violence in the social and educational experiences of many of the people interviewed'.[11] This underlines the importance of educating Belgian students about African history, including an examination of the colonial process from an African perspective, and how colonial mechanisms, institutions, and attitudes are at the root of present-day racism.[12] As Antoine Tshitungu Kongolo reminds us, Belgium is still engaged in a 'memorial conflict', and examining history uniquely through the lens of White colonial figures is misleading.[13] Planned revisions to colonial history teaching have been announced, with new secondary textbooks due to be brought in from 2026.[14]

The much-needed critical interrogation of Belgium's colonial past only began in earnest from the late 1990s. Matthew Stanard traces four phases of memory in Belgium: a period of silence from the mid-1960s to the mid-1980s; a period of commemoration and nostalgia from 1985 (the centenary of the creation of the Congo Free State) to 1994; a reinterrogation of relations following the genocide in 1994 until 2010; and from 2010 onwards a period characterised by increasingly frank recognition of the colonial heritage, particularly led by the younger generations, including Afro-descendants.[15] This shift in attitude was accompanied by an increase in academic research, particularly in the 2000s following the publication of Adam Hochschild's *King Leopold's Ghost* (1998) and Ludo De Witte's *The Assassination of Lumumba* (1999),[16] a wave of interest that Idesbald Goddeeris and Sindani Kiangu refer to as 'Congomania in academia'. Nonetheless, the authors remark that 'there is little dialogue between Congolese and Belgian historians', limited both by language and lack of means: 'no Congolese historian has been translated into Dutch and the greatest part of their Belgian collaboration is channelled to the French-speaking part'.[17] Denise Bentrovato and Karel Van Nieuwenhuyse observe a 'notable imbalance in historical research', with 'the predominance of Belgian over Congolese perspectives'.[18] This is closely linked to the ongoing divisions and differing interpretations of the colonial past within Belgium itself: Goddeeris and Kiangu conclude – perhaps somewhat gratuitously – that 'Flanders has largely come to terms with its colonial past, but that the French-speaking community has a more problematic memory'.[19]

But what of Rwanda in all this? There is a small but significant Rwandan diaspora, with just over 32,000 Rwandans living in Belgium, of which approximately 4,500 are under the age of eighteen.[20] In terms of academic research, there has been little consideration of the colonisation of Ruanda-Urundi in comparison to that of Congo. We can also observe similar linguistic divides, with most academic research on the region published in French and English, with little translated into Dutch. Scholarship on recent Rwandan history greatly increased following the 1994 genocide, although there still appears to be limited dialogue between Rwandan and Belgian historians. Nevertheless, a growing number of publications by genocide survivors living in Belgium have helped to increase the visibility of Rwandan voices in the public sphere.[21] At the political level, a parliamentary commission of inquiry was conducted in 1996–97 regarding the events in Rwanda in the months leading up to the genocide.[22] As a result, in 2000, the then prime minister of Belgium, Guy Verhofstadt, presented his apologies to Rwanda for Belgium's failure to stop the massacres in 1994. On the occasion of Rwandan President Paul Kagame's visit to France in 2011, Belgian Minister of Foreign Affairs Louis Michel recalled these important steps as a means of testifying 'to the manner in which my country has turned the page on its past relationship with Rwanda to look towards the future'.[23] And yet there is still no apology forthcoming for – nor sufficient interrogation or acknowledgement of – Belgium's colonial policies that contributed to the ethnicisation of the Rwandan people, a key factor in the genocidal ideology of 1994.

This chapter will show that, beyond the imbalance in academic historiography, Rwanda remains largely absent in colonial history education in Belgium. The chapter will proceed in three parts. The first will briefly examine how colonial history has been taught in Belgian schools, paying particular attention to scholarship focusing on curricula and textbooks in order to situate the teaching about Rwandan history in the broader context. The second will examine specific examples of teaching materials developed by education-focused Belgian memory groups and Rwandan community organisations to promote the teaching of Rwandan history – and specifically the teaching of the history of the genocide against the Tutsi – in Belgian schools. The final section will then situate these initiatives within broader networks of memory activism in Belgium that have emerged in recent decades.

Colonial History Teaching in Belgium

A 2008 study found that one in four students finishing secondary education in Belgium did not know that Congo had been a Belgian colony.[24] Writing on the fiftieth anniversary of Congo's independence, Gratia Pungu remarks that 'it is quite possible today in Belgium to finish secondary education without having studied the colonisation of the Congo'.[25] Romain Landmeters is equally worried to note 'the absence in school history textbooks – beyond a simple mention – of the colonial link that existed between the present-day countries of Burundi and Rwanda'.[26] This reticence to critically engage with Belgian colonial history is due in part to the fact that 'Belgian colonialism still seems to be considered – mistakenly – as a "separate history", that of "Others" at the regional level.'[27] As Landmeters explains, the only mention of colonial history in the Fédération Wallonie-Bruxelles's 2017 *Pacte pour un Enseignement d'Excellence* is revealing in this regard: 'the authors put on an equal footing – as part of the measures towards greater social diversity – the history of colonisation (or of immigration) and access in schools to a vegetarian menu for people of different faiths'.[28]

In terms of the ways colonial history is represented in history textbooks, the focus has traditionally been on Leopold II and his personal rule of the Congo Free State. The Belgian king was initially depicted as a hero and later as an anti-hero – due to his 'greed' and the atrocities committed in the Congo Free State. This shift in public opinion has in turn enabled the creation of the myth that Congo was 'saved' from this despotic king by the Belgian state in 1908, allowing more recent Belgian governments to sidestep the truth that the violence and exploitation of Congolese people and resources continued during the period of Belgian colonial rule. Moreover, there are marked differences between these representations in the francophone and Flemish communities. In her detailed study of representations of Leopold II in secondary school textbooks published between 1960 and 2007, Stéphanie Planche observes that the changing attitude in public opinion began to be reflected in Flemish textbooks in the 1980s, but it wasn't until the 1990s that the representations in francophone textbooks began to shift from the myth of 'génie' ['genius'] to 'gêne' ['shame'].[29] Planche argues that this is perhaps less an engagement with the history of colonialism but rather 'an opportunity to address the polemical question of the preservation of the monarchy in Belgium',[30] attitudes towards which differ widely between the north and the south of the country.

Unlike other European countries grappling with national memory and their colonial histories, there are two factors that are specific to Belgium: 'the issue of the monarchy and the language tensions gradually tearing apart the fabric of the nation'.[31] There is a high emotional and political cost to acknowledging Belgium's role as colonial perpetrator, and public debate on Belgium's colonial legacy has long been determined by the problematic national framework. According to Geert Castryck, 'Belgium, being a bi-national state, started to disintegrate around the same time it lost its (African) colonies, and education was one of the first domains to be split'.[32] Federalisation of the Belgian state led to a 'dispersion of national memories', and increased tension between the language communities 'undermined the national account of the past'.[33] As a result, colonisation became an issue of contention between the language communities, which has led to a certain 'communitarisation' of the country's colonial heritage. Valérie Rosoux and Laurence van Ypersele point to the 'tacit consensus' of silence and deliberate amnesia that has consequently developed across the language communities in Belgium in relation to colonial history.[34] As Geert Castryck observes:

> Contrary to most nation-states, Belgium survived the past few decades by *not* constructing a national identity, by avoiding national history. [...] the

neglect of history has been a conscious policy for a long time, and in the 1970s the Belgian government even seriously considered abolishing the teaching of history altogether.³⁵

It was not until 1990, when education was formally devolved to the Belgian communities, that history as a school subject regained a more prominent and stable position in both Flemish and francophone education and came to belong to the basic curriculum in secondary education. Nevertheless, what I would describe as a consensus of avoidance still exists, where '[n]either national nor subnational history are extensively focused upon in history education on both sides of the linguistic boundary. The basic frame of reference is European'.³⁶

In line with Stanard's observations about the phases of colonial memory in Belgium, Karel Van Nieuwenhuyse identifies two broad trends in education curricula: a period of colonial amnesia that occurred after Congolese independence in 1960, which endured until the 1990s, after which debates have become more critical and an 'increasing perspectivism' on colonial history has made its way into the education system. However, as Van Nieuwenhuyse reminds us, the societal changes and shifts in public opinion take much longer to be applied in secondary history education. Textbooks in Belgium are based on and written according to guidelines from standards established by the Flemish and francophone ministries of education. These standards were introduced in both communities in 2000 and delineate the minimal final attainment targets that history education should achieve. While there are some common general trends, separate curricula operate in the main school systems within each language community. According to Van Nieuwenhuyse:

> The issues of (de)colonization and (post)colonialism are not explicitly addressed in the Flemish standards. […] The francophone standards on the other hand do contain explicit references. In the so-called key moments in history, which must be dealt with in history class, both imperialism and decolonization, and north-south relations are explicitly mentioned.³⁷

That said, it is important to remember that the textbooks themselves are commercial products, neither subsidised nor controlled by the government. They are written predominantly by history teachers rather than academics and, as a result, 'often do not conform to the academic history discipline, but form a relatively autonomous "vulgate"'.³⁸ Idesbald Goddeeris has likewise observed the public/academic divide, noting how the majority of historical scholarship happens in isolation from Belgian society, with historians largely failing to translate their findings into more accessible language.³⁹

Similar issues continue to plague representations of Belgian-Rwandan colonial and postcolonial history. In a highly problematic yet revealing article, Danielle de Lame points to a unique form of nostalgia – or 'mourning' – for the former Belgian colony, particularly among the older generations and former missionaries,[40] as well as the difficulty Belgians continue to experience in facing the 'stigma' placed on the Belgian colonial past in the wake of the 1994 genocide against the Tutsi:

> The Rwandan genocide has been a shock beyond any consideration of nationality or affiliation. However, as the media were understandably eager to provide their audience with some simple explanation for the terrible images they dispatched, Belgium and its colonial past came quickly to the fore as the tentative explanations. [...] Belgium, quite unprepared for this, was forced to discover the unexpected hatred of which she was the object.[41]

It would seem, then, that the challenges concerning knowledge of Rwandan history in Belgium echo those identified by Castryck in the Congolese context:

> there is a generational difference in Belgium concerning knowledge of colonial history: the youngest half of the population does not know colonial history because they never learned about it in school, and the oldest half of the population... does not know colonial history because they only learned the colonialist propaganda.[42]

This underscores the urgency in critically revising the Belgian curriculum, in particular incorporating colonial history teaching into secondary education, drawing on the expertise of both historical scholarship and grassroots memory organisations, and giving priority to African perspectives. The following analysis of specific teaching materials thus focuses primarily on initiatives driven by members of the Rwandan diasporic community, foregrounding their voices and lived experiences.[43]

Sample Teaching Materials

In this section, I will present three recent examples of teaching materials that have been developed to aid Belgian teachers when addressing the topic of the 1994 genocide against the Tutsi in Rwanda in their classrooms at the secondary level. Rather than focusing in detail on the specific content of these materials, it is germane to examine the main actors involved in developing these materials, their accessibility, and which classes they aim to teach. To some extent, this analysis also attempts to identify who is teaching this material, although it remains difficult to obtain accurate information about how – and how widely – these resources are currently being used by Belgian teachers in the classroom. This study nevertheless gives us some indication of the possible impact of these materials, which, while this currently remains very limited, does point to a growing impetus for initiatives of this kind.

La Promesse faite à ma sœur – Espace Nord

The first example is the *carnet pédagogique* developed by the Fédération Wallonie-Bruxelles in collaboration with the Belgian publishing house Espace Nord to accompany the 2018 re-edition of Joseph Ndwaniye's novel *La Promesse faite à ma sœur* [2006].[44] The forty-page *carnet* devotes seven pages to the history of Rwanda and the genocide,[45] while the remainder presents the author and the novel in more depth, concluding with an exploration of broader themes such as responsibility, guilt, and forgiveness. As Nicki Hitchcott observes in her chapter in this volume, the key failing of the *carnet* is that it glosses over the role that Belgian colonial policy played in laying the groundwork for genocidal ideology to take root in Rwanda. A paragraph on the final page of the *carnet* invites students to prolong their engagement with this topic by visiting the Musée Royal de l'Afrique Centrale (RMCA) in Tervuren, which acknowledges the link between this resource and the broader structures of colonial memory in Belgium, although representations in the museum of Belgium's responsibility in Rwanda remain problematic.[46]

The *carnet* is freely available to download as a PDF from the Espace Nord website, along with an accompanying folder of images, maps, and documents.[47] It was also distributed to teachers in printed format along with copies of the novel at the Journée de réflexion pédagogique autour de la transmission de l'histoire du génocide des Tutsi au Rwanda en 1994 [Day of pedagogical reflection around the transmission of the history of the 1994 genocide against the Tutsi in Rwanda], organised by the Cellule Démocratie ou Barbarie in Brussels on 20 March 2019.[48] This coincided with the twenty-fifth anniversary of the genocide and was also an important event for understanding the memory and education networks in Belgium, to which I will return in more detail in the next section.

The *carnet* was compiled by Valériane Wiot, a French and history teacher and the 'responsable pédagogique' [educational manager] for the Espace Nord collection. It is difficult to tell whether Ndwaniye himself was involved in the development of the *carnet*, although the 'avant-propos' states that the *carnet* draws on the postface and the interview with the author that form part of the paratextual material to the novel, suggesting that Ndwaniye had little direct input. At the Journée de réflexion pédagogique (at which Ndwaniye was not present), Wiot explained that the *carnet* had been designed for use in French classes but that it could easily be adapted for history classes. This raises interesting questions about the use of this teaching aid in the classroom. The introduction to the *carnet* emphasises that the activities are intended to familiarise students with the history of the genocide. Nevertheless, while literature can undeniably be a powerful means to address historical responsibility, teaching this material in the context of a French class rather than a history class may well be a possible way of sidestepping the confrontation with the difficult issues of Belgian colonial history in the classroom. This is further implied in the description about the *carnet* on the Espace Nord website, which draws attention to more universal questions of 'humanity', 'the transmission of identity', as well as highlighting the tools for literary analysis, such as understanding auto-fictional writing, that the *carnet* provides.[49]

The Espace Nord collection is contributing to the trend of relaunching important literary works with pedagogical accompaniments. Ndwaniye's novel therefore falls under the rubric of the publishing house's 'Espace pédagogique', which is intended to provide teachers with 'all the necessary tools to develop lessons on Belgian francophone literature for secondary students of all levels. [These tools are] designed to be a direct support for teachers who want to help students discover Belgian authors in their French classes.'[50] It is perhaps surprising that a novel that went relatively 'unremarked' for many years was chosen as part of this initiative, but the timing of the publication of this re-edition and the *carnet pédagogique* ahead of the twenty-fifth anniversary of the genocide against the Tutsi in 2019 is certainly a contributing factor here. Nevertheless, it seems that Ndwaniye's novel – and the Rwandan history it presents – perhaps loses some of its specificity under the banner of 'Belgian francophone literature', with Ndwaniye himself designated as a 'Belgian author'.

'D'ici et d'ailleurs' – Muyira Arts et Mémoire

The second example is a pedagogic resource produced by Muyira Arts et Mémoire asbl, a small genocide survivor organisation based in Brussels that was founded in 2014. While their primary concern is preserving and transmitting the memory of the genocide against the Tutsi, Muyira 'has extended its activities to the fight against all forms of racism, xenophobia, sexism and homophobia'.[51] The association has produced one pedagogic resource to date: 'D'Ici et d'ailleurs: Témoignages des survivants du génocide des Tutsi du Rwanda vivant en Belgique' (2016) [From here and there: Testimonies of Survivors of the genocide against the Tutsi in Rwanda living in Belgium], which takes the form of a film and a *livret pédagogique*.⁵² The film presents the testimonies of five genocide survivors living in Belgium.⁵³ The *livret* is divided into four parts: the first provides a relatively brief historical context of the genocide (twelve pages in total); the second provides information about five survivors and short summaries of their stories; the third suggests questions about the 'before', 'during', and 'after the genocide' as well as more general questions to work on with students in the classroom; and the final section presents a number of 'fiches thématiques' [thematic factsheets], including a chronology and key issues linked to the genocide against the Tutsi and its aftermath, as well as information on other genocides in history, including the Herero in Nambia, Armenia, and the Shoah. Unlike the *carnet* discussed above, the *livret* pays more attention to the role of Belgian administration in codifying ethnic identities in Rwanda and the tensions created in the movement towards independence, but the tone remains largely factual rather than critical.

This example is particularly relevant to discussions on colonial and postcolonial history education, as it specifically considers the experiences of Rwandan survivors living in Belgium. As the description on the Muyira website emphasises:

> Since the end of the 1994 genocide against the Tutsi in Rwanda, many survivors have immigrated to Belgium for a variety of reasons: professional, familial, economic; others to escape the emptiness left by the total or partial extermination of their families. They bring with them the memory of the genocide, their wounds and their dreams.⁵⁴

Consequently, this is an important resource in raising awareness and developing understanding among Belgian students of Rwandans' lived experiences and why so many Rwandans immigrated to Belgium after the genocide, which is also key to understanding contemporary Belgian society. As outlined above, foregrounding African voices and experiences over the White (colonial) perspective is crucial, and engaging directly with their testimonies should be a central part of Belgian education. In terms of accessibility, however, the resource is not available online. A hard copy can be requested directly via the Muyira website or from the Cellule Démocratie ou Barbarie, but only a limited number of the film and *livret* have been produced, so they are reserved for teachers. Copies were also distributed to teachers at the Journée de réflexion pédagogique run by the Cellule in March 2020.

The *livret* is clearly designed for use in history classes, although its focus on understanding 'genocide' as a concept and linking the Rwandan case to other genocides around the world means that it is not necessarily intended to be used as part of colonial or postcolonial history curricula. Rather, it could be taught as part of the curriculum focusing on the Holocaust. In the French-speaking community, teaching the history of the Shoah tends to come under the banner of 'citizenship education' (and 'remembrance education' in the Flemish-speaking community), which has been part of the cross-curricular objectives of secondary education since 2010.[55] The goal of this type of education is to consider pupils as members of society and to develop their historical consciousness, cultural training, identity-building, and social resilience.[56] As Karel Van Nieuwenhusye and Kaat Wils note, '[r]emembrance education thus becomes a general umbrella for education about "dark chapters" from the past'.[57] While citizenship education draws on Holocaust remembrance and other periods of violent global history – such as the world wars and European imperialism – it does not include a critical historical interrogation of Belgium's national colonial past specifically. Indeed, the focus is on building social transformation but, as Van Nieuwenhuyse and Wils remind us, 'the absolute moral standards and the present-centred character of remembrance education is far removed from the more historical and contextual thinking of history education'.[58]

'Rwanda 1994' – Centre Pluridisciplinaire pour la Transmission de la Mémoire

The final example is the *dossier pédagogique* 'Rwanda 1994', prepared by the Centre Pluridisciplinaire pour la Transmission de la Mémoire (CPTM), part of the non-profit association MNEMA asbl.[59] The *dossier* is available to download freely from both the MNEMA and Cité Miroir websites.[60] However, given the volume of information on both websites, it is not easy to locate the document without prior knowledge of the organisations and their specific educational activities. Moreover, it has been difficult to determine where this initiative originated, who was responsible for compiling the dossier, or what the aims were in developing it, although a clear goal of the *dossier* is to raise awareness of the genocide commemorations in Belgium and is explicitly tied to remembrance education. As the introduction to the *dossier* emphasises, 'in the framework of the commemoration of the genocide against the Tutsi, during the month of April, MNEMA asbl proposes a pedagogic dossier for teachers wishing to study the subject with their students'.[61]

Again intended to be incorporated into history education, the *dossier* is much more prescriptive about the way it should be used in the classroom, as set out in the introduction:

> The proposed activities are accessible for audiences aged 15 and over. The document is organised around a global research question to which students must respond through exploring more specific research questions. A sum-

mary is then provided at the end of the dossier, which serves as an evaluation of the correct integration of the different concepts newly acquired.[62]

As well as establishing a pedagogic template to approach the subject, the *dossier*'s formulation of the global research question is of particular note: 'How can we explain this phrase: "There is no genocide without neighbours"?'[63] The implication here is that through studying the history of genocide and the particularities of the genocide against the Tutsi in Rwanda, students can arrive at a better understanding of citizenship and the need for solidarity with different groups in contemporary society, regardless of their background.

Following a cultural introduction – including song lyrics by Stromae and Gaël Faye, as well as an extract from Faye's 2016 novel *Petit pays*[64] (see Hannah Grayson's chapter in this volume) – the *dossier* confronts Belgium's uncomfortable historical ties with Rwanda head-on, with nineteen pages devoted to the historical context of Rwanda, providing a wide range of documents that enable a critical examination of Belgium's colonial administration and its consequences post-independence. These documents show how the Belgian authorities measured the physical characteristics of Rwandan subjects as part of their attribution of 'ethnic' identity and explain the introduction of the now infamous *cartes d'identité*, as well as protest from the Rwandans themselves against these measures. Three key research questions in this section directly situate racism as being rooted in colonialism: 'Why is Rwanda linked to Belgium?'; 'How was racism spread in Africa?'; 'How did racial hatred evolve under the successive republics in Rwanda?'. A later section in the *dossier* also addresses the memory work in Belgium and France, including drawing attention to the memorials in Brussels and Paris, Guy Verhofstadt's 2000 apology, and the ongoing debates around France's responsibility in the events of 1994. A further large section of the *dossier* is dedicated to justice and memory, as well as discussions of the repercussions of the war in the DRC in the years following the genocide.

In many ways, the *dossier* is far more comprehensive than both the *carnet* and *livret* discussed above, but at the risk of trying to be exhaustive. The full document is eighty-one pages in total, which could be a textbook for an entire history course in its own right; students are given extensive documents to analyse, exercises to undertake, and numerous research questions to answer. The *dossier* also includes a large sixteen-page bibliography that may well be intimidating to students and teachers alike. It is therefore unclear how this resource could be used effectively in the classroom, especially where teachers are only able to devote a few hours to the topic overall. Nonetheless, this is an important example of the type of nuanced and critical teaching materials that are sorely needed to address Rwandan colonial and contemporary history in any meaningful way in the Belgian classroom.

Memory Networks

While it could be argued that the materials created by Rwandan organisations appear to be more critical of Belgian colonial history, it is important to note that all the pedagogical tools discussed above have been developed with the support of the Fédération Wallonie-Bruxelles (FWB), the governmental body for the French community in Belgium.[65] The FWB is at the heart of numerous memory networks operating across the French-speaking region of Belgium, and it is important to understand these networks and their multiple initiatives in the context of history and 'citizenship' education, particularly pertaining to the memory of difficult pasts (including international conflicts, global imperialism, genocide, and crimes against humanity). Several *cellules* operate within the FWB, including the Cellule Démocratie ou Barbarie (DoB), which focuses on crimes against humanity and genocide. Importantly, the Conseil de la Transmission de la Mémoire was instituted to advise the government of the Cellule DoB following the FWB's 2009 decree relating to the transmission of the memory of these crimes.[66]

In light of this decree, the Cellule DoB's mission is 'to rise to the challenge of sensitising teachers and students to citizenship education through the values of mutual respect, equal rights and a commitment to building a more peaceful, just and unified world'.[67] To achieve its goal of awakening a sense of citizenship, the Cellule DoB regularly organises training days and produces and distributes pedagogical materials, as well as providing reference documents for teachers. The Journée de réflexion pédagogique autour de la transmission de l'histoire du génocide des Tutsi au Rwanda en 1994 organised in March 2019 is an important example. This Journée brought together teachers, academic researchers, community members, and genocide survivors. The dialogues established and the distribution of materials to teachers during the event were intended to coincide with the twenty-fifth anniversary of the genocide with the aim of encouraging more teachers to introduce the topic in their classrooms during this landmark anniversary – and equipping them with the relevant tools to do so.

Vital information is still needed as to how these pedagogic resources are being used, how many teachers are using them, and whether teachers find them to be effective tools. To gain further insights, I have recently begun to work with a group of ten Belgian history teachers who participated in an educational trip to Rwanda in April 2019 and have committed to teaching about the genocide against the Tutsi in their classrooms.[68] This trip was led by the genocide survivor organisation Ibuka Mémoire et Justice Belgique asbl, in collaboration with the Centre Communautaire Laïc Juif (CCLJ) in Brussels, with the aim of educating the teachers about the genocide – through visits to memorials and discussions with survivors and educators in Rwanda – in order to develop methods of transmitting this knowledge to young Belgian audiences.

A deeper understanding of the collaborative, multidirectional links across different organisations and memory networks is essential here. The collaboration with the CCLJ is very important for the Rwandan community, and Ibuka is using elements of the work of the CCLJ as a model for their own initiatives. For example, the CCLJ has published an illustrated book based on the story of a genocide survivor, *Sophie, l'enfant cachée*,[69] aimed at younger children aged ten to thirteen years, and Ibuka is currently developing a similar publication for the Rwandan context. Further interrogation is needed of initiatives aimed at younger children, for, as a recent survey of families in Rwanda shows, Rwandan parents have to carefully consider at what point they should disclose information about their experiences of the genocide to their children,[70] an issue that is perhaps even more sensitive in the Rwandan diaspora where children are not exposed to the history at school and have fewer opportunities to participate in public commemorative activities.

It is also important to note several new initiatives aimed at encouraging Belgian teachers to engage with Rwandan history. First, the Belgian non-profit organisation RCN Justice & Démocratie, which was created in the aftermath of the genocide against the Tutsi, launched a call for six Belgian teachers to take part in a knowledge-exchange project in Rwanda in autumn 2021, comparing approaches, methods, and good practices in education on memory.[71] RCN Justice & Démocratie also offers a series of courses for secondary school students on themes such as discrimination and stereotypes, international justice, global citizenship and solidarity, using testimony from Rwanda, Congo, Burundi, Cambodia, and Bosnia.[72] Similarly, Ibuka ran another *voyage d'études* in July 2021, in collaboration with the CCLJ, for a small group of Belgian teachers 'who want[ed] to more deeply understand the history of Rwanda, the tragic reality of 1994 and the issues arising in the post-genocide context'.[73] A condition of participating in the trip was that teachers would then be committed to delivering a historical and memorial programme to their students in the academic year 2021–22. The trip was advertised via Ibuka, the CCLJ, MNEMA, and the Fondation Auschwitz, which suggests that, while the 2019 trip involved teachers primarily from the Brussels area (Uccle and Woluwé Saint-Lambert) and Tournai, they are now attempting to reach teachers from other parts of Wallonia.

Nevertheless, these educational trips can only accommodate a small number of participants. Moreover, the cost of the trips, much of which teachers must fund themselves, may well be an obstacle to participation.[74] But above all, as the CPTM *dossier* and the select educational programmes emphasise, given the lack of coherent, systematic educational policy, these initiatives must target teachers who are personally and independently motivated to work on the subject of the genocide against the Tutsi with their students. It therefore becomes the choice of individual teachers, based on their own interests, background, and perceived capabilities, that determines who takes part in these initiatives and, ultimately, in which schools Rwandan history is taught.

Conclusions

The growing number of education-focused memory initiatives aimed at training Belgian teachers and designing effective teachings materials gives weight to the case for incorporating the history of the genocide against the Tutsi into the Belgian curriculum. It also raises crucial questions about where the teaching of this history fits into the broader history curriculum and how Belgian national colonial history is taught in schools (if at all). As Sabrina Parent, Véronique Bragard, and Maurice Amuri Mpala-Lutebele observe:

> the history of Belgian colonisation and the decolonisation of knowledge, while still not a compulsory part of the secondary education programme, is progressively finding its place in the University, in the classes aimed at future secondary school teachers who, upon discovering this hidden history, confess to not understanding the reasons for the national omission and often feel a certain shame because of this.[75]

Overcoming this sense of shame is still a major obstacle to developing a nuanced and critical education of colonial history in Belgian secondary schools. Without adequate specialist training or the provision of comprehensive teaching materials, teachers often do not feel comfortable addressing the subject in their own classrooms. Shame at their own lack of knowledge combined with the difficulty of addressing such a complex subject with young students can potentially be further compounded if there are students from the African diaspora or Afro-descendants in the classroom.

The teaching materials addressed in this study attempt to find a balance between educating students about universal values – in line with broader trends of 'citizenship education' and teaching about global imperialism, decolonisation, and anti-racist values – and the specific history of the 1994 genocide against the Tutsi. Yet teaching about, or developing materials to aid teachers in their teaching about, the genocide in Belgian schools still seems to be the work of motivated individuals and collectives. There is a prevailing lack of cohesion in the initiatives that have been or are being developed, led by a range of disparate (and mainly charitable or non-profit) organisations. Practical issues such as funding also play a key role here: charitable organisations are especially reliant on funding to be able to move forward with new initiatives or to maintain their current activities. The educational trips taking Belgian teachers to Rwanda, for example, seem to be organised on an ad hoc basis and are heavily dependent on funding or subsidies.[76]

This is linked to the historical development of education in Belgium where individual schools have retained a great deal of academic freedom – a flexibility introduced to appease heterogenous factions (Catholic versus state schools, different linguistic communities, etc.) – and raises important questions about the teaching of Belgian colonial history more broadly and the limited efficacy of the efforts to decolonise the curriculum in Belgium to date. It will be interesting to see what recommendations will be made by the Congo Commission, and whether these will extend to the Rwandan context or will remain focused on Congolese history. Moreover, this commission has been extremely divisive in the Rwandan diaspora, as the only Rwandan selected to join the commission's panel of experts is Laure Uwase, a lawyer and self-proclaimed human rights activist associated with a prominent genocide-denial organisation, Jambo asbl.[77] In an open letter published in the Flemish newspaper *De Standaard* on 17 August 2020, fifty-eight Belgian historians also heavily criticised the commission on decolonisation, claiming that the commission's primary goal of 'historic truth' is not enough and that a much broader multidisciplinary team of experts, including members of the African diaspora, is needed:

> the current debate concerning Belgian colonialism will never be resolved as long as historians continue to organise their discipline as they have done for the past several decades: maintaining their distance from public debate in the name of 'independence' all while proclaiming their exclusive rights to the discourse on the past.[78]

This points to the ongoing separation between academic historical research and the teaching of history in schools in Belgium, as well as stressing the need for more critical historical engagement in broader public debates. While the examples analysed here are valiant initiatives, it is clear that, without widespread official policy, such resources can only have a limited impact on the education curriculum in Belgium. In a climate where genocide denial and revisionism are increasingly visible and virulent (particularly in the Flemish region of Belgium, despite the 2019 law banning denial of the 1994 genocide against the Tutsi), a critical and nuanced engagement with colonial history in the education system has never been more crucial.

Notes

1. The newly rebranded AfricaMuseum in Tervuren reopened in December 2018 after an extended period of renovation and 'decolonisation' of its collections. For a critical assessment of these efforts, see, Dónal Hassett, 'Acknowledging or Occluding "The System of Violence"?: The Representation of Colonial Pasts and Presents in Belgium's AfricaMuseum', *Journal of Genocide Research*, 22.1 (2020), 26–45.
2. For example, statues of King Leopold II were removed in Brussels, Antwerp and Ghent in June 2020.
3. See, for example, the declaration by Caroline Désir, Minister of Education for Wallonie-Bruxelles, on 8 June 2020: <https://www.rtbf.be/info/societe/detail_caroline-desir-reaffirme-son-projet-de-rendre-obligatoires-les-cours-sur-l-histoire-du-congo-et-de-la-colonisation?id=10519014> [accessed 30 April 2021].
4. Most notably the introduction of identity cards, which contributed to the 'fixing' of ethnic identities in Rwanda. See, Timothy Longman, 'Identity Cards, Ethnic Self-Perception, and Genocide in Rwanda', in Jane Caplan and John Torpey (eds.), *Documenting Individual Identity: The Development of State Practices in the Modern World* (Princeton and Oxford: Princeton University Press, 2001), pp. 345–57 (p. 352–53).
5. United Nations Assistance Mission for Rwanda. The force was reduced from approximately 2,500 to 270.
6. I use the term 'implication' in line with Michael Rothberg's concept of 'implicated subjects', subjects who, without being direct agents of harm, 'help propagate the legacies of historical violence and prop up the structures of inequality that mar the present'. Michael Rothberg, *The Implicated Subject: Beyond Victims and Perpetrators* (Stanford: Stanford University Press, 2019), p. 1.
7. This can be seen, for example, with the creation in July 2020 of the special parliamentary commission examining Belgium's colonial past, informally referred to as the 'Congo Commission'.
8. United Nations OHCHR, 'UN experts challenge Belgium to confront its colonial past', 11 February 2019 <https://www.ohchr.org/en/NewsEvents/Pages/DisplayNews.aspx?NewsID=24155&LangID=E> [accessed 30 April 021].
9. Quoted in Axel Mudahemuka C. Gossiaux, 'L'éducation permanente en lutte contre le racisme et la colonialité en Belgique francophone?', Étude, FUCID (2020), pp. 1–32 (p. 16). All translations from French are my own.
10. Romain Landmeters, 'L'histoire de la colonisation belge à l'école: décentrement, distanciation, déconstruction', *BePax* (22 December 2017), pp. 1–4 <https://bepax.org/publications/l-histoire-de-la-colonisation-belge-a-l-ecole-decentrement-distanciation-deconstruction.html> [accessed 3 February 2021].
11. Sarah Demart, et al., *Des citoyens aux racines africaines: un portrait des Belgo-Congolais, Belgo-Rwandais et Belgo-Burundais* (Bruxelles: Fondation Roi Baudouin, 2017), p. 165. More than 800 Afro-descendants aged 18 and above were interviewed in this quantitative study.
12. Ibid., p. 166.
13. Antoine Tshitungu Kongolo, 'Belgique: une mémoire coloniale sélective', *Politique: revue belge d'analyse et du débat*, 65 (June 2010) <https://www.revuepolitique.be/belgique-une-memoire-coloniale-selective/> [accessed 30 April 2021].
14. See, Eric Burgraff, '(Dé)colonisation: les référentiels d'histoire sont déjà réécrits, mais pas encore enseignés, *Le Soir* 10 June 2020 <https://plus.lesoir.be/306401/article/2020-06-10/decolonisation-les-referentiels-dhistoire-sont-deja-reecrits-mais-pas-encore?> [accessed 30 April 2021].
15. Matthew Stanard, *The Leopard, the Lion, and the Cock: Colonial Memories and Monuments in Belgium* (Leuven: Leuven University Press, 2019), pp. 22–31.
16. Adam Hochschild, *King Leopold's Ghost: A Story of Greed, Terror and Heroism in Colonial Africa* (Boston: Mariner Books, 1998); Ludo De Witte, *The Assassination of Lumumba*, translated by Ann Wright and Renée Fenby (London and New York: Verso, 2001 [1999]).
17. Idesbald Goddeeris and Sindani E. Kiangu, 'Congomania in Academia: Recent Historical Research on the Belgian Colonial Past', *BMGN-LCHR*, 126.4 (2011), 54–74 (71).
18. Denise Bentrovato and Karel Van Nieuwenhuyse, 'Confronting "Dark" Colonial Pasts: a Historical Analysis of Practices of Representation in Belgian and Congolese Schools, 1945–2015', *Paedagogica Historica*, 56.3 (2020), 293–320 (295). One notable exception is Isidore Ndaywel è Nziem's *Histoire générale du Congo: De l'héritage ancien à la République Démocratique* (Paris; Brussels: Duculot, 1998), the first comprehensive history of Congo written by a Congolese academic based in Congo but published in Belgium and France.
19. Goddeeris & Kiangu, 'Congomania in Academia...', p. 54.

20. Sean O'Dubhghaill, 'Mapping the Rwandan Diaspora in Belgium', International Organization for Migration (2019) <https://publications.iom.int/books/mapping-rwandan-diaspora-belgium> [accessed 5 May 2021], p. 15.
21. For example, Félicité Lyamukuru's testimony *L'Ouragan a frappé Nyundo* (Mons: Éditions du Cerisier, 2018). The popularity of Belgian-Rwandan artists such as Stromae, whose father was killed during the genocide, has also increased public awareness of this history in Belgium.
22. See <https://www.senate.be/english/rwanda.html> [accessed 30 April 2021].
23. Louis Michel, 'Quand la Belgique présentait ses excuses au peuple rwandais', *Libération*, 12 September 2011 <https://www.liberation.fr/planete/2011/09/12/quand-la-belgique-presentait-ses-excuses-au-peuple-rwandais_760468/> [accessed 30 April 2021].
24. Nico Hirtt, *Seront-ils des citoyens critiques? Enquête auprès des élèves de fin d'enseignement secondaire en Belgique francophone et flamande* (Brussels: Appel pour une école démocratique, 2008), p. 8.
25. Gratia Pungu, 'Mémoire, stéréotypes et diaspora. Introduction', *Politique: revue belge d'analyse et du débat*, 65 (June 2010) <https://www.revuepolitique.be/le-congo-dans-nos-tetes-memoire/> [accessed 30 April 2021].
26. Landmeters, 'L'histoire de la colonisation belge à l'école…', p. 2.
27. Ibid., p. 1.
28. Ibid. The 2017 *Pacte pour un Enseignement d'Excellence* can be accessed the Fédération Wallonie-Bruxelles website: <http://www.enseignement.be/index.php?page=28280>.
29. Stéphanie Planche, 'Le "Roi colonisateur" à l'école: portrait ambivalent d'un (anti)héros', in Vincent Dujardin, et al (eds.), *Léopold II: Entre génie et gêne. Politique étrangère et colonisation* (Bruxelles: Racine, 2009), pp. 269–84 (p. 276).
30. Ibid., p. 279.
31. Valérie Rosoux and Laurence van Ypersele, 'The Belgian National Past: Between Commemoration and Silence', *Memory Studies*, 5.1 (2011), 45–57 (53).
32. Geert Castryck, 'Whose History is History? Singularities and Dualities of the Public Debate on Belgian Colonialism', in Csaba Lévai (ed.), *Europe and the World in European Historiography* (Pisa: Pisa University Press, 2006), pp. 71–88 (p. 78).
33. Rosoux & van Ypersele, 'The Belgian National Past…', p. 52.
34. Ibid., p. 54.
35. Castryck, 'Whose History is History?...', p. 76.
36. Karel Van Nieuwenhuyse, 'Increasing Criticism and Perspectivism: Belgian-Congolese (Post) Colonial History in Belgian Secondary History Education Curricula and Textbooks (1990–Present)', *Yearbook of the International Society of History Didactics*, 36 (2014), 183–204 (191).
37. Ibid., p. 191.
38. Ibid., p. 198.
39. Idesbald Goddeeris, 'Postcolonial Belgium: The Memory of the Congo', *Interventions*, 17.3 (2015), 434–51 (446).
40. Florence Gillet observes a comparable phenomenon among former Belgian colonisers in Congo and their disconnect from contemporary Belgian society. See, Florence Gillet, 'Congo rêvé? Congo détruit… Les anciens coloniaux belges aux prises avec une société en repentir. Enquête sur la face émergée d'une mémoire', *Cahiers d'histoire du temps présent*, 19 (2008), 79–133.
41. Danielle de Lame, '(Im)possible Belgian Mourning for Rwanda', *African Studies Review*, 48.2 (2005), 33–43 (35).
42. Castryck, Whose History is History?...', p. 79.
43. The analysis is limited to examples drawn from the francophone context due to my own language abilities and field of interest, combined with the fact that there are significantly more materials available in French than in Dutch.
44. Valériane Wiot, *Joseph Ndwaniye, La Promesse à ma sœur. Carnet pédagogique*. Ndwaniye's novel was first published in 2006 with Les Impressions Nouvelles.
45. Primarily taken from the Didier-Hatier textbook *Construire l'Histoire*, from Documents 63, 'l'Afrique des Grands Lac', aimed at students in Secondary 6. See <https://view.publitas.com/averbode/construire-lhistoire_manuel_6/page/3> [accessed 30 April 2021].
46. Note the usage of the museum's old 'colonial' name rather than the new 'AfricaMuseum'.
47. See <https://www.espacenord.com/fiche/carnet-pedagogique-sur-la-promesse-faite-a-ma-soeur/> [accessed 16 September 2020].
48. A summary of the *Journée de réflexion pédagogique* is available on the Cellule's website: <http://www.democratieoubarbarie.cfwb.be/index.php?id=21394> [accessed 16 September 2020].
49. The final section of the *carnet* also includes a set of exercises intended to develop students' core French language skills (speaking, writing and reading). See, Wiot, pp. 35–37.
50. See <https://www.espacenord.com/espace-pedagogique/> [accessed 16 September 2020].
51. See <https://www.muyira.be/muyira-asbl> [accessed 16 September 2020].

52. Uwindekwe P. Rwayitare and Florence Caullier, *D'Ici et d'ailleurs. Témoignages des survivants du genocide des Tutsi du Rwanda vivant en Belgique* (Brussels: Muyira asbl, 2016).
53. Spéciose Mugorewera, Félicité Lyamukuru, Justine Mudahogora, Uwindekwe P. Rwayitare and Dorcy Rugamba. Most of these are prominent members of the Rwandan diaspora community; in particular, Lyamukuru, author and President of Ibuka Mémoire et Justice (Belgique), and Rugamba, an internationally renowned author, actor and playwright.
54. See <https://www.muyira.be/d-ici-et-d-ailleurs-film-et-livret-> [accessed 16 September 2020]. It is important to note that the Muyira website has recently been updated and is now advertising a *Centre de documentation*, based in Liège, which boasts an extensive list of resources for consultation. It is possible to make a reservation online to visit the centre: <https://www.muyira.be/copie-de-bibliothèque> [accessed 14 December 2021].
55. For more information, see <http://www.enseignement.be/citoyennete>.
56. See, Karen Van Nieuwenhuyse and Kaat Wils, 'Remembrance Education Between History Teaching and Citizenship Education', *Citizenship Teaching & Learning*, 7.2 (2012), 157–71 (161).
57. Ibid., p. 160.
58. Ibid., p. 168.
59. MNEMA was originally founded in 2004 as a genocide survivor organisation based in Liège, which now manages the education and cultural centre *Cité Miroir* in Liège. For more information on the mission of MNEMA and the CPTM, see: <http://www.mnema-cptm.be/transmission-de-la-memoire>.
60. <http://www.mnema-cptm.be/dossier/rwanda-1994>; <https://www.citemiroir.be/fr/en-pratique/ecoles> [both accessed 30 April 2021].
61. CPTM, *Rwanda 1994. Dossier pédagogique* (MNEMA Editions, 2019), p. 3. The element of choice pointed to here is of crucial importance.
62. Ibid., p. 3.
63. Ibid., p. 8.
64. Gaël Faye, *Petit pays* (Paris: Editions Grasset, 2016).
65. See <http://www.federation-wallonie-bruxelles.be/a-propos-de-la-federation/apropos/> [accessed 30 April 2021].
66. The objectives of this decree are linked to the transmission, commemoration, education and critical reflection. For more information, see <http://www.democratieoubarbarie.cfwb.be/index.php?id=7800> [accessed 16 September 2020].
67. See <http://www.democratieoubarbarie.cfwb.be/index.php?id=7762> [accessed 16 September 2020].
68. Surveys have been sent out to the teachers and more in-depth follow-up interviews will be conducted in due course, although at the time of writing this data has yet to be collected. There are more details about this trip on the Ibuka. app website, including the programme, information about the sites visited, and short videos of the teachers describing their initial reactions at the end of their visit: <https://www.ibuka.app/paroles-de-profs-et-de-participants/> [accessed 14 December 2021].
69. Véronique Ruff, Florence Caulier, and Audrey Elbaum, *Sophie, l'enfant cachée* (Brussels: CCLJ, 2013).
70. Caroline Williamson Sinalo, Pierre Claver Irakoze, and Angela Veale, 'Disclosure of Genocide Experiences in Rwandan Families: Private and Public Sources of Information and Child Outcomes', *Peace and Conflict: Journal of Peace Psychology*, advance online publication (2020) <https://doi.org/10.1037/pac0000521>.
71. The project consisted of a one-day workshop in Belgium followed by a visit to Rwanda from 28 October to 6 November 2021. See <https://rcn-ong.be/appel-a-candidat-e-s-visite-denseignant-e-s-belges-au-rwanda-echange-de-bonnes-pratiques-en-matiere-de-transmission-de-la-memoire-du-28-octobre-au-6-novembre-2021/> [accessed 5 May 2021].
72. See <https://rcn-ong.be/que-faisons-nous/nos-outils-pedagogiques/> [accessed 5 May 2021]. Similarly, the Cellule DoB offered a series of online webinars in February and March 2021 for history teachers on the topic of teaching Belgian colonial history. One of the sessions focused specifically on using testimony as part of colonial history education. See <https://histoireestelle77.wixsite.com/communicationdobcaf> [accessed 5 May 2021].
73. See <http://www.mnema-cptm.be/activite/voyage-detudes-au-rwanda> [accessed 5 May 2021]. This educational trip took place from 3 to 18 July 2021, and the overarching theme was 'From colonisation to the genocide against the Tutsi in 1994'.
74. The advertised cost of the RCN trip was only €250 per teacher, as it was subsidised by the FWB and Wallonie-Bruxelles International, whereas the Ibuka trip cost €1,000 per teacher.
75. Sabrina Parent, Véronique Bragard, and Maurice Amuri Mpala-Lutebele, 'Entre évitement et ressassement: le spectre colonial belge dans les productions littéraires, artistiques et culturelles', *Revue Belge de Philologie et d'Histoire*, 97 (2019), 677–88 (681).

76. For example, the educational trip organised by Ibuka in 2019 was a response to a call for projects launched by the FWB linked to the transmission of memory.
77. See, Colette Braeckman, 'Une association rwandaise dénonce déjà le groupe d'experts sur la décolonisation', *Le Soir*, 9 August 2020 <https://plus.lesoir.be/318060/article/2020-08-09/une-association-rwandaise-denonce-deja-le-groupe-dexperts-sur-la-decolonisation> [accessed 16 September 2020].
78. Berber Bevernage et al., 'Commission Congo: la peur paralysante de l'historien', *Le Soir*, 24 August 2020 <https://plus.lesoir.be/320703/article/2020-08-24/commission-congo-la-peur-paralysante-de-lhistorien> [accessed 16 September 2020].

PART 2
International Resonances

Imperial Entanglements of the Congo/African Institute, Colwyn Bay, Wales (1889–1911)

Robert Burroughs

Introduction: Britain's Congo Free State

'Britain's' Congo Free State? My starting point might sound like counterfactualism, but I hope it makes a provocative point about Britain's position of power and influence in a colony beyond the formal bounds of its own empire. Both scholarly and popular histories have often failed to capture the many connections of Britain to the early colonial Congo, and twenty-first century remembrances tend to fall back on oversimplified understandings that square Britain's imperial role in Central Africa with humanitarianism. After establishing a critical perspective on Britain's part in the early colonial history of the Congo, my chapter will focus on a study of the Congo/African Training Institute, a school for young Africans in late nineteenth-century north Wales. Situated in a rural part of Britain, in a principality that has its own conflicted relationship to British imperialism, I explore how this institute mediated questions of race, nationality, religion, politics, and ideas about the imperialist-civilising self in general, and consider how and to what effect this case history of Britain's past entanglements in the Congo has been represented in more recent remembrances.

In its inception, the Congo Free State (1885–1908) was an international endeavour, drawing colonial administrators, traders, soldiers, missionaries, and more from throughout Europe (Belgium, Britain, France, Greece, Italy, Sweden, Denmark, and elsewhere) and the United States (see Pierre-Philippe Fraiture's chapter in this volume). Britons were at the fore of initial developments. The early years of military and environmental infrastructural advance into the Upper Congo was overseen by the Welsh American Henry Morton Stanley, and supported by several young British officers known personally to Stanley. Britain was foremost among the nations that approved Leopold II's rule of Central Africa after he promised that the imperial powers might practise free trade and religious instruction there. British businesses and missions gladly entered the region, pledging to help Leopold banish slavery and overcome Islamic influence from the east. To build its railway and to grow its armed forces, the early colony also relied on imported labour from other colonies in western and eastern Africa. Thousands of British colonial subjects from West Africa migrated to labour in the Lower Congo in the late 1880s and early 1890s, many of them joining, or being conscripted into, service in so-called wars of pacification in the Central African interior.

As Leopold sought to increase his personal profits, other trading interests were squeezed out of the Congo. Migrant labour was deprioritised and new methods of working the region's own populations were established. Many peoples of the upper-river basin were enlisted unknowingly into systems of debt bondage, to be repaid through menial labour under a threat of violent reprisal that was all too often realised. The monarch's actions soured relations between the Congo administration and its European supporters as well as with the various parties, who identified themselves as critics of Leopold. Economic interests fused with humanitarian concern as reports emerged of extraordinary violence exacted on peoples of the Upper Congo in pursuit of rubber and ivory. A Congo Reform Movement arose in Liverpool, spearheaded by the journalist E. D. Morel and the consul Roger Casement. Much of this movement's thrust came from Britain, though it, too, quickly became international in scope, as recently emphasised by Dean Pavlakis.[1] This campaign connected brutal methods of colonialism to Leopold's drive towards monopolies on trade. As Morel once indignantly quipped, in reference to the bodily mutilations for which the colony would be remembered, for both the rubber gatherer and the independent trader the Congo now meant 'hands off!'.[2]

Both scholarly and popular historians have often charted Britain's founding role in Congo colonialism and its shift to humanitarian watchdog.[3] They generally delineate too clear a transition, however, neglecting to note that Britain remained invested in the Congo. This is literally the case for businesses and missions whose stay in the region began before or outlasted Leopold's rule. The notorious Anglo-Belgian India Rubber Company, for example, was founded with British capital and maintained British shareholder investment until 1898, by which time its violent stranglehold on the peoples of the Lopori-Maringa river basin was established.[4] A number of British- and American-based Protestant missionary societies had built chains of stations up the river by this time, too. The cautious response to an unfolding scandal by mission leaders, and some rank-and-file evangelists, reflected a desire to maintain their footing in the face of mounting Catholic mission interest and competition.[5]

British 'investment' also existed in the sense of the nebulous cultural fascination in the region, as a site of colonial adventure and enterprise (even utopian thinking, as Stephen Donovan has examined), of scientific experimentation and of general interest in the supposedly exotic.⁶ Even as a popular campaign petitioned the British government to impose itself on Leopold, in the hope of humanitarian relief of his colonial subjects, Britons applauded scientists from the Liverpool School of Tropical Medicine whose findings from their sleeping sickness surveys of 1903–05 effectively exonerated the colonial regime of its part in an epidemic outbreak, a view challenged by later scientists.⁷ While British audiences turned out in large numbers to see Congo Reform lantern lectures displaying maimed Congolese bodies, British audiences flocked to see exotic performances by Ituri Forest 'pygmies' laid on by Colonel James J. Harrison, a defender of Leopold's regime, as they toured Britain between 1905 and 1907.⁸ Though reports of colonial violence and the ensuing controversy infiltrated numerous British cultural fields, others were insulated from – resistant or oblivious to – the iconography of atrocities and 'red rubber'. Emphasis upon humanitarian reaction in recent research conceals numerous ways in which sectors of British society and culture remained absorbed, often complexly and paradoxically, in a region coming to be defined by its colonial atrocities.

Acknowledging the interweaving of British imperial interests in another nation's atrocious regime is valuable for a few reasons. Without losing sight of those who were most responsible for bloodshed – a king and an international cast of officials, officers, and soldiers – this focus incorporates those lesser-known 'beneficiaries' in distant societies and cultures that gave licence to violent acts before and even amid overseas humanitarian outcry. As Bruce Robbins observes, the history of humanitarian thought has permitted privileged onlookers' indignation at the suffering of others without always requiring that those onlookers consider too deeply how their own privileges are rooted in the suffering of distant others.⁹ Locating Britain in the Congo's past calls for a more multifaceted understanding of the relations between humanitarianism and imperial violence, as well as history and memory. In Britain today, the Congo Free State represents a part of the past in which well-informed, critically minded readers, including those who wish to encourage better engagement with Britain's own colonial history, still routinely cite Adam Hochschild's *King Leopold's Ghost* (1998) and its account of British and American 'heroism' and Belgian 'greed' and 'terror'.¹⁰ To train a spotlight on those who distantly profited from the crimes of the Congo challenges this simplistic narrative, and reminds us of the difficulties of extracting the 'good' from the 'bad', and the perils of the 'balance sheet approach'.¹¹ The often unacknowledged status of the distant beneficiaries of colonialism is a measure of how far historians have been willing or able to go in understanding the full complexity of the past, and of the ways in which simple designations of 'perpetrator' or 'witness' status have been emphasised over time to ideological and political ends.

This chapter reflects upon the submerged position of Britain as beneficiary of Congo colonialism, and how this positioning affects historical knowledge and memories of the relations between these two countries. Owing to limitations of space my discussion will centre on a single case study, emerging out of Britain's evangelical interests in the colony, the Congo/African Training Institute, Colwyn Bay. Besides recovering a little-known instance of British involvement in Leopold's colony in the late 1880s and 1890s, my aim is to analyse how this school was entangled in wider debates connecting imperial Britain to Congo. Further, drawing on recent historical writings and other creative interventions, I consider how scholarly and other accounts have been shaped by the prevailing narrative of Britain's opposition to Leopold, as a result of which the Congo/African Training Institute has been regarded benignly to exist outside of wider debates on humanitarianism, violence, and African agency under colonial rule. By situating the institute in contexts of residual evangelical concerns for Central Africa, recent historical accounts and acts of memory have failed fully to discuss some of its arguably more progressive entanglements, such as its connections to histories of nascent pan-Africanism in Britain and West Africa.

The Congo/African Training Institute, Colwyn Bay

Between 1890 and 1911, the small town of Colwyn Bay, a holiday resort in north Wales, played host to an unusual experiment in imperialism, charity, and race relations. The school known initially as Congo House, or the Congo Training Institute, and later rebranded the African Training Institute, was the invention of Rev. William Hughes, a Baptist pastor who had served as a missionary in Central Africa in the early years of its colonisation by Europeans. Hughes's spell in the Congo was defined by the death of colleagues, his own sickness, and his struggles to preserve and extend a fledgling group of youths whom, he felt, were amenable to Christian instruction. Ill health forced him to abandon his mission station, and with it, so it transpired, his missionary career. But he took two youths with him from Africa. Once returned to Wales with these boys, Hughes struck upon an idea to import young Africans for practical education and religious training in what he regarded as the medically and morally healthier climes of his native north Wales. By preparing his students both as catechists and as artisans, he expected them to return to their homelands as self-supporting missionaries who could spread the word of God without recourse to financial backing from Britain's mission bodies. By 1890 he had formed a committee to oversee his work and to help attract support from subscribers, upon whose generosity his plans depended. He founded a school in a large residential building, which he renamed Congo House. In 1891 he secured patronage from the two most eminent figures in the European partition of Central Africa, Henry Morton Stanley and King Leopold II. His ideas clearly chimed with these figures' explanations of colonialism as a means of civilising philanthropy.

Hughes was greatly influenced by pervading images of Central Africa as a place of cultural and religious desolation, and he went further than many contemporary missionaries in concluding that it would be impossible for Europeans to convert Africans to Christianity on African soil. He felt that the negative influences there were too many and too great. Europeans were frequently degraded by their exposure to the climate, while elder generations of Africans could not, in his view, be saved. They 'were in such profound ignorance and darkness, that they could not thoroughly grasp anything that was said to them'.[12] His attempts to distance children from their communities were thwarted, a problem he repeatedly explained in terms of 'ignorant and superstitious' mothers.[13] The only way 'to get proper hold of the young people', as he saw it, was to 'separat[e] them as much as possible from former friends, old superstitions, and other injurious influences'.[14] Young Africans therefore were best removed entirely from their home environment. Kinkasa, the youth whom Hughes reports mysteriously to have 'found' on his way to his mission station, and taken with him, had shown the way for Hughes.[15] Moved far from his own mother, Kinkasa's loyalty was secured free of her interference. At around age ten, he was taken overseas along with one other boy, the eight-year-old Nkanza, whose mother had agreed to his departure after Hughes had paid to redeem him from enslavement.

Besides the influence of bestselling narratives of Central Africa such as Stanley's, Hughes was inspired by a work on British social reform – itself directly informed by Stanley –William Booth's *In Darkest England and the Way Out* (1890).[16] The title of Hughes's book about his own scheme, *Dark Africa and the Way Out* (1892), acknowledges this debt. From Booth, Hughes drew a belief in the morally and materially restorative benefits of the British countryside where, in 'farm colonies', the destitute might be redeemed through honest labour and devotional practice. Congo House was Hughes's project in Christian redemption through extreme relocation. In Colwyn Bay, Hughes planned a 'farm colony' of his own populated not by the British labouring poor but by Africa's so-called heathens. In drawing equivalences between metropolitan squalor and African savagery, Hughes's scheme takes its place among several other cultural developments of the fin de siècle, through which the line between imperial and domestic space became blurred, in part as a means of justifying colonialism in terms of European development. Located in north Wales, a part of Britain long identified as both part of the metropolitan centre and yet peripheral ('England's oldest colony', as it is sometimes described), Hughes's school for Africans was situated in between apparently opposed spheres – colonial and imperial, metropolitan and urban, African and European, politics and religion, domestic and international, and more – allowing or demanding that those who took interest in it situate themselves in the same nexus.

In his reminiscences, Hughes attempts to instil confidence that he had gained the consent of his young recruits. Depicting their families, in particular mothers, in terms of an incorrigible 'darkness' helped Hughes and his readers believe in his strategies as labours on behalf of a higher authority seeking the salvation of innocent young souls. On the earthly plane, in taking Kinkasa and Nkanza, Hughes acted on little authority other than his own. He had taken the children while employed by the Baptist Missionary Society, but his exit from Africa effectively signalled his retirement from this organisation. If short of institutional backing, however, Hughes's actions had considerable historical precedent. There had been a steady flow of educational migrants from Africa to Britain in the nineteenth century, many under mission auspices. As an example of the potential benefits of his plans, Hughes pointed to the story of the Yoruba Samuel Ajayi Crowther, who, as a child, had been rescued from the middle passage by HMS *Myrmidon* and educated in Sierra Leone and Britain before returning to Africa as a pioneering missionary, later becoming the first Black bishop of the Church of England.[17]

From the Congo Free State, too, educational migration had become common. The Catholic White Fathers had established the Institut des Jeunes Noirs in Malta in 1881, which received at least five pupils from the Congo plus more from other African territories. Dozens of pupils, boys and girls, arrived at Abbot Van Impe's Institut St.-Louis de Gonzague in east Flanders between 1888 and 1900.[18] In Britain, too, Baptist missionaries, including individuals known to Hughes, brought their young charges from the Congo to Europe on periods of furlough in the late 1880s and early 1890s. Further afield, Congo-born students were enrolled in institutions created primarily for African American education. A handful of young male intakes at Wayland Seminary, Washington corresponded with the students at Congo House, while in Atlanta, Georgia, Spelman Seminary received young women sent by the American Baptist Missionary Union.[19]

Missionaries believed that exposure to 'civilisation' would be of benefit to African trainees. Their time overseas was usually carefully circumscribed, and confined to limited roles. Often employed as personal servants, they were also involved in publicising the work of the mission to audiences of potential donors. As well as sometimes receiving schooling themselves they could help missionaries in learning African languages and in preparing printed language texts.

Despite this productivity, and the modesty of the opportunities availed to them, however, the travels of young mission converts were a source of anxiety among mission leaders of various denominations, including the baptists with whom Hughes was closely affiliated. Subscribing to racialised ideas about the moral infirmity of Africans, they speculated that exposure to European civilisation might lead individuals to become conceited and proud, unable to reintegrate among their own people as productive parts of society.

When outlining his own relocation scheme, Hughes conceded that too often earlier generations of young converts had been spoiled by the hospitality they received in Britain.[20] Nonetheless, Nkanza and Kinkasa travelled in north Wales with Hughes. They participated in his public lectures and sermons as specimens of African life and as examples of the potential of African youth for education and Christianity. They recited hymns in their own language, Welsh, and English, danced to African music, and wore African dress over the top of their suits. They were thrust into a public spotlight, though there is little sense from the available reportage that they were overly indulged by Hughes or their hosts. Their experiences should be situated in the wider context of colonised peoples' performative communication of colonial and racial ideologies, and their time as what Sadiah Qureshi terms 'peoples on parade' seems to have been laborious.[21]

However generic and stereotypical, the students' performances of African culture and customs took on specific meanings in the context of north Wales. In parading the benefits of his scheme before Welsh audiences, Hughes's students not only reflected upon the 'Dark Continent' but also the communities that received them. If lectures on the missionary movement in Africa had become a standardised means by which the British public established its evangelical credentials, then the presence of young Africans among British congregations, praying and participating in alms alongside one another, disclosed with unusual explicitness that the goal of civilising 'others' was intimately bound up in the mission to civilise the British self, in all its social, cultural, and geographical diversity. Their presence among the Welsh flocks spoke to ideas about exceptional zeal among the people of north Wales for the church and the missionary movement. The school's appeal, in other words, also was constituted by how the British, and in particular the Welsh, saw themselves, and in promoting the specific tonic of residence in north Wales, Hughes's school entered implicitly into a debate on the civilisational fitness of Britain, and the need for social uplift in British society.

Between 1888 and 1893, European missionaries sent a further nine students to north Wales from the Congo, as well as some from the Cameroons with connections to missions in the Lower Congo. By then, the school had been established in Colwyn Bay, and the pupils' lives became more sedentary. Schoolwork became routine, and many of the male students were entered into apprenticeships with local tradespeople. Some of the youths from this period emerged as star pupils who were keenly supported by the local community during their stay and in preparation for their return to Africa. Frank Teva Clark kept up correspondence with Hughes as well as other families in Colwyn Bay after his successful four-year residence in Wales, at the end of which Teva Clark voyaged on to Central Africa for a new career as missionary. His achievements were among the stories of success fondly recalled by Hughes in public writings seeking to attract support for the scheme.[22] His time in the limelight was explained as the natural consequence of personal qualities, which marked him out as a potential trailblazer for Christ in Africa. Individuals such as Hughes successfully negotiated the demands and expectations made upon the students to appear as living proof of redemptive power of cultural transformation in line with the same ideologies and race and empire that justified Europeans' violent acquisition of African resources.

But not all students experienced Colwyn Bay in this way. Life there imposed specific, racialised behavioural expectations on the students, and where they did not conform to these, British society judged them harshly.[23] Those students who won less local support, whose spell in Wales ended with little fanfare, have left behind a scant archival record, the quietness of which speaks suggestively of the demands placed upon Black migrants to Britain in this context. Time in Congo House was further significantly gendered.[24] The few female students were more closely associated with family life, and their educational experience channelled them towards futures as missionaries' wives. While the male students received donors' gifts that prepared them for professions – writing equipment or formal clothing, for example – Ernestina Francis, one of the female students, received 'sewing things' among her presents.[25] Hers was the longest of all residences at Congo House, one which was ended finally by marriage to another student, the African American Joseph Morford. Having arrived in 1891 at age eight, Ernestina Francis embarked to join Morford in West Africa in 1906.

Congo House was also a place of illness and death – for Hughes's own family as well as for his students. Among the students who died while in Colwyn Bay was both Kinkasa, whose death at age twelve was, according to a local surgeon, owing to a residual bout of sleeping sickness in 1888, and Nkanza, who succumbed to heart failure on 3 April 1892, aged fifteen.

In spite of the hardships, surveying the achievements of Nkanza, Teva, and other students, Hughes felt able to declare his plans a success by 1890.[26] Almost immediately, however, he was forced to acknowledge that his plans were in peril owing to political developments in the Congo and the Cameroons.[27] While relations with the independent churches in the Cameroons would continue in spite of German rivalries, the Congo Free State authorities' ban on educational migration from the Congo, also affecting the schools in Malta and Flanders, soon thwarted the recruitment of students from its European missions.[28]

After initially drawing all his intakes from the Congo, in 1893 Hughes established recruitment depots in the German-occupied Cameroons, the Republic of Liberia, and the British Niger Coast Protectorate. In other parts of British West Africa, including Sierra Leone, Lagos, and the Gold Coast (Ghana), African supporters of Hughes's venture formed subcommittees that provided financial assistance and publicity, and helped select new trainees. The subcommittees also subscribed (in all senses) to advancing their own interests through the narrative of civilisational uplift via imperial education.

In the 1900s the catchment of Congo House expanded further to include small numbers of arrivals from southern Africa, the United States, and the Caribbean. Brought together by their shared racial heritage, this student body was quite diverse in terms of social and cultural background, age, and place of origin. Backed by wealthy patrons or parents in Africa, these students often regarded Congo House as a kind of finishing school to prepare them for university study. While some would enter into clerical careers, others moved on to careers in industry, teaching, medicine, and law. When resident in Britain, some pursued short careers as what Hakim Adi describes as 'student politicians', petitioning the authorities and the public on colonial injustices that affected them and their compatriots.[29] Where these appeals won support from donors of Congo House, they can be said to have shifted the focus of humanitarian culture. Traditional depictions of 'darkest Africa' at times made way for more progressive accounts, by the students themselves, of their progress and their aspirations, often in spite of hostile attitudes and official policies. Some of the later arrivals would be associated with early Ethiopianist and pan-Africanist organisation in Britain, of a kind that continued to attract support from much the same people as had backed the school in its earlier phase.

In total, eighty-seven students, including three girls and young women, attended Congo House, according to lists published by Hughes. However, the overall number is debatable, as Hughes seems both to have overlooked individuals and to have nominated others whose relations to the institute were ambiguous.[30] This indeterminacy is significant because of what it suggests about Hughes's own practices. The school collapsed in 1911 amid racist uproar in the British press concerning the 'black scoundrel' John Lionel Franklin, a man with a chequered past registered as a student, who had fathered a child with a White woman in Colwyn Bay.[31] Hughes claimed libel, and the subsequent trial exposed his own questionable bookkeeping under severe financial pressure over several years. Hughes had falsified some accounts, misled donors on details of student registrations, and even misappropriated the bequest of one of the female students. The trial ruined Hughes. In 1917 he sought to return to Africa for a third time, this time as a missionary in the Cameroons.[32] Ironically, he inverted the logic of his earlier scheme, positioning himself as one in need of redemption from those to whom he had previously imagined himself to offer it. Despite some of his old students coming to his aid, the plan was soon aborted. He died in the Conwy workhouse in 1923, leaving relatively few traces of his endeavours.[33]

Remembering Congo House

The school disappeared. Beyond the local milieu, few remembered Hughes, or Congo House. The fictional statue 'of the great Welshman (1856–1924) who sacrificed himself for the planting of Christianity in Darkest Africa', which watches cold-eyed over the events of the Guyanese author Denis Williams's experimental novel set in Wales, *The Third Temptation* (1968), seems not only to resemble Hughes but also to capture the obsolescence of his story in the midtwentieth century.[34] That story would be recovered, albeit briefly, in major studies of the historic Black presence in Britain.[35] Substantial academic studies appeared in the 1980s and early 1990s, moreover, including research by the Congolese Belgian historian Mathieu Zana Aziza Etambala.[36] These have been recently supplemented by accounts by local historians in Wales, including Christopher Draper and John Lawson-Reay's *Scandal at Congo House: William Hughes and the African Institute, Colwyn Bay* (2012).[37] But while the latter are replete with anecdotal detail and local history, they are largely based around defensive accounts of Hughes's actions, which are cast as progressive in comparison to the opinions of his contemporaries. Hughes's story is furthermore foregrounded at the expense of his students or their African supporters. As a result, *Scandal at Congo House* risks a 'white saviour' optic in which Hughes's actions are key to the fates of his students, while, as individuals, their significance to him is as walk-on actors in a rise-and-fall narrative that means little to their lives. For example, when weighing up the success of Hughes at the end of the book, the authors of *Scandal at Congo House* dubiously point to some of the later achievements of the students as evidence of the value of Hughes's venture.[38]

The story of Congo House has been deftly woven into a more critical discussion of British society and its imperial past, *Sugar and Slate* (2002), by the academic and author Charlotte Williams. In a number of publications and initiatives, Williams has enriched understanding of Wales's multicultural past. *Sugar and Slate*, which won Wales Book of the Year in 2003, is a memoir of growing up as a mixed-race child and young adult in Wales, Guyana, and Africa. As a work of life-writing, *Sugar and Slate* consciously takes an imaginative approach to its historical source materials. Bonds of kinship are sought with earlier generations not literally but creatively, in the acts of remembering and writing that traverse the time and space of the Black Atlantic. For Williams, '[w]hen I visit the graves of the Congo boys I feel just like those pilgrims to the slave fortresses at Elmina in Ghana who stand in ancestral spaces and recreate the past in the present'.[39] In contrast to the straightforward reproduction of a paternalistic image of Hughes, Kinkasa, and Nkanza on the cover of *Scandal at Congo House*, Williams 'studie[s] the old photos to see if I could see anything of the spirit of the boys'. Though unable to penetrate their 'bland and lifeless' faces, she does identify personal connections: 'The Reverend stands between them in the picture looking like my Uncle John'.[40] Identifying herself with Hughes, rather than the boys, at this juncture, Williams situates herself between histories and identities.

Exploration of the self, rather than the archive, leads this writer to claim of Hughes's pupils: 'I feel that I know something about their voyage across the Atlantic'.[41] Williams is of course also informed by the work of local historians, in particular her friend Ivor Wynne Jones, which perhaps encourages her particular focus upon Kinkasa and Nkanza, 'the Congo boys'. And just as the photograph of Hughes recalls her British affiliations, there are times when the language used by Williams repeats that of her local informants, and even their nineteenth-century sources. Of an early reference to the 'Dark Continent', of her speculation as to the 'pigmy' identity of Nkanza, and of her statement that Kinkasa and Nkanza 'carried the memory of the power of their witchdoctor deep inside them long after they reached Wales', it might be said that the desire to understand their inner lives beyond their 'bland and lifeless' portrait photographs leads Williams ambiguously to deploy the same exoticising language as characterises many nineteenth-century sources on the subject.[42]

In certain passages this text betrays further affinities to the White patrons who had originally taken interest in the Congo boys. A literal echo of Hughes himself is apparent in one passage, which begins by borrowing his words. In his book *Dark Africa and the Way Out*, Hughes had observed of Nkanza that '[t]he idea of going home grew in his heart as he grew'.[43] Williams repeats and elaborates on this idea:

> As Nkanza grew, so the desire to return to his homeland grew in his heart. The edges of his dreams were fringed with sadness. As he slept his spirit roamed the forests listening to the roar of the lion in the distance, he heard the hum of the songs of his ancestors on the lips of the huntsman, he heard the women's stories as they planted manioc and he yearned for home.[44]

While Williams's memoir incorporates the story of Congo House into a wider, imaginative pan-African framework, one in which British racism and the violence of imperialism are explored, and the personal histories of the author mediated, it also betrays some of the same deference to essentialising nineteenth-century sources as is evident in local historians' accounts. These parts of *Sugar and Slate* are symptomatic of deep, cultural ensnarement, which other parts of the book consciously diagnose. Williams's focus, moreover, is largely upon the early, Congo phases of the school, despite her having spent part of her childhood in regions of Nigeria, which would become one of the largest suppliers to Congo House in its later years (the Nigerian territories are omitted from Williams's list of places from which Hughes drew students[45]). In this sense, too, her book takes its cue from earlier historical perspectives on the school.

Connections between Africa and Wales, past and present, have also been forged through the work of Norbert X. Mbu-Mputu. Mbu-Mputu moved to London as an asylum seeker, having been arrested for investigating political corruption in Congo-Kinshasa. Having previously visited this European capital as part of a successful career, which included work for the United Nations, he found himself homeless. Eventually immigration services relocated him to Wales, where he continued his career as a journalist, activist, researcher, and charity worker.[46] Serendipitously, the move to Wales provided Mbu-Mputu with a connection to his homeland. He is from the same region of Congo as the first recruits to Congo House, a connection which enables him to pursue extraordinary knowledge of their lives. Working between Britain and Africa, he has investigated the historic links between Wales and Congo. On a journey to Colwyn Bay, he spoke to the locals, found the graves of the African students, and learned of their stories. With support from the Heritage Lottery Fund, Mbu-Mputu led a project to help young people in south Wales explore the shared heritage of Congolese and Welsh communities. One outcome of this work was his book *Bamonimambo (the Witnesses): Rediscovering Congo and British Isles Common History* (2012), which draws upon oral sources to further document Congo House and its students.[47] At each turn, Mbu-Mputu's work has forged opportunities for sharing and understanding across the divides of community, race, age, and language. With support from community historians, he has been involved in a visit by a delegation from the Democratic Republic of Congo's UK Embassy to Colwyn Bay and to Bangor, where the largest archival holding for Congo House is kept.[48] These encounters inspired another delegation from the same embassy to travel to Colwyn Bay for a day of celebration, in which the graves of the Congo boys were reconsecrated. Moving amateur footage of this event is available on YouTube.[49]

For much of the 2010s, local historians continued to recover the history of Congo House as part of an African Institute Research Group. Their work continues in much the same spirit established by Mbu-Mputu: seeking to connect communities across continents through shared history. While much of this work is admirable, a film made by members of this group in association with Crefft Media, *The Remarkable Reverend William Hughes and the African Institute of Colwyn Bay* (2018), is too uncritical and apologetic in its discussion of Hughes and his motives to be of use to students and researchers.[50]

Conclusion

Looking across these recent retrievals of the story of Congo House, there has been a general focus on local history, and a reluctance to delve into critical frameworks of colonial history. A concentration on those initial voyagers from Central Africa, as opposed to later arrivals from western and southern Africa, and further afield, is another noticeable element of this historical framing. In many ways this emphasis is understandable. (My own discussion is similarly focused on the Congo, of course.) The early years of Hughes's venture are the better documented ones. Many of Hughes's own accounts cater to popular interest by recalling his encounters with Kinkasa and Nkanza, and by highlighting the successes represented by the likes of Frank Teva Clark. As later generations arrived in greater numbers, they received rather less individual coverage. And because those later arrivals travelled from parts of Africa that had, and would continue to have, several other points of connection to Britain and British history, their stories are less central to those nations' diasporic histories in Europe than is the case for the 'Congo boys' of Colwyn Bay. That Congo House is a rare but rich chapter in relations between Britan (or Wales) and Congo is precisely the claim of much of the recent coverage.

However, the focus upon the early years of the school does of course shape our understanding of it in significant ways, and is linked to the anodyne and apologetic tone of recent coverage. The recruits from Congo are in fact distinct among all the students of Congo House (excepting a small number of early recruits from the Cameroons) in that they were brought to Europe exclusively under the auspices of European missionaries. Later generations secured their place with important patronage from members of the 'mediated classes' of Africa, in particular leaders of the African-initiated or Ethiopianist church movement. Recent coverage loses sight of the ways in which Congo House changed over time under these forces, catering to its supporters from among the African elites by rethinking its own evangelical aims in favour of enabling matriculation for young Africans bound for university education and professional careers in medicine and law. It is instructive to situate the prospects of those Congo-born youths who survived their time in Colwyn Bay, each of whom moved on to mission service, alongside those alternative career paths afforded to later arrivals. It is also important to note, as Hazel King does in her excellent scholarly accounts, that in bringing together educated young people from across Africa, the school briefly became an early pan-African meeting ground.[51] Some of the Congo-born intakes remained in north Wales to share their experiences with classmates from western Africa, and eminent visitors such as the independent church leader Mojola Agbebi, a follower of E. W. Blyden, though this aspect of their lives is obscured by the focus on Hughes, White patrons, and evangelical networks.

While the African supporters were navigating their own identities vis-à-vis colonial discourses on darkness and enlightenment, and perhaps problematically conforming to European racist ideals of civilisational difference, just like Hughes's Welsh patrons, it is important to give full consideration of their outlooks, which were also complex and which could differ from European mission agencies in important ways. It can be said that the Ethiopianist convergence on Colwyn Bay in the early 1900s did expose not only the students but also their audiences to different lines of Christian and imperialist thought. Placing the spotlight on the Congo travellers, then, emphasises the White evangelical networks through which paternalistic authority was maintained, at the expense of knowledge of the Afrocentric networks, which provided not only students but also financial support for and interests in Hughes's scheme. In de-emphasising Black patronage of Congo House, one of the truly unique aspects of its history, recent accounts have underemphasised African agency in British humanitarian culture. The inaccessibility of these pan-African networks to Congolese owing to particularly oppressive education policies in the early colonial period also becomes apparent when the historical lens is broadened.

Besides the early history of pan-Africanism, it is possible also for the past voyages of Congolese to late nineteenth-century Britain to be placed in the more critical framework with which I began this paper, that of Britain's ongoing imperial relation with the Congo Free State. Students of Congo House show how a charity and its small community of donors, organisers, and aid recipients existed at the same time as, but largely avoided crossing over with, the emerging debate on human rights in Central Africa. Indeed, the ban on Congolese educational migration to Europe was a symptom of the mounting oppressive character of colonialism, which Hughes responded to by looking further afield for his students. But Hughes did not abandon support for Leopold, and Hughes continued to court the monarch's favour even after serious concerns about the Congo Free State were raised in the British press.[52] The lives of the early, Congo-born intakes of his school were shaped by Britain's formative role in the founding of that colony, as well as those channels that maintained links between it and Britain even as humanitarian concerns grew.

It was possible for Hughes and his school to coexist with the scandal in the Congo because Congo House was founded in a residual alternative version of humanitarianism based around evangelistic, paternalistic deference to a higher authority. Even if some progressive voices in Britain were considering alternatives to this form of rule, many instead, or nonetheless, remained invested in the old ways of seeing Africa. This bifurcated understanding of Central Africa has allowed historians to neglect that residual strain of evangelical humanitarian culture, instead attending to, and even celebrating, the Congo Reform Movement as ushering in a new and more secular understanding of human rights. Whether or not it did so, it was those contemporaneous, traditional forms of evangelism that marked the lives of the students of Congo House, as well as other Congolese travellers to Britain in this period. The fact that Congo House continues to be remembered apologetically in an evangelical framework, while British contributions to Congo reform are lionised, suggests Britain's understanding of its past investments in the Congo remains bifurcated. In recovering the evangelical side of Britain's past relation to the Congo Free State, it is vital to think critically about it, and to situate the lives of the 'Congo boys' outside of it, including in pan-Africanist networks of the time.

Notes

The author thanks Yvette Hutchison, Pierre-Philippe Fraiture, and Norbert X. Mbu-Mputu for commentary on an earlier draft of this chapter.

1. Dean Pavlakis, *British Humanitarianism and the Congo Reform Movement* (Farnham: Ashgate, 2015), pp. 157–74.
2. E. D. Morel, *King Leopold's Rule in Africa* (London: Heinemann, 1904), p. 295.
3. Scholarly accounts include S.J.S Cookey, *Britain and the Congo Question, 1885–1913* (London: Longmans, 1968); Roger Anstey, *Britain and the Congo in the Nineteenth Century* (London: Longmans, Green and Co, 1982). Popular accounts include Adam Hochschild's hugely influential *King Leopold's Ghost: A Story of Greed, Terror and Heroism in Colonial Africa* (Boston: Houghton Mifflin, 1998); Dan Snow's *History of Congo*, dir. Robin Barnwell (BBC Northern Ireland: This World, 2013).
4. Robert Harms, 'The World Abir Made: The Margina-Lopori Basin, 1885–1903', *African Economic History*, 12 (1983), 125–39.
5. For a discussion of how this caution shaped an individual missionary's life, see my article, which is forthcoming in *Cultural and Social History*: 'The Redeemed Life of Lena Clark, Christian Missionary and Humanitarian in the Congo Free State'.
6. For an array of European cultural interests in the Congo, see 'Europe Made in Africa: The Congo Free State in Literature and Culture, 1885–1920', a special issue of *English Studies in Africa*, 59.1 (2016), 1–86, ed. by Stephen Donovan, which includes Donovan's article 'Congo Utopia', 63–75.
7. Maryinez Lyons, *The Colonial Disease: A Social History of Sleeping Sickness in Northern Zaire, 1900–1940* (Cambridge: Cambridge University Press, 1992).
8. Jeffrey Green, 'Edwardian Britain's Forest Pygmies', *History Today*, 45.8 (1995) <https://www.historytoday.com/archive/edwardian-britains-forest-pygmies> [accessed 18 December 2020].
9. See Bruce Robbins, *The Beneficiary* (Durham, NC: Duke University Press, 2017).
10. I refer to the subtitle of Hochschild, *King Leopold's Ghost: A Story of Greed, Terror and Heroism in Colonial Africa*.
11. Alan Lester, 'Time to Throw Out the Balance Sheet Approach', Snapshots of Empire: University of Sussex, 26 January 2016 <https://blogs.sussex.ac.uk/snapshotsofempire/2016/01/26/time-to-throw-out-the-balance-sheet/> [accessed 18 December 2020].
12. William Hughes, *Dark Africa and the Way Out; or, A Scheme for Civilizing and Evangelizing the Dark Continent* (London: Sampson Low, Marston, 1892), p. 98.
13. Ibid., p. 39. See also pp. 41–43.
14. Ibid., p. 8.
15. Ibid., p. 90.
16. General [William] Booth, *In Darkest England and the Way Out* (London: Salvation Army 1890); see Felix Driver, *Geography Militant: Cultures of Exploration and Empire* (Oxford: Blackwell, 2001), pp. 170–98.
17. Hughes, *Dark Africa*, p. 5. For a pertinent discussion of this African cleric, see V.Y. Mudimbe, *The Invention of Africa: Gnosis, Philosophy, and the Order of Knowledge* (Bloomington and Indianapolis: Indiana University Press; London: James Currey, 1988), p. 49.
18. Barbara A. Yates, 'Educating Congolese Abroad: An Historical Note on African Elites', *The International Journal of African Historical Studies*, 14.1 (1981), 34–64 (38). Mathieu Zana Aziza Etambala, *Des Écoliers congolais en Belgique 1888–1900: Une page d'histoire oubliée* (Paris: Editions L'Harmattan, 2011).
19. Mathieu Zana Aziza Etambala, 'Congolese Children at the Congo House in Colwyn Bay (North Wales, Great-Britain), at the End of the 19th Century', *Afrika Focus*, 3.3–4 (1987), 237–85 (238–39); Hughes, *Dark Africa*, p. 27; Burroughs, 'Redeemed Life'.
20. Hughes, *Dark Africa*, pp. 25–26.
21. Sadiah Qureshi, *Peoples on Parade: Exhibitions, Empire, and Anthropology in Nineteenth-Century Britain* (Chicago: University of Chicago Press, 2011). See also Pascal Blanchard et al, eds. *Human Zoos: Science and Spectacle in the Age of Colonial Empires* (Liverpool: Liverpool University Press, 2008).
22. For example, Hughes, *Dark Africa*, pp. 106–08.
23. I detail a racist backlash against one of the students in the national press in Robert Burroughs, 'The Racialisation of Gratitude in Victorian Culture', *Journal of Victorian Culture*, 25.4 (2020), 477–91.
24. For a more detailed discussion of discussion of gender, education and Congo colonialism, see Burroughs, 'The Redeemed Life'. For wider context, Victoria K. Haskins and Claire Lowrie (eds.), *Colonization and Domestic Service: Historical and Contemporary Perspectives* (New York: Routledge, 2015).
25. [William Hughes], *Report of the Congo House Training Institute for African Students, Colwyn Bay, N Wales* (Colwyn Bay: Rev RE Jones and Bros [1893]), p. 60.

26. [William Hughes], *Report of the Congo House Training Institute for African Children, Colwyn Bay, North Wales* (Colwyn Bay: H.W. Powlson, 1890), p. 9.
27. [William Hughes], *Report of the Congo House Training Institute for African Students, Colwyn Bay, North Wales* (Colwyn Bay: H.W. Powlson, 1891), p. 54.
28. Yates, 'Educating Congolese Abroad'.
29. Hakim Adi, 'Bandele Omoniyi: A Neglected Nigerian Nationalist', *African Affairs*, 90 (1991), 581–605 (581).
30. Eighty-seven names are listed in the final Annual Reports for the school, which are the most authoritative records available. These are the basis for the list in Christopher Draper and John Lawson-Reay, *Scandal at Congo House: William Hughes and the African Institute, Colwyn Bay* (Llanwrst: Gwasg Carreg Gwelch, 2012), pp. 214–17. At other times, however, Hughes claimed that '[u]pwards of a hundred students have now passed through the Institute and gone their ways'. [William Hughes], *Annual Report of the British and African Incorporated Association, Otherwise Known as the African Training Institute, Colwyn Bay, North Wales* (Colwyn Bay: African Training Institute, 1909), p. 12.
31. 'A Baptist Mission Scandal. II', *John Bull*, 23 December 1911.
32. [William Hughes], *Third Visit of the Rev. W. Hughes, Colwyn Bay, to the West Coast of Africa, brief Account of the Cameroons, the Native Hymn and Tune Book, and the Native Churches of that Land* (Wrexham: Hughes and Son, 1917).
33. Draper and Lawson-Reay, *Scandal at Congo House*, pp. 265–67.
34. Denis Williams, *The Third Temptation* (Leeds: Peepal Tree Press, 2010), p. 43.
35. Congo House is noted in Peter Fryer, *Staying Power: The History of Black People in Britain* (London: Pluto Press, 1984), p. 438, for example; and Jeffrey Green, *Black Edwardians: Black People in Britain 1901–1914* (London: Routledge, 1998), pp. 139, 141, 232, 241, 265.
36. Yates, 'Educating Congolese Abroad'; Hazel King, 'Mojola Agbebi: African Church Leader', in Rainer Lotz and Ian Pegg (eds.), *Under the Imperial Carpet: Essays in Black History 1780–1950* (Crawley, England: Rabbit Press, 1986), pp. 84–108; Hazel King, 'Cooperation in Contextualization: Two Visionaries of the African Church: Mojọla Agbebi and William Hughes of the African Institute, Colwyn Bay', *Journal of Religion in Africa*, 16.1 (1986), 2–21; Etambala, 'Congolese Children at the Congo House'.
37. Draper and Lawson-Reay, *Scandal at Congo House*. See also Neil Evans and Ivor Wynne Jones, 'Wales and Africa: William Hughes and the Congo Institute', in Charlotte Williams, Neil Evans, and Paul O'Leary (eds.), *A Tolerant Nation? Revisiting Ethnic Diversity in a Devolved Wales* (Cardiff: University of Wales Press, 2015), pp. 106–27.
38. Draper and Lawson-Reay, *Scandal at Congo House*, p. 278. I am attempting a study focused on the students' experiences in a forthcoming monograph, *Black Students in Imperial Britain: The African Institute, Colwyn Bay, 1889–1911* (Liverpool University Press).
39. Charlotte Williams, *Sugar and Slate* (Ceredigion: Planet, 2002), p. 26.
40. Ibid., p. 29.
41. Ibid., p. 33.
42. Ibid., pp. 8, 26, 27.
43. Hughes, *Dark Africa*, p. 114.
44. Williams, *Sugar and Slate*, p. 32.
45. Ibid., p. 28.
46. 'Building Bridges', Croeso I Gymru, BBC Wales <http://www.bbc.co.uk/wales/audiovideo/sites/yourvideo/pages/norbertx_mbumputu_01.shtml> [accessed 18 December 2020].
47. 'Young Africans Explore Congo Roots', BBC Local: South East Wales <http://news.bbc.co.uk/local/southeastwales/hi/people_and_places/arts_and_culture/newsid_8234000/8234119.stm> [accessed 18 December 2020]; Norbert X Mbu-Mputu et al., *Bamonimambo (the Witnesses): Rediscovering Congo and British Isles Common History* ([Newport]: South People's Projects, 2015).
48. 'Town Council Welcomes Congolese Delegation', Bay of Colwyn: Town Council <https://www.colwyn-tc.gov.uk/town-council-welcomes-congolese-delegation/ https://www.dailypost.co.uk/news/local-news/bangor-universitys-historic-congo-link-11569154> [accessed 18 December 2020].
49. 'Minutes of a Meeting of the Bay of Colwyn Town Council [...] on Monday 17th October 2016' <https://www.colwyn-tc.gov.uk/wp-content/uploads/2016/12/MIN-Council-17.10.16.pdf> [accessed 18 December 2020]; Black History Month North Wales <http://www.bhmnw.com/index.asp?pageid=580958> [accessed 18 December 2020]; '19 11 16 Return of the Congolese', YouTube <https://www.youtube.com/watch?v=Dp-4jBhQIzXo> [accessed 18 December 2020].
50. *The Remarkable Reverend William Hughes and the African Institute* (Llangefni: Crefft Media [2018]).
51. King, 'Mojola Agbebi'; King, 'Cooperation in Contextualisation'.
52. Hughes to Leopold, 18 May 1903, rpt. in Draper and Lawson-Reay, *Scandal at Congo House*, pp. 161–62.

Performative Challenges to Belgium's Colonial Amnesia
Mobilising Archives and Resonant Spaces

Yvette Hutchison

Colonial amnesia, the choice to forget or remember certain aspects of colonial history in specific ways, is often experienced simultaneously as déjà vu because the violence and traumas of a past keep returning to haunt the present. Ann Stoler's edited book has usefully tracked some of the durable traces on the material environment and people's bodies and minds that continue to revisit the present.[1] To address this haunting, many countries have set up truth commissions to 'promote reconciliation, outline needed reforms, allow victims a cathartic airing of their pains, and represent an important, official acknowledgement of a long-silenced past'.[2] In July 2020 the Belgium parliament appointed 'a "special commission" [...] to look into Belgium's colonial past in Congo, Rwanda and Burundi'.[3] This commission tasked historians, political scientists, and lawyers to scope both 'the known fundamentals and historical consensus on colonization, but they will also mention the grey areas, the aspects on which they disagree among themselves, the historical gaps'.[4] That this was set up as a special commission, not a commission of inquiry or a truth commission that would formally investigate a period of history, suggests that Belgium acknowledges a need to engage with its colonial past, but is not prepared to fully interrogate it. In this chapter I argue that artists and performances, not included in this process officially, can play a particular role in challenging colonial amnesia and negotiating sensitive colonial histories and archives. I analyse how they can and have engaged visual memories of the past critically by connecting archives of the past with Belgium's present particularly through the use of resonant spaces to challenge the 'known fundamentals and historical consensus on colonization' before this commission was constituted.

In my approach to resonance, I draw on two ideas: the idea of sympathetic resonance observed in musical instruments, which occurs when one string starts to vibrate and produce sound after a different one is struck; and the phenomenon of echolocation, a physiological process used by humans or animals to locate distant or invisible objects (such as prey or an obstacle) by sound waves reflected back to the emitter (a blind person's cane) from the objects. Thus, resonance can involve a sympathetic response evoked in recognition of a stimulus played back to one – in this case, histories of the past provoke an awareness of behaviours or attitudes that continue to impact the present. The sense that a sound can both orient a person and provoke further sounds frames my analysis of the ways in which artists have used archival material and spaces that have particular associations with the past to facilitate predominantly European audiences positioning themselves critically in relation to diverse colonial histories. This positioning can then produce further awareness regarding how these pasts are affecting the present and could define our futures.

But what is meant by 'an archive'? There is much debate about the relationship between memory and archive. The director of the networking, advocacy, and research initiative Archival Platform, Jo-Anne Duggan, has suggested that:

> The act of exteriorising, or sharing, shifts memory from the private realm of the individual into the public domain. But this does not necessarily mean that it enters the archive. As with records, memory enters the archive when it is both exteriorised and deemed to be of archival value. Deemed memories enter the archive because they are considered to be potentially valuable to us when we think about the past. As valued resources, they demand preservation so that they can be accessible to others, in the present and in the future.[5]

Thus, archives are not so much about presenting facts as defining a shared understanding of the past in the present. Derrida refers to 'the social and political power of the archive, which consists in selecting the traces in memory, in marginalising, censoring, destroying, such and such traces through precisely a selection, a filter',[6] in order to constitute a collective, formal version of the past in service of narrating the nation and its core values coherently.[7] An archive is established, made visible, and disseminated through written historical narratives, literature, monuments, museums, and exhibitions. These processes can be compared to Austinian performative utterances,[8] which not only describe a given reality, but at the moment of their utterance ('I do'), they change the social reality that is being described ('I am now married'). Thus, a material formulation of a narrative constitutes it into social being as an accepted reality.

Belgium's official remembering of King Leopold II's colonisation of the Congo from 1885 to 1908, and the Belgian state's engagement with the colony thereafter, exemplifies this clearly. As Julien Bobineau[9] and Matthew Stanard[10] convincingly demonstrate, official Belgium colonial records have tended to emphasise Leopold II's mission and the Belgian state's involvement in the colonial Congo areas as being 'civilisational' and 'philanthropic'.[11] Bobineau notes

Figure 1. Statue of King Leopold II, Ostend, Belgium, 1931. Photo: Georges Jansoone.

that from 'the 1910s Belgian historians gradually began to glorify the deceased king in order to justify the purchase of the colony', by convincing the public that the 'wild Africans' needing 'to be dressed, missionised and civilised'.[12] Castryck suggests that even 1970s school textbooks continued to present this image of 'Belgian heroism, until Congo disappeared from history courses altogether'.[13]

Given this silence or disavowal of Belgium's colonial history, visual memorials are particularly significant as mnemonic embodiments of how the state has remembered this past for the nation. There are many monuments of Leopold II, ubiquitously sitting astride a horse, looking powerful. However, I want to consider an unusual rendering of him in the Royal Galleries, built to protect the bourgeois from the rain and wind when they went to the Royal Palace racetrack by the beach in Ostend. The monument was sculpted by Alfred Courtens and unveiled in 1931. (Fig. 1)[14] At the centre and top of the bridge is a quintessential representation of Leopold II, in military dress on a horse, represented as a dignified European leader. In such commemorations, colonised subjects are usually absent, but below and on one side of the plinth, Courtens has sculpted the 'grateful Congolese people'. The plaque states that Leopold II had 'liberated them from the slavery by the Arabs', and the scene on the other side is entitled 'the homage by the Ostend fishermen to its brilliant protector'. Juxtaposing these images in effect suggests an equivalent comparison of the subjugated Congolese peoples to local fishermen, patronised by a kind and benevolent king. Visually, this monument exemplifies one of the four strategies Antoon Van den Braembussche suggests are used to cope with historical taboo – namely, 'ideological historical falsification'[15] – whereby Belgium continues to present itself as having been 'reluctant imperialists',[16] intent on saving and civilising its colonial subjects, rather than plundering and murdering millions of people.[17]

However, the protests against these amnesiac versions of Belgium's past in the early 2000s illustrate what happens when an '*archive* of supposedly enduring materials (i.e. texts, documents, buildings, bones [monuments])', interacts with 'the so-called ephemeral *repertoire* of embodied practice/knowledge (i.e. spoken language, dance, sports, ritual)'.[18] In 2004, when the members of the Flemish group De Stoeten Ostendenoare [The Bold Ostenders] sawed off the left hand of a Congolese slave figure that featured in the Congolese group that accompanied the Ostend statue of Leopold II,[19] the group performatively undermined the officially constituted history and made visible the disavowed memory of the cutting off of hands as part of the regime's rule of brutality and terror.[20] The group's subsequent offer 'to return the hand, but only if the royal family and the Belgian state apologised for their colonial history'[21] insists on both those currently in power acknowledging this disavowed past and the importance of symbolic reparation in addressing a violent past. The royal family have refused to perform this act to date, even though King Philippe I, in a letter addressed to Félix Tshisekedi (the Congolese premier) to mark the sixtieth anniversary of Congo's independence expressed "'my deepest regrets for the injuries of the past'".[22]

Performative resistance to Belgium's accepted history continued in 2010, when the group Collectif Memoires Coloniales et Luttes contre les Discriminations marched to this monument at Ostend on the anniversary of the assassination of Congo's first prime minister, Patrice Lumumba, and symbolically replaced the cut off hand with a hand made of chocolate. They then cut the chocolate hand into pieces, which they distributed to the Congolese participants present as symbolic reparation.[23] This performance resonated in many ways: first, it extended De Stoeten Ostendenoare's making visible Belgium's disavowed history to metaphorically reference the colonial exploitation of raw materials in the Congo, and the ongoing need for restitution. Second, the hand cast in chocolate suggested that Belgium's exploitative history is not past history but involves ongoing exploitation. Belgian chocolate is a key national symbol and a significant contributor to the economy; by '2013, the last year of data, Belgium was exporting more than 500,000 tons of chocolate worth more than 500 million euro'.[24] This may seem unrelated to colonialism, but there is evidence of ongoing trafficking and slavery of African children as part of the European chocolate industry,[25] despite the Harkin Engel Protocol of 2001 that was set up to eliminate child labour in the growing and processing of cocoa beans and their derivative products. This performance insisted that people see the past in the present and acknowledge European complicity in ongoing colonial resonances.

And such protests have escalated with the Black Lives Matter movement, which has included various performative interventions on social media platforms. Hezbon Mureithi's Twitter post entitled 'THIS BELGIAN BRUTE',[26] for example, juxtaposed the ubiquitous image of civilised Leopold II to archival images of colonial brutalities, thereby publicly challenging official memory and history. These posts link the past to the present directly, as they were narrated by the children of colonised peoples who continue to experience the resonances of colonialism in present global policies and everyday racism.

It is thus no surprise that growing public criticism of and dissatisfaction with Belgian colonial amnesia has motivated museums like the Royal Museum for Central Africa in Tervuren, renamed the AfricaMuseum, to rethink their exhibits (see Dónal Hassett's chapter in this volume). Thompson quotes director general of the museum, Guido Gryseels, on this project: "'decolonisation is a process. We're certainly moving toward the direction of a decolonised museum, and I think a lot of things could be a lot better," he says, citing the involvement of the African diaspora',[27] which is key to challenging amnesias in this increasingly mobile, transnational world.

Performance engagements with the past: *Exhibit B* and *De Waarheidscommissie*

This leads to the question of how we situate diverse bodies in performances when renegotiating memories. It is clear that individual performative acts have made national amnesia visible to the public to a limited extent. However, I suggest that artists can mobilise archives to engage publics more closely with these contested pasts. I have chosen to analyse two performance installations that interrogated disavowed Belgian history in resonant spaces in 2012–13:[28] *Exhibit B* (2012–13) by South African artist Brett Bailey, and *De Waarheidscommissie* (*The Truth Commission,* 2013) by Flemish-Tunisian theatre-maker Chokri Ben Chikha with the Flemish intercultural group Action Zoo Humain.[29] Both these productions mobilise specific archives in resonant spaces to facilitate what sociolinguist and anthropologist Johannes Fabian called a coeval approach to time and space to create a sense of 'intersubjective time',[30] which he argues anthropological accounts specifically deny. By inhabiting the same physical space in the present that resonates a specific past, as framed by the constituted archive, the observer is implicated in the installation. Thus, the aesthetic chosen can facilitate an active intersubjectivity that brings 'them' and 'us', 'there' and 'now' together, making the viewer aware that they are complicit in the accepted renderings of other peoples, times, and places, while resisting anthropological allochronism.

Brett Bailey's *Exhibit B*

Brett Bailey creates provocative work that combines community projects with 'an eclectic mix of spiritual forms: trance dance, African *sangomas* (diviners/shamans), consciously structuring the plays in the form of *intlombe*, a play within a ritual'.[31] He constructs his plays in this way to facilitate a critical engagement with an audience's perceived realities. In particular, he seeks to highlight the source of fear that manifests itself in rape, murder, and other acts of violence in South African society.[32] He never attempts to facilitate an authentic African ritual, but rather Bailey layers his performances, juxtaposing authentic rituals with highly performative melodrama to provoke thought about where our beliefs and values come from, and the implications of cultural frames for these. These provocations are evident in the titles of his plays that engage overtly with particular historic moments: *Zombie* (1995) that was reworked as *Ipi Zombie?* (1998), *iMumbo Jumbo* (1997), and *The Prophet* (1999).[33]

Ipi Zombie? dramatises events that took place in Kokstad, a town in the Eastern Cape, in 1995 when three women were accused of being witches that caused a road accident resulting in the death of twelve boys travelling in a minibus, and then turning them into zombie slaves. *iMumbo Jumbo* stages the quest by Chief Nicholas Gcaleka to retrieve the head of his ancestor, King Hintsa kaPhalo, paramount chief of the AmaXhosa, from Scotland. The title suggests how confusing such negotiations can be, but also the terms used to dismiss the returning colonised subject who comes to claim colonial reparations. *The Prophet* (1999) tells of Nonqawuse, a fifteen-year-old girl who persuaded the Xhosa people to sacrifice all their livestock to overcome the British in the midnineteenth century, suggesting the horrifying consequences of believing impossible prophecies. These plays all use highly theatricalised aesthetics, which Bailey calls Afro-Kitsch, to address specific horrors. Here Bailey engages Hannah Arendt's argument regarding the banality of evil and thoughtlessness in connection with the Eichmann trial in Germany in 1961, where she questions whether

> the activity of thinking as such, the habit of examining and reflecting upon whatever happens to come to pass, regardless of specific content and quite

independent of results, could [...] be of such a nature that it 'conditions' men against evildoing?[34]

Both Arendt and Bailey insist that revising violence requires more than an intellectual excavation of facts. Bailey suggests that it requires people to perceive and acknowledge that the source of social imbalance and violence is not external but begins with something within themselves, often fear of the unknown or the inexplicable. Bailey uses theatrical frames to move audiences between subjective and interrogative modes of experience and thought to acknowledge their complicities[35] and so begin a secular exorcism of past and present violences.

In 2009 Bailey shifted from creating theatrical plays dealing with violent events to interactive installations, beginning with the one-off performance *Blood Diamonds: Terminal*, a work that 'rests contextually on the history of the city, and the massive divide and bloody fault-lines which separate the obscenely wealthy from the obscenely poor, in this country in general, but Grahamstown in particular'.[36] In this performance, audience members were ushered into the ticket office and then waited on the platform of the old Grahamstown station, before a young 'street child' led them individually by the hand down the platform, over the railway bridge, into the graveyard, and beyond into the Xhosa areas of the town. The silent journey was punctuated by a series of performance installations that illustrated the fault lines that continue to divide the colony and Africa. This marked the beginning of Bailey's engagement with disavowed histories through installations. Bailey's *Exhibit Series*, which deals with disavowed European colonial histories, began in 2010. Bailey says, 'what I'm looking at in this work is how Europeans have represented the African body and how those distortions have led to a particular sequence of actions and legitimized some of the most terrible atrocities'.[37]

Exhibit A (2010–11)[38] explored German colonial South West Africa, now Namibia. *Exhibit B* (2012–13)[39] considered atrocities under the Belgian and French colonial regimes in the two Congos. *Exhibit C* was planned to expose British colonialism in Africa, but this was replaced by a reworked *Exhibit B* (2014),[40] which addressed general European colonial histories, and was specifically aimed at European audiences, so they were not performed in Africa beyond Namibia and South Africa. The installations, *Exhibits A & B*, exhibits were set up as a series of individual rooms, which audience members entered one by one and were confronted by twelve to fourteen fixed tableaux vivants that depicted images of colonial atrocities taken from archives or contemporary images of racism by European nations towards African asylum seekers. These included images of the genocide of the Herero and Namaqua by the German colonisers in 1904 in German South West Africa, now Namibia, with images of individuals, such as a Black woman who sits on the edge of a bed in chains, waiting to be raped by her master, alongside examples of contemporary incidents of racism by European nations towards African asylum seekers, like the deportation from Schiphol airport of an illegal immigrant who suffocated on the aeroplane. The performers silently stared back at the spectators as they paused to sit and look at them in the chairs provided, read the accompanying plaques, or passed on.[41] These installations were clearly designed to parody the human zoos of the nineteenth and early twentieth centuries, where Europeans could look at individuals or groups of people brought from various colonies as exhibits. Bailey used local performers and immigrants in each city the installations were staged to embody the disavowed images and ask what we know, how we know it, and how far we are postcolonial.

After a successful run of *Exhibit A*, Bailey researched and mounted *Exhibit B* at the Kunstenfestivaldesarts (KFDA) in partnership with the Koninklijke Vlaamse Schouwburg KVS (Brussels) [Royal Flemish Theatre] in 2012. Initially the work was received positively. Part of the success of the early exhibitions was Bailey's careful choice of resonant found spaces in which the work was performed: in Brussels it was staged in the monumental but destitute Gesù church; later in 2012 it was staged at the Berliner Festspiele in the daunting old water towers on Prenzlauer Berg, once the site of an early Nazi concentration camp. In an interview on the Brussels exhibition Bailey said,

> I was looking for a location in Brussels I first considered the magnificent Palais de Justice, because it was built under Leopold II and represents justice in a disputable way. I also thought of the public Galeries Saint-Hubert, but I soon realised that unless you frame a performance like this very carefully, informed looking and reflection becomes very difficult. The Gesù church is interesting because it was squatted for many years by undocumented people who today are still living in the adjacent monastery. Indeed, another thing I look at is the present policy of the European Union towards African immigrants: the deportation centres, the racial classification based on DNA profiling, people without documents, etc.[42]

Bailey's choice of venues facilitated audience members perceiving the connections between different pasts and present struggles: linking by association colonial violence, the Holocaust, and contemporary policies and behaviours towards migrants in Europe. Bailey intensified these associations in his casting strategy by recruiting local performers and immigrants without acting experience to perform alongside the Herero performers who travelled with the show and sang in the final tableaux. These Namibian performers were juxtaposed against German professor of medicine, anthropology, and eugenics Dr Eugen Fischer's ethnographic photographs.[43] This overtly suggests comparisons between his field research in German South West Africa in 1906, which included medical experiments on the Herero and Namaqua people that resulted in interracial marriage being prohibited throughout the German colonies from 1912 and later legislation on race including the Nuremberg laws, with the medical experiments conducted on Jews in Nazi Germany and recent deportations of immigrants that have led to their deaths. The uncomfortable question arises: how postcolonial is contemporary Europe?

Re-engaging the past is never easy or simple, nor do intentions always translate into the desired effect, as seen by responses to later performance installations: some historians and individuals of former colonies applauded the exhibits, and others roundly condemned them, all in quite emotional terms.[44] Protests against *Exhibit B* began in Berlin in 2012. Members of Buehnenwatch[45] were outraged about the aesthetic form Bailey had chosen to use, and Black activists joined demonstrations at the Kleiner Wasserspeicher, where the work was programmed as part of the Foreign Affairs Festival. Sandrine Micosse-Aikins stated, 'This is the wrong way to discuss a violent colonial history'.[46] In a post-performance public debate in Berlin, South African-born spoken-word artist Philipp Khabo Koepsell challenged Bailey directly, saying:

> If you have a white South African director giving orders to black performers to tell their story voicelessly, you're not breaking the legacy [...] You are enforcing and reproducing it. You can call it whatever you like, but the fact is that you as a white, privileged person are sitting there and ordering black people around.[47]

Race features centrally in these protests: Bailey was challenged not only for his choice of aesthetics but also for being a White stage director, which gave him specific 'privilege' and access to spaces and archives, not available to Black immigrants or subjects. However, performers like Collivan Nsorockebe Nso, who played Aamir Ageeb, a twenty-year-old Sudanese asylum seeker who was suffocated on a passenger flight in 1999, alongside the names of fourteen immigrants who died while resisting deportation from Europe between 1991 and 2010, said:

> This is my story [...] I'm a Cameroonian, and I've been in Germany since 2002. I should have been deported in 2006. I hate talking about it. It's so painful. I don't want sympathy; this is how we live every day. There is this silence, but we need to talk about these things.[48]

These diverse responses opened a space with great potential to engage publics not only with what was being remembered but by whom, for what purpose, and on what terms. They particularly suggested that certain aesthetics may or may not be appropriate to engage violences of the past and questioned how power dynamics can be made visible without replicating them. These exhibits literally staged silence and the power of the gaze, using these strategies to implicate each audience member, who had to choose whether to look or look away, and think about what they did or did not know about the histories or contemporary incidents cited.

However one evaluates *Exhibit B*, not working with local communities whose histories were involved and not including images of everyday racism significantly affected this works' reception.[49] Later protests in the United Kingdom and Paris exposed how disconnected major cultural institutions like the Barbican were from communities beyond their regular audience members. Paul Richards from the UpRise anti-racism campaign and BrazenBunch arts collective said regarding protests in the United Kingdom:

> The people who created, commissioned and staged Exhibit B did not grasp the gravity of the issues it tackled and the impact it would have. The Barbican did not consult the black British or African communities [...]. There was no cognitive or cultural diversity in the conversation. Something like this has to be in consultation, or have informed decisions, with the community.[50]

This argument about consulting local communities regarding *Exhibit B*, which was cancelled due to protests, is fascinating because these same groups did not insist on being part of the decisions about how archives are being negotiated in the British Museum or programming in the Barbican's mainstream venues, where Bailey's adaptation of Verdi's *Macbeth*, which includes similarly provocative images of Africa's colonial and postcolonial history, had been staged the preceding week. This anomaly suggests that there is something about the way in which specific spaces, here The Vaults, a maze of disused railway arches under Waterloo station in London, and physical repertoires of remembering expressed through embodied performances of oppression, can trigger deeply emotional responses. This juxtaposition illustrates Diana Taylor's argument for dialogic interaction between archives and repertoires when negotiating memories and histories, highlighting the importance of key players situating themselves carefully in relation to the narratives, experiences, memories, and histories that are invoked in these restagings of contested pasts.[51] Form is key – despite Bailey's insistence that, 'This is not a human zoo [...] It's performance theater',[52] this was not what audiences and local Black communities perceived. The sense of outrage at a White South African highlighting issues of Black African suffering in Europe using an aesthetic they felt replicated the violence was outrageous to many.

Action Zoo Humain: *De Waarheidscommissie/The Truth Commission*,[53] Ghent 2013

Action Zoo Humain is an intercultural artistic collective formed around brothers Chokri and Zouzou Ben Chikha.[54] Since 2017, the company has been funded by the Flemish government; and from the 2018–19 season, it has had artist-in-residence status at NTGent, the city theatre of Ghent and one of the biggest theatres in Belgium. However, I am going to look back at the play that launched this company in Ghent in 2013. I begin with the geopolitical context from which this play by Morroccan-Flemish Belgians working with other immigrants emerged. The context creates two layers for the work: first, it explores how Flanders positions itself in relation to Belgium in terms of different cultural hegemonies, particularly vis-à-vis language, and second, in relation to wider immigration issues. Bobineau notes that

> [a]ccording to a joint survey of the [French-language] newspaper *La Libre Belgique* and the Flemish newspaper *De Standaard* in 2010, almost half of Flemings (46%) generally rejected the Belgian monarchy while only 26% of the Walloons demanded a republic without a royal house'.[55]

Based on the perceived shared linguistic and sociopolitical struggles against the dominant French Belgian administration, Flemings tend to associate themselves with the subjugated colonised rather than with those involved in the colonial endeavour, despite many missionaries having been recruited to the Congo from Flanders. In part, this play critiques this positioning of Flemish Belgians as solely victims, and suggests they are implicated in both Belgium's past and the legacies of its colonialism that continue to resonate in the present, particularly in its immigration policies.

De Waarheidscommissie took as its specific topic the one hundredth anniversary of the Ghent World Fair, while noting wider engagements with similar events:

> Flanders and Belgium were champions of human zoo for millions of visitors until a century ago. Think of the 144 Congolese in Antwerp (1894), the 270 Congolese in Brussels (1897) or the 128 Senegalese and 60 Filipinos at the Ghent World Exhibition (1913), who were literally or imaginatively placed in a cage.[56]

Figure 2. Ousmane N'Diaye performing in the former Court House on Koophandelsplein, Ghent, Belgium, 2013. Photo: Kurt van der Elst.

The play set out to interrogate how Ghent officially positioned itself in relation to this aspect of Belgium's colonial past. The website *Ghent, 1913–2013 the Century of Progress* described the original exhibitions of Filipino and Senegalese peoples as 'the 28th in a long row of exhibitions which had been organized in Europe and America since 1851', where visitors came to 'gaze at "these savages" with their bizarre way of life'.[57] It noted the scale and backing of the exhibit in positive terms, 'by pacesetters from the private sector, by eminent industrials and representatives of the social elite in Ghent'. The section entitled 'Ark of Mamon' defended its place in the nineteenth-century scramble for Africa, suggesting that 'Belgium showed the world that it was absolutely right to seize the enormous territory in Central Africa from the hands of the severely contested "owner" King Leopold II'. Action Zoo Humain felt that the terms of this remembering of Belgium's colonial past was inappropriate and thus they created a performative critique, pitting the archive against various embodied repertoires of remembering this past.

Like Bailey, Chokri and Zouzou Ben Chikha chose resonant spaces for their critical performances: in Belgium it premiered in April 2013 in the former courthouse on Koophandelsplein in Ghent (Fig. 2); in South Africa it was performed in February 2014 in the Senate building at the University of the Western

Cape,[58] which was the former 'coloured' Chamber of the Tricameral Parliament of South Africa between 1984–1994.[59] These spaces reminded audiences of the venues' legal, judicial, and sociopolitical roles both in the past and present. The spatial arrangements for the performances denied audiences the comfort of passively watching the proceedings; in both contexts, audiences faced one another: on the traverse in Ghent, and on three sides in Cape Town. This forced audiences to watch both the staged performance and one another's reactions to the proceedings.

The play's titular reference to the South African Truth and Reconciliation Commission (TRC, 1996–98) signals the company's intention to use this play to engage critically with Belgium's colonial history and its contemporary resonances. The South African TRC extended its mandate beyond investigating the acts and patterns of violence and gross human rights violations that took place during a specified period of time, as are the usual parameters of such commissions, to 'restore victims their human and civil dignity by letting them tell their stories and recommending how they can be assisted'.[60] This placed the personal narratives of both survivors and perpetrators at the heart of the commission, thereby challenging previous versions of South African history and its legal processes.[61]

By invoking the TRC, the artists signalled their intention to move away from traditional fiction towards verbatim or documentary theatre, which blurs the boundary between what is 'real' and what is fictional. This form provokes questions about how we access truth and ascertain veracity, again echoing some of Bailey's concerns.[62] Traditionally, verbatim theatre cites actual people and their words to interrogate an event, in this case the 1913 World Fair in Ghent, to challenge the findings and archives formally adopted by the state. Simultaneously, this form facilitates a collective exploration of the trauma for survivors, in this case descendants of the Senegalese people exhibited, and by association, other formerly colonised peoples. In this piece, the commission is chaired by a significant public figure, Herman Balthazar, an academic and former governor of Flanders. In South Africa his co-commissioners were Mrs Josiane Rimbaut, a news reporter; Mrs Marijke Pinoy, an actress, dancer, and mother of five; Christopher Kudyahakudadirwe, an African historian and activist; and Ilse Marien, who was responsible for the social inclusion of immigrants in Belgium. Those testifying include a descendant of a Senegalese man who died in the Ghent exhibition, Madi Diali, played by Michael Olabode Hyslop in Cape Town and Ousmane N'Diaye in Ghent. He comes to the commission to petition the Belgian government to repatriate his ancestor's remains, represented materially in South Africa by a skeleton, and in Belgium by moulded heads. Dr Verdoolaege (University of Ghent) is a researcher who presents 'facts' regarding the conditions and experiences of the Senegalese people in the 1913 exhibition. Tom Lanoye, Flanders's best known and highly acclaimed playwright, plays the role of Cyriel Buysse, a Flemish naturalist and playwright who fought for the rights of the Flemish language, but whose writing includes racist passages. This mixture of identifiable people and actors representing historical characters and contemporary figures indicates various positions in this debate regarding Belgium's colonial past and how colonial attitudes continue to resonate in the present, as exemplified by references to Belgium's programmes for integration and language policies for immigrants.[63]

Both the spatial arrangements and testimonial form invited audiences to 'bear witness', a term that conjures a law court, where witnesses' testimonies become the basis for a verdict; a community support group where individuals publicly acknowledge faith or a taboo secret, like substance abuse or alcohol dependence; or where one is called upon to report on a significant event at which one has been an agent or bystander. All these instances require individuals to actively speak out and to take a position regarding an issue or event. Action Zoo Humain overtly invited audience members 'to take part in the Truth Commission [to] watch and listen to the witnesses to [sic] the dubious event of 1913, testifying in word, image and movement'.[64] This invitation also overtly signals their intention to shift away from privileging spoken testimony, as is the case in most commissions,[65] to include embodied repertoires of remembering. Once again, the archive of formal documentation is juxtaposed against repertoires of memory held in peoples' bodies, including those of the audience, who are asked to interpret what they see and hear in relation to what they already do or do not know or believe.

For example, Diali's ritual drumming, performed by Ousmane N'Diaye in Ghent (Fig. 3), or Chantal Loial's dance (Fig. 4), which visually references Sarah Baartman, can only be interpreted against knowledge that audience members already have of these specific histories and cultures. Thus, the performances themselves invite audiences to question what they know about Africa and Belgian colonialism, how, and why this is so. The manner in which these performances blurred specific temporal-spatial referents of here and now, there and then, invoked Fabian's intersubjective temporality to destabilise how audiences believe they make meaning of the past in relation to the present. For example, after Loial's dance, the actress-commissioner raised concerns about this performance, which left her feeling 'disturbed, confused, like a voyeur'. She suggested that 'this dance was maybe not in the right place as it was not a theatre or museum, but a commission'. She objected to the dancer being re-objectified by a male choreographer for the sake of his reputation and the audience's pleasure. This response suggested that the embodied mode of performance

Figure 3. Ousmane N'Diaye performing in Ghent, Belgium, 2013.
Photo: Kurt van der Elst.

both evoked the colonial period and demonstrated the ethical issues involved in re-representing subjugated people from the past in the present, as the past and its representations segue into the present, and issues of representation and reproduction converge, as they might do in dramatic reconstructions in court proceedings. The embodied performance created much greater disturbance than images of Sarah Baartman in a history textbook. The physical repertoire and the performer's insistence on her own agency challenged colonial notions of the fixed, passive colonial subject.

The play further conflates the past and present by means of Mourade Zeguendi's participation as a contemporary Moroccan immigrant to Belgium. Throughout the piece he constantly interrupted proceedings with requests for a translation of what was being said, or by objecting to Belgium's current immigrant integration programme, which irritated the Belgian commissioners. These interventions highlighted how language is at the heart of much of Belgium's politics, as the status of French and Dutch has long been debated. It also serves to draw parallels between African colonial issues of the past with contemporary cultural hegemonies experienced by European minority groups and immigrants, further complicating narratives of the 'past', 'progress', and 'post-coloniality'.

Figure 4. Chantal Loïal performing in Ghent, Belgium, 2013.
Photo: Kurt van der Elst.

Zeguendi also highlights broader assumptions about what is African and the complexities involved in interpreting unfamiliar embodied performances when he, as a Moroccan, objected to the Senegalese man's impassioned ritual dance between the first and second hearings. Zeguendi accused him of dancing 'like a monkey' for White people, as his ancestors did in the zoo. The irate Diali responded by insisting that neither the audience nor Zeguendi had understood the ritual he had performed for his ancestor, and that he neither wants to perform for Whites nor does he need anyone to defend or moderate him, as he can choose how and for whom he performs. This heated interchange forced the audience to reconsider the idea of a homogenous Africa, and how even Africans' own specific knowledge of various African performances and cultures can influence their various understanding of resistances and histories being engaged.

These challenges regarding audience positionality and their processes of interpretation are important, as they demonstrate how a performance can offer more than a polemical viewpoint on complex colonial issues if the aesthetic is significantly nuanced. South African theatre director Mark Fleishmann suggests that performance can involve a kind of transformation when 'a physical action or gesture begins as one thing and metamorphoses into something else passing through a range of possibilities in between'.[66] This is most evident in the embodied performances, which remain ambiguous in this play. The physical action 'opens up a plural field of possibility for the spectator. Each image is in this sense dialogical: a play of open-ended possibilities interacting between two fixed poles which exist in some form of dialogue with each other'.[67] These two fixed poles could include spectators' perceptions of their own identity and history, and the spaces between these perceptions and what is being performed could open up an awareness of alternative possibilities and perspectives on the past, and these resonances allow us to resituate ourselves relationally.

This production questioned everything, even its own documentary form, which suggests the performance as live and authentic, despite its being clearly scripted (with translations projected onto the screen in South Africa). The limits of performance are also raised when, at the end, the commission handed over specific recommendations regarding the processing of African artists' visas, reparations of wages for Senegalese descendants of those in the Human Zoo of 1913, and the inclusion of this aspect of Flemish history in the school curricula (see Catherine Gilbert's chapter in this volume) to Belgian government officials. This act raises questions regarding the potential efficacy of theatre beyond facilitating awareness, to suggest that it could influence cultural policymaking regarding the colonial past.[68] Although seemingly utopian, this may be an extension of documentary theatre's attempt to 'construct the past in service of a future the authors would like to create'.[69]

Theatre's role in facilitating a dialogic re-engagement of contemporary audiences' senses of accepted history and how this relates to their current values was most obvious when Chokri and Zouzou Ben Chikha requested the audience actively support their insistence that the African performers hand over their passports to prevent their illegal disappearance at the end of the show. The debates between audience members that followed in Ghent and Cape Town became quite heated. This move from documentary theatre to invisible theatre forced audience members to analyse their attitudes towards contemporary 'others' against the backdrop of the show's engagement with the Ghent human zoo, thus demonstrating the possible gap between values articulated in theory and those tested in a highly charged context, which further complicates processes of re-evaluating actions, views, and values of the past.

However, both pieces raise the question of where such work needs to be done – as neither has been performed in the areas of the two Congos discussed. They primarily address the European coloniser from the perspective of supposedly previously colonised subjects who continue to face the legacies of colonialism as immigrants or post-apartheid subjects. This suggests that addressing colonial amnesia is shifting from national histories to more transnational perspectives, as people continue to move from the Global South to the Global North, and thus unavoidably insist on disavowed stories being heard. These works indicate the ways in which performance can 'open the space between analysis and action, and [...] pull the pin on the binary opposition between theory and practice',[70] and thereby make visible silences in archives and demonstrate how colonialism continues to resonate in the contemporary world. However, it also exemplifies the potential impact aesthetic choices and resonant spaces may have on people for whom these images and experiences may be painful. Thus, it underscores the critical importance of cultural institutions involving subjugated peoples in the processes of negotiating contested or disavowed histories and memories. Arranging these kinds of mediated encounters between colonial archival material, embodied audiences, and performers in significant resonant spaces can play a crucial role in facilitating transnational echolocation that allows us to lay our colonial ghosts to rest by finding appropriate cultural expressions that 'promote reconciliation, outline needed reforms, allow victims a cathartic airing of their pains, and represent an important, official acknowledgement of a long-silenced past'.[71]

Notes

1. Ann Laura Stoler, 'Introduction: "The Rot Remains" From Ruins to Ruination', in Ann Laura Stoler (ed.), *Imperial debris: On ruins and ruination*. (Durham, NC: Duke University Press, 2013), pp. 1–36.
2. Priscilla Hayner, 'Commissioning the Truth: further research questions', *Third World Quarterly*, 17.1 (1996), 19–29 (19). See also Priscilla Hayner, 'Fifteen Truth Commissions – 1974 to 1994: A comparative study', *Human Rights Quarterly*, 16 (1994), 597–655.
3. Gaëlle Ponselet, 'Belgium's colonial past: ten experts to set the scene', *Justiceinfo.Net*, 24 July 2020 <https://www.justiceinfo.net/en/truth-commissions/44974-belgium-colonial-past-ten-experts-to-set-the-scene.html> [accessed 06 January 2021].
4. Ibid.
5. Jo-Anne Duggan, 'From memory to archive', editorial for *Archival Platform*, 26 July 2011 <From memory to archive | Archive & Public Culture (uct.ac.za)> [accessed 18 August 2011].
6. Jacques Derrida, 'Archive Fever in South Africa', in Carolyn Hamilton, et al. (eds.), *Refiguring the Archive* (Cape Town: David Philip Publishers; Dordrecht: Kluwer Academic Publishers, 2002), pp. 38–80, even pages only, (p. 44).
7. See Benedict Anderson, *Imagined Communities: Reflections on the Origins and Spread of Nationalism*, rev. ed. (London: Verso, 2006); Nadine Holdsworth, *Theatre & Nation* (Basingstoke/New York: Palgrave Macmillan, 2010); John McLeod, *Beginning Postcolonialism* (Manchester: Manchester University Press, 2000).
8. J. L. Austin, *How to Do Things with Words* (Oxford: Clarendon Press, 1962), p. 5.
9. Julien Bobineau, 'The Historical Taboo: Colonial Discourses and Postcolonial Identities in Belgium', *Werkwinkel: Journal of Low Countries and South African Studies*, 12.1 (2017), 107–23.
10. Matthew G. Stanard, Stanard, Matthew G., *Selling the Congo: a History of European Pro-Empire Propaganda and the Making of Belgian Imperialism* (Lincoln: University of Nebraska Press, 2011), Nebraska press ebook.
11. In the post-colonial period, critical voices have emerged, particularly from the 1980s onwards, see Jean Stengers, *Congo, mythes et réalités. 100 ans d'histoire* (Paris; Louvain-la-Neuve: Éditions Duculot, 1989).
12. Bobineau, 'The Historical Taboo...', p. 110.
13. Geert Castryck, 'Whose History is History? Singularities and Dualities of the Public Debate on Belgian Colonialism', in Csaba Levai (ed.), *Europe and the World in European Historiography* (Pisa: Pisa University Press, 2006), pp. 71–88 (p. 78).
14. Statue of King Leopold II, Ostend, Belgium, 1931. Photo: Georges Jansoone <https://commons.wikimedia.org/wiki/File:Oostende.Leopold_II_(01).jpg> [accessed 14 August 2020]
15. Antoon Van den Braembussche, 'The Silenced Past. On the Nature of Historical Taboos', in Wojciecha Wrzoska and Jerzy Topolski (eds.), *Świat historii. Prace z metodologii historii i historii historiografi i dedykowane Jerzemu Topolskiemu z okazji siedemdziesięciolecia urodzin* (The world of history: works on the methodology of history and history of historiography dedicated to Jerzy Topolski on the occasion of his 70th birthday) (Poznań: Inst. Historii UAM, 1998), pp. 97–111 (pp. 106–09).
16. Stanard, *Selling the Congo*, p. 167.
17. Ibid., p. 30.
18. Diana Taylor, *The Archive and the Repertoire: Performing Cultural Memory in the Americas* (Durham, NC: Duke University Press, 2007), p. 19.
19. See detail of the statue with the missing hand in Ostend. Photograph: Emilie CHAIX/Getty Images/Photo nonstop RM, in Daniel Boffey, 'Reappearance of Statue's Missing Hand Reignites Colonial Row', *The Guardian*, 22 Feb 2019 <https://www.theguardian.com/world/2019/feb/22/statue-missing-hand-colonial-belgium-leopold-congo> [accessed 21 August 2020].
20. This is a huge historic debate. About this aspect of colonial rule, see *Congo, Mythes et réalité* by Stengers.
21. Boffey, 'Reappearance of Statue's Missing Hand...'.
22. Cited by Béatrice Delvaux, in 'Colonisation du Congo: enfin ce geste si nécessaire, qui grandit le Roi et son pays', *Le Soir*, 30 June 2020. My translation.
23. Bobineau, 'The Historical Taboo...', p. 113.
24. Garrone, Maria, Hannah Pieters and Johan Swinnen, 'From Pralines to Multinationals: The Economic History of Belgian Chocolate', in Mara P. Squicciarini and Johan Swinnen (eds.), *The Economics of Chocolate* (Oxford: Oxford University Press, 2016), pp. 88–115 (p. 94).
25. Miki Mistrati and U. Roberto Romano, 'The Dark Side of Chocolate – Child Trafficking & Slavery', YouTube, 2012 <https://www.youtube.com/watch?v=7Vfbv6hNeng> [accessed 25 August 2020]
26. Hezbon Mureithi, 'THIS BELGIAN BRUTE', 10 march 2020, @HezMureithi, https://twitter.com/HezMureithi/status/1237411467118477312 [accessed 10/08/20]

27. Linda Thompson, 'Africa Museum Renovation allows Critical View of Colonial Past', *The Bulletin*, 6 December 2018, para 10 <http://www.flanderstoday.eu/africa-museum-renovation-allows-critical-view-colonial-past> [accessed 10/08/2020].
28. The performances overlapped with *Exhibitions. L'invention du sauvage* at the Quai Branly Museum in Paris (29 November 2011–3 June 2012), where Pascal Blanchard and Nanette Jacomijn Snoep intended to highlight the history of women, men, and children from Africa, Asia, Oceania, or America that were exhibited in circus acts, theatre performances, cabaret reviews, fairs, zoos, parades, reconstituted villages, or in universal and colonial exhibitions from the end of the fifteenth to the beginning of the twentieth centuries in Europe, America, and Japan. (Groupe de recherche Achac – Colonisation, immigration, post-colonialisme, 'Zoos Humains – Exhibitions. L'invention du sauvage', 2011 <https://www.achac.com/zoos-humains/exhibition-linvention-du-sauvage-2/> [accessed 07 January 2021]); and the refurbishment of the Royal Museum for Central Africa in Belgium.
29. Other work engaging in similar explorations include European Attraction Limited's controversial restaging of a human zoo in Oslo from May to August 2014, to mark the hundredth anniversary of the Norwegian Jubilee Exhibition of 1914; and Swedish filmmaker Göran Hugo Olsson's 2014 documentary *Concerning Violence, which juxt*aposes images from multiple African subaltern histories against verbatim extracts from Fanon's *The Wretched of the Earth*, that are delivered by singer, songwriter and activist Lauryn Hill, see *Concerning Violence* Press Kit, 2014 <http://dogwoof.com/films/concerning-violence> [accessed 12 May 2014].
30. Johannes Fabian, *Time and the Other: How Anthropology Makes its Object* (New York: Columbia University Press, 1983), p. 24.
31. Brett Bailey, 'Performing So the Spirit May Speak', *South African Theatre Journal*, 12.1/2 (1998), 191–202 (193).
32. See Anton Krueger, *Experiments in Freedom: Explorations of Identity in New South African Drama* (Newcastle upon Tyne: Cambridge Scholars Publishing, 2010), pp. 151–66 and Daniel Larlham, 'Brett Bailey and Third World Bunfight: Journeys into the South African Psyche', *Theater*, 39.1 (2009), 7–17, for close analysis of these plays.
33. See Third World Bunfight <http://thirdworldbunfight.co.za/> and Brett Bailey, *The Plays of Miracle and Wonder – Ipi Zombi?, iMumbo Jumbo, The Prophet* (Cape Town: Double Story, 2003).
34. Hannah Arendt, *Eichmann in Jerusalem: A Report on the Banality of evil* (New York: Penguin Books, 1979[1963]), p. 418.
35. Miki Flockemann, 'Facing the Stranger in the Mirror: Staged complicities in Recent South African Performances', *South African Theatre Journal*, 25.2 (2011), 129–41.
36. Robyn Sassen, 'Bailey Rocks Grahamstown Divide', CUE ON LINE, 2009 <http://www.thirdworldbunfight.co.za/files/PRESS_from_National_Arts_Festival.pdf> [Originally accessed 28 December 2011, most recently 07 August 2020]
37. Bailey in Anton Krueger 'Gazing at Exhibit A: Interview with Brett Bailey', *Liminalities: A Journal of Performance Studies*, 9.1 (2013), 1–13 (p. 7).
38. Staged in 2010: Wiener Festwochen (Vienna), Theaterformen Festival (Hannover); 2011: Kiasma Centre (Helsinki).
39. Staged in 2012: Kunsten Festival des Arts in partnership with KVS (Brussels), National Arts Festival (Grahamstown, SA), Berliner Festspiele (Berlin); 2013: Holland Festival (Amsterdam), Vooruit Centre (Ghent), Avignon Festival, Le 104 (Paris), le Maillon (Strasbourg).
40. Staged in 2014: Edinburgh – Edinburgh International Festival, Playfair Library, London – Barbican Theatre, Moscow – Museum of Modern Art, Territoria Festival, Poitiers – TAP, Paris – Théâtre Gérard Philipe de Saint-Denis, Paris – Le 104.
41. For images and details on the Exhibits see Third World Bunfight. 'Exhibit B' <http://thirdworldbunfight.co.za/exhibit-b/>, 'Exhibits A, B, and C' <https://www.thirdworldbunfight.co.za/productions/exhibit-a-b-and-c.htmln> [accessed 10 August 2020].
42. Quoted in Michaël Bellon, 'KFDA012: Brett Bailey Takes to the Courtroom', *Agenda magazine*, 3 May 2012, paragraph 4, KFDA012: Brett Bailey takes to the courtroom | BRUZZ [accessed 18 July 2014 and 2 September 2021].
43. On this notorious figure, see Elise Fontenaille-N'Diaye's *Blue Book* (Paris: Calman-Lévy, 2015).
44. Compare responses, for example, in BBC article 'Exhibit B: Is Controversial Art Show Racist?', 24 September 2014 <http://www.bbc.co.uk/news/entertainment-arts-29344483> [accessed 24 September 2014].
45. Buehnenwatch is an association of people from the arts, science and journalism established in 2011 that keeps watch over German theatre perforamances and speak out against perceived racist practices or performances. https://www.facebook.com/buehnenwatch/ [accessed 1 August 2022].
46. Quoted in Shirley Apthorp, 'Black "Human Zoo" Fury Greets Berlin Art Show', *Bloomberg News*,

3 October 2012 <http://www.businessweek.com/news/2012-10-03/black-human-zoo-fury-greets-berlin-art-show> [accessed 18 July 2014]
47. Cited by Apthorp in 'Black "Human Zoo"…'.
48. Ibid.
49. For a full analysis of this point, see Katrin Sieg, 'Towards a Civic Contract of Performance: Pitfalls of Decolonizing the Exhibitionary Complex at Brett Bailey's Exhibit B', *Theatre Research International*, 40.3 (2015), 250–71.
50. In BBC, 'Exhibit B: Is Controversial Art Show Racist?'.
51. See Nathanael M. Vlachos's comparison of Bailey's staging of *Exhibit B* in South Africa with how he approached it in Germany: 'Brett Bailey's Traveling Human Zoo: Fragmentations of Whiteness Across Borders', in Lucy Michael and Samantha Schulz (eds.), *Unsettling Whiteness* (Leiden: Brill Publishers, 2014), pp. 59–67.
52. Quoted in Apthorp, in 'Black "Human Zoo"…'.
53. Chokri Ben Chikha, *De Waarheidscommissie/The Truth Commission*, unpublished, 2013.
54. Action Zoo Humain <https://www.actionzoohumain.be/nl> [accessed 14 July 2020].
55. Bobineau, 'The Historical Taboo …', pp. 115–16.
56. *De Waarheidscommissie* production notes (my translation from Flemish), *De Waarheidscommissie*, Aktion Zoo Humain website, 2013 <https://www.actionzoohumain.be/nl/productie/de-waarheidscommissie> [Accessed 22 January 2021]. See also Arnaut's analysis of postcolonial reproductions of human zoos; reinventions or reworkings of human zoos and artistic 'parodies' thereof in Karel Arnaut's 'The Human Zoo as (Bad) Intercultural Performance', in Pascal Blanchard, Gilles Boetsch and Nanette J. Snoep (eds.), *Exhibitions: the Invention of the Savage* (Paris: Musée du Quai Branly; Arles: Actes Sud, 2011), pp. 345–63.
57. '"Ghent, 1913–2013", the century of Progress' <http://1913-2013.gent.be/en/ghent-wants-have-largest- world-fair> [accessed 22 July 2014]. See also: A virtual reconstruction of the 1913 World Fair at STAM – Ghent city museum | MWF2014: Museums and the Web Florence 2014 [accessed 13 January 2022].
58. And when performed again in 2018 (in Dutch and French), it took place in the Plenary Session Room of the Belgian Senate with RMCA historians and anthropologists participating, see 'The Truth Commission', 7 and 8 December 2018, Belgian Senate, Brussels <https://www.africamuseum.be/en/news/waarheidscommissie> [accessed 14 August 2020]
59. The VDE photographs were taken in Belgium by Kurt van der Elst. All photographs are reproduced with permission of Action Zoo Humain.
60. TRC Pamphlets, *The Committee on Amnesty*, *The Committee on Human Rights Violations*, and *Truth. The Road to Reconciliation* (Rondebosch: Justice in Transition, 1995).
61. There is a vast literature from various disciplines that analyses the form and impact of South Africa's TRC, and it is well beyond the scope of this chapter, see Yvette Hutchison, *South African Performance and Archives of Memory* (Manchester and New York: Manchester University Press, 2013).
62. See Alison Forsyth, and Chris Megson (eds.), *Get Real: Documentary Theatre Past and Present* (Basingstoke and New York: Palgrave Macmillan, 2009) and Carol Martin, *Dramaturgy of the Real on the World Stage* (Basingstoke and New York: Palgrave Macmillan, 2010) for discussions of verbatim theatre in USA, Europe and South Africa.
63. Jérémy Mandin, 'INTERACT Research Report: An Overview of Integration Policies in Belgium'. Co-financed by the European Union, 2014 <https://cadmus.eui.eu/bitstream/handle/1814/33133/INTERACT-RR-2014%20-%2020.pdf?sequence=1> [accessed 24 August 2020]
64. Personal Invitation (print), February 2014, Cape Town.
65. Although the South African TRC did include songs and hymns, dramatic gestures, crying, etc., these were not included in the official transcriptions of the events that formed the basis of the final report and recommendations – the version formally archived.
66. Mark Fleishman, 'Physical Images in the South African Theatre', *South African Theatre Journal*, 11.1/2 (1997), 199–214 (p. 204)
67. Fleishman, p. 205.
68. Literature and performances have a definite role to play in this exercise. In France, for instance, the 'loi Taubira', a parliamentary bill which recognised slavery as 'crime against humanity', was the product of extensive debates between policy makers and writers such as Edouard Glissant, Patrick Chamoiseau and Maryse Condé. See Johann Michel's 'Esclavage et réparations. Construction d'un problème public', *Politique Africaine*, 146 (2017), 143–64.
69. Martin, *Dramaturgy of the Real*, p. 10.
70. Dwight Conquergood, 'Performance Studies – Interventions and Radical Research', *The Drama Review* 46.2 (2002), 145–56 (p. 145).
71. Priscilla Hayner, 'Commissioning the Truth', (19).

Writing in Ciluba
From Colonial Extirpation to the Challenge of Globalisation

Albert Kasanda

In the framework of the reflection on *Empire and Postcolonial Resonances*, it seemed appropriate to me, as a Luba and native of the former Belgian colony (the Democratic Republic of the Congo), to explore the relationship between colonisation and Ciluba literature. I am aware that the debate on the relationship between colonisation and literature in African languages is by no means new. I would like to take up this issue, since it remains a permanent quest concerning the relationship between the different cultures of humankind, and it constantly addresses the way we live together and build society.

I examine the statement according to which colonisation constitutes the ruthless gravedigger of languages of colonised people, at least as far as Belgian colonisation is concerned. Therefore, after sketching the genesis of Belgian colonisation, I explore Belgian colonial language policies to show how far Ciluba, as a literate and literary language, resulted from colonisation and was used to reinforce the colonial mission. Second, I analyse the post-colonial language policies to shed light on the role and achievements of Congolese leaders regarding the fate of national languages including Ciluba. Third, in view of the challenges generated by globalisation and the homogenisation of cultures, I examine how far the Luba community manage both the Luba language and culture. This section concludes with a short exploration, as a case study, of an essay in Ciluba by François Kabasele, 'Ndi muluba', which addresses Luba identity in the current era of people mobility and cultural mutations around the world.[1]

The Colonial Background of Writing in Ciluba

The Genesis of the Belgian Empire

The Berlin Act (1884–85) materialised the dream of colonial expansion of Leopold, the Belgian king, by granting him the territory of the Congo Free

State (CFS), now the Democratic Republic of the Congo (DRC). This acquisition depended on the will of the sovereign who, without any national support, engaged himself in an adventure whose profitability was a real challenge. Anthopologist Frank Wesseling observes that

> After ascending to the throne, Leopold realized that his country [...] did not want to hear about colonial expansion. *Fortiter in re, suaviter in modo*, he remained faithful to his dream, but changed his method. He would now act as an individual. He would obviously be adorned with his monarchical prestige, and he would have his family's fortune in reserve, but he should not be accountable to either the government or the parliament. Constitutional ruler in Belgium, independent entrepreneur beyond state borders, such was Leopold's new strategy.[2]

King Leopold managed the CFS according to an oppressive method guided by an unrestrained desire for maximum profitability. Two postulates determined the way he ran the colony: the idea of the colonial surplus and the premise of mandatory cultures.[3] The principle of the colonial surplus considered the metropolis as the beneficiary of colonial dividends. This postulate enabled the king to launch, thanks to the profit generated by the CFS, various architectural projects of public interest and to carry out sumptuous works throughout the kingdom.[4] This initiative earned him the qualification of the king-builder.

However, this recognition hardly concealed the brutality of the system of exploitation that was set up in the CFS. Adam Hochschild's famous diatribe against the CFS counts among the harshest critiques of the Leopoldian's exploitation system.[5] Years before the publication of Hochschild's book, Aimé Césaire had already denounced, in his *Discours sur le colonialisme*, the iniquity and dehumanising aspects of colonialism.[6]

The principle of mandatory cultures is approached here in a broader meaning. It includes the dispossession of colonised people of their lands and resources, but also evokes the eradication of their cultures considered as primitive. This perception echoed the theory of the civilising mission that was used to legitimise colonialism. By the same token, Western civilisation was presented as superior to other civilisations, and thus considered as an exclusive reference for all meaningful discourse on God, humankind, and the world. Following Césaire, I can observe that this claim to universalism was accompanied by a deep contempt towards non-Western cultures and traditions. In other words, it represented a denial of alterity and difference.[7]

The annexation of the CFS to the Kingdom of Belgium (1908) embodies the paradox of change in continuity. Without losing sight of the original purpose of colonisation initiated by the king, both the Belgian government and parliament restored the image of their country, as it had been tarnished by the brutal methods of exploitation used in the CFS.[8] They set up a tripartite alliance to rule the colony –the government, the church, and the market – that is, financial institutions and concessionary companies.[9]

This form of collaboration was already used during King Leopold's management. The added value of its update consisted in highlighting the henceforth national character of Belgian colonialism. This arrangement made it possible to replace the sporadic and often abusive presence of CFS's agents – formerly recruited by the king himself[10] – by a strict administrative network and a rational control of the colonial territory.

Colonising the Luba Land

The management of the colony was entirely contingent on the colonisers' objectives. By this logic, the welfare of the colonised took second place. Regarding the region of Kasayi, the coloniser preferred large towns and cities to small villages scattered over large areas. These settlements were clustered around Catholic or Protestant missionary stations.[11] Colonial cities were designed as administrative areas and regulated according to a discriminatory policy separating modern spaces from indigenous zones.[12] The former were reserved for White people, while the later were assigned to Black people. Following Frantz Fanon, this principle of regulation reveals the unequal balance of power governing society.[13] Paradoxically, this division of the city has survived, except that now wealthy people have taken the place of White people, while the poor have been allocated to the euphemistically named 'popular' areas.

Fearing the slave raids launched by Tippu Tip,[14] most Baluba moved to zones under colonial authority to be protected. A decree of the general administration of CFS, dating from 1895, granted them permission to settle in the vicinity of existing administrative localities and missionary stations. Aimé Van Zandijcke recalls the settlement of the first Luba migrants as follows:

> In early 1896, a first and small group of migrants presented themselves to Kalamba. [Kalamba] took them to Father Cambier at the Mission of Luluabourg St Joseph (Mikalayi). [Father Cambier] received from the ruling authority of Luluabourg-Malandi the permission to house these migrants in the surroundings of the missionary station, where they founded a small village.[15]

This excerpt sheds light on one of the dark sides of the Luba exodus during the colonial era. Hunted down by slave traders, the Luba abandoned their ancestral lands to join a new existential economy in which the power relationship was not in their favour. This situation reinforced their uprooting and the reconfiguration of their identity. José Tshisungu observes that

> The colonial authorities replaced the [precolonial] society, in which barter dominated, by an industrial structure based on a monetary economic system. They replaced orality and the educational system based on rites of initiation by a written language and modern school instruction. This educational system, which initially did not take women into consideration, promoted people who were able to read, count, and write in Ciluba.[16]

This short reminder of the genesis of Belgian colonialism and the occupation of the Luba region helped to define the context in which Ciluba acquired both the status of literate and literary language. Before examining the effects of writing in Ciluba both for the coloniser and the colonised, let us examine how Ciluba became a literate language.

Colonial Language Policy Assessment

Ciluba Language: From Orality to Writing

Orality was (and is today) the predominant way of communication in the Luba community. It is the channel through which collective memory and knowledge are recorded and transmitted from a generation to another. The Luba writing system was created recently compared to languages such as Ge'ez (Ethiopia) or Swahili in eastern Africa.[17] For Crispin Maalu-Bungi, Ciluba became a literate language at the end of the nineteenth century thanks to the work by Western explorers and Christian missionaries. It also became a literary language in the first quarter of the twentieth century thanks to the dynamism of Luba people and locutors, as well as to the commitment of both Catholic and Protestant missionaries regarding evangelisation and educational duties.[18]

The Ciluba spelling relies on the Latin alphabet. Its codification was carried out by German explorers including Paul Pogge and Hermann Wilhelm von Wissmann. These figures arrived in Kasayi in October 1881 from Angola.[19] Laying the ground for the European conquest of Africa, they set up a system of linguistic notation of Ciluba. Their work benefitted from the expertise of their Angolan guides and interpreters whose mother tongue was Kimbundu. This language, which had already been codified by the Portuguese, belongs to the same linguistic group as Ciluba, in other words, the Bantu languages group according to Malcolm Guthrie's classification.[20] The work of Pogge and Wissmann was supplemented by other explorers and philologists, including Ludwig Wolf and Carl Gotthilf Büttner. The codification of Ciluba was accompanied by the compilation of a Ciluba grammar, the earliest of which was published in 1897, under the title *La Grammaire de la langue des Bena Lulua*.[21] Tshisungu observes that '[this] first draft [...] was descriptive and normative [...] and was used as a reference book in elementary education'.[22]

The Society of Congolese (Zairian) linguists contributed to the improvement of Ciluba codification and spelling. As will be developed further, this society took advantage of President Mobutu's nationalist agenda and promotion of Zairian authenticity to propose a new approach to Congolese languages.

According to Tshisungu, the process whereby Ciluba became a literate *and* literary language coincided with the entry of Luba society into modernity.[23] This development may suggest the idea that Luba people uncritically reproduced Western schemes. For me, this process enriched Luba culture and communication. Luba people can use it to capture their reality, and to record their memory. Writing in Ciluba represents an important milestone in Luba historiography and culture because it is the starting point of a new self-perception and self-expression. In other words, Ciluba writing revolutionised Luba culture, and here, I fully endorse Tshisungu's view:

> The introduction of colonial structures in Congo implied the modernisation of Ciluba. This modernisation was possible thanks to the codification of this language. This process made meaningful the act of writing and it transformed the way Ciluba speakers remember and store perceptible reality. This codification is a kind of power.[24]

The blossoming of Ciluba as a literary language depended on language policies implemented by the ruling authority. In this respect, three different periods can be noted, including the colonial rule, the post-colonial period, and the globalisation era. Before exploring their related policies and effects on Ciluba writing, let us underline the already evoked transformation of Luba society generated by the new status of Ciluba as follows:

> [Now] writing in Ciluba is to domesticate the word, which, in essence, rises in prominence. Memory tames speech only partially, and for a limited period. Writing materialises the word, makes it perceptible through the mediation of symbols. Formally, writing [in Ciluba] is the equivalent to implementing a codification technique acquired thanks to an apprenticeship.[25]

Luba Writers under Colonial Rule

Language is an essential asset, as it allows human beings to reveal themselves to each other and to build a community. As Frantz Fanon observed, 'to speak is to exist absolutely for the other'.[26] The predominance of the colonisers' language reflected their desire to wipe out or, at best, to assimilate the colonised into the ruling culture and system. Some colonised considered that it was important to master the language of the coloniser for them to be recognised as human beings. Fanon denounces the violent premise of this way of thinking, since it both generates the discrimination and inferiority complex of colonised people. Commenting on the Martinican situation, he notes that:

> Every colonised people [...] finds itself face to face with the language of the civilizing nation; that is, with the culture of the mother country. The colonised is elevated above his jungle status in proportion to his adoption of the mother country's cultural standards. He becomes whiter as he renounces his blackness, his jungle.[27]

Various African writers also denounced this policy. In this respect, Ngũgĩ wa Thiong'o can be viewed as one of the leading figures because of his choice to write and to publish in his mother tongue. By this choice, Ngũgĩ expressed his desire to make visible his native language and culture in a context of struggle for recognition. He addressed the British colonial system and literary elite for which African writers are expected to write in English to be acknowledged and to access literary recognition. Like in the French colonial situation described by Fanon, the mastery of the coloniser's language is set as a condition for the recognition of the colonised as human beings and writers. As will be explained later, Belgian language policies were different from the policies underpinning the French assimilation system, since they favoured vernacular languages over Western ones and made it difficult for the locals to learn European languages.[28]

As a matter of fact, Belgian language policies in the CFS were ambiguous and confusing. Colonial authorities relied on a kind of empiricist attitude,[29] as they rejected preconceived systems and rigid theories. They adopted a day-to-day attitude that changed according to ever-changing priorities. French was declared the official language of the CFS in 1887. As Barbara Yates observes:

> It is thus recommended to officials to use, as much as possible, only French terms in their official dealings with State soldiers and workers in a manner to have in each post a nuclear of men knowing the rudiments of language and who will in turn propagate it among natives.[30]

The implementation of this policy was complex because of various factors, including national ethnolinguistic conflicts, missionary rivalries, and the multiple origins of the CFS colonial agents recruited by King Leopold. Barbara Yates remarks that

> Leopold's policy of attempting to diffuse French throughout the Congolese population was a failure. His three principal goals – Belgianisation, adequate manpower, and a humanitarian, international image – offset each other. Many officials did not themselves speak French, and although political considerations precluded the teaching of any other modern European language, the subsidised Catholic schools did not actually propagate French, and the colonial Government did not support Protestant schools that did teach French.[31]

In addition, Belgian authorities themselves were reluctant to teach European languages to the locals. The conservative Parti catholique was one of the standard bearers of this policy that was based on paternalistic considerations aiming at protecting indigenous from Western subversive ideas, keeping them submissive, exploited, and far away from the White community. The following statement by Edouard Kervyn, a pro-Catholic director of justice and education in the Congo central headquarters in Brussels, can attest to this attitude:

> First, in the opinion of very experienced colonials, all negroes knowing French refuse to do manual labour, especially in urban areas. Secondly, missionaries and colonial officials were especially irked when Africans wanted to imitate the dress, behaviour, and language of whites. Colonialists noted derisively that, in knowing a few words of French, an African imagined himself as *civilisé* who should be accorded special liberties; indeed, the idea of African assimilation continued to upset Belgian colonialists. Thirdly, to have all Congolese study French was 'to risk the creation of a generation of *déclassés* and anarchists.[32]

After complex debates, which also touched on financial considerations and the profitability of the colony, the Belgian administration allowed the use of indigenous languages, including Kikongo, Swahili, Lingala, and Ciluba. This option contrasted with British policy, for example, which opposed the teaching of English to Kenyans.[33] For the advocates of the separatist policy, this refusal to provide education in European languages was a strategy to maintain a demarcation between the colonisers and the colonised. For the defenders of the colonised people's dignity and emancipation, this policy expressed the coloniser's racial contempt. I personally go beyond these two attitudes, as I consider that this reluctancy to teach foreign languages (French or Flemish) to Baluba constituted an opportunity for the development of Ciluba, which benefitted from the attention of the colonial authorities *and* local intelligentsia. Both the Catholic and Protestant missionaries were involved in its modernisation and dissemination through education and evangelisation. They engaged with the translation of the Bible into local languages, and spearheaded the publication of textbooks and magazines in Ciluba, for which locals received some basic training in the art of writing. Magazines such as *Nkuruse, Lumu lua Bena Kasayi,* and *Dibeji dia balongi bakale* represented an important stage in the development of Ciluba literature and the book industry.[34]

Earlier Luba writers were shaped by the colonial *and* missionary ideologies.[35] They were not highly educated since the coloniser limited the education of Congolese youth to a basic and vocational level. The happy few willing to make a career in the Church were taught philosophy and theology under the strict supervision of Church clerics. While developing their own cultural heritage and individual abilities, most of these pioneers and writers often worked in close collaboration with missionaries and colonial staff who initiated them into the art of writing.[36]

Pioneering Luba writers such as Emery Ngoyi and Mundadi Samuela started writing in the interwar period and made use of various literary genres including poetry, theatre, the novel, and the essay.[37] Their aim was to shed light on two aspects: first, they celebrated the triumph and the consolidation of missionary Christianity (and by extension Western civilisation) in Luba land; second, they set out to announce the defeat of Luba traditions perceived as the legacy of paganism.[38] This double consideration reflects the Manichaeism at the heart of their works. They denounce Luba precolonial culture while praising missionary Christianity and Western civilisation without any critical distance.

François Kabasele, the author of *Ndi muluba*, disagrees with this proselytism. For him, the Luba precolonial heritage was by no means synonymous with paganism, as it was predicated on humanist values and relied on a monotheist doctrine considering God as the Creator (*Mvidi-Mukulu*) of both visible and invisible realities.[39] Tshisungu also denounces the crusade carried out by this first generation of Luba writers against their own culture. For him, these writers fought against their ancestral beliefs because they were faced with a foreign ideology and religion. Subsequently, they focused on creating a new Luba identity based on Christian and Western values. Tshisungu wrote:

> [For these writers] to write is to affirm (their) Christian belief. The author, and later the writer, defines himself as a person carrying a Christian message intended to influence their conscience.[40]

Martin Kalulambi Pongo expresses the same concern in *Être Luba au XXe siècle*.[41] For him, missionary magazines published in Ciluba contributed to shaping a new Luba identity marked by Christian values. The Catholic magazine *Nkuruse* can be considered as one of the most active platforms in this respect. This first generation of Luba writers were submissive, and they served as a sounding board for colonial and missionary ideologies. An analysis of works by Emery Ngoyi and Mundadi Samuela would confirm this statement.[42] In sum, from the perspective of Luba colonial historiography, it can be noted that this generation of writers attests to Fanon's postulate about colonised people's self-alienation and self-hatred.

Finally, it is worth noting that colonial language policies generated a paradoxical outcome. At first, it created favourable conditions for the development of vernacular languages, including Ciluba. Thus, these languages developed from their original status as oral languages into literate and literary languages. Second, this policy turned out to be a trap to control and stifle Luba culture, as suggested by Barbara Yates:

> [The Belgian language policy] was, thus, an 'admirable' agent of social control of the African population. Colonialists were quite aware that, by discouraging the learning of a European language, the extent and nature of ideas could be limited or expanded at their discretion.[43]

As already mentioned, this policy reinforced the alienation of Luba people and their submission to the ruling order. As a result, most of the works written in Ciluba during the colonial period were marked by this paradox.

The Ciluba Literature in the Postcolonial Era

Congolese Emancipation and Language Policies

Following the euphoria of Congolese emancipation in 1960, and in the wake of the new nationalist momentum created by this event, French became the official language and the main language of instruction at all levels of formal education. The first Congolese president, Joseph Kasa-Vubu, officialised this choice through his presidential ordinance of 17 October 1962.[44]

Various postulates have been evoked in support of this language choice, including national unity and development, the efficiency of European languages of wider communication, and their cost-effectiveness. The idea of national unity relies on the fear that the use of a vernacular language as an official language in a Congolese context marked by multilingualism would lead to ethnic conflicts, and that this situation would subsequently compromise the fragile national unity in progress. To prevent such an upheaval, the government privileged a European language (French) viewed as neutral and free of any ethnic background. The argument of national development referred to the idea that progress – understood as catching up with Western modernisation – would only be possible if European languages of wide communication were used as media of instruction. In other words, African (Congolese) languages were viewed as an obstacle to progress. They are perceived as less developed than European languages and therefore unsuitable as media of instruction. By the same token, it was also thought that the adoption of an indigenous language would be very expensive, as it would have required the translation and writing of textbooks, reference tools, and the training of teaching personal.

These arguments have already been the subject of multiple studies, and it is not the purpose of this chapter to revisit them.[45] However, it seems enlightening for my purpose to underline their counterproductive effects both for Luba-speaking people and their literature. The imposition of French as the country's official language and the language of education at all levels distorted people's self-representation, and it affected their relationship to vernacular languages. Indeed, this decision devalued people's self-esteem and upset the way they negotiated their relationship to the world. Henceforth, to access a valuable education and a successful career, one would have to adopt a foreign language, French, in this case. As a result, many people lost trust and motivation towards their own mother tongue, since it was classified as a second-class language and seen as nonessential to access modernity. This situation generated an inferiority complex among vernacular-speaking people towards French speakers, and vice versa. A social and cultural divide was thus created between the educated elite and the uneducated lower classes. The former considering the later as the incarnation of conservatism and underdevelopment. As a reaction to such contempt, the vernacular-speaking community cultivated a kind of resistance that consisted in making fun of the elite's eagerness to learn and speak French in everyday-life situations. Therefore, they employ the following humoristic assertion that is still in use today: *Mfwalansa ki mfwalanga to* literally translated as 'French does not produce money', which means 'learning and speaking French is not enough to earn a living'.

Despite this situation, Luba writers have carried out remarkable works. Using different literary genres, such as poetry and the essay, they have explored new topics away from colonial and missionary ideologies. They have focused on social and political conflicts including, for example, the ethnic violence between the Luba and Lulua communities and the expulsion of the Luba community from the Katanga province. Mabika Kalanda's essay 'Tabalayi bama betu'[46] is symptomatic of this period. From the outset, Mabika Kalanda states why he writes in Ciluba. For him, writing in Ciluba represents a straightforward and easy way to tell the truth to his people, and to be understood unequivocally by them. In other words, he seeks direct communication with his readers, free of all kinds of intermediaries and obstacles. This motivation is far from coinciding with Ngũgĩ wa Thiong'o's decision to go back and write in Gikuyu. For the former, the desire to touch and to be in touch with his Luba readers has come first, while the latter has denounced the British and ruling systems and their marginalisation of vernacular languages.

Instead of using the language of the elite, Mabika Kalanda made use of Ciluba to encourage the Luba to reflect and make adequate choices in a complex and conflictual political situation. Indeed, he wrote this book shortly after independence at the right moment when the Luba community was in turmoil facing a variety of challenges including, for example, the ethnic war opposing the Lulua to the Baluba, the internal antagonism between the Luba of the East and those of the West (*Bena Mukuna ne bena Cibanda*), the race for power between local and national political leaders.[47]

The African Authenticity and the Standardisation of Ciluba

The change of regime in 1965 under the aegis of President J. D. Mobutu ushered in a new era characterised by the quest for African authenticity. The philosophical premise of this quest dealt with the rehabilitation of African culture and identity, seen as the principle of African dignity and national development. This ideology included various topics such as the struggle against the alienation resulting from colonialism, the expression of a way of being and living according to the aspiration of African (Zairian) people, and the enhancement of ancestral customs and values.[48]

President Mobutu tried and brought this project into reality through various political and administrative measures including, for example, the replacement of names of Western origin by those of Congolese origin. These measures applied to Congolese nationals (who became Zairians), to the country (from Congo to Zaire), to cities and various institutions in the country. By the same token, it can also be mentioned that even the dress code was readjusted by replacing the suit and tie with the abacost (for males) and the prohibition of women from wearing dresses, trousers, and miniskirts. The monuments built in memory of the colonisers were also removed from public spaces all over the country (on this issue, see Bambi Ceuppens's chapter in this volume). In addition, this ideology contributed to the legitimisation of authoritarian political power, and to the truncation of the complex history of exchanges between cultures. Its fundamental postulate relied on a culturalist view of the world and the relationships between humankind as antagonistic, opposing indigenous people to foreigners, the authentic to the alien, and 'us' to 'them'.

The anxiety elicited by this rehabilitation of African culture constituted a favourable background for the reconsideration of Congolese language policies, particularly regarding vernacular languages. In this respect, the first seminar of Congolese (Zairian) linguists, held in Lubumbashi in 1974, represented an important milestone in raising awareness of the country's linguistic questions, including the teaching of and in vernacular languages, and the standardisation of these languages. André Mbula Paluku observes that

> [t]he theme of this seminar was the promotion of the Zairean languages [...] it aimed at both asserting the citizen's cultural identity as concerning the linguistic level, and at bringing major languages of the country to the status of modern languages capable of conveying both scientific and technological knowledge. At the end of this seminar, the government decided to reintroduce the four national languages as vehicles and subjects in primary education.[49]

The reintroduction of national languages in the education programme was an attempt to offset the damages created by the previous language policy consecrating French as the predominant language of the administration and education in a country where more than 70 per cent of people can hardly speak French and have only received basic education. This decision represented a new start for national languages and their (re)enhancement. An output of this seminar is also that it encouraged the standardisation of spelling of literate national languages, particularly Ciluba. Specialists in Luba linguistics proposed various improvements regarding the pioneering work achieved by Paul Pogge and Hermann Wilhelm von Wissmann. As Crispin Maalu-Bungi remarks, these changes concern the transcription of the semivowels 'y', 'w', and the replacement of the trigraph ('tsh') with the sign 'c'. He identifies 'the adoption of the semi-vowels y and w instead of I and u [...]; the systematic notation of tones and vowel quantity [...]' and 'the transcription of the deaf palatal affricate by the sign c to replace the trigraph "tsh"'.[50]

However, the implementation of the conclusions from this historic seminar suffered from vagaries impeding the political and economic development of the country. The Zairian supporters of Ciluba faced significant obstacles, particularly concerning the development of a successful book industry. Among other things, there was a scarcity of centres for the publication and dissemination of literature in national languages and hence a general erosion of the body of available readers and writers. What is more, vernacular languages are still held in suspicion and regarded as inferior by French users.

Despite this difficult transition, Luba literature has resisted. In addition to its ever-dynamic poetry, other literary genres – the essay, the novel, and the comic book – have been developed. This generation of Luba writers explored new issues including, for example, the critique of Mobutu's dictatorship,[51] the love for Luba culture,[52] power, Luba aesthetics and ethics, and Luba historiography. Thanks to this dynamism, Luba literature is propelled to the heart of debates on the ability of African languages to match modernity and to transcend local considerations. In this respect, it is worth underlining the remarkable work of Pius Ngandu Nkashama on Ciluba plasticity, morphology, and semantics.[53] Via an analysis of two Luba verbs, *Ku-twa* and *Kw-ela*, he shows how far, through a meticulous articulation of both the morphology and syntax, these verbs include multiple meanings and can be applied to various contexts.

Ciluba Literature in a Globalised World

Beyond the (Post)Colonial Stereotypes

Postcolonial thinking can be viewed as a critical discourse concerning norms established by the colonial system and aiming at consolidating a hierarchical relationship between the metropolis and the colony. This discourse denounces the philosophy structuring the relationship between the centre and the periphery.[54] It applies to a variety of fields including political, social, religious, artistic, and literary areas. In the area of literature, this criticism has consisted in denouncing the occultation and marginalisation of literatures in non-Western languages, especially those published in African languages, a central point in this chapter. The postulate behind this attitude is that protagonists of Western hegemony consider literature in African languages to be literature with a local vocation, a kind of second-class literature. The African languages themselves are perceived as incapable of grasping and formulating the challenges of modernity. In addition, many of these protagonists think that African writers have no choice but to write in Western languages in their pursuit to publish rational works and access universal readerships.

This contemptuous dogmatism about African languages and literature in African languages has been widely questioned by both anglophone and francophone African thinkers. Ngũgĩ wa Thiong'o is one of the recent and virulent critics of this dogmatism. It is worth recalling that decades before Ngũgĩ wa

Thiong'o's rebellious cry, Cheikh Anta Diop had already expressed the need to revalorise African languages in his project of intellectual emancipation.[55] Writing in African languages – especially in Ciluba as is the focus of this chapter – amounts to participation in the struggle for emancipation and development of Luba people.

I personally think that Ngũgĩ wa Thiong'o is right to call for the decolonisation of literature through language. My statement relies on the following postulates. At first, I refer to the importance of language as a communicational process, since it can be viewed as a way people call each other into existence and build a community, as suggested by Fanon, 'to speak is to really exist for the other'. One's language is the most beautiful, most secure, and easiest way to approach truth and beauty. Given this premise, it is my belief that writing in one's own language constitutes the very assertion of one's existence and interactions with others. Communication through one's language represents the epiphany of the other, or the revelation of 'oneself as another', to make use of Paul Ricœur's hermeneutical expression.[56] Such a revelation disrupts colonial patterns and calls for the renewal of our own vision of the world and that of the others.

Next, I take into consideration the idea that literature in African languages is by no means a literature from the margins and forever enclosed in such a framework. This literature transcends geographical, political, cultural, and linguistic barriers, and tries to match current humankind challenges. Through their respective publications in their native languages, writers like Ngũgĩ wa Thiong'o and Boubacar Boris Diop demonstrate how rich and creative their mother tongues are to express modern experiences. Regarding Ciluba, writers such as Pius Ngandu Nkashama, Mabika Kalanda, and François Kabasele have also demonstrated through their respective works how far Ciluba can create and extend concepts to match all kinds of reality and contexts.[57]

I am of the view that Ciluba literature belies the idea according to which Afrophone literature operates in a cultural ghetto and fails to promote any universal messages. This literature is not tied to Luba land, the Kasai region. Given the 'circulation of worlds'[58] and the subsequent emergence of new configurations, it travels all over the world and addresses multiple challenges and themes. Ciluba literature is disseminated in the world by the Luba diaspora, which, while facing challenges related to migration, unemployment, and social and cultural integration, refuse to enclose themselves into Afrocentrist or ethnic debates. This community negotiates on the basis of its participation in the world. It addresses new topics while calling for the renewal of Luba culture regarding current mutations. Via Afrophone literature, it is possible to underline the role played by the diaspora in the dissemination of Ciluba literature:

'This diaspora contributes greatly to relocating languages. [...] This is why an important part of the literary production in Ciluba is currently published in Canada, Belgium, and France'.[59]

It is worth revisiting here some relevant works published during this period in the diaspora and in the DRC: Pius Ngandu Nkashama's *Bidi ntuilu bidi mpelelu*,[60] François Kabasele's *Ndi Muluba*, Bertin Makolo Musuasua's *Munanga wanyi*, Tshisungu wa Tshisungu's *Cimvundu* and *Kuanyi kuamba*, Therese Tshiadua Kandala's *Bumfumu bua kabukulu* and Kapajika Kamudimba's *Kanyingela*.[61]

Before exploring my proposed case study, *Ndi muluba* by François Kabasele, I would like to point out the relevance of Pius Ngandu Nkashama's novel *Bidi ntwilu bidi mpelelu* as a critique of the contempt towards Afrophone literature. Crispin Maalu-Bungi notes that this novel is a translation into Ciluba, by the author himself, of a novel (*Le pacte de sang*[62]) previously published in French. I firmly believe that the passage from French to Ciluba does not affect the originality and the literary value of the Ciluba version. On the contrary, by translating his own work into his mother tongue, Pius Ngandu Nkashama wrote a new novel that is far from a mere copy of the French original, as it involves various nuances and rhythms unknown in French. I can say that approaching reality and formulating it in Ciluba is not the same thing as doing it in French. Indeed, there is no room here for a simple equivalence of words. This process requires the author's ability to handle, like a seasoned artist, the morphology and syntax of Luba terms, to give them additional semantic capacity and extent. He explains this by introducing his other book on *Sémantique et morphologie du verbe en Ciluba*, as follows:

> The project for this study of the morphology and syntax of Ciluba was inspired by the work of writing a novel, *Bidi ntwilu, bidi mpelelu*. During this literary experience, it appeared that with each paraphrase, the language was discovered from within, displaying its lexical resources and its semantic expressivities. [...] But by the contextualised situations and locutions, the demands of discursivity as much as those of narrativity turned out to be more important than they seemed at first glance.[63]

Concerning the use of the verb *Kw-ela*, for example, he notes:

> By using the only verb *Kw-ela* and its derivatives, all the meanings of violence, struggle, combativeness of the protagonists, as well as actions carried out around the battle between two people are rendered. And this, without the speaker having to resort to approximate, analogies, synonymous, and metaphors.[64]

As already suggested, relying on the demonstration by Pius Ngandu Nkashama of how the articulation of morphology and syntax of verbs in Ciluba can create new meanings and extend concepts, I can note the inconsistency of the colonial stereotype considering that African languages including Ciluba 'are weak, poor, incapable of expressing abstract notions, unsuitable for logical reasoning or simply philosophical thinking, incompatible with mathematical concepts and symbols'.[65] Xavier Garnier expresses a similar argument about the way in which postcolonial and francophone theorists disregard Afrophone literature.[66] For him, these two categories of scholars consider Afrophone literature with contempt, as local, popular, and didactic literature. As already suggested, this perception needs to be rectified, because publications in vernacular languages – particularly in Ciluba – are far from being locked into such a theoretical rut. In addition to its ability to grasp and express an infinite number of situations, Luba literature is spread throughout the world thanks to the 'circulation of worlds',[67] and the dynamism of the Luba intelligentsia and diaspora who largely contribute to the production and dissemination of Ciluba writings by setting up appropriate publishing houses,[68] promoting Luba cultural activities, and expanding Luba networks and meeting spaces.

François Kabasele, Between Conservatism and Renovation

François Kabasele is a theologian and liturgy specialist. In addition to his involvement in higher education in the DRC and abroad, he has carried out work on the inculturation of Christianity in Kasayi. He perceives inculturation from a dual perspective: on the one hand, this notion is ideological and, following the reflection conducted by negritude figures, refers to the emancipation and de-alienation of African people, and the rehabilitation of their cultures and traditions. On the other, Kabasele believes that his concept includes a normative dimension aiming at educating, rehabilitating, and forging a new Luba society in accordance with Luba traditions and Christian values. Linking the word to the deed, Kabasele himself tried to bring this project into reality through his teaching and his pastoral activities in the diocese of Mbuji-Mayi, where he has also been responsible for the liturgy office.[69] Kabasele also cooperates with the Congolese diaspora in Brussels – particularly with the Sangalayi association – to set up a Luba cultural archive. The book to be introduced here, *Ndi muluba*, can attest to this commitment. This book is an essay whose style is concise and clear. Through his writing, Kabasele complies with the guidelines by Congolese (Zairian) linguists' society aiming at standardising Ciluba spelling. Therefore, he counts within few Luba writers engaged for the renewal and standardisation of their language.

The book focuses on Luba identity. Kabasele claims that identity is constantly changing while preserving what is essential. Without specifying what this essential element is made of, Kabasele engages with the enumeration of multiple features that, for him, constitute Luba identity. In other words, Kabasele relies on a broader concept of identity to express the convergence of different factors including music, art, religion, territory, language, to mention but a few. Since the scope of this chapter does not allow an extensive analysis of these factors, I will limit myself to mentioning some of their main aspects. The book is divided into three sections: Luba identity, the encounter of Luba people with Christianity, and the challenges facing Luba identity regarding the future.

Starting from a poorly substantiated premise that the Baluba are a migrant people, Kabasele contends that elements such as the Luba world view, beliefs, and aesthetics, including sculpture and traditional music, social and religious rites, and political organisation, are constitutive of the Luba identity. He also mentions the unflattering aspects of the Baluba – their selfishness, greed for power, pride, complacency, and ostentation. In his sketch of Luba identity, Kabasele is prone to amplify some traits so much that he gives the impression of being disconnected from their real existence. As Tshisungu observes, this propensity has the collateral effect of disembodying and weakening his purpose:

> The Muluba (singular of the term Baluba) that the author describes seems disembodied, withdrawn from the constraints of the environment. Socially speaking, such a Muluba does not exist.[70]

The second section of the book analyses the Christianisation of Luba. This issue is important because it was through evangelisation that Ciluba achieved the status of a written and literary language. Modern education, infrastructure, and Luba daily life were shaped through the colonial and missionary economy.[71] While recognising these achievements, Kabasele denounces the anti-paganist crusade considering precolonial Luba culture as a legacy of paganism. For him, Luba people had always believed in God. Their Christianisation can be viewed as an opportunity for both Christianity itself and Luba heritage to flourish. From this postulate, he focuses on various Luba religious beliefs, practices, and rituals[72] that he connects to the Christian doctrine as expressed in the Bible and Church documents, essentially from the Second Vatican Council to today.

The last section focuses on the challenges of being Luba today. Kabasele informs his readers about the dissemination of the Luba diaspora around the world in the United States, Canada, Belgium, France, and the United Kingdom,[73] to mention but a few. Without losing sight of risks associated with this dissemination, including the erosion of Luba cultural identity, he calls for a moral and intellectual effort to maintain Luba values and traditions. He insists on the importance of solidarity and the responsibility of Luba diasporic communities about the future. They should kindle the fire of Luba identity. This last point is the leading idea of Kabasele's research as expressed in this book. Therefore, it can be considered as an important contribution, from the Luba-speaking world, to recurrent debates on acculturation, inculturation, interculturality, and hybridity.

The fact that Kabasele broaches some of these debates in Ciluba is important, because, following Mabika Kalanda's project, he addresses first and foremost the Luba, the people who are involved in and concerned by these issues. As I have already commented on the importance of one's mother tongue in the framework of communication, I believe that Kabasele's message in Ciluba reaches and affects his readers. In this respect, he has genuinely contributed to the revival of Luba literature in recent years. He has created an inventory of elements from Luba culture and has found them resonant with post-Vatican II Christianity, which he considers free from colonial and missionary shortcomings. Although Kabasele barely questions the structures of power inside the Catholic Church, nor challenges the social and political structures of contemporary society, he is fully absorbed by the issue of Luba identity. However, his perception of the Luba cultural legacy is based on a monocultural and past-oriented basis. The Luba identity is depicted as pure and static, and in this discussion, he mainly focuses on precolonial Luba communities. As I have already suggested, Kabasele's book acts as a compass in the current context of globalisation, but it suffers from a disconnect between the reality of Luba people and their ascribed identity, which seems to be much more normative than existential and pragmatic.

Conclusion

This chapter has relied on the postulate that writing in Ciluba is linked to the colonial and postcolonial history of the Luba community. In the wake of early explorations and the work of linguistic codification carried out by figures such as Paul Pogge and Hermann Wilhelm von Wissmann, Belgian colonialism contributed to making Ciluba both a literate and literary language. The language policies of the Belgian coloniser and those of the Congolese leaders after independence have shaped the standardisation of Ciluba and influenced its diffusion.

The existence of Luba literature can be viewed as a critique of colonial and elitist contempt towards vernacular languages. For the pioneers of this literature – e.g. Emery Ngoyi, Lazare Mpoyi, Mundadi Samuela – writing in Ciluba was a means to reject precolonial paganism and sing the praise of Christian modernity. This chapter has also demonstrated how far this literature has escaped literary ghettoisation, examined modern themes, and explored them with appropriate concepts. In this respect, the contributions of authors like Pius Ngandu Nkashama, Mabika Kalanda, and François Kabasele have been crucial because, while exploring the multifaceted aspects of Luba identity, they have also revealed the linguistic riches of Ciluba. Luba literature, like most Afrophone literatures, suffers from a lack of standardisation and publishing infrastructures; however, the dynamism of the Luba diaspora is a reason for hope.

Ciluba as both a literate and literary language aims at approaching the world and dialoguing with it from a Luba point of view. This perspective can be considered as that of the powerless and the 'wretched of the earth' because, from the colonial era until now, Luba people have belonged to the category of impoverished people, even though, paradoxically, their homeland is rich in natural, human, cultural, linguistic, and spiritual resources. From their daily struggle for survival, they perceive the flaws of our globalised world, and they call for the establishment of another possible world. To this end, I believe that Luba writers can be seen as dawn watchers.

Notes

1. François Kabasele Lumbala, *Ndi muluba* (Louvain-la-Neuve: Éditions Panubula, 2004)
2. Henri Wesseling, *Le partage de l'Afrique* (Paris: Denoël, 1996), p. 151. All translations are mine unless otherwise stated.
3. Pierre-Philippe Fraiture, *Le Congo belge est son récit francophone à la veille des indépendances. Sous l'empire du royaume* (Paris: L'Harmattan, 2003), pp. 25–26.
4. See works such as the African Museum of Tervuren (now AfricaMuseum), L'arc du cinquantenaire, the Brussels Courthouse, to mention but a few. On this process, see Matthew G. Stanard, *The Leopard, the Lion and the Cock: Colonial Memories and Monuments in Belgium* (Leuven: Leuven University Press, 2019).
5. A. Hochschild, *The Ghosts of King Leopold: A Story of Greed, Terror, and Heroism in Colonial Africa* (Boston: Mariner Books, 1998).
6. Aimé Césaire, *Discourse on Colonialism*, trans. Joan Pinkham (New York: Monthly Review Press, 1972), p. 41.
7. Albert Kasanda, 'Les figures de l'autre. Prismes et gestion de la différence en Afrique', in Albert Kasanda (ed.), *Dialogue interculturel. Cheminer ensemble vers un autre monde possible* (Paris: L'Harmattan, 2013), pp. 197–243.
8. See Matthieu Zana Etambala, *Congo veroverd, bezet, gekoloniseerd 1876-1914* (Gorredijk: Sterck & De Vreese, 2020).
9. See Fraiture (2003), pp. 32–33.
10. In the earlier stage of colonisation, Leopold was obliged to recruit administrators, army officers, traders, missionaries, and other workers from various Western nations, since Belgian people manifested very little interest in his African venture. They came from all over the world: the United States, the United Kingdom, Finland, Norway, Denmark, Sweden, Russia, Switzerland, Italy, and Portugal.
11. See V. Y. Mudimbe, *The Idea of Africa* (Bloomington and Indianapolis; James Currey: Indiana University Press; London, 1994).
12. See Johan Lagae and Jakob Sabakinu Kivilu, 'Infrastructure, paysages urbains et architecture: témoins du «développement» ou instruments de « mise en valeur »?', in Idesbald Goddeeris, Amandine Lauro and Guy Vanthemsche (eds.), *Le Congo colonial: une histoire en questions* (Waterloo: Renaissance du Livre, 2020), pp. 183–95.
13. F. Fanon, *Les Damnés de la terre*, introduction by Gérard Chaliand, preface by Jean-Paul Sartre (Paris: Gallimard, 1991 [1961]), pp. 68–71.
14. See Leda Farrant, *Tippu Tip and the East African Slave Trade* (London: Hamish Hamilton, 1975).
15. Aimé Van Zandijcke, *Les Baluba dans la tourmente* (Kananga: Éditions de l'Archidiocèse, 1989), p. 7.
16. J. Tshisungu wa Tshisungu, *La Littérature congolaise écrite en Ciluba* (Ontario: Glopro, 2006). p. 14.
17. On these precolonial African alphabets, see Alain Ricard, *The Languages & Literatures of Africa* (Oxford: James Currey, 2004), 'The Manuscript Heritage', pp. 46–74.
18. Crispin Maalu-Bungi. 'Quand la pratique lexicographique se modernise en RD Congo. Note sur *Nkongamyaku Ciluba-Mfwalansa*, dictionnaire bilingue de Ngo Semzara Kabuta', *Lexikos* 21.1 (2011), 320–36 (324).
19. Marcel Scheitler, *Histoire de l'Eglise catholique du Kasayi* (Kananga: Éditions de l'Archidiocèse, 1991), p. 9.
20. See Introduction to bantu languages (bantu-languages.com) [accessed 22 December 2021].
21. Mgr August De Clercq, *La Grammaire de la langue des bena Lulua* (Brussels: Polleunis et Centerick, Imprimeries, 1897).
22. Tshisungu (2006), p. 19.
23. Ibid., p. 15.
24. Ibid., p. 16.
25. Ibid., p. 19.
26. Frantz Fanon, *Black Skin, White Masks*, trans. Charles Lam Markmann (London: Pluto Press, 1986 [1967]), p. 17.
27. Ibid., p. 19.
28. See Michael Meeuwis, 'Bilingual Inequality: Linguistic Rights and Disenfranchisement in Late Belgian Colonization', *Journal of Pragmatics*, 43 (2011), 1279–87.
29. Mukala Kadima-Nzuji, *La Littérature zaïroise de langue française (1945-1960)* (Paris: ACCT/Karthala, 1984).pp. 9–10.
30. Barbara Yates, 'The Origin of Language Policy in Zaire', *Journal of Modern African Studies*, 18.2 (1980), 257–79 (258).
31. Ibid., p. 260.
32. Ibid., p. 272. Edouard Kervyn quoted by Yates.
33. Makim M. Mputubwele, 'The Zairian Language Policy and Its Effect on the Literatures in national languages', *Journal of Black Studies*, 34. 2 (2004), 272–92 (278).
34. The proliferation of these magazines in local languages can also be explained by the support offered by Belgium to missionary institutions searching for a better knowledge of the colonised. See: Martin Kalulambi Pongo, *Être luba au XXe siècle. Identité chrétienne et ethnicité au Congo Kinshasa* (Paris: Karthala, 1997), pp. 231–32.

35. In this chapter, I only focus on Luba native writers. This does not imply the concealment or underestimation of works in Ciluba carried out by many foreigners including missionaries and colonial agents. In his book (pp. 43–45), Tshisungu (2006) provides a list of these individuals.
36. See V. Y. Mudimbe, *Tales of Faith: Religion as Political Performance in Central Africa* (London; Atlantic Highlands, NJ: Athlone Press, 1997).
37. Crispin Maalu-Bungi, *L'inconnue de l'histoire. La littérature créative en langues congolaises* (Paris: Présence Africaine, forthcoming), see particularly chapter 6.
38. The following statement by Lazare Mpoyi is instructive: 'Bankambwa beetu bavwa batuutubuja kudi Dyabolo' (Our ancestors were subjugated by the devil). See: Lazare Mpoyi, *Histoire wa Baluba* (Mbuji-Mayi: Institut Saint Jean-Baptiste de la Salle, 1966), p. 17. Quoted in Kabasele, *Ndi muluba*, p. 89.
39. Kabasele Lumbala, *Ndi muluba*, pp. 89–91.
40. J. Tshisungu (2006), pp. 23–24.
41. Kalulambi Pongo, *Être luba au XXe siècle*.
42. For a substantial introduction to these writers and their works, see: Maalu-Bungi's *L'inconnue de l'histoire* and Tshisungu wa Tshisungu's *La littérature congolaise écrite en ciluba*.
43. Yates, 'The Origins of Language Policy in Zaire', p. 278.
44. Mputubwele, 'The Zairian Language Policy…', pp. 280–81.
45. See for example: Ayo Bomgbose, *Language, and the Nation: The Language Question in Sub-Saharan Africa* (Edinburgh: Edinburgh University Press, 1991). Eyamba G. Bokamba, 'Arguments for Multilingual Policies in Public Domains, in Eric A. Anchimbe (ed.), *Linguistic Identity in Postcolonial Multilingual Spaces* (New Castle: Cambridge Scholars Publishing, 2007), pp. 27–65.
46. Mabika Kalanda, *Tabalayi bana betu* (Léopoldville: Concordia, 1963).
47. For an overview of works published during this period, see: Tshisungu (2006), pp. 35–65.
48. Bob White, 'L'incroyable machine d'authenticité: l'animation politique et l'usage public de la culture dans le Zaïre de Mobutu', *Anthropologie et sociétés*, 30.2 (2006), 43–63. https://www.erudit.org/fr/revues/as/2006-v30-n2-as1445/014113ar/ accessed 10/05/2022.
49. André Mbula Paluku, 'L'enseignement des et en langues nationales au Zaire', *Revue Tranel*, 26 (1996), 15–32 (23).
50. Crispin Maalu-Bungi, 'Quand la pratique lexicographique se modernise en RD Congo, p. 323. However, the Ciluba standardisation process is far from over, as both the old and new spelling are still in use.
51. Kadiebwe Muzembe Nyunyu, *Tshibula tshia mujangi* (Kananga: Ciam-Kasayi, 1998).
52. Bertin Makolo Musuasua, *Kanyi kalambo* (Kananga: Éditions de l'ISP, 1979). Crispin Maalu-Bungi, *Mwakulu wa ciluba, leelu ne makelela* (Sudburry: Editions Glopro, 2004).
53. Pius Ngandu Nkashama, *Sémantique et morphologie du verbe en Ciluba. Etude de ku-twa et kwela* (Paris: L'Harmattan, 1999).
54. This is a vast field. Some of its most prominent figures include Edward Said, Homi Bhabha, Robert J.C. Young, Dipesh Chakrabarty, Gayatri Spivak but also Helen Tiffin, Gareth Griffiths, and Bill Ashcroft. In this scholarship, the influence of French thought – and of thinkers such as Michel Foucault, Jacques Derrida, and Jacques Lacan – has been significant.
55. See Pierre-Philippe Fraiture, *Past Imperfect: Time and African Decolonization, 1945–1960* (Liverpool: Liverpool University Press, 2021), pp. 173–96.
56. P. Ricœur, *Oneself as Another*, trans. by Kathleen Blamey (Chicago: University of Chicago Press, 1992).
57. See particularly the following works: Pius Ngandu Nkashama, *Bidi ntuilu, bidi mpelelu* (Lubumbashi: Editions Impala, 1998), Mabika Kalanda, *Tabalayi bana betu*, Francois Kabasele, *Ndi muluba*. Concerning a theoretical analysis of the deployment of both the Ciluba morphology and syntax, see: Pius Ngandu Nkashama, *Sémantique et morphologie du verbe en Ciluba*.
58. Achille Mbembe, *Sortir de la grande nuit. Essai sur l'Afrique décolonisée* (Paris: La Découverte, 2010). See Chapter 6, 'La Circulation des mondes: l'expérience africaine', pp. 203-37.
59. Xavier Garnier, 'Les littératures en langues africaines ou l'inconscient des théories postcoloniales', *Neohelicon* 35.2 (2008), 87–99 (89). See also X. Garnier, *The Swahili Novel: Challenging the Idea of 'Minor Literature'*, trans Rémi Tchokothe and Armand and Frances Kennett (Woodbridge, Suffolk: Boydell & Brewer; James Currey, 2013).
60. Ngandu Nkashama, *Bidi ntwilu, bidi mpelelu*.
61. For further comments about these works, see: Crispin Maalu-Bungi, *L'inconnue de l'histoire*, particularly chapter 6 on Luba Literature.
62. Ngandu Nkashama, *Le pacte de sang* (Paris: L'Harmattan, 1984).
63. Ngandu Nkashama, *Sémantique et morphologie en Ciluba*, p. 18.
64. Ibid.
65. Ibid., p. 13.
66. X. Garnier, 'Les littératures en langues africaines…'.
67. See Mbembe, *Sortir de la grande nuit*.

68. Such as Panubula (Louvain-la-Neuve), Éditions Glopro (Ontario), Ciam-Kasayi, and Mabiki (Brussels/Kinshasa).
69. Kabasele, 'L'inculturation comme antidote à la violence en Afrique', in *Revue des sciences religieuses*, 85.3 (2011), 427–46, https://journals.openedition.org/rsr/1752 [accessed 22 December 2021].
70. Tshisungu wa Tshisungu, *La littérature congolaise écrite en ciluba*, p. 130.
71. Kalulambi Pongo Martin, *Être Luba au XXe siècle*.
72. Such as the ancestor worship, birth ceremonies and the welcoming of children into the community, reconciliation, and wedding.
73. See Kabasele, *Ndi muluba*, pp. 297–312.

PART 3
Imperial Practices and Their Afterlives

Media Representations of Burundi's 2020 Elections in Belgium and Burundi

Caroline Williamson Sinalo

On 20 May 2020, Burundians went to the polls to elect a new president. This was the first election since the 2015 political crisis, when President Pierre Nkurunziza announced that he would violate the Arusha Accord by running for a third term. Following his 2015 re-election, Nkurunziza and his wing of the ruling party, the National Council for the Defense of Democracy – Forces for the Defense of Democracy (CNDD-FDD) proceeded to consolidate power, securing 'almost complete control over state and society'.[1]

Although Nkurunziza announced that he would not run in 2020, many of the underlying issues of the 2015 conflict persisted. As predicted, the 2020 elections were marred by irregularities including reports that members of the opposition party, the National Congress for Liberty (CNL), led by Agathon Rwasa, were threatened, beaten, arrested, and even killed by the police and *Imbonerakure*.[2] International observers were prevented from entering the country while internal journalists faced intimidation.[3] Despite the irregularities, however, the violence never reached the scale of the 2015 crisis, and the CNDD-FDD candidate, Évariste Ndayishimiye, won with 68.72 per cent of the popular vote. The elections also took place during the Covid-19 pandemic, which was downplayed by the CNDD-FDD. Less than three weeks after the poll, however, President Pierre Nkurunziza died unexpectedly from complications linked to Covid-19, although his illness was denied by the authorities, who claimed he died from a heart attack.

This chapter investigates domestic and Belgian media narratives of events surrounding the 2020 election. It explores opposing sides of the country's media conflict through an analysis of coverage by the state-run *Radio Télévision Nationale du Burundi* [Burundi National Radio and Television] (RTNB) and the independent online news outlet *SOS Médias Burundi* and compares this to coverage found in *La Libre Belgique* and *Le Soir*, outlets from Belgium, the former colonial power. International media often downplay the legacy of historical colonialism in favour of essentialist stereotypes when representing conflict in

Central Africa, and the Belgian press is no exception.[4] Drawing on theories of framing and narrative, the chapter will scrutinise the varying constructions of the 2020 elections for different sets of Burundian and Belgian audiences.[5]

Belgium's Historical Role in Burundi

While much has changed in Burundi since independence, the legacy of Belgian colonialism cannot be understated, particularly its role in racialising social identities. In precolonial times, the economic system was based on a form of clientelism (*ubugabire*) between Tutsi patrons and Hutu clients, and it is generally agreed that this system provided the basis for later ethnic classification although the politics surrounding the terms Hutu and Tutsi, and the nature of precolonial social and political relationships, is highly contested.[6] Colonial domination, first by Germany (1897–1916) and then by Belgium (1916–62), brought about significant changes in Burundian society, particularly in relation to the construction of Tutsi and Hutu identities.

Like the Germans before them, the Belgians 'entered Burundi with entrenched ideological preconceptions of racial and class superiority which they used to interpret the sophisticated hierarchical political and economic structures of the society'.[7] They believed that the Tutsi were evolutionarily closer to Europeans and thus superior to the Hutu. This belief, based on the now discredited Hamitic hypothesis, stemmed from the idea that Tutsi were descendants of Noah's son Ham who had migrated to Africa from the Middle East. According to the myth, Tutsi eventually arrived in Rwanda from Somalia or Ethiopia and conquered the Hutu and Twa as a result of their natural superiority.[8] Tutsi, Hutu, and Twa were considered to be of completely different racial groups, and the Belgians subsequently translated these beliefs into racist policies. For example, the colonial education system was designed to educate a Tutsi elite while Hutu were completely evicted from positions of power.[9]

The education system was run by the Catholic Church, which played an important role in promulgating the Hamitic hypothesis (see Chantal Gishoma's chapter in this volume). Not only did the hypothesis determine education policy, but it also dominated the Church's evangelisation strategy. Cardinal Charles Lavigerie, who established the Society of African Missions, believed that the conversion of non-Christian peoples would be most successful if evangelistic efforts focused on political leaders and so set about converting the ruling (Tutsi) class in the expectation that the (predominantly Hutu) masses would follow suit.[10] Such a policy solidified the ethnic hierarchy and also forged a direct relationship between church and state.[11]

In summary, Tutsi were reinvented by the colonial state and Catholic Church as a non-native group that was elevated above Hutu but was 'still lower down the racial hierarchy from the master [European]'.[12] According to Alexandre Raffoule, colonial rule effectively ethnicised the state and all of its institutions.[13] Indeed, Patricia Daley argues that 'Belgian colonialism laid the conditions for the traditions of genocide' in Burundi (and, moreover, in the broader Great Lakes region).[14]

The Legacy of Colonial Racialisation

Burundi gained independence in 1962 when the Belgians handed over power to Tutsi-dominated politico-military institutions. Within the first decade following independence, ethnic-based conflict was planned and executed by the state security institutions, claiming the lives of around two hundred thousand Hutu.[15] Indeed, ethnic violence would continue for the next four decades, as the Tutsi-led Union for National Progress (UPRONA) dominated the political landscape and retaliated with heavy force to localised Hutu uprisings in 1965, 1969, 1972, and 1988.[16] This force reached a genocidal scale in 1972, which left around three hundred thousand dead.[17]

The Tutsi-dominated military dictatorship lasted until 1993 when, in the country's first democratic elections, the Hutu Melchior Ndadaye of the Hutu-dominated Front for Democracy in Burundi (FRODEBU) was elected. Just a few months later, however, Ndadaye was assassinated by Tutsi military officers who opposed the political power shift, triggering a twelve-year civil war between a Tutsi-dominated government under Pierre Buyoya and several Hutu militias.[18] The conflict claimed the lives of about three hundred thousand people. Signed in August 2000, the Arusha Peace Agreement paved the way for democratic elections in 2005, ensuring ethnic quotas in the two chambers of legislature that enabled the de-ethnicisation of politics.[19] The extent to which such de-ethnicisation has been achieved for the long term is, however, hotly debated.

Raffoule considers that Arusha successfully reduced ethnicist discourse in Burundian politics in the period 2000–15.[20] He notes that many Tutsi political candidates joined the CNDD-FDD to increase their chances of being elected, and there was a decrease in ethnic voting, particularly among Tutsi voters.[21] Raffoule also argues 'ethnicity was not widely re-politicised' during the 2015 crisis.[22]

Nevertheless, the term 'genocide' started to circulate among national and international NGOs to refer to the increased state violence since 2015.[23] In an analysis of these warnings, Andrea Purdeková argues that the 'ethnic genocide frame obfuscates the nature of the conflict in Burundi'.[24] According to her, the 'genocide reticence-turned-logorrhoea witnessed in this crisis is directly tied to the perceived close resemblance of Burundi and Rwanda and hence the pressure not to repeat the mistakes of the past'.[25] In her view, the overuse of the 'genocide' label to refer to Burundi 'has increased regime isolationism and emboldened the regime'.[26] More broadly, she observes that this framing of the political crisis 'maintains African conflict in the representational straightjacket of ethnic conflict'.[27] Similar observations have been made about media narratives surrounding the 2015 events, with news outlets, including Belgian ones, discussing the risk of events 'taking an "ethnic turn" and/or becoming genocidal' and adopting expressions such as 'ethnic enmities' or 'ethnic hatred', and, in some cases, comparing the crisis with events in Rwanda in 1994.[28]

While the alarm of genocide, ethnic enmities, and comparisons with Rwanda in 1994 may have been overblown and oversimplified, a number of observers have noted a re-ethnicisation of politics in Burundi since 2015. Daley and Rowan Popplewell argue, for instance, that 'recent violence appears to be political in nature, [however] we cannot dismiss ethnicity entirely from the analysis. There are growing fears in Burundi that ethnicity will emerge as a major fault line as the political crisis progresses'.[29] These authors note that 'parts of the former Tutsi elite, while accepting the ethnic split in government, are increasingly alarmed by their marginalisation from power by the current regime, especially since, for historical reasons, they constitute the bulk of the educated people in Burundi'.[30] Furthermore, analysts of Burundi's media and civil society have noted an increasing ethnicism in politics.[31] Stef Vandeginste argues, for example, that the introduction of non-consensual ethnic quotas in the international NGO sector 'puts ethnicity back at the heart of political contestation' and that this 'contributes to a re-ethnicisation of society'.[32]

Belgium's (Non)Recognition of Colonial History

It is clear that the construction of ethnicity under Belgian colonialism has marked Burundian politics and continues to a play a fundamental if contested role. Meanwhile, Belgium seems to have difficulty acknowledging its colonial past.[33] Castryck considers the problem to be threefold:

(1) the silent majority is basically not interested – and never was – in Congolese or colonial affairs,
(2) African studies in Belgium are extremely minimal and the academic attitude in general attaches little importance to informing broader society, and
(3) the political situation causes a preference for keeping history unknown.[34]

On the other hand, the death of George Floyd on 25 May 2020 and subsequent global Black Lives Matter (BLM) protests gained significant media attention in Belgium, raising questions about the country's colonial past and its relationship with contemporary forms of racism.[35] The movement resulted in the removal of statues of King Leopold II in Brussels, Antwerp, Leuven, and Ghent, and on 30 June 2020, Belgian King Philippe I addressed a letter to President Tshisekedi of the DRC in which he expressed regret for 'acts of violence and cruelty' committed under the Congo Free State[36] (see Yvette Hutchison's chapter in this volume). There has yet to be any formal recognition of Belgian's role in Burundi, however, and despite the proliferation of discussions about racism and Belgian's colonial past since Floyd's death, Burundi remains peripheral if it is mentioned at all. As the analysis presented in this chapter suggests, many of the issues regarding Belgian's relationship to the past persist.

All the outlets analysed in this chapter present Nkurunziza and his successor Évariste Ndayishimye as religiously inspired leaders who trivialise the pandemic and conceal Nkurunziza's death as the result of Covid-19. This narrative is presented as legitimate in the state-run *RTNB* but is highly criticised in *SOS*, *La Libre*, and *Le Soir*, which also note the increasing authoritarian nature of the government and highlight the electoral irregularities. The principal difference between the coverage in *SOS* and that found in the Belgian outlets is that *SOS* reports the use of the reformulated Hamitic hypothesis to discredit the main opposition candidate, Rwasa, as a Tutsi accomplice, despite him being a Hutu who had previously participated in anti-Tutsi massacres. In the final discussion, this chapter argues that this ethnicist discourse reveals a sophisticated political manoeuvre, highlighting the socially constructed, rather than essential, nature of ethnicity in Burundi. Surprisingly, references to ethnicity are mostly absent in the Belgian media depictions of events. The 'ancient hatreds' stereotype, which was used in media accounts of 2015, fails to capture the construction of Rwasa as a Tutsi collaborator.[37] In their depictions of the 2020 elections, the Belgian outlets therefore opt for silence on issues of ethnicity and turn instead to alternative clichés such as irrational dictators and desperate poverty. It is argued that if they were to recognise this political use of ethnicity, the Belgian outlets would need to confront the historical nature of these constructions and, consequently, Belgium's role in current Burundian affairs. The choice to focus on dictators and poverty, on the contrary, exonerates Belgium's role in ongoing conflicts and suggests the need for Belgian support. This discussion highlights the need for further decolonisation of the Belgian media.

Methodology

Le Soir and *La Libre* are Belgium's most popular francophone newspapers. *La Libre* is generally considered more conservative than *Le Soir*, a liberal and progressive news outlet. *RTNB* is Burundi's national broadcaster that, according to Jean-Benoît Falisse and Hugues Nkengurutse, 'gives a preponderant place to spokespersons of the regime'.[38] *SOS Médias* is an online newspaper that was established following the big shutdown of independent media in Burundi in 2015. While many journalists fled in exile, some remained in the country and continued to operate. A few who had worked at Radio Bonesha, a former private, multi-ethnic radio station known for its reconciliation-oriented programmes, established *SOS Médias Burundi* by disseminating information online through social networks.[39]

The majority (thirteen) of articles published in *Le Soir* analysed here are attributed to Colette Braeckman, Central African specialist and the outlet's editor for Central Africa. Without doubt, Braeckman has elsewhere contributed to discussions of Belgian's historical role in the region through her many publications on the subject.[40] On the other hand, scholarly analyses of *Le Soir*'s past coverage of the region show that the outlet adopts stereotypical representations as do some of Braeckman's independent publications.[41] The remaining *Soir* articles are attributed to Agence France Presse (AFP), Belga, the Belgian press agency, and other in-house journalists. *La Libre* attributes thirteen articles to Marie-France Cros, Central African specialist and the outlet's Africa editor. The remaining articles are attributed to AFP, Belga, and other in-house journalists. Stories in the Burundian *RTNB* and *SOS Médias* are exclusively authored by in-house journalists. The outlets were selected because they offer insights into the differing ways in which the story of these events was constructed for different sets of Burundian and Belgian audiences. All articles were retrieved using keyword searches via the outlets' online search facility.[42] The total number of articles analysed for each outlet can be found in Table 1.

	Le Soir	La Libre	RTNB	SOS Médias
Total	23	28	25	61

Table 1: The number of articles analysed for each news source

The analysis that follows draws on the concept of framing found in narrative analysis. According to Robert Entman, framing selects 'some aspects of a perceived reality and make(s) them more salient [...] in such a way as to promote a particular problem definition, causal interpretation, moral evaluation, and or treatment recommendation'.⁴³ Mona Baker argues that the concept of framing can best be understood through narrativity, describing narratives as 'stories that are temporally and causally constituted in such a way as to allow us to make moral decisions and act in the real world'.⁴⁴

The analysis investigates the framing of the 2020 election by applying Margaret Somers and Gloria Gibson's narrative concepts of *causal emplotment* and *selective appropriation*, which are particularly useful for identifying frames in social texts. According to them, emplotment 'translates events into episodes. As a mode of explanation, causal emplotment is an accounting (however fantastic or implicit) of why a narrative has the story line it does'.⁴⁵ As Baker explains, causal emplotment can override chronological or categorical order to 'turn a set of propositions into an intelligible sequence about which we can form an opinion, and thus charges the events depicted with moral and ethical significance'.⁴⁶ Causal emplotment also enables us to make evaluative judgements, demanding and enabling the selective appropriation of constituent elements. It would be impossible to include every detail of experience into a narrative. Selective appropriation refers to the selection of 'events or elements from the vast array of open-ended and overlapping events that constitute experience'.⁴⁷

The analysis is divided into three sections, each examining the narration of the central elements of the story: 1) Nkurunziza's government prior to the election, 2) the government's handling of the pandemic and Nkurunziza's death, and 3) the post-Nkurunziza government. The final discussion considers the outlets' use of hermeneutic composability, a narrative feature identified by Jerome Bruner that describes how elements of a story are reconstituted to form a new whole for readers in different cultural contexts.⁴⁸

Analysis

Nkurunziza's Government Prior to the Election

In *RTNB*, Nkurunziza is primarily framed as a legitimate, peaceful, and democratic president and also as the country's spiritual leader, reinforcing the colonial legacy of a close relationship between church and state. In one article, for example, *RTNB* focuses on a speech made by the president to the Église de Rocher in Buye, the evangelical church at which his wife, Denise Bucumi-Nkurunziza, is an ordained minister.⁴⁹ The outlet describes the president as assuring the crowds that '[...] since 1962, no leader completed his term without there being internal conflicts'. The establishment of peace and democracy is, according to Nkurunziza, thanks to Burundians' having 'reserved the first place for

God'. The outlet thus frames Nkurunziza as a clerical, even sacred, figure who is able to instil faith in the people, which in turn results in peace and democracy.

For all the outlet's emphasis on democracy, however, coverage of the elections is limited to a few procedural issues, with almost no discussion of the opposition candidate, Rwasa, or the alleged electoral irregularities. The only mention of the 2015 election in the outlet is in an article covering Nkurunziza's speech on Labour Day in which he 'welcomed the contribution made by the population to the elections from 2015 until 2020. "May this good practice continue in Burundi in order to cut off foreign aid", the Head of State noted'.[50] This statement reflects the trend of isolation seen in Burundi since 2015, notably the cutting of international aid. Since independence, Burundi has been heavily dependent on aid money, particularly from Belgium, other Western countries, and the European Union. Belgium was the first international donor to withdraw aid following the 2015 crisis, but it was soon followed by the Netherlands, the United States, and the European Union, which consequently pushed the country into an economic crisis.[51] This statement in *RTNB*, however, suggests that the move away from foreign aid is Burundi's intention rather than a decision imposed from outside.

SOS Médias reports the same Labour Day speech in its coverage, albeit with a different emphasis. According to this outlet, Nkurunziza

> largely drew up a positive assessment of his 15 years in power. He took the opportunity to explain that the first 10 years of his rule were 'painful because of political parties and civil society organizations that served the interests of the colonisers'.[52]

Like *RTNB*, *SOS* shows Nkurunziza's positive appraisal of his own presidency here, but the outlet also includes his suggestion that members of the opposition, civil society, and between the lines, those who opposed his third term, held him back until he was finally free following the 2015 elections. Moreover, he overtly accuses these actors of working in the interests of the 'colonisers'. This insinuates the decision of former colonial powers such as Belgium to cut aid following the events of 2015; however, unlike *RTNB*, here it seems that Nkurunziza is expressing disapproval of the decision and blaming the opposition for causing it. This may be because, rather than simply cutting aid, Belgium and other former donors decided to redirect money towards international NGOs, UN agencies, and national development agencies, many of whom work with local NGOs.[53]

Like *RTNB*, *SOS* highlights the government's use of religious discourse, however, such discourse is presented by the outlet as the government's attempt to consolidate power rather than provide spiritual leadership. For example, in an article about a party meeting, a party activist recites the following prayer:

> Oh Lord! Walk alongside Évariste. Direct our Rock, his steps [...] make him sit in the palace of Ntare (the presidential palace), give us Burundians the spirit to respect him as we respect our eternal Pierre Nkurunziza. [...] Our Rock, we ask this of you. Make sure that the enemies of Burundi who are currently in lockdown remain so. And until the end of our elections. May Kagame watch us without reaching us, may the United States observe us with their weapons without reaching us, may European Union meetings about Burundi be doomed.[54]

While the outlet highlights in the same way as *RTNB* how Nkurunziza is presented by his party as a spiritual leader, the more extremist elements of his speech (referring to Rwanda, the United States, and the European Union as state enemies) do not appear in the *RTNB*. SOS notes in the same article how 'since 2015, the CNDD-FDD has banned Rwandan gospel music during its large gatherings'. Burundian and Rwandan relations deteriorated significantly following the events of 2015, largely because both states accuse the other of supporting each other's opponents.[55] Given that the 2015 protestors, educated people, civil society, and members of the opposition were considered by the regime to be constituted primarily of Tutsi, and that Rwanda is ruled by Tutsi President Paul Kagame, the singling out of Rwanda in this way could be construed as a subtle form of ethnicism, reinforced – much like in Burundi's colonial past – using religious discourse. Explicit ethnic politics are also reported in *SOS Médias*.

For example, in response to 'extensive human rights violations' committed by the *Imbonerakure*, *SOS* reports allegations by the main opposition candidate, Rwasa, that the CNDD-FDD and its allies 'spread messages inciting ethnic hatred, [Rwasa] then deplored the fact that he is considered a tool of the Tutsi, particularly the Hima'.[56] This is an interesting characterisation of Rwasa given his history as a Hutu rebel during Burundi's civil war in which he was allegedly involved in the massacre of over 150 Congolese Tutsi refugees in Gatumba.[57]

The Belgian outlets generally take a similar stance to *SOS Médias*; however, such explicit discussions of ethnic politics are altogether absent. The Belgian outlets also differ in their adoption of a somewhat paternalist tone, as can be seen in the *Soir* article discussing 'miracles' in need of explanation.[58] Framing the president in terms of his religious discourse, the article opens by asserting that 'the president of Burundi proudly proclaims that if it has been spared relatively, it is because "his country has put God first"'. Rather than a miracle, Braeckman intimates that the limited impact of the pandemic on Burundi is more likely explained by the lack of credible statistics, the youthful population, and the rupture with the international community.

The real 'miracles' of the situation, according to Braeckman, are the fact that the election took place in relative calm, that Nkurunziza was not running, and that Rwasa was allowed to organise successful rallies. Rwasa's mobilisation of the population, she notes, 'has started worrying the authorities and the *Imbonerakure* (the government's militia) are on the war footing and are already harassing Rwasa's supporters. We are therefore waiting for a miracle, or a coup d'état on the eve of the elections'. Maintaining the irony, Braeckman concludes that the one miracle needed is to save flood victims in Gatumba, where over 28,000 people remain without housing. As the author notes, 'Since international aid has deserted Burundi, these poor people live in catastrophic conditions'. Braeckman's suggestion that the country needs a miracle in the absence of Western assistance has an air of paternalism.

References to Burundi's poverty appear elsewhere in *Le Soir*'s coverage, with one article highlighting that 'Burundi is ranked among the three poorest countries in the world'.[59] The same article cites the World Bank 'which estimates that 75% of the population live below the poverty line, against 65% when Mr. Nkurunziza came to power in 2005'. *La Libre* likewise adopts a paternalist tone (grouping Nkurunziza together with other world dictators without historical context) and also makes reference to Burundi as one of the three poorest countries in the world, quoting the same poverty statistic while emphasising Burundi's reliance on international aid.[60]

In summary, all outlets highlight the government's use of religious discourse. However, while *RTNB* presents Nkurunziza as a benevolent, democratic, spiritual leader, *SOS Médias* and the Belgian outlets offer a reversed pattern of causal emplotment, suggesting that such discourse is a means to consolidate authoritarian control.

There are also narrative differences between *SOS Médias* and the Belgian outlets. While they all include discussions of the government's human rights violations, use of intimidation, and other voting irregularities, the Belgian outlets are alone in emphasising Burundi's increased poverty and dependence on international aid. The selective appropriation of these themes suggests that impoverished Burundians are left at the mercy of an authoritarian dictator and in need of Western assistance.

SOS Médias makes a different use of selective appropriation, excluding the theme of poverty but introducing that of ethnicity. This outlet highlights the government's enmity with the West, civil society, Rwanda, and the opposition, who, the outlet suggests, are all accused of allying with each other.

The outlet also includes allegations that the government incites ethnic hatred and accuses the opposition of collaborating with Tutsi, particularly the Hima. Such an accusation demonstrates the persistence of the Hamitic myth and its reformulation, which positions Tutsi as a power-hungry collective bent on dominating the region, the same myth that underpinned the 1994 genocide against the Tutsi. *SOS Médias* thereby offers an altogether different use of causal emplotment to the other outlets by narrating the CNDD-FDD's leadership not only as a dictatorship but also as a potentially genocidal government.

The Government's Handling of the Pandemic and Nkurunziza's Death

While the colonial legacy of an alliance between church and state is maintained by the Burundian government under Nkurunziza, the response to the Covid-19 pandemic is quite different to former colonial methods. Motivated by economic, scientific, and humanitarian interests (even if marred by racist condescension), Belgian colonial responses to previous disease outbreaks, such as the sleeping sickness epidemics of 1900–40, involved a coercive approach. Influenced and often administered by the Catholic Church, this involved controlling people's movements and herding those suspected of infection into camps where they were permanently separated from their families, lived in poor conditions, faced a lack of food, and were injected with atoxyl, an arsenic compound that caused blindness in up to 20 per cent of patients.[61]

Rather than adopting such a heavy-handed, medical approach, in a bid to gain popularity, the Nkurunziza government instead mobilised the legacy of African scepticism of Western medicine by trivialising the pandemic and ridiculing international public health advice. The narration of this response and the death of Nkurunziza varies across the outlets. For example, reflecting the government's position, *RTNB* discusses the pandemic considerably less than the others, mentioning the terms Covid, coronavirus, or pandemic just 19 times compared to 120 mentions in *SOS*, 62 in *La Libre*, and 84 mentions in *Le Soir*. The few discussions of the pandemic in *RTNB* are paired with religious reassurances and authoritative advice, suggesting that the government is in control while minimising the potential danger of the virus.[62] Significantly, there is no mention of Covid-19 in the outlet's coverage of Nkururnziza's unexpected death, which is reported as the result of 'a heart attack'.[63]

In contrast, *SOS Médias* frames the government's handling of the pandemic in reference to its general authoritarianism, reporting, for instance, how the government expelled the team of WHO experts who were in Burundi to support the country's coronavirus response.[64] The same article highlights the government's minimisation of the pandemic, noting that 'Burundi refuses to recognize the threat posed by this virus'.

Nkurunziza's personal views on the virus are revealed in an article that appeared following the elections in which he reportedly ridiculed wearing a mask: 'God controls the atmosphere in Burundi so that those [pandemics] do not reach us. Who wears a mask among you? No one. And yet you are doing well. There you go, God works miracles'.[65] When Nkurunziza died less than two weeks later, *SOS Médias* counters official reports of a heart attack, claiming that 'he succumbed to respiratory complications linked to Covid-19'.[66] The outlet reveals that people in both his government and family were also Covid positive, including his wife, who was sent to Kenya for treatment, although her illness was denied by the government as part of its Covid-denial campaign.[67]

The Belgian outlets present events similarly to *SOS Médias*, mentioning the government's ejection of the WHO, Nkurunziza's religious appraisals and denial of the threat posed by the virus, and that his death was eventually caused by the virus. One significant difference in *Le Soir*'s coverage relative to *SOS* is the outlet's explicit attribution of Nkurunziza's death to his government's denial of the pandemic:

> The denial of the coronavirus epidemic has had dramatic consequences in Burundi: it is confirmed that the outgoing president, Pierre Nkurunziza, was carried away by the virus and that the only ventilator available in the country, which was in the hospital King Khaled in Bujumbura, was sent in vain to Karusi, in the centre of the country.[68]

As can be seen here, *Le Soir* also highlights the lack of infrastructure in the country. The article goes on to note that 'King Khaled Hospital can no longer cope with the influx of patients, reagent products are lacking, Covid-19 patients are accommodated in the old maternity ward but beds are starting to run out'.

La Libre does not attribute responsibility to the government quite so explicitly as *Le Soir*, but it does also emphasise the country's relative poverty as a hinderance to dealing with the pandemic.[69] As seen elsewhere, the outlet highlights Burundi's need for Western (Belgian) assistance, with an article discussing how the King Baudouin Foundation raised over €200,000 to assist with the pandemic in the DRC and Burundi.[70]

In summary, *RTNB* makes only scarce reference to the pandemic, no mention of the government's ejection of the WHO, and no mention of Covid when reporting Nkurunziza's death. The few references to Covid are paired with religious and political reassurances, suggesting that the pandemic is under control. The other outlets all accentuate the potential seriousness of the virus in Burundi and highlight the government's trivialisation of the pandemic and its ejection of the WHO. They also all report that Nkurunziza died as a result of contracting the virus and that the government attempted to conceal this. Overall, these outlets offer a reversed pattern of causal emplotment to *RTNB* by presenting the pandemic as out of control.

There are, nonetheless, some differences in these outlets' use of narrative features. For example, only *Le Soir* directly attributes the death of Nkurunziza to the government's handling of the pandemic, adopting a similar but more explicit line of causal emplotment compared to *SOS* or *La Libre*. Both Belgian outlets stand alone in emphasising Burundi's poverty and lack of infrastructure, adopting a distinct line of causal emplotment that implies Burundi's need for Western/Belgian assistance to handle the pandemic, maintaining the paternalist view that Burundi still relies on its former colonisers.

Representations of the Post-Nkurunziza Government

Following Évariste Ndayishimiye's inauguration in Gitega on 18 June 2020,[71] *RTNB* reports the new president delivering a consolation prayer:

> it will be remembered that the late President Pierre Nkurunziza campaigned for dialogue between religions, cemented the links between the bureaucracy and the common people through community development and instilled in Burundians the love of God and prayer, the love of work, of the country and of mutual aid to unite society. [...] By continuing in this way, you will have shown to the world that you are his disciples.[72]

As can be seen, Nkurunziza is still depicted as a spiritual leader after his death and is credited with developing the country. Maintaining the colonial church-state relationship, Ndayshimiye, whose speech was 'punctuated with biblical references', appears to follow in these footsteps. In an article describing his inauguration, Ndayishimiye sets out a range of policy priorities yet makes no reference to the coronavirus pandemic, suggesting that, like for his predecessor, Covid-19 is not a primary concern.[73]

SOS Médias offers an altogether different appraisal of the former regime, running the headline: 'Nkurunziza's disappearance: "he leaves without the truth about his crimes being known"'.[74] The article cites Lewis Mudge, Human Rights Watch director for Central Africa, who highlights 'the extrajudicial executions, tortures, disappearances and harassment of opposition' during Nkurunziza's 'reign'. *SOS Médias* refrains from taking a position on the new president, however, and instead presents a range of views about the new regime from Burundian refugees and international observers. Overall, *SOS Médias*'s coverage on the new regime is fairly neutral within the time frame studied.

La Libre, in contrast, takes an unequivocally pessimistic stance. In one article, Cros notes that 'Mr Ndayishimiye was proclaimed the winner by the Constitutional Court, despite extensive fraud that the "independent" National Election Commission had to remove the election results from its website because they were so implausible'.[75] Considering the candidate himself, the outlet suggests that Ndayishimiye is 'a man deemed malleable, dominated by the half-dozen CNDD-FDD generals who actually rule Burundi'. Having been placed in power by these generals, the outlet predicts that it is unlikely for him to oppose them since he never took action against previous abuses by the *Imbonerakure*. In contrast, *Le Soir* offers an overall positive appraisal of the election outcome. Unlike Cros and *La Libre*, Braeckman reports on the peaceful nature of the election and its impressive turnout, presenting Ndayishimiye as a moderate with a reputation for integrity.[76]

In summary, *RTNB* and *La Libre* both project a continuation of Burundi's pre-election trajectory, seeing in Ndayishimiye similar traits to Nkurunziza. However, while this is appraised positively by *RTNB* (selectively appropriating elements of the narrative that make both presidents seem like peaceful, democratic, and spiritual leaders), *La Libre* depicts them in negative terms (appropriating elements such as their use of religion to consolidate power, their indifference to criminal activity, and their overseeing an authoritarian system of governance). *Le Soir* and *SOS*, like *La Libre* selectively appropriate similar elements about the former regime, but *Le Soir* includes altogether different elements in its depiction of Nadyishimiye, portraying him as moderate and principled. Only *SOS*, which does not hesitate in its critique of Nkururnziza's regime, remains neutral in its stance about the new regime, including both positive and negative appraisals of his electoral victory.

Conclusions and Discussion

Overall, the outlets offer four distinct narratives of events. *RTNB* selectively appropriates elements of the narrative that depict Nkurunziza and Ndayishimiye as spiritual leaders who have brought Burundi peace and democracy. Despite the infection of the government's inner circle with Covid-19 and Nkurunziza's death, the outlet limits the discussion of the pandemic and minimises its impact. *SOS*, *La Libre*, and *Le Soir* also selectively appropriate the government's religious discourse; however, they include other narrative elements and offer a different pattern of causal emplotment to *RTNB*. These outlets portray Nkurunziza as an authoritarian leader who downplayed the Covid-19 pandemic, which eventually took his life. *SOS* is the only outlet to selectively appropriate the re-ethnicisation of Burundian politics in its coverage while the Belgian outlets are alone in inserting Burundi's poverty into the story. This ultimately leads to quite different patterns of causal emplotment: the *SOS Médias* narrative is about the politicisation of ethnic tensions in a country with a history of ethnic conflict caused by colonialism and an ongoing refugee crisis. In contrast, the narrative in *La Libre* and *Le Soir* is about a poor country with a dictatorial regime that still needs the support of former colonial powers and their aid money. The main difference between the two Belgian outlets is that *La Libre* projects a negative future for Burundi, while *Le Soir* assesses the new government in relatively positive terms.

To understand why these narratives differ, it is useful to turn to Bruner's concept of hermeneutic composability. Bruner highlights two issues affecting narrative interpretation: author intentionality and contextual factors (such as the background knowledge of both the storyteller and the listener).[77] As he writes, narratives are not '"unsponsored texts" to be taken as existing unintentionally'.[78] As the state broadcaster, it is unsurprising that *RTNB* generally portrays both Nkurunziza and Ndayishimiye in positive terms, and acts largely as a government mouthpiece. As independent media organisations, *SOS Médias*, *La Libre*, and *Le Soir* are freer to adopt a critical stance; however, this is not to say that their editors are without intentionality.

As an organisation with a tradition of reconciliation and one that remained in the country in order to continue reporting on politics and human rights, it is understandable that *SOS Médias* would draw attention to the use of extremist ethnic politics. Where the outcome of the situation is unclear, such as the future under Ndayishimiye, *SOS Médias* maintains its orientation towards peace and reconciliation by depicting voices from a range of opinions, without pre-empting possible future abuses of power. In more recent coverage, however, the organisation continues its commitment to human rights, reporting about deaths and arrests during Ndayishimiye's first one hundred days in office,[79] and highlighting the renewed ethnic violence of his regime. This includes reports about *Imbonerakure* attacks against Tutsi families,[80] police encouraging the denouncement of Tutsi Kinyarwanda speakers within the country,[81] and accusations of ethnicism within government institutions.[82]

As independent media, the omission of ethnic politics in the Belgian outlets is intriguing given the Western tendency to present conflict in the Great Lakes region as 'ethnic'.[83] The ethnic frame was rolled out in representations of the 2015 conflict by both human rights organisations and the media, including in Belgium.[84] *Le Soir*, for example, reported 'fear of an ethnic turn' just a day after the first protests began and made multiple comparisons with Rwanda in 1994.[85] So why, in this case, do the Belgian outlets remain silent on the issue of ethnicity, preferring instead to emphasise poverty?

The answer to this question may lie in the main victim of the government's 'ethnic discourse'. As discussed above, Rwasa is a Hutu and former rebel allegedly responsible for the mass murder of Tutsi but who has since rebranded his public profile as a figure of peace and reconciliation.[86] The complexity of this 'ethnic' story thus goes well beyond the essentialist 'ancient hatreds' arguments, which presuppose irrational violence within an atavistic group.[87] In this case, Tutsiphobia is applied by a Hutu who is relatively innocent of crimes (i.e. Ndayishimiye) to discredit a Hutu who is allegedly responsible for mass-murdering Tutsi. Thus rather than constituting essential characteristics of Hutu or Tutsi people, the case demonstrates a highly sophisticated political strategy to socially construct the opposition as a dangerous 'Other' by drawing on a racist ideology that was first brought to Burundi by the Belgians.

To explain the CNDD-FDD's weaponisation of the ethnic (Hamitic) discourse would be difficult without recalling the colonial history of this ideology and Belgium would, therefore, have to acknowledge a role in contemporary Burundian affairs. Instead, the Belgian outlets turn to an alternative cliché: that of a poor African country in the hands of an authoritarian, ostentatiously religious dictator.[88] Such a framing highlights Burundi's ongoing need for Western assistance and enables the outlets to portray Belgium in a positive light, providing readers with a sense of cultural superiority.

Interestingly, this story unfolded around the same time as the death of George Floyd. During the time frame covered in this study, the Belgian outlets published a series of articles in response to the BLM protests, offering discussions about decolonising public space,[89] creating positive relations with former colonies,[90] initiating a parliamentary committee on the Belgian colonial past,[91] as well as a discussion about ongoing racism in Belgium.[92] These articles focus almost exclusively on the DRC, however. Despite the BLM movement, it seems that substantial discussions surrounding decolonisation and Burundi are yet to take place in these Belgian outlets. Based on this analysis, decolonised coverage would need to avoid essentialisations, stereotypes, and paternalist discourses that imply Burundi's need of the West. It would also need to include a greater acknowledgement of the link between Burundi's colonial past and its political present, explaining the background behind such phenomena as the church-state alliance or medical scepticism in Burundi.

In the spirit of this volume, which recognises that overly pessimistic conclusions about African affairs are yet another representational pitfall, some final comments are reserved for the laudable commitment to reconciliation and responsible reporting observed in *SOS Médias*. Before the big shutdown of independent media in 2015, Burundi was praised for the freedom of expression and professionalism of its journalists.[93] This vibrant media sector was forced into a rapid reconfiguration online as broadcasting centres were burned down and many journalists fled in exile.[94] While this change limited popular access (on account of relatively low levels of literacy and internet access), the ongoing commitment of outlets like *SOS Médias* demonstrates the resilience of local journalism. By calling out the government's use of colonial ethnic-religious discourse to consolidate power, while avoiding the essentialisms and dependency discourse presented in the Belgian outlets, media like *SOS* clearly play an important role in resisting the internal and external legacies of colonialism in Burundi. There are also signs that Ndayishimiye's government is rekindling the media sector, suggesting that the future of Burundian journalism looks promising.[95]

Notes

1. Stef Vandeginste, 'Ethnic Quotas and Foreign NGOs in Burundi: Shrinking Civic Space Framed as Affirmative Action', *Africa Spectrum*, 54. 3 (2019), 181–200 (183).
2. *Imbonerakure* in Kirundi means 'Those who see far'. The name refers to the youth wing of the CNDD-FDD party, which was reportedly involved in threatening and intimidating people into voting for them.
3. Leila Keza, 'Burundi-Élections: Le Ministre de la Communication Exige la Radiation de Certains Journalistes de la Synergie des Médias', *SOS Médias*, 16 May 2020 <https://www.SOSmediasburundi.org/2020/05/16/burundi-elections-le-ministre-de-la-communication-exige-la-radiation-de-certains-journalistes-de-la-synergie-des-medias/> [accessed 03 March 2021]
4. Sophie Pontzeele, 'Le Schème de la « Guerre Ethnique » dans la Médiatisation des Crises Africaines: Burundi 1972 et Rwanda 1994', *Les Cahiers du Journalisme*, 18.1 (2008), 166–182; Caroline Williamson Sinalo, 'Narrating African Conflict News: An Intercultural Analysis of Burundi's 2015 Coup', *Journalism*, (2020), 1–16.
5. Jerome Bruner, 'The Narrative Construction of Reality', *Critical Inquiry*, 18 (1991), 1–21; Mona Baker, 'Reframing Conflict in Translation', *Social Semiotics*, 17. 2 (2007), 151-169; Margaret Somers and Gloria Gibson, 'Reclaiming the Epistemological "Other": Narrative and the Social Constitution of Identity', in Craig Calhoun (ed.), *Social Theory and the Politics of Identity* (Oxford: Blackwell, 1994), pp. 37–99.
6. Early accounts written by Europeans such as Jacques Maquet and Tutsi such as Alexis Kagame have been challenged by more recent work e.g. Jan Vansina, *Antecedents to Modern Rwanda. The Nyiginya Kingdom* (Madison: University of Wisconsin Press, 2004). Most scholars acknowledge, however, the relative fluidity of these identities. Patricia Daley, *Gender and Genocide in Burundi: The Search for Spaces of Peace in the Great Lakes Region* (Oxford: James Currey, 2007), p. 46.
7. Ibid., p. 49.
8. Timothy Longman, 'Identity Cards, Ethnic Self-Perception, and Genocide in Rwanda', in Jane Caplan and John Torpey (eds.), *Documenting Individual Identity: The Development of State Practices in the Modern World* (Princeton, New Jersey: Princeton University Press, 2001), pp. 345–59 (p. 351).
9. Alexandre Raffoule 'The Politics of Association: Power-Sharing and the Depoliticization of Ethnicity in Post-War Burundi', *Ethnopolitics*, 19. 1 (2020), 1–18 (10).
10. Timothy Longman, *Christianity and Genocide in Rwanda* (Cambridge: Cambridge University Press, 2010), p. 39.
11. Ibid., p. 25.
12. Patricia Daley, *Gender and Genocide in Burundi: The Search for Spaces of Peace in the Great Lakes Region* (Oxford: James Currey, 2007), p. 50.
13. Raffoule, 'The Politics of Association…', p. 10.
14. Daley, *Gender and Genocide*, p. 13. The Hamitic myth lies behind genocidal ideologies in the region. In Burundi, it justified the mass killing of Hutu. In Rwanda, it was reformulated to construct Tutsi as inherently evil foreign conquerors, justifying the 1994 genocide.
15. Ibid., p. 34.
16. Raffoule, p. 10. Vandeginste, 'Ethnic Quotas…', p. 182.
17. Raffoule, p. 10.
18. Vandeginste, p. 183.
19. Ibid.
20. Raffoule, p. 11.
21. Ibid., p. 12.
22. Ibid., p. 13–14.
23. E.g. FIDH, 'Repression and Genocidal Dynamics in Burundi', 15 November 2016 <https://www.fidh.org/en/region/Africa/burundi/repression-and-genocidal-dynamics-in-burundi> [accessed 3 March 2021].
24. Andrea Purdeková, '#StopThisMovie and the Pitfalls of Mass Atrocity Prevention: Framing of Violence and Anticipation of Escalation in Burundi's Crisis (2015–2017)', *Genocide Studies and Prevention: An International Journal*, 13. 2 (2019), 22–37 (23 & 30).
25. Ibid., p. 22.
26. Ibid., p. 23.
27. Ibid., p. 30.
28. Williamson Sinalo, 'Narrating African Conflict News…', p. 5.
29. atricia Daley and Rowan Popplewell, 'The Appeal of Third Termism and Militarism in Burundi', *Review of African Political Economy*, 43.150 (2016), 648–57 (563).
30. Ibid., p. 563.
31. Marie-Soleil Frère, 'Silencing the Voice of the Voiceless: The Destruction of the Independent Broadcasting Sector in Burundi', *African Journalism Studies*, 37.1 (2016), 137–46 (139–40); Vandeginste, pp. 194–95.
32. Vandeginste, pp. 194 & 195.
33. Axel Mudahemuka C. Gossiaux, 'L'éducation Permanente en Lutte Contre le Racisme et la

Colonialité en Belgique Francophone?', *Fucid*, (2020) <https://www.fucid.be/wp-content/uploads/2020/10/2020.ET-de%CC%81colonisation-EP.pdf> [accessed 3 March 2021].

34. Geert Castryck, 'Whose History Is History? Singularities and Dualities of the Public Debate on Belgian Colonialism', in Sven Mörsdorf (ed.), *Being a Historian. Opportunities and Responsibilities: Past and Present* (Pisa: Cliohres.net, 2010), pp. 1–18 (p. 6).

35. Gossiaux, 'L'éducation Permanente…', p. 14. These events coincided with the 2020 Burundian elections.

36. The Belgian government had already apologised for its role in the 1994 genocide against the Tutsi in Rwanda in 2000. Ibid., p. 16. This and all subsequent translations from French are my own.

37. Williamson Sinalo, 'Narrating African Conflict News…', p. 13.

38. Jean-Benoît Falisse and Hugues Nkengurutse, 'From FM Radio Stations to Internet 2.0 Overnight: Information, Participation and Social Media in Post-Failed Coup Burundi', in Maggie Dwyer and Thomas Molony (eds.), *Social Media and Politics in Africa: Democracy, Censorship and Security* (London: Zed, 2019), pp. 171–94 (p. 179).

39. Frère, 'Silencing the Voice of the Voiceless…', p. 142.

40. E.g. Colette Braeckman, *Rwanda, histoire d'un génocide, 1994* (Paris: Fayard, 1994); Colette Braeckman, *Congo, Rwanda-Burundi: les racines de la violence, 1996* (Paris: Fayard, 1996).

41. For analyses of *Le Soir*, see Pontzeele, 'Le Schème de la « Guerre Ethnique »…', p. 175; Williamson Sinalo, 'Narrating African Conflict News…', p. 13. Braeckman's book about Congolese gynaecologist, Dr Denis Mukwege, adopts the troubling 'man who fixes women' discourse. Colette Braeckman, *L'homme qui répare les femmes: Le combat du Docteur Mukwege* (Waterloo: La Renaissance du livre, 2016).

42. 'Burundi' and 'Nkurunziza' were used to search the Belgian outlets; 'Election' and 'Nkurunziza' were used to search the Burundian ones.

43. Robert Entman, 'Framing: Towards clarification of a Fractured Paradigm', *Journal of Communication*, 43.4 (1993), 51–58 (52); see also Denis Chong and James Druckman, 'Framing Theory', *Annual Review of Political Science*, 10 (2007), 103–26 (104).

44. Baker, 'Reframing Conflict in Translation', pp. 156 & 155.

45. Somers and Gibson, 'Reclaiming the Epistemological "Other"…', p. 28.

46. Baker, p. 155.

47. Baker, p. 155; Somers and Gibson, p. 29.

48. Bruner, 'The Narrative Construction of Reality', p. 7. The same concept is described as 'relationality' by Somers and Gibson, p. 25.

49. Raphaël Bigirimana, 'Le Chef de l'Etat s'associe aux fidèles de l'église du Rocher de Buye dans la prière dominicale', *RTNB*, 3 May 2020 <https://rtnb.bi/fr/art.php?idapi=4/1/131> [accessed 03 March 2021]

50. *RTNB*, 'Le Burundi célèbre la journée internationale du travail et des travailleurs', *RTNB*, 1 May 2020 <http://www.*RTNB*.bi/fr/art.php?idapi=4/1/128> [accessed 03 March 2021]

51. International Crisis Group, 'Soutenir la population burundaise face à la crise économique', Report 264, 31 August 2018 <https://www.crisisgroup.org/fr/africa/central-africa/burundi/264-soutenir-la-population-burundaise-face-la-crise-economique> [accessed 21 June 2021]

52. Adam Ntwari, 'Fête du travail: Nkurunziza défend son bilan et énumère les boucs émissaires', *SOS Médias*, 1 May 2020 <https://www.SOSmediasburundi.org/2020/05/01/fete-du-travail-nkurunziza-defend-son-bilan-et-enumere-les-boucs-emissaires/> [accessed 03 March 2021]

53. International Crisis Group, 'Soutenir la population burundaise'.

54. Jean Ntumwa, 'Elections 2020: ces prières du CNDD-FDD qui s'attaquent aux occidentaux et au Rwanda', *SOS Médias*, 1 May 2020 <https://www.SOSmediasburundi.org/2020/05/01/elections-2020-ces-prieres-du-cndd-fdd-qui-sattaquent-aux-occidentaux-et-au-rwanda/> [accessed 03 March 2021]

55. Jill Craig, 'Relations Between Burundi, Rwanda Deteriorating', *VOA*, 14 October 2015 <https://www.voanews.com/africa/relations-between-burundi-rwanda-deteriorating> [accessed 03 March 2021]

56. Eric Irambona, 'Burundi-élections: Agathon Rwasa demande aux Imbonerakure de changer de comportement' *SOS Médias*, 15 May 2020 <https://www.sosmediasburundi.org/2020/05/15/burundi-elections-agathon-rwasa-demande-aux-imbonerakure-de-changer-de-comportement/> [accessed 03 March 2021]

Referring to Rwasa as Hima is significant because the officers who overthrew the monarchy in 1962 and went on to monopolise power in Burundi were Tutsi-Hima. Raffoule, p. 10.

57. HRW 'Burundi: 15 Years On, No Justice for Gatumba Massacre', 13 August 2019 <https://www.hrw.org/news/2019/08/13/burundi-15-years-no-justice-gatumba-massacre#> [accessed 03 March 2021]

58. Colette Braeckman, 'Burundi: quelques «miracles» qui méritent une explication…', *Le Soir*, 13 May 2020 <https://plus.lesoir.be/300616/article/2020-05-13/burundi-quelques-miracles-qui-meritent-une-explication?referer=%2Farchives%2Frecherche%3Fdatefilter%3Dlastyear%26sort%3Ddate%2Bdesc%26start%3D10%26word%3Dnkurunziza> [accessed 03 March 2021]
59. Le Soir, 'Élections présidentielles au Burundi: le candidat du pouvoir élu', 25 May 2020 <https://plus.lesoir.be/302888/article/2020-05-25/elections-presidentielles-au-burundi-le-candidat-du-pouvoir-elu?referer=%2Farchives%2Frecherche%3Fdatefilter%3Dlastyear%26sort%3Ddate%2Bdesc%26start%3D0%26word%3Dnkurunziza%22> [accessed 03 March 2021]
60. Marie-France Cros, 'Comment la situation au Burundi, un des trois pays les plus pauvres du monde, s'est encore aggravée depuis 2015', *La Libre Belgique*, 20 May 2020 <https://www.lalibre.be/international/afrique/comment-la-situation-au-burundi-un-des-trois-pays-les-plus-pauvres-du-monde-s-est-encore-aggravee-depuis-2015-5ec3ffbad8ad581c5400d923> [accessed 03 March 2021]
61. Daniel R. Headrick, 'Sleeping Sickness Epidemics and Colonial Responses in East and Central Africa, 1900–1940', *PLoS Neglected Tropical Diseases*, 8.4 (2014) <https://journals.plos.org/plosntds/article?id=10.1371/journal.pntd.0002772> [accessed 22 June 2021]
62. E.g. *RTNB*, 'Le Burundi célèbre'.
63. *RTNB*, 'Décès inopiné du Président de la République Pierre Nkurunziza', 10 June 2020 <https://RTNB.bi/fr/art.php?idapi=4/1/205> [accessed 03 March 2021]
64. SOS Médias, 'Burundi-elections: un orage se prépare selon Human Rights Watch', 15 May 2020 <https://www.SOSmediasburundi.org/2020/05/15/burundi-elections-un-orage-se-prepare-selon-human-rights-watch/> [accessed 03 March 2021]
65. Jean Ntumwa, 'Gitega: le CNDD-FDD et Pierre Nkurunziza (guide suprême) défient la covid-19', *SOS Médias*, 29 May 2020 <https://www.SOSmediasburundi.org/2020/05/29/gitega-le-cndd-fdd-et-pierre-nkurunziza-guide-supreme-defient-la-covid-19/> [accessed 03 March 2021]
66. Eloge Willy Kaneza, 'Le Président Nkurunziza a été emporté par le virus covid-19 (sources concordantes)', *SOS Médias*, 12 June 2020 <https://www.SOSmediasburundi.org/2020/06/12/le-president-nkurunziza-a-ete-emporte-par-le-virus-covid-19-sources-concordantes/> [accessed 03 March 2021]
67. E.g. Joelle Kamikazi, 'Mort de P. Nkurunziza: son épouse se confie lors d'une prière', *SOS Médias*, 13 June 2020 <https://www.sosmediasburundi.org/2020/06/13/mort-de-p-nkurunziza-son-epouse-se-confie-lors-dune-priere/> [accessed 03 March 2021]
68. Colette Braeckman, 'Burundi: le Covid-19 décapite la classe dirigeante et plonge le pays dans l'angoisse', 12 June 2020 <https://plus.lesoir.be/306777/article/2020-06-12/burundi-le-covid-19-decapite-la-classe-dirigeante-et-plonge-le-pays-dans?referer=%2Farchives%2Frecherche%3Fdatefilter%3Dlastyear%26sort%3Ddate%2Bdesc%26start%3D0%26word%3Dnkurunziza> [accessed 03 March 2021]
69. Marie-France Cros, 'Comment la situation au Burundi…'.
70. *La Libre Belgique*, 'La Fondation Roi Baudouin a récolté 15 millions d'euros pour 1.100 acteurs de terrain: "Avec ces soutiens, des besoins urgents ont pu rapidement être satisfaits"', 5 June 2020 <https://www.lalibre.be/belgique/societe/la-fondation-roi-baudouin-a-recolte-15-millions-d-euros-pour-1-100-acteurs-de-terrain-avec-ces-soutiens-des-besoins-urgents-ont-pu-rapidement-etre-satisfaits-5eda0cc5d8ad58250fa92560> [accessed 03 March 2021]
71. It took place two months ahead of schedule because of Nkurunziza's death.
72. *RTNB*, 'Gitega/Prière d'action de grâce: le Chef de l'Etat livre un message de consolation', 25 June 2020 <http://www.*RTNB*.bi/fr/art.php?idapi=4/1/231> [accessed 03 March 2021]
73. *RTNB*, 'Investiture du nouveau Président de la République: Gén Maj Evariste Ndayishimiye prend les rênes du pouvoir', 18 June 2020 <http://www.*RTNB*.bi/fr/art.php?idapi=4/1/213> [accessed 03 March 2021]
74. David Irakoze, 'Disparition de Nkurunziza: "il part sans que la vérité sur ses crimes soit connue" (HRW)', *SOS Médias*, 10 June 2020 <https://www.SOSmediasburundi.org/2020/06/10/mort-de-nkurunziza-il-part-sans-que-la-verite-sur-ses-crimes-soit-connue-selon-hrw/> [accessed 03 March 2021]
75. Marie-France Cros, 'Burundi: pourquoi le nouveau président n'amènera que peu de changements?', *La Libre Belgique*, 18 June 2020 <https://www.lalibre.be/international/afrique/burundi-pourquoi-le-nouveau-president-n-amenera-que-peu-de-changements-5eeb74ca7b50a66a598c7db9> [accessed 03 March 2021]
76. Colette Braeckman, 'Burundi: une élection contestée, mais un vainqueur qui n'est pas le pire', *Le Soir*, 25 May 2020 <https://plus.lesoir.be/302952/article/2020-05-25/burundi-une-election-contestee-mais-un-vainqueur-qui-nest-pas-le-pire?referer=%2Farchives%2Frecherche%3Fdatefilter%3Dlastyear%26sort%3Ddate%2Bdesc%26start%3D0%26word%3Dnkurunziza> [accessed 03 March 2021]

77. Bruner, p. 10.
78. Ibid., p. 10.
79. Jean Ntumwa, 'Cent premiers jours du gouvernement Ndayishimiye: un bilan controversé', *SOS Médias*, 18 September 2020 <https://www.sosmediasburundi.org/2020/09/18/burambi-des-familles-tutsis-de-plus-en-plus-ciblees-par-des-imbonerakure/> [accessed 03 March 2021]
80. Jean Ntumwa, 'Burambi: des familles Tutsi de plus en plus ciblées par des Imbonerakure', *SOS Médias*, 18 September 2020 <https://www.sosmediasburundi.org/2020/09/18/burambi-des-familles-tutsis-de-plus-en-plus-ciblees-par-des-imbonerakure/> [accessed 03 March 2021]
81. Leila Keza, 'Gitega: plusieurs réfugiés Banyamulenge expulsés de la ville de Gitega', *SOS Médias*, 9 October 2020 <https://www.SOSmediasburundi.org/2020/10/09/gitega-plusieurs-refugies-banyamulenge-expulses-de-la-ville-de-gitega/> [accessed 03 March 2021]
82. Jean Ntumwa, 'Makamba-Rumonge: les décisions de la CNTB divisent', *SOS Médias*, 10 November 2020 <https://www.SOSmediasburundi.org/2020/11/10/burundi-makamba-rumonge-les-decisions-de-la-cntb-divisent/> [accessed 03 March 2021]
83. Daley, *Gender and Genocide*, p. 5.
84. Purdeková, '#StopThisMovie and the Pitfalls…', p. 31; Williamson Sinalo, Narrating African Conflict News…', p. 5.
85. Williamson Sinalo, Narrating African Conflict News…', p. 5.
86. Eric Irambona, 'Burundi-élections: Agathon Rwasa'.
87. Daley, *Gender and Genocide*, p. 2.
88. The outlets make no mention of Belgium's role in bringing Christianity to Burundi.
89. Colette Braeckman, 'Bruxelles, capitale du Congo de grand-père? Le parlement régional veut décoloniser l'espace public', *Le Soir*, 29 May 2020 <https://plus.lesoir.be/303946/article/2020-05-29/bruxelles-capitale-du-congo-de-grand-pere-le-parlement-regional-veut-decoloniser?referer=%2Farchives%2Frecherche%3Fdatefilter%3Dlastyear%26sort%3Ddate%2Bdesc%26start%3D50%26word%3Dburundi> [accessed 03 March 2021]
90. *La Libre Belgique*, 'Organisons un débat mature et intégral sur le Congo et favorisons un menu de démarches positives', 19 June 2020 <https://www.lalibre.be/debats/opinions/organisons-un-debat-mature-et-integral-sur-le-congo-et-favorisons-un-menu-de-demarches-positives-5eec71a27b50a66a598c7e91> [accessed 03 March 2021]
91. Martine Dubuisson, 'Une commission parlementaire sur le passé colonial belge dès la rentrée', *Le Soir*, 18 June 2020 <https://plus.lesoir.be/art/d-20200617-GGMA5C?referer=%2Farchives%2Frecherche%3Fdatefilter%3Dlastyear%26sort%3Ddate%2Bdesc%26start%3D40%26word%3Dburundi> [accessed 03 March 2021]
92. Lorraine Kihl, 'Belgique: un niveau de discrimination à l'embauche similaire aux Etats-Unis pour les afrodescendants', *Le Soir*, 15 June 2020 <https://plus.lesoir.be/307408/article/2020-06-15/belgique-un-niveau-de-discrimination-lembauche-similaire-aux-etats-unis-pour-les?referer=%2Farchives%2Frecherche%3Fdatefilter%3Dlastyear%26sort%3Ddate%2Bdesc%26start%3D40%26word%3Dburundi> [accessed 03 March 2021]
93. Frère, p. 138.
94. Falisse and Nkengurutse, 'From FM Radio Stations to Internet…', pp. 175–81.
95. Jean Ntumwa, 'CNC vs Médias: une rencontre prometteuse', SOS Médias, 1 February 2021 <https://www.sosmediasburundi.org/2021/02/01/cnc-vs-medias-une-rencontre-prometteuse/> [accessed 03 March 2021]

Living with Ruination
Rural Neglect and the Persistence of 'Grey' Colonial Architecture in Kongolo, Tanganyika, DRC[1]

Reuben A. Loffman

Introduction

Demands to tear down colonial monuments greatly accelerated after the death of George Floyd on 25 May 2020. Protestors around the world deemed statues of imperialists, such as Cecil Rhodes, as an important visible means by which racist ideologies were publicly legitimised and even celebrated.[2] Removing or defacing controversial statues, known as 'urban fallism', was a graphic and sensational means by which the 'Black Lives Matter' and 'Rhodes Must Fall' campaigns attempted to challenge this very public aspect of racial injustice.[3] The desire on the part of activists to remove monuments to controversial figures from the past in the present is more than mirrored in a burgeoning literature on statues of historical figures and their place in public life.[4] Yet this chapter departs somewhat from this scholarship by highlighting how colonial influence or 'coloniality' in the contemporary built environment exists in the form of more than simply statues of deceased imperialists. Although the more mundane aspects of colonial influence on present-day landscapes are not as sensational as statues in public places, they nevertheless represent the dead hand of colonial-inspired influence on people's daily lives today. This paper concentrates on the economic and social lives of such built colonial environments. In short, David Morton's characterisation of Maputo's architecture that, in essence, 'much of the past remains embedded in the present and keeps a tight grip on possibilities for the future' resonates strongly with the Democratic Republic of the Congo's (hereafter DRC) built environment in rural places.[5]

The built environment in this context will be limited to what has commonly been termed 'grey architecture'. Traditionally, this term has been understood to mean administrative and commercial buildings. Yet this chapter will have a dual focus on sacred as well as secular buildings. The rationale is twofold. First, ecclesiastical architecture, such as churches and schools built by Catholic missionaries in the colonial period, continues to play a very important role in the daily lives of Congolese people today. Given that the Belgian administration outsourced education and health to missionaries to a large extent, there are historical reasons why a definition of 'grey' architecture in the specific Congolese context should include ecclesiastical buildings.

Colonial buildings, be they of secular or sacred provenance, continue to determine relations of space in much of contemporary provincial DRC, which has seen little government investment, as state resources are showered on the country's capital, Kinshasa.[6] Indeed, nearly all the most visible forms of post-colonial architecture in the Congo have been based in the capital, not least the RTNC[7] Congo Building and the Gécamines Commercial Building. Post-colonial Congolese leaders, notably Mobutu Sese Seko, saw cities, in particular Kinshasa, as *the* crucibles in which their version of modernity would be forged.[8] Ironically, this view of modernity as manifested in urban spaces was not vastly dissimilar to their colonial predecessors. And Congolese architecture undertaken after independence in 1960 generally reflects a top-down emphasis on urban architectural investment. As Filip De Boeck so aptly put it: 'Kinshasa is the city that was permeated for decades by the Word of the Dictator [Joseph Mobutu], and the all-pervasive aesthetics of the Mobutist animation politique which accompanied that word.'[9]

It is worth noting, though, that even in Kinshasa, where the Mobutist aesthetic reigned supreme, buildings with a colonial heritage remain to shape a good deal of post-colonial life in the capital. De Boeck, for instance, has written about the Cielux Office Congolais de Poste et Télécommunication site, commonly known as 'The Building', which was first constructed in the 1950s.[10] Likewise, the Hôpital Mama Yemo, whose lifespan dates as far back as 1922, has also been studied.[11] Yet provincial Congo is far more illustrative of the continuing influence of colonial 'grey' architecture. This chapter focuses on a hinterland territory in the south-east of the DRC called 'Kongolo'. And nearly all the buildings in Kongolo's town centre, which is also known as 'Kongolo', date from the colonial period. As such, this chapter will focus primarily on the central business district (CBD) while making some references to some buildings in the territory's rural hinterland.

Colonial buildings in Kongolo are a good illustration of what Ann Laura Stoler describes as the 'rot that remains' given the preponderance of decaying colonial 'grey' architecture there.[12] In using this phrase, Stoler has borrowed in part from Derek Walcott's poem 'Ruins of a Great House'[13] and this reference, in turn, points to the trans-post-colonial dimension of colonial legacies, a point of utmost significance when considering the relationship between Belgium and the DRC. In *Imperial Debris*, Stoler usefully defines her approach to exploring imperial artefacts – namely *ruination* – as follows: 'to think with ruins of empire is to emphasize less the artefacts of empire as dead matter or remnants of a defunct regime than to attend to their re-appropriations, neglect, and strategic positioning within the politics of the present'.[14]

Rather than seeing the presence of colonial architecture as serving only to reproduce the era of Belgian rule in Congo, this chapter reads the built environment in Kongolo through Stoler's concept of ruination. While it identifies the ways in which these buildings have presented post-colonial governments and their citizens with a limited repertoire of difficult choices to make, it also emphasises the fact that the 'rot' has also occurred in a literal sense because of a lack of provincial investment in the DRC. Nancy Rose-Hunt's argument that aspects of colonial phenomena can repeat themselves on occasion will also be useful here.[15] Rather than gender-based violence, as per Rose-Hunt's chapter, the prevalence of class hierarchies, albeit without the presence of Europeans who often dominated colonial relations of production, continue to dominate spatial relations in Kongolo town and territory. Altogether, then, I understand debris and ruination both in a very literal sense, for example, surviving colonial buildings being in a dilapidated state, as well as a figurative one, as in the class hierarchies and lack of investment that dominate manifestations of the built environment.

The chapter makes an original contribution inasmuch as it does not focus on one of the DRC's major cities, such as Kinshasa or Lubumbashi, which have traditionally attracted the bulk of the literature on the built environment in the country.[16] Despite the colonial heritage of many rural buildings, it is unlikely that these will be redeveloped soon given, first, how little international attention is focused on them and, second, the little interest post-colonial governments in general have in investing in the African hinterland. Yet scholars, notably Fassil Demissie, have noted how Africans have reinvented colonial architecture in a multiplicity of new ways, beyond imperial and post-colonial nation-building efforts.[17] This chapter, however, is much less optimistic about the ways in which colonial spaces can be reshaped. Although generalised state poverty has hindered coercive nation-building projects, and has likewise paved the way for some post-colonial African reinvention of colonial ruins, the urban remains of Belgian rule have been easily co-opted by class hierarchies of colonial and post-colonial heritage.

Finally, by way of introduction, the source material that forms the basis of this chapter is varied. It includes oral history interviews, conducted largely over mobile telephone given that much of the research here was undertaken as the Covid-19 pandemic limited global travel. Aside from oral history interviews, photographic evidence forms another important part of this article's methodological repertoire. The Service Photographique at the AfricaMuseum took a large number of pictures of colonial buildings, among other things, from the early twentieth century onwards and these represent valuable sources. No doubt, colonial administrators and their allies wanted to present their work in the best possible light and so photos of buildings are often presented without much reference to their wider role in Congolese society or general context. But the photos are important given that they evince the dates for the construction or existence of buildings if nothing else. Likewise, they also give an impression of their scale and significance in relation to the built environment at large – if only on occasion. Finally, my own observations from fieldwork conducted in 2008, 2009, and 2015 also play an important part in this chapter.

'Like a Sort of Archive': Colonial Administrative and Industrial Constructs

It is unclear when the first post called 'Kongolo' was created by the Belgian colonial administration. But it was likely around the time that the Katanga Company (KC) was given rights to much of south-eastern Congo in 1891. At that time, the Congo was under the rule of Léopold II's nefarious Congo Free State (CFS). The KC were relatively uninterested in the rural north given that they were much more concerned with prospecting for mineral deposits in the central and southern regions of south-eastern Congo. While some chiefs were installed in Kongolo during the lifetime of the KC and its erstwhile successor concession company, the Special Committee for Katanga (1900–10), very little if any infrastructure was actually erected during the fin-de-siècle period given that the Free State did not invest much in the Congo. The lack of architecture was emblematic of what the pre-eminent historian of the colonial Congo, Jean-Luc Vellut, described as the 'conquest state' that generally showed little interest in civilian rule.[18] Some of the only European architecture to emerge at this time in what was to become northern Katanga was of the ecclesiastical variety. Yet even the churches that religious communities, such as the Holy Ghost Fathers (or Spiritans) and the Society of Missionaries of Africa, more commonly known as the 'White Fathers', constructed were generally flimsy. Many of these rudimentary structures would need replacing later in the period of Belgian rule.[19]

Serious, long-standing colonial constructions in Kongolo date only from the period after *la reprise* or the transference of the CFS to the Belgian parliament that was completed in 1908. Colonial officials began to see Kongolo, named after the mythical eponymous founder of the Luba-Katanga ethnic group, much more as a labour reserve than as a centre of capital accumulation in its own right. Put another way, the Belgian administration was more interested in recruiting

Figure 1. Chief Engineer's Residence, Kongolo, Belgian Congo, 1913. Photo: L. Burgeon.

labour *from* the territory than drawing labour *into* it during the early colonial period. As well as its status as a potential pool of labour, whose population typically disappointed recruiters such as the Katangese Labour Exchange, Kongolo became a railway junction for the Great Lakes Railway Company (Compagnie des Chemins de Fer du Congo Supérieur aux Grands Lacs Africans, CFL). The CFL first built a station in Kongolo in 1910 and this was an important moment as far as the history of its relationship with Belgian colonialism was concerned given that this greatly intensified European presence in the territory.[20] Aside from missionaries, more colonial administrators, for example, were stationed in the region after the construction of the railway junction.

Given the importance of the railway, Kongolo's town centre and arguably its hinterland too is a railscape par excellence.[21] One of the first buildings to be constructed in Kongolo, for example, was the chief engineer's residence in the city centre (Fig. 1). There are a number of features of this building that mark out its special importance over and above the fact that it is situated close to the town centre. First, the building is detached from every other one – which demonstrates its individuality and importance. Second, it is the tallest building

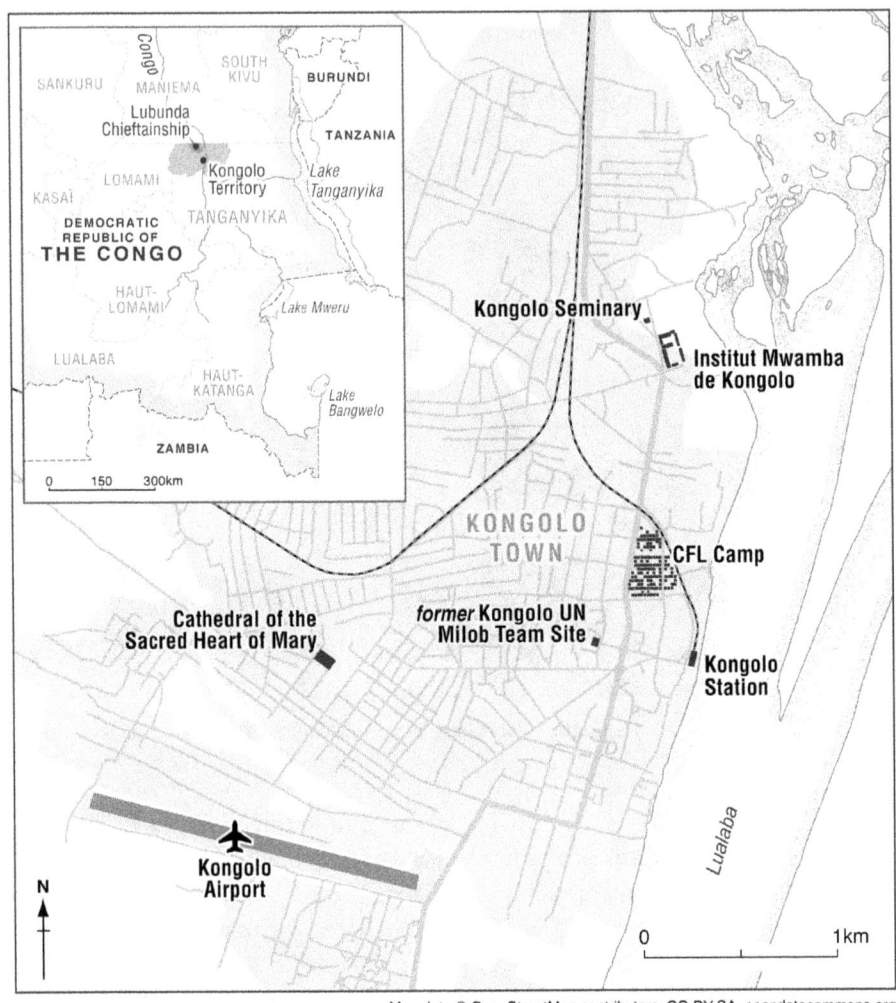

Figure 2. Map of Kongolo, DRC, and its Regional Context.

in Kongolo town centre. As Figure 1 suggests, the residence has a balcony on each level, so the chief engineer could survey the hinterland even if that was not necessarily the function of this aesthetic.

The features of the chief engineer's residence are important not least because the building still stands, even if the interior is now severely compromised by damp and decay. For a long time after the colonial period, the building served as the headquarters of the United Nations Organization Stabilization Mission in the Democratic Republic of the Congo in Kongolo (Fig. 2). As opposed to the early twentieth century, it is true that there are now many houses as well as itinerant market traders who operate around this building. Yet this is not emblematic of a wider pattern of local recapturing of a formally colonial space. For example, a ring of barbed wire separates the building and its surroundings from market stalls and the population at large. So, there were distinct echoes of colonialism here, even if the UN was not a colonial institution per se. For example, the UN was, with the exception of the Church, the best-resourced institution in Kongolo and was also staffed by itinerant operatives whose relationship to the people resident in the territory can best be described as fleeting.

The remnants of the CFL architecture therefore provided powerful institutions, in this case the UN, with an important means by which to survey and operate within the territory of Kongolo. There was little room for local residents of Kongolo to appropriate this space even if they can use the surrounding area. Rather, the house and gardens are gated with only those given clearance allowed in. In 2020, the chief engineer's residence was sold to a private individual, however, so it is no longer the preserve of the UN though it still remains out of the reach of the majority of Kongolo's population.[22] It remains unclear if the aforementioned private investor will resuscitate the building beyond its current decaying state. But, if they do, they have some work ahead of them – and monies to invest – to arrest the building's structural decline.

The dominance of Kongolo's built environment by colonial-era CFL architecture, which in turn serves to limit the agency of local peoples, is further underlined by the unmissable presence of the workers' camp (Fig. 3).

Oral sources suggest that the CFL camp was actually completed in the 1920s, but work began on it much earlier, from the first time the railway entered Kongolo in 1910 as the introduction suggested. The photo below (Fig. 3) – of the CFL façade – conveys the sheer scale of the building and, at the same time, the importance it has in the context of Kongolo's town centre. No other construction approaches its scale even if the chief engineer's residence equals or even exceeds its height. The size of the CFL camp, which encompasses around half an acre of the town centre, serves not only to underline the importance of the rail industry to Kongolo as a whole (see map in Fig. 2) but also to remind the viewer of the number of workers it housed during the early twentieth century. For example, archival sources suggest that 198 people lived there on the eve of the Great Depression in 1929.[23]

There is a rich historiography on the development of workers' camps in general in the Belgian Congo.[24] To summarise, though, these were panoptical spaces of discipline, not unlike the mission outstations run by the White Fathers, in which workers would be surveyed by their erstwhile employers for the duration of their contracts, usually around three years.[25] Although labour

Figure 3. The Façade of the CFL Workers' Camp, Kongolo town centre, DRC, 23 April 2009. Photo: Reuben A. Loffman.

disputes could be arranged in these spaces, and this happened in Kongolo at least during the late colonial period, they were generally easy to survey and so were never a focus of armed rebellion against the colonial state – even if the latter was often nervous about them acting as such.[26] As a result, the CFL camps falls firmly into Demissie's understanding of colonial architecture as serving to 'control and regulate spatially the existence of Africans in urban areas'.[27] Given the CFL's organisation of space, Demissie's thinking could equally apply to provincial areas as well, such as Kongolo's town centre.

The photo in Figure 3, taken in 2009, demonstrates that the structure of the workers' camp remains even if it is dilapidated. What is more, it is still used as a residence for a number of retired SNCC workers in Kongolo to this day.[28] Although around sixty years have passed since decolonisation, the old CFL camp still boasts some of the only concrete residencies available to people living in Kongolo and, likewise, is located conveniently in the centre of the town. Yet the railway has ceased to be the town's main employer, so the camp's purpose has changed somewhat since the colonial period. To understand why the railway no longer constitutes such a major part of the economic life of Kongolo, it is important to give some brief historical context to it in south-eastern Congo as well as the country as a whole.

The CFL's 'concessionary authority was ended in 1965' with the firm finally being nationalised in 1974, in line with Mobutu's policy of nationalisation that formed the backbone of the president-for-life's Zairianisation campaign.[29] Zairianisation was a system that was rhetorically justified to Zairian citizens as a means of Africanising key industries. It was presented as an act of corrective justice. It was in fact a means by which Mobutu rewarded his political allies and occasionally bought off his rivals.[30] Shortly after nationalisation, the CFL came to be part of a sprawling and badly run national network called the Société Nationale des Chemins de Fer Zaïrois (SNCZ), along with the other colonial rail companies that had served the Belgian Congo.[31] Once Mobutu fell, the SNCZ became the Société Nationale des Chemins de Fer du Congo (SNCC). The SNCC was, if anything, even more poorly resourced than its SNCZ predecessor had been.[32] The dilapidation of the SNCC is a fact that, unfortunately for researchers, is reflected in the lack of an informative website about it.[33] For all its disrepair and underinvestment, however, the CFL camp continues to host relatively prosperous Congolese people who can afford to live there. Just as under colonial rule, the CFL camp, an important example of Belgian colonial debris, plays host to a relatively privileged aggregate.

Given that the SNCC can no longer afford a large labour force, many of the houses in it lie empty save for those who are retired from the company or those who rent property there. However, somewhat remarkably given its lack of capital, the camp site is still owned and regulated by the SNCC. So the camp's existence continues to constrain the possibilities available for those living in its remnants. Most obviously, while the camp hosts those who can afford to live there, the facilities available to its residents are threadbare (Fig. 4). Given its material decline, the camp enjoys little access to electricity and other resources such as running water and internet connection. As the facilities are so sparse and the state of the housing is poor, it is not a surprise that many potential residents choose not to live there. However, there are some Congolese who continue to reside in the camp's housing. There are two major ways in which people can access this housing, such as it is. First, residents tend to be those who have retired from the SNCC who may have even worked at one time for the SNCZ.[34] Indeed, the camp is retained primarily for housing retired workers rent-free as a reward for their service, not least given the fact that it cannot afford to actually pay them a pension.[35] As well as retired SNCC workers, it is possible for non-railway workers to apply for housing in the camp, but these applicants must pay rent.

The housing contained in the camp is a mixture of residencies with three or six rooms, the latter being more expensive than the former.[36] The monthly

Figure 4. Houses in the CFL Camp, Kongolo, DRC, 7 May 2009.
Photo: Reuben A. Loffman.

cost of renting a six-room house in the CFL camp is around 30,000 Congolese Francs (CFs) whereas a house with three rooms costs fifteen thousand for the same period. Given that two thousand CFs are equivalent to $1, the accommodation in the camp ranges from $8 to $15 a month.[37] But this figure, which might appear cheap by Western European standards, would absorb half of the average monthly wage of a teacher in as of 2006 – only three years before the photo in Figure 4 was taken.[38] As such, most residents of Kongolo and its environs could simply not afford to live there.

The situation is, admittedly, far better for the former SNCC workers who can live in the camp for free. However, as Figure 4 demonstrates, the camp hardly provides ideal living spaces. Moreover, there is nothing occupants can do to alter the structure or even to some extent the form of these houses.[39] The government has decreed that these are historic buildings and so cannot be substantially altered. Even if one did have the money and time to renovate, therefore, there is little that can actually be done to make these spaces more appealing beyond the fact that they are durable and they are close to Kongolo's town centre. My friend Juvenal Paipo, who lived in Kongolo for many years, put it best when he said to me: *Ils sont comme une sorte d'archive* [they are like a sort of archive].[40] The camp is therefore considered an integral part of the colonial heritage of the DRC, hence why the state has declared that the buildings within cannot be substantially altered.

Given the emphasis currently placed by both the SNCC and the Congolese government on preservation, or even conservation, the camp's continued existence means that other buildings that could house more people there cannot be built. Renovation is largely impossible. The camp is in many respects, therefore, a lived-in museum of sorts. The state's keeping the CFL camp in this way might suggest that it has invested in at least promoting some aspects of its history, yet it has not done this. As such, it is difficult to escape the conclusion that preservation is being used as a rhetorical means of masking underinvestment in this case. Despite falling into disrepair and ruination, the CFL camp continues to push out poorer people from the town centre while educating few if any about the history that surrounds it. It is true that CBDs are inaccessible to most of the world's poorest people, yet the camp's role in enforcing class divisions still deserves remark.

Rather than being able to easily appropriate buildings in the wake of neoliberal decay, Congolese people continue to have to negotiate the remnants of colonial buildings and the limitations they impose on their daily lives. Correspondingly, literal ruination is a very real concept for those living in the former CFL camp even if they are among a privileged aggregate who get to live in Kongolo's CBD. Stoler's subtle understanding of the concept of ruination is nonetheless helpful in this context. Stoler problematises the easy historical linkage between present-day suffering and colonialism and seeks to explain in more detail why certain spaces and peoples continue to suffer after the formal end of most European colonialism. Correspondingly, the ruin that has befallen the CFL camp is not simply the result of the dilapidation of a set of colonial buildings but is also a result of the choices of the post-colonial government and its donors. The government has chosen to maintain the structure of the camp as a living museum yet refused to invest in a properly funded exposition of its history that might justify such constrictions on current renovation. Rather than Belgian imperialism alone contributing to 'the rot that remains', contemporary Congolese governments are content for their citizens to live with it and within it.

Outside the former CFL railway infrastructure, one of the main hangovers from the colonial bureaucratic infrastructure is found in the form of the Territorial Bureau in Kongolo town centre itself. One of the most important points to note about the office is that it is not as tall as the chief engineer's residence (Fig. 1), nor is it as expansive as the CFL camp (Fig. 3). It is not smaller than other territorial bureaus in similar territories in the DRC, such as Nyunzu, Kongolo's contiguous eastern neighbour, but it ironically demonstrates yet again how important the CFL was to Kongolo's colonial political economy. The building itself is a largely whitewashed structure consisting mainly of a square, one-floor building with a gabled roof and a modest portico constructed from corrugated iron. The interior is split by a corridor that separates two main offices, with one being where the territorial administer conducts their *public* business.

Unlike the CFL camp, the exterior of the bureau is generally maintained in that paint, for example, is reapplied to it on a semi-regular basis to prevent it looking too dilapidated to the casual observer. The interior is also cleaned on occasion although this is – to be clear – merely cosmetic. To a great extent, cleaning occurs because the territorial administrator conducts business within the bureau, and this includes meetings with citizens as well as the chiefs that administer the hinterland. To ensure that business can be conducted without impediment, the Territorial Bureau cannot fall *too* far into ruin. Moreover, the office is explicitly associated with the Congolese state, and this provides even more motivation to make the building appear well maintained. For example, there is a very visible Congolese flag outside the bureau to signal its importance to the general population. I was told that the flag was saluted at 4 p.m. every day by one of my informants, but I saw no evidence of this on any of my stays in the territory. Either way, the bureau is the most auspicious sign of the presence of statehood in Kongolo and can at least lay some claim to the national purse – though how much it gets exactly and when it gets it is difficult to say and is likely fairly erratic in any case.

For all the pageantry that may or may not surround it, the bureau lacks electricity and, but for the occasional repaint, looks like it has changed relatively little since the colonial days. The bureau, like the camp, has suffered from a lack of sustained and significant investment by the state. Stoler's concept of ruination is useful here because it illustrates the literal dilapidation of the building and suggests how the state has continued to underinvest in building the capacity of the provincial state.[41] As she suggests:

> At least one challenge is not to imagine the 'postcolony' or the postcolonial imperium as replicas of earlier degradations or as the inadvertent, inactive leftovers of more violent colonial relations. It is rather to track how new de-formations and new forms of debris work on matter and mind to eat through peoples' resources and resiliencies […].[42]

One of the most obvious manifestations of the lack of resources available to territorial administrators is the dearth of digital information available to them in their offices given the lack of electricity. The poor resourcing of this government building represents in many respects the way that colonialism haunts many different sectors of society in Kongolo today in that government elites as well as poorer citizens are hamstrung by it. Colonial officials famously used typewriters to author their reports, and little has changed in terms of the format of the bureau to suggest any technical upgrade has recently been done. In his path-breaking history of the Kuba under Belgian rule, Jan Vaninsa suggested that Congolese people in Kasaï considered the typewriter 'the chosen instrument of the administration' and evinced this claim using Djilatendo's famous image of the 'Administrator at Work' (1930–31).[43] It is ironic, therefore, that an instrument so indelibly associated with the Belgian administration should continue to dominate in the post-independence era.

What is more, unlike slave forts, such as Elmina in Ghana whose purpose is in part to convey the horrors of the transatlantic slave trade for a burgeoning tourist industry, there is no intellectual or aesthetic reason why buildings like the bureau should not be renovated if they continue to stand.[44] It is useful to conserve the structure of Elmina as close as possible to the structure that would have interned slaves so as to preserve the public memory of the slave trade, in other words, but this does not apply to the territorial bureau, which serves a far more functional purpose. If the Congolese state wishes to make a point about the horrors of Belgian colonialism, then the territorial bureau might help fulfil that role with the right curation. But, much like the case of the CFL camp, the administration shows little interest in doing so. As such, the limited facilities available to territorial administrators are as much a symptom of the state's fiscal neglect of areas outside its major cities as colonial 'rot'.

Fiction in the Buildings: Ecclesiastical Imaginaries and Education

Aside from the surviving state and industrial buildings, some of the other major examples of early colonial architecture that withstood the post-independence violence in Kongolo were those built by the Catholic Church. Although not traditionally counted as 'grey' architecture, the preponderance of ecclesiastical buildings in Kongolo means that those who live there interact with them on a near daily basis. The Catholic Church competed with the CFL, along with the Belgian administration, for social primacy in Kongolo throughout the colonial period.[45] Indeed, missionaries generally viewed the CFL camp with deep suspicion. They especially worried about its potential to inspire materialism and ultimately proletarianisation in what they wanted to be a 'Christian kingdom'.[46] The CFL, for example, marked the start of a secular modernity demonstrated in the emergence of a new temporality: the train timetables.[47] Ironically, therefore, the majority of Catholic missionaries in Kongolo arrived with the advent of the railway in 1910. One set of missionaries, the Spiritans, concentrated on evangelising the town centre while the other, the White Fathers, focused on the hinterland. Both sets of missionaries arrived in Kongolo intent on building a substantive network of facilities.

Catholic missionaries saw an important opportunity to carve out a state-like presence given the large-scale absence of infrastructure built by the colonial administration itself. Yet while both the Spiritans and the White Fathers believed they were locked in an ideological competition with the CFL, paradoxically it was the spiritual geography of local African groups that determined the locations of the first churches in Kongolo rather than the railway.[48] The Bayazi ethnic group, for example, wanted a particular mound in the town centre to be used solely for ancestor worship rather than as the site of a new Spiritan cathedral that would, as they put it, "'reach the sky'".[49] The White Fathers had more luck early on in the hinterland, principally in a place called 'Sola', in which they began to erect what they described as 'hangars'.[50] These were rudimentary structures of thatched roofs and wooden poles. Needless to say, few of these from that era exist today even if examples of this architectural style are still present in Kongolo. Hangars were gradually replaced by brick structures and churches also remade in more durable materials. Much of this building work could only happen after the First World War, though, since wartime privations not only affected the materials available to the missionaries but also the social and political climate in which they worked.

When Catholic missionaries, such as Emilio Callewaert of the Spiritans, created lasting structures in the interwar period, these were designed with a strong moralistic purpose in mind, since Catholic missionaries wanted to engineer pristine Christian communities. To do this, the White Fathers in particular borrowed from their colleagues, the Jesuits, who had worked in Lower Congo and fashioned *écoles-chapelles* or 'school chapels'.[51] The school chapel system was designed to cut children off from their ancestral traditions to make them perfect Christians. A strong system of discipline was imposed on potential converts, with punishments ranging from beatings to expulsion. Ben Knighton found that Victor Roelens, the leader of the White Fathers in what was northern Katanga, loved a revealing quote about education: 'The rod was born in paradise'.[52] Such love for 'the rod' was far from uncommon among Catholic missionaries in their early and even to some extent their later years in Kongolo.[53] The Sola complex, in which a large-scale primary school was based, remained the most important for the White Fathers in terms of their encounters in Kongolo while that of Lubunda ironically outshone the Spiritans' work in the town centre. The school chapel system, in which the discipline was so fierce, retained a central place within church education in south-eastern Congo.

Scholars such as Marvin Markowitz have written at length about the fact that the Church was granted considerable subsidies to educate Congolese people, thereby saving the colonial administration having to erect school buildings and hire teachers.[54] The Church fought throughout its colonial lifetime to retain control of Congolese education. While missionaries' grip on control of schooling had lessened by the end of the colonial period, with the introduction of non-religious education in many parts of the Congo, there was no questioning the continued primacy of Catholic education in the newly independent country.[55] Much as scholars have already suggested, but for a brief period when Mobutu completely nationalised education in the Congo (1974–77), the Church has retained a dominance over education in the DRC, and Kongolo is no exception.[56] Indeed, the primacy of the Church over matters of education is one of the most visible colonial hangovers in the DRC as a whole.

To properly understand the continued importance of ecclesiastical institutions such as the Catholic Church to schools in Kongolo, it is worth adumbrating the history of the Church's role in education in the post-independence DRC. Once it became clear that the economic state of Mobutu's Zaire was imperilled by the fall in copper prices in 1974/75, the autocrat largely withdrew from his battle with the Church over schooling. In 1977, Mobutu signed the National Schools Management Convention. This agreement mandated that the state would be the 'organising power of all the approved schools [...] and [provided] their financing'.[57] But 'the Church is the managerial power of the national schools [...] This management concerns the internal organisation of the schools, the functioning of the schools, staff management, financial management, and the organisation of the social life of the pupils'.[58] What is more, the teaching of religion in schools accelerated.[59] Most schools in Kongolo, as elsewhere in rural Congo as a whole, are therefore Catholic Convention Schools (Écoles Conventionnées Catholiques) (ECCs).

There are a variety of ECCs in Kongolo, but arguably one of the most striking is the École Normale in the Lubunda chieftainship in the north of the territory (Fig. 5). The École Normale functions as a teacher-training college, primarily for primary school teachers, and so it has an important part to play not merely in the life of Kongolo but in the wider region of what is now the Province of Tanganyika. Its status has changed in that it is now what is known as an *école moderne* in that graduates need to spend more time in school to become a teacher.[60] Yet, as is normal in the case of ECCs, the school is still staffed by Catholic clergy.

Other schools, established by the Spiritans in particular during the colonial period, dominate the educational scene in the CBD. One of the most auspicious examples of a school that continues to function from the early colonial era is that of the Institut Mwamba de Kongolo, another ECC (see map in Fig. 2). The

Figure 5. École Normale, Lubunda, DRC, 21 April 2009.
Photo: Reuben A. Loffman.

institute started life as the Collège Liberman, yet changed its name to Mwamba by the time that the Congo's ill-fated First Republic ended. The institute is staffed by clergy.[61] Thus, although the curriculum has most likely changed since the College Liberman days, the importance of Catholic clergy to its day-to-day functioning has remained an important characteristic of the facility. The Institut Mwamba is a vitally important secondary school given that it teaches approximately two thousand pupils every year.[62] It would be interesting to see exactly how much Catholic religion gets taught within the current curriculum and more research in this area would be welcome.

Given its size, the Institut Mwamba looks, at least from the outside, as if it has attracted enough funding from the state to avoid the kind of ruination present in, say, the houses in the CFL camp. This is not to say, however, that investment would be unwelcome. A better example of a school in need of some repair would be the Ngongo Ramazani primary school in Sola, a town in the chieftainship of Bena Nkuvu outside of Kongolo's town centre. A sign above one of the classrooms in the school suggests, incorrectly, that Ramazani was the first Congolese White Father.[63] The first ordained Congolese priest, who was in fact

Figure 6. Ngongo Ramazani Primary School in Sola, Bena Nkuvu, DRC, 1 August 2015. Photo: Reuben A. Loffman.

sponsored by Victor Roelens, was Stefano Kaoze in 1917.[64] What this incongruous sign indicates about Ramazani remains unclear. My oral history research suggests that Ramazani, who lived from 1935 to 1969, was the first African to become a White Fathers missionary in Kongolo.[65] Whether he was ordained or not, however, is unclear. Either way, the dilapidation of the primary school that bears his name is inescapable (Fig. 6). Figures for state expenditure on this school, as others, are very difficult to come by. However, just from a glance at the building itself, one can see the level of literal ruination that has befallen it. Likewise, having been in the school, I can say that its interior matches its exterior decay.

It is clear that, given the lack of state funding for education, the oversight of schools by the Catholic Church is in many ways a good thing in that it ensures they remain open. If schools were left to the state to manage, furthermore, the situation could be perilous given that 'the education sector has virtually disappeared from the Congolese state budget since the mid-1980s'.[66] Yet the importance of the Church in education is nonetheless a continuity with the colonial period. In effect, it means that the Church enjoys a great deal of day-to-day control over what happens in schools. While the importance of the relationship between the Church and the state has remained in the context of education, the buildings that have historically sustained it are in a state of disrepair and, in the case of Ngongo Ramazani, quite profoundly so. Again, Stoler's nuanced reading of ruination is useful here. While the primary school was constructed during the colonial period, there was nothing to say that it should have been left to dilapidate during the post-colonial period. On the other hand, the importance of the Church in the educational life of the Congolese has remained undimmed.

This section on ecclesiastical imaginaries has focused on the more numerous Catholic schools than those built by Protestant missionaries and has highlighted how the buildings in which pupils of these schools are taught are tangible examples of ruination. They might not prevent pupils being educated, but they do little more than the bare minimum required of school buildings in that they mostly provide some sort of shelter for learning – though even this largely depends on the weather. In some ways, these buildings are historically significant in that they tell of an important colonial mission encounter or series of encounters and how these were spatially situated. They come, in other words, not from the educational context of the twenty-first century but from the early twentieth. The conservationist case is in some ways moot here in that investment is required either to renovate or start again from scratch.

Conclusion

This chapter has hardly scratched the surface of the range of different buildings dating from the colonial period that remain in Kongolo and that – in many cases – continue to function in different ways to this day. Rather, the array of buildings that residents in Kongolo continue to engage with that date from the period of Belgian rule is staggering. What I have done in this chapter is highlight some of the most conspicuous examples of colonial architecture on show in the territory. For example, I have examined the former CFL chief engineer's residence, the CFL camp, the Institut Mwamba, and the École Normale. I have read these buildings through Stoler's concept of ruination.

So, on the one hand, I have highlighted how colonial-era buildings, despite playing an important part in the daily lives of, in some cases, hundreds of Congolese people, are in a state of decay. At the same time, some of the colonial buildings that remain, in the case of the CFL camp for example, have served to reproduce the dominance of a labour aristocracy, albeit one with severely attenuated means, over a provincial town in the contemporary DRC. Alongside the fact that some buildings have served class interests not dissimilar to those witnessed during the colonial period, they also bear testament to the continuing importance of religion in post-colonial education, in the case of the schools surveyed here, for example.

On the other hand, however, and in keeping with Stoler's reading of ruination, there is not a straight line of continuity between the rotting colonial-era buildings and the limitations they place on contemporary Congolese life. The buildings as a whole bear witness to the continuing lack of state and donor investment in provincial DRC. The state of the buildings used for educational purposes in Kongolo alone is a scandalous indictment not just of the colonial state but its post-colonial successor. The insistence of keeping the CFL camp as a living museum is interesting but has not actually manifested in a greater understanding of the DRC's past as the dilapidation of the residencies in the facility suggest. Rather, the evocation of history as a justification for preserving the structure of decaying colonial monuments and limiting local strategies of co-opting these ruins serves, if anything, to mask considerable underinvestment.

Admittedly, the postcolonial history of neglect of Kongolo is complex. The United States Agency for International Development invested a good deal in the territory and neighbours in the 1970s and the early 1980s.[67] But this US investment was chiefly the product of Cold War imperatives on the part of the United States. America did not want to see major revolts in what was then northern Katanga threaten its supply of uranium in the south of the then province. As such, it sought to stabilise Mobutu's regime in the south-east, which saw the onslaught of the Shaba Wars in the late 1970s, to ensure its continuing access to nuclear bomb-making minerals. For his part, Mobutu was disinterested in investing in Kongolo. As such, once US funding ran out, buildings and infrastructure were once again left to decay. Unsurprisingly, the Congo Wars of the late 1990s and early 2000s did nothing to arrest the decline of Kongolo as the major agricultural centre it had been in the late colonial period. If anything, this chapter has served as a cri de cœur both for a more equitable balance of state spending vis-à-vis urban and rural/town Congolese environments as well as more scholarly and donor attention to be paid to provincial Congo as a whole. Without adequate investment, colonial structures might well fall but not in a way that empowers the communities in which they are situated.

Notes

1. All translations from French are mine unless otherwise stated.
2. Simukai Chigudu, 'Rhodes Must Fall in Oxford: A Critical Testimony', *Critical African Studies*, 12.3 (2020), 302–12.
3. Sybille Frank and Mirjana Ristic, 'Urban Fallism', *City: Analysis of Urban Change, Theory, Action*, 24.3/4 (2020), 552–64; BBC News, 'Black Lives Matter: Bristol's Colston Protest Police 'Didn't Lack Courage', *BBC*, 10 June 2020, https://www.bbc.co.uk/news/uk-england-bristol-52993995 [accessed 5 September 2020].
4. Aleksandra Hadzelek, 'Spain's "Pact of Silence" and the Removal of Franco's Statues', in Diane Kirkby (ed.), *Past Law, Present Histories* (Canberra: Australian National University E-Press, 2012), pp. 153–76; Mahunele Thotse, 'Contesting Names and Statues: Battles Over Louis Trichardt/Makhando "City-Text" in Limpopo Province, South Africa', *Kronos*, 36.1 (2010), 173–83; Nicole M. Elias, Sean McCandless, and Rashmi Chordiya, 'Administrative Decision-Making Amid Competing Public Sector Values: Confederate Statue Removal in Baltimore, Maryland', *Journal of Public Affairs Education*, 25.3 (2019), 412–22.
5. David Morton, *Age of Concrete: Housing and the Shape of Aspiration in the Capital of Mozambique* (Athens: Ohio University Press, 2019), p. 226.
6. Theodore Trefon, 'Introduction: Réforme et Désillusions', in Theodore Trefon (ed.), *Réforme au Congo (RDC): Attentes et Désillusions* (Paris: L'Harmattan, 2009), p. 28.
7. RTNC stands for Radio Télévision nationale congolaise.
8. Margaret A. Turner, *Housing in Zaire: How the System Works and How People Cope* (Madison: University of Wisconsin Press, 1985), p. 241.
9. Filip De Boeck and Sammy Baloji, *Suturing the City: Living Together in Congo's Urban Worlds* (London: Autograph ABP, 2016), p. 236.
10. Filip De Boeck, '"Poverty" and the Politics of Syncopation: Urban Examples from Kinshasa (DR Congo)', *Current Anthropology*, 56.11 (2015), 146–58 (149).
11. Simon De Nys-Ketels, Johan Lagae, Kristien Geenen, Luce Beeckmans, and Trésor Lumfuankenda Bungiena, 'Spacial Governmentality and Everyday Hospital Life in Colonial and Postcolonial DR-Congo', in Daniel E. Coslett (ed.), *Neocolonialism and Built Heritage: Echoes of Empire in Africa, Asia, and Europe* (London: Routledge, 2020), pp. 147–67.
12. Ann Laura Stoler, 'Introduction: "The Rot Remains": From Ruins to Ruination', in Ann Laura Stoler (ed.), *Imperial Debris: On Ruins and Ruination* (Durham: Duke University Press, 2013), pp. 1–35 (p. 1).
13. Derek Walcott, 'Ruins of a Great House', in *Collected Poems 1948–1984* (New York: Noonday Press, 1986).
14. Stoler, p. 11.
15. Nancy Rose Hunt, 'An Acoustic Register: Rape and Repetition in Congo', in Ann Laura Stoler, (ed.), *Imperial Debris: On Ruins and Ruination* (Durham NC: Duke University Press, 2013), pp. 39–66.
16. Manuel Herz, Ingrid Schröder and Hans Focketyn (eds.), *African Modernism: The Architecture of Independence: Ghana, Senegal, Côte d'Ivoire, Kenya, Zambia* (Zürich: Park Books, 2015); Fassil Demissie, *Postcolonial African Cities: Imperial Legacies and Postcolonial Predicament* (London: Routledge, 2013) and Filip De Boeck and Marie-Françoise Plissart, *Kinshasa: Tales from the Invisible City* (Leuven: Leuven University Press, 2014).
17. Demissie, *Postcolonial African Cities*, p. 6.
18. Jean-Luc Vellut, 'La Violence armée dans l'État Indépendant du Congo: Ténèbres et Clartés dans l'histoire d'un État conquérant', *Cultures et Développement*, 16.3/4 (1984), 671–707.
19. Reuben Loffman, 'In the Shadow of the Tree Sultans: African Elites and the Shaping of Early Colonial Politics on the Katangan Frontier', *The Journal of Eastern African Studies*, 5.3 (2011), 535–52.
20. Jean-Luc Ernst, 'La Compagnie des Chemins de Fer du Congo Supérieur aux Grands Lacs Africains ou CF: Aperçu Historique', https://www.stanleyville.be/cfl.html [accessed 14 May 2021].
21. Matt Thompson, 'Modernity, Anxiety, and the Development of a Popular Railway Landscape Aesthetic, 1809–1879', in Steven D. Spalding and Benjamin Fraser (eds.), *Trains, Literature, and Culture: Reading/Writing the Rails* (New York: Lexington Books: 2012), pp. 119–56 (p. 120).
22. Interview with Juvenal Paipo, by telephone, 5 February 2021.
23. Ministère des Affaires Étrangères, Brussels (AAB), Archives Africaines et de la Main-d'œuvre (AIMO), 'Rapport Général de l'Administration (RGA)', 1929, 20.
24. Bruno De Meulder, *De Kampen Van Kongo: Arbeid, Kapitaal, en Rasveredeling in de Koloniale Planning* (Amsterdam: Meulenhoff; Antwerp: Kritak, 1996); Benjamin Rubbers, 'Mining Towns, Enclaves, and Spaces: A Genealogy of Worker Camps in the Congolese Copperbelt', *Geoforum*, 98 (2019), 88–96; Bogumil Jew-

siewicki, 'The Great Depression and the Making of the Colonial Economic System in the Belgian Congo', *African Economic History*, 4 (1977), 153–76.
25. Valentin Yves Mudimbe, *The Idea of Africa* (Bloomington: Indiana University Press, 1994), pp. 105–53.
26. Loffman, *Church, State, and Colonialism in Southeastern Congo, 1890–1962* (Basingstoke: Palgrave Macmillan, 2019), pp. 194–95.
27. Demissie, *Postcolonial African Cities*, p. 5.
28. Interview with Juvenal Paipo, by telephone, 5 February 2021.
29. Thomas Turner and Crawford Young, *The Rise and Decline of the Zairian State* (Madison: University of Wisconsin Press, 1985), p. 285.
30. Ibid., p. 328.
31. Roland Pourtier, 'Transports et Développement au Zaïre,' *Afrique Contemporaine*, 29.153 (1990), 3–26.
32. Emizet François Kisangani and Scott F. Bobb, *Historical Dictionary of the Democratic Republic of the Congo* (Lanham: Scarecrow Press, 1999), p. 484.
33. The official website's link, e.g., http://sncc.cd/, has been broken for as long as the present author can remember.
34. Interview with Juvenal Paipo, by telephone, 5 February 2021.
35. Ibid.
36. Ibid.
37. Figures from Google and correct as of 9 February 2021.
38. Kristof Titeca and Tom De Herdt, 'Real Governance Beyond the "Failed State": Negotiating Education in the Democratic Republic of the Congo,' *African Affairs*, 110.439 (2011), 213–31 (221).
39. Interview with Juvenal Paipo, by telephone, 5 February 2021.
40. Ibid.
41. Stoler, 'Introduction,' in Stoler (ed.), *Imperial Debris*, p. 29.
42. Ibid.
43. Jan Vansina, *Being Colonized: The Kuba Experience in Rural Congo, 1880–1960* (Madison: University of Wisconsin Press, 2010), p. 232.
44. Ishmael Mensah, 'The Roots Tourism Experience of Diaspora Africans: A Focus on the Cape Coast and Elmina Castles', *Journal of Heritage Tourism*, 10.3 (2015), 213–32.
45. Loffman, *Church, State, and Colonialism*, pp. 63–118.
46. Allen F. Roberts, 'History, Ethnicity, and Change in the "Christian Kingdom" of Southeastern Zaire', in Leroy Vail (ed.), *The Creation of Tribalism in Southern Africa* (Berkeley: University of California Press, 1991), pp. 193–214.
47. I am grateful to Pierre-Philippe Fraiture for this observation.
48. Loffman, 'In the Shadow of the Tree Sultans', p. 541.
49. Ibid.
50. Nestor Ngoy Katahwa, *Initiation des Jeunes Hemba: Tradition et Modernité* (Kinshasa: Facultés Catholiques de Kinshasa, 2009), p. 44.
51. Flavien Nkay Malu, *La Mission Chrétienne à l'Épreuve de la Tradition Ancestrale – (Congo Belge, 1891–1933)* (Paris: Éditions Karthala, 2007), p. 179.
52. Ben Knighton, 'The Determination of Religion in Africa', *African Affairs*, 109.435 (2010), 325–35 (333).
53. Abbot Molisho Jérôme was a pupil of a mission school in Kongolo during the late colonial period and, in conversation with me, remembered not the 'rod' as such but rather the whip. Data from: interview with Abbot Molisho Jérôme, Caritas, Kongolo town centre, 31 July 2015.
54. Marvin Markowitz, *Cross and Sword: The Political Role of Missionaries in the Belgian Congo, 1908–1960* (Stanford: Hoover Institute, 1973).
55. Patrick M. Boyle, 'School Wars: Church, State, and the Death of the Congo', *The Journal of Modern African Studies*, 33.3 (1995), 451–68 (455).
56. Wyatt MacGaffey, 'Education, Religion, and Social Structure in Zaire', *Anthropology and Education Quarterly*, 13.3 (1982), 238–50.
57. Archdiocèse de Bukavu, 'Coordination Diocésaine et Provinciale des Écoles Conventionnées Catholiques,' available at: http://www.archidiocesebukavu.com/diocese/commissions-diocesaines/coordination-diocesaine-et-provinciale-des-ecoles-conventionnees-catholiques/ [accessed 10 February 2021].
58. Ibid.
59. Ibid.
60. Interview with Juvenal Paipo, by mobile telephone, 5 February 2021.
61. Ibid.
62. Ibid.
63. From fieldwork observation by author on 1 August 2015.
64. Roberts, 'History, Ethnicity, and Change in the "Christian Kingdom" of Southeastern Zaire', p. 201.
65. Interview with Juvenal Paipo, by telephone, 21 May 2021.
66. Tom De Herdt and Kristof Titeca, 'Governance with Empty Pockets: The Education Sector in the Democratic Republic of the Congo', *Development and Change*, 47.3 (2016), 472–94.
67. Reuben Loffman, 'An Obscured Revolution? USAID, the North Shaba Project, and the Zaïrian Administration, 1976–1986,' *Canadian Journal of African Studies*, 48.3 (2014), 425–44.

Cash Crops and Clichés
Agriculture, Contact Zones, and Afterlives of Belgian Colonialism

Sarah Arens

Imperialism after all is an act of geographical violence through which virtually every space in the world is explored, charted, and finally brought under control.[1]

The writing of new spatial relations (territorialization) was, ultimately, tantamount to the production of boundaries and hierarchies, zones and enclaves; the subversion of existing property arrangements; the classification of people according to different categories; resource extraction; and, finally, the manufacturing of a large reservoir of cultural imaginaries. These imaginaries gave meaning to the enactment of differential rights to differing categories of people for different purposes within the same space; in brief, the exercise of sovereignty. Space was therefore the raw material of sovereignty and the violence it carried with it.[2]

In a chapter entitled 'Land Reforms in the Democratic Republic of Congo (DRC)', Tukumbi Lumumba-Kasongo traces land rights and land reforms from the precolonial to the postcolonial period and writes, on the impact of Belgian colonial occupation of the Congo, that '[l]and, as an integral element of the process of production, was a structuring element of the "colonial modernization"'.[3] He goes on to demonstrate how, '[t]his so-called modernization is referred to as the beginning of the system of deconstruction of the Congo through Europeanization of the system of control and production, as well as the introduction of the new religious and capitalistic value systems'.[4] In doing so, Lumumba-Kasongo emphasises the centrality of land for the exercise of civilian and economic control – under the pretext of 'modernisation' – for Belgian colonial rule, both during the so-called Congo Free State and the Belgian Congo.[5] With the renewed rise in interest in questions of decolonisation within and beyond the academy, questions of land use and land rights, reparations and restitution (also of land) have moved to the forefront of discussions about the long-term impact of European colonialism again, and it is specifically within the national context of the present-day Congo that these issues resonate. Against the background of the kleptocratic Mobutu rule (1965–97), and this regime's continuation of colonial policies under the guise of a decolonisation through 'Africanisation' and 'authenticity', Lumumba-Kasongo's call for putting the land issue at the centre 'of Congolese debates and research activities on and/or about political decolonization' registers as particularly pertinent.[6]

While issues of land use are crucial considerations in all colonial contexts, agriculture appears as a significant issue to understand the long-term detrimental impact of Belgium's colonial occupation of the present-day DRC, Rwanda, and Burundi. Focusing on agriculture in the Belgian Congo between 1930 and 1960, this chapter highlights agriculture and agrarian science's unique function for the Belgian colonial system and the central part it has played for its harmful post-colonial legacies. Analysing its complex role as applied science and means of control enables us, first, to gain a more accurate understanding of exploitation of both human labour and non-human resources and the successes and failures of exercising hegemonic control in the last decades of the Belgian Congo. Second, departing from Lumumba-Kasongo's notion above that land was a 'structuring element of [...] "colonial modernization"', this chapter argues that colonial agriculture emerges as an important element in Belgium's aspiration to be acknowledged as a 'modern' coloniser by other imperial powers, as one that had 'moved on' from the atrocities of the 'Free State' era under King Leopold II.[7] 'Modernisation', as well as its intellectual dimension of 'modernity', are, of course, always already fraught categories, particularly in a (post)colonial context. 'Modernity' is a contested and vaguely defined term, as Pierre-Philippe Fraiture argues with reference to Anthony Giddens.[8] In this discussion, Fraiture identifies conversion to Christianity, new modes of capitalist production, and the imposition of the European idea of the nation-state as the hallmarks of Belgian colonial modernity.[9] Colonial agriculture becomes part and parcel of this coercive modernising process, as the practical dimension of 'modernity' that can be seen as the infrastructures, tools, and processes elicited by Belgian colonialism. In the post-colonial period, this process continues under a different, even more extended guise, from 'foreign aid' to global commodity chains, as I discuss later in this chapter.

Agriculture also appears as a particularly visible site that demonstrates the ongoing detrimental impact of Belgian colonialism in Central Africa. While the continuing conflict in Kivu (eastern Congo) is inextricably connected to land issues, in colonial 'Ruanda-Urundi' in particular, colonial land management and agricultural policies appear as a contributing factor to the developments that led to the 1994 genocide against the Tutsi in Rwanda. For example,

Koen Vlassenroot and Chris Huggins explain how unequal access to land in the border region of Eastern Congo, a 'result of a longer historical process of colonial land reforms and post-colonial patrimonial rule', has led to 'intensified local competition', which 'was transformed into disputes and violence between ethnic communities when local elites from the early nineties started to mobilise entire communities on the basis of ethnic belonging and collective land rights'.[10] Part of colonialism's legacy is the connection between ethnic conflict and conflict over land: Jan Vansina explains specifically for Rwanda that, while the distinction and conflict between Hutu and Tutsi already existed by the time the first Europeans arrived in the region, the German colonisers were unable to understand the conflict in terms other than inflexible and simple ethnic categories and falsely attributed the notion of 'racial hatred' to it, which was subsequently adopted by the Belgians after Ruanda-Urundi became a Belgian League of Nations mandate following World War I. This demonstrates how this inability to comprehend a conflict outside of the prism of European racism fundamentally shaped the policies and practices of subsequent colonial occupation.[11]

While Osumaka Likaka has already pointed to the link between racist ideologies, colonial (agricultural) policies, and 'myth making', to which I return at a later point, I consider agriculture as an integral colonial contact zone, to use Mary Louise Pratt's oft-quoted term.[12] Pratt describes the contact zone as treating 'the relations among colonizers and colonized [...] not in terms of separateness or apartheid, but in terms of copresence, interaction, interlocking understandings and practices, often within radically asymmetrical relations of power'.[13] Reinvestigating the agricultural contact zone offers a range of insights into the country's colonial cultures: namely, into the way in which the colonial state perpetrated violence not only through a forced-labour system, but also in a geographical and epistemological sense, by overwriting indigenous knowledge and knowledge systems about land use.

The Belgian Congo constituted an immense occupied territory in Central Africa, including people of several hundred different ethnicities, languages, religious, and cultural practices; many different forms, epistemologies, cosmologies, and traditions of agriculture, land use, and land rights. This chapter does not claim in any way that this plethora of indigenous knowledge systems can be represented in a unified way, nor that that the Belgian colonial occupation had the same impact and was experienced in the same way across these vastly different regions. Instead, it is important to deconstruct the colonial state's multitude of clichés and myths to better understand colonialism's complex contact zones. These stereotypes produced oppression and violence, while, at the same time, they opened up opportunities for resistance and change. Likaka has described the colonial state's manufacturing of stereotypes as part of a larger process of integrating African subjects into colonial administration and economy.¹⁴ Analysing harmful, ethnicity-based stereotypes of Africans, such as the idea of the 'gift of imitation' that denies all African creativity, he demonstrates how this discourse played an equally important role for the colonial state's recourse to violence as economic factors, such as the lack of capital.¹⁵ What is more, Likaka identifies agriculture, which integrates most Congolese into the colonial economy, as a crucial site for the fabrication of stereotypes:

> the agronomists of the territory collected information from the agricultural supervisors [...] and the African chiefs who attentively observed [other] Africans. Each agronomist or administrator interpreted the information obtained from an African chief or agricultural instructor according to his [own] ideology, his class [background] and his conception of society and this mediation often gave rise to clichés.¹⁶

Before moving on to analysing the use of stereotypes in the work of Edmond Leplae (1868–1941), agronomist and director general at the Belgian Ministry of the Colonies, who was described by Likaka as the 'architect of forced cotton cultivation', Likaka insists on the important aspect of mediation in the Belgian colonial administrators' production of clichés, through the projection of their horizon of experience onto the indigenous population.¹⁷ I am taking a lead from Likaka here and argue that this production of clichés can also be considered on a much larger scale: Belgian agriculture – as seen from abroad, by other European imperial powers, such as Britain – allow us to consider colonial clichés about both coloniser and colonised in conjunction. These 'other' imperial perspectives enable us to complicate any easy assumptions and stereotypes about Belgian colonialism such as its 'belatedness' vis-à-vis Europe's 'more established' imperial powers that ignore both earlier colonial ambitions under Leopold I and modernisation efforts that characterised both the Congo Free State and the Belgian Congo.

This chapter suggests how to use these stereotypes to read archival material 'against the grain' to pay attention to the voices of 'hidden' actors, such as Congolese agricultural labourers who opposed directives within the colonial system.¹⁸ I join Benoît Henriet, who, in his work on rural resistance in the interwar Belgian Congo, has emphasised the possibility to highlight 'workers' agency [...] through the strategies implemented by the Europeans to achieve their own goals, be they profit maximisation or territorial control' when studying imperial archival sources.¹⁹

In the second part, I draw more directly from materials on Belgian colonial agriculture produced between the 1930s and 1960. However, its origins, and 'natural' sciences more broadly, reach back further, as some examples from earlier texts show. Marc Poncelet connects the development of colonial sciences in Belgium to the country's struggle for 'legitimacy' to be taken 'seriously' as an imperial power on the world stage but also by its own citizens. This is important for two reasons: first, while there is little doubt that Belgium's status as a 'serious' imperial power was certainly established by the erection of the Congo Free State, Belgian imperial expansionism started significantly earlier, with Leopold I, for example during the short-lived Belgian colonial presence in Santo Tomás de Castilla in Guatemala (1843–54).[20] While the scope of this chapter does not allow for an in-depth analysis of Belgium's early colonial ambitions, it is important to consider the struggle that Poncelet describes as part of a longer development of establishing, maintaining, and promoting an empire with the support of scientific research.

Second, Poncelet identifies what he calls – not unproblematically – a 'brief golden era of colonial science' that he locates loosely in a period stretching from the 1930s until after the end of World War II and that is tied up with the myth of the 'model colony'.[21] He mentions this 'golden age' several times in the introduction to his book on Belgian colonial sciences and eventually locates it 'at the end of the crisis of the 1930s and extended until the end of the Second [World] War'.[22] This is quite surprising given the intensification and, indeed, professionalisation of colonial cadres in the last decades of Belgium's colonial occupation of the Congo and specifically after World War II. This was provided by institutions that had been formed after the end of World War I, particularly in the 1920s and 1930s, such as the Université Coloniale de Belgique (1920),[23] the Institute of Tropical Medicine (1923), as well as the Académie royale des Sciences d'Outre-Mer [Royal Academy of Overseas Sciences] (1928), but also the establishment of research institutions in the Belgian Congo, such as the Institut national pour l'étude agronomique du Congo belge (INEAC) [National Institute for Agronomic Studies of the Belgian Congo] in Yangambi in 1933. In his chapter on the INEAC, Poncelet states that the first organised research missions of the Congo Free State were in the field of botany and that agronomic research tools did not exist prior to 1895.[24] However, according to Poncelet, they develop rapidly, and in 1908, the agricultural services already include 113 engineers and technicians, five veterinarians, and about ten thousand 'collaborateurs africains' [African co-workers].[25] While these numbers still suggest a certain 'belatedness' of Belgium 'catching up' in erecting agriculture as an effective means of colonial exploitation and control, the development of agrarian science appears accelerated in comparison to other European imperial powers, such as Britain.[26] When we consider the last couple of decades of Belgian colonial occupation of the Congo, this view of Belgium 'catching up' is then rendered a lot more complex.

The external acknowledgement of Belgium's 'modern' colonial rule represents a direct consequence of the support of agrarian research and education in the Belgian Congo, spearheaded by the aforementioned Edmond Leplae.[27] Yet, at the same time, this increased investment in agriculture and attempts at augmenting productivity, combined with the well-documented racist policies, led to growing resistance and radicalism in rural areas.[28] While at first glance, these momentary 'slippages' in colonial control might seem insignificant, they can help to uncover the voices of actors erased from the colonial archive. For instance, Henriet shows how studying imperial sources, such as letters written by local administrators, enables us to get a better understanding of the colonial state's inability to control palm-fruit cutters' migratory movements in the largest palm-oil concession during the interwar period and how this allowed the workers to avoid 'administrative surveillance'.[29]

Coming back to Leplae, Poncelet briefly mentions the 'scientific tensions' of the 1920s between him and Emile Auguste de Wildeman (1866–1947), the influential botanist and director of the botanic garden in Brussels.[30] He describes these 'tensions' as rooted in their different approaches to exploiting the colony's natural resources – that of a botanist, who is interested in the cataloguing and categorisation of plants and that of an agronomist, whose primary concern is the maximising of agricultural export profits.[31] While their disagreements are certainly fuelled by their different functions in the colonial system, this chapter problematises the binary ideological opposition between these two figures to arrive at a better understanding of the long-term resonance of their work in the postcolonial period.

Paying attention to Belgium's (self)representation as a 'modern' coloniser makes it possible to better articulate how the centre of power becomes dependent on its 'others' to know itself.[32] Pratt writes:

> While the imperial metropolis tends to understand itself as determining the periphery [...] it habitually blinds itself to the way in which the periphery determines the metropolis – beginning, perhaps, with the latter's obsessive need to present and re-present its peripheries [...] to itself.[33]

In the case of Belgian colonial agriculture, this appears as one of the primary areas that the colonial state weaponises. This is done not only for power and profit but also to represent itself to the nation 'at home' and to the outside world as an 'innovative' imperial force at the forefront of optimistic post-war progress, culminating in the 1958 Brussels World Fair, the first major post-war world fair. Indeed, this more abstract notion of 'modernity' that figures in the Belgian state's self-representation clearly overlaps with the infrastructures, tools, and processes of 'modernisation' deployed by the colonial regime. By focusing on agriculture and the way it is narrated by scientific and political discourses alike,

I highlight its crucial role for the Belgian colonial regime's production of stereotypes and their impact in the post-colonial era.

Indeed, these stereotypes, such as its 'delay' to enter the imperial competition and the ideological caesura in 1908, underpinned Belgium's rule and played an important role for the contested space that the colonial period occupies in Belgian public memory.[34] Re-reading the writings by colonial-era scientists like de Wildeman enables us to better understand the link between violent epistemological and cultural consequences generated by the introduction of 'modern' agriculture and how colonialism generated these specific stereotypes in the field of agriculture – as analysed in Likaka's work. I continue to build on Likaka by arguing that a new 'contact zone' emerges here: there are echoes and traces of Leplae's and de Wildeman's ideologies that can be perceived in the academic works by Poncelet, Lumumba-Kasongo, and Likaka. They speak from different epistemological standpoints, disciplines, institutions, and have different approaches to agriculture, yet their critical engagement with colonial-era scholarship and the dialogue across time they create shows how colonial viewpoints and principles still resonate now in the twenty-first century.

Tensions and Tropes of Empire

Poncelet describes the argument between Emile de Wildeman and Edmond Leplae, whose professional careers began during the 'Free State' era and continued well into the administration of the Belgian Congo, as being rooted in de Wildeman's role as the 'father of Congolese botany' and 'tireless advocate of the development of indigenous cultures on indigenous soil, a *global option* reinforced by the idea of prioritising the maintenance of the vegetation cover'.[35] Poncelet's phrasing here is interesting for several reasons. First, he illustrates two apparently fundamentally different scientific ideologies of the interwar period. Already in 1910, Leplae had become the director general of the agricultural service at the Ministry of the Colonies. According to Jean Lebrun:

> Over the course of the next 23 years, Leplae implements a fruitful policy through which science is used to benefit the economic productivity of the colony. This policy is based on large-scale farming and, from 1917 onwards, on forced crop growing and forced labour of indigenous people.[36]

While the 'forced labour of indigenous people' was not a phenomenon exclusive to the Belgian empire, less than ten years after the end of the Congo Free State, such policies in the name of agricultural 'development' and 'improvement' evoke memories of its abject violence. The Cessation of the CFS in 1908 and its 'conversion' into the Belgian Congo does *not* represent a total caesura in terms of policies and practice and appears rather as a continuation of certain forms of violence under a different guise. The differentiation between the two periods was part of a significant propaganda effort to present the 'Free State' to the international community as an aberration to be then contrasted with the new 'model colony'.[37] For instance, the 'notes of an address at a meeting of the Royal African Society' of Maurice Lippens, former governor general of the Belgian Congo, state that '[s]ince 1908, that is in 30 years, we may boast of having abolished the most barbaric customs of the country [the Congo], entirely pacified it, and put a curb to the epidemics which reigned there'.[38] Interestingly, Lippens immediately ties his praises of Belgian colonialism to presumed successes in medical sciences. It is important to carefully nuance these continuities and to be precise of where certain forms of violence prevailed in agriculture and where they did not (or to a lesser degree). For instance, the small-scale introduction of the 'paysannat indigène',[39] and the full application of the scheme in the 1940s and 1950s is assessed by Reuben Loffman as representing a significant improvement of 'peasant household income', while also having 'substantial downsides'.[40] And while there is a hiatus in rubber production after the official end of the Congo Free State and a 'less brutal' return after World War I, the introduction of the violent system of forced cotton cultivation has had a long-term impact on Congolese farming that still continues today: Sara Lowes and Eduardo Montero show how the use of violence and forced labour, and the appropriation of local systems of governance within the CFS's rubber concession economy, still cause wealth inequality and stifled physical development among present-day inhabitants of historical concession areas.[41]

Coming back to Lebrun, he highlights here the colonial state's instrumentalisation of science in service of maximising the colony's profits through the deliberate exploitation of human workforce and unfree labour as key to Leplae's 'modernization' of the agricultural service.[42] Sven van Melkebeke has identified 'agronomical science and coerced labor […] [as] entangled dimensions' of cotton cultivation in the Belgian Congo.[43] Contrary to Leplae's position, de Wildeman opposes the introduction of European crops and methods of farming, as well as, more generally, the clearing of the soil for (European) cultivation purposes.

Second, while Poncelet does not define what he means by his rather opaque notion of a 'global option', especially in connection to the 'developing indigenous cultures on indigenous soil' – which might have been a universally applicable option, even favoured by colonial administrations across the globe – this invites further questioning of de Wildeman's approaches. They represent a divergent insight into the colonial state's employment of different fields of science in the Congo more broadly, rather than simply a quarrel between two researchers in two different disciplines.

This does not mean, however, that de Wildeman did not have a strong interest in agriculture: in 1908, two years before Leplae would become the director general of the Ministry of the Colonies' Agricultural Service, de Wildeman published a new version of his 1902 *Les Plantes tropicales de grande culture* [Tropical Agricultural Crops], aimed at agronomists and Belgian settlers in the Congo. The title is reminiscent of the French agricultural botanist Henry Lévêque de Vilmorin's 1892 work *Les Plantes de grande culture: céréales, plantes fourragères, industrielles et économiques* [Agricultural Crops: Grains, Fodder, Industrial and Economic Crops]. De Vilmorin is well known for his contributions to research into the 'modernisation' (i.e. the modification) of wheat through breeding to 'enhance' its qualities for a rapidly growing population during the Industrial Revolution. It is no coincidence, then, that de Wildeman describes the purpose of his book in much the same utilitarian terms:

> We can only hope for industrial development, especially in the tropics, after a long agricultural period. The mere exploitation of plant wealth is not sufficient, as is unfortunately too often believed, to bring about the lasting prosperity of a colony. If, for centuries, the native plants of a country have been abundantly sufficient for the needs of its inhabitants, they will not be able to satisfy for a long time an intensive export trade, unless, by artificial means, by cultivation, we do manage to increase and especially to regularise the output.[44]

With his opposition to the introduction of non-native plants or other non-sustainable forms of farming, de Wildeman might at first glance appear as an advocate of 'modern' agricultural sustainability *avant la lettre* and it is important to note that he will later move away again from this stance favouring industrial development in the Congo.[45] However, what becomes clear when looking at his writing published before the end of the CFS is that his earlier view of agriculture's function for the colonial system is quite similar to Leplae's. While his scholarly approach might differ, botany and agronomy are not depicted as rivalling disciplines; he simply describes 'tropical agronomy' and 'colonial botany' as 'new and difficult fields'.[46] De Wildeman presents agriculture as an instrument of the colonial 'modernisation' effort, the aim of which is the European-style industrialisation and exploitation of natural resources and human labour for exclusively European gain. He, too, advocates a dismissal of indigenous epistemologies and practices, because he does not consider them to be 'scientific', which is also why he opposes the 'mere exploitation of plant wealth' and promotes 'cultivation'. He thus considers European science a necessary accelerator for the introduction of the Congo into global trade as part of the Belgian colonial project of 'modernity', a perspective very much in line with Leplae's policies and rooted in evolutionism and its particular vision of 'history'. According to Anthony Giddens, evolutionism's view of history 'can be told in terms of a "story line" which imposes an orderly picture upon the jumble of human happenings' and considers 'the emergence of modern societies in the West' as a logical conclusion of the development from 'isolated cultures of hunters and gatherers […] to the formation of agrarian states'.[47] This 'totalising' vision of history also implies the impossibility of coexisting different 'histories'.[48] Giddens's take on evolutionist history also connects with Dipesh Chakrabaty's analysis of Western historical narratives, who pointedly notes that

> Crudely, one might say that it was one important form that the ideology of progress or 'development' took from the nineteenth century on. Historicism is what made modernity or capitalism look not simply global but rather as something that became global over time, by originating in one place (Europe) and then spreading outside of it. […] Historicism thus posited historical time as a measure of cultural distance (at least in institutional development) that was assumed to exist between the West and the non-West.[49]

The absence of anything other than the 'master narrative' and the '"first in Europe, then elsewhere" structure of global historical time' that Chakrabarty describes, then resonate strongly with colonialism's 'civilizing mission' and the relegation of the colonised (and their histories) to a place 'outside' of time.[50] Coming back to Poncelet's passage mentioned above, it draws attention to a commonly employed stereotype in the historiography about Belgian colonialism's presumed 'belatedness' and that Poncelet himself employs: '[t]his social history of colonial knowledge in Belgium is a very localised exercise regarding the *belated and limited fate of a small country*'.[51] This cliché, an oversimplified shorthand, is rooted in Belgium's comparatively brief colonial presence in Africa. I argue, however, that this perspective of Belgium 'catching up' with other European powers is falsely limited. It does not account for the specific history of Belgian colonial (agricultural) ideologies of 'improvement' and 'development' against the backdrop of the CFS and its reckless exploitation of human life, labour, and natural resources. It thus ignores the fact that the Belgian Congo did not emerge out of a vacuum but a longer process of 'modernisation' that had started decades earlier during the 'Congo Free State' period and which resulted in the 'nervous state' diagnosed by Nancy Rose Hunt in her landmark study, which carefully unpacks the afterlives of Free State violence in the Belgian Congo, resulting in a coexistence of 'modern' medical infrastructures and punitive colonial state.[52] Moreover, this perspective also obscures the long-term impact of these ideologies. For example, de Wildeman's belief in the linear development from 'pastoral' farming to industrialised agriculture that partakes in global capitalism with the aid of scientifically 'enhanced' cash crops still resonates within a broad variety of contemporary discourses. As Robert Young wrote in 1991 on 'neocolonialism':

> The means of administration may have often moved from coercive regiments to regimes supported by international aid and the banking system, the 'white man's burden' may have been transformed by the wind of change into the TV appeal for famine in Africa. But the burden of neocolonialism remains for all those who suffer its effects; and responsibility cannot be ignored by those who find themselves part of those societies which enforce it.[53]

Young's framing of post-Cold War neocolonial practices mentioning the 'TV appeal for famine in Africa', implying agricultural shortcomings, such as crop failure, is of particular importance here, as it refers to the exploitative marketing of Western charity organisations that regularly depict malnourished Africans as having no agency. Beyond representation as well, there is little reckoning with the West's role in many postcolonial armed conflicts on the African continent – such as the precarious situation of the ethnic minority of Batwa following the expulsion from their ancestral lands in Virunga National Park in 1952 – as well as the calamitous impact on climate change that European industrialisation and colonialism have had (see Matthias De Groof's chapter in this volume).[54] What Elizabeth Fortin calls the 'globalization of agriculture', the 'increasing technological industrialization of food production with the growing integration of international, or global, production structures' is a direct product of colonialism and shaped by 'interventions', such as the policies of the World Bank.[55]

At the same time, this transnational perspective that is required to understand present-day agricultural globalisation is, in turn, already necessary to deal adequately with colonial legacies and to grasp Europe's shared complicity in colonialism in Africa and its long-term political, social, and environmental impact. Moving beyond the centre–periphery binary and applying a 'transcolonial' perspective, to employ Olivia Harrison's use of the term, opens up broader contexts, which have received relatively little academic attention so far.[56] Transcolonial practices of agriculture can thus be considered a multilayered contact zone: between different colonial empires and scientists, between coloniser and colonised, between different epistemologies and practices, between different ideologies of colonialism, between colonial state and citizens 'at home' and narratives of benevolent and technical 'improvement'. It is through these transcolonial contact zones that we can better comprehend the resonances of ideologies like de Wildeman's and Leplae's in the continuing exploitation of the Congo by multinational corporations, unethical academic research and 'charity' work, and international policymaking.

'Sustainable' Stereotypes

As initially mentioned, to improve our understanding of Belgian colonialism's ideologies and stereotypes, such the ones discussed here, its perceived 'belatedness' or the myth of the 'model colony', its transcolonial intersections, and afterlives in the postcolonial era, this second part turns our attention to developments in the last three decades of Belgian occupation. Leplae's lasting impact on the final phase of Belgian colonial agriculture is marked by the inauguration of the INEAC. INEAC itself consisted of a number of different research divisions, which, in turn, maintained several research centres. For instance, by 1955, the Division Forestière included seven separate research centres and employed, according to the visiting British ecologist H. C. Dawkins of the Uganda Forest Department, '100 to 150 indigenous workers of all grades'.[57] The institute played a central role not only for Belgian agricultural research activities, but was also of international significance: for instance, a Semaine Agricole [Agricultural Week] was held here (1947), which brought together scientists from all over colonial Sub-Saharan Africa.[58] Just a year later, a follow-up event, the Conference Africaine des Sols [African Soil Conference] was held in Goma in eastern Congo. It was attended by 150 participants from Belgium, Portugal, the United Kingdom, and what was then Rhodesia, the Union Française, and the South African Union. The institute thus became an important international hub of knowledge exchange and gained a favourable reputation abroad, further highlighting the need for transcolonial approaches. This is apparent, for instance, in a 1950 article on 'The Agricultural Development of the Belgian Congo' in *The World Today*, the magazine published by the Royal Institute of International Affairs (today better known as Chatham House):

> An international meeting of comparable interest was the 'Semaine Coloniale', held in 1949 at the Université Coloniale de Belgique at Antwerp, which enabled visitors to see for themselves the strong current of interest in colonial affairs in the motherland, reflected in the very thorough training given to recruits for the Colonial Service at this institution.[59]

This article, providing a British perspective on the period of most intensely practised agriculture in the Congo, offers some interesting insights into agriculture's role for the Belgian colonial project in its 'last phase', but also as a 'concern' about what there is to come. First, this is reflected by mentioning the rising interest among the general population in Belgium in the colonial territories overseas – a point that is also frequently being made in more recent historiographies.[60] The article goes even further by explicitly tying this cliché of the Belgian populations' perceived 'disinterest' in their country's colonial endeavour to a development in understanding Belgium as a 'national' coloniser:

> Right up to the recent war the Belgian public at home remained in the mass apathetic about their colonial possession; but since the war there has been a tremendous revival of interest, apparent in many directions, not least in the sphere of agricultural research and development.[61]

The remits of this chapter do not allow for a discussion of the development that led to the Belgian population's rising interest in its 'empire' after World War II, including an analysis of propaganda, exhibitions, and school curricula. However, the increased investment into scientific research and practice, initiated by Leplae's policies, which forms part of this larger propaganda endeavour of representing the colonial project to both 'home' and international audiences, can certainly be considered a factor for this intensified interest.[62] This is the case as late as 1958, at the World Fair in Brussels, which has become notorious as a late example of featuring a so-called human zoo.[63] Matthew Stanard notes, quoting from the fair's catalogue, that '[t]he creators of the agriculture pavilion drew a contrast between the "condition of the primitive native" and his ancestral tools and utensils displayed under glass and the Belgian activities which had "brought Congolese agriculture to its current state of development"'.[64] From de Wildeman's 'tropical crops' to the 'Expo 58', this imperial logic of agricultural 'modernity' pervades the Belgian Congo throughout its fifty-two years of existence.

Interestingly, the *World Today* article also employs the stereotype of Belgium's 'belatedness' amid the more 'advanced' imperial nations of Europe. It criticises the Belgian colonial state overall as an outdated, top-down administrative structure:[65]

> While it is quite typical of their [Belgian] system that coffee-planting has been enforced by administrative order rather than encouraged by agricultural extension services, it must be remembered that similar methods were quite frankly employed in developing early exports in several British territories when at a similar stage of development.[66]

At the same time, this common cliché of Belgian 'belatedness' in the article is somewhat countered when it identifies Belgian agricultural *science* as advanced in comparison to other colonial empires' endeavours in the same field:

> The Dutch, formerly the most painstaking of tropical agricultural scientists, have seen their technical activities in Indonesia sadly curtailed by political events; but their mantle seems to have fallen in no small measure upon their neighbours the Belgians. It is with surprise and envy that visiting British agriculturists, used only to tiny staffs for research work, find, as at Yangambi, an experimental station staffed by over a hundred university graduates of first-class calibre.[67]

Finally, the article offers a brief glimpse into how a focus on indigenous agricultural practices and property relations can function as a way to read archival material 'against the grain' – as a way of working towards a decolonial methodology that recovers, reassesses, and amplifies the voices and agency of those not included in the Western archive. Nathan Sowry suggests that '[t]his practice of reading archival records against the grain has a large impact on archival practice as well, as it enables archivists and users to re-think and re-interpret the documents in their care'.[68] While Sowry invites a renewed assessment of the presentation (and contextualisation) of archival materials, I suggest that this method not only requires institutions once celebrating the 'achievements' of empire to do the same, but also that assuming a transcolonial perspective aides to uncover the 'slippages' of colonial rhetoric and control. The *World Today* article describes the introduction of 'corridor settlements' by the Belgians as method of growing crops. On the one hand, the author notes that

> [t]he system has been claimed to combine ingeniously the advantages of collective farming with those of individual tenure; certainly it is of the greatest interest to British administrators experimenting with various forms of "group farming" to find the method best suited to African conditions

and that '[s]uch advantages appeal to the Belgians, who in some parts of the Congo have long grouped the cultivators compulsorily in villages for administrative reasons'.[69] On the other hand, however, the author states that tensions in implementing this new policy have arisen due to, for example, '[…] the problem as whether a bachelor should be given the same sized holding as a man with two wives'.[70] It is useful to engage with Likaka's work again at this point; he demonstrates how these moments of rural resistance, which he analyses within the context of cotton cultivation, can also function as a resource for the administration's 'fabrication' of clichés about the indigenous population.⁷¹ In particular, he mentions Leplae's involvement and demonstrates how the latter employed stereotypes to facilitate control and the production and distribution of propaganda materials via the *Bulletin Agricole du Congo belge*.⁷² Likaka traces the evolution of Leplae's stereotypes and how they change according to the latter's agenda. For instance, Likaka quotes Leplae as describing Africans as 'indigenous farmers endowed with sufficient qualities [...] and capable of relatively rapid development' in front of a budgetary commission in 1914,⁷³ while the reduced purchasing power and growing resistance following the Great Depression in 1929 prompt him to use a very different vocabulary and paints them as 'incapable' and that 'the authorities have to think in their place'.⁷⁴

The agricultural contact zone thus emerges as a space of 'myth making', from which various clichés emerge, both racist and harmful when targeting the indigenous population or to aggrandise the colonial state and its 'achievements' in an attempt to fashion the Belgian colonial project as an ostensibly 'modern' one. In the case of Belgian colonialism, that is the persistent stereotype of the 'model colony'. Agriculture, as a means of control, provided the Belgian colonial administration with a large repository of imaginaries of 'modernity', an asymmetrical space where ideologies and epistemologies converged, with usually brutal consequences for the Congolese farmers and labourers. However, as Likaka reminds us, agriculture and land issues also represent key issues and opportunities for (anti-colonial) resistance. It is here that the colonial state had to concede to local legislation, such as the division of cultivable land to avoid social conflict, and change its policies resulting from what the *World Today* article describes as 'the problem as whether a bachelor should be given the same sized holding as a man with two wives'. From decolonial resistance to contemporary rural activism and locally founded NGOs focusing on land rights and refugees in the DRC, such as Solidarité des Volontaires pour l'Humanité in the South Kivu region, a genealogy of defiance emerges, which warrants further research to continue troubling the colonial archive. In this way, a focus on 'reading against the grain' also helps challenge what Hunt has described as the

> reduction of Congo's history in public memory [...] [that] suggests a single trajectory with two hinges: first 'red rubber,' then Lumumba's assassination (now often extended by a third point: terrible rape and war in Congo's east since 1996). Such a storyline of continuity and repetition has history moving from violence to violence, malfeasance to malfeasance.⁷⁵

Moving away from a focus on 'the horror, the horror' and instead towards these genealogies of defiance that testify to the importance of understanding resistance as a constant across the colonial and postcolonial periods – and not just reduced to those moments that have received academic attention thus far. Instead, paying attention to those 'slippages' in control and sovereignty challenge received understandings in existing historiography of Belgium's colonial occupation of Central Africa.

Conclusion

Focusing on Belgian colonial agriculture and agrarian science, its practices, scholarship, and evaluation from afar (both from imperial contemporaries and from the vantage point of the late twentieth- and early twenty-first century) invites us to revisit and to question repetitive stereotypes of Belgian imperialism and its legacies after 1960. For instance, the cliché of Belgian 'catching up' in erecting a 'modern' colonial empire like other European imperial powers is challenged by the Belgian state's support for agrarian research and research activity in the Belgian Congo (and which is recognised from abroad), as the analysis *The World Today* article has shown, while forced cotton cultivation and the mixed results of the 'indigenous peasantry scheme' raise questions about the received idea of the Belgian Congo as 'model colony' and further reinforces Hunt's work on the 'afterlives' of Free State violence.[76] Most importantly and pressingly, however, as Osumaka Likaka's path-breaking work has shown, research in critical cultural and historical studies into agriculture and agrarian science (and by extension into any other area of colonialism) needs to focus on those voices left out of the official colonial archive. For instance, as I suggest, by engaging with the already developed method of reading sources 'against the grain' to uncover moments of resistance and rebellion for which agriculture has emerged as a primary site. Focusing on the 'culture' in 'agriculture', what emerges is also its long-term (and multifaceted) impact on present-day diasporic Belgium: from contemporary armed conflict and grassroots activism for land rights to Belgium's ban on halal and kosher slaughtering practices that disproportionately impacts the country's postcolonial and diasporic communities. Discourses like these show how important a focus on colonial agriculture is, even for life in the ex-imperial metropolis of the twenty-first century.

Notes

1. Edward Said, *Culture and Imperialism* (London: Vintage, 1994), p. 271.
2. Achille Mbembe, 'Necropolitics', trans. by Libby Meintjes, *Public Culture*, 15.1 (2003): pp. 11–40 (pp. 25–26).
3. Tukumbi Lumumba-Kasongo, 'Land Reforms in the Democratic Republic of Congo (DRC): A Study of the Political Economy of Underdevelopment and Nation-State Building', in Tukumbi Lumumba-Kasongo (ed.), *Land Reforms and Natural Resource Conflicts in Africa: New Development Paradigms in the Era of Global Liberalization* (New York: Routledge, 2015), pp. 150–79 (p. 170).
4. Ibid.
5. Ibid.
6. Tukumbi Lumumba-Kasongo, 'Land Reforms in the Democratic Republic of Congo (DRC)', p. 156. See also for example Georges Nzongola-Ntalaja, *From Zaire to the Democratic Republic of the Congo* (Uppsala: The Nordic Africa Institute, 1999) and *The Congo from Leopold to Kabila: A People's History* (London: Zed Books, 2002); Frank van Acker, 'Where Did All the Land Go? Enclosure and Social Struggle in Kivu (D.R. Congo)', *Review of African Political Economy* 32.103 (2005), 79–98.
7. Importantly, Lumumba-Kasongo points out that '[p]hilosophically, there are no essential differences between the administration of the Congo Free State and that of the Belgian colony with regard to how the land was conceived and how the land policy was formulated. The land practice used by Leopold II was also adopted into the colonial dogmas' (p. 169).
8. Namely: Anthony Giddens, *The Consequences of Modernity* (Cambridge: Polity Press, 1990).
9. See P.-P. Fraiture, 'Modernity and the Belgian Congo', *Tydskrif vir Letterkunde*, 46.1 (2009), 43–57 (43).
10. Koen Vlassenroot and Chris Huggins, 'Land, Migration and Conflict in Eastern D.R. Congo', in Chris Huggins and Jenny Clover (eds.), *From the Ground up: Land Rights, Conflict and Peace in Sub-Saharan Africa* (Pretoria: Institute for Security Studies, 2004), pp. 115–94 (p. 116).
11. See, in particular, Jan Vansina, *Antecedents to Modern Rwanda: The Nyiginya Kingdom*, trans. by Jan Vansina (Madison: University of Wisconsin Press, 2004), p. 138 and Timothy Longman, 'Identity Cards, Ethnic Self-Perception, and Genocide in Rwanda', in Jane Caplan and John Torpey (eds.), *Documenting Individual Identity: The Development of State Practices in the Modern World* (Princeton: Princeton University Press, 2002), pp. 345–57 (p. 351).
12. See O. Likaka, 'Colonialisme et clichés sociaux au Congo Belge', *Africa: Rivista trimestrale di studi e documentazione dell'Istituto italiano per l'Africa e l'Oriente*, 52.1 (1997), 1–27 (2–3).
13. Mary Louise Pratt, *Imperial Eyes: Travel Writing and Transculturation* (London: Routledge, 1992), p. 7.
14. See Likaka, 'Colonialisme...', p. 1.
15. Ibid., p. 3.
16. Ibid., p. 8; my translation. All translations are mine unless otherwise stated.
17. Osumaka Likaka, *Rural Society and Cotton in Colonial Zaire* (Madison: The University of Wisconsin Press, 1997), p. 61.
18. See, for instance, Osumaka Likaka, 'Rural Protest: The Mbole against Belgian Rule, 1897–1959', *The International Journal of African Historical Studies*, 27.3 (1994), pp. 589–617; Benoît Henriet, '"Elusive Natives": Escaping Colonial Control in the Leverville Oil Palm Concession, Belgian Congo, 1923 –1941', *Canadian Journal of African Studies / Revue canadienne des études africaines*, 49.2 (2015): pp. 339–61; Benoît Henriet, *Colonial Impotence: Virtue and Violence in a Congolese Concession (1911–1940)* (Berlin: De Gruyter, 2021).
19. Henriet, '"Elusive Natives"...' (2015), p. 340. Due to the constraints imposed on producing this chapter by the ongoing Covid-19 pandemic and the resulting restricted access to archives and fieldwork, examples of applying this method are limited but hopefully demonstrate its importance for future research.
20. The critical analysis of Leopold I's colonial ambitions remains an under-researched area. See, for example: Jan Anckaer, *Small Power Diplomacy and Commerce: Belgium and the Ottoman Empire during the Reign of Leopold I (1831–1865)* (Istanbul: The Isis Press, 2013); Robert R. Ansiaux, 'Early Belgian Colonial Efforts: The Long and Fateful Shadow of Leopold I' (doctoral thesis, University of Texas, Arlington, 2007) <https://rc.library.uta.edu/uta-ir/handle/10106/382> [accessed 12 August 2021]; André Lederer, 'La colonie belge au Guatemala', *Collectanea Maritima*, 6 (1968), pp. 243–59; n.a., *Expansion Belge/Belgische Expansie 1831–1865* (Brussels: Académie Royale des Sciences d'Outre-Mer/Koninklijke Academie voor Overzeese Wetenschappen, 1965); Albert Duchesne, *A la recherche d'une Colonie belge: Le Consul Blondeel en Abyssinie (1840–1842) – Contribution à l'Histoire précoloniale de la Bel-*

gique (Brussels: Institut Royal Colonial Belge, 1953).
21. See Marc Poncelet, *L'Invention des sciences coloniales belges* (Paris: Karthala, 2008), p. 17.
22. Ibid., p. 18.
23. Renamed the *Institut universitaire des territoires d'outre-mer* (INUTOM) [University Institute for Overseas Territories] in 1949.
24. See Poncelet, p. 312.
25. See Ibid.
26. Ibid. p. 2–3.
27. Osumaka Likaka, *Rural Society and Cotton in Colonial Zaire* (Madison: The University of Wisconsin Press, 1997), p. 61.
28. Ibid., p. 56, and Osumaka Likaka, 'Colonialisme…'.
29. See Henriet, '"Elusive Natives"…', p. 340.
30. See Poncelet, p. 312.
31. Ibid.
32. See Pratt, *Imperial Eyes*, p. 7.
33. Ibid., p. 6.
34. See, for instance, Goddeeris, 'Postcolonial Belgium: The Memory of the Congo'; Matthew Stanard, *Selling the Congo: A History of European Pro-Empire Propaganda and the Making of Belgian Imperialism* (Lincoln: University of Nebraska Press, 2011); Sarah Arens, 'Memory in Crisis: Commemoration, Visual Cultures and (Mis)representation in Postcolonial Belgium', *Modern Languages Open* 1 (2020): n.p. <http://doi.org/10.3828/mlo.v0i0.328> [accessed 20 May 2021].
35. Poncelet, p. 312; my emphasis.
36. Jean Lebrun, 'Leplae (Edmond)', in *Biographie Nationale*, 1967–68, Vol 34, col. 565–71. Forced labour was briefly banned and then quickly re-introduced in the Colonial Charter; on this issue, see Julia Seibert, 'Travail forcé', in Idesbald Goddeeris, Amandine Lauro and Guy Vanthemsche (eds.), *Le Congo Colonial: Une histoire en questions* (Waterloo: Renaissance du Livre, 2020), pp. 141–54 (p. 143).
37. See, for instance, Matthew Stanard on the effort made at the 1910 World Fair to distance the Belgian Congo 'from its EIC forebear' (Stanard, *Selling the Congo*, p. 52).
38. Count Lippens, G.C.V.O., 'The Belgian Congo', *African Affairs*, XXXVIII.CLIII (1939), 419–26 <https://doi.org/10.1093/oxfordjournals.afraf.a101237> [accessed 20 May 2021].
39. The 'indigenous peasantry scheme' was developed following Crown Prince Leopold's study visit of the Congo in 1933, which aimed to improve the economic position of impoverished families or clans. Piet Clement assesses that, '[o]n paper, it looked as if the indigenous peasantry scheme would offer the Congolese rural population, for the first time since the onset of colonization, the freedom to adopt a government-sponsored agricultural system that would allow it to improve its relative income position on a permanent basis' (Piet Clement, 'Rural Development in the Belgian Congo: The Late-colonial "Indigenous Peasantry" Programme and its Implementation in the Equateur District (1950s)', *Bulletin des Séances de l'Académie Royale des Sciences d'Outre-mer*, 60.2 (2014), 251–86 (259)). Interestingly, Clement highlights that '[f]or the colonial administration the project was also a matter of prestige, as it was meant to demonstrate to the Congolese and to external observers such as the United Nations that rural development was being taken seriously' (ibid., 265).
40. Reuben Loffman, *Church, State and Colonialism in Southeastern Congo, 1890–1962* (London: Palgrave Macmillan, 2019), p. 208.
41. Sara Lowes and Eduardo Montero, 'Concessions, Violence, and Indirect Rule: Evidence from the Congo Free State', *National Bureau of Economic Research – Working Paper 27893* <https://www.nber.org/papers/w27893> [accessed 1 August 2021].
42. Likaka points to the fact that Leplae was indeed very well aware of the human cost of exploitation (see Likaka, *Rural Society*, p. 19).
43. Sven van Melkebeke, 'Science as the Handmaiden of Coerced Labor: The Implementation of Cotton Cultivation Schemes in the Eastern Congo Uele Region, 1920–1960', in Johan Heinsen, Martin Bak Jørgensen and Martin Ottovay Jørgensen (eds.), *Coercive Geographies: Historicizing Mobility, Labor and Confinement* (Leiden: Brill, 2020): pp. 169–91 (p. 169).
44. Emile de Wildeman, *Les Plantes tropicales de grande culture* (Brussels: Maison d'édition Alfred Castaigne, 1908), p. v.
45. See Poncelet, p. 312–13.
46. De Wildeman, *Les Plantes*, p. vi.
47. Giddens, *The Consequences of Modernity*, p. 5.
48. Ibid.
49. Dipesh Chakrabaty, *Provincializing Europe: Postcolonial Thought and Historical Difference* (Princeton: Princeton University Press, 2000), p. 7.
50. Ibid., p. 7–8.
51. Poncelet, p. 14; emphasis added. For a substantial overview on the historiography of Belgian colonialism, see Guy Vanthemsche, *Belgium and the Congo, 1885–1980*, trans. Alice Cameron and Stephen Windross (Cambridge: Cambridge University Press, 2012). See also: Matthew G. Stanard, *The Leopard, the Lion, and the Cock: Colonial Memories and Monuments in Belgium* (Leuven: Leuven University Press, 2019).
52. Very much in the sense of Nancy Rose Hunt's 'nervous state', the long-term effects and after-

lives of the Congo Free State in the Belgian Congo, see Nancy Rose Hunt, *A Nervous State: Violence, Remedies, and Reverie in Colonial Congo* (Durham, NC: Duke University Press, 2016).

53. Robert Young, 'Neocolonial Times', *The Oxford Literary Review*, 13.1 (1991), 2-3 (p. 2).

54. See n.a., 'New Law in DRC to finally protect Indigenous Peoples Land Rights', *International Land Coalition* <https://africa.landcoalition.org/en/newsroom/new-law-drc-finally-protect-indigenous-peoples-land-rights> [accessed 10 August 2021]. See also, for instance, Mark Langan, *Neo-Colonialism and the Poverty of 'Development' in Africa* (London: Palgrave, 2018); Meera Sabaratnam, *Decolonising Intervention: International Statebuilding in Mozambique* (London: Rowman & Littlefield, 2017); Eyal Weizman and Sheik Fazal, *The Conflict Shoreline: Colonialism as Climate Change* (Göttingen: Steidl, 2015); Jason C. Young, 'Environmental Colonialism, Digital Indigeneity, and the Politicization of Resilience, *Environment and Planning E: Nature and Space*, 4.2 (2019), pp. 230-51; Phoebe Okowa, 'The Pitfalls of Unilateral Legislation in International Law: Lessons from Conflict Minerals Legislation', *International and Comparative Law Quarterly*, 69 (2020), 685-717.

55. See Elizabeth Fortin, 'Reforming Land Rights: The World Bank and the Globalization of Agriculture', *Social & Legal Studies*, 14.2 (2005), 147-77 (149).

56. Olivia Harrison, *Transcolonial Maghreb: Imagining Palestine in the Era of Decolonization* (Stanford: Stanford University Press, 2015), p. 2. I have made the argument for a broader perspective before, see Sarah Arens, 'Memory in Crisis…'.

57. See H.C. Dawkins, 'INEAC in the "Forêt Dense", Impressions of some High-Forest Research in the Congo', *Empire Forestry Review*, 34.1 (1955), 55-60 (56). See also J. Sémal, 'Camille DONIS', *Bulletin des Séances - Académie Royale des Sciences d'Outre-Mer/Mededelingen der Zittingen - Koninklijke Academie voor Overzeese Wetenschappen - Jaarboek - 1990 - Annuaire*, 36.1 (1990), 57-60.

58. *Comptes rendus de la Semaine Agricole 1947: Yangambi, Congo* (Brussels: Institut national pour l'étude agronomique du Congo belge, 1947).

59. G.M.B., 'The Agricultural Development of the Belgian Congo', *The World Today*, 6.8 (1950), 348-54 (354).

60. See, for example, Vanthemsche (2012) and Stanard (2019), who both demonstrate the long-lasting effect Belgium's colonial activities have had on Belgium itself, socially, politically, economically, and culturally.

61. G.M.B., p. 348.

62. This, together with Leplae's notoriety in Britain is also echoed by Leplae's obituary in *Nature*: see E.J. Russell, 'Prof. Edmond Leplae', *Nature* 147 (1941), 738-39.

63. See, for instance, Pascal Blanchard and Maarten Couttenier, 'Les Zoos humains', *Nouvelles Études Francophones*, 32.1 (2017), 109-15; Pascal Blanchard et al, *Human Zoos: Science and Spectacle in the Age of Colonial Empires* (Liverpool: Liverpool University Press, 2008); Sarah van Beurden, '"Un panorama de nos valeurs africaines": Belgisch Congo op Expo 58', in Bambi Ceuppens, Vincent Viane, and David Van Reybrouck (eds.), *Congo in België. Koloniale cultuur in de metropool* (Leuven: Leuven University Press, 2009), pp. 299-311. Another notorious example of or at least very closely reminiscent of a 'human zoo' took place in Yvoir, Belgium, in 2002.

64. Matthew G. Stanard, '"Bilan du monde pour un monde plus déshumanisé": The 1958 Brussels World's Fair and Belgian Perceptions of the Congo', *European History Quarterly*, 35.2 (2005), 267-98 (274).

65. See G.M.B., p. 349; however, not without referring to the inhabitants of the Congo area as 'a very primitive population whose development over large areas is behind that of most of the rest of the continent' (ibid.).

66. Ibid., p. 350.

67. Ibid., p. 348.

68. Nathan Sowry, 'Silence, Accessibility, and Reading Against the Grain: Examining Voices of the Marginalized in the India Office Records, *InterActions: UCLA Journal of Education and Information Studies*, 8.2 (2012) <http://dx.doi.org/10.5070/D482011848> [accessed 14 August 2021].

69. Ibid., p. 350.

70. Ibid., p. 354.

71. See Likaka, *Rural Society*.

72. See Likaka, 'Colonialisme', pp. 8-9.

73. Edmond Leplae, *Documents relatifs à l'agriculture du Congo Belge: L'agriculture coloniale dans la discussion du budget du Congo Belge pour 1914; Le programme colonial agricole de l'institut Solvay* (Louvain: F. Ceutrick, 1914), n.p., qtd. in Likaka, 'Colonialisme', p. 8.

74. Edmond Leplae, 'Les cultures obligatoires dans les pays d'agriculture arriérée', *Bulletin agricole du Congo Belge*, 4 (1929): p. 458, qtd. in Likaka, 'Colonialisme', p. 9.

75. Hunt, p. 3.

76. See Hunt, p. 3.

The Legacy of Alexis Kagame
Responses to Conceptions of Colonisation and Evangelisation in Rwanda

Chantal Gishoma

Among the Rwandan authors of the colonial and post-colonial periods, one author, Alexis Kagame (1912–1981), seems to stand out as central, even essential. His name represents the entire history of a scientific, literary, and cultural movement in Rwanda since the Belgian colonial period when he became a priest and was thus subjected to the norms and rules of the Belgian clergy.

In Europe, streets often bear the names of great personalities. This living archive is inscribed throughout cities and districts as a testimony of the legacy for the inhabitants whose conception of history is mediated through great artists, politicians, and writers. The identity of the place is merged with the actions of men and women who have marked their history, as Matthew Stanard has shown in a book on colonial memory.[1] Likewise, it is inconceivable to think or speak of Rwanda without speaking of Alexis Kagame. Even so, no building, neighbourhood or street has been named after him despite the central place he occupies in our understanding of his native country, not only in Rwanda but also Africa as a whole and Belgium.

The present chapter intends to look back at this complex, hard-to-pin-down character and to analyse his response to the colonial enterprise through his intellectual production. This provides an opportunity for us to better understand the Belgian colonial ideology (1916–62) in Rwanda as well as the political and cultural shifts that occurred during the post-colonial era to the present day, a period fundamentally reshaped by the 1994 genocide against the Tutsi.

What does the immense work of this author, who grew up and worked while Rwanda was under Belgian rule, a system which purported the inability of the colonised to either think for themselves or govern themselves,[2] signify for us today? How did he react against this colonial framework that sought to overturn ancient habits and customs, introduce new practices designed to establish a modern administration, and teach a new wisdom substantiated by the Christian religion? What strategies did he adopt to counter this situation?

Alexis Kagame's response to the Belgian colonial system will be divided into three parts, including the revalorisation of Rwanda's cultural models by reappropriation of cultural riches obscured or poorly explained by Europeans, and the examination of some of Kagame's little-known works on Rwandan culture produced to alleviate the shocks and sudden changes engendered by colonialism. But first, it is essential to broach the context in which this author emerged.

Alexis Kagame's Era and the Birth of His Consciousness

The arrival of the colonisers and missionaries in Rwanda brought about many changes on different levels and their respective actions were consistently complementary.[3] It was in a rapidly changing society that young Kagame evolved and worked. Catholic missionaries taught him how to read and write before entering the minor seminary in 1928, then the major seminary of Kabgayi in 1933. During this period, the evangelising mission,[4] which had begun under the German colonisation in the years 1887–1915, continued successfully in the Belgian period.[5] These two opposing forces continued to infuse changes that were to lead, as Kagame observes in a eulogy to this new modernity,[6] to profound 'economic, social, political and artistic changes'.[7]

Father de Decker, rector of the major seminary, who had noticed this societal transformation and cultural revolution, oriented the studies of the seminarians towards research on the traditional riches of Rwanda. Every year, he organised cultural evenings during which the seminarians presented the fruits of their investigations before the guest of honour, the king of Rwanda, Mutara III Rudahigwa. During one of these events, Alexis Kagame recited poems so eloquently that the king was impressed by this young man unknown by the aristocrats and the families of the royal court poets. He summoned him and asked him where the poems came from; Kagame replied that he had learned them from Sekarama,[8] and hearing this, Mutara III Rudahigwa promised to send him more and better ones. Henceforth, his research career began with the collection and study of the oral heritage of Rwandan culture and history: 'stories, tales, panegyric texts and genealogical stories of dynastic poetry'.[9] From then onwards, the bards continued to come in droves, but he 'became the first Rwandan intellectual, without doubt the first and the last, to have (direct) access to the source of Rwanda's history [...]; and to be graciously served by those who were the living reservoirs of this source'.[10]

It is in this context that the young Alexis Kagame, supported by the Rwandan monarchy, the Catholic Church, and anthropologists who were often the missionaries themselves,[11] found a role to play in the history of Rwanda. He acquired and was fascinated by Rwandan oral traditions while, at the same time, he received training from the missionaries, which allowed him to discover European civilisation: its history, philosophy, religion, technology, the arts, the conquest of the world and space. This discovery created in him an incredible awareness as well as intellectual and artistic ferment:

> My first step was learning to write; then, I learned the French language through which I encountered French culture. Knowing their culture has helped me better understand mine. [...] Once I understood their culture, I realized that mine had to hold its own against theirs.[12]

Kagame was amazed to discover that one truly understands one's own culture when compared to another's, in this case, the coloniser's. The comparison was a dangerous exercise because, in the comparative logic of the 1920s–30s – a period dominated by the Hamitic ideology[13] – some cultures regarded themselves as more advanced than others. Nonetheless, the comparison generated a will to define Rwandan identity, to resist and to refuse to be taken for a jigsaw puzzle with pieces waiting to be created and arranged by outsiders. This resistance was not to be relished by the Belgian colonialists (such as Jean-Paul Harroy) who consequently labelled Kagame a dangerous nationalist.[14]

Fortunately, the above-mentioned comparison became the source of a multidimensional work and a coherent architecture founded in Kinyarwanda, Kagame's first language. Thus, he took Kinyarwanda as a starting point to deduce the existence of a history, a culture, and a Rwandan Bantu philosophy. The Belgian colonial system used Kinyarwanda neither in the administration nor in education because the new school system favoured the coloniser's language:

> [T]his new language, taught in schools, is understood by less than 4% of the population [...]. French is the language of prestige and social advancement; and it is used in the so-called higher functions, while Kinyarwanda remains, at the national level, the language of social communication.[15]

Kinyarwanda and French divided the national life into two domains, thus establishing a certain diglossia: Kinyarwanda being the language of the domestic and intimate sphere while French was the language of the administration, the outside world, and ostentatiousness.

Against this hierarchy of languages, cultures, and men, Kagame advocated the dismantlement of this colonial hegemony by highlighting ignored aspects of his own heritage and by creating original models adapted to the Rwandans. From 1943 to 1966, he wrote in Kinyarwanda to disseminate the wealth of Rwandan literature and translated into this minority language to provide it with new lexicons and concepts of modernity. The idea was that Kinyarwanda was able to convey all national life experiences and possessed significant lexical resources in different professions and human relations. Following the dynamics of modernity, his writing provided Kinyarwanda with the possibility to borrow or coin its own terminologies, so much so that in the post-colonial period, Kinyarwanda has become the language of instruction at primary level, while French has maintained its status at secondary and university levels but has now been superseded by English since 2008.

The Valorisation of Rwanda's Little-Known Cultural Models

Under Belgian colonisation, religious congregations focused primarily on education. With young people, their teachings not only replaced traditional systems of thought with a new religious system but also ensured a certain homogeneity between the colonial school and the metropolitan school. These schools gradually introduced in the school curriculum the results of studies carried out on Rwanda by the Europeans. Alexis Kagame's work served to fill in the gaps on certain aspects of Rwandan culture explored by previous researchers and missionaries.[16] In this process, he published scientific works and revisited pre-existing literary genres.

On Languages

Alexis Kagame's contribution here consisted in rejecting the idea of the language hierarchy developed by the colonial system and disproving the Eurocentric reading of Kinyarwanda and Kirundi.[17] He started with the grammatical description of Kinyarwanda, followed by literary creations and translations, as his ambition was to remove Kinyarwanda from the domination of European languages and put measures in place for it to become a language of instruction.

Initially, Kagame critiqued the linguistic and grammatical studies written for non-Rwandans by Eugène Hurel,[18] the French White Father, and André Coupez, the Belgian anthropologist and linguist based at the Tervuren Museum.[19] In 1960, Kagame wrote *La langue du Rwanda et du Burundi expliquée aux autochtones* [The Language of Rwanda and Burundi Explained to the Natives] and offered seventy-eight lessons on Kinyarwanda and Kirundi.[20] From within the language, he made an anatomical description of the language they – the natives – speak without prior knowledge of the grammatical structures.[21]

The description and knowledge of this language enabled him to correct errors related to a poor understanding of Kinyarwanda and Kirundi grammatical rules proposed by Hurel, in particular. For Kagame, these past studies focused on the systematisation and arrangement of linguistic materials by following categories of the European languages despite the differences in structure between these languages and the Bantu language.[22] From a perspective that is both descriptive and pedagogical, he responded to statements such as: 'there are no articles in Kinyarwanda and Kirundi', 'the search for the past participle in Kinyarwanda and Kirundi according to the French model', 'the identification of the relative pronoun in Kinyarwanda outside the verbal framework', and 'the poverty of Bantu languages in qualifying adjectives'.[23] Kagame's work evokes that of Moussa Travélé, the Malian linguist who also carried out research on his own language during the colonial period. Both were opposed to the approach adopted by European linguists who explained Afrophone languages via categories operating in the language of the other.[24]

Furthermore, Kagame proposed to reformulate the structure of the word in Kinyarwanda,[25] and this structure is still acknowledged by linguists today.[26] Others like André Coupez opted for a deletion of the roots' prefixed elements or for the omission of the classifier preceding the root designating, among others, Bantu languages and nationalities. Yet these are the unique elements that indicate, with some degree of precision, the meaning of the word's root in Kinyarwanda. The omission of these elements is illustrated by the title of Coupez's book, *Grammaire Rwanda simplifiée* [Simplified Rwanda Grammar].[27] This should have been Ki-nya-rwanda Grammar. For Kagame, this is the result of the colonialist contempt for other countries, including Rwanda and Burundi:

> What would happen if I allowed myself to write or say: Belgium Army? England Fleet? France citizens? Germany industry? [...] Don't you believe, that an independent country has the right to the same treatment, in this respect, as the European nations, especially when this country is clearly resistant to the form persistently imposed by the unrepentant colonialists? Hutu, Tutsi and Twa, nor Rundi for that matter, nor Shi, nor Hunde, nor Luba, [...] I will make up my mind only when you would have written Gium, Rance, Many for Belgium, France and Germany. As long as these bizarre forms are presented to you, as they are elsewhere too – my demand for respect of the African denominations will never cease.[28]

Omitting the classifier or the prefixed elements to the radical stems is a perpetual cultural or epistemological violence given that the identity cards established by the Belgian Tutelage in the 1930s transcribed the ethnic references by the words *Hutu, Tutsi* and *Twa*, instead of 'Umuhutu, Umututsi and Umutwa'. Hence, the nature of the written term can only be guessed through the context. This official transcription of word, from their roots and by omitting the initial vowel and the classifier (*u-mu*) is taken up blindly in expressions such as 'the genocide of the Tutsi' or the 'Revolution of the Hutu', for 'genocide of the Batutsi' and the 'Bahutu Revolution'. Even though Kagame's work is remarkable from this viewpoint, this quest for liberation has partially failed, since the terms *Hutu*, *Twa*, and *Tutsi* have prevailed.

Finally, Alexis Kagame refuted studies presenting the alleged poverty of African languages, routinely described by Westerns as languages poor in qualifying adjectives, or incomplete languages having neither the verb 'to be', nor abstract terms, and future markers.[29] In response to this ignorance, it is through writing that Kagame would deploy his efforts in extremely varied fields to highlight the riches of Kinyarwanda, a language with little writing during the colonial era.[30] Writing and translating scientific and literary texts in Kinyarwanda was to lay the basis for future linguistic majority status. Translating also puts Kinyarwanda and French on the same footing.

His efforts were rewarded after Rwanda obtained independence and he saw the change of status of Kinyarwanda shift from a minority language in education during the colonial era to that of official language. More recently, in August 2017, the translation into Kinyarwanda of *Petit pays* by Gaël Faye (see Hannah Grayson's chapter in this volume) was the strategy adopted to communicate literary news from France in a language spoken by the majority of Rwandans but insufficiently represented in writing. If Kinyarwanda has become a written literary language, it is undoubtedly because of Alexis Kagame's intuition.

Without having received formal linguistic training, Kagame attempted, with nuance, to dialogue with European linguists. The latter contributed to 'the fetishization of African languages, a process, which, in turn, led Africans to de-fetishize them'.[31] Beyond the linguistic description, the use of Kinyarwanda as a scientific and literary tool participated in the deconstruction of the Belgian colonial conception of hierarchising languages of the colonised countries.[32] This operation was achieved through translation and the restoration of Kinyarwanda as a language of science and creation. Thus, he refuted the idea that there are complete languages (imperial) and incomplete languages (primitive).[33] For Kagame, these African languages are not neutral; they are, on the contrary, bearers of history and philosophy.

On History

Before 1900, Rwanda was a non-literate society, and its history was written by missionaries using information collected from traditional informants.[34] In addition to the work done by the missionaries, Alexis Kagame greatly contributed to making the kingdom of Rwanda, its inhabitants, its different institutions and customs better known. He specialised in the analysis of the cultural heritage transmitted by the monarchy and the valorisation of the precolonial Rwanda oral literature that he himself had transcribed, with the authorisation of King Mutara III Rudahigwa. He first decided to write *Inganji Kalinga*[35] [Kalinga the Victorious[36]], the history of Rwanda in Kinyarwanda from the mythical origins of this country to historical times. The introduction to this book sets the tone and purpose for his work in history:

> This book will remind us of what we are! Before adopting what comes from the West, let's first know our own achievements and what we add to it! It will remind us that we are not wanderers that God has carelessly thrown into nature. It will show us that Rwanda is a country with roots and a long history. It will show us that we have ancestors who created this country for us and who forged the culture they bequeathed to us! In short, it calls out to us: 'Look at the achievements of your ancestors! They created Rwanda and made it bigger! And now there is peace: There are no more wars for its expansion! But if you do not deny your ancestors, bring your stone to the completion of its construction; try to enrich it in spirit!'[37]

While reflecting the author's revolt, this extract is in fact intended for his compatriots trained in missionary schools, suffering from an inferiority complex, and more attracted by European civilisation. Kagame's goal was to

> [e]ducate Rwandans about the values of their country, warn Rwandans against mistakes, call on Rwandans to develop their country, to complete the action of the ancestors, to be the worthy descendants of these brilliant ancestors and lead Rwanda towards the optimal and global fulfilment.[38]

Kagame's vision of history is progressive. In this context, progressiveness signifies the ability to draw on the benefits of Western and African cultures, in other words, to combine Rwandan values and what was regarded as the positive contributions of the Belgian colonisers. Although he insisted that Rwanda had a valid culture and robust institutions, his first books were published in French.[39] He then wrote the epics inspired by traditional poetry and historical narratives in the three volumes of *Isoko y'amajyambere* [The Source of Progress][40] published successively in 1949, 1950, and 1951.

The first two volumes of this epic describe the actions taken by each of the mythical and historical kings in their mission to contribute to the glory of the monarch. They detail their political projects aimed at putting the well-being of the Rwandan population at the forefront. Apart from certain monarchs, the majority achieved their mission thanks to their military, administrative, political, and diplomatic qualities. These two volumes seem to mean 'they have not carefully thought this out. Those who have dared to imagine that there could be a People without a history, without a Civilisation. [...] have confused civilisation itself with one of its elements: technical advancement?'[41] The last volume only highlights positive contributions of colonisation in its missionary form. The action carried out by Bishop Léon Classe as a civilising hero is hailed in the same way as that of the Rwandan kings: he carries within himself the same royal qualities in the sense that he advances Rwanda towards a technical and spiritual development by building schools and setting up training centres, health centres, and churches.

However, although praised by Kagame, Léon Classe was far the embodiment of perfection, especially because of his decisive role in dealing with the ethnic problem of Rwanda. Critics agree that the French prelate reinforced the idea that there is the noble Tutsi and the commoner Hutu and that power is one of the factors of ethnic categorisation. Mahmood Mamdani contends that

> [f]or Father Léon Classe, the future bishop of Rwanda and the key architect of missionary policy, the Tutsi were already in 1902 'superb humans' combining traits both Aryan and Semitic, just as for Father François Ménard, writing in 1917, a Tutsi was 'a European under a black skin.' If the Church heralded the Tutsi as 'supreme humans' in 1902, the same Church would turn into a prime site for the slaughter of Tutsi in 1994. The colonial state called upon missionary knowledge from early on. Soon after colonization, the Belgian state ordered a reflection on Rwanda from the White Fathers. The purpose was to elaborate and implement "race policies." In response, Fathers Arnoux, Hurel, Pagès, and Schumacher – Church fathers with expertise – prepared anthropological treatises. A consolidated document was then drawn up by Léon Classe, the head of the Catholic Church in Rwanda, and then presented to government authorities. This 1916 document had a wide readership. Not surprisingly, it gave vent to the kind of race thinking that the Church hierarchy had come to hold as a deeply felt conviction. 'Race policy' became such a preoccupation with the colonial power that from 1925 on, annual colonial administration reports included an extensive description of the 'races' in a chapter called 'race policy'.[42]

Therefore, colonial and missionary literature accredited as a faith dogma the thesis that the Tutsi was of foreign origin and had come to civilise the indigenous Hutu and Twa. From this hypothesis the Tutsi was associated with the Belgian coloniser. In the period leading to independence, the same racist ideology would continue to be adopted by Belgium when it was decided that independence would be given to the Hutu who, by then, were regarded as the real Rwandans and the martyrs of a system that hitherto had favoured the Tutsi. Jean-Paul Harroy and Guy Logiest would be the main agents in restoring the country to its purported real owners, and the alleged Tutsi colonisers would be driven out of the country.[43]

Curiously, this dark aspect of Léon Classe's action was not evoked by Alexis Kagame's various contributions, and his silence still stirs up controversy. Moreover, since 1961, historical critiques target Kagame's sources and regard their interpretation as partisan or manipulated by different ideologies expressed by the royal court, Eurocentric figures, and nationalists. While arguing that Kagame was more a politician than a historian,[44] Jan Vansina, the famous Belgian anthropologist, argued that before Kagame, historians had used only a fraction of the available sources and that his merit had been to explore all the sources capable of shedding light on the history of the country. Consequently, their research diverged on several points.

Other critics agree with Vansina in that history written by Kagame, taught in Rwandan schools, is the history of the reigning dynasty, which overlaps, knowingly or not, with the social history of Rwanda. First, for Ferdinand Nahimana, the history of Rwanda

> is therefore lived through the history of the Nyiginya dynasty and its abami [kings]. [...] Kagame concealed certain historical realities and even went so far as to deny historical facts to allow the Nyiginya dynasty and its abami [kings] to shine on their own and to be perceived as the sole architects of the history of Rwanda.[45]

Two fundamental reasons can potentially explain this conception of the history of Rwanda. The first reason, little mentioned by historians critical of Kagame, is that his version of history is largely influenced by the history of European kingdoms (before the end of the eighteenth century and the first half of the nineteenth century), as was the case for other African intellectuals of the same period (like Cheikh Anta Diop). The second reason is that Kagame was probably influenced by the royal court and particularly by the solicitation and confidence of King Mutara III Rudahigwa, who introduced him to the college of official holders of the esoteric code of royalty and whom he asked to make oral texts available to him.

Next, Roger Heremans, a White Father of Belgian origin, doubts the reliability of Ubwiru,[46] one of Kagame's sources:

> Ubwiru is not objective. He is so linked to royalty that he must have often misrepresented the facts. [...] as interpreters of history, the Abiru have distorted the past, either by projecting current situations anachronistically into

the distant past or by interpreting history according to the current ideology of kingship.[47]

Finally, in 2011, lecturers, researchers, and historians from the National University of Rwanda collectively rewrote the new version of the *History of Rwanda*.[48] The authors of this book comment on the approach adopted by historians before the genocide:

> They were motivated by the manipulation and distortions which were at the very heart of propaganda that preceded and accompanied the 1994 genocide. Now, Rwandans want an objective, truthful, extensively research-based, non-biased and serenely recorded history.[49]

Indeed, while acknowledging Alexis Kagame's immense contribution, various contributors to this collective work contend, on the one hand, that he remained subjective in his treatment of oral traditions and tethered to the colonialists' and missionaries' theses. For them, Kagame supported the centralising vision of power that fuelled an elitist project, which at times, has led to historical distortion. On the other hand, Kagame's work adhered to the Hamite/Bantu myth and nineteenth-century evolutionary and diffusionist theories. These critics support Mahmood Mamdani's view:

> It took Belgian rule a little over a decade to translate its vision of a civilizational mission in Rwanda into an institutional imprint. Central to that translation was the Hamitic hypothesis.[...] Belgian power turned Hamitic racial supremacy from an ideology into an institutional fact by making it the basis of changes in political, social, and cultural relations. The institutions underpinning racial ideology were created in the decade from 1927 to 1936. These administrative reforms were comprehensive. Key institutions – starting with education, then state administration, taxation, and finally the Church – were organized (or reorganized, as the case may be) around an active acknowledgment of these identities.[50]

Now that the post-colonial period has perpetuated these identity prejudices through education or in political ideologies, the new Rwandan historiography finds itself faced with a duty to find true history, without colonial or nationalist manipulation. The great challenge of the current generations, not itself immune to the consequences of these endured and assimilated deformations, is that of shedding the colonial imprint and succeeding in building a Rwandan history without markers or residues of colonial and racial ideologies.

Kagame's Little-Known Original Works on Rwandan Culture

In addition to valorising little-known Rwandan cultural practices, Alexis Kagame looked at possible foundations for building a post-colonial Rwanda: first by drawing on the old precolonial institutions whose functioning he describes and then by the creation of epics intended to *kinyarwandiser* [kinyarwandise] evangelisation. These creations and commentaries by Kagame continue to inspire Rwandan society now although they were imagined as responses to the dominant features of Belgian colonialism.

On Political Institutions

Alexis Kagame liked to say 'I played politics by saying nothing, by simply taking care of the sources that I introduced to Rwanda'.[51] These sources create a portrait of Rwanda where a social, political, economic, and military order has been prevailing for centuries.

Indeed, *Le Code des institutions politiques du Rwanda pré-colonial* [The Code of Political Institutions in Precolonial Rwanda] et *Les organisations socio-familiales de l'Ancien Rwanda* [Socio-familial Organisations in Ancient Rwanda] dissect the military training, the herds of cattle associated with them, as well as the territorial organisation of precolonial Rwanda. At the time of their publication in the early 1950s, the will for independence was widespread in colonial Africa. One might think that Kagame wished Rwanda to be ready for this event and at the same time hoped that these two books would constitute a working basis for those responsible for the ten-year plan (1951–61).[52] This plan was supposed to generate the country's new political organisation, which avowedly was to combine elements of Belgian origin with those that had for centuries proven their worth in the traditional system. The ambition was to protect Rwanda from the possible dangers of a misconstrued transition. Once again, starting from the lessons of European history, Kagame sought to show the world and Rwandans in particular their capacity to take charge of themselves and to do so by drawing on truly Rwandan achievements, which were, he suggested, as remarkable as Belgian ones.

The period 1950–1961 coincided with the administrative reconfiguration of Ruanda-Urundi by the Belgian colonial administration. The key architects of this ill-fated process were Vice-Governor Jean-Paul Harroy, Colonel Guy Logiest, and Bishop André Perraudin. Faced with the annihilation of the Rwandan institutions, Kagame used his knowledge to prove that 'Rwanda is a great kingdom whose institutions had nothing to envy from other monarchies, be they Western: a kingdom in which social and moral sense were very high with intelligent people that only lacked technical knowledge'.[53]

He contended that the cause of Rwanda would be best served by the strengthening of its constitutional monarchy, a monarchy that, in the future, would be treated as favourably as in Belgium. This stance engendered various feelings towards him.[54] On the one hand, the king and other local officials saw him as 'the convinced defender of their cause occupying a strategic position', although 'no document, no testimony confirms that Kagame was assigned by the Royal Court with such a mission, the abbot behaved as if this mission came first'.[55] On the other hand, Kagame reported that his opponents regarded him as a dangerous nationalist.

The 1950s also saw the Hutu elite begin to demand more justice and equality and question the monarchical political system. The Church, headed by Bishop Léon Classe, and the colonial administration, once won over to the cause of the reigning aristocracy, were gradually led to change sides and to lend their support to the new Hutu movement.[56] In 1959, the new republican political regime replaced the monarchical system. The events surrounding this transition from a feudal system to a republican regime resulted in a bloodbath. These troubled and bloody periods, from the revolution to independence, forced a large part of the population, including Alexis Kagame's family, to go into exile.[57] How did this author, seen as a servant of the powerful, managed to get through these periods when he was identified as the champion of the old ruling class? Could this be attributed to the 'general respect for his thinking and his scholarly qualities'?[58] Could his work have been rich enough to be used by the political regime dominated by the Hutu? I have just noted that he is a benchmark author, a unifier with the ability to reconcile the past and the present. His work, apart from a few troubling aspects, is still revered. As a result, from primary education to university, school and academic curricula introduce the results of his research into various and varied subjects and courses (history, literature, and philosophy). However, from 1995 to 2011, history lessons were removed from school curricula and were only reintroduced when the *Histoire du Rwanda des origines à la fin du XX^{ème}siècle* was completed.

On a political level, post-colonial Rwanda will often draw inspiration from traditional structures whose function has been sufficiently documented by Alexis Kagame, and it uses them to deal with current political events, especially at the civic education level, for reconciliation or justice. Given its absolute neutrality, this work inspires different political actors who use it in various ways. Three examples deserve to be highlighted: that of the militias, the Itorero, and the Gacaca.[59]

The first example concerns the manipulation of the 'militias', which have plunged Rwanda into mourning during various political crises. The Rwandan precolonial militias (1963) were required to perform war service or other services to be provided to the court. They were not intended only for combat and could form a sort of social army, or 'A vast corporation with social and economic rights and duties. The respective members of this "Social Army" could be mobilised to defend different causes. Rights and duties were of far greater importance than war obligations'.[60]

Post-colonial Rwanda saw the revival of the militia phenomenon, especially in the years 1990–94, a period of the implementation of resolutions adopted by the La Baule conference (June 1990) at the Franco-African summit, which imposed political pluralism. With regards to the dissemination of ideologies, all political parties competed in the mobilisation of youths and supervised them in accordance with the model of precolonial militias as to their creation and their denomination.[61] However, their missions were hijacked, as the militias were no longer defending a national cause against a foreign country, but targeting their own countrymen. The best-known militias were Interahamwe and Impuzamugambi. They were respectively linked to political parties, the Mouvement révolutionnaire National pour le développement [National Revolutionary Movement for Development] (MRND) and the Coalition pour la Défence de la République et de la Démocratie [Coalition for the Defense of the Republic and Democracy] (CDR), that played an active role in the violence that shook the country from 1992 to 1994.

The militias acted under the manipulation of political leaders whose speeches incited irregular acts of violence and hatred against Tutsi and Hutu political opponents. From April 1994, the militiamen joined forces with the Presidential Guard to track down, arrest, and kill Tutsis and Hutus. In their murderous madness, they were also supported by local leaders, communal police officers, certain members of the army and the gendarmerie as well as simple peasants. The precolonial militia whose original mission was to protect has been abused since the colonial period because the racist principles used in Ruanda-Urundi and in the Belgian Congo have, like a time bomb, exacerbated the hierarchy of ethnic groups and created frustrations.

Next, in traditional Rwanda, young adults learned essential values (generosity, courage, and tolerance) in a traditional school known as Itorero and received civic education.[62] Since 2007, the National Commission for Unity and Reconciliation reintroduced Itorero as a civic education programme for students and professionals of all levels. Itorero mainly addresses the themes of the history of Rwanda, the cultural values that can be used for improved coexistence. In this same framework, in 2013, the Ndi Umunyarwanda, or 'I'm Rwandan', programme was created to reignite and strengthen the Rwandan spirit and contribute to the 'national identity' that Belgian rule had destroyed through the dissemination of ethnic stereotypes and clichés of all kinds.

The third example is Gacaca, which was a traditional legal institution intended to judge neighbourhood disputes only, but which, in its original form, was not employed to adjudicate blood crimes. However, faced with the nature and scale of the massacres of Tutsi, the government encouraged Rwandan researchers and experts to explore the Gacaca solution alongside the classic judicial system and the International Criminal Tribunal for Rwanda. Subsequently, a law was promulgated to allow the alleged culprits to be brought to justice in September 1996.[63] Across the country[64] Gacaca has been rekindled and has been used to settle genocide disputes by drawing inspiration from the means of conflict management of traditional Rwanda. To strengthen the unity of Rwandans and the reconstruction of the social fabric, the new mission of Gacaca is to reveal the truth about the genocide, to carry out speedy trials, and to eradicate impunity by involving the population in the punishment of those responsible for the crimes.

The sources of these precolonial institutions have constantly inspired the solutions that different generations have brought to the sociopolitical problems of post-colonial Rwanda. Differently appreciated, his status constantly discussed, his commitment variously interpreted, the echo of Kagame's work is constantly resonating.

On Theology and Evangelisation

In his capacity as priest of the Catholic Church of Rwanda, Alexis Kagame was concerned with the transmission of the Christian message by multiplying initiatives and strategies to envisage the encounter of Rwandan and Christian cultures. Not only did he translate from French into Kinyarwanda a multitude of liturgical texts and the New Testament,[65] but he also put his talent at the service of creating models of evangelisation appropriate to the traditional mentality, which had its own *pierres d'attente de la foi* ['stepping stones of the faith'] and which should not be rejected without further examination. Poetry in Kinyarwanda became immediately a constitutive component of his strategy, because his firm conviction was that Christianity transcended cultures and that it can be transmitted to either culture without unnecessarily affecting the cultural elements of the populations concerned.[66] Thus, to inculcate an intelligible Christianity within the reach of Rwandans, he composed in Kinyarwanda the biblical epic *Umulirimbyi wa Nyili-Ibiremwa* [The Cantor of the Master-of-Creation] from 1941 to 1966. Inspired by biblical revelations, this epic tells the story of humanity: from all eternity, from the evolution of humanity in the universe to the period of the two World Wars and the creation of the United Nations. Kagame's theological approach was noticed by Pope Pius XII, who congratulated him on the task completed and praised him for the orthodoxy of this work and for the value it represented in Christian literature.

Along with this biblical epic, Kagame spoke of progress made by the missionaries in terms of the development of Rwandan society through *Isoko y'amajyambera* (vol III). This progress idealises the foundation of a Rwandan Christian culture based on two projects of complementary societies: that of the Rwandan monarchs to achieve the objectives relating to the well-being and the education of the population and to the organisation and expansion of the country, as well as that of Monsignor Léon Classe, who gave himself the mission of Christianising Rwanda and fostering its technological advancement.

Léon Classe's mission thus came to complete the civilisation started by Rwandan actors, and his work reached its climax in 1943 with the baptism of King Mutara III Rudahigwa. He received Christian first names (Charles Léon Pierre) and accepted to administer his country in accordance to the examples of the Christian and humanist kings of Europe.[67] Here the link and resonance between Rwanda and Belgium are highlighted by the integration into the Rwandan epic of Léon Classe, the humanist kings of Europe, new elements (baptism, consecration of Rwanda to Christ the King). This story highlights the hitherto unexplored poetic potentials that served as a foundation for multicultural values, openness, and adherence to the new Rwandan Christian culture.

Let us also highlight that this focus on poetry to service Christian thought is not coincidental. At a literary level, this innovative method gave Kagame the opportunity to immortalise in writing traditional poetry while bypassing the formal codes of traditional genres by introducing thematic variations. On the other hand, poetry, as a communication tool employed by the monarchy, always occupied an important place in disseminating political ideologies. It is therefore a functional and efficient channel for several reasons. It has the privilege of connecting with Rwandans on an emotional level; it represents a sort of storehouse of Kinyarwanda lexicon that, when faced with European civilisation, loses its footing. Above all, it is also the politically correct means by which disputes are formulated in a subtle manner.

Kagame used poetry to express his indignation against methods of evangelisation based on colonial ethnocentrism. He deplored the actions of some disguised missionaries who not only set out to remove the cultural elements incompatible with the Christian doctrine but also took it upon themselves to implant, at all costs, their own cultural elements. With *Umulirimbyi wa Nyili-Ibiremwa*, he reiterates the principles of equality and freedom of human races:

> God created us with Intelligence; at the same time, he flooded us with the Will; both engender Liberty, one of the characteristics of the human nature.

> Liberty is by no means the result of the race in which we are born. Whether you are European, Black, or another skin colour. We are all conceived for Liberty.⁶⁸

This same freedom cannot allow one language or culture to override another on the pretext of belonging to a human group considered superior or inferior. In this process, we must therefore put Kinyarwanda at the service of a Christian philosophy through literary creation and translation, not only to oppose the one-sided view that was held by some but also to respond to those who brought Christianity to Rwandans in a

> Western packaging and under historical and sociological conditions that did not allow missionaries to indigenise it. The African collective conscience, now awakened, is not opposed to the Christian message but to the attitude of those who imagine it is synonymous with European civilisation.⁶⁹

In addition to Kinyarwanda poetry, Alexis Kagame's theological quest can also be seen in his contribution through scientific articles. In 1957, in *Des Prêtres noirs s'interrogent* [Black Priests ask Questions], Alexis Kagame, and the young African priests studying in Europe (Vincent Mulago, Meinrad Hebga, and Englebert Mveng), who were undeniably receptive to the Negritude movement, demanded a real Africanisation of the Church.⁷⁰ They were convinced that '[t]he Church will be African in Africa otherwise it should not be in Africa'.⁷¹ Furthermore, Kagame expressed himself in *Le Colonialisme face à la doctrine missionnaire à l'heure de Vatican II* [Colonialism and the Missionary Doctrine at the Time of Vatican II], challenging the domination of missionaries and the destructive effects of this presence on the local clergy.

The criticism subtly initiated by Kagame in written poetry has served as a model for post-colonial poets, such as Rugamba Cyprien and Gasimba François-Xavier, who address different subjects of current political, social, or economic interest.

Conclusion

Alexis Kagame's work is crucial to reflect on Rwanda's colonial past and the resonance of this past in post-colonial Rwanda. Faced with the universalism advocated by Belgian colonisers in Rwanda who considered Belgium to be the source of administrative and economic policy, religion, education, and territorial division, Kagame opted for a more open-ended and open-minded brand of universalism – that is, a posture embracing the plurality of languages and cultures and the search for a 'dialogical horizon based on diversity'.[72]

Seen as a nationalist by some critics, ambiguity may arise about this Catholic priest, cultural broker, and intellectual regarding his positions as a convinced defender of the culture and the people of Rwanda who also championed the universalism of the Christian religion. What is most paradoxical is his silence regarding Bishop Léon Classe's missionary policy, which he praised despite the catastrophic results of his actions in Rwanda and Classe's active role in the dissemination of the racial prejudices that became constitutive of a murderous political ideology. However, he anticipated with remarkable prescience that Rwandan culture was being threatened to extinction by the domination of civilising and universalising projects such as colonisation and Christianisation. Confronted with these, his choice was to receive and to give in order to move towards a common horizon.

Alexis Kagame's response to Belgian colonisation in Rwanda was of paramount importance and its resonance is still pervasive in Rwanda now. Despite certain grey areas, he was driven by an ambition to produce a context in which Belgium and Rwanda would work together to achieve a pluriracial and pluricultural coexistence and create a collective conscience purged of any form of domination and unconscious submission. Although the constancy of his optimism did not produce all the desired results, his logic (adding rather than erasing) strove to tirelessly challenge the rationale behind colonial knowledge production.

Notes

1. Matthew Stanard, *The Leopard, the Lion, and the Cock: Colonial Memories and Monuments in Belgium* (Leuven: Leuven University Press, 2019).
2. See Colette Braeckman, *Rwanda. Histoire d'un génocide* (Paris: Fayard, 1994).
3. V. Mahmood Mamdani, *When Victims Become Killers: Colonialism, Nativism, and the Genocide in Rwanda* (Princeton: NJ: Princeton University Press, 2001), pp. 85–108.
4. The Protestant missionaries arrived in Rwanda before the Catholic missionaries and left at the same time as the German troops after their defeat in the First World War. Thereafter, the resumption of the Lutheran missionaries became very challenging given the monopolistic intents of the Catholic missionaries.
5. Paul Rutayisire, *La Christianisation du Rwanda (1900–1945). Méthode missionnaire et politique selon Mgr Léon Classe* (Fribourg, Éditions universitaires, 1987).
6. See the flattering portrait of Léon Classe for his action in Rwanda by Alexis Kagame in the historiographical poem *Isoko y'amajyambere*, Vol III (Kabgayi: Éditions Morales, 1951).
7. Alexis Kagame, *Un Aperçu panoramique de la culture rwandaise* (Butare: unpublished, 1971), p. 1.
8. Sekarama is one of Rwanda's great poets known for his important role in the memorisation and transmission of Rwanda's history, in particular, the reigns of Kigeli IV Rwabugiri and Mutara III Rudahigwa.
9. Claudine Vidal, *Sociologie des passions* (Paris: Karthala, 1991), p. 52.
10. Ferdinand Nahimana, 'La conception de l'Histoire du Rwanda d'après Alexis Kagame', in Joseph Nsengimana (ed.), *Alexis Kagame: L'homme et son œuvre* (Kigali: Education, science et culture, 1987), pp. 255–71, (261).
11. See Friedrich Stenger, *White Fathers in Colonial Central Africa: a Critical Examination of V.Y. Mudimbe's Theories on Missionary Discourse in Africa* (Münster; Hamburg; London: LIT Verlag, 2001).
12. Gérard Gahigi, *Kagame: le fond d'une vie et le cheminement d'une pensée de l'homme libre et serein* (Butare: unpublished, 1976), p. 29.
13. Jean-Pierre Chrétien and Marcel Kabanda, *Rwanda, racisme et génocide: l'idéologie hamitique* (Paris: Belin, 2016).
14. Gérard Gahigi, *Kagame*, p. 29.
15. Laurent Nkusi, *Le Kinyarwanda peut-il devenir un instrument de communication scientifique Moderne?* (Butare: unpublished, 1980), p. 1.
16. See, for example, Père Paulin Loupias, 'Tradition et légende des Batutsi sur la création du monde et leur établissement au Ruanda', *Anthropos*, 3.1 (1908), 1–13; Albert Pagès, *Un Royaume hamite au centre de l'Afrique* (Bruxelles: Marcel Hayez: 1933); et Léon Delmas, *Généalogie de la noblesse (les Batutsi) du Ruanda*, (Kabgayi: Vicariat Apostolique du Rwanda, 1950); Louis de Lacger, *Le Ruanda ancien*, Vol I; *Le Ruanda moderne* Vol II (Namur: Grands lacs, 1939).
17. On this derogatory approach to African languages, see Alain Ricard, *The Languages and Literatures of Africa* (Oxford: James Currey, 2004).
18. E. Hurel, *Grammaire kinyarwanda* (Kabgayi: Édition Morales, 1951).
19. A. Coupez, *Grammaire rwanda simplifiée, méthode rwanda à l'usage des Européens* (Usumbura: Éditions du service d'information, 1961).
20. National and official language of Burundi.
21. Laurent Nkusi, 'Kagame et la problématique du langage', in Joseph Nsengimana (ed.), *Alexis Kagame, L'homme et son œuvre*, (Kigali:Education, science et culture, 1987), pp. 122–42 (p. 125).
22. Alexis Kagame, *La langue du Rwanda et du Burundi expliquée aux autochtones* (Kabgayi: Édition Morales, 1960), p. 7.
23. Hurel, *Grammaire kinyarwanda*, p. 129.
24. See Cécile Van den Avenne who partly focuses on Travélé dans *De la bouche même des indigènes. Echanges linguistes en Afrique coloniale* (Paris: Vendémiaire, 2017), p. 125.
25. The initial vowel (*indomo*), the noun class marker/classifier (*indanganteko*), the root (*igicumbi*) et la désinence (*umusozo*).
26. See Yves Cadiou, 'La structure du mot en kinyarwanda', in Francis Jouannet (ed), *Le Kinyarwanda, études linguistiques* (Paris: SELAF, 1983), pp. 181–95 (pp. 186–87).
27. A. Coupez, *Grammaire rwanda simplifiée: méthode rwanda à l'usage des Européens* (Usumbura: Éditions du service de l'information, 1961).
28. Alexis Kagame, *Réponse au pamphlet boomerang de M. André Coupez* (Butare: unpublished, 1972), p. 10.
29. On this derogatory description of African languages and Swahili in particular, see Johannes Fabian, *Language and Colonial Power: The Appropriation of Swahili in the Former Belgian Congo 1880–1938*, Foreword by Edward Said (Berkeley; Los Angeles; Oxford: University of California Press, 1986).
30. From 1941 to 1966, Kagame became the creator of his own literary texts through the inspiration of diverse traditional literary genres which he collected, transcribed and translated.

31. Anastase Gasana et Nkiko Munyarugerero, 'Alexis Kagame et la problématique du langage: le cas des langues bantu', in Joseph Nsengimana (ed.), *Alexis Kagame, l'homme et son œuvre* (Kigali: Ministère de l'enseignement supérieur et de la recherche scientifique, 1987), pp. 143–48 (p. 143).
32. This policy of prioritising languages by the Belgians has been studied by various authors [on Swahili]: Johannes Fabian, *Language and Colonial Power*; and also Michael Meeuwis, 'Bilingual Inequality: Linguistic Rights and Disenfranchisement in Late Belgian Colonization', *Journal of Pragmatics*, 43 (2011), 1279–87.
33. See Souleymane Bachir Diagne's conference 'Quand traduire est un acte de décolonisation, Souleymane Bachir Diagne (Columbia University), « Quand traduire est un acte de décolonisation » – YouTube [accessed 15 Septembre 2021].
34. Paulin Loupias, 'Tradition et légende des Batutsi sur la création du monde et leur établissement au Ruanda', *Anthropos*, 3.1 (1908), 1–13; Albert Pagès, *Un royaume hamite au centre de l'Afrique* (Bruxelles: Marcel Hayez, 1933); Léon Delmas, *Généalogie de la noblesse (les Batutsi) du Ruanda* (Kabgayi: Vicariat Apostolique du Rwanda, 1950) and Louis de Lacger, *Le Ruanda ancien*, Vol I; *le Ruanda moderne*, Vol II (Namur: Grands lacs, 1939).
35. Alexis Kagame, *Inganji Kalinga*, vol I (Kabgayi, Éditions Royales, 1943); *Inganji Kalinga*, vol II (Kabgayi, Éditions Royales, 1959).
36. *Kalinga* is the name of the emblem drum of the Rwandan dynasty. *Inganji Kalinga* is the title of the book, the first volume of which was published in 1943, the second in 1950, and then the two volumes together in 1959.
37. Alexis Kagame, *Inganji Kalinga*, p 5. (Translated from the original text in Kinyarwanda).
38. Ferdinand Nahimana, 'La conception de l'Histoire du Rwanda…', p. 259.
39. See, Alexis Kagame, *Le Code des institutions politiques du Rwanda pré-colonial* (Brussels: Institut Royal Colonial Belge, 1952); *Les organisations socio-familiales de l'Ancien Rwanda* (Brussels: Académie royale des sciences coloniales, 1954); *Les Milices du Rwanda précolonial* (Brussels: Académie royale des sciences d'Outre-mer, 1963).
40. Alexis Kagame, *Isoko y'amajyambere*, vols I-III (Kabgayi, Éditions Royales, 1949–51).
41. Alexis Kagame, *Un Aperçu panoramique de la culture rwandaise* (Butare: unpublished, 1971), p. 3.
42. Mamdani, *When Victims Become Killers*, pp. 95–96.
43. Paul Rutayisire, 'Le Tutsi étranger dans le pays de ses aïeux', *Les Idéologies, Evangile et Société*, 4 (1996), 42–56 (49).
44. Jan Vansina; *L'Évolution du royaume Rwanda des origines à 1900* (Brussels: Académie royale des sciences d'Outre-mer, 1962), p. 7.
45. Ferdinand Nahimana, 'La conception de l'Histoire du Rwanda…', p. 262.
46. Ubwiru was an important esoteric-political institution, subsidiary to the kingdom, having the duty to preserve and adapt the sacred kingdom in the form of a monarchy. The Abiru (royal advisers) were responsible for taking care of the rites the king set about to resolve the country's major problems.
47. R. Heremans, *Introduction à l'Histoire du Rwanda* (Kigali: Éditions Rwandaises, 1973), p. 9.
48. Déo Byanafashe and Paul Rutayisire (eds.), *Histoire du Rwanda des origines à la fin du XXème siècle* (Huye: Université Nationale du Rwanda, 2011).
49. Ibid., p. 9.
50. Mahmood Mamdani, *When Victims Become Killers*, pp. 95–96.
51. Gérard Gahigi, *Kagame*, p. 3.
52. Ministère des Colonies, *Plan Décennal pour le Développement économique et social du Ruanda-Urundi* (Brussels: Éditions De Vissher, 1951).
53. Jean de Dieu Karangwa, 'L'Abbé Alexis Kagame: un érudit engagé', *Congo-Meuse* ('Figures et paradoxes de l'Histoire au Burundi, au Congo et au Rwanda', ed. by Marc Quaghebeur), 2 (2002), 401–33 (418).
54. See Claudine Vidal, *Sociologie des passions*, p. 52 and Ian Linden, *Christianisme et pouvoir au Rwanda (1900–1990)* (Paris: Karthala, 1999), p. 293.
55. Claudine Vidal, *Sociologie des passions*, p. 52
56. Joseph Jyoni wa Karega, 'Le Rwanda sous la 1ère et 2ème République' in Déo Byanafashe and Paul Rutayisire (eds.), *Histoire du Rwanda des origines à la fin du XXème siècle*, pp. 422–516 (p. 474).
57. Some members of his family are refugees in Uganda, Burundi, Kenya and others in Belgium and Switzerland. After the 1994 Tutsi genocide, some returned to Rwanda; others still live in Europe.
58. Jean de Dieu Karangwa, 'L'Abbé Alexis Kagame …', p. 403.
59. Alexis Kagame, *Le Code des institutions politiques du Rwanda pré-colonial*; *Les organisations socio-familiales de l'Ancien Rwanda*; *Les Milices du Rwanda précolonial*.
60. Alexis Kagame, *Les Milices du Rwanda…* (1963), p. 8.
61. The militias have eulogised names bearing their missions/objectives.

62. Roger Heremans, *Introduction à l'Histoire du Rwanda*, pp. 43–44.
63. Organic law n°8/96 of August 30, 1996 on the organisation of the prosecution of offenses constituting the crime of genocide or crime against humanity committed in Rwanda on October 1, 1990.
64. The Gacaca courts follow the administrative division. Their number is around 10.684 (instead of the 12 specialised chambers provided by the organic law of 1996) with approximately 260,000 men and women who exercise the functions of Honest Judges called Inyangamugayo. (See Faustin Rutembesa, 'Le génocide perpétré contre le Tutsi, Avrit-Juillet 1994', in Déo Byanafashe et Paul Rutayisire (eds.), *Histoire du Rwanda, des origines à la fin du 20^{ème}siècle*(2011), pp. 518–77.
65. See Chantal Gishoma, 'Une facette méconnue d'Alexis Kagame: un poète auto-traducteur', *Etudes littéraires Africaines* (La question de la poésie en Afrique aujourd'hui'), 24 (2007), pp. 42–47.
66. Alexis Kagame, 'Conscience chrétienne et conscience africaine', *Revue diocésaine:Foi et Culture*, 26 (1969), 23–45 (29).
67. Alexis Kagame, *Isoko…* (1951).
68. Alexis Kagame, *Umulirimbyi wa Nyili-Ibiremwa* (Butare: unpublished, 1966), translated from Kinyarwanda, p. 179.
69. Alexis Kagame (1969), 'Conscience chrétienne…', p. 53.
70. Albert Abble [et al.], *Des Prêtres noirs s'interrogent*, Preface by Monsignore Lefebvre; published under the aegis of Présence Africaine (Paris: Éditions du Cerf, 1957).
71. Bruno Chenu, *Théologies chrétiennes des tiers mondes, latino-américaine, noire américaine, noire sud-africaine, africaine, asiatique* (Paris: Éditions du centurion, 1987), p. 126.
72. See Souleymane Bachir Diagne & Jean-Loup Amselle's dialogue: *En quête d'Afrique(s): universalisme et pensée décoloniale* (Paris: Albin Michel, 2018).

PART 4
Trans-African Entanglements

'Depuis la Flamandchourie'

Legacies of Belgian Colonialism in
Sony Labou Tansi's Kinshasa

Sky Herington

Introduction

Novelist, poet, and playwright Sony Labou Tansi (1947–1995) is best known as a writer of the celebrated 'phratry' of Brazzaville, the Republic of the Congo (RC).[1] While a fierce critic of the country's one-party regime, which endured from 1964 to 1991, Sony rejected readings of his work as a denunciation of African dictatorships alone,[2] with his satirical attacks being directed as much towards French (neo)colonialism as the authoritarianism of the Congolese government. At the same time, he was skilled at both avoiding government censorship and securing support through the patronage of various French cultural figures and institutions.[3] This complicated relationship with the government of the RC and the institutions that represented the ongoing French presence in the country arguably obscures the more subtle references to the (post)colonial history of the neighbouring Democratic Republic of the Congo (DRC) in his work. Such allusions take various forms, with references made to the political events of the 1960s, to Mobutu Sese Seko, president from 1965 to 1997, and to the legacies of Belgian colonialism. One such example is found in the novel *L'État honteux* [The Shameful State] in which the president bemoans the condition his (fictional) country has been left in by the Belgians and, in a neologism typical of Sony's writing that gives this chapter its title, complains of the former colonisers' 'Flamandchourie'.[4]

Dominic Thomas reads Sony's use of some of these references as a strategy for attacking authoritarianism without the risk of naming the RC, the 'interconnectedness of the respective colonial and postcolonial histories' of the two countries being 'close enough for criticism to apply to both spheres'.[5] Indeed, their similarities, particularly along the shared border imposed by European colonisation that divides part of what was once the Kongo Kingdom, and intertwined histories have resulted in the two capitals being considered 'mirror cities'.[6] Furthermore, from an artistic perspective, the larger-than-life figure of

Mobutu arguably made for a more fruitful model for satire than the more austere president Marien Ngouabi in the RC.[7] The critiques of Belgian colonialism might also be explained by Sony's desire not to be pigeonholed as a critic of one particular colonial power, since his aim was to write about 'man's barbarism in all its possible forms'.[8] These various explanations for Sony's references to the DRC and its (post)colonial history in his work overlook, however, his own experience of growing up in the Belgian Congo. Born in Kimwenza, south of what was then Léopoldville, to a father from the DRC and mother from the RC, Sony studied at the regional Protestant school where he was educated in Kikongo, before being sent, aged twelve, to the RC, where he was taught in French at a Catholic school.[9] His first-hand experience of colonialism was, then, at least in theory, limited to those childhood years he spent under Belgian rule. As he later said: 'I was never colonised by France, but rather by Belgium. I come from Congo-Leo'.[10]

Sony's experience is not unique given the migratory flux between these two countries, and he is not the only author to have written on the Belgian Congo/DRC from across the border in Brazzaville.[11] However, in what follows, I hope to show, through a study of the different depictions of Kinshasa in Sony's work, how his sustained interest in this real setting across a number of texts (in an oeuvre otherwise almost exclusively set in fictional locations) allows for a particularly fruitful examination of the changing city between the colonial and post-colonial eras, which, I argue, is reflected in a transformation in his very writing style.[12] I explore the legacies of Belgian colonialism in Sony's portrayals of Kinshasa in three little-known works set over a period of some forty years: in two unpublished plays, *Marie Samar* (1970)[13] and its sequel *Le Bombardé* [The Bombed] (1971),[14] both written for a French competition for African radio plays, and in the short story, 'Le Sexe de Matonge' [Matonge's Sex] (1984).[15] The diptych format of the plays, set respectively in 1963 Léopoldville and 1999 Kinshasa, along with the 1984 setting of 'Le Sexe de Matonge', allows for an analysis of different relationships to the former colonial power over time, and an exploration of the different temporalities produced in each text. Indeed, both temporality and space are foregrounded in this comparative study. The focus on the capital city as a setting in these works attests to Sony's own interest in, and ambivalent relationship to, urban space, deemed a 'hell necessary to life', and highlights the significance of the city space to the Belgian colonial project.[16] Furthermore, despite the fact that these early plays appear never to have been performed on stage, the specific city space of Kinshasa is, I argue, important to the development of Sony's creative process given its reputation as a 'theatrical and exhibitionist city', continually reinventing itself in a vast 'public theatre'.[17] The strategies of *débrouillardise* [getting by] and artistic innovation of its inhabitants are mirrored in 'Le Sexe de Matonge' and used as a model for moving towards a decolonised space, place, and mode of writing. This progression towards a future Kinshasa, free from the influence of the Belgian colonial past and authoritarian present, is reflected in the movement of the Congo River, which, I conclude, offers a symbol of escape from colonial legacies and a source of inspiration for a new style, which might be described, following Céline Gahungu, as a form of 'meandering writing'.[18]

1963: *Marie Samar* and the Dreams of the Independence Era

In the comic play *Marie Samar*, two middle-aged men – Simon Samar, a middle-class man of Portuguese and Congolese heritage, and Bernard Baroza, his witty valet – form a humorous double act. Samar is obsessed with keeping his teenaged daughter, Marie Clara (also known as Clara), in isolation, determined to marry her to a minister likely to bring wealth and glory in the uncertain times of early independence. He devises a series of increasingly ridiculous strategies to ensure her confinement, including sending her to a convent in Luluabourg (Kananga), building a wall around the house, and amassing guard dogs to ward off potential intruders. Eventually, however, he is persuaded to allow Clara to marry her lover, Patrice, convinced by Baroza that his soon-to-be son-in-law might himself become a minister of the new political elite, and the play ends with a cheery toast to the couple and their future children imagined as little ministers.[19]

The references to Belgium in *Marie Samar* reflect the ongoing presence of the former colonial power in a supposedly postcolonial Congo. This continuity is reflected in the names of the cities of the play (Léopoldville, Luluabourg), which, although already renamed by the time of writing in 1970, in the 1963 setting are yet to be changed from their Belgian names and replaced with the new ones that would later, as Sony writes elsewhere, 'kill those left by the Belgians'.[20] Several characters whose names suggest Flemish identity and are therefore, as Thomas writes, 'essentially interchangeable with the Belgian colonizers' in Sony's work, are mentioned, but never appear on stage, constituting rather a lingering, shadowy presence in the background of the city and play.[21] Samar speaks, for instance, of a Mr Vandermatch, from whom he plans to buy yet another guard dog to add to his collection.[22] This example of ongoing financial interaction can be interpreted as a symbol of the continuing economic profit drawn from the country by Belgium in its determination to transfer public debts to the newly independent Congolese state while also protecting its own lucrative investments held with private companies,[23] an interpretation that is reinforced by an earlier version of the play in which one character reports having been short-changed by a Belgian shopkeeper.[24] The sale of guard dogs in particular evokes trade in surveillance and defence systems, and recalls the associated interests and involvement of the Belgian military in the unfolding of the Congo Crisis, particularly in the unsolicited return of Belgian troops to Léopoldville just days after Congolese independence.[25]

The characters' attitudes to these colonial legacies reflect their political allegiances based on class and racial identities. Samar is part of the Congolese social class of so-called *évolués* created by the Belgian colonial project, while his White Portuguese heritage associates him with the beginnings of colonialism in the fifteenth century in the Kongo Kingdom, the ongoing Portuguese colonisation of the neighbouring country of Angola, and the small number of Portuguese *petits blancs*, or lower-class White community in colonial Léopoldville, considered inferior to the generally wealthier Belgian settlers. He occupies a position bridging rigid social and racial categorisations but, himself a fervent believer in the colonial racial hierarchy who behaves, according to Baroza, 'like a white man when his own mother was Black',[26] Samar also demonstrates the lasting legacy of colonial anxiety regarding miscegenation in his desire to 'protect' Clara's 'Portuguese blood'[27] and improve his position in the postcolonial order through securing a supposedly advantageous marriage for her, defined in racial terms.[28] He embraces the values of the civilising mission, repeatedly attempting to educate Baroza by correcting his French and admonishing him for his mistakes, as when Baroza misspells *attention* [caution] as *attansion* when making a sign to deter trespassers.[29] Samar is nostalgic for a colonial past that he perceives as a time of order and efficiency: while waiting for Clara to return from the convent on a train that is delayed, he daydreams about the days 'when the Belgians were still here!'.[30] The selective nature of this memory is highlighted by the reference to the railway, frequently used in Congolese literature to reflect on colonial history, as in, for example, Fiston Mwanza Mujila's *Tram 83* (see Pierre-Philippe Fraiture's chapter in this volume). In this play, the railway is a symbol of European modernity but also, in the Congolese context, connotes Leopold's brutality and the exploitation involved in its construction,[31] as well as its purpose as a means of extracting resources and creating wealth for the coloniser.[32] Ironically, however, Samar's nostalgia also unwittingly draws attention to the paucity of the material colonial legacy when he remarks that Polar beer is 'all that is left of the 80 years during which we were Belgian!'.[33] With such comments he inadvertently undermines discourses on the disinterested generosity and modernising impact of the colonial endeavour that brought, according to King Baudouin in his address to the people of the Congo at independence, the 'railways, roads, shipping and air lines which, in putting [their] populations in contact with one another, promoted their unity'.[34]

A Black Congolese servant, Baroza challenges Samar's selective nostalgia, countering his recollection with another memory of having to undergo bodily checks because of his race to be allowed, he tells Samar, to buy a hat at the local branch of the Belgian retail chain, Sarma.[35] This retort draws attention to Belgian scientific racism and the colonial control of and violence towards the Congolese population, manifested in the operation of surveillance and scrutinisation of the colonised Black body made into what V. Y. Mudimbe describes in Foucauldian terms[36] as the 'African docile body'.[37] It also recalls Patrice Lumumba's powerful riposte to King Baudouin's speech and his evocation of the racism of colonialism.[38] However, in the play, it is in fact the cunning Baroza who controls and manipulates his master. Recalling the many forms of resistance to colonial authority by Congolese people in his subtle tricks and asides to the audience,[39] Baroza is skilled in the art of strategy, defending with irony his misspelling of the sign on the basis that it will make the warning 'more savage',[40] or appeasing Samar with flattery, mockingly complimenting his having 'the teeth of Leopold II'.[41] He advocates on Clara's behalf, securing at least the promise of her marriage to Patrice, and thereby creates a conclusion to the play that constitutes a double rejection of the colonial values espoused by Samar: Clara will marry her young Black lover, disregarding the socio-racial hierarchy that Samar advocates. The promising ending suggested by the imminent marriage implies a bright future free from the chokehold of these imposed values dictated by the father and the current political elite, and instead to be determined by the young man as a representative of the new generation.

1999: Postcolonial Disillusionment in *Le Bombardé*

Yet *Le Bombardé*, the sequel to *Marie Samar* set nearly forty years later in December 1999, unsettles this hopeful ending from the outset. The sound of barking dogs that opens *Marie Samar* is here replaced by the sound of protesters, the symbolic representations of militarised defence now transformed into real, armed political agents.[42] The setting in the bloody butchers' quarter of what is now Kinshasa signals the country's descent into conflict and violence in a jarring change of scene from the domestic celebrations and champagne toasts that closed the first play. Here, Baroza, now an ex-valet, takes over as the president of the Congo in the midst of a civil war over Katangese secession. He has in fact married Clara himself, although she also has a teenaged daughter, Elva, fathered by Patrice, who is now fighting in Angola. Advocating peace, unity, and a refusal of military assistance from abroad, Baroza is opposed by Ndolo, the prime minister, whom he suspects of working under the orders of foreign 'masters'.⁴³ Throughout the play, Baroza is the target of a number of attempted assassinations in the form of mysterious letter bombs, which drive him to take increasingly dramatic, but ultimately ineffective, precautions to avoid them. These bombs leave him with a new injury each time he appears onstage, the injuries reflecting the war raging around him. Eventually, he is admitted to hospital, and the play closes in uncertainty as to whether he will survive, his whole body now in plaster and the hospital itself under threat of attack.

Such a portrayal of the state of Kinshasa and the Congo more generally reflects the postcolonial disillusionment in the years following independence. As Sony later joked in one interview:

> After the Belgians: then what? Independence. Well! We were all joyous, we danced and then, I think two or three, or maybe four, years later, someone says [...]: 'Hey! Hey! Kids, when is this independence of yours going to end?'⁴⁴

Marred by political unrest, violence, and corruption, the independence era is revealed to be yet another traumatic period of destruction following on from colonisation that the population wants to escape. The implied continuity between these periods is made explicit in the similarities between the two plays, with little having changed since 1963. The city's new name only emphasises its other continuities with the past, especially in the context of Mobutu's project of renaming as part of the 'authenticity' campaign, which contradicted his continuation of the imperial monopolisation of wealth for the political elite. A sense of stasis is created through the reappearance of the main characters who, for the most part, have not aged, or who have aged less than the forty years that have passed. The violent situation can be read as an inheritance of colonialism in terms of the difficult political and economic conditions in which the country was left by Belgium to begin its independence, in the repetition of violence once employed by its forces and, through the references to Katanga, in Belgium's involvement in supporting the claims to secession which, Baroza laments, are throwing the population into civil war.⁴⁵ Ndolo, who tries to claim that the Belgians should be left alone now they have been gone for forty years, is quickly reminded by Baroza's guard that they did not depart 'without leaving a trace',⁴⁶ with the guard going on to accuse Ndolo of wanting 'to call them back to teach us how to kill our wives and children'.⁴⁷ Significantly, Ndolo, who like the Belgian characters in the first play is 'always in the shadows', here appears in disguise, as if to emphasise the underhand strategies and implications of Belgium in the politics of the country.⁴⁸

Any change seems then to be illusory, and the apparent impossibility of achieving real transformation is most striking in the character of Baroza. While his life is dramatically different, and he is now a businessman, politician, and the sole protagonist of the play, his behaviour in his new roles connects him to the ruling elite and bourgeoisie of *Marie Samar*. Ironically, as Clara's husband, he has himself now become the minister Samar always wanted as a son-in-law. Where once he played, often strategically to his own advantage, the role of the uncivilised servant, here he has seemingly adopted the values of his one-time employer, in many respects becoming a clone of his father-in-law, particularly in the way in which the master-servant dynamic is repeated in his relationship with his own employee. Having hated Samar's guard dogs in *Marie Samar*, he now has his own and is determined to use his political position to accrue personal capital: as journalists complain, he 'holds meetings to sell his beers which he has decreed national drinks'[49] and makes 'millions' from his supporters.[50] A Belgian framework of social organisation also continues to structure society and delimit the political roles occupied by Congolese actors: if Baroza, trained as a cook, is a politician perceived as cunning and motivated by financial interests, involved as he is in what Ndolo describes as a politics of 'recettes'[51] (signifying both 'recipes'[52] and 'receipts'), this is because, his guard responds, 'those are the categories that the Belgians made for us'.[53] Seemingly ruling in the interests of his personal finances then, Baroza, in his new position, appears to symbolise a mere change of guard of the previous order, and, especially in this theatrical context, which makes use of disguise and impersonation, embodies Frantz Fanon's warning of the potential for the post-independence state to become a farcical imitation of Europe.[54]

The 'Apocalyptic Interlude': Memories of a Postcolonial Future

Heroes and villains are, however, scarce in Sony's work. Baroza is an ambiguous character who, while adopting a lifestyle of luxury and potential financial corruption, is also committed to his political principles. He is dedicated to the people, regularly reminding them of the hopes they once had in the early independence years, and frustrated by the continued interference of an anonymous 'them' – which would seem to include the former colonial power – as he exclaims in a phrase repeated throughout the play: 'why won't they leave us in peace?'.[55] Determined to prevent all foreign military intervention and to ensure the Congo's independence, he interprets potential external aid as self-interested and more concerned with attacking Katanga's factories than suppressing the rebels. 'Military assistance', he tells Ndolo, is a euphemism for the importation of plunderers and murderers.[56] At the end of the play, Baroza's suspicions are confirmed when, while he is critically injured and in hospital, foreign military intervene and destroy the factories.⁵⁷ Outraged upon later hearing this news, he exclaims, 'No. Stop! Stop. You can't ask them to kill our forty years of work. [...] No'.⁵⁸ His determination to honour the promises of the early independence years complicates an interpretation of his character as a straightforward reproduction of his former master in a series of imitations of colonial ideals.

Baroza's insight into the motives behind the foreign aid and his anticipation of what would happen in Katanga should external forces intervene mark him as a visionary, however flawed.⁵⁹ While his new life enjoyed in the 'dazzling luxury' of a house decorated with animal skins recalls Mobutu's taste for opulence, Baroza's beer sales, his commitment to genuine independence and liberation, his political position on unification, and his (here, attempted) assassination seemingly at the hands of Belgian-backed secessionists also align him with the figure of Lumumba.⁶⁰ If this portrait of Baroza appears contradictory, it is worth noting that the image that Sony paints of Lumumba elsewhere is equally ambiguous: he is simultaneously presented as a fellow visionary⁶¹ and of little interest to Sony, having been, Sony claims, too influenced by the Belgians.⁶² In the ambiguous character of Baroza, Sony imagines the complex figure Lumumba might have become and how the country might have been shaped in an alternate version of Congolese history in which he survived. This hypothetical survival is emphasised in the play's final tableau in which Baroza is on the verge of death and surrounded by devastated family and remorseful political adversaries, in an image evoking representations of Lumumba as a Christlike figure.⁶³ The doctor's closing statement that 'he might not be dead'⁶⁴ and his hope of being able to save Baroza suggest the character's potential survival beyond the play's boundaries, and beyond the grave. This possibility of resurrection recalls the afterlives of many Congolese prophets and their enduring position in the collective memory and imaginary alongside Lumumba, following similarly suspicious disappearances or deaths at the hands of colonial authorities.⁶⁵ The reappearance of various characters named Patrice who haunt both plays, often in a repetition of previous events, as when Elva announces her intention to marry her lover Patrice just as her mother did in *Marie Samar*, reconfigures the temporality of death as ending.⁶⁶ Indeed, Clara expresses her continued love for the original Patrice and ardent belief in his imminent return.⁶⁷ Through the cyclical temporality of these evocations, the present is permeated with reminders of past political ideals, embodied by Lumumba, which now seem increasingly elusive in the context of civil war. However, Clara also berates Baroza for his paranoid obsession with his rival, criticising his failure to try 'to see beyond Patrice', and thereby also suggesting a need to see beyond the individual saviour as a means of (re)imagining the future.⁶⁸

Le Bombardé creates further resonances and echoes that contribute to this circularity, contrasting with the relatively linear narrative trajectory of *Marie*

Samar. It incorporates and collapses different time frames, with the epilogue, for example, shifting back from the futuristic play setting to ask: 'What will we be in 1999 if we fail to take seriously what we are today?'.[69] A gesture is made to the audience's present when one character tries to tell Baroza that what is currently, in 1999, happening to the president is obscurely linked to events of 1970.[70] Indeed, in addition to the inconsistencies in the characters' ageing between the two plays, here, events of a real-life past are transposed into a future world: while Katangese secession and the Congo Crisis were absent from 1963 Léopoldville in *Marie Samar*, here they appear to be playing out in late 1999. The spectator's past is thus repeated and made into an imagined future reflected on stage.

The complex temporalities of the play would also appear to unsettle the linear temporality of Western modernity, characterised by what Sony terms, in the context of Western art, 'the straight line'.[71] Their coexistence might be understood by reference to what Filip De Boeck calls the space-time of the 'apocalyptic interlude' in Kinshasa, in which various phases of the Book of Revelation collapse into one another in a 'confusing present' that explodes the linear chronology of this part of the Bible.[72] Just as in *Le Bombardé*, where past and future merge, this temporality simultaneously holds within it a better future, both near and distant, and a judgement day that has both already happened and is yet to come. Engaging with this religious time as it plays out in the place of Kinshasa, Sony foregrounds local lived experiences of time, destabilises the 'post' of the postcolonial, but also, arguably in contrast to these religious notions of time, emphasises the role of the people who must look to their own present ('what *we are* today') to find a future, rather than to the figure of the individual saviour, if that future is to be different from the disturbing image of the new millennium presented in the play. Baroza, evoking both Mobutu and an imagined future Lumumba, often seen as representing divergent possibilities for the independent DRC, demonstrates in his ambiguity the need to go beyond a reliance on past or revenant national heroes in the reshaping of a better tomorrow.

From Haunted Houses to the Living City

The engagement with Kinshasa's temporalities in *Le Bombardé* is mirrored in the plays' representations of the specificities of the city's spatial and architectural configuration. As suggested in the introduction, urban space was central to the colonial project, particularly in the case of Belgium, which attempted to re-programme Central Africa in its own image.[73] It made Kinshasa into a centre of economic activity, which also conveyed its ideology through the creation of a 'dichotomized city' in which the 'Ville' (urban) and 'Cité' (suburban) were rigidly segregated by race.[74] In the plays, the city does not feature as a vast metropolis but is instead characterised by this segregation, with the dimensions of the characters' lives largely reduced to their domestic environments. Although other regions of the country are important to Baroza's politics of unification in *Le Bombardé*, these other spaces, as well as any details of different areas of Kinshasa, are absent: the focus is static and remains on the small world of the new elite, physically, and by implication politically, distanced from the populace. The grand houses of both Samar and Baroza are contrasted only with the anonymous 'street', metonym for the people who occupy the space outside these confines. Johan Lagae contends that the existence of gated communities in Kinshasa is one example of the persistence of the racial segregation ingrained in the colonial urban planning of the city,[75] and this legacy appears in *Marie Samar* in the separation of Samar's house from the outside world by a four-metre wall.[76] Indeed, Clara's life is defined by the enclosure of both convent and home, to the extent that, near the end of the play, she exclaims, exasperated, 'I loathe walls. Loathe dogs! Loathe all enclosed spaces, all convents, all prisons, all schools'.[77] Elsewhere, in a short essay on Kinshasa, Sony himself explains how this architectural legacy conveys colonial values:

> I don't like Binza because of its houses which grip onto the hills like strange mushrooms. They're called villas. But nobody sees them really because of their forbidding walls which form all-powerful lines around them like forests, and which are purposefully erected in opposition to the African tendency towards communitarianism. You might even call it the proof that we have chosen any old door through which to enter civilisation with a bang – that civilisation which has resolutely chosen to botch [*bâcler*] humanity and the whole universe.[78]

If the houses here are likened to natural phenomena – 'mushrooms', 'forests' – they nonetheless appear as parasites on the land and are removed from the reach of the people. Symbolising the entrance into colonial civilisation, imitating, as Lagae explains, what was considered the very best in the wealthy residential neighbourhoods of the Zoute, or of Wépion and Koekelberg in Brussels, the villa stands as a symbol of Western modernity and individualism in opposition to more community-minded ways of living.[79] However, as one stage direction in *Le Bombardé* demonstrates, the price of this 'entry into civilisation' is high: here, Baroza's 'ultramodern house' is surrounded by the 'remnants of an explosion'.[80] Colonial ideology is represented by the house, where time and space combine in a symbol of the evolution between 'primitive' and 'modern', but the intrusion of the devastation wrought by war into this space suggests the human cost of this supposed 'development'. The striking juxtaposition here is also echoed in the extravagance of Baroza's garden. This outdoor space, known as the *barza* in colonial jargon, in an echo of Baroza's own name, is presented by the protagonist for journalists in a tour recalling the exhibitions of the colonial garden in Belgium and elsewhere.[81] This includes a glasshouse that protects his precious plants, a symbol of the fragility of his power, which is only emphasised when the house is burned down at the end of the play by the 'anti-Barozards'.[82] Yet, though the proximity of the signs of a 'botched' universe in the form of war reveals the true legacy of colonial urban planning and architecture, the eventual destruction of the house itself suggests the possibility of a future end to this colonial influence.

This possibility is developed in a more expansive and imaginative portrait of the city space in Sony's later text, 'Le Sexe de Matonge', first published in 1984. Recounting a single night out in the Matonge neighbourhood of Kinshasa, in contrast to the accounts of the individual house that epitomised the legacy of segregation in the independence years in the plays, the narrator continually moves around this heart of the city and beyond, offering a more detailed exposition of its different areas. Here there is no explicit mention of the former colonial power, and the city's colonial buildings are described as remnants of an ancient past; they are white concrete giants that remind the narrator of the 'old skeletons of prehistoric monsters' and of 'coffins' that watch over the city's famous main road, renamed the Boulevard du 30 juin, the date of Congolese independence.[83] These lifeless but nonetheless haunting remains of the colonial past reflect the scenes of violence and death that the narrator witnesses during the night. He is haunted by the image of a girl whom he earlier saw being run over in the Barumbu neighbourhood and whose inert body is left lying on the tarmac while, it is said, in a reformulation of the phrase spoken in *Le Bombardé*, the person responsible for the accident has likely 'gone without leaving a trace'.[84] Later, the narrator comes across a man being attacked by a group of 'kaki helmets',[85] in a scene of violence recalling colonial repression in the segregated city, and leaving the victim barely alive and likened to a 'corpse'.[86] In this text, then, the Belgian influence on the city, both in its architecture and the control of and violence towards its inhabitants, remains a haunting, deathly presence.

Yet, in contrast to this portrait of the wider city haunted by the violence and death of state brutality past and present, the focus on the specific area of Matonge offers another perspective on Kinshasa. This neighbourhood has its own subjectivity and is very much alive; Matonge takes on a life of its own as the heart of the whole urban space with 'its flesh, blood, sweat and smells'.[87] Represented as an eroticised body, as conveyed by the text's title, this part of the city pulsates with life and seems itself to become a creative, generative force, bringing bodies together in its bars through music and dancing, and connecting people across various borders. It is noteworthy that the narrator reflects here on the piece of paper that serves as his identity card and the checks to which he was subjected on his arrival from Brazzaville, and that he is reminded by one woman he meets that he dances 'in the CFA style'[88] – that is, like someone from the French colonies.[89] Despite his acquaintance's comment, Matonge provides the setting for this (re)connection after the divisions created by the borders of European colonialism, in much the same way as its namesake in Brussels is transformed into another meeting place by and for the Congolese diaspora.[90] Matonge thus represents a quarter of Kinshasa that is both alive and life-*giving*, becoming a space of freedom, creativity, and connection.

Decolonising (Writing) Kinshasa

This shift towards a new part of the city promising life and connection, gradually but determinedly moving away from the violence and segregation of *Le Bombardé*, is mirrored in Sony's development of an idiosyncratic authorial voice, well-established and recognisable by the time of the publication of 'Le Sexe de Matonge'. Indeed, this process had already begun in *Le Bombardé*, which was the first of a number of works to be set in the future, marking a new direction in his writing. Gahungu has argued that this play signals a decisive transformation in his theatre, marking a 'definitive break from the first plays'.[91] Compared to *Marie Samar*, *Le Bombardé* presents a more performance-oriented style of writing, and diverges from classical French models such as Molière, Beaumarchais, and Marivaux, whose influence is immediately obvious in the earlier play.[92] In this change in style, Sony begins to move towards a writing practice that might be described as decolonised, and which he explores in the play's epilogue, writing:

> We must say what we say where we're from with our own mouths, think what we think where we're from just as we think it there […] and see what we see where we're from with our own eyes.[93]

Le Bombardé symbolises in its writing style a step towards this decolonisation not yet achieved within the diegesis of either play. This is developed in 'Le Sexe de Matonge', which combines French and Lingala and incorporates the voices of various, often anonymous, Kinois, whose speech punctuates the narrative, with snippets of their lives revealed as they pass by. The narrator's physical journey through the spaces of the city, where, as Sony writes elsewhere, there are neither addresses nor road signs, is mirrored in this text by a stylistic wandering characterised by enumeration.[94] The focus on a few hours of one night and first-person narration in the present tense also seem to produce what De Boeck calls the 'excessive temporality of a neverending "now," a euphoric postindependence space' created by arenas of popular culture.[95] Coloured by music, dance, crowds, and sexual suggestion, this depiction, in its positive image of the city in the present, reflects the simultaneous spatial move that is occurring through the city's rapid growth, away from the 'place' of colonialism, that is, 'from the mimetic reproduction of an alienating model of colonialist modernity, imposed by the colonial and the Mobutist state'.[96] At the same time, the writing folds the past into the present, particularly in its references to Congolese rumba music, which at once embodies this present in its live performance in the text and conveys a nostalgia for the heyday of this style that once symbolised the hope of the whole continent in the anthem 'Indépendance Cha Cha'. This is underscored here in the (re)appearances of real legendary musicians such as Docteur Nico (here the 'ex-doctor'), once a member of the renowned bands Grand Kalle et l'African Jazz and African Fiesta, who was left destitute when his Belgian record company collapsed.[97] In 'Le Sexe de Matonge', published a year before Nico's death in Brussels, he is found languishing in a bar, mourning his wife. The narrator tries to bring Nico back to the present, urging him, in Lingala, to join him in dancing. While, as discussed earlier, death lingers in both the city's architectural legacy and violence past and present, the text depicts a city with a powerful 'now', embodied by the rumba that might serve as 'life, future, present, past and provisional eternity', and offers a tentatively hopeful writing of Kinshasa.[98]

In the interview quoted earlier in which Sony discusses the aftermath of independence, he also speaks about the necessity of finding new ways of writing to 'change the content of independence'.[99] In 'Le Sexe de Matonge', he makes a gesture towards this newness:

> Our cities, conceived as monsters, which function just like monsters, have suddenly begun to produce a life, a system of knowledge, a philosophy: other needs than the initial need to consume like the West. It's a lovely, incredible transformation.[100]

The possibility of recreation despite the physical constraints of the Belgian colonial legacy demonstrates the extent to which this production of life is a mental process, as is the case in many forms of art emerging from Kinshasa. Arguably, the 'neverending now' is, as in the colonial-era narratives of 'reverie' studied by Nancy Hunt, both an 'aspiration' and 'revendication' – that is, an imagined future free from both Belgian colonialism and postcolonial dictatorship that is brought into the present tense.[101] This dream is as much about the imaginative possibilities of the city as a defiance of the past restrictions of physical movement created by segregation, which is here captured by the conditional mood. Kinshasa is not only where one is or has been, but where one could go next, since, as the narrator reflects here, 'we could go to Niva's place, to Ndolo or else to Matete', in a gesture towards a future that is constantly unfolding.[102] In Sony's vision of this Kinshasa, which 'is beginning to be born' (literally, 'to come into the world'), the city's future, symbolised by this image of (re)birth on its own terms, demands delivery, and begins to be summoned into being by the process of writing itself.[103]

Conclusion

This chapter has sought to examine, through a close analysis of three fictional works depicting Kinshasa, the representations of continuity and change in terms of Belgian influence on the city between the colonial era and the post-colonial period. With a focus on references to a continued Belgian presence in the city and conceptions of temporality, spatial organisation, and architecture, I have explored these colonial legacies as they influence the urban setting of the capital. I have observed shifts in relation to this colonial history within the diegeses of the three works, arguing that the desire to escape these past influences, while not achieved within the narrative of *Le Bombardé*, is more fully realised in 'Le Sexe de Matonge', in which Sony's new style, coming some fourteen years after the writing of *Marie Samar*, most resolutely reconfigures the city and its inhabitants free from both a traumatic past and repressive present. The realisation of this freedom is achieved through an imaginative practice of renewal, also found in Kinshasa's arts scene, where the everyday of, and in, the city is regularly reinvented by its own inhabitants.

If, as I have implied, the city can at times represent an ambiguous space – promising human connection but also threatening the possibility of violence – this creative depiction of Kinshasa succeeds in reimagining the urban setting through the inclusion of the natural world in the writing of the city, in the form of the Congo River that flows between Kinshasa and Brazzaville. Reflecting the wandering movement of the narrator of 'Le Sexe de Matonge', this impressive, expansive river symbolises a meandering that contrasts with a landscape divided by the West's conceptual 'straight line', defies containment, and acts as a connecting force that reconstitutes a former kingdom divided by the border imposed by French and Belgian colonisation. As Gahungu has written of Sony's novels, 'the meandering of the river [...] sketches out a political project, as if [this site] constituted the fragments of an ideal country, the famous Kongo, claimed by the author as the "metaphysical homeland"'.[104] While evoking the colonial project through the travels and writings of such figures as Henry Morton Stanley, Joseph Conrad, and André Gide, the river also appears to evade the forces of this history, seemingly unaffected by the events occurring around it, as is suggested elsewhere in a poem by Sony: 'They're dancing-Belgium and jumping-France/ On the two banks of the Kongo river'.[105] In 'Le Sexe de Matonge', this indifference is emphasised when the monstrous buildings left by the Belgian colonial project are diminished by the river next to them so that looking out over it, they project only 'the laughable image of the frog who wants to make himself as large as a cow'.[106] Sony's Kinshasa is, then, a space and place repeatedly brought into being through an act of imagination inspired by the Congo River, in its symbolism of connection, its meandering movement, and its evasion of the legacies of Belgian colonialism.

Notes

1. Sylvain Bemba, 'La phratrie des écrivains congolais', *Notre Librairie*, 'Littérature congolaise', 92–93 (1988), 13–15. Countries and cities are hereafter referred to by their present-day names, except where they appear differently in the source texts. Translations from French are my own, unless otherwise stated.
2. Édouard Maunick, 'Sony Labou Tansi, l'homme qui dit tous les hommes', *Demain l'Afrique*, 40 (1979), 81–84 (83).
3. On Sony's circumvention of censorship, see Dominic Thomas, *Nation-Building, Propaganda, and Literature in Francophone Africa* (Bloomington: Indiana University Press, 2002). On his relationship with French cultural institutions see Céline Gahungu, *Sony Labou Tansi: naissance d'un écrivain* (Paris: CNRS Éditions, 2019).
4. Sony Labou Tansi, *L'État honteux* (Paris: Éditions du Seuil, 1981), p. 142. This neologism appears as a portmanteau of the adjective 'flamand' (Flemish) and the verb 'chourer' (to rob or nick) but also evokes the region of 'Mandchourie' (Manchuria), arguably in an allusion to the invasions of and political tensions in the region in the second half of the twentieth century, as well as the increasing influence of China in Central Africa.
5. Thomas, *Nation-Building*, p. 60.
6. Charles Didier Gondola, *Villes miroirs: migrations et identités urbaines à Kinshasa et Brazzaville, 1930–1970* (Paris: L'Harmattan, 1996). There are also of course stark differences, particularly in the colonial tactics employed in each city and their urban landscapes. As Gondola shows, colonial Brazzaville was perceived as a sleepy, leafy city in comparison to the industrial Léopoldville (p. 67), and less socially restrictive (Charles Didier Gondola, *Tropical Cowboys: Westerns, Violence, and Masculinity in Kinshasa* (Bloomington: Indiana University Press, 2016), p. 221n11).
7. For example, in comparison to both Mobutu, whose lavish lifestyle is well-documented, and Denis Sassou Nguesso, who took over the presidency in 1979 following Ngouabi's assassination in 1977 and was known as the 'Cardin-communist', Ngouabi appeared to have less appetite for the ostentatious, typically appearing in public in a 'drab' uniform. David Eaton, 'Diagnosing the Crisis in the Republic of Congo', *Africa: Journal of the International African Institute*, 76.1 (2006), 44–69 https://www.jstor.org/stable/40026156 [accessed 28 October 2018] (63).
8. Maunick, 'Sony Labou Tansi', p. 83.
9. This move seems to have happened in 1959/60 rather than in 1964 as suggested by Phyllis Clark-Taoua. See Sony Labou Tansi, *Paroles inédites*, ed. by Bernard Magnier (Montreuil-sous-Bois: Éditions théâtrales, 2005), p. 48; Sony Labou Tansi, *Cercueil de luxe/La Peau cassée*, ed. by Bernard Magnier (Montreuil-sous-Bois: Éditions théâtrales, 2006), p. 57; Phyllis Clark[-Taoua], 'Passionate Engagements: A Reading of Sony Labou Tansi's Private Ancestral Shrine', *Research in African Literatures*, 31.3 (2000), 39–68 http://www.jstor.com/stable/3820872 [accessed 10 June 2020] (49).
10. Sony Labou Tansi, 'Je soussigné cardiaque' [interview], *Le Journal de Chaillot*, 25 (1985), 39, Limoges, Bibliothèque francophone multimédia de Limoges (BFM), Fonds Sony Labou Tansi (FSLT), SLT 150 A.5.
11. On migration between the two capitals, see Gondola, *Villes miroirs*. Henri Lopes was also born in the DRC and Tchicaya U'Tamsi's *Le Bal de N'dinga*, for example, is set in colonial Léopoldville. Tchicaya U Tam'si, *Le Bal de N'dinga*, online audio recording, Radio France internationale, 31 August 2018, https://www.rfi.fr/fr/emission/20180902-tchicaya-tamsi-congo-bal-ndinga-ca-va-le-monde-rfi [accessed 25 February 2021].
12. *La Gueule de rechange* and *L'Anté-peuple* are perhaps the only other of Sony's major works to feature real settings, respectively set in France and between Brazzaville and Kinshasa.
13. Sony Labou Tansi [Sony Tendra], 'Marie Samar', 1970, Limoges, BFM, FSLT, SLT 68.
14. Sony Labou Tansi [Marcel Sony], 'Le Bombardé', 1971, Limoges, BFM, FSLT, SLT 60.
15. Sony Labou Tansi, 'Le Sexe de Matonge', *Politique africaine*, 100.4 (2005) [1984], 118–22 https://doi.org/10.3917/polaf.100.0118.
16. Jean-Claude Blachère, 'Sony Labou Tansi – La Ville et demie', *Francofonía*, 8 (1999), 121–36 (123).
17. Filip De Boeck and Sammy Baloji, *Suturing the City: Living Together in Congo's Urban Worlds* (London: Autograph, 2016), p. 297.
18. Céline Gahungu, 'Poétique du paysage dans *L'Anté-peuple* et *La Vie et demie* de Sony Labou Tansi', *Études littéraires africaines*, 39 (2015), 79–89 https://doi.org/10.7202/1033133ar (89).
19. Sony LT, *Marie Samar*, p. 45.
20. Sony Labou Tansi, 'Kinshasa ne sera jamais', in *L'Autre monde: écrits inédits*, ed. by Nicolas Martin-Granel and Bruno Tilliette (Paris: Revue noire, 1997), pp. 21–23 (p. 23). These cities were among those whose names were changed by Mobutu in 1966, in an early example of the project of Zairianisation which would be developed over the following years.
21. Thomas, *Nation-Building*, p. 59.
22. Sony LT, *Marie Samar*, p. 16.

23. John Kent, 'Lumumba and the 1960 Congo Crisis: Cold War and the Neo-Colonialism of Belgian Decolonization', in *The Ends of European Colonial Empires: Cases and Comparisons*, ed. by Miguel Bandeira Jerónimo and António Costa Pinto (London: Palgrave Macmillan, 2015), pp. 218–42 (p. 220).
24. Sony Labou Tansi, [Untitled manuscript], Limoges, BFM, FSLT, SLT 36.
25. Kent, 'Lumumba and the 1960 Congo Crisis', p. 226.
26. Sony LT, *Marie Samar*, p. 4.
27. Ibid., p. 22.
28. Filip De Boeck and Marie-Françoise Plissart point out that in the colonial era, most '[m]ixed African-European households set up by Portuguese or Greek traders and shopkeepers, formed a buffer zone between African and European neighbourhoods', but his description of the colonials, who 'restricted their contact with indigenous worlds to a functional minimum' appears, as will be seen, a better summary of Samar's behaviour and movement in the play. *Kinshasa: Tales of the Invisible City* (Leuven University Press, 2004), pp. 52–53.
29. Sony LT, *Marie Samar*, p. 23.
30. Ibid., p. 26.
31. In *The Rulers of Belgian Africa, 1884–1914* (Princeton University Press, 1979), Lewis Gann and Peter Duignan unjustifiably conclude that Belgian colonialism was overall beneficial to the Congo, despite showing the extent of forced labour and deaths amongst the Congolese population in the construction of various railways (see p. 71; p. 124). On railway construction in the RC, see Ieme Van Der Poel, *Congo-Océan: un chemin de fer colonial controversé* (Paris: L'Harmattan, 2006).
32. Charles Didier Gondola, *The History of Congo* (Westport: Greenwood Press, 2003), p. 85.
33. Sony LT, *Marie Samar*, pp. 15–16.
34. 'Les Trois discours du 30 juin 1960', *Mbakamosika*, 1 June 2010. http://www.mbokamosika.com/article-les-trois-discours-du-30-juin-1960-51503127.html [accessed 29 July 2020].
35. Sony LT, *Marie Samar*, p. 26.
36. Michel Foucault, *Surveiller et punir: naissance de la prison* (Paris: Gallimard, 1975), pp. 137–71.
37. V.Y. Mudimbe, *Tales of Faith: Religion and Political Performance in Central Africa* (London; Atlantic Highlands, NJ: The Athlone Press, 2016 [1997]), p. 51. See also Nancy Hunt, *A Nervous State: Violence, Remedies, and Reverie in Colonial Congo* (Durham: Duke University Press, 2016).
38. 'Les Trois discours'.
39. Bogumil Jewsiewicki, 'Political Consciousness Among Peasants in the Belgian Congo', *Review of African Political Economy*, 7–19 (1980), 23–32 http://doi.org/10.1080/03056248008703438 (29).
40. Sony LT, *Marie Samar*, p. 23.
41. Ibid., p. 26.
42. Sony LT, *Le Bombardé*, p. 3.
43. Ibid., p. 43.
44. Sony Labou Tansi, 'Conférence à Lomé, le 15 février 1988', *Riveneuve continents*, 1 (2004), 152–71 (161).
45. Sony LT, *Le Bombardé*, p. 26.
46. Ibid., p. 40.
47. Ibid.
48. Ibid., p. 2.
49. Ibid., p. 45.
50. Ibid.
51. Ibid., p. 39.
52. On the significance of cooking in Sony's work see Dominic Thomas, 'From the Grotesque to the Fantastic: Sony Labou Tansi's *Qui a mangé Madame d'Avoine Bergotha?*', in *New Francophone African and Caribbean Theatres* by John Conteh-Morgan with Dominic Thomas (Bloomington: Indiana University Press, 2010), pp. 131–40.
53. Sony LT, *Le Bombardé*, p. 39.
54. Frantz Fanon, *Les Damnés de la terre* (Paris: La Découverte, 2002 [1961]), p. 304.
55. Sony LT, *Le Bombardé*, p. 8 (*passim*). As demonstrated by the allusions Baroza makes to different foreign powers in the play, this 'they' also implicates other nations beyond Belgium, notably the USA, Russia and the United Kingdom, reminding us of Sony's interest in condemning abuse in all its forms.
56. Ibid., p. 42.
57. Ibid., p. 76.
58. Ibid., p. 79.
59. Ibid., p. 43.
60. Ibid., p. 55. Cf. Aimé Césaire's portrait of Lumumba in *Une Saison au Congo* (Paris: Éditions du Seuil, 1966).
61. Sony Labou Tansi, 'Je soussigné cardiaque', BFM, FSLT, SLT 22.
62. Sony LT, *Paroles inédites*, p. 55. In this interview, Sony contrasts Tchicaya U Tam'si's concept of the Congo with that of Lumumba, arguing that the latter's idea of the country was inspired by the Belgians. This ambiguous portrait appears in other Congolese writing, such as Sylvain Bemba's *Léopolis*. See Marie-José Hoyet, 'Quelques images de Patrice Lumumba dans la littérature du monde noir d'expression française. Un panorama', in *Patrice Lumumba entre Dieu et diable: Un héros africain dans ses images*, ed. by Pierre Halen and János Riesz (Paris: L'Harmattan, 1997), pp. 49–80.
63. Bogumil Jewsiewicki, 'Corps interdits: la représentation christique de Lumumba comme rédempteur du peuple zaïrois', *Cahiers d'études africaines*, 36:141/142 (1996), 113–42 www.jstor.org/stable/4392672 [accessed 12 August 2020].

One famous example discussed by Jewsiewicki is the work of artist Tshibumba Kanda-Matulu.
64. Sony LT, *Le Bombardé*, p. 80.
65. See Martial Sinda, *Le Messianisme congolais et ses incidences politiques: kimbanguisme, matsouanisme, autres mouvements* (Paris: Payot, 1972); Charles Didier Gondola, *Matswa vivant: anticolonialisme et citoyenneté en Afrique-Équatoriale française* (Paris: Éditions de la Sorbonne, 2021), pp. 421-34. Available online: https://doi.org/10.4000/books.psorbonne.82720.
66. Sony LT, *Le Bombardé*, p. 58.
67. Ibid., p. 31.
68. Ibid., p. 30.
69. Ibid., p. 81.
70. Ibid., p. 13.
71. Sony Labou Tansi, 'Donner du souffle au temps et polariser l'espace', in *Encre, sueur, salive et sang: textes critiques*, ed. by Greta Rodriguez-Antoniotti (Paris: Éditions du Seuil, 2015), pp. 65-71 (p. 66).
72. Filip De Boeck, 'The Apocalyptic Interlude: Revealing Death in Kinshasa', *African Studies Review*, 48.2 (2005), 11-32 http://doi.org/10.1353/arw.2005.0051 (23).
73. See De Boeck and Plissart, *Kinshasa*, pp. 28-35.
74. Thierry Nlandu, 'Kinshasa: Beyond Chaos', in *Under Siege: Four African Cities, Freetown, Johannesburg, Kinshasa, Lagos*, ed. by Okwui Enwezor (Ostfildern-Ruit: Hatje Cantz, 2002), pp. 185-99 (p. 185).
75. Johan Lagae, 'Kinshasa. Tales of the Tangible City', *ABE Journal*, 3 (2013), https://doi.org/10.4000/abe.378.
76. Sony LT, *Marie Samar*, p. 5.
77. Ibid., p. 33.
78. Sony LT, 'Kinshasa ne sera jamais', p. 21. On the place of Binza in relation to the rest of the city in the early independence years, see Jean Sybil La Fontaine, *City Politics: A Study of Leopoldville, 1962-63* (Cambridge University Press, 1970), p. 43.
79. Johan Lagae, 'Modern Living in the Congo: the 1958 Colonial Housing Exhibit and Postwar Domestic Practices in the Belgian Colony', *The Journal of Architecture*, 9.4 (2004), 477-94 https://doi.org/10.1080/1360236042000320332 (487).
80. Sony LT, *Le Bombardé*, p. 8.
81. Lagae, 'Modern Living in the Congo', p. 478.
82. Sony LT, *Le Bombardé*, p. 75.
83. Sony LT, 'Le Sexe de Matonge', p. 118.
84. Ibid., p. 119.
85. Ibid., p. 121.
86. Ibid.
87. Ibid., p. 118.
88. The reference is also a reminder of the continued financial dependency of the RC on France through the currency of the CFA. See Fanny Pigeaud and Ndongo Samba Sylla, *L'Arme invisible de la Francafrique: une histoire du franc CFA* (Paris: La Découverte, 2018).
89. Sony LT, 'Le Sexe de Matonge', p. 118.
90. On this 'postcolonial mirror', see, for example, Sarah Demart, 'Histoire orale à Matonge (Bruxelles): un miroir postcolonial', *Revue Européenne des Migrations Internationales*, 29.1 (2013), 133-55 https://doi.org/10.4000/remi.6323.
91. Gahungu, *Sony Labou Tansi*, p. 121.
92. Ibid., pp. 110-12 and p. 121. The relatively minimal influence of Belgian literature on his work in comparison to these French influences, despite his identification with the Belgian Congo, is arguably due in part to the pervasiveness of French cultural ideology in its colonial project (and beyond), which, as Sony's own education in the two countries shows, was, and is, particularly focused on the promotion of French language and literature. See, for example, John Conteh-Morgan, *Theatre and Drama in Francophone Africa: A Critical Introduction* (Cambridge University Press, 1994), p. 51.
93. Sony LT, *Le Bombardé*, p. 81.
94. Sony LT, 'Kinshasa ne sera jamais', p. 23.
95. De Boeck and Plissart, *Kinshasa*, p. 95.
96. Ibid., pp. 33-34.
97. Sony LT, 'Le Sexe de Matonge', p. 121.
98. Ibid., p. 119.
99. Sony, LT, 'Conférence à Lomé', p. 162.
100. Sony LT, 'Le Sexe de Matonge', p. 120.
101. Nancy Rose Hunt, 'Espace, temporalité et rêverie: écrire l'histoire des futurs au Congo belge', *Politique africaine*, 135:3 (2014), 115-36 http://doi.org/10.3917/polaf.135.0115 (116).
102. Sony LT, 'Le Sexe de Matonge', p. 120.
103. Ibid., p. 122.
104. Gahungu, 'Poétique du paysage', p. 83. The river is a recurring image in work by Congolese authors from both countries, as Nicolas Martin-Granel shows in '"Le Fleuve commence ici", choix de textes', *Continents manuscrits*, 11 (2018), http://doi.org/10.4000/coma/2890. See also, Nicolas Martin-Granel, 'D'une rive l'autre: questions de génétique et poétique', *Continents manuscrits*, 15 (2020), http://doi.org/10.4000/coma.6277.
105. Sony Labou Tansi, [Untitled], in *L'Autre monde: écrits inédits*, pp. 54-58, (p. 56).
106. Sony LT, 'Le Sexe de Matonge', p. 118.

Landscaping and Escaping the Colony in Mudimbe's, Ruti's, and Nayigiziki's Works'[1]

Maëline Le Lay

Introduction

The description of space is a constant feature of colonial and colonialist literature. First of all, if this element is central in colonialist literature, it is because explorers in the service of imperial states were concerned with mapping the territory to be colonised, indexing it to control it for further exploitation. This would then be carried out by the settlers, be they planters or engineers, whose talent for pioneering was measured by their impact on the landscape, their ability to transform it, to shape it for profit. As Pierre Halen reminds us, 'the colonist appears as a "surveyor of spaces" [...]. His first actions will be cartographic, gestures of exploration and measurement, but also of neglect, if it is true that maps neglect places by abstracting them'.[2]

The nuance that Halen brings out is a significant one: the colonialist authors' gesture of inhabiting and arranging space neglects places by rendering them abstract and failing (though not systematically) to consider their aesthetic features without any preconceived agenda; it is even more rare for colonial authors to recognise a metaphysical dimension in the landscape. However, a close reading of francophone African colonial literature reveals that these authors – at least those from Belgian (and French) colonies, which will be our focus here – deal differently with places.

Pioneers of African francophone literature – writers such as Camara Laye, Paul Lomami-Tshibamba, and Léopold S. Senghor – learned early in their careers to represent and valorise the places they knew. They were also able to demonstrate that the natural environment had shaped their cultures. Published even earlier than some of the pioneering novels by these classical authors, *Mes Transes à Trente ans (Escapade ruandaise)* by Saverio Naygiziki (1950) shows a clear sensitivity to landscape that reflects, in a romantic way, the protagonist's moods.[3] But the text also lends itself to a political reading; its point of view is squarely situated within colonial ideology, although it is not without some discreet criticisms. Indeed, like Lomami Tshibamba's tale *Ngando*,[4] *Mes transes à trente ans* depicts the childhood landscape and its surroundings as a beautiful, even mystical space, but also, more circumspectly, as a space under surveillance.

This colonial autobiographical novel (the subtitle of the first edition is *Histoire vécue mêlée de roman* [A Lived Story with Novelistic Features] will be compared to two texts published after independence: an autobiography, *Les Corps glorieux des mots et des êtres* by Valentin Yves Mudimbe (1994)[5] and *Le Fils de Mikeno* by Antoine Ruti.[6] Even though the latter presents itself as a work of fiction, it was likely inspired by the author's own experiences in Rwanda, where he was born, and Congo, where he settled.

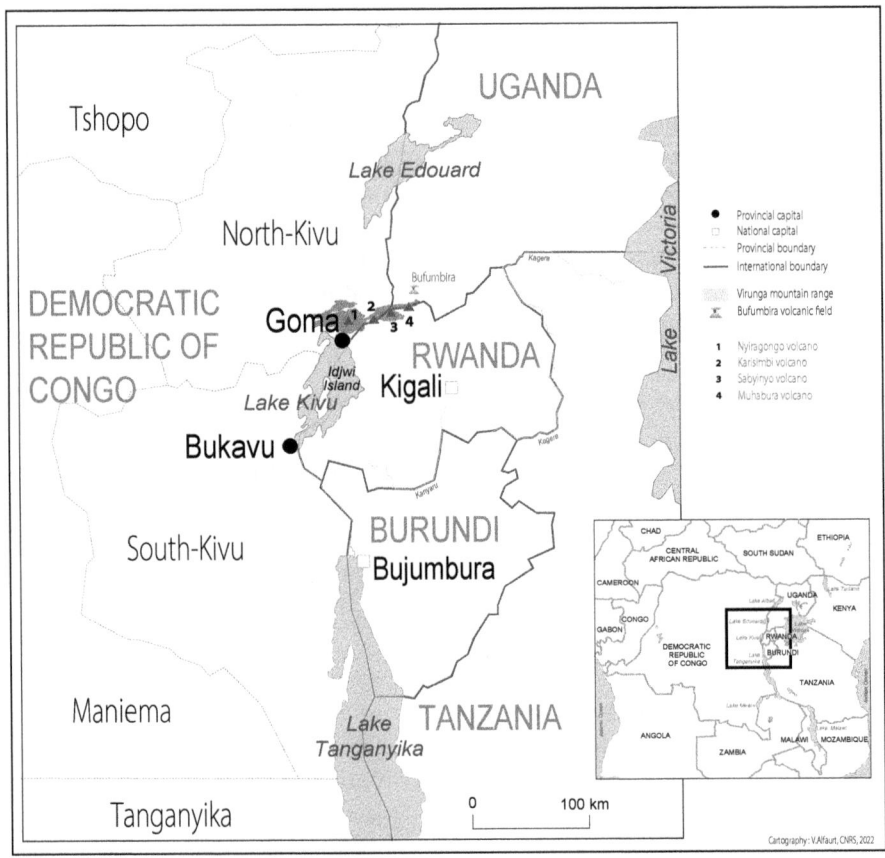

Figure 1. Map of Rwanda, Burundi, Congo, and Uganda with elements of natural geography. Cartography: V.Alfaurt, CNRS, 2022.

Although these texts are characterised by a strong emphasis on the landscapes of the Great Lakes region (Rwanda, Congo, Uganda, and Burundi), which are surveyed by characters living under the colonial regime, only Nayigiziki's work was written during the colonial period. We shall attempt to highlight how this temporal difference affects the writing and the experience of place as depicted in these works. As we shall see, Ruti and Mudimbe show the domestication and constriction of the landscape by colonial rulers more acutely than Nayigiziki does. Political territorialisation is implemented through the presentation of a dual landscape, a palimpsestic landscape made of two layers: the natural landscape and the political landscape. This intrinsic duality of landscape under colonial control generates an ambivalent understanding of certain places constantly traversed and transgressed by the protagonists.

The Experience of Palimpsestic Landscape

Our three stories unfold in four countries (five, if we count Kenya, where the *Fils de Mikeno* character Apollinaire briefly goes): Rwanda, Burundi, Congo, and Uganda. The region and the countries comprising it are bounded by elements of natural geography: Lake Kivu and Ijwi Island; Lakes Victoria and Tanganyika (and other smaller lakes); the volcanoes Nyiragongo, Karisimbi, Muhabura, and Savinyo; the Bufumbira volcanic field, the Virunga mountain range, and various rivers such as Kanyaru and Kagera (Fig. 1).

The places described in these narratives are approached in different ways by their protagonists. They are sometimes experienced (especially through walking), sometimes imagined (through reflective analysis of past experiences of places), and sometimes expressed through a specific toponymy that often leads to interpretation.

Experiencing Places

These characters wander throughout the region, but they do not all attach the same importance to travel. While Apollinaire Silimu (in *Le Fils de Mikeno*, henceforth *FM*) merely goes from one place to another without dwelling on the journey that makes this movement possible, Justin (in *Mes Transes à trente ans*, henceforth *MT30*) and Mudimbe (in *Les Corps Glorieux des mots et des êtres*, henceforth *CG*) are walkers. Silimu, despite often opting not to mention his movements, does not eschew the description of the places he visits, which resonate with him in a specific way. A few passages will give a sense of the way the configuration of places influences him and introduces his unique encounter with the landscape:

> What a radiant day! Here, from the summit of the Nyamiyaga, I feel as though I'm living a kind of transfiguration. The blue above, where the wild swallows frolic, and the green below, where streams snake by, awaken curious thirsts within me. The joy extends on into infinite space. The month of May is the most beautiful of the year. Flowers without number, dominated by yellow, create a festive atmosphere. On the horizon, beyond the expanses draped in green and gold, Mount Karisimbi towers with its snowy peak. Our ancestors saw that same peak, and perhaps our fathers today see it too, as a bouquet of lilies laid down at the summit of the volcano, an offering to the Lord. Fever arrives, a fever like those you catch on a grand occasion, and which electrify you. (*FM*, p. 47)

Justin (from *MT30*) is a tireless walker, one who criss-crosses the region and its many borders. He traverses it from top to bottom, from hill to stream, paying attention to the natural elements he encounters. He describes every space he walks through, focusing on the topography (by means of strictly informative commentaries) or the climate, weather, and atmosphere:

> Sometimes, questioning the unnerving horizon with a disoriented glance, always avoiding running into anyone, I continue my hallucinated race across vast fields of manioc, pass hills and valleys and around noon, I collapse, weak with exhaustion, thirsty and panting, in what must be Mayaga, in the middle of the steppe, on the steep crest of who knows what hill, – Kibirizi perhaps, or Matara? – where brambles, nestled next to wild shrubs, grow under God's attentive hand in the ungrateful soil of rock and stone. (*MT30*, pp. 72–73)

His descriptions are often interspersed with a series of introspective remarks, references to colonial propaganda, and aspects of political history and sociology. Notwithstanding, as informative as these landscape descriptions in Ruti's and Nayigiziki's writings may be, the authors' subjectivity (through the expression of what they feel while travelling) is not the only source of these descriptions; they also emanate from their spirituality, as they undergo a process of conversion. The first passage might be read as a succinct statement of the traces and remnant of ancestor worship in a society being gradually evangelised. To begin with, Silimu speaks of an experience of 'transfiguration', of a 'fever' that 'electrifies' him in the manner of a trance. Then Mount Karisimbi is described syncretically. Indeed, the character observes it first through the eyes of his ancestors, and then through his father's generation; the narrator assumes that these men had all admired the mountain's snowy peak, which would have reminded them of a bunch of lilies, reminiscent of a divine offering to the Lord. Moreover, in the Christian tradition, lilies are a symbol of royalty as well as of the divine – in any case, of those chosen by a higher power. Interestingly, the term *ancestor* is used here in its purely genealogical sense (of 'forefather') and not in its spiritual sense (related to the worship of ancestors), which attests to an epistemic break with a precolonial cosmogony. This passage of *MT30* thus bears witness to a successful Christianising process, which nevertheless does not completely do away with all signs of previous spiritual forms.

While Mudimbe pays attention to the landscapes through which he travels, he is far from a wandering pilgrim like Justin, who walks without stopping. For Justin, indeed, the walking represents a kind of headlong rush forwards, which by his own admission, he transforms into an adventure ('Are not visions the adventurer's only joys?', *MT30*, p. 279). Mudimbe retains his seminarist's habit of seeing walks in nature as meditation in motion. Several passages of *CG* describe occasional walks, provoked by some pragmatic quest – such as collecting a parcel containing books – but which turn into opportunities to meditate on nature and life.

In these three stories, the protagonist's progression through the landscape is recounted as an experience that is just as sensory as it is meditative and introspective. It is through the intervention of the senses, awakened by physical contact with the landscape, that the protagonist experiences places, immerses himself in their appearance and scale. He then retreats within himself to listen to what this experience elicits: emotions and sentiments (nostalgia, joy, plenitude, danger, sadness, and melancholy) as well as scattered reflections.

Thinking Places

In these stories, places are sometimes first imagined before being experienced or interpreted. Landscape thought can be expressed by representations that immediately arise in the protagonist's mind, or by a reflective gaze on a given place via an object-witness of that place, an object that recalls this landscape.

In Ruti's work, reflectivity is almost absent, at least in the sense of a reflective re-evaluation of a place, or even of the past: the character exists completely in the moment, without a pre-established plan, and seems to make completely spontaneous decisions about where he will go and how he will act next. An attitude of this type obviously does not encourage any theory of places mediated by a transitional object, as occurs in Mudimbe's text. *CG* is indeed made up exclusively of back-and-forth movement between different periods, and it is precisely one of these journeys that provokes his contemplation of the Rwandan landscape in which he briefly lived. This made him think of how he became a novice in the Church:

> A Sunday in September. [...] It does not undo anything in this beautiful season. It simply validates an effort: my work to lose myself in the Benedictine Rule. The dry season stretches on. Soon, the rains will be here. After the high mass, Brother Hildebrand puts the spotlight on me; he takes photographs [...]. That photo is before me now. It's been over thirty years since the day I gave myself up to this dubious exhibitionist's exercise. Since then, I've learned to decode the signs. And I reread this photograph with displeasure. [...] The tilt of my head is proud, the tilt of a conqueror's head. Essentially, the photo represents a symbol: I believe I've made it, I've reached a goal. Only my gaze lost in the middle distance reconciles me with what I have in fact become: someone anxious, someone agnostic. The person in the photograph is contemplative, lost in these hills whose beauty I only truly discovered years after having left Gihindamuyaga, thanks to the book by Marie Gevers. It's true, I am reinventing that Sunday, now. Brother Hildebrand has made me a gift of a complete set of these photos. I travel through them, seeking the trajectories of my gaze and my dreams in the distance. I see anew the imprecise waves of the hills, with their scattered and frail trees against a brilliant green; small hamlets protected by banana trees, dark spots pointed out by streaks of light-coloured smoke. All around us, silence. Or no, rather a green peace, that our white robes violate. I remember, saying to Brother Hildebrand: 'September, in Rwanda, is truly a lovely month.' He gave me his timid smile. We left the fence and advanced into the garden. [...] Through the trees, I can see, halfway along the slope and the road leading to Astrida-Butare, the roof of the convent of our Benedictine Sisters. The hour spreads itself out. [...] I take up this test again thirty years later, in the Americas, on this 30th of March 1990, and I rediscover familiar alleyways and the Rwandan hamlets on the hillsides. In essence, propositions on the virtues of a cultural conversion. (*CG*, pp. 53–54)

This excerpt is a key passage in Mudimbe's autobiographical narrative. For one thing, it embodies – via the body seen and considered in the landscape – the idea of cultural conversion (an idea that, for Mudimbe, is inscribed in the colonial organisation of space). But it also indicates a conversion from one career to another, from Catholic novice to thinker and university scholar. And this major idea in Mudimbe's thought gains precision and strength from the memory of a specific instant, in the encounter with the photographic representation of the man he once was. His thought is thus born from a retrospective reading of the landscape. The representation of his then self in the then landscape is interrogated by today's gaze. The photograph acts as the negative of the landscape, giving it its full significance. In other words, it is the act of looking today at yesterday's photograph that allows Mudimbe to decode the signs, to construct a philosophy from this emblematic landscape of the Great Lakes region during the colonial period. Here, photography perfectly fulfils its role of catalysing imagination and reflection; interweaving these together generates new schemas of meaning. Stéphane Ledien notes something similar in his reading of *Le Scribe et son ombre* by Abdelkebir Khatibi:

> A 'machine', as Khatibi phrases it, 'to go back in time and fabricate both a past and a virtual memory', photography in fact projects 'the object in a beam of apparently fixed images'; but this fixity is but 'pure illusion, for it is the person looking who justifies it by depositing in it the meaning he or she desires'.[7]

This Rwandan landscape presents itself as a complex network of representations: the passage evokes, on the one hand, Mudimbe's mental representation of the landscape at the time the photograph was taken (he already had an aestheticising view of the landscape, since he had commented on its September loveliness), and on the other hand, the representation he acquired later with the help of work by the Belgian writer Marie Gevers.[8] *Des Mille Collines aux Neuf Volcans* is a travel narrative belonging to the corpus of colonial literature, which was first published in 1953 and then republished in 2002 with a preface by Mudimbe.[9] In this short text, the author recalls how striking this reading had been for him both when he read it for the first time while in Gihindimuyaga, and later in America. He acknowledges the powerful empathy of a book in which Gevers strives to understand Rwandan people while at the same time speaking consciously from where she stood, as a Belgian, as exemplified by her depictions of the country and her reliance on a personal set of cultural references. He also points out how perceptive she was of the political tensions already building up in Rwanda during this period, pioneering Ruti's sharp critiques of Rwandan society. Mudimbe also admires how observant she was of the beautiful diversity of the Great Lakes region's landscapes around Rwanda, from South Kivu to Uganda. Her attention to the people, the landscape transformations, and the political movements still resonates powerfully in Mudimbe's mind in the early 2000s. This later – and literary – idea of the landscape helps him appreciate it more fully in retrospect. And there is even a third aspect: the socio-politically inflected re-reading he performs at the time of writing.

In *CG*, the landscape is no sooner summoned than it is theorised or interpreted. While for Silimu in *FM* the landscape is never a pretext for giving oneself up to reverie or contemplation, Nayigiziki represents a kind of intermediary between Mudimbe and Ruti. He is all at once intensely present in the immediate experience of the landscape, describing it at the moment of its perception, and ready to share his representations of places by means of symbols he invokes, and other untheorised bodies of knowledge that the landscape evokes in his mind; with these elements, Nayigiziki then gives free rein to the reveries and emotions that the landscape elicits. His departure from Nyanza, the land of his childhood, just before his long escapade through the region, offers an opportunity to evoke the entire set of collective representations attached to that place (even before turning to his childhood memories or the sentiments that tie him to Nyanza):

> In the street I find myself more at ease and gaze one last time at the beautiful views of Nyanza. A Sunday in Nyanza is always a celebration! Dear Nyanza, a hill chosen among all others to be the residence of our kings, the capital of a country now pacified and already subjugated, a city restless and Rwandan above all others, where foreigners are only ever passing through; a city one hates at first and loves at length! How I struggle to tear myself away from you! How I miss you before even leaving you! (*MT30*, p. 58)

Speaking and Interpreting Places

What strikes the reader of these three narratives is their geographical character, the abundance of place names. Because the characters are in constant movement, they regularly describe the places through which they travel, and give them their right names. However, it seems that beyond the desire to inform and to ensure that the narrative remains intelligible, the quantity of topographical indications corresponds to a deliberate accumulation effect, a true semiotics of place to which the narrators aim to awaken their readers.

Without explicitly formulating this intention, Ruti's and Nayigiziki's narratives reveal the phenomenon of 'activating toponymy', as Mudimbe says (*CG*, p. 44). By designating places by their indigenous *and* colonial names, the protagonists open a window onto the process of colonisation in their countries' spaces, exposing the act of a third party rewriting a country by de-baptising and re-baptising places for their appropriation.

The narrator of *FM*, who introduces himself as a bastard, only defines himself in this way by assigning his biological origins to different landscapes – real and imagined – in Rwanda. Thus, he not only alludes to Lake Kivu and to the various hills and mythical cities of Rwanda (Nyanza, royal capital) but also regularly to Egypt, from where the Tutsi have allegedly descended. He himself, because of his hazy lineage, is not in a position to identify with any of the three groups: neither Tutsi, nor Hutu, nor Twa:

> From the side of the Nyamiyaga, where since early morning I have allowed our meagre fortune to graze aimlessly, I overlook this pastoral region where, almost alone among the Tutsis, my father is this poor. Zachée Mikeno, such is his name, but people mockingly call him 'Citizen Mikeno', meaning Mikeno the anonymous, the nobody. He goes everywhere, as if he had not a single right, even the right to trod on the earth of the roads. Anonymous in appearance most of all, with a dull and undistinctive face. In this country with three ethnic groups, no one would know in which one to place him. Is it really possible that I was born of such a person? (*FM*, p. 15)

From beginning to end, *FM* deploys an imaginary geography made up of two opposite poles: Lake Kivu and its islands, in the western fringes of the Kingdom of Rwanda, where young women pregnant from undesirable unions were locked away, and an imagined and distant Egypt, from where the forefathers of the Tutsi are said to have migrated to Rwanda after the Hutus. With this genealogy comes the obvious characteristics denoting grandeur and all the historical corollaries that this implies. In its evident adherence to the Hamite ideology, which flourished during the colonial era, and has been thoroughly analysed by Jean-Pierre Chrétien,[10] this narrative brings uneasiness to today's reader, but allows us to grasp this schema and its consequences on the experience of the Great Lakes landscape. Saddled with such an ideology (as a persistent pattern inherited from colonial ideology) in the late colonial and early post-colonial Rwanda he depicts, it is unsurprising that the narrator should feel nowhere at home. So, he traverses the region indefatigably, meeting sometimes his compatriots, sometimes members of ethnic groups known to him (Tutsi, Hutu), seeking without pause to save his skin, or at least not to miss a single opportunity for survival.

The most abundant crop of place names can be found in Nayigiziki's work. Many passages highlight the double toponymy that reflects the double possession of the landscape – indigenous and colonial:

> From Gihogwe, where on our right we see, in Buhoro across from Leremacu, a beautiful view of the century-old 'Byimana', the last remains of a vast Mwami residence, we find ourselves in Bitsibo, tumbling into the Kizuba swamp which originates in the steep slopes of Rugobagoba hill. At the top of this hill, in the middle of a grove that looks sacred, we see, temple-like, an old brick cottage flanked by an alley of cacti. This cottage, so old but still

standing, which might still be in use, was used more than 20 years ago as a lodging for Mr. Joseph Dardenne or 'Zezefu', the valiant pioneer, so well-known and so deservedly famous, who built the present-day Kigali-Astrida road. [...] In this region, with its wild contours, between gaunt Nduga and haughty Ndiza, between jagged, desert-like Bumbogo, forested Bulima and defiant Bwanacyambwe, the single village of Rukoma, below the Nyabarongo which snakes along majestically at its feet, appears as a genuine jewel. And the Protestant missionaries who, in the time of the Germans, had already set up camp in this oasis, had a good eye, for the old Mission, called the Lemera Mission, which was passed on to the Belgian Protestants twenty years ago, has few equals, even seen from afar, for location or beauty. (*MT30*, 225–26)

As shown by this excerpt, these passages are often an opportunity to praise the colonial enterprise. This quote is particularly rich in historical strata, for no fewer than three reigns are evoked: those of the Mwami but also those of the German and Belgian colonisers. It is clear that for the narrator – whose voice is indistinguishable from that of the author, a clerk in the colonial administration employed in both Rwanda and Congo – politics validates his perception of the location's exceptional character, since those in power inhabit this landscape and consequently shape it. The landscape, already remarkable for its splendour, acquires supplementary value as the place chosen by the region's governing authorities, from the Mwami to the Belgian missionaries and colonisers.

CG offers the most distinct display of the different strata of landscape, since Mudimbe chooses them as an object of analysis. The long passage devoted to his walk from Kapolowe to the Mpala mission in South Katanga on 30 June 1960, is another crucial section of the narrative. Reading it makes clear the extent to which this experience of walking in a landscape at nightfall – on the very day of the independence of the Congo – was a foundational experience for Mudimbe's understanding and theorisation of the process of 'conversion' that constituted Belgian colonisation in Africa:

So, I walk toward Kapolowe. [...] I walk slowly. I am *in situ* and I advance, happy to be able to name concrete connections. They bring together the order of a conquest and the metamorphosis of the space through which I move. On another level, the marks or traces of a past in this night ought to be able to repeat and give new voice to their own differences as brutalized experiences. In the name 'Belgian Congo', for instance, the adjective that disappears on this thirtieth of June 1960 is a perfect artefact. The space it leaves is, from this moment on, inscribed in the new history opening its doors. Yet the fact is clear that the proof of the rupture, if the rupture is indeed fact, is in no way

> in the erasure of the adjective, nor even in the new signs that this elimination might authorize, but, rather, in the body that lives (survives) as end and letter of the metamorphosis. Kapolowe is a space reminding me, and powerfully so, of another place: Mpala. [...] Between these two zones, there is an empty space [...] It is neither garden nor forest. All in all, it is neither an arrangement of flowerbeds, nor total chaos. It irritates by what it reveals: separation. [...] The symbolism established by this distance and this separation into black and white seems paradoxically to invoke the marriage of the two extremes. In a sense, then, the South might, someday, become the North. And yet we know that, geographically, such a thing is impossible. (*CG*, pp. 43–44)

In the end, Ruti's geography is just as imaginary as Mudimbe's. While Ruti can be said to extend the borders of Rwanda all the way to Egypt and Kivu (which he claims as a province of Rwanda, a subject of great controversy[11]), Mudimbe imagines a new geography ensuing from the policy of racial segregation, beginning with the vacant zone of the *cordon sanitaire* (see Pierre-Philippe Fraiture's chapter in this volume) set up by the Belgians to separate the White and Black populations. Imagining the empty space filled with union is what the 'new' name for the area promises: 'Kapolowe-Saint Gérard', a hyphenated name that is a 'symbolic conjunction' (*CG*, p. 44).

Just as the photograph acts as the negative of a landscape that hosts memories, the new place name acts as a negative of the past, which can reveal, by means of the reversible pivot constituted by the hyphen, the strata beneath and their reversed reflection: the new superimposed strata. The photograph catalyses memories – images and sensations of a bygone time; the name 'activates toponymy' (*CG*, p. 44) and the history of the place it contains, in the manner of a metonymy. This very paradox, of a landscape that represents both separation and union, is what Mudimbe experiences in his walk to Kapolowe/Mpala on that thirtieth of June. The paradox appears to him by way of his walk through a landscape one has to name to decipher:

> The proper name, wrote my late friend, Michel de Certeau, [...] gives meaning to a space. The best way to illustrate this would be to use walking. To quote Michel de Certeau, walking is fundamentally paradoxical. Walking constitutes, on one hand – because of external demands that impose themselves on the person advancing in space [...] – the act of going outside of oneself, outside of one's home. But walking is also – according to inner convictions that the act can make visible – to renew and extend an inner space: this is my garden, my street, my village, my region, etc., and I can name them. (*CG*, p. 42)

The three narratives, then, offer a description of the Great Lakes region as a palimpsestic landscape whose different layers of appropriation and representation can be stripped away and examined in turn. Reading a landscape is in fact an eminently political act, and allows the reader to grasp the process of colonisation in action, inscribed in physical space. This conversion is also carried out by dint of statements and by the signage of the landscape's territorialisation. In other words, one might speak of a performative toponymy, in the sense that describing a landscape and enunciating its toponymy perform not only the possession but also the reappropriation of all its layers and remnants.

On a Few Significant Topoi

Several places capture this landscape and its multiple strata – the landscape that people seek with equal passion to absorb, master, and abstract themselves from – and many of these are what we might call domesticated places, that is to say, places where the territory undergoes a transformation into inventory or heritage. These places reveal the profound ambivalence of the narrators' relationship to a landscape that they inhabit under colonial control.

The Garden

The garden occupies a unique position in Mudimbe's work. In *CG*, we find figurative deployments of the trope of the garden – that is, domesticated nature. Once again, the garden acts as a metaphor for ploughing and organising ideas, representations, and perceptions as if they were living essences. Recounting the beginning of his psychoanalytical treatment, Mudimbe refers to the trope of the 'secret garden', a notion designating an intimate space of self-containment and self-expression: 'Since then, two or three times a week, I live in a setting where kindly, she obliges me to name the flowers and brambles of my garden, as well as my unsatisfied desires' (*CG*, p. 27). This is because, as Pierre Lepape insists, 'the art of gardening is nominalistic, and its primary relationship to nature, its first taking of possession, the first act of initiation invariably takes place through words. The gardener first plants names, not seeds'.[12] For Mudimbe, it is as if the performativity of the landscape's architecture leads to an 'archi-texture' of self, of his most intimate being, as underscored by this later remark about his psychoanalysis: 'My childhood resurfaces, an art, a vocation. I emerged from it, and since then I turn in circles in a garden, astonished' (*CG*, p. 158).

The garden is also represented as a refuge in Mudimbe's novel *Shaba Deux*,[13] a book that can be read in continuity with *CG*. This continuity is both thematic and historical: *CG* relates different episodes from the colonial period and the independence period, while *Shaba Deux* takes places eighteen years after independence, but in a convent whose habits have barely changed since independence. Like *Shaba deux*'s main character, Mudimbe regularly takes refuge in the garden to reflect and meditate while walking. The garden presents itself as a synecdoche for nature, as a vehicle for symbolically recreating either a miniaturised version of wild nature or its reassuring substitute fulfilling the narrator's needs:

> And I returned, later, through the wood, an artificial one, but blessed with a lovely beauty [...] I was thinking of a friend from Africa. It was the ideal moment for a conversation. I had the right words. They imposed themselves on me. I think, she would have liked them. They were taking shape, literally, in my mind. The surrounding trees marked a permanence of things. The strength of nature, the rationality of a continuity of natural life. A continuity since when? I know: this wood is a creation of the last century. It was what it signified as natural reason that mattered to me (*CG*, p. 137).

The enclosed, organised space of the garden seeks to fulfil the human desire for beauty (Alain Roger speaks of nature's 'artialisation', a concept that considers the landscape as intrinsically springing from art) and the human need[14] for security all at once. But in an African context, the garden is first and foremost a Western invention, transmitted principally by the clergy and their missions. Reading between the lines, we can see this expressed in Mudimbe's disappointment when he reaches La Procure at Usumbura (Burundi) and fails to find there the outside garden he had expected:

> After the evening prayer, I wanted to get some air: to melt into the night, to feel around me, silent and welcoming, the life of trees, plants, the presence of nature. So, I went out. Five minutes later, I was in my room once more. There was no garden. All around, I had found nothing but trucks, cars, tractors. In essence, the splendour of the mission and of conquest (*CG*, p. 22).

Here, then, is no beauty created by sculpted nature, but civilisation at its most industrial: engines and machines. The same sentiment is expressed in no uncertain terms by Ruti when describing the city of Nairobi on his first visit. He plainly associates the public gardens with the planning and arrangement of the territory by the Europeans whose loose morals he deplores:

> A city in every way European, planted in the heart of Africa: that's Nairobi. The European, omnipresent, is on top. Even the Asian only occupies the out-

skirts. As for the Black, you won't see him at all, except in uniform. […] More modern yet than Kinshasa, Nairobi stands out for his numerous imposing buildings and daring architecture. Public gardens of a tender green are scattered throughout the city. There come strolling white women flanked by a bevy of servants pushing prams. Drunk on idleness, wearing but a hint of underwear and a flimsy bra, they wallow in the well-kept lawn (*FM*, p. 211).

The Mission

The garden is the microcosm of the mission, as suggested by Mudimbe. It is also the ultimate place representing the appropriation of a country and its territorial reorganisation is the Christian mission. It is striking to notice the extent to which mission buildings delineate the landscapes journeyed over by the narrators in each of our three works. *MT30* contains the most frequent appearances of the mission. Nayigiziki offers poetic and deeply felt descriptions of the Great Lakes region and shows how this area has been combed by rivers and moulded by mountains. His reading is also political, interpreting the cross-border space organised around the colonial administrative posts belonging to different imperial states (Belgium, Britain) and to Christian missions.

The mission is always presented as the epicentre of a given district. It is the rallying point of its inhabitants, the centre of civilisation, conveying order and meaning in the midst of vast, underdeveloped expanses of nature of raw beauty but ominous silence. The presence of the mission reassures our characters; the cloister acts as a refuge for pilgrims, where they can rest their hearts, refocus on themselves, and above all return to the path of virtue and rectitude, through song and prayer. The following passage shows how deeply the mission shapes the landscape:

> Beneath a tawny red, spotted sky – like a serval's skin – thin clouds, a cold wind, in the timid morning, destroy the last vestiges of the night. In Savé, to the coppery sound of the old bell, the old mission starts to bustle with life. Beyond, on the hillside with the gentle slope, by a slanted path that leads to the church, children run like little spots, and slow women bearing crowns, a scattering of men dressed in muddy clothing emerge, appear, and disappear, like shadows sliding in the milky fog, through the old, full cemetery, toward the house of God. (*MT30*, p. 44)

Faced with the existential anguish brought by the realisation that life runs its ineluctable course in the villages and in nature, only the Church offers solace to the narrator:

Before us, beyond the insalubrious valley, the city of Nyanza awakens and stretches out for the sordid comings and goings of the high market days. [...] This renewal of things touches and terrifies me all at once. Alone, radiant and calm, resplendent in its morning beauty, with her stained-glass eyes enlivened by the red fires of a straightforward sun, the church gives me heart. How starkly she contrasts with the vulgarity of all these things that dance in the wind, that distract the eyes and shimmer like waves! Up there, on the bank of a plateau covered in paths, houses and fields; between two green-tinted hills, she emerges, maternal and good-natured, as a shelter for rest and peace, as a divine warehouse of hope open to all, where anybody may find sustenance for an indigent heart and for a naked soul, a pure white cloak. (*MT30*, p. 50)

This paean notwithstanding, the perception of missions in Nayigiziki's work contains more contrast than this would tend to suggest. Indeed, despite the novel's propagandistic tonality, which means that it occasionally reads as a defence of the evangelisation of Rwanda as well as of colonisation in general, the lyrical description of the Nyanza mission includes a tinge of cynicism vis-à-vis the signs and effects of its recent Christianisation. Thus, he begins by describing the natural environment in which the Nyanza mission is nestled, which was initially the seat of the kingdom, the sacred ancestral capital of Rwanda:

It's a grassy, high-perched plateau which, from behind, overlooks the city of Nyanza hidden away in the tall greenery of the eucalyptus, and on the right, the royal palace, barely visible in a thick wood. There we see, from above, all the legendary nearby hills. Here, Mugandamure, Gasoro, Mutende, Mukingo, in Nduga where a few smoky huts are lost in the pale foliage of scattered banana groves. And in Kabagari, we first see the Nyamagana hill which still carries the gigantic vestiges of an ancient Mwami kraal; domed huts and old models are in construction there, for a princess: the eldest daughter of Musinga. [...] In Bufundi, past the muddy Mwogo, the formidable links of the Congo-Nile line. (*MT30*, pp. 30–31)

In a second stage, the narrator's eye comes to rest on the mission proper, on the life unfolding around the Church and its offices. The description of the inhabitants of Nyanza is clearly disparaging. We can identify a biting critique of the game of appearances and the servile obedience of the common people:

In the sky stripped of its mourning, the sun of just before 8 laughs riotously like a baby who has finished crying. The bell, intoxicated by its Sunday joy, calls with all its might, all the way to the horizon. From every corner, the roads vomit up the faithful who rush toward the church. High mass in Nyanza, more than elsewhere perhaps, takes on a singularly formal aspect on the part of the faithful. It's the mass of high society. For the poor of Nyanza, despite being neat and clean, are ashamed, like elsewhere, to mingle their Sunday rags with fine suits. (*MT30*, p. 58)

Ruti, whose pen is more acidic, explicitly criticises the co-opting of the sacred nature of the ancestral Nyanza hill by the Church, and then by its worshippers, who are ridiculed here:

Nonetheless, the current king – a conclusion added by the priest, unbeknownst to the poet – will be known as greater than his predecessors, for his role as artisan of the most glorious of victories. By dedicating the land to the Christ-King, he turned Nyanza into one of the capitals of Christendom. Nyanza, that bastion of the monarchy, carrier of opulent symbols, shines brightly on this eve of ceremony. From all corners of the country, and from abroad, colourful crowds flood the streets; the lowliest lackey has donned his festive garb [...] Neither landscape, though they appear grandiose to many, can match this centre of the country, so artistically fluffed, and whose numberless hillocks bear poetic names that come always in twos (*FM*, p. 76).

The reorganisation of the territory provoked by the missions is perceived with ambivalence in these texts. In the case of Nyanza in particular, the narrators seem to recognise the coherence and strategic intelligence of the colonists' policy of employing an already sacred site, and fully investing a high place of power in order to install their own authority. At the same time, however, this colonial strategy of co-opting seems to exasperate them. The transmutation of power on the same site has the effect of absorbing the original signifiers (the power of the Mwami). Between the lines, a discreet critique of this act of imposition and substitution is being put forward, masked by the two authors' sarcastic critique of the ritualistic pomp displayed in this religious celebration.

The Road and the Paper

Roads, because they structure a territory as much as mission buildings, are one of the central instruments employed in the transformation of the colonial landscape. The construction of thoroughfares, and the subsequent social change elicited by this process, is a recurring topos of colonial and postcolonial African literature exploring the imperial period: we need only think of the *Bouts de bois de Dieu* (1960) by Ousmane Sembène, which describes the construction of the

Dakar-Niger railway line. More recently, *Tram 83*, a novel by Fiston Mwanza Mujila (2014) describes the railway connecting Lubumbashi to the Kasaï province and former Rhodesia, and *Dance of the Jakaranda* by Peter Kimani (2017) is a novel organised around the construction of the Mombasa-Nakuru railway, the backbone of British East Africa.[15]

The descriptions of landscapes in Belgian Africa in the texts by Ruti and Nayigiziki bring out the structuring importance of roads for the proper functioning of the colony and for its economic organisation, both internal and external. Indeed, the advent of the road concentrates within itself all the violence of colonial exploitation. The first pages of *FM* express this point neatly while revealing the central organisation of the territories administered by Belgium:

> The chill of the night still lingers when the echoes vibrate from the cacophony of horns. The *barkers* ring in the signal to gather for the colonial State's chores: 'Pickaxe and basket! […] On the road!' This road is the territorial administrator Joseph Demal's obsession and is intended to shorten the way from Astrida to Bukavu, across an uneven and jagged landscape. (*FM*, p. 7)

As it is associated with forced labour and with the subjugation of colonised populations for the (commercial) benefit of the coloniser, the road is also a potentially threatening place for our fugitive characters. As a point of passage, the road exposes them to the surveillance of the authorities, who are likely to interrupt their journey and block their access to certain parts of the territory, declare their movements illegitimate, or even deport them (the term, as illustrated in the example below, is not excessive) to places where they will be forced to work for the colonisers. In the next quote, Justin, on his way to Uganda, meets a Murundi who provides him with information on such places (a plantation):

> – Hi there ! What's the fighting for ?
> – Listen, he said hurriedly, these four trucks over here belong to the 'Gasamvu', which is to say the Gakira Sugar Company. They come here, with the authority, apparently, to take workers by force for the sugar cane plantations. You're badly paid and badly treated there; people die constantly. You almost never come back. We don't want to get in the truck, nor to sign on to work for the Gasamvu. And the drivers with their helpers want to take us by force. […] The four Gasamvu trucks will be held under surveillance; the Baganda, who own the trucks, are absolutely forbidden to take any Burundi passengers in their vehicles who have not yet stayed in English territory for three months or who do not come recommended or protected by a native of the Tanganyika Territory. (*MT30*, pp. 92–93)

The sugar company discussed here by Justin, which is today the Ugandan company Kakira, a historic leader in the East African sugar industry ('Sweetening Uganda since 1930'), bases its foundation story on the construction of this very road, in 1940, as the backbone of the extractivist industry.[16]

The road is also the way that one seeks out to flee, or just the place one wants to avoid so as not to be too visible. When characters have no choice but to use the road, they must equip themselves with an official document that can act as a permit or pass. Such a paper might be a letter of recommendation penned by a benevolent member of a religious order, hoping to ensure the protégé's safety, as Justin recounts during one of his many escape episodes; or it might be, as in the following episode, a 'tax token', no doubt meant to demonstrate the characters' diligence with regard to their duties to the state:

> In the afternoon, I say a sad goodbye to my aunt, my cousin, to this sunny hill: the land of my father. Rusiribana, my beloved, devoted uncle, as sad as I am, gives me his 1945 tax token under the pretext of safekeeping, and accompanies me. My *boy* follows us, bearing a little parcel under his arm: our parcel for the journey, into which my cousin has slipped provisions for tonight and tomorrow. (*MT30*, p. 77)

On multiple occasions in *MT30*, and to a lesser extent in *FM*, a piece of paper acts as a key: an object that opens the way and authorises free movement on the road, which can in that case fulfil its primary role of guaranteeing connection between different places. These roads form part of the geography of the country that they shape in response to the colonial government's policies. In this sense, we may say that thoroughfares do tell a historical story, and allow our characters to move within their region and cross borders, but they also transmit a construction of historical memory, which is an agent of division. Roads can thus give concrete form to psychological borders when they become symbolic vehicles for describing mythical lands and the glorious, dream-fuelled geography of the country before foreign presence. Ruti is more radical and aggressive than Nayigiziki in the geographical representation of his country: in Ruti's work, a kind of claim can be heard, an insistence on driving back certain borders and strengthening others. It is therefore not surprising that his novel was, in all likelihood, written during the early 1990s, and is the work of a Tutsi exiled in Congo, for we know that one of the effects of prolonged exile is the exacerbation of national sentiment and the promotion of the mystification of one's home country; this effect became even more pronounced in the context of the war that severely plagued the entire Great Lakes region at that time.

Conclusion

In his *Court traité du paysage,* Roger speaks of landscape (*paysage*) as a well-behaved land (*pays sage*) – in other words, as a domesticated space, or at least a mapped and inventoried space, noticed for its exceptional attributes.[17] Might it be justified to say that these texts bear witness to a colonial invention of the African landscape?

Describing landscapes allows authors to express a strong individual subjectivity. This subjective dimension had not been expected nor desired by the European 'tutors' who nurtured the first generation of African writers (such as Nayigiziki). As a result, the landscape is above all emotional and intimate. Each of the narrators pours forth their mental and emotional states within the landscape, projecting them onto these natural spaces. Obviously, this does not correspond to the 'documentary' expectations of their European mentors. This synaesthetic relationship to landscapes exists in Mudimbe's work; is abundantly present in Nayigiziki's, as demonstrated by the numerous passages cited here; and also in Ruti's novel but to a lesser extent.

In addition, the narrators decipher the landscapes they cross via a political frame of reference. Travelling and crossing borders are, for them, vital and existential operations, for these figures are fundamentally nomads: uncategorisable, eternal sceptics (if not cynics), Mudimbe no less than Silimu (the bastard) and Nayigiziki (the fugitive).

This prevalent scepticism might be explained by the narrators' discoveries, as they progress through their crossings and re-crossings of this (colonial) landscape. Their nomadism leads them

> toward places where the 'sacramental' conception of space is increasingly being undone, that is to say, towards a horizon where grace is more and more foreign to each place and where the relative hope of finally locating the meaning and the expanse is more and more 'senseless'.[18]

as the focus on the mission *locus* has shown. Indeed, these religious places are inhabited by a strong power where the pomp of the Christian rite prevails over the sacred.

Consequently, the narrators are characters who seek to escape the colony and its coercive aspects by means of a *praxis* of the territory, that is to say, a reflexive dialogue with landscape through travel. In that respect, these narrators behave like many of their counterparts in the Great Lakes region characterised by 'itinerant territoriality', as Gillian Mathys argues in her study about identities and territories in the precolonial Lake Kivu region.[19]

Ultimately, they are defectors, in the sense in which Bridet employs the word:

> As a figure of disidentification, the defector (decivilised, white Negro or adventurer king) calls into question the idea of a solid kernel of identity that resists change, and opens the possibility of a labile in-between (between two, three or four), always in a state of becoming.[20]

These defectors participate in the construction of the colony's landscape; by their praise-filled descriptions and their deciphering of historical and political signs, they landscape the colony, while ceaselessly attempting to escape it.

Notes

1. I am grateful to the translator, Emelyn Lih, and to the editor of this book for his very helpful comments.
2. Pierre Halen, 'Paysage exotique et paysage colonial', Françoise Chenet (ed.), *Le Paysage et ses grilles* (Paris-Montreal: L'Harmattan, 1996), pp. 51–70, (p. 10).
3. Saverio Naygiziki, *Escapade ruandaise: journal d'un clerc en sa trentième année*, preface by J.-M. Jadot (Brussels: G.-A. Deny, [1950]). In this chapter, I will refer to the reedition of this text: *Mes Transes à trente ans. Escapade ruandaise*, complete text introduced and edited by Jean-Paul Kwizera (Metz: Centre Écritures, 2009).
4. Paul Lomami Tshibamba, *Ngando (Le crocodile)*, preface by Gaston-Denys Périer (Brussels: Éditions Georges A. Deny, 1949).
5. V-Y Mudimbe, *Les corps glorieux des mots et des êtres. Esquisse d'un jardin africain à la Bénédictine* (Montreal/Paris: Humanitas/Paris, 1994).
6. A. Ruti, *Le Fils de Mikeno* (Lubumbashi: Éditions Impala, 1997). Posthumously published but most probably completed in the early 1990s.
7. Stéphane Ledien, 'Entre médiation, tiraillement et éclatement, la crise identitaire de l'écrivain-narrateur d'autobiographie intellectuelle', *Itinéraires. Littérature, textes, cultures*, 2020–23 (2021), http://journals.openedition.org/itineraires/8859 [accessed 13 December 2021].
8. Marie Gevers, *Des Mille Collines aux Neuf Volcans* (Paris: Stock, 1953).
9. Marie Gevers, *Des Mille Collines aux Neuf Volcans (Ruanda)*, preface by Valentin-Yves Mudimbe (Brussels: AML Éditions, 2002).
10. Jean-Pierre Chrétien and Marcel Kabanda, *Racisme et génocide. L'idéologie hamitique* (Paris: Belin, 2016).
11. On this contentious issue, see Gillian Mathys, 'Bringing History Back in: Past, Present, and Conflict in Rwanda and the Eastern Republic of Congo', *Journal of African History*, 58-53 (2017), 465-87.
12. Pierre Lepape, 'La pensée de la plate-bande', *Traverses*, 5–6 (1976), 28–36 (32), quoted by Maryline Cettou, 'Jardins d'hiver et de papier: de quelques lectures et (ré)écritures fin de siècle', *A contrario*, 11 (2009), 99–117, (99).
13. V. Y. Mudimbe, *Shaba Deux. Les Carnets de Mère Marie Gertrude* (Paris: Présence Africaine, 1989).
14. Alain Roger, *Court traité du paysage* (Paris: Gallimard, 1997). For a critical enquiry of the artialisation concept, see: Alain Nadaï, '*Degré zéro. Portée et limites de la théorie de l'artialisation dans la perspective d'une politique du paysage*', *Cahiers de géographie du Québec*, 51.144 (2007), 333–43.
15. Ousmane Sembène, *Les Bouts de bois de Dieu* (Paris: Pocket, 1960); Fiston Mwanza Mujila, *Tram 83* (Paris: Métailié, 2014); Peter Kimani, *Dance of the Jakaranda* (New York: Akashic Books, 2017).
16. See http://www.kakirasugar.com/?q=content/our-history [accessed 15 December 2021].
17. Alain Roger, *Court traité du paysage* (Paris: Gallimard, 1997).
18. Bertrand Lévy, *Hermann Hesse, une géographie existentielle* (Paris: José Corti, 1992), pp. 401–02. The works of Hermann Hesse and those of Mudimbe feature startling points of convergence.
19. '"Itinerant" territoriality refers to territoriality determined by movement and change. Precisely because of this "itinerant" characteristic, the frontier provided opportunities to escape the control of political authorities': Gillian Mathys, 'Questioning Territories and Identities in the Precolonial (Nineteenth-Century) Lake Kivu region', *Africa: The Journal of the International African Institute*, 91-3 (2021), 493–515 (497).
20. Guillaume Bridet, 'Introduction', in Guillaume Bridet (ed.), *Passeurs, alliés et transfuges à l'époque coloniale* (Paris/Pondicherry: Kailash Éditions, 2019), pp. 9–45 (37).

Récit d'enfance, récit de distance
Gaby as implicated subject in Gaël Faye's Petit Pays

Hannah Grayson

Introduction

Gaël Faye's award-winning 2016 novel *Petit Pays* has received critical acclaim for its lyrical depiction of a childhood universe set alongside the violence of Burundi's civil war and the genocide against the Tutsi in Rwanda. Translated into over forty languages, the novel has been hailed varyingly as an ode to a lost paradise of childhood in Burundi, and a contemporary oral tale of political realism. The focus of this reading will be on Faye's interweaving of a child's perspective with a sustained focus on proximity and distance, and how these shed new light on this historical experience. The figure of the child is a vehicle for exploring subjects implicated in violence; and alongside this, distance draws our attention to how intricately different actors remain involved. In this way we can start to inch beyond the binaries of innocence/guilt, victim/perpetrator that dominate discussion of this period when transitional justice frameworks remain the primary approach to episodes of extreme violence. Combining both these elements, Faye's novel brings Gaby's position to the fore and reveals such subjects as complexly implicated in systemic injustice. As such, the insight is not on those larger-than-life political figures so dominant in Great Lakes history, but rather on the childhood of an ordinary figure.

Michael Rothberg's umbrella category of 'implicated subject' helps us read Gaby as protagonist in *Petit Pays* in numerous ways. The term refers to a subject who participates in injustice but in indirect ways, and thus gives us a more complete picture of violence, exploitation and domination.[1] Foregrounding implication rather than victimhood gives us insight into the interplay between subjectivity, structural inequality, and historical violence, and enables us to see figures who are more complexly entangled than more common descriptors may suggest.[2] It also opens up the discussion to the lesser discussed actors within this history: in this case children and Burundi. Especially true in writing about life after the genocide is what Rothberg identifies as anchoring most explorations of traumatic violence: a conceptual framework based on the stable categories of victim/perpetrator.[3] This imaginary, essential to the work of transitional justice, can skew our vision of subjectivity by limiting our analysis to a legalistic, individualistic, and I would argue, adult framework. But where does the child fit into such categories? Or a resident of a neighbouring country, such as Burundi (which until now remains understudied, particularly in literary studies)?[4] An understanding of systemic injustice requires looking at the everyday reproduction of certain conditions, which are to be found in small actions by multiple actors who may *appear* removed from any violence that is perpetrated. This chapter examines a number of such small actions to argue that Faye's text presents the kind of agency and subjectivity that requires Rothberg's different kind of vocabulary.

Though Rothberg's focus on responsibility does not address childhood as a category, his focus on implication as a subject position embedded in diachronic and synchronic relationality accurately describes how Gaby's ties to injustice are due to current circumstances and inherited privilege. Further, Gaby's development as a character underscores that implicated subjectivity is not a fixed ontological identity, but rather a dynamic position liable to shift. This comes in the novel against a backdrop of Burundi's shifting political landscape. Central to my reading of the text will be the reconsideration of guilt and innocence that is created through the narrative of a child who moves closer to and further away from the violence of the genocide and civil wars as he grows older. This analysis reveals how situations of conflict position us in morally and emotionally complex ways, while still calling out for political engagement.[5] Such a reading then influences the way we consider the ongoing entanglements of other actors – namely, Belgium and its former empire, as discussed in this volume.

The fictional representation of violence, trauma, and memory during and in the wake of the genocide has been treated by a number of scholars within the field of francophone studies.[6] A specific focus on the child's perspective comes in two works of fiction: Tierno Monénembo's *L'Aîné des orphelins* (2000)[7] and Scholastique Mukasonga's *Notre Dame du Nil* (2012),[8] and I will refer to these in what follows. The experience of child soldiers in African conflicts has also been the subject of several critical works, most commonly on the better-known fiction of writers such as Ahmadou Kourouma and Emmanuel Dongola.[9] The perspective tends to be first-person and the tone, as in *Allah n'est pas obligé*, often pessimistic and resigned. These focus on children as explicit agents of violence who are identified as innocent victims turned gun-wielding killers operating under the influence of drugs. Faye's text presents a more nuanced account of childhood than these two extremes. At first glance his protagonist is ostensibly a 'good boy'. Yet, in the way Faye uses distance and proximity to shape the story, we see that child's closeness to and implication in various forms of injustice. The text shares with *Notre dame du Nil* and *L'Aîné des orphelins* a certain remove from the violence of the genocide that sets them apart from more direct acts of witnessing, but in this way provides fresh insight into the wider temporal and geographical scope of that particular crisis. By addressing these two facets of the text together (childhood and distance), my aim is to avoid reductive readings of childhood as ignorant/innocent, or accounts of participation in injustice as clichéd or polarised. What I seek to show is the way this perspective underscores the conflation of child and adult perspective, in broader terms how the past lingers on in the present and what traces of Burundi's colonial past can be found in this fictional account of the 1990s. The importance of vehicles and movement draws our attention to the longed-for but near-impossible wish to set oneself at a distance from violence.

Petit Pays tells the childhood story of Gabriel (or Gaby) as he comes of age in Burundi. We are given a picture of his everyday life, and gradually the disruption and destruction of various forms of violence, not least the genocide against the Tutsi in neighbouring Rwanda. The novel has the eponymous title of one of Faye's autobiographical rap songs, and though the author has spoken clearly against this being his own story, in ways it suggests some crossover.[10] Both Faye and Gaby are born of a French expatriate father and a Rwandan refugee mother, and raised in Burundi during the years leading up to the 1994 genocide in Rwanda and the concurrent tragedy that unfolds in Burundi. The plot runs from 1992 to 1995, and its circular structure begins and ends in France, following the family's expatriation there. The past does not vanish but remains present in far more than nostalgia in the text. *Petit Pays* is narrated from a dual perspective of Gaby as a reminiscing adult and Gaby as child, giving access to both life stages but also revealing the ways they are conflated. I disagree with critic Marie-Odile Ogier-Fares who sees the two voices as distinct, marked always by shifts in the syntax, claiming that 'It's the child who brought and spoke of the wonderful Small country all through the first part of the novel'.[11] The transitions between these narrative voices occur throughout the novel and are not always obvious, and I would argue, deliberately so. These happen at sentence rather than chapter levels, and act as small-scale interruptions of the adult perspective to disrupt and overlay any notions of 'pure' childhood naivety. This has the effect of blurring boundaries between life stages, underscoring the presence of the past, and demonstrating the grey zones where innocence and responsibility overlap. Illustrations of this provide the main body of this chapter.

When we first meet the adult Gaby at the novel's opening, he is obsessed with a return to Burundi. He describes himself as unadapted to the world, unable to settle though at moments decidedly established 'in France'.[12] The return journey lingers with inevitability, but his sense of a temporary locatedness goes beyond that:

> Except that I no longer live anywhere. Living somewhere involves a physical merging with its landscape, with every crevice of its environment. There's none of that here. I'm passing through. I rent. I squat. My town is a dormitory that serves its purpose. My apartment smells of fresh paint and new linoleum. My neighbours are perfect strangers, we avoid each other politely in the stairwell.[13]

In this way, our initial encounter is with a subject self-consciously uncertain of his position. What is more, his entanglement in structures of racial injustice is penned in the prologue when the founding stereotypes of Hutu-Tutsi difference are uttered to the child Gaby by his French father. On the opening page of the novel, the informal dialogue of a family embeds him in those myths. The child Gaby is positioned within that structural injustice when he is told, "'Take you, Gabriel,' he said, pointing at me, "you're a proper Tutsi: we can never tell what you're thinking'".[14] Gaby's uncertainty about his position and identity, which I discuss later on, hinges on this marker. Not only does he receive this label from a French father married to his Rwandan mother, and thus charged with the significance of that categorisation from the Rwandan context. But also, given that there was no Hutu social revolution in Burundi and that the Tutsi remained in control there after independence in 1962, Gaby lives with that label in a context where the Hutu/Tutsi dichotomy carries very different meaning. His coming of age (and political consciousness) coincides with the Hutu-majority Frodebu victory of 1993.[15] The trans-African significance of the term 'Tutsi' is mobile, therefore, and as a child, Gaby's murky understanding of these dynamics comes across loudly throughout the novel.

This understanding of dynamic and embedded positioning is crucial to a move beyond a victim/perpetrator binary in thinking through what Rothberg describes as the complex subjectivities of life after violence.[16] What is more, the coming-of-age story shows an increasingly independent child nonetheless persistently intertwined with his past, his peers, and his parents. Faye's dual and overlapping narrative voices get to the heart of this in the violence of genocide and civil war, gesturing as such to the multiple entanglements of decolonisation. By unpacking the complexities of Gaby's position as a child shifting closer to and further away from that violence, we better understand his and other subjects' relationship to it. I am by no means presenting the child as an allegory for Burundi, but rather inviting us to see him as an illustration of the implicated nature of subjecthood that does of course affect a whole range of actors in this region's history of injustice.

Childhood as Innocence

Readings of childhood narratives of violence in contemporary African literature fall into the trap of framing childhood as a period of ultimate bliss and, crucially, absolute innocence, interrupted and ruined by episodes of violence.[17] When violence, of varying kinds, is described by critics as 'erasing childhood'[18] or 'depriving [one] of childhood',[19] it belies a naive vision that conflates childhood with absolute innocence or freedom from pain. This results in an overwhelming stereotyping of children only as innocent victims. My approach here does not follow that of scholars such as Aline Lebel, whose examination of *Petit Pays* frames the tale as a case of 'lost paradise', where Gaby's childhood, as well as the land he leaves, is a lost and longed-for Eden. Although she mentions the adult narrator's challenge to any idealised view of the past, Lebel nonetheless argues that the childhood presented in the book is a time of happiness, and she equates this with innocence.[20] Ogier-Fares does similarly, asserting that 'the child narrator has guaranteed innocence'.[21] Though the author himself was taken by the notion of a lost paradise,[22] an overemphasis on this myth risks overlooking the far more ambivalent nature of Gaby's childhood. I argue instead that far from offering a clichéd view of childhood as innocent and pure, the text itself holds such a reading up as naive by blurring the boundaries between childhood and adulthood, and between guilt and innocence.

What Faye's text gives us is a picture of childhood that moves beyond the absolutist descriptions of perfection turned to horror. There is an ambivalence and strain to Gaby's memories, even in the chronological period before the civil war in Rwanda. Where Lebel contrasts Mukasonga's work to Faye's for the way the former shows that 'violence has always formed part of her world',[23] the critic overlooks the backdrop of violence in Gaby's domestic and regional situation. This comes through vividly, for example, in the soundscape of his parents' conflict:

> That night, the walls of our house trembled with Maman's rage. I heard the sounds of breaking glass, of windows being shattered and plates smashing on the floor [...]
>
> Their voices were indistinguishable, distorted by the high and low notes bouncing off the tiles and reverberating in the false ceiling, I could no longer tell what was French and what Kirundi, what was shouting and what were tears, whether these were my parents battling or the neighbourhood dogs fighting to the death.[24]

Such perception – characteristic of the impression Faye builds through what Gaby sees, hears, and thinks – disquiets readings of the child as 'enchanted' and thus blissfully unaware.[25] It is reminiscent of the young protagonist Faustin in Monénembo's *L'Aîné des orphelins*, who is under no illusions and whose tone often reflects the violence he is witness to. What is more, *Petit Pays* directly undoes notions of this period as Edenic by pointedly using associated images to underscore the horror, ironically drawing attention to the mythical nature of such descriptions: 'Mais le Rwanda du lait et du miel avait disparu. C'était désormais un charnier à ciel ouvert'[26] [But the Rwanda of milk and honey had disappeared. It was now a mass grave, open to the skies].[27] The internal echo of *miel* and *ciel* enclosing the shocking *charnier* at this chapter-end mark the emptiness of those Edenic ideals, and the danger of surrounding places and ideas with such language. Gaby's relatives return to Rwanda after thirty years in Burundi, having fled after the first episodes of ethnic cleansing in 1959. But their dreamed-for return instead becomes a search for the dead. The incoherence of a romanticised view fuelled by vocabulary of utopic bliss is underscored by the words' proximity. Typical of the blurred-double narrative, these words come in a voice that blends the semi-awareness of a child (who writes of 'this thing that wasn't war'[28]) with the astute language of an adult. There is no way for the child Gaby to remain 'enchanted' or 'carefree' due to the repeated interruption of the adult narrative voice in the text, the backdrop of small and large-scale violence, and his own everyday experiences of growing up.

There are certainly moments of ease and happiness. As the narrator describes time with his four best friends:

> It was in that VW Combi that we plotted our futures, from small outings to grand excursions. We were full of dreams and it was with impatient hearts that we imagined the joys and adventures life held in store for us. In short, we felt at one with the world, in our hideout on the patch of wasteland by our street.[29]

Yet during this period, what Lebel characterises as 'insouciance' [carefreeness] is accompanied with the ordinary childhood struggles of pride, jealousy, and belonging.[30] Ogier-Fares also describes the childhood world as 'a radiant and extraordinary world',[31] which seems at odds with Gaby's experiences. Faye's text brings to the fore the ambivalent actions and subjectivity that are at the heart of an ordinary childhood.[32] So where Lebel describes an 'innocence enfantine' [childish innocence] ruined by the rupture of extreme violence, she overlooks the ambivalence of the everyday realities of coming of age.[33] It is not so much a clear-cut case of the two narrative perspectives being distinguished by guilty (adult) vs innocent (child). Rather, their blurring highlights the impurity of Gaby's position where Faye draws particular attention to the moral dilemmas that the protagonist faces. As Rothberg outlines, 'opening up the more ambiguous space of the implicated subject between and beyond the victim/perpetrator binary paradoxically provides a more precise picture of the production of damage'.[34] This question of responsibility allows us to examine the grey zones of indirect participation in injustice, even in childhood.[35]

Two instances where Gaby's innocence is under scrutiny illustrate this, providing insight into the kind of spectrum of culpability along which multiple subjects hover. These episodes are more ambiguous than the more direct act of violence when Gaby sets fire to the taxi killing the man inside, yet are linked into the same web of implication.[36] When the boys take mangoes from neighbours' yards their childish play is amusing, but when this is followed by selling them back to Mme Economopoulos and being beaten up by Francis, the lines between fun, exploitation, and violence are blurred.[37] Faye draws our attention here, first in Francis's patronising remarks, 'You shouldn't steal from other people's gardens. Didn't your parents ever teach you that?' and then in Gaby's panic at finding himself, for the first time, directly victim to violence, 'So was this what violence meant? Raw fear and disbelief'.[38] Any apparent childhood innocence is already marked by inequality and violence, remarked on here with adult astuteness. The fact that the giver of this lesson, Francis, is a Banyamulenge marks another specific trace of violence and marginalisation where ethnicity and its horrific implications reverberate from one generation to the next.[39] Gaby's growing understanding of this marks him out as more complex than a child naively pursuing fun with friends.

Gaby's consciousness around crime grows in an episode surrounding the theft of his bicycle. This episode is one example of where the dual narrative perspectives of *Petit Pays* converge. When the child Gaby learns his bicycle has been stolen by the family's guard, we read: 'No way. Surely Calixte would never do something like that? I was crying real tears now. It felt as if the whole world was against me'.[40] Eight-year-old Gaby is obviously distressed that a man he trusted has committed this theft, but the overwhelming feeling is of having been victimised. Nearing the end of their rural search for the stolen bicycle, Gaby spots Calixte in a crowd of curious onlookers who then give chase. Yet the tone again here is one of a philosophising adult where simile and reflections on language signal a perspectival shift away from the wronged child:

> The entire town ran after him, as if chasing a chicken whose neck needed wringing in time for lunch. There's nothing like a spot of blood sport during the midday lull to kill time in the sleepy provinces. Popular justice is the

name they give to lynching, it has the benefit of sounding civilised. Luckily, the crowd didn't have the last word that day.[41]

The shift is away from an emotional stance of victimhood (Gaby in tears, as above), but this is marked as a conscious shift in agency, not just emotion. Indeed, Gaby is then given the choice to leave his bicycle with its current owner, a farmer's son who until this point is none the wiser to its origins. His dilemma is whether to regain possession of his BMX, or to leave it with the boy to avoid 'breaking a child's heart'.[42] To underscore his conflicting feelings, Gaby's companions each echo a different stance vis-à-vis the right solution. Donatien, not wanting the farmer's son to be deprived in turn of 'his' bicycle, pleads with Gaby to let him keep it, 'to help a poor child'.[43] The less patient Innocent – deliberately named – is set against such Robin Hood moves, and against lying to Gaby's father, and loads the bicycle into the truck.[44] Ultimately, Gaby is left with heightened consciousness of his agency, and his implication, but still in a state of remorse: 'I'd been feeling vain, selfish and generally ashamed of the whole episode: I had gone from victim to executioner, simply by wishing to retrieve something that belonged to me in the first place'.[45] Faye's use of the words *victime* and *bourreau* belies the child's simplified thinking, at the very moment the author also draws attention to his complex and layered emotions. As Gaby looks for reassurance, he articulates the anxious shift in positioning between agency and powerlessness.[46]

Gaby's playful thieving, assault at the hands of Francis, and his pursuit for justice for stolen bicycle reveal the limitations of fixed and mutually exclusive categories of guilty/innocent. He is responsible but not fully, and naive but not ignorant. As such his 'impure' positions of implication both challenge reductive readings of childhood and provide insight into the complexities of subjectivity and agency in and after violence, supplementing absolutist moral ascriptions with a more nuanced account of power.[47] This has implications for how we consider other actors in the genocide, and in particular those who might be considered, for various reasons, innocent at first glance. I come back to these intricacies of involvement below.

Each of these scenarios is of course also taking place within a system of powers and privileges that structure Gaby's life, including the way he is racially and socially positioned by others, as the opening page of the novel established. Gaby as protagonist is the focus of this chapter, but he is not an individual removed from community. Hannah Arendt's writing on communities and collective responsibility – as another move away from the individualised (Western) sway of 'guilty perpetrator' or 'ideal victim' – is pertinent to this analysis and is discussed by Rothberg.[48] The example below reveals Gaby as member of a rich family, employing others, but Gaby is also a member of a gang, an active pen pal, a neighbour, friend, and school pupil. Each of these communities sees him enter into different networks of relatedness and therefore implication. None of this action takes place in a vacuum of power relations, and this is where Rothberg's account of systems of privilege that engender both synchronic and diachronic implication is most clearly relevant. For Rothberg, it is about far more than individuals and their morality, and more about the collective responsibilities of those who are implicated in events in which they are not active, criminally culpable participants.[49] Indeed, while not ignoring individual crimes, it becomes crucial to reposition subjects in their political, social, and economic structures. As one reviewer describes him:

> Gabriel is in fact a privileged little boy: he is sent to the French school in Bujumbura (the capital of Burundi), he lives in a beautiful villa where he is served by domestic servants, and he has but one goal: to have a good time with his friends and gorge themselves on mangoes in their hideout, an old VW Combi.[50]

Gaby's entanglement in a system of powers is obvious in the stolen bicycle episode, where his parents' household employees spend the day chasing down the bicycle, involving police and a crowd of onlookers, only for Gaby to conclude that he will never ride it again. At this, Innocent's exasperated 'Enfant gâté' [spoiled brat] highlights Gaby as superior to the 'pauvre enfant' [poor child] who had been found with his bike.[51] The short, contrasting phrases underscore Gaby's position of privilege, and this is all the more emphatic coming from an employee paid to look after his family. It is not only through class that he occupies this privilege, but by the intersection of other privileges from his wealth, French education, mixed race, and large, gated home. What is more, in terms of inherited privilege, this epithet (of 'enfant gâté') also echoes Gaby's mother insulting his father when he dismisses her desire to live safely in Europe: 'L'histoire dont je parle ne t'intéresse pas, Michel, elle ne t'a jamais intéressé. Tu es venu ici chercher un terrain de jeux pour prolonger tes rêves *d'enfant gâté* d'Occident'[52] [You've never been interested in my version of the story, Michel…You came here from Europe in search of a playground where you could eke out the dreams of your spoilt childhood in the West].[53]

The oversimplified conception of childhood as but a linear, temporal category characterised as innocent and pure neglects both the ambivalence of childhood experiences *and* the way they endure. Such a reading also points to the need to interrogate other actors involved in the genocide. The reach and persistence of Gaby's childhood into the adult life maps equally onto our reading of Belgium's colonial past in this region: ambivalent and persistently entangled (see Nicki Hitchcott's chapter in this volume). Rothberg's simultaneous focus on the diachronic draws our eyes to the colonial legacy that lingers in the text. Hierarchical relationships are reflected in the status of the various inhabitants of the cul-de-sac and their domestic staff, but also class distinctions between this neighbourhood and the plight of Rwandan refugees and rural poor beyond Bujumbura. This comes both as a synecdoche of where they stand historically, and a geographical inscription marking a kind of sociopolitical dead end. The slow days where Gaby and his friends drag their feet through the oft-cited 'impasse' (cul-de-sac or no-through road) underscore the permanent traces of such colonial stratifications. The author thus points to the legacies of colonialism in poverty and social fracture, as well as the more direct damage caused by European states' involvement (and lack thereof) in the genocide.[54] When Ruanda-Urundi was taken over by Belgium as a result of the Treaty of Versailles, the new administration adopted the evolutionist and racist criteriology – the infamous Hamitic hypothesis – used by the Germans to map out the ethnic boundaries of their colony.[55] Like the Belgian Congo, this League of Nations Trust territory was managed by paternalistic administrators who exacerbated ethnic differences – between the Hutu and the Tutsi – to impose colonial rule.[56]

Most explicitly, the colonial past is embodied in Jacques, an older Belgian man whom the family regularly visits in Bukavu (DRC). Enduring racism in this encounter points to material and immaterial traces of that past as explored elsewhere in this volume. Jacques's racist jokes are met with laughter from everybody but Gaby and Ana, whose confusion here is part of their ongoing exposure to injustice they don't understand: 'Don't make fun of me, you baboon! [...] And to think I couldn't hold onto a good woman for more than three days', Jacques went on, 'but I've been lumbered with this chimpanzee for thirty-five years!'[57] We see again here that violence and injustice are embedded in everyday relations, as the complexity and coercion of Belgium's history is drawn out. Another place the novel undermines utopic visions of life is where Jacques's property (the stage for these racist insults) is described as a quasi-paradise: 'a sort of Garden of Eden on the banks of Lake Kivu [...] At Jacques's house the table had already been laid to welcome us'.[58] In this way, the Great Lakes horrors of the 1990s are set in a longer history of systemic violence.[59] Faye uses the family's border crossing to underscore the traces of territorialisation and expropriation that have been so divisive and demeaning in the region's history from 1885 onwards.[60] This renders even more problematic any notion of Burundi pre-1990 as Edenic (see Lebel above), pointing at the same time to the entangled histories of justifying European religious and political 'missions' in the region.[61] Tropes that risk whitewashing Belgium's bloody-handed history are satirised, as Faye contests such discourses with this caricature of colonial pomposity. And yet, the children's bemused state at the same time highlights the blurred lines of implication.

In these ways this chapter speaks to three 'silences' that Mahmood Mamdani outlines as common to many accounts of the genocide, and by extension accounts that surround both Burundi and Rwanda's civil wars.[62] The nuancing I see in Gaby's characterisation corresponds to a silencing around the *agency* where top-down initiatives behind the genocide can dominate at the expense of recognising its subaltern and 'popular' character. Mamdani describes the large-scale civilian involvement as the genocide's 'uniquely troubling aspect', since the majority of those involved were ordinary citizens. Hence the value of unpacking Gaby's 'ordinary', ambivalent childhood. Second, the contextualisation in the workings of systemic injustice over time speaks to a recurring silence around the *history* of the genocide. That is to say, the way the genocide has been described as without precedent both in terms of colonialism (and the way it politicised indigeneity) and preceding waves of violence (to which the generations in Gaby's family bear witness). Last, the albeit crucial focus on Rwanda as the nation in which the genocide was perpetrated can risk silencing the *geography* of processes that led up to, and shaped responses to, the atrocities. The border crossing in Faye's novel points not least to the fact that 'Ruanda-Urundi' was one single 'trust' territory managed by the Belgians from 1923 onwards. These dynamics went far beyond the boundaries of Rwanda and are addressed by the spectres of Belgian colonialism I have described above, but more so in Faye's attention to approaching, crossing, and communicating over borders and boundary lines. Neighbouring countries and households are navigated by Gaby, as Faye hints at the tense, complex relationships such 'neighbours' have known in Central Africa's recent past. In a region where neighbours and moving over borders holds particular resonance, the thematic of distance calls for attention, and I turn to this for the remainder of the chapter.

Distance and Proximity

Central to the novel's dynamics is the notion of distance, which Faye plays with as he shifts the focus from individual to national and international and small-scale interactions presage political tensions and large-scale violence. Subjects' implication in injustice is in *Petit Pays* repeatedly examined by this presence of distance, both spatial, temporal, and ethical. Distance dominates far more than any sense of 'reconciliation' as described by Ogier-Fares: 'We can thus reread the whole novel in the light of this epilogue of reconciliation between the adult and the child, between the adult and the country of his childhood'.[63] Rather, from the novel's opening there is a strong sense of detachment between the narrator and his home setting, but also a painful distance felt from Burundi and from a painful past. There is a sense in which the adult perspective views the past with the guilt-tinted spectacles of the émigré. Within the frame of the return journey that encloses the rest of the novel (introduced at the beginning of this chapter), there are multiple comings and goings; in other words, a drawing apart and together that points to relationships more strained than reconciled. This tension is partly (in the retrospective narrative) the weight of guilt at never having been at the very centre of the most horrific violence, even as a child. Nor is it a case, as I have demonstrated, of a childhood totally protected from hardship that is suddenly interrupted by that brutality, from the genocide in neighbouring Rwanda. Rather, Gaby's proximity to violence creeps and shifts, just as he also attempts to withdraw from it in different ways. The narrative maintains a climate of tension that affects him throughout: from the domestic to the international, it proves impossible for him to remain removed.

In his own positionality, as we have seen, Gaby embodies the trans-African entanglements explored in this volume. As protagonist, he is at the centre of the story. But as a child, and living in Burundi, he is simultaneously at a double remove from the intense violence of the genocide in Rwanda. Though Burundi was intensely tied up in the genocide violence,[64] as the narrator describes, 'From April to July 1994, at a distance and between four walls, next to a telephone and a radio, we lived through the genocide'.[65] At a more local level, Gaby is allowed, by his position of privilege for quite some time, to snooze, like the cul-de-sac, only partially awake to villages being ravaged and clashes beyond Bujumbura in the political turbulence of elections and ethnic conflict. Despite the need for curfew, '[f]rom the womb-like safety or our house, all of this seemed unreal. The *impasse* was as sleepy as ever'.[66] In relation to his sister Ana, too, Gaby is kept further from violence. Free to roam the streets with his gang, the vehicles so central to his escapades hint at the degree of freedom he has as a young man to truant and travel. In one episode the group of boys commandeer a taxi to take them to a college swimming pool during school hours. It is no coincidence they drive down 'chaussée Prince Louis Rwagasore', as they carve out their own path of independence.[67] Instrumental in the creation of the Uprona and an enduring symbol of Burundian independence, Prince Rwagasore was assassinated in the early stages of the decolonising process. He still stands for national unity – echoed in this episode at the band of brothers' togetherness as they drive past his tomb, emblazoned with the country's motto 'Unity Work Progress'.[68] Diving from the highest board, then laughing their way back to the taxi 'bare-bottomed', the 'band of brothers' revel in their friendship and freedom: 'We had never felt so free, so alive from head to toe, all of us as one, joined by the same veins, the same life-force flowing through us'.[69] This access to money, vehicles, movement, and even nudity is Gaby's partly due to being male. Unlike his sister, Ana, Gaby is not tied to the domestic space in the same way, both due to her gender and due to being subject to the complex demands of their volatile mother.[70]

Gaby's relationship with his mother is one of suspicion, increased hostility, and distance. Her own absence is preceded by her distress at being far from her homeland and members of her family, and by her brother Pacifique's departure to join the RPF offensive. Distance is at once what structures and propels the plot. What is more, Faye's overall approach to narrating the genocide is to use this removed perspective, where – in a similar vein to Monénembo and Mukasonga – a young narrator is exposed to snippets of violence, rather than a plot that takes it as a sensationalised central subject. Faye describes these two levels: 'And I tried – just as the character keeps violence at a distance, in my role as writer at that moment – I tried for as long as possible to keep this violence at a distance and not to describe it too much'.[71] Though Gaby's experience of distance/as distanced is made central in this way, he nonetheless moves closer to the heart of physical violence as the plot progresses. At each of these junctures, the adult and child perspective are conflated as young Gaby tries to make sense of what he sees and hears, and the overlaid adult voice pierces that naivety with dark realism.

As Gaby's family are directly affected, so is he. His uncle Alphonse is killed in an RPF offensive, then his mother's other brother Pacifique leaves to join the fighting. There is at this point a shift in his consciousness:

> My home? But that was here. Yes, I was the son of a Rwandan woman, but my reality was Burundi, the French school, Kinanira, our street. Nothing else existed. Still, with the death of Alphonse, and now Pacifique's departure, there were times when I felt as if politics did affect me.[72]

Once again we read the self-consciousness of a child realising his position (torn as his family is between Rwanda and Burundi), alongside the maturity of an adult reflection. Here the text's lingering inevitability (of violence coming closer to home) is articulated explicitly. Gaby's reading of the political backdrop is apt not only on a personal front, since the novel unfolds against the backdrop of the 1993 multiparty parliamentary elections (the first since 1965). Melchior Ndadaye's win saw an end of military rule and the victory of Frodebu (Front for Democracy in Burundi), crucially a Hutu majority party that sees a political landscape tracing previous (colonial) ethnic mapping. The weight of this remains unknown to the child Gaby, of course, whose written summary of the election focuses on the president's 'presentable and clean' appearance: 'This matters! Because soon he'll have his portrait hung throughout the country, so nobody forgets about him'.[73] The young boy is at that point ignorant of Ndadaye's impending assassination, where the scene is set for the horrors of an unfurling civil war across Burundi, as well as fractious tensions with Rwanda.

That same sense of inevitability is shown with acute fear, as the family are stopped at a roadblock on the way from Kigali to Gitarama for Pacifique's wedding to Jeanne. The car trip in Rwanda starts with joyful dancing along to a Papa Wemba song. Wemba's transnational fame is a symbolic nod, perhaps, to the power of culture to reach beyond political and ethnic divisions, on the part of musician author Faye. But the limitations of that transcendent potential are bitingly clear as the family approach a roadblock hushed into silence at threats to the 'inyenzi' [cockroaches] on the same radio. The mood turns sour as Gaby's aunt lies about the purpose of their trip:

> 'I've never seen a Frenchwoman with a nose like yours. And as for that neck…'
> He ran his hand down the nape of Maman's neck. She sat there, rigid with fear. Over on her side, Aunt Eusébie was negotiating with the other soldier. She was desperately trying to hide her nervousness. 'We're going to Gitarama to visit a sick relative.'[74]

The realism of the harassment in the name of checking identity brings to life the persistent and insidious racism suffered, as well as the policing of movement known by so many, especially Tutsi, and the gendered nature of that violence. But where this is clear to the reader, the child narrator sits in the car with the sick feeling of simultaneously exposed and compromised innocence. There is a clear sense of alienation as he understands 'the soldier's innuendoes, the fear in Aunt Eusébie's gestures, the fear that had taken hold of Maman' and yet remains an observer in 'a ringside seat for this spectacle of hatred'.[75] All eyes are focused on the vehicle during this episode of racist violence that foreshadows the later arson and recalls Gaby's truanting in the taxi and Combi – revealing his shifting proximity to violence and guilt. It is once again his youth, gender, and race that keeps him in the back seat (or indeed in the boot of the car where he is sat) here, ill at ease as his mother is harassed. Gaby's sense of alienation is only heightened then at the family wedding where he and Ana are unable to answer their relatives' questions in Kinyarwanda, and feel uneasy and conspicuous, 'at a loss with [their] clumsy bodies'.[76]

This is a key moment in the text for the way it draws attention to the intertwined histories of Burundi and Rwanda (as well as the DRC) as exemplified in the bouts of violence which follow this moment: the genocide in Rwanda, civil war in Burundi, the overthrow of Mobutu in the DRC three years later.[77] The text, always playing with the notions of return and distance, thus looks both backwards to the colonial past and forwards to its violent trans-African traces.

Once again it is Faye's novel pairing of childhood with this focus on distance that sheds new light on the experience of violence. For Gaby, there are repeated attempts to escape. These come in play, in friendship, and in reading and writing; all are pursued with a child's imagination. Whether in the stationary Combi with his gang of friends, or writing to his pen pal, or spending time reading borrowed novels from the neighbour Madame Economopoulos, Gaby's imagination provides a temporary remove from the bleaker realities of daily life. Ogier-Fares frames this as a more positive development of individualism that suggests another society to come in future: 'The act of writing has a redemptive role, as much for the individual as for the society. His metamorphosis and his search are closely intertwined'.[78] Yet ultimately the child awakes from reveries and dreams when the noise of gunshots reaches his house – he cannot escape the violence: 'But no matter how much hope I held out, my dreams were fettered by reality. The world and its violence were closing in on us a little more each day'.[79]

In each of these there is an attempt to get away from the various forms of violence that surround him, ('forgetting [him]self entirely')[80] but an inevitability that each escape is short-lived or limited. This dynamic permeates the text in such a way that I see Faye highlighting not only the interwoven nature of different sites and scales of violence in Central Africa, but the localised, personal experience of those violences as varyingly held at a somewhat safe distance, then inescapably up close, in repeated cycles of unpredictability. Gaby's mother is an embodiment of this close then distant volatility, and the novel's concluding scene, where her voice haunts the returned adult son, marks the ultimate trace of the past: *'That voice, a voice from beyond the grave, cuts me to the quick. It mutters something about stains on the floor that won't go'*.[81]

It is through Gaby's vain attempts at escape that Faye underscores the impurity of the character's position. What becomes clear is that his 'petit pays' – the world of his street and friends – is always already connected intricately to other people and places. He cannot extricate himself from his parents' origins, for example, or the tensions of the civil war. And as he moves inevitably closer to violence – without possibility of permanent escape – we see him not as an ideal victim but more as a morally compromised subject. It should not go unnoticed that the key episodes involving Gaby are all to do with vehicles (a bicycle, taxis, and a car). His entanglement with those vehicles speaks to a more general determination to escape from hostile circumstances, as well as the pressing, dangerous significance of travel and border-crossing. His everyday journeys are foregrounded against subtle but significant references to the men who have shaped both Gaby's family and wider Great Lakes history (see mention of his uncles, Ndadaye, and Rwagasore above). There is a progression, as Gaby comes of age, from two wheels to four, but as a child, his access to and control of those vehicles is dependent on others. His relationships of trust, envy, dependence, and desire shape his positions in each scene: whether confused in the back seat en route to the wedding, or forced forwards by jeering peers towards the petrol-soaked taxi. In Gaby we see moral compromise as he is pushed and pulled around, his very movements subject to wider social rules of belonging and loyalty.

What Faye's pairing of childhood and distance provides is a new access point for the impure positions of less likely subjects in this episode of historical injustice. At once seeking distance and feeling guilty for it, Gaby navigates his political, social, and ethical positioning as a confused child. The ambivalence of his involvement in the episodes discussed in this chapter speaks to the multiple ways in which ordinary citizens are caught up in webs of implication. Faye's description of the various departures and returns, halted by borders and roadblocks, maps onto the region's wider scarring of territorial division. Gaby's fraught episodes with vehicles, trying and failing to escape multiple violences, demonstrate that political impasse suffered by the region as prolonged effects of empire. The parallel adult perspective throughout the novel augments the picture of complex implication in small- and large-scale violence, by overlaying self-conscious positionality that goes beyond so-called victim or perpetrator roles. In this way the chapter has demonstrated the need to go beyond established categories that dominate scholarship on agency in extreme violence, in order to train our eyes to areas that are central to the ongoing production of systemic injustice.

By shedding light on this period of Great Lakes history, Faye works to counter the three silences around agency, history, and geography that Mamdani identifies. This in turn counters representations of Central Africa as the heart of darkness that have in the past led to decades of violent interventions in the name of civilising a primitive chaos. Contesting the political consequences and preconceptions that come as legacies of such outdated images of Africa requires new angles on history, and new vocabulary. Discussions of memory and historical injustice have in large part overlooked implication and implicated subjects, and yet this kind of focus can open up new forms of memory work.[82] It has been my argument in this chapter that *Petit Pays* provides a new access point on the impure position of a child in this period of violence. Such a focus is necessary for confronting the material and symbolic dimensions of inequality that persist as postcolonial traces in Burundi, Rwanda, and beyond. This wider volume takes steps to explore the complex entanglements of other 'lesser-seen' actors, such as those European states who are implicated subjects – historicised through dominant discourses as distant and removed from this period of violence, but embedded in its systemic injustice in multiple ways which are yet to be fully acknowledged. What Faye's text does through Gaby's trajectory is demonstrate the ways those countries (Burundi and Rwanda on the one hand, Belgium on France on the other) do not sit in any neat dichotomy of proximity/distance. Implication on trans-African and transnational scales is revealed as the involvement in injustice of these bordered zones is held under scrutiny. Faye's expert conflation of child/adult, past/present, and innocent/guilty is thus extended also to these nations, revealing them to be complexly entangled spaces of postcolonial resonance.

Notes

1. Michael Rothberg, *The Implicated Subject* (Stanford: Stanford University Press, 2019), p. 20.
2. Ibid., p. 35.
3. Ibid., p. 7.
4. See for example Juvénal Ngorwanubusa, *Le Regard étranger: L'image du Burundi dans les littératures belge et française* (Oxford: Peter Lang 2014).
5. Rothberg, *The Implicated Subject*, p. 19.
6. See Virginie Brinker, *La Transmission littéraire et cinématographique du génocide des Tutsis au Rwanda* (Paris: Classiques Garnier, 2014); Alexandre Dauge-Roth, *Writing and Filming the Genocide of the Tutsis in Rwanda: Disremembering and remembering traumatic history* (Lanham: Lexington, 2010); Nicki Hitchcott, *Rwanda Genocide Stories: Fiction After 1994* (Liverpool: Liverpool University Press, 2017); Zoe Norridge, *Perceiving Pain in African Literature* (Basingstoke: Palgrave Macmillan, 2012).
7. T. Monénembo's *L'Aîné des orphelins* (Paris: Seuil, 2000).
8. S. Mukasonga's *Notre Dame du Nil* (Paris: Gallimard, 2012).
9. See Éloïse Brezault, *Johnny chien méchant d'Emmanuel Dongola* (Paris: ACEL-Infolio, 2012); Odile Cazenave, 'Writing the Child, Youth and Violence into the novel from sub-Saharan Africa: the impact of age and gender', *Research in African Literatures* 36.2 (2005), 59–71; Pius Ngandu Nkashama, 'Les "enfants-soldats" et les guerres coloniales: A travers le premier roman africain', *Etudes littéraires*, 35.1 (2003), 29–40; John Walsh, 'Coming of Age with an AK-47: Ahmadou Kourouma's Allah n'est pas obligé', *Research in African Literatures* 39.1 (2008), 185–97.
10. See Catherine Fruchon-Toussaint, 'Petit pays n'est absolument pas mon histoire', interview with Gaël Faye, RFI, 8 September 2016, https://www.rfi.fr/fr/culture/20160908-gael-faye-petit-pays-absolument-pas-histoire [accessed 8 August 2020].
11. Marie-Odile Ogier-Fares, 'L'enfant, voix de la terreur et de la beauté, une figure énonciative de la réconciliation dans *Petit Pays* et *En attendant Bojangles*', *Revue Critique de Fixxion Française Contemporaine*, 17 (2018), 17–25 (23). (All secondary text translations in this chapter are my own.)
12. Gaël Faye, *Small Country*, transl. by Sarah Ardizzone (London: Hogarth, 2016), p. 3. All primary text references are from the English translation unless otherwise stated.
13. Ibid.
14. Ibid., p. 1.
15. René Lemarchand, *Burundi: Ethnic Conflict and Genocide* (Washington, D.C.: Woodrow Wilson Center Press; Cambridge; New York, NY: Cambridge University Press, 1996), pp. 178–79.
16. Rothberg, *The Implicated Subject*, p. 33.
17. Childhood and coming-of-age stories set in Africa are doubly subjected to these absolutist clichés when they are overlaid with the all-too-common narrative of Africans as only victims of tragedy.
18. Edgar Nabutanyi, 'Archives of Troubled Childhoods in Contemporary African Fiction', unpublished doctoral thesis, Stellenbosch University, 2013, p. 6.
19. Odile Cazenave, 'Writing the Child, Youth and Violence into the Novel from sub-Saharan Africa: the Impact of Age and Gender', *Research in African Literatures* 36.2 (2005), 59–71, p. 62.
20. Aline Lebel, 'Le récit d'enfance au prisme du génocide et de la violence politique: le motif du "retour" vers la terre d'enfance chez Gaël Faye et Scholastique Mukasonga', *Revue Critique de Fixxion Française Contemporaine*, 17 (2018), 100–16, p. 104.
21. Ogier-Fares, 'L'Enfant…', p. 24.
22. See Fruchon-Toussaint, 'Petit Pays…'.
23. Lebel, 'Le récit d'enfance…', p. 105.
24. Faye, *Small Country*, pp. 21–22.
25. See Ogier-Fares, 'L'Enfant…'.
26. Gaël Faye, *Petit Pays* (Paris: Grasset, 2016), p. 167.
27. Faye, *Small Country*, p. 136.
28. Ibid., p. 135.
29. Ibid., pp. 57–58.
30. Lebel, 'Le récit d'enfance…', p. 105. For instance, Gaby resists the addition of Francis to their friendship group, and he envies his friend Gino who 'spoke fluent Kinyarwanda and knew exactly who he was' (Faye, p. 65).
31. Ogier-Fares, 'L'Enfant…', p. 23.
32. The horror of the genocide was in large part due to the scale of involvement by ordinary citizens who participated in the killings, as Mahmood Mamdani discusses (p. 7).
33. Lebel, 'Le récit d'enfance…', pp. 100; 106; 109.
34. Rothberg, *The Implicated* Subject, p. 34.
35. Ibid., pp. 37–39 where Rothberg discusses Primo Levi's notion of grey zones.
36. Faye, *Small Country*, p. 173.
37. Ibid., p. 78; p. 130.
38. Ibid., p. 103.
39. This Kinyarwanda speaking group, established in South Kivu, DRC, and in Burundi, was persecuted after the Rwandan genocide. See Mahmood Mamdani, *When Victims Become Killers: Colonialism, Nativism and the Genocide in Rwanda* (Princeton: Princeton University Press, 2001), pp. 238–51.

40. Faye, *Small Country*, p. 26.
41. Ibid., p. 42.
42. Ibid., p. 45.
43. Ibid.
44. Ironically named since he uses the context of the war to perpetrate his own crimes. See also Gaby's uncle, named Pacifique, who fights for the RPF.
45. Faye, *Small Country*, p. 51.
46. The focus Faye provides in this episode is far more on Gaby's internal shifts than any sense of an epic boys' adventure, as presented by Ogier-Fares, that helps Gaby bounce back from his mother's departure (p. 23).
47. Rothberg, *The Implicated Subject*, p. 35.
48. Ibid., p. 50
49. Ibid., p. 44.
50. Mel Teapot, 'Petit pays: l'histoire d'un paradis perdu', *L'Envolée Culturelle*, 9 May 2017 http://www.lenvoleeculturelle.fr/petit-pays-lhistoire-dun-paradis-perdu/ [accessed 23 July 2020], n.p.
51. Faye, *Small Country*, p. 46.
52. Gaël Faye, *Petit Pays* (Paris: Grasset, 2016), p. 30 (my emphasis).
53. Faye, *Small Country*, p. 17. The fact that Yvonne sees Michel in Gaby becomes crystal clear later on in the novel when, following her breakdown, she refuses to speak to either of them and repeatedly shows a preference for her daughter Ana.
54. See for example Roméo Dallaire, *Shake Hands with the Devil: The Failure of Humanity in Rwanda* (Toronto: Random House Canada, 2002).
55. See for example Jean-Pierre Chrétien et Marcel Kabanda, *Rwanda, racisme et génocide: l'idéologie hamitique* (Paris: Belin, 2013).
56. See Pierre Ryckmans, *Dominer pour servir* (Brussels: Librairie Albert Dewit, 1931).
57. Faye, *Small Country*, p. 14.
58. Ibid., p. 12.
59. Colette Braeckman, *Terreur africaine. Burundi, Rwanda, Zaïre: les racines de la violence* (Paris: Fayard, 1996).
60. See for example Bas De Roo, 'L'État indépendant du Congo, une machine à piller au service d'un Léopold II impitoyable?', in Idesbald Goddeeris, Amandine Lauro and Guy Vanthemsche (eds.), *Le Congo Colonial: une histoire en questions* (Brussels: Renaissance du Livre, 2020), pp. 33–49.
61. See Gale Kenny and Tisa Wenger, 'Church, State, and "Native Liberty" in the Belgian Congo,' *Comparative Studies in Society and History*, 62.1 (2020), 156–85.
62. Mamdani, *When Victims Become Killers*, p. 8.
63. Ogier-Fares, 'L'Enfant…', p. 23.
64. See Mamdani, *When Victims…* and Lemarchand, *Burundi: Ethnic Conflict and Genocide*.
65. Faye, *Small Country*, p. 135.
66. Ibid., p. 101.
67. Ibid., p. 126.
68. Ibid. See Christine Deslaurier, 'Rwagasore for ever? Des usages contemporains d'un héros consensuel au Burundi', *Vingtième Siècle. Revue d'histoire*, 118.2 (2013), 15–30, for detailed analysis of Rwagasore's significance as a site of memory and ongoing figure of significance in postcolonial Burundi.
69. Faye, *Small Country*, p. 129.
70. Ibid., p. 159 and p. 255 for examples.
71. Fruchon-Toussaint, 'Petit Pays…', n.p.
72. Faye, *Small Country*, p. 66.
73. Ibid., p. 79.
74. Ibid., p. 119.
75. Ibid.
76. Ibid., p. 120.
77. Kevin Dunn, *Imagining the Congo: The International Relations of Identity* (New York: Palgrave Macmillan, 2003), p. 3.
78. Ogier-Fares, 'L'Enfant…', p. 24.
79. Faye, *Small Country*, p. 165.
80. Ibid., p. 153.
81. Ibid., p. 182.
82. Rothberg, *The Implicated Subject*, p. 57.

PART 5

The Emergence of Diasporic Agents

'Without Art Congo Is Just a Mine'
Art as the Restoration of Shattered Bodies[1]

Bambi Ceuppens

Introducing Congoism

Johnny Van Hove uses the term Congoism to describe the ways in which American and European intellectuals have represented DRC (henceforward Congo) since the nineteenth century as the ultimate antidote to Western 'civilisation', a place of decontextualised radical alterity.[2] The pervasiveness of the trope is in no small part related to the fact that so many Westerners were caught up in various ways in Leopold II's colonisation of the Congo Free State, from the Polish-British Joseph Conrad and the Anglo-Irish Roger Casement to the many Scandinavians who played a crucial role in the king's colonial project. The latter fact helps explain why the Senegalese, who were exhibited in Oslo at the 1914 Jubilee Exhibition, were presented to the Norwegian public as 'Congolese'.[3]

Van Hove traces Congoism back to contradictory American descriptions of enslaved Angolans and Congolese as either weak and docile and therefore only fit to be house slaves, or as rebellious, likely to escape and best suited as field slaves.[4] A similar polarising logic characterises Joseph Conrad's representation of the Congo Free State as 'the Heart of Darkness': a place where Congolese are victims of atrocities inflicted upon them by Europeans, while being little more than beasts themselves. Post-independence representations likewise show Congolese simultaneously as cruel perpetrators and pitiful victims of gruesome violent acts.[5]

In his novel *Congo*, Michael Crichton writes that the moment his protagonists left their aircraft and arrived in the country:

> They also left civilization, and all the unquestioned assumptions of civilization. They were jumping not only through the air, but through time, backward into a more primitive and dangerous way of life – the eternal realities of the Congo, which had existed for centuries before them.[6]

While the idea of Congo as the ultimate 'other', out of time and out of sync with the rest of the world has remained stable since the nineteenth century, the elements that supposedly characterise its 'otherness' have changed over time.[7] In 1965, journalist Richard West described the country as

> [A] place of cannibalism, slavery, crocodiles, gorillas, driver ants and the black mamba snake, which has been known to chase and kill a galloping horse and rider. [...] the classic country of raped nuns and stewed missionaries, of pygmies and poisoned blow-darts, of voodoo and leprosy.[8]

Nowadays, Congo is routinely and erroneously described as the 'rape capital of the world'[9] and a place of grinding poverty epitomised by photographs of adults and children risking their lives for a pittance extracting raw materials for new technologies in artisanal mines.

Poor People, Rich Culture

The title of the memoir by French journalist Edward Behr, *Anyone Here been Raped and Speak English?*, derives from a query a BBC reporter addressed to rescued Europeans who had been taken hostage during the siege of Stanleyville in Congo in 1964.[10] The question is indicative of ongoing preconceptions about Congo as a 'rape country' and for the casual and callous cruelty with which Western journalists, photographers, and humanitarian workers feed on real crises in the country. The controversial film *Episode III – Enjoy your Poverty* by Renzo Martens was based on the premise that poverty is Congo's major export product, making the fortune and reputation of film-makers and photographers while leaving Congolese out of pocket.[11] Film-makers associated with Yole!Africa in Goma (see Matthias De Groof's chapter in this volume) try to counter stereotypical representations of eastern Congo by foregrounding young artists in the region. Sammy Baloji has criticised the proliferation of NGOs in conflict zones in that part of the country in the exhibition, *Hunting and Collecting* (MuZee, Ostend, 2014). More recently, Pamela Tulizo's photo series *Double Identity* denounces Western media representations of women in eastern Congo by showing the tensions between their global media image as eternal victims of sadistic Congolese men[12] and their self-image as elegant, proud, self-confident, strong, and talented.

Sammy Baloji is widely considered one of the world's most important contemporary artists. In 2020, Pamela Tulizo won the third edition of the prestigious Dior Photography & Visual Arts Award for Young Talents. Baloji and Tulizo are part of a roster of Congolese artists whose works have captivated Western art lovers since the nineteenth century. If, as has been argued, Congoism was developed to legitimise colonisation and justify the plundering of

Congo's immense natural resources,[13] it should be noted that after the end of the transatlantic slave trade, Western interest for Congolese natural resources went hand in hand with the development of trade in Congolese artworks.[14]

Such artworks by mostly anonymous artists now form part of the core collections of the best known so-called ethnographic museums and museums for world cultures.[15] The African object that first fascinated Pablo Picasso was a wooden figurine made by a Vili artist who lived on the Loango coast in the region of the ancient Kongo kingdom, which covers parts of Angola, DRC, Gabon, and the Republic of Congo.

The pioneering role that Congolese artists have played in modern and contemporary art (contemporary art only starts from the 1970s onwards) world is less known. The first sub-Saharan African painters to make watercolours were the Congolese Albert Lubaki and his wife Antoinette and Tshyela Ntendu during the 1920s. In 1968 the painter Pierre-Victor Mpoy became the first African artist to have works of art exhibited at the Venice Biennale. In 2018 Bodys Isek Kingelez was the first African artist to get a solo show in the Museum of Modern Art in New York. Also in 2018 Sotheby's in London announced that Congolese artists did particularly well at their second sale of modern and contemporary art: twelve of the fourteen works on offer were sold at a price that represented just under a third of the total sale price for all artworks. Between July 2018 and June 2019, the list of contemporary African artists who had achieved the highest prices at sales was dominated by Congolese: Cheri Samba at numbers 1, 2, 5, 8, and 9, and Eddy Kamuanga Ilunga, who is only thirty years old, at number 3.[16]

Congo is not only known for its outstanding classical artists and contemporary visual artists. Kinshasa is the capital of comics in Africa and of Congolese rumba. In 1960, *Indépendance Cha Cha* by Joseph Kabasele and African jazz became the unofficial national anthem of all newly independent African countries. In the words of the Congolese guitarist Felly Pepe Manuaku,[17] Congolese rumba subsequently colonised the whole of sub-Saharan Africa with the exception of South Africa.[18] In 2008 the group Konono No. 1 got a Grammy nomination for their album *Live at Colour Café*. One year later the group Staff Benda Bilili received the prize for best musicians at Womex (World Music Expo). In 2012 Rachel Mwanza won the Silver Bear for best actress at the Film Festival in Berlin for her role in the Canadian film *Rebelle*. In 2017 Dieudo Hamadi won the Grand prix du cinéma du réel at the Festival du Réel in Paris for his film *Maman Colonelle*. In 2019 Nelson Makengo accumulated international awards for his films *E'ville* and *Rising Up at Night*. Together with Sammy Baloji choreographer and dancer Faustin Linyekula is Congo's most celebrated artist.

This list, while not exclusive, not only upsets the Congoist notion of Congo as a place of eternal savagery, it also throws up an apparent paradox: how can one of the poorest countries in the world manage so systematically to punch above its weight artistically? In an interview with Filip De Boeck, André Yoka Lye Mudaba, novelist, playwright, and director general of the Institut National des Arts in Kinshasa gave the following explanation:

> We have lost everything; we no longer have economic or political power. We have lost our family ties and we no longer know what the fixed values are. Artistic development is the only possibility that remains to express something together and it is a kind of lifebuoy in the hope of giving a meaning to this existence.[19]

In the documentary *The Rumba Kings*, Yoka describes Congolese rumba as being not only dance but a state of mind and the joy of living. In the same film, Manda Tchebwa, an expert on Congolese music, describes the history of Congolese rumba as the story of a people who decided to fight against oppression through music. Paul Mwanga, who formed part of the first wave of urban Congolese musicians during the colonial era, confirms this by stating that he and other musicians created music out of love for their country: in the face of White colonisers who insulted them by calling them *macaques*, they decided to show them that they were going to create something to restore their dignity.

Against the idea that art would be a luxury that poor people cannot afford, these Congolese describe artistic creativity as their ultimate weapon in their fight against dehumanisation. Journalist and author Vincent Lombume Kalimasi goes so far as saying that 'suffering, despite its negative side, has something beautiful about it: it is what propels us upwards'.[20] When one reads Russian literature of the Golden and Silver Age or listens to the glorious rumba played during Mobutu's dictatorship, one would indeed be tempted to conclude that autocratic regimes are conducive to the creation of great art—which does not mean that suffering is a necessary condition for artistic creativity.

Writing from the Caribbean, Derek Walcott described art as the restoration of shattered bodies.[21] In the Congolese context, the most extreme example of defiant artistic creativity is possibly that of the man who at the start of the twentieth century made mural paintings with a plantain-stalk brush in his mouth held in his teeth, having had both his hands cut off.[22]

Kinshasa, Congo's postcolonial capital has been described as an urban theatre,[23] a tableau vivant,[24] a city of performers,[25] a place where 'everything is ART. City or art installation, in the open air, where each inhabitant of Kinshasa plays his or her part or gives his or her "performances" under a scorching sun. Despite the hunger that constricts their bellies'.[26] The Kinois author and artist

Sinzo Aanza reacted angrily when the French cineaste Renaud Barret described Kinshasa as being characterised by incredible political and social chaos without paying any attention to its history and current context.[27] Barret's Congoist representation of Kinshasa is reminiscent of Western representations of classical Congolese objects created by people living in an eternal, unchangeable tradition and goes against the explicit recommendation of Black curators and scholars to take into account postcolonial conditions when describing and analysing contemporary black art.[28]

Striving for Freedom in the Face of Colonial Violence

Most Congolese are more invested in the actual living conditions in their country than in Congo as a trope. Against ahistorical Congoist perspectives, many Congolese describe the relations between their country and the outside world as defined by predation since the time of the transatlantic slave trade, depriving the country first of its human resources and subsequently from its many natural resources: ivory, rubber, wood, copper, gold, diamonds, uranium, coltan, cobalt, and so on. The sense of constituting a community of suffering,[29] cursed for the abundance of their human and natural resources, coveted by the outside world,[30] is an important source of national identity. An immense sense of pride in Congo's rich cultural heritage in general and Congolese popular music in particular is another.

If making art is what makes human beings human, for many Congolese, Congolese popular music is what makes them Congolese. This idea is far removed from Johann Joachim Winckelmann's notions of an essentialised national genius,[31] but grounded in a Congolese reading of Congolese history: Congolese realise that rumba was forged in a context of colonial oppression and extraction, even as it was largely developed outside of Belgian control. The musicians were self-taught, but for the Belgian jazz musician Bill Alexandre who introduced the electric guitar. The music industry was dominated by Greeks from mainland Greece and Rhodes (which was ruled by Italy between 1911 and 1947) who gave the musicians free rein. The colonial authorities considered rumba harmless dance music and the lyrics mostly innocent and inoffensive.

Zoë Strother has shown that some Pende masks created during the colonial period referred specifically to the colonial context while colonial violence and poverty led to an artistic flowering, including a rebirth of masquerades from the 1940s onwards: as the colonial government had replaced legitimate political leaders with stooges, dancing became a unique way for young men who refused to collaborate with the colonial administration to gain prestige and excel in their own society. It could be argued that in the face of colonial violence, both ritual masquerades in the countryside during the 1940s and urban rumba during the 1950s allowed young men (and in the case of rumba also women) to create an alternative world in which they, not the colonisers, could rule supreme. But whereas Pende masquerades remained local, rumba could become a national genre because the Belgian authorities allowed for it to be broadcasted on Radio Congo belge throughout the colony.

There are also analogies to be drawn between the parallel universes of Pende masquerades and rumba music on the one hand and late nineteenth-century to early twentieth-century Congolese figurines, grafted gourds, and mural paintings that made fun of Europeans on the other. Losing oneself in dances, be it in the context of rural masquerades or city bars, and mocking White people may only offer a brief respite from violence without producing a real alternative, but to dismiss such pleasure and laughter as hedonist escapism is to deny the humanity of individuals striving to experience an exhilarating sense of freedom under the most difficult circumstances.[32]

The Mobutu Years: Academic and Urban Art

There was never a formal music school in Belgian Congo and little formal art education. In 1943, the Belgian missionary Marc Wallenda set up Saint Luc de Gombe Matadi, based on the Belgian Saint Lucas Academies. The institution moved to Léopoldville in 1949 and was officially recognised as the Academy of Fine Arts for higher education in 1957. During that same year, a private art school founded by the Belgian artist Laurent Moonens in Elisabethville was officially recognised as the Official Academy of Fine Arts at secondary school level. To this day, these remain the only institutions for art education in the whole of Congo. Since, in the absence of bursaries, few parents can afford to send their children to study art in Kinshasa, the number of academically trained artists in the country is very small compared to those who received little or no formal academic training, especially outside of the capital.

In 1971, Mobutu proclaimed his official ideology of authenticity: Zairians had to reconnect with the supposedly authentic precolonial culture from which they had been alienated as a result of colonisation. Mobutu was neither a purist nor a man who had thoroughly studied precolonial Zairian cultures. The first ordinary congress of his party, the Popular Movement of the Revolution, instructed the National Executive Council in 1972 to 'focus Zairian culture on a process of permanent recourse to authenticity rooted in the heritage of traditional cultural values or, to accept external cultural contributions'.[33] Congolese 'authentic' culture turned out to be a mixed bag. A few examples may suffice: the native tongue of the self-proclaimed 'Bantu chief' was a non-Bantu language; the traditional wrapper he obliged women to wear was industrial cotton cloth based on the Indonesian wax technique; *l'abacost*, the suit men were supposed to wear, was based on the suit worn by Mao (whose Little Red Book inspired Mobutu's Little Green one) while its name came from the French *à bas le costume* [down with the suit]; the Lingala in which Mobutu used to address his fellow citizens had developed during the colonial era, as was the case for the rumba music, which formed a core part of his political propaganda; rumba musicians could continue to play electric guitars and other imported instruments while traditional orchestras could amplify their music; Mobutu's major building projects in Kinshasa and the region in which he grew up were largely modernist and drew no inspiration from precolonial architecture.

In 1973, some ten young male artists affiliated with the Academy of Fine Arts in Kinshasa published the manifesto of the Congolese avant-garde, which inscribed itself in the authenticity ideology. The artworks (mostly statues and paintings) created by these avant-gardists did not draw inspiration from specific precolonial Congolese artistic traditions, but combined a generalised and idealised vision of 'traditional' Congolese culture with the academic formalism in which students of the institution had been trained since the colonial era.[34]

Like rumba music, academic art transcended ethnic differences. But in a curious way, it mirrored the displays in colonial museums like the Royal Museum for Central Africa, which systematically ignored objects that showed the influence of the European presence on material culture and only exhibited so-called authentic Congolese objects as if colonialism had never taken place.[35] Both in terms of form and content, the artists ignored tensions and strove for harmony instead. Themes that referred to the alleged authenticity of Zairian culture – such as 'mother and child', 'the market', 'the family', and 'the palaver'[36] – kept the realities of both colonial history and Mobutu's Zaire firmly out of sight. Academic art was in essence purely decorative.[37] It lacked the performative quality that characterised the use of ritual power objects such as statues and masks, as well as the mass spectacles with music and dance that Mobutu organised for propaganda purpose. And being firmly apolitical, it also set itself apart from the contemporary art that developed elsewhere at the time. While Mobutu used academic art as part of his political propaganda, Western connoisseurs qualified it as retrograde, exoticising, trading in stereotypes, a poor imitation of Western art, and so on.[38]

By contrast, self-taught male urban painters had a different approach to the colonial past and, from the 1980s onwards, found their way to the international art market. During the 1950s, some Congolese painters without formal training who made oil paintings (as opposed to the aquarelles made by the Lubakis and Tshyela Ntendu) drew the attention of Europeans;[39] little is known about those catering for a Congolese clientele. I am aware of only two such paintings (a great many colonial paintings made for Western patrons survive), both in private collections in Belgium: one made in Léopoldville in 1959 with reference to the second trip of King Baudouin, the other created in Elisabethville in November 1960, at the time of the Katangese secession, depicting a party at the occasion of Congolese independence on 30 June 1960. During the 1970s, expatriates first began to collect and describe urban paintings in Lubumbashi.[40] Bogumil Jewsiewicki bought his first painting in Mbandaka in 1968 and went on to collect some two thousand paintings in Beni, Bukama, Bunia, Goma, Isiro, Kananga, Kikwit, Kinshasa, Kisangani, Kolwezi, Lubumbashi, Matadi, Mbandaka, and Mbuji-Mayi; they now form part of the collections of the Royal Museum for Central Africa.[41]

Some urban painters like Cheri Samba started out as comic book artists; others, like Cheri Cherin and Cheri Benga, initially made mural publicity paintings. Thus, they tend to combine pictures and texts. Urban paintings are not so much objects as images[42] or conversation pieces[43]: they must be put into action through human interventions, prompting and stimulating reflection and debate among those who contemplate them in the social setting of the living room in which they are displayed, and they are abandoned once they have lost their power to set discussions in motion. As such, these secular commodities retain the performative nature of ritual power objects[44] and in a similar way draw inspiration from an oral culture that makes abundant use of allegories, fables, innuendos, metaphors, metonymies, puns, and symbols. The aim is not to obscure certain subjects by avoiding the use of plain language, but to stimulate discussion, advising, or teaching.[45] This means that urban paintings can have different meanings: on the one hand, artists rely on the public's ability to read symbolic signs at the deepest level;[46] on the other hand, the paintings have a certain open-endedness, which allows and even encourages people to give them their own meanings. They share this characteristic with many rumba songs. Franco Makiadi Luambo, one of the greatest rumba stars, used to say that his songs were only half composed, and that the listener had to add meaning.[47] He was a recognised master of *mbwakela*, lyrics in a coded language, rich in metaphors and symbols that attack tyrants, oppressors, or rivals, which allowed him to record songs in which he criticised Mobutu and his henchmen indirectly, alongside songs in which he praised him. If the open-endedness that characterises many urban art forms is reminiscent of Umberto Eco's *opera aperta*[48] the development of such open works in DRC preceded that of a new scientific paradigm and postmodernism in the West. It can also be used to great advantage under an oppressive regime in a context of colonial or postcolonial censorship. In this respect, Pierre-Philippe

Fraiture suggests that Mudimbe's early books criticised the Mobutu regime but escaped censorship because they were so abstruse.[49]

Paintings representing the colonial past do not have the dense meanings that those representing contemporary society have, because the painters do not have the same knowledge about the urban culture at the time (the songs that were popular, the rumours swirling around Radio Trottoir) that make contemporary urban painting so difficult to interpret for those who are not familiar with current urban cultures in Congo. Nevertheless, some are open to different interpretations. During the 1970s, the colonial period and the Congo crisis were prominent themes. The most ubiquitous image was called *Colonie belge (1885– 1960)*. Not distinguishing between the Congo Free State and Belgian Congo, the painting focused on a Congolese soldier whipping a chained Congolese prisoner under the watchful eye of a Belgian officer. Usually, other enchained prisoners were shown in the background and sometimes, at the right-hand side, two women would be seen weeping over the prisoners' plight. The territory of the prison usually referred to the region from which the purchaser hailed.

When Mobutu came to power in 1965, he was popular because he had put an end to the Congo Crisis. His ideology of authenticity inspired in many Zairians a deep sense of pride in precolonial cultures. Even ardent critics of his dictatorial regime have told me in interviews and personal conversations that he was right to urge Congolese to reconnect with precolonial cultures. I've already mentioned that academic artists drew inspiration from precolonial cultures in their artworks. Kasereka Kavwahireri has analysed authenticity as framework for writers and thinkers during Mobutu's rule.[50] In his African philosophical bibliography, Father A. J. Smet records twenty-eight texts by and interviews with Congolese philosophers that deal with authenticity, and this list is far from complete.[51] In his 1973 address to the United Nations, Mobutu asked the General Assembly to vote on a resolution to ask the former colonial powers to return the cultural heritage they had appropriated. It inspired the popular painter Tshibumba Kanda Matulu to make a painting of the event, which he called *The Most Applauded Discourse at the UN*: 'So he spoke, and we all agreed; not a single thing was disputed'.[52] Mobutu had tried to foster a national identity by establishing institutions such as the Théâtre national congolais (1970) and the Ballet nationale du Zaïre (1974). A national poll among students conducted in 2010 established that the majority described Congo as a unitary and indivisible state, a pluri-ethnic, multilingual, and pluricultural nation, and defined Congolese identity as characterised, among other things, by its music and theatre.[53]

But over time, Mobutu and his cronies ran the economy into the ground, and his rule became increasingly repressive. An awareness of the fact that he reintroduced punishment by *chicotte* for prisoners allows for a different reading of the *Colonie belge* paintings executed during his dictatorship. A painting by Gabriel Londe, *Colonie belge*, currently held in the RMCA's collections, takes on a specific meaning when one knows that he was imprisoned and possibly whipped during the Mobutu years.

Apart from King Baudouin on Independence Day, few historical Belgian persons figured in urban painting. Next to local cultural heroes who had contested colonial rule, Patrice Lumumba, the first prime minister of Congo, emerged as a national cultural hero. Some paintings referred to Lumumba's speech on 30 June 1960, which could be represented as having the power to make independence happen that and subsequently drive away Belgians, bearing testimony to the power of the human voice in transforming the world.[54]

During the 1840s, sculptors on the Loango Coast carved ivories that included representations of shackled enslaved persons being transported across the Atlantic Ocean; during the 1950s, colonial scenes on gourds grafted by Benoît Madya and Laurent Bumbu included shackled prisoners. In urban painting, shackles represent colonialism as a transformation of the slave trade. Thus, Lumumba is often represented as a Christlike figure who sacrificed his life for his countrymen's freedom: having casted off the shackles that symbolise colonisation on Independence Day, he was stripped of his shirt and vest and shackled after his capture and ended up dying between two companions, like Christ and the two thieves on Mount Golgotha. Through its diffusion on the 20 makuta bill, the image of Lumumba breaking the chains of colonialism gained national currency.[55]

On one level, the academic art and urban paintings produced during Mobutu's reign seemed to be each other's opposite in their treatment of the colonial past: in line with Mobutu's ideology of authenticity, academic artists effaced the colonial past while urban painters preserved it. However, both types of art works were produced for a Congolese clientele. Ownership of such art orks became a mark of belonging to the upper middle class in the case of the former and of the lower middle class in the case of the latter.

The Post-Mobutu Years

After the fall of Mobutu, international researchers and cultural institutions returned to Congo. In 1996, Daniel Shongo, the new director of the Academy of Fine Arts in Kinshasa, offered great freedom to students and created exchanges with international schools. Students started revolting against their teachers. In 1997, a number of students and alumni, including Francis Mampuya, founded an art collective called Librism [Freedom]. Next came an art collective called Synergic Librism, which included Vitshois Mwilambwe Mwendo, Steve Bandoma, and Freddy Mutombo, followed by the art collective Eza Possibles [It Is Possible] to which Vitshois Mwilambwe, Francis Mampuya, Mega Mingiedi, Pathy Tshindele, Eddy Ekete, Kura Shomali, Kennedy Dianga, Freddy Mutombo, and Iviart Izamba belonged.[56]

In 2003 the Academy of Fine Arts set up a partnership with the Haut école des arts du Rhin de Mulhouse – Strasbourg. A number of students from Kinshasa graduated from there. Rare were those who, like Steve Bandoma, could afford to individually fund further education abroad, in his case in South Africa. Other students expressed their dissatisfaction with the teaching at the Academy of Fine Arts in different ways. After graduating, Freddy Tsimba did an apprenticeship with a blacksmith; JP-Mika did an apprenticeship with the urban painter Cheri Cherin. Alumni like Gosette Lubondo followed master classes organised by international cultural institutions in Congo. Other students, such as Eddy Ilunga Kamuanga, dropped out. Artists with no formal academic training like Sammy Baloji received training from Western artists. The international cultural institutions Wallonie-Bruxelles International, L'Institut Français, and the Goethe Institut started organising exhibitions with works by young artists. Some found their way to the international art market. As a result of the economic decline that had set in during Mobutu's regime, urban painters lost their Congolese clientele and became all but wholly dependent upon foreign clients to survive, while academic artists, deprived of Mobutu's patronage, no longer got commissions and continued to fail to find buyers outside of the country.

Unlike Mobutu, none of his successors saw culture as a priority. Although this means that many artists struggle to survive, like musicians during the colonial era, they have great artistic freedom. But as during the colonial era, they must be careful not to fall foul of the censors, as some artists have found out to their cost (cf. Faustin Linyekula.[57] Contemporary art, whether made by academically trained or self-taught contemporary artists is inherently political, although as far as I am aware, Steve Bandoma is the only one who has ambitions of following in the footsteps of his politician father. Contemporary artists started out experimenting with forms before addressing the situation of Congolese society, in much the same way that urban painters after the end of Mobutu's rule started painting his demise, the economic crisis, and its consequences (the disintegration of families, street children, the rise of evangelical churches, the arrival of Laurent-Désiré Kabila, the two Congo wars, and so on) in paintings that were often dense with meanings.

Escaping the Hole

Congolese often cite the fictitious fifteenth article of the constitution, 'Débrouillez-vous' [Fend for Yourselves], which has inspired urban paintings, to express how they have to make do by any means necessary. Artworks such as *Ici on crève* [Here We Die], visual artists such as Aimé Mpane, and the song 'Nini Sali tè' by the group Mouvement Populaire de la Musique evoke the struggles of ordinary Kinois trying to survive. Four days after it came online in November 2021, the clip of the song racked up eight hundred thousand views on YouTube. It was quickly, albeit only briefly censored. Its lyrics clearly struck a chord with many Congolese:

> Study! We did it.
> Fasts and prayers! We did it.
> We have even undone family ties.
> Fight and persevere! We did it.
> But what have we not done?[58]

The Kikongo word *kiesse* originally meant 'designated the happiness/madness brought on by spirit possession'.[59] For the inhabitants of the capital, the transformation of *Kin Kiesse* or *Kin la Belle* [beautiful Kinshasa] to *Kin la poubelle* [Kinshasa, the garbage bin] remains emblematic of the ruin that the country became during Mobutu's reign. Kinois now also describe their city as *libulu* [a hole]. But if they live in a hole, they might as well dance in it.[60] However, the famous Kinois *ambiance*,[61] a (post)colonial transformation of the kind of madness associated with precolonial ritual,[62] is not purely escapist pleasure: apart from allowing Kinois to forget their daily troubles, it lets them escape the darkness at home when there are electricity cuts.

The parallel world that Kinois nightlife offers for many of its inhabitants resembles similar worlds created by Kinois artists such as Bodys Isek Kingelez and Pume Bylex. In 1985, on the occasion of the twentieth anniversary of Mobutu's coup on 24 November 1965, Bodys Isek Kingelez made the sculpture *Kinshasa: Cité du 24 Novembre de l'Authenticité Africaine*.[63] But as he became disillusioned with Mobutu's rule, he started creating the models of ideal clean cities on which his reputation rests. Their empty silent streets and empty harmonic buildings stand in sharp contrast to the actual realities of his home city, a metropolis with twelve million inhabitants, slums, endless noise, garbage heaps, open gutters, pollution, and potholes.

The model of the tourist city created by Pume Bylex, another Kinois and self-taught artist who is twenty years younger than Bodys Isek Kingelez, also presents an ideal, clean world that is far removed from his hometown. Curiously, the utopic cities that both artists create share the totalitarian nature of Mobutu's dictatorship even as they mirror the hole that Kinshasa became under his reign. Unlike the ambiance that characterises Kinshasa's nightlife, the artistic projects of both artists leave no room for dialogue: they turn their back to the city and its inhabitants by withdrawing into their own minds. In the words of Pume Bylex:

> Your mind does not need to take public transport. Your mind does not have to get on a plane to return to your room in Kinshasa or Brussels when you are somewhere else. The mind is free, and even in captivity it cannot be confined. Consider a prisoner. Lock him up in a cell somewhere. What do you see? If the prisoner feels the need to see his house or his room, he doesn't need permission from the guard. A guard would never allow my mind to see my room! But my mind can get out even without the guard's permission, and go to see my room. By this I mean that the mind is the basis, for in your mind there are relations far more complex than those outside, in the visible world. That is the power of the mind, and this power is a victory.[64]

As such, the artworks by Bodys Isek Kingelez and Pume Bylex do not appear to confirm Andre Lye Yoka Mudaba's insight that '[a]rtistic development is the only possibility that remains to express something together'.[65] On the one hand, it is fair to say that these artists try to find individual freedom from an oppressive reality. On the other hand, it is rare for Congolese artists to represent the situations they criticise by reproducing them. Urban painting is unusual in its attempt to represent city life as chaotic as it appears to be. But on the whole, like precolonial Congolese art, (post)colonial Congolese art tends to eschew realism for idealised forms of representation. As such, Bodys Isek Kingelez and Pume Bylex place themselves in a long tradition, as do other contemporary artists.

Kiripi Katembo photographed the Kinois cityscape in the reflection of the stagnant water pools that abound in the city (it may have led to his untimely death as a victim of cerebral malaria). The drawing *Kin Délestage* by Mega Mingiedi and the film *Nuit debout* by Nelson Makengo present power cuts in a poetic way. In her photography series *Imaginary Trip*, Gosette Lubondo staged travellers in a disused train, evoking the atmosphere of the colonial era when the trains operated. In her next series, *Imaginary Trip II*, she staged schoolchildren in uniform in an abandoned school set up by a missionary congregation in 1936. In a sense, many contemporary Congolese artists are like Perseus who did not look the Medusa in the eyes, but severed her head while looking at her reflection in the mirrored shield given to him by the goddess Athena. This staging aspect recalls the nature of ritual performances.

Other artists leave earth altogether to create parallel worlds in outer space: Balufu Bakupa Kanyinda in his movie *Nous avons aussi marché sur la lune* (2009), Monsengo Shula's recent space paintings, and the performers who are part of the Collective Kongo Astronauts, for example. This fascination with outer space has many sources: the Christian faith shared by many Congolese, the popularity of Hergé's 1964 comic book *On a marché sur la lune* [Destination Moon], the visit of Apollo 11 astronauts to Kinshasa in 1969, and Mobutu's failed space programme.

However, once again it would be wrong to dismiss such fascination with outer space as pure hedonist escapism. Monsengo Shula has named one of his paintings of a classical Congolese sculpture in space *Ata Ndele*, the title of a song recorded by Adou Elenga in 1954. Its lyrics 'Ata ndele mokili ekobaluka' [Sooner or later the world will change] got the record taken out of circulation by the colonial authorities. The painting's title thus leaves open the question whether the predicted change refers to Congo's colonial past or to its future. *Après Schengen*, a series of photographs and a performance created by Kongo Astronauts in 2019 after the closure of the Maison Schengen in Kinshasa where Congolese have to obtain a visa to visit the European Union, suggests that if Congolese cannot escape their living conditions in their homeland they can only go to outer space.[66]

Making Art Out of Dirt

Kongo Astronauts create their robots by means of motherboards, cables, and batteries that contain minerals mined in Congo in difficult and often dangerous circumstances.[67] As such, they are among an increasing number of artists who make artworks out of recycled objects. The Kinois Freddy Tsimba was one of the first visual artists to make extensive use of recycled materials. The nickname given to his fellow Kinois and colleague Emmanuel Botalatala, *Le Ministre des poubelles* [the Minister of Garbage], speaks for itself. Also in Kinshasa, the group Fulu Muziki make their own musical instruments with what they find in the street. In their animated films, which criticise the sacrifice of Congolese workers and their environment for economic exploitation, the Lushois Tétshim and Frank Mukunday bring workers and miners, represented by stones from the subsoil, to life by stop-motion before they are destroyed by machines and turned into dead stones again.

In Kinshasa, Eddy Ekete, one of the co-founders of the annual performance festival KinAct in 2015, created the mask *The Can Man* to criticise pollution. In its wake, many more masks have been created. They owe more to precolonial masquerades than to contemporary performances, not only formally (e.g. masks resembling those worn during Pende masquerades) but also because the masks render the alternative personalities the artists (now including street children) create visible. Most such masks are made with recycled materials to criticise Kinshasa's environmental problems: *The Electric Woman* by Falone Mambu draws attention to power cuts; Junior Mvunzi created a mask of a traditional warrior by means of cans to denounce Western multinationals exporting mountains of waste to African cities; New-mama Mobando warns of the dangers of deforestation; *Tshombo* [Telephone] by female artist Nada Tshibwabwa refers both to the exploitation of coltan and the high cost of mobile phones, which are indispensable in a megalopolis like Kinshasa; Sarah Ndele's *Plastic Woman* points to the dangers of microplastics; Junior Longalonga (also known as Savant Noir) pays tribute to Congolese who lost their lives during the brutal rubber exploitation in the Congo Free State with the mask *The Rubber Man*.[68]

All these artists seem to operate according to the logic that if they have to live in a hole, they may as well try to turn in into art. As such, they can be compared to alchemists trying to turn lead into gold—and more often than not, succeeding in doing so.

Carrying the Past on One's Back and in One's Body

Just like the colonial system tried to erase the precolonial past and Mobutu, in response, tried to erase the colonial period, when Laurent-Désiré Kabila replaced Mobutu in 1997, he tried to reconnect with independence. His son and successor, Joseph Kabila, was the first president to honour his predecessors:[69] he had a monument built for his father and statues erected for Patrice Lumumba and President Kasa-Vubu, and proclaimed Simon Kimbangu and Laurent-Désiré Kabila national heroes. However, this official recognition of the colonial past alone cannot explain the increasing interest of contemporary artists in that era.

Faustin Linyekula who is, in his own words, obsessed with Congolese history, has said that for a long time he avoided the colonial past for fear of using it as justification for Africans' inability to govern their countries today, preferring to identify and emphasise Africans' own responsibility for their misery and for the ruins they created after independence.[70] He finally confronted the colonial past in his choreography *Congo* in 2019. In an interview at the opening of an exhibition with photographs of his series *Kolwezi* in Brussels in 2017, Sammy Baloji said that, growing up, he did not know colonial history: 'I went to a Catholic school where we were mainly taught to forgive'.[71] Describing why he makes robots, Précy Numbi says that he does not want to go back to the past because Congolese already carry the past on their backs.[72] Nevertheless, his robot Lumumba is a clear reference to the past. For many Congolese, Lumumba represented the hope for the future of their country. With his assassination, Congo died in some ways. And as he was never properly buried, his ghost continues to haunt the country. Many young Congolese bitterly reproach their elders for betraying the independence Lumumba fought for, as their road towards upwards social mobility is blocked. Georges Senga's *Une vie après la mort* is based on Kayembe Kilobo, a Lushois man who dresses up like Lumumba.[73] I once found on Facebook a photograph of a man tied to a tree on what appeared to be the Avenue du 30 juin in Kinshasa similar to representations on urban paintings, in clear reference to Lumumba's imprisonment before he died. Balufu Bakupa Kanyinda fruitlessly tried to get a film about Lumumba off the grounds for years, but his figure looms large over Congolese film.[74]

Contemporary artists seldom directly express anger vis-à-vis their parents or grandparents who are responsible for the ruins they created after independence.[75] Instead, many retrace these ruins to the shaky foundations upon which colonial society was built. While urban painters tried to retrieve and remember the past during the Mobutu years of which they retained personal memories, contemporary artists who were born after independence turn to the colonial past to find clues to explain the postcolonial condition. Unlike urban painters, Tshibumba Kanda Matulu eminent among them, they do not try to recount the colonial past in a narrative sequence. Instead, it emerges in relation to problems affecting contemporary society. As such, these artists are on the whole less concerned with individual persons and historical events than with the structures that continue to shape Congolese society since the colonial era. Aimé Mpane's work *Congo: L'ombre de l'ombre*, which contains the date of the Berlin Conference, is unusual in that regard.[76]

Through his robot, Numbi wants to show Lumumba as a twenty-first century superhero. Like other robots and some masks, Numbi's Lumumba also references the fact that new technologies developed in the West depend upon Congolese natural resources. In that sense, there is a clear connection with the shackles that Lumumba threw off on Independence Day and that he was forced to wear again after his imprisonment. In a similar way, the animation films made by Tétshim and Mukunday about labourers and miners toiling in Katanga's industrial centres can be interpreted both in relation to colonial and postcolonial society. In Congo, history repeats itself, but it is history, not simply a throwback to 'the eternal realities of the Congo, which had existed for centuries before them'.[77]

There appears to be some truth in Barly Baruti's observation that in Congo, the wounds of colonialism are still so fresh that it is impossible for Congolese to make fun of colonisation the way the French do in the comic book series *Asterix*. One could counter that it took the French almost two thousand years to satirise the Roman colonisation of Gaul or point to the fact that Ernest Lubitsch made his satire on the Nazis, *To Be or Not to Be*, during World War II. Congolese certainly made fun of Belgians during the colonial era, not only through artworks but also by giving them nicknames and mocking them when they were sure Belgians could not understand them, for example. Since the end of Mobutu's dictatorship, they have started joking about *mobuitude* or *mobutuité*.[78] Nelson Makengo's short film *Théâtre Urbain*, in which Barbie and Captain America go looking for the special belt that survived when Kimpa Vita was burned at the stake in 1706, certainly has the light touch one associates with many Congolese encounters. But it is true that postcolonial art tends not to treat colonial history lightly.

Faustin Linyekula initially wanted to become a poet, but after the Congo Wars that hit Kisangani where he studied and now lives and works particularly hard, he wondered how he could dream of poetry amid ruins and decided to dance instead.[79] He considers the body an archive that expresses the traumatic legacy of colonialism and postcolonial wars:

> The body also reveals the violence that was done to us. The hands that were chopped off because the Congolese did not work hard enough on the rubber plantations. The whippings that left scars on my grandfather's back. The wars, the rapes, up to and including the acts of cannibalism during the latest civil wars. That whole history of physical violence must be reflected in the physical forms of culture, in dance especially.[80]

While Sammy Baloji deals systematically with the colonial past, all his art is in fact informed by the ethnic cleansing of Baluba in Katanga during the early 1990s, which had its origins in the colonial past. Increasingly, he draws inspiration from precolonial art forms, including scarification, Kongo textiles, the Luba *lukasa* memory board that serves as a mnemotechnic device, and the Luba *kasala*, a sung or recited ceremonial poem. Artists like Steve Bandoma and Freddy Tsimba refer to Kongo *minkisi* in a similar way.[81] If, as David Van Reybrouck writes, 'the body is [...] a site of revolt, of refusal, of rebellion',[82] this would go some way to explain the enduring importance of music, dance, performance, and the interest in ritual performative objects in contemporary Congolese art.

Conclusion

My brief description of the ways in which a number of postcolonial Congolese artists represent the colonial past or draw inspiration from older art forms suggests that the lines between 'ritual', 'urban', and 'contemporary' art and between self-taught and academically trained artists, between artists who (in)directly address the colonial past or ignore it through hedonistic escapism are not clear cut.

In 2021 Aimé Mpane became the first artist of Congolese descent to have an individual show at the Royal Museums of Fine Arts in Brussels. One of his works of art on display, *Or* [Gold], refers simultaneously to the fact that Congolese power objects could not stop colonisation or soften its harsh nature and the ongoing exploitation of Congo's natural resources by foreigners.

Possibly more than any other country in the world, Congo confronts us with the stark contrast between relentless ongoing human exploitation and human creativity. Unlike capitalism, however, culture is not a zero-sum game: even as colonialism brutally disrupted and destroyed Congolese cultures, Congolese (like colonial subjects elsewhere) created new ones. In the words of the French Cameroonian author Léonora Miano: when one's worlds disappear, one doesn't die; one invents a new one,[83] albeit it not from scratch. Many Congolese postcolonial artists struggle with the phantom pain of colonialism, while defiantly holding on to performative practices that the colonial regime tried to supress.

But since Congo's contacts with the West at the end of the nineteenth century, its artworks have been resources for foreigners as much as the country's rich natural resources. There is a certain irony in the fact that the ahistorical academic art produced under Mobutu's rule never found many buyers abroad, whereas Western private collectors and museums are willing to pay hefty sums for artworks that oppose Western Congoist visions on Congolese history and culture by exposing and denouncing the ways in which foreign powers and enterprises continue to exploit Congo's natural resources at the detriment of the population. Like classical art, most urban and contemporary Congolese art is now to be found in private and public collections outside of the country. If, as Sinzo Aanza wrote on Facebook on 19 May 2020, without art Congo is nothing but a mine, it is of the essence that Congolese have the opportunity to come face to face with the various art forms Congolese artists continue to create as they stubbornly refuse to be dehumanised and represent Congolese as victims.

The fact that they continue to make art in the face of financial hardship and political and societal opposition (artists like Géraldine Tobe and Freddy Tsimba have been accused of witchcraft) can be interpreted as a refusal of victimhood. In that regard, the name of the artistic collective *Eza possibles* is revealing, all the more so when taken into consideration with the often-used expression, *L'impossible n'est pas congolais* [the impossible is not Congolese]. Paraphrasing Lord Darlington in the third act of Oscar Wilde's play *Lady Windermere's Fan*, it can be said of many Congolese (artists) that even if they are in the gutter, they keep looking at the stars.

Notes

1. Apart from the authors whose texts I quote, I am indebted to the many Congolese artists and musicians it has been my privilege to meet and get to know these past years.
2. J. Van Hove, *Congoism: Congo Discourses in the United States from 1800 to the Present* (Bielefeld: transcript Verlag, 2017), p. 28.
3. Mohamed Ali Fadlabi and Lars Cuznor in personal conversation in 2014: https://www.dailymotion.com/video/x1tw6sz
4. Van Hove, p. 27.
5. Frits Andersen, *The Dark Continent? Images of Africa in European Narratives about the Congo*, trans. William Frost & Martin Skovhus (Aarhus: Aarhus University Press, 2016), pp. 17–18.
6. M. Crichton, *Congo* (London: Arrow Books Ltd., 1980), p. 163.
7. Van Hove, p. 29.
8. R. West, *The White Tribes of Africa* (London: Jonathan Cape, 1965), p. 129.
9. See Chloé Lewis, 'The Making and Re-Making of the "Rape Capital of the World": On Colonial Durabilities and the Politics of Sexual Violence Statistics in DRC, *Critical African Studies*, (2021), 1–18; and Charlotte Mertens, 'Sexual Violence in the Congo Free State: Archival Traces and Present Reconfigurations', *The Australian Review of African Studies*, 37.1 (2016), 6–20.
10. E. Behr, *Anyone Here Been Raped and Speaks English?* (Hodder & Stoughton General Division, 1987).
11. Renzo Martens, *Episode III – Enjoy Poverty* (Imagine Film Distribution, 2009.)
12. For a discussion on the gender-related aspects of this question, see Gayatri Chakravorty Spivak, 'Can the subaltern speak?', in Cary Nelson and Lawrence Grossberg (eds.), *Marxism and the interpretation of culture* (Urbana: University of Illinois Press, 1988), pp. 271–313.
13. See Van Hove, p. 28; Andersen, p. 13; Sindre Bangstad & Bjørn Enge Bertelsen, 'Heart of darkness reinvented? A tale of ex-soldiers in the Democratic Republic of Congo', *Anthropology Today*, 26.1 (2010), 8–12; Sarah De Mul, 'The Congo as Topos of Dystopic Transgression in Fin-de-Siècle Literature, *Tydskrif vir Letterkunde*, 46.1 (2009), 95–108 (95–96).
14. Zoë S. Strother, *The Invention of Masks: Agency and History in the Art of the Central Pende* (Chicago & London: The University of Chicago Press, 1988), pp. 41–42.
15. For a critique of the concept of ethnography as an 'othering' device, see Johannes Fabian, 'On Recognizing Things: The "Ethnic Artefact" and the "Ethnographic Object"', *L'Homme*, 70 (2004), 47–60; and Tim Ingold, 'That's Enough about Ethnography!', *Journal of Ethnographic Theory*, 4.1 (2014), 383–95, https://www.haujournal.org/index.php/hau/article/view/hau4.1.021
16. See https://www.artprice.com/artprice-reports/the-contemporary-art-market-report-2019/african-artists-breaking-through [accessed 6 January 2022].
17. Cited in Alan Brain's documentary film, *The Rumba Kings* (No Distributor, 2021). See: https://afropop.org/articles/alan-brain-on-the-rumba-kings [accessed 12 January 2022].
18. See Tom Salter, 'Rumba: From Congo to Capetown', unpublished PhD thesis, University of Edinburgh, (2007).
19. Quoted in Filip De Boeck, Koen Van Synghel & Vincent Lombume Kalimasi, *De gesproken stad: gesprekken over Kinshasa* (Kessel-Lo: Literarte, 2005), p. 202. All translations are mine unless otherwise stated.
20. Cited in Brain's *The Rumba Kings*.
21. Cited in Bogumil Jewsiewicki, in 'Leaving Ruins: Explorations of Present Pasts by Sammy Baloji, Freddy Tsimba and Steve Bandoma', *African Arts*, 49.1 (2016), 6–25.
22. Enid Schildkrout and Curtis A. Keim, *African Reflections: Art from Northeastern Zaire* (Seattle and London: University of Washington Press; New York: American Museum of Natural History, 1990), p. 105.
23. As argued by Nelson Makengo in his short film *Théâtre Urbain* (Pantin: Sudu Connexon, 2017).
24. Renaud Barret, cited in Julie Peghini, 'Représenter Kinshasa', *Critique*, 5/6/7 (2020), 563–74.
25. Olivier Marboeuf, cited in ibid.
26. Jean Kamba, cited on https://www.e-flux.com/announcements/176349/megalopolis/ [Accessed 6 January 6, 2022].
27. Cited in Peghini (2020), p. 569
28. See Okwui Enwezor, 'Between Localism and Worldliness, *Art Journal* 57.4 (1998), 29–36 (32–33); Okwui Enwezor and Chika Okeke-Agulu, 'Situating Contemporary African Art: Introduction', in Enwezor & Okeke-Agulu, *Contemporary African Art since 1980* (Bologna: Damiani, 2009), pp. 8–17 (pp. 11–12); and Stuart Hall, 'Black Diaspora Artists in Britain: Three "Moments" in Postwar History', *History Workshop Journal*, 61.1 (2006), 1–24 (23).
29. Pnina Werbner, 'Rich Man Poor Man: or a Community of Suffering: Heroic Motifs in Manchester Pakistani Life Histories', *Oral History* 8.1 (1980), 43–48.
30. See Dirk-Jan Koch, *The Congo codes* (Amsterdam: Prometheus-Bert Bakker, 2014).

31. Brian Vick, 'Greek Origins and Organic Metaphors: Ideals of Cultural Autonomy in Neohumanist Germany from Winckelmann to Curtius', *Journal of the History of Ideas*, 63.3 (2002), 483–500 (584)
32. Mary Douglas, cited in Zoë S. Strother, *Humor and Violence: Seeing Europeans in Central African Art* (Bloomington: Indiana University Press, 2016), p. 69.
33. Cited in Badi-Banga Ne-Mwine, *Contribution à l'étude historique de l'art plastique zaïrois moderne. Fin XVe siècle ? – 1975* (Kinshasa: Editions Malayika, 1977), p. 95.
34. Jean Kamba. 2014. 'Kinshasa contemporain: Les arts visuels. 1ère partie' http://jeankamba.centerblog.net/1-kinshasa-contemporain-un-article-de-jean-kamba [accessed 6 January 2022]; and Sarah Van Beurden, *Authentically African: Arts and the Transnational Politics of Congolese Culture* (Athens, Ohio: Ohio University Press, 2015), pp. 152–53.
35. Bambi Ceuppens, 'From Colonial Subjects/Objects to Citizens: The Royal Museum for Central Africa as Contact-Zone, in Francesca Lanz and Elena Montanari (eds.), *Advancing Museum Practices* (Turin: Umberto Allemandi & C., 2015), pp. 129–47.
36. See Kamba (2014).
37. Steve Bandoma, cited in Chantal Tombu (ed.). *Papiers de société: Kura Shomali, Raymond Tsham et Steve Bandoma* (Neufchâteau: Weyrich Edition, 2020), p. 92.
38. Van Beurden (2015), p. 192
39. See Joseph-Aurélien Cornet, Rémi de Cnodder, Ivan Dierickx and Wim Toebosch (eds.), *60 ans de peinture au Zaïre* (Brussels: Éditions d'Arts Associés, 1989); and Jean-Luc Vellut, et al., *La naissance de la peinture contemporaine en Afrique Centrale, 1930 – 1970* (Tervuren: Royal Museum for Central Africa, 1992).
40. Ilona Szombati-Fabian and Johannes Fabian, 'Folk Art from an Anthropological Perspective, *Studies in the Anthropology of Visual Communication*, 3.1 (1976), 1–21.
41. Jewsiewicki, in Ceuppens and Baloji (2016).
42. Ibid.
43. Johannes Fabian, 'What is African Popular Art Doing in a Museum? Keynote Speech Symposium 'Popular Imagination: Fiction with a Message', Amsterdam: Tropenmuseum, 22 September 2011.
44. Z. Strother, 'From Performative Utterances to Performative Objects: Pende Theories of Speech, Blood Sacrifice, and Power Objects', *Anthropology and Aesthetics*, 37 (2000), 49–71.
45. B. Jewsiewicki, 'Popular Painting in Contemporary Katanga: Painters, Audiences, Buyers, and Sociopolitical Contexts', in Bogumil Jewsiewicki (ed.) *A Congo Chronicle: Lumumba in Urban Art* (New York: The Museum for African Art, 1999), pp. 13–27; Jewsiewicki, in Ceuppens and Baloji; Jean Kennedy, *New Currents, Ancient Rivers: Contemporary African Artists in a Generation of Change* (Washington: Smithsonian Institute Press, 1992), p. 14; Szombati-Fabian and Fabian (1976), p. 18.
46. Benedetta Jules-Rosette, 'Aesthetics and Market Demand: The Structure of the Tourist Art Market in Three African Settings', *African Studies Review*, 29.1 (1986), 41–59 (49).
47. Gary Stewart, *Rumba on the River: A History of the Popular Music of the Two Congos* (London: Verso, 2003), p. 231.
48. U. Eco, *The Open Work*, trans. Anna Cancogni (Cambridge, Mass., Harvard University Press, 1989).
49. P.-P. Fraiture, *V. Y. Mudimbe: Undisciplined Africanism* (Liverpool: Liverpool University Press, 2013), p. 51.
50. Kasereka Kavwahireri, 'L'authenticité comme cadre de pensée et d'écriture au Congo-Kinshasa entre 1970 et 1982', in Isidore Ndaywel è Nziem and Elisabeth Mudimbe-Boyi (eds.) *Images, mémoires et savoirs: Une histoire en partage avec Bogumil Koss Jewsiewicki* (Paris: Karthala, 2009), pp. 625–48.
51. A. J. Smet, *Bibliographie de la philosophie africaine/bibliografie van de afrikaanse [sic] wijsbegeerte*, https://sites.uclouvain.be/sisp/sites/philafr/M.html [accessed 8 June 2022]. Among the texts not mentioned is the following: Nkombe Oleko, 'Méthode et point de départ en Philosophie africaine: Authenticité et libération', *La philosophie africaine. Actes de la 1ère Semaine Philosophique de Kinshasa*, 1 (1977), 69–87.
52. J. Fabian, *Remembering the Present: Narrative and Paintings by Tshibumba Kanda Matulu* (Berkeley and Los Angeles: University of California Press, 1996), p. 170.
53. Luc Reychler and Jean Migabo Kalere (eds.), *RD Congo: pays de l'avenir. Construisons ensemble une paix durable pour un Meilleur destin. Livre ouvert, 87* (Leuven: KU Leuven Centre of Peace Research and Strategic Studies, 2010), pp. 90–91.
54. B. Jewsiewicki, 'Popular Memories of Patrice Lumumba, in Jewsiewicki (ed.) *A Congo Chronicle*, pp. 59–69; and Strother (2000), 67–68.
55. Jewsiewicki, 'Popular Painting in Contemporary Katanga…', p. 25.
56. Kamba (2014); Jean Kamba, 'Kinshasa: Decolonising Arts Education I. Towards an Open Approach or a Dead Letter?' (2016) https://www.contemporaryand.com/magazines/towards-an-open-approach-or-a-dead-letter/ [Accessed 6 January 2022].

57. Faustin Linyekula, cited in Gie Goris, 'Congolees kunstenaar neemt KVS over' *Mo**, 22 April (2008), https://www.mo.be/artikel/congolees-kunstenaar-neemt-kvs-over [Accessed 6 January 2022].
58. https://www.youtube.com/watch?v=KqzEwuv-VvYs [Accessed 6 January 2022].
59. Wyatt MacGaffey, cited in Joe Trapido, *Breaking Rocks: Music, Ideology and Economic Collapse from Paris to Kinshasa* (New York & Oxford: Berghahn Books, 2020), p. 32.
60. Filip De Boeck, '"Illuminating the Hole": Kinshasa's Makeovers Between Dream and Reality' [n.d.], https:// humanitiesfutures.org/papers/illuminating-the-hole-kinshasas-makeovers-between-dream-and-reality [Accessed 6 January 2022].
61. Biaya, T.K., 'La culture urbaine dans les arts populaires d'Afrique: Analyse de l'ambiance zaïroise', *Canadian Journal of African Studies / Revue Canadienne des Études Africaines*, 30.3 (1996), 345–70.
62. Trapido, p. 32.
63. Sarah Suzuki, 'Kingelez "visionnaire"', in Sarah Suzuki (ed.), *Bodys Isek Kingelez* (New York: MoMA/ Brussels: Mercator, 2018), pp. 9–30 (p. 11).
64. Cited in De Boeck, '"Illuminating the Hole"…'.
65. Quoted in De Boeck et al. (2005), p. 202, my emphasis.
66. Dominique Malaquais 2020, p. 514. 'Sans pathos. Des Kongo Astronauts, de Lamyne M, *Critique Editions de Minuit*, 513–25 (514) https://halshs.archives-ouvertes.fr/halshs-03100460/document [Accessed 6 January 2022]
67. Ibid., p. 516.
68. Anonymous, 2021.
69. Katrien Pype, 'Political Billboards as Contact Zones: Reflections on Urban Space, the Visual and Political Affect in Kabila's Kinshasa', in Richard Vokes (ed), *Photography in Africa. Ethnographic Pespectives* (Woodbridge: Boydel & Brewer and James Currey: 2012), pp. 187–204.
70. Mélanie Drouère, 'An Interview with Faustin Linyekula' (2019) https://www.theatregaronne.com/dossier/congo) [accessed 14 January 2022]
71. Cited in Bettina Hubo, 'Over de wereldwijde crisis en de creuseurs in Kolwezi' (2012) https://www.bruzz.be/culture/expo/over-de-wereldwijde-crisis-en-de-creuseurs-kolwezi-2012-05-18 [accessed 6 January 2022]
72. See https://www.youtube.com/watch?v=LEcDzytYb2M [accessed 14 January 2022]
73. For an analysis of *Une vie après la mort*, see Gabriella Nugent, *Colonial Legacies*, pp. 85-118.
74. Matthias De Groof and Alessandro Jedlowski, 'Congolese Cinema Today: Memories of the Present in Kinshasa's New Wave Cinema (2008 – 2018)', *Francofonia: studi e ricerche sulle letterature di lingua francese*, 76 (2019), 117–35 (128–30).
75. See Drouère.
76. Van Beurden (2016), p. 326.
77. Crichton, p. 163.
78. Gauthier de Villers, 'Confusion politique au Congo-Kinshasa', *Canadian Journal of African Studies / Revue Canadienne des Études Africaines*, 33.2/3 (1999), 432–47 (434). 'Special Issue: French-Speaking Central Africa: Political Dynamics of Identities and Representations'.
79. David Van Reybrouck, 'My Only True Country is My Body' (2006) http://www.kabako.org/txt-entretiens/mybody.html [accessed 6 January 2022]
80. Linyekula, quoted in Goris (2008).
81. Jewsiewicki, 'Leaving Ruins…' (2016).
82. Van Reybrouck (2006).
83. See https://www.dailymotion.com/video/x18cdad (03:01).

From Leopold III's Masters of the Congo Jungle to Contemporary Congolese Eco-Cinema
Postcolonial Resonance

Matthias De Groof

In this chapter, I will have two films resonate with each other: a 1958 colonial film initiated by Leopold III called *Les Seigneurs de la forêt* [The Masters of the Congo Jungle], and a 2020 post-colonial Congolese film, *Mother Nature*, by Maisha Maene, produced by Yole!Africa in Goma. Both films were shot in eastern Congo, an area where ecological disasters were caused by colonial relations to nature and compounded by socio-economic and political conflicts. I will question how the films themselves are part of these relations, escape them, or provide alternatives.

The Masters of the Congo Jungle and *Mother Nature* could not be more different. The former is an international blockbuster and high-budget feature film from the late colonial period, while the latter is a local low-budget postcolonial short that sits completely outside the margins of canonical film history. What connects them, however, apart from the fact that they were both shot in eastern Congo, are the complex questions they raise about representations of nature that precede its colonisation. This analysis will be informed by (postcolonial) film theory and by the theoretical frameworks developed by Philippe Descola and Malcom Ferdinand in *Par-delà nature et culture*[1] and *Une écologie décoloniale*.[2] While the former helps us to understand different approaches to nature, the latter offer useful pointers to discern the residues of coloniality in these approaches.

By highlighting the echoes created by these two films, I am interested in discovering how the descendants of the people featured in Leopold's film direct the camera towards their surroundings and, in doing so, exercise their media sovereignty today, even though *Mother Nature* does not constitute a direct response to the 1958 film. Can the animism attributed to the *Masters of the jungle* become a cinematic method allowing their descendants to transcend the coloniality of the 1958 film? And is *Mother Nature* an example of this? These are some of the main issues that I investigate in this chapter, which will be structured as follows:

Figure 1 Two posters from *Les seigneurs de la fôret* [The Masters of the Congo Jungle], 1958. Courtesy of Cinematek (Royal Film Archive). Copyright: Asbl Fondation Internationale Scientifique.

the first, and main ipart, focuses on *Masters of the Congo Jungle*, the context surrounding its creation, its characteristics and contradictions. This focus, however, will allow me, in the second part, to extend my analysis to eco-cinema in Congo (and specifically in Kivu) and draw useful lessons from *Mother Nature*.

Masters of the Congo Jungle

Masters of the Congo Jungle is a 1958 film initiated by King Leopold III. He wished to see a film that would capture the splendours of the Great Lakes region and the Virunga National Park in the former Belgian colonies. Originally called the Albert Park, this nature reserve is situated in the eastern part of the Democratic Republic of the Congo. It was created in 1925 and is among the first protected areas in Africa. It covers an area of 8,090 km² and is listed in the List of World Heritage in Danger.[3] Justin Mutabesha, the programme director of the Association of Young Visionaries for the Development of the Congo, says this park is home to a wealth of biodiversity, not just for Congo, Africa, or his community, but for the whole world.[4]

Masters of the Congo Jungle is the first major Belgian production in CinemaScope. The filming took eighteen months and cost more than 60 million Belgian francs, which is the equivalent of 12 million euros and sixty times more than the average Belgian documentary today. Twentieth Century-Fox distributed the film in twenty-two languages and enjoyed immense success on its release. The film was referred to as 'The Anti-Walt-Disney' in the press. *The Daily Herald*, for instance, reported on 11 December 1959: 'Leopold of the Belgians beats Disney at his own game and becomes KING OF THE JUNGLE FILMS […] Leopold makes Disney's efforts look like a collection of old shots of the London Zoo taken with a box Brownie'.[5] This statement, however, does not take on board the fact that Walt Disney was invited to a private screening in the Castle of Laeken in 1958 and admired the film, according to Leopold's daughter Esmeralda.[6]

The film was accompanied by a photobook[7] with fold-out pages and images both in colour and black and white, designed by Yves Delacre, written by Jacques Bolle, and initiated by the International Scientific Foundation, over which Leopold III presided. Although most of the pictures in the book were taken by the film's two directors, five were taken by Leopold III, who joined the film expedition. By then, Leopold III had been forced to abdicate in favour of his son Prince Baudouin because of the controversy about Leopold's alleged unconstitutional surrender to occupying Nazi Germany, his visit to Adolf Hitler, and his lack of gratitude towards allied forces and the resistance.[8]

Nazi

The film was initiated by Leopold III, directed by Heinz Sielmann and Henry Brandt, narrated by Orson Welles and William Warfield, and produced by Henri Storck,[9] after he took over from Gerard De Boe who was the initial co-director and executive producer of the film. According to his son Christian,[10] Gerard De Boe was confronted during the shooting in the Belgian Congo with situations and practices he could not accept. After he repeatedly but fruitlessly urged his commissioner to settle matters, he handed in his resignation: 'On the field things deteriorated. Having lost all control over Sielmann's operations, De Boe and his main collaborators resigned as a group', writes Francis Bolen.[11] However, Frédéric Sojcher[12] remarks that de Boe resigned because of the Nazi past of Ernst Schäfer (1910–1992),[13] who was, alongside Leopold III, the film's other spiritual father. Schäfer was also the film's screenwriter and the scientific leader of the expedition. Before moving to Venezuela, he had been a German Nazi officer, working closely with Reichsführer Heinrich Himmler.[14] Himmler ordered the execution of Leopold III and his family, but this didn't happen because General George Patton's troops had destroyed the telephone lines and the message never arrived. As a SS-Sturmbahnfürher, Schäfer photographed medical experiments in Dachau and human skulls supporting Nazi racial theories.[15]

After the war, Schäfer met Leopold on an excursion in the Orinoco in Venezuela. Little is known about this encounter. What is known, however, is that the idea of *Masters of the Congo Jungle* arose there. Schäfer was invited to Belgium to prepare the film and was a permanent guest at the Royal Castle of Laeken. He also had a luxurious workplace in the Royal Castle of Villers-sur-Lesse.[16] Part of Belgian public opinion – especially among resistance circles – found Schäfer's participation in the film unacceptable. Thus, the film was controversial from its premiere, which was intended to take place at the Brussels' world fair of 1958. The political scandal took on an international dimension. At the gala premiere in Amsterdam, the appearance of Leopold III and his wife Lilian de Réthy, who had been invited by the Dutch Queen Juliana and Prince Bernhard, was cancelled due to so-called 'unforeseen circumstances'.[17]

Colonial

The film is highly colonial. Orson Welles's omniscient, authoritarian, White, and slightly paternalistic narrative voice takes the viewer to a nostalgic Rousseau-like era of virginal pristine wilderness that has not been part of Western 'progress'. The camera objectifies, exoticises, and eroticises nature and culture under the guise of science. *The Daily Herald* of 11 December 1959 states:

Leopold wanted to film the traditional love-dance of the girls of the Watutssi tribe. This [choreography] imitates the mating procedure of a bird called the crown crane. He decided that the best girls for the job were the sixth-form Watussi pupils of a convent. Leopold wanted them to dance in traditional costume. And he talked the authorities into it – quite a feat, since 'traditional costume' is a cotton skirt and nothing else. And these girls are normally muffled up to the eyebrows.[18]

Landscapes are regarded as relics of deep time and prehistoric past that are embedded in stories of human evolution. The human, then, is seen as a de-historicised 'noble savage', 'closer to nature', or 'in balance with nature'.[19] In the park – a living museum – 'contemporary ancestors' were invented as living fossils who provided access to humankind's biological and cultural past.

The very idea of the film is hyper-colonial: a salvage ethnography combined with a salvage biology. What is in danger of being lost should be recorded while completely being part of the system (i.e. imperialism) that accelerates the threat. 'The world is evolving so fast nowadays that I thought it desirable to record the remains of the thousand-year-old Congo on audio and film', writes Leopold.[20] Malcom Ferdinand[21] calls these salvages iterations of the colonial environmentalism of Noah's ark, in contrast to decolonial and ecological perspectives from the enslaved persons in the hold of the slave ship. Whereas the former narrowly focuses on 'nature', the latter thinks social and environmental justice together, while focusing on the world as a whole. Ferdinand indeed makes a distinction between, on the one hand, environmentalism that focuses on conservation but perpetuates the colonisation of nature (see Maëline Le Lay's chapter in this volume) through its instrumentalisation of non-humans, its nature/culture dichotomy, and its universalist position, which occults colonial, patriarchal, and the slavery foundations of modernity; and, on the other hand, an ecology that addresses the colonial roots of ecocide, and proposes a living-together that sees social justice as inseparable from ecological justice.[22]

The film presents the territory *as if it were not occupied* and as if it remained outside of the colonial endeavour of appropriation. This approach entirely serves colonial self-imagery. The cinematic construction of a fictional outsideness that remains untouched is fundamentally colonial as a necessary propagandistic counterpoint to the annexation, land clearing, and massacres outside of the 'reserve'. It serves as the necessary opposite to what Malcom Ferdinand calls 'matricide', the colonial assassination of Mother Earth.[23] This *eco-logical* matricide includes epistemicide (the destruction of logos, cosmogonies, and mythopoesis, which the film now promotes) as well as infanticide (the uprooting and displacement of first land defenders from their *oikos*, and the erasure of the idea that the inhabitants of these lands) – which the film now portrays – are the children of these lands.[24] This matricide was never the subject of colonial filmmaking, but appeared unintended in some films.[25]

The 'taxidermy'[26] of *Masters of the Congo Jungle* constructs a dichotomy between, on the one hand, the depicted Lega, Nyanga, Komo, and Twa protagonists who are called *seigneurs de la forêt* [the masters of the jungle] in the film, and Belgian audiences, on the other. The latter are comforted with the idea of being the veritable masters of the jungle. After all, the Congo was then the Belgian Congo, and Virunga was still called Albert Park. Cinema not only brought the colony home but also increased the self-perception of the users who now realised they were part of the colonial power. The immersive widescreen format of CinemaScope and the intended setting of the film's premiere – the 1958 Brussels world fair[27] – makes this meta-message even more convincing for the viewer.[28] Essentially, the film celebrates fifty years of the Congo's annexation to Belgium. But more importantly, and like all world and universal exhibitions, the '58 fair made the ideology of progress tangible and contrasted it with a fictitious construction of savagery in order to legitimise the brutal intervention. In 1958, a 'human zoo' was located right below the Atomium, the 102-metre-high icon of the 1958 world fair depicting atoms and expressing a faith in scientific progress (see Sarah Arens's chapter in this volume). Both aspects were also mediated by films like *Masters of the Congo Jungle*. CinemaScope technology embodies the idea of scientific progress and privileges an (albeit aesthetic) access to the 'real', a reality and alterity constructed in opposition to the idea of progress, which thereby makes this very idea even more palpable. Through *Masters of the Congo Jungle*, the world became once again more visible, viewable, and accessible, albeit staged. The contrasting construction of otherness in space, and its denial of coevalness was painfully repeated in 2002 in Belgium, when Baka peoples from Cameroon were exposed in an animal park. The entrance ticket for adults was 6 euros and 3.5 euros for children. The exhibition was severely criticised by the Belgian-African League for the Restoration of Fundamental Freedoms in Africa[29] and the New Migrants Movement[30] who wondered if there is compatibility between humiliation and humanitarian action.[31]

Pangolin

Masters of the Congo Jungle attributes a central place occupied by the pangolin (*ikaga* in Lega and *Manis Smutsia Gigantea* in Latin), a contradictory animal, just as the film itself is contradictory, as we will see. The film tells the story of this sacred animal that was never to be hunted. Yet a pangolin accidentally died during a hunt:

> The sacred animal, coming from the depths of time, is the unexpected victim of the trap set by the young men. The forest becomes silent; nothing will take place anymore, all activities are suspended, because the pangolin is an animal full of omens.[32]

The prohibited and taboo animal was dead. To ritually dispose of the pangolin, the presence of all clans is required. The pangolin is placed on a few branches and laid out 'like a king'. A noble and intense dance follows. The dancers show that the leaves acting as tiles of their houses are arranged as suggested by the superimposition of scales on the back of the pangolin. To violate the pangolin taboo is to expose oneself to the serious disapproval and sanctions of public opinion. Most often, a hunter would be forced to leave his group, writes the Belgian anthropologist Daniel Biebuyck who was part of the film crew in charge of its ethnography.[33] The pangolin is taboo because of the animal's contradictions. The pangolin is an anomaly and an in-betweenness. It does not neatly fit into categories. It has scales but it's not a fish. It looks like a lizard but is actually a mammal; unlike other small mammals, but like humans, it produces mostly one offspring at a time. So it's sort of partly fish and partly human, but it also climbs trees. When threatened, it rolls itself into a ball rather than running away.[34] The pangolin is an animated person. Like the human animal, the pangolin owns a mind. This is the reason why eating one outside a ritual context is unimaginable in the Lega communities. Today, the pangolin – who got much attention as one of the possible carriers of Covid-19 and thought of as a possible origin of the pandemic[35] – is the most illegally trafficked mammal in the world and is threatened with extinction. Between five hundred thousand and 2.7 million pangolins are captured each year in the forests of Central Africa.[36]

The Film's Contradictions: Colonial Anticolonialism

Like the pangolin, the film is itself fraught with contradictions. The most apparent of these, on which I shall focus here, is that this colonial film is actually also anti-colonial – because it criticises the civilising mission – while, at the same time, *not* applying to itself the lessons it teaches. By juxtaposing the myth of progress with that of savagery, *Masters of the Congo Jungle* is situated at the heart of an ideological fantasy of empire. Simultaneously, however, this film explicitly denounces these myths by combining anticolonial and anti-extractivist discourses. The central aim of the film was to raise awareness of the role humans play in disrupting the natural balance, and the film makes clear that this disruption is caused (or at least accelerated) by colonial extractivism: 'Thoughtlessly, civilisations [...] have taken without restraint from natural resources, and we see destruction accompanying opulence'.[37] In the photobook, we furthermore read that the balance in nature

> cannot be modified with impunity. Today, at great expense, attempts are being made to repair the faults of the past; very often, one is forced to be satisfied with limiting the damage because it seems that in the twentieth century, man can do anything, except rebuild what he has destroyed in Nature.[38]

Elsewhere, Leopold III says:

> The unbridled capitalism of our society, coupled with rampant individualism, will one day plunge us into a serious crisis. [...] The way of life of those peoples, whose ancestral traditions and culture are so rich, give us much food for thought.

Leopold III contrasts Western 'civilisation' (historic modes of capital accumulation, slavery, colonialism, empire, extractivism, productivism, and consumerism, or in short, the project called 'the West'[39]), with the civilisation of the *seigneurs*, thereby presenting their way of life as a salvation.[40] 'The communion of the man of the forest with nature, which he respects', Leopold wrote, 'constitutes for us a great lesson and a spiritual heritage'.[41] The 'salvation', or antidote for this malpractice, are the *seigneurs*: the Lega, Nyanga, and Twa who offer new non-European imaginaries, epistemologies, ontologies, and counter-narratives that would now be qualified as decolonial ecologies,[42] and presented as key to ecological challenges today as they were in 1958. Indigenous knowledge being key to the environmental struggle today is a reversal we also observe during colonial times and which states that the West should be developed and educated by the indigenous, rather than the other way round.[43]

As answer to colonial ways of inhabiting the earth, *Masters of the Congo Jungle* proposes a decolonial ecology as a world-making that is situated prior to the colonial/environmental fracture. The film therefore starts and ends with cosmology and mythology even though the accompanying book states that 'Our understandings of the people of the forest only reach the vulgar stage'.[44] Nevertheless, the film advocates a *matricial* relationship to the Earth and a communion between man and nature. This communion, beyond the (naturalist) culture/nature dichotomy, is part of what French anthropologist Philippe Descola calls animism.[45] The shared interiority[46] entails a relationship to lands, places, non-humans in which humans do not occupy the centre of creation to order the structures for their benefit through commodification, exploitation, or extraction. This idea is somehow romanticised and simplified in the film in a normative way:

> For [*Les Seigneurs*], the animal is not [...] that thing which one sees at the end of a gun, or in the bottom of a dish; but it is, full of complex meanings, a sort of intermediary, between LIFE, in the universal sense, and humankind.[47]

(De)Colonial Ecologies in *Masters of the Congo Jungle*

On 14 December 1959, *The Times* reported that there were nature films that denied the existence of man, others that made sensitive people feel like apologising for belonging to the human race, and still others that made the public feel that all kinds of creatures – from lions to insects – 'are being prodded and provoked into unnatural combats'.[48] *Masters of the Congo Jungle*, *The Times* continued, was none of those. The communion between the man of the forest and his natural surroundings, a point evidenced in every second of the film, implies (rather than asserts) a deliberate cry of protest against the brutal greed of men. The accompanying photobook confirms this view by stating that the poetry of the film owes nothing to 'the inspiration of a vulgar anthropomorphism, so widespread in books and films of scientific appearance, where man and animal alike are scorned'.[49] That's why the film was referred to as 'The Anti-Walt-Disney' in the press.[50]

Nevertheless, I argue that the decolonial ecologies as described above are diluted or even nullified by the framing of the film and its colonial grammar:

> Factually, writes Ferdinand, the environmentalist perspective of a return to nature has often been translated by a *colonial* grammar aimed at violently appropriating a space and forcefully projecting the fantasies and modes of occupation of one group onto another. This was the case with the ideology of *wilderness*, where the creation of parks was synonymous with the expulsion, not only of Native Americans in the United States, but also of local communities in India, Tanzania or South Africa.[51]

An ever-increasing literature denounces environmental colonialism,[52] including on Virunga, specifically. But what interests us here is *Masters of the Congo Jungle*'s specific filmic grammar. Is the film similar to a museum, which, as Aimé Césaire describes, 'present for our admiration, duly labeled, [...] dead and scattered parts [of non-European civilizations, for] smug self-satisfaction [and] secret contempt?'[53] Is the film, in Audre Lorde's words, a 'Master's House', exhibiting the results of its 'hunting and collecting'?[54] Is this film '*cynema*', that is, filmmaking that hunts?[55] We have already discussed the ways in which this film is a classic example of colonial representation. I would add that this colonial dimension is also noticeable in its production, sponsors, commercial intent and in the fact that animals were captured to facilitate the shooting process. What retains our attention is how the film contradicts – and even cancels out, neutralises, and annihilates – the animist proto-filmic 'communion between man and nature' as described by *The Times*, by an opposing 'ontology' that, however, remains off-screen. In his vast production, Descola called this the 'naturalist' ontology. Here, the non-human is not an animal but a beast without a mind. The human becomes human in contradistinction to the beast (which it can then domesticate or consume as mere resource). 'Enlightened' humans elevate themselves above an artificial boundary called 'nature', but those who do not adopt this naturalisation of difference are denied full humanity.[56] Now, the artificial border, however, is also already inscribed in the cinematographic medium itself.[57] Challenging that border by different modes of filmmaking may require its opposing ontology, namely animism, since animism makes this nature/culture border porous.

Congolese Eco-Cinema Today

How to explain the contrast between the pangolin taboo that existed in 1958 and the fact that this animal is now the most illegally trafficked mammal in the world? This radical switch points to an abandonment of the world view as depicted in the 1958 film in which, for the *seigneurs*, hunting should never exceed the needs of life.

One possible answer is green imperialism. Turning land into 'nature reserves' was a reformist measure to the rapid and alarming decline of ecosystems due to colonial destruction by extractivist activities, ranging from plantations to mining. Even though this salvage is accompanied by the cinematic exoticisation and romanticising of indigenous life forms as being in harmony with 'nature' and presented as salvation of decadent modernity, the communities themselves were often expelled from the parks. In the case of the Virunga, chiefs signed treaties, which are questioned again today. The Congo Research Group writes:

> As documented by several scholars, including Paul Vikanza and Joseph Nzabandora, the creation of the park was characterized by contestations, which partly resulted from the displacement of populations without compensation, and several extensions of the park without much consultation of

local stakeholders. [...] While the idea of nature conservation is generally supported, and people are proud of the park, seeing the wildlife as their heritage, many feel that the park has expropriated their ancestral lands.[58]

Historian Raf De Bont confirms:

> Although the transnational network of conservationists often represented the area as an empty wilderness, it contained substantial human populations, particularly after the park's enlargement in 1929. To restore the park's primitive character, its administration set up eviction schemes, affecting thousands of individuals from the local [...] population. A small group of Twa—represented as noble savages—were allowed to stay, but their freedom to use the park's resources was increasingly restricted over time.[59]

In the twenty-first century, similar buyouts have occurred within the Emission Trading System, offsetting the emissions of big polluters that land-grab territories, reclassify them as carbon sinks, and push the forest-dependent peoples out of their previous – often sustainable and low carbon intensive – ways of life.[60] These forest-dependent communities understand very well that the violence inflicted upon them is the flipside of a corporate disregard for the earth's ecosystems.[61] But unable to defend their *oikos*, these new ways, then, include the destruction of that same *oikos* through illegal poaching (e.g. of the Pangolin), working on the adjacent monocultural plantation, cutting trees to sell charcoal, and trafficking minerals, thereby contributing to the ecological degradation of their land. If not made into scapegoats by privileged city dwellers who perform labour that is seemingly less directly devastating, those still living in the vicinity of the park (rather than being confined to suburbs) are re-educated by NGOs advising them against cutting trees or poaching. Both ways help to distract attention from the industrial extractivism that was the cause of ecological destruction in the first place. In a context where climate change has become a crucial issue, these industries ironically continue to mine strategic minerals that are essential to post-carbon growth. A 2020 report from the European Commission states:

> For electric vehicle batteries and energy storage, the EU would need up to 18 times more lithium and 5 times more cobalt in 2030, and almost 60 times more lithium and 15 times more cobalt in 2050 compared to the current supply to the whole EU economy.[62]

Given this predicament, is present Congolese eco-cinema produced by the descendants of the Lega, Nyanga, and Twa protagonists – who are not the *sei-*

gneurs anymore – able to forge a *matricial* bond with the earth, in contrast to the aforementioned matricide of the colonial habitat? Can this cinema recreate a 'Mother Earth' that constitutes the womb of existence and give rise to a matrigenesis through new world-makings that advances environmental justice as an extension of the struggle against coloniality? Or, conversely, is present Congolese eco-cinema more 'environmental' than 'ecological', and, as such, unable to denounce the colonial causes of this disruption while remaining focused on the symptoms that allow to scapegoat local communities? Either way, to answer the first question, whether this body of work is *environmental cynema* or *ecological cinema*, one needs to add a second question: do these films escape fulfilling a 'salvage' role for mere scopophilic surplus value of audiences that enjoy environmental privilege in the Global North (and in the north of the South)? If contemporary Congolese eco-cinema *does* succeed in transcending the contradictions of *Masters of the Congo Jungle*, how do spectators avoid seeing the films as salvation of a (yet accelerated) decadent consumerist 'modernity'? In sum: how do these films resonate with the past?

Given the limited number of Congolese eco-films, and since the corpus is still increasing, it is not our goal to give definitive answers to these questions. Congolese films with an explicit or implicit ecological message or films offering or producing eco-perspectives on the relations between the human and non-human include *Machini* (2019) by Tétshim and Mukunday, which shows how mines extract life from bodies;[63] *Kapita* (2020) by Petna Ndaliko Katondolo, which reveals how colonial film camouflaged this violent extractivism in the mines from which multinationals obtain their supplies;[64] *Pungulume* (2016) by Sammy Baloji, which shows social and cultural disruption as consequences of this industrial colonial extraction; and *Postcolonial Dilemma: Parts I–III* (2021) by Kongo Astronauts, which represents waste and pollution through electronic debris as aesthetic tropes.[65] Other Congolese eco-films exist,[66] and ecocritical analysis could be unleashed on virtually any Congolese film.[67] Furthermore, I will not discuss 'Green Savior Complex' videos;[68] NGO films such as *Fossil Free Virunga* (2021), a story of climate activists fighting for social and environmental justice in the DRC; or the Western films on Congolese environment that repeat the salvage ecology, such as *Virunga* (Orlando von Einsiedel, 2014).

Instead, I will briefly focus on the experimental short film *Mother Nature* (2020) by Maisha Maene. Through its aesthetics of bodies drenched in oil, the film explicitly refers to the threats facing the Virunga Park, as it is being turned into a huge oil field by corporate businesses such as Eni, Efora, Total, SOCO, and Dominion Petroleum with the help of the Congolese Ministry of Hydrocarbons, which has granted exploration permits covering 85 per cent of the park's area. The extraction of its vast quantities of untapped oil risks provoking an

Figures 2-4. Stills from the film *Mother Nature*. 6'14", 6'46", 8'00". Copyright and courtesy: Maisha Maene.

ecocide on a regional level, which can spill over as far as the Mediterranean Sea and cause the displacement of entire communities. Furthermore, by speculating on the financial return of not already running but *proposed* plants, and thus by willing to take global warming beyond two degrees,[69] these companies precipitate the death sentence of countless of people across the world, especially in the most vulnerable areas, such as the DRC, which is one of the countries that has least contributed to global carbon emissions.[70]

The film *Mother Nature* was selected at festivals such as Congo in Harlem (New York), Digital Gate International Film Festival (Algeria), Leida Internationale Art Film Festival (Spain), Congo International Film Festival in Goma, and AfroBrix (Italy). Maene is part of the Komo community whose chiefdom is located at the foot of the Nyiragongo volcano in the Virunga Park. The film is produced by Yole!Africa and Alkebu Film Productions, founded by acclaimed filmmaker Petna Ndaliko Katondolo in 2000. Through its film and media institute and its projects ALT2TV, ART, on the FRONTLINE and Alkebu Film Productions, Yole! gathers Congolese activists and filmmakers to create awareness through film. Throughout its two decades of existence, Yole!Africa has influenced government, public health, journalism, and other initiatives in non-violent resistance. Yole!Africa operates from Goma, the capital of North Kivu province, bordering the Virunga National Park. The Kivu region is particularly relevant in terms of extractivism, armed conflict, ecological disasters, and social disruption. And Yole!Africa represents innovative ways in which films deal with colonial legacies and their paradoxes, such as the so-called green economy but also a context in which extractivism continues to produce environmental ravages. Their films are made in places where activists continue to defy extractive industries, protest against logging, mining, and pollution and block land seizures that are violently pursued to produce goods commonly consumed in the Global North.

The film opens with a reflection of a boy in a puddle (Fig. 5). This image – which typifies the aesthetics of Congolese photographer and filmmaker Kiripi Katembo – is an ambiguous one, in which the foreground and background seem to be interchangeable. Due to the anthropocentrism of the viewers, they interpret a human being in a first moment while the perception of another element precedes this interpretation. The perception of what is considered the background is actually the foreground, and this element makes the interpretation possible in the second instance. An ecological relation is thus represented within an ecology of relations between foreground and background. Then, the boy looks in the puddle, holding a ball.

A second image shows Nuru. She is looking straight into the camera. This direct visual address is a second form of reflexivity and breaks through the cin-

Figure 5. Still from the film Mother Nature. 0'36".
Copyright and courtesy: Maisha Maene.

ematic fourth wall[71] because it makes contact with the viewer. The woman walks with the steering wheel as if she was driving a car, but without any direction. Continuing to steer without a car stands for the illusory belief in 'progress'. She 'drives' between the chunks of coagulated lava that the Nyiragongo spat out. A little later, she is soaked in fossil fuel and walks with a burning oil lamp in broad daylight. She feels like she is already in a devastated world. A pair of sunglasses obscures her gaze. Armed blue helmets pass by, and surrounding people take pictures of Nuru. On the way, she stops to observe an artist, performed by Primo Mauridi. The artwork shows a chained man holding a globe and looking at it. He is chained among polluting industries. On the hills, only one tree remains, but pangolins are all extinct. At the bottom we see a timeline towards the future: 2050, 2100, ... The man turns out to be the boy who was looking at his ball. This ball was made of scrap and rags and represents the damaged planet. We see accelerated urban landscapes with automated traffic controllers. The man looks through the puddle to a nocturnal Afrofuturistic scene in which a woman with visible power ornaments and traditional costume is flanked by two people looking directly at the camera. According to Maene, her hands in front of her belly indicate the possibility of being reborn when taking matters into one's own hands. Finally, the man leaves the puddle, walks away, and arrives in a green, lush, and thriving environment. A plant with roots is offered to him. Planting the tree is planting consciousness.

Although the film does not offer a clear analysis of environmental injustice, eco-colonialism, green imperialism, climate apartheid, or environmental racism, it nevertheless provides an antidote to the hegemony of the coloniality of nature by relating to the plant as nucleus of a future. Interestingly, this process is mediated through precolonial cosmologies as reshaped by Afrofuturist aesthetics. In contrast to a colonial heart-of-darkness environmentalism,[72] *Mother Nature* does not desperately try to find solutions in the militarisation of parks,[73] or reduce the habitat to carbon sinks.[74] Nor does it prioritise Western environmental knowledge or further the exploitation of nature through techno-fixes. On the other hand, the film does not reproduce the nativist and revivalist idea of a 'nature people' in which the 'ancestors' are presented as immune to capitalist civilisation. On the contrary, Nuru is literally drenched in the dark side of industrial capitalism. Also, the film does not reduce Mother Nature to the caring and reproductive functions often ascribed to this Mother Earth trope. Of course, the maternal vision of earth is normatively gendered, as are Ferdinand's derived notions such as 'matricide', 'matrigenesis', and 'matricial'. However, it is not translated into a binary patriarchal or phallocentric construct, let alone matriarchy.[75]

The aesthetic tropes in *Mother Nature* of being soaked in oil (and its derivates) and life-giving plants are shared by Extinction Rebellion (XR) Goma whose activists reconnect the environment with population and environmental justice with social justice. 'We cannot pretend to protect the Virunga National Park if we do not want to respond to the clear demands of the populations bordering the park', says Pascal Mirundi, one of the founders of XR Université de Goma.[76] In addition to raising awareness among the population, XR also lobbies for a participatory management plan between the population and the parks.

It seems thus that, at least for this case in point of contemporary Congolese eco-cinema, *Mother Nature* does transcend the contradictions of *Masters of the Congo Jungle*. But does the film nevertheless risk fulfilling a 'salvage' role? As for this concluding question, Maene contests the idea of the film as a disengaged and comforting spectacle, since it was used to spark discussion in the first place. These interactions, in contrast to the screenings of *Masters of the Congo Jungle* in 1958, cannot be determined by a metanarrative that constructs a naturalist dichotomy between here/now and there/then, which neutralised the on-screen animist communion. The interactions are different, not primarily because the people on-screen who take pictures of Nuru are the same people that engage in discussions on the film and on pollution. The dichotomy is removed first and foremost because of the pollution itself. As is increasingly evident, pollution is present in every cell of what was previously called nature. When this pollution is due to historic colonialism or to the broader colonisation of the non-human, we can safely say (from ecocritical, political ecological, or environmental

Figures 6-7. Extinction Rebellion Goma. Copyright and courtesy: Guerchom Ndebo. Photos: Guerchom Ndebo.

humanities perspectives) that postcolonial resonances are omnipresent. Since anthropogenic pollution automatically makes the border between 'human' and 'nature' porous, the artificial boundary that was constructed through films such as *Masters of the Congo Jungle* to distinguish (on-screen) 'nature' from audiences who feel they 'master' nature and can partake in its colonisation become obsolete in *Mother Nature*.

Nature is not imagined, invented, or constructed *outside* of industrial and colonial pollution. Can we still speak of animism here as the way to transcend the naturalist artificial boundary between nature and culture, a boundary that was still materialised by the silver screen on which *Masters of the Congo Jungle* was projected? Or should we speak of *in*animism as lacking the quality of life due to pollution? (In)animist shattering the nature/culture divide is even more clearly thematised in Tétchim and Mukunday's short *Machini*. In that film, rocks from which humans are made are extracted by a machine whose pollution contaminates the humans who are consumed by that machine, which eventually extracts life from bodies. In any case, Maene's filmic gesture ascribes agency to nature, and makes human and non-human worlds permeable, and in this manner, Maene conveys the two key components of animism. As such, the animist gesture is an antidote to the objectification, exploitation, and alienation that characterise colonial relationship with nature in the so-called 'Anthropocene'.[77] In the words of Japanese filmmaker Miyazaki Hayao, 'Animism will be an important philosophy for humanity in the 21st century [...] because it can address profound scepticism about modern civilization [...] limitations to the materialistic aspects of human society, and the poor condition of the earth'[78].

In sum, it seems that *Mother Nature* reveals the choice between *animate* plants and thus giving future a life, breath, soul,[79] and the *inanimate* fossil fuel as 'decayed remnants of long-dead life-forms'[80] destroying life. Or to put it in Naomi Klein's words: between a society of grave robbers and a society of life amplifiers.[81] Filmmaking in the 'Congocene'[82] returns to animism as described by Sergei Eisenstein as reconciliation of humanity and nature:

> the 'animation' of nature emanates from here: nature and the I are *one and the same*, further along they are identical, even further they are similar. Up to the stage where the difference is sensed, they all work on the animation of nature, on animism.[83]

Conclusion: (In)animist Pollution

Masters of the Congo Jungle is an example of the naturalist representation of the relations between humans and nature in the late colonial era. Despite the representation of other ontologies such as animism, naturalism is dominant on-screen through an othering, a salvage narration, and objectifying visual registers. The context of the 1958 screenings, where audiences are constructed as the real masters, reinforced this dimension. The screen itself literally became the border that, like a mirror, is both constitutive and critical of the myths of progress. The range of resonances between, on the one hand, this colonial/modernist myth and, on the other, its self-critique, which instrumentalises non-Western paradigms, corresponds to the different dominant modes of dealing with the ecological crisis today and provides the scope in which dissensus is allowed.

With *Mother Nature*, however, we go further. Pollution, in its indiscriminate contamination, negates binaries and makes the naturalist hyper-separation between culture and nature superfluous. Animism as challenging the Western dualistic view of the world and the interrogation and disruption of the fundamental assumptions of modernity, here, is distinct from the communal animism as represented in *Masters of the Congo Jungle*, which remains framed within the nature/culture divide. Whereas *Masters of the Congo Jungle* translates a Eurocentric understanding of animism in which it is modernity's antithesis,[84] *Mother Nature* conveys the idea of a critical brand of animism that is meshed *within* modernity. Animism as a way to survive modernity is linked to the inevitable shattering of the nature/culture dichotomy due to pollution. This critical animism is thus at the same time *in*animating, as became clear with the pangolin's fate and the ensuing pandemic. The postcolonial resonances, then, consist in a historic reversal: whereas the West constructed an idea of nature through representation that allows nature to be colonised, contaminated nature now colonises us.

Notes

1. Philippe Descola, *Par-delà nature et culture* (Paris: Gallimard, 2015).
2. Malcom Ferdinand, *Une écologie décoloniale: penser l'écologie depuis le monde caribéen* (Paris: Éditions du Seuil, 2019).
3. https://whc.unesco.org/en/danger/ [accessed 19/11/2021].
4. Michael B. Kalamo and Hugo Duchesne, *Fossil Free Virunga*, 350.org and MNKF Productions (350.org and MNKF Productions, 2021).
5. 'King of the Jungle Films', *The Daily Herald*, 11 December 1959.
6. Maria Esmeralda and Philippe De Gryse. *Mijn vader, Leopold III* (Tielt: Lannoo, 2001), p. 71.
7. Jacques Bolle, *Les Seigneurs de la forêt* (Paris: Arthaud, 1958).
8. See Martin Conway, *The Sorrows of Belgium: Liberation and Political Reconstruction, 1944–1947* (Oxford: Oxford University Press, 2012).
9. Ten years later, in 1968, Henri Stock edited a new film, *Forêt secrète d'Afrique*, from the footage of *Masters of the Congo Jungle*.
10. Johan J. Vincent, Paul Geens, André Vandenbunder, Rudolf De Muynck, and Anton Wilsens, *Naslagwerk over De Vlaamse Film: ('Het Leentj')* (Brussels: C.I.A.M., 1986), p. 176.
11. Francis Bolen, *Histoire authentique, anecdotique, folklorique et critique du cinéma belge depuis ses plus lointaines origines* (Brussels: Memo & Codec, 1978), p. 394.
12. Frédéric Sojcher, *La Kermesse héroïque du cinéma belge* (Paris: L'Harmattan, 1999), p. 74.
13. Patricia Van Schuylenbergh, 'Entre science et spectacle: « Les seigneurs de la forêt », le film initié par Léopold III', *Museum Dynasticum*, 2 (2002), 17–23 (22).
14. On the relation between Schäfer and Himmler, see: https://www.ifz-muenchen.de/archiv/zs/zs-1405.pdf [accessed 24 August 2021].
15. Thierry Debels, *Kroongeheimen: Waarheid en leugens over het Belgisch koningshuis* (Manteau: Antwerpen, 2013).
16. 'Der Anti-Disney', *Der Spiegel*, 24 March 1959, pp. 60–62.
17. Ibid., 60–62.
18. 'King of the Jungle Films'.
19. Raf de Bont, 'A World Laboratory: Framing the Albert National Park', *Environmental History*, 22 (3) (2017), 404–32.
20. Esmeralda and De Gryse, *Mijn vader*, p. 138. All translations are mine unless otherwise stated.
21. Ferdinand, *Une écologie décoloniale*, p. 461.
22. Although Ferdinand's book rethinks ecology from the Caribbean world, and his examples are mostly drawn from this context, the aforementioned distinction is applicable on a planetary scale, and thus also to Congo.
23. Ibid.
24. Ibid., p. 76
25. Matthias De Groof, 'Review: Kapita.' In *Ultradogme*, 13 May 2021, Review: 'Kapita' (2021) dir. Petna Ndaliko Katondolo – ULTRA DOGME [accessed 17 May 2021].
26. This morbid metaphor, which I borrow from Fatimah Tobing Rony and its understanding by An Van Dienderen, points to an imagery that immobilises and objectifies its subjects, turning them into taxidermic objects, while fetishising truth claims. T. Bellinck and A. van Dienderen, 'That's My Life Jacket! Speculative Documentary as a Counter Strategy to Documentary Taxidermy', *Critical Arts* (2019), 1–15.
27. Other films specially made to be shown at the World Expo '58 (like *Masters of the Congo Jungle*) are Paul Haesaerts' *Under the Black Mask* and *Congorama*, a film intended to be shown on two screens in the Congo pavilion.
28. See Colin MacCabe's film theory on Classic Realist Text, in C. MacCabe, 'Realism and the Cinema: Notes on Some Brechtian Theses', *Screen*, 15 (1974), 7–27.
29. La Ligue belgo-africaine pour le rétablissement en Afrique des libertés fondamentales.
30. Mouvement des nouveaux migrants.
31. Pacifique Mukumba, 'Escroquerie humanitaire du 21ème siècle. Les pygmées Baka du Cameroun exposés dans un parc animalier en Belgique', *Dossier. KMMA* (2002), 1–12.
32. Bolle, *Les Seigneurs de la forêt*, p. 117.
33. Daniel Biebuyck, 'Répartitions et droits du pangolin chez les Balega', *Extrait de Zaire*, 9 (1953), 899–924.
34. Mary Douglas, *Purity and Danger: An Analysis of Concepts of Pollution and Taboo* (London: Routledge, 1966) and Helen King, 'What is it About the Pangolin?', *Wondersandmarvels*, 2015, in: https://www.wondersandmarvels.com/2015/07/what-is-it-about-the-pangolin.html [accessed 14 November 2021].
35. Amy Y. Vittor, Gabriel Zorello Laporta, and Maria Anice Mureb Sallum, 'How deforestation helps deadly viruses jump from animals to humans', *The Conversation*, (2020), in: theconversation.com/how-deforestation-helps-deadly-viruses-jump-from-animals-to-humans-139645 [accessed 14 November 2021].
36. Julie Lacaze, 'Le pangolin d'Afrique est le mammifère le plus braconné du monde', *National Geographic*, 9 (2017), in: www.nationalgeographic.fr/animaux/le-pangolin-dafrique-est-le-mam-

mifere-le-plus-braconne-du-monde [accessed 14 November 2021].
37. Bolle *Les Seigneurs de la forêt*, p. 7.
38. Ibid., p. 8.
39. Édouard Glissant, *Le Discours antillais* (Paris: Seuil, 1981), p. 503.
40. Esmeralda and De Gryse, *Mijn vader*, p. 12.
41. Bolle, *Les Seigneurs de la forêt*, p. 5.
42. Ferdinand, *Une écologie décoloniale*, p. 461.
43. See Georges Balandier, *Afrique ambiguë* (Paris: Seuil, 1957), Chapter III, 'Traditions'.
44. Bolle, *Les Seigneurs de la forêt*, p. 67.
45. Philippe Descola, and Pierre Charbonnier, *La Composition des mondes: entretiens avec Pierre Charbonnier* (Paris: Flammarion, 2014). Philippe Descola, *L'Écologie des autres: l'anthropologie et la question de la nature* (Versailles: Quæ, 2011).
46. Philippe Descola, *Par-delà nature et culture* (Paris: Gallimard, 2015), p. 247, p. 229. Philippe Descola, *Une écologie des relations* (Paris: CNRS, 2019), p. 41.
47. Bolle *Les Seigneurs de la forêt*, p. 68.
48. *The Times*, Dec 14th 1959.
49. Bolle *Les Seigneurs de la forêt*, p. 11.
50. Ironically, anthropomorphism is one of the reasons why Soviet film theoretician and filmmaker Sergei Eisenstein attributes animism to the films by Walt Disney. See: Serge Eisenstein, *Eisenstein on Disney*, ed. by Jay Leyda, trans. Alan Y. Upchurch (Calcutta: Seagull Books, 1986).
51. Ferdinand (2019), p. 326.
52. See also: Mark David Spence, *Dispossessing the Wilderness: Indian Removal and the Making of the National Parks* (Oxford: Oxford University Press, 1999); Ramachandra Guha, 'Radical American Environmentalism and Wilderness Preservation: A Third World Critique', *Environmental Ethics*, 11.1 (1989), 71–83; Roderick Neumann, *Imposing Wilderness in Africa* (Berkeley: University of California Press, 2008); David McDermott, *From Enslavement to Environmentalism Politics on the South African Frontier* (Seattle: University of Washington Press & Weather Press, 2006); Bernhard Gissibl, *The Nature of German Imperialism: Conservation and the Politics of Wildlife in Colonial East Africa* (New York: Berghahn Books, 2016); Robert H. Nelson, 'Environmental colonialism, "Saving" Africa from Africans"', *The Independent Review*, 8.1. (2003), 65–86.
53. Aimé Césaire, *Discours sur le colonialisme* (Paris: Présence Africaine, 2004 [1955]), p. 65.
54. Sammy Baloji, Lotte Arndt, Asger Taiaksev, Sandrine Colard, Yasmine van Pee, Patricia van Schuylenbergh, *Hunting & Collecting* (Ostend: Kunstmuseum aan Zee, 2016).
55. "To hunt" is derived from "hound", κυν- (kun-), stem of κύων (kúōn, "dog").

56. Dehumanisation is premised on these divisions and became fully developed in colonialism, and culminated in Nazism. Alain Renaut, 'Le crime contre l'humanité, le droit humanitaire et la Shoah', *Philosophie*, 67 (2000), 19–32, cited in Didier Durmarque, 'Le Nazisme est-il un humanisme?' *Philosophie de la Shoah*, 2014, in http://didier.durmarque.com/2014/07/le-nazisme-est-il-un-humanisme/ [accessed 14 November 2021]. For literature on links between Nazism and colonialism, see Hannah Arendt, Nikita Dhawan, Max Silverman, Aimé Césaire, Jürgen Zimmerer, Dirk Moses, and Sven Lindqvist, among many others.
57. Cinema served as a tool for the desire to master time, space, nature and life. The names of the precinematic devices (Zoopraxiscope, Zoetrope, Kinetoscope, Mutoscope, Vitagraph, Vitascope, etc.) attest to this. Jennifer Fay, *Inhospitable World: Cinema in the Time of the Anthropocene* (Oxford: Oxford University Press, 2018).
58. Congo Research Group, Trouble in Virunga: the challenges of conservation amidst conflict, violence and poverty, in http://congoresearchgroup.org [accessed 14 August 2015].
59. R. de Bont, 'A World Laboratory…', p. 417.
60. "Many of the Nande but also a few Hunde and Hutu peasants that formerly cultivated illegally in the area feel 'trapped', as they are now forced now to work for large-scale land-owners under exploitative agreements." Ibid.
61. Ferdinand, *Une écologie décoloniale*, p. 308.
62. Critical Raw Materials Resilience: Charting a Path towards greater Security and Sustainability, European Commission, 2020.
63. Matthias De Groof, 'CONGOCENE. Congolese Cinema in / on / against the Anthropocene', in Marina Gržinić and Sophie Uitz (eds.), *Rethinking the Past for a New Future of Conviviality: Opposing Colonialism, Anti-Semitism, Turbo-Nationalism* (Cambridge: Cambridge Scholars Publishing. 2019), pp. 87–109.
64. De Groof, 'Review: Kapita'.
65. Dominique Malaquais, 'Postcolonial Dilemma: Parts I–III', *Ellipses: Journal of Creative Research*, (2016), www.ellipses.org.za/project/postcolonial-dilemma-parts-i-iii/ [accessed 16 May 2021].
66. These include David Shongo's *A62* (2019). This film, whose title sounds like "acide" in French, gives voice to kids who turn out to be completely aware of the toxic environment they live, work and play in. *Mines de Rien* by David-Douglas Masamuna Ntimasiemi (2015) explores child labour in the mines of Katanga, giving further voice to the victims of the mining area. Kiripi Katembo also deals with these topics in *Après-Mine* (2010). See also: *Entreprise de consommation* (2021) by Elise Sawasawa, *Derrière nos portables* (2017) and *Kishimpo* (2018) by Eli Maene.

67. Matthias De Groof and Alessandro Jedlowski, 'Congolese Cinema Today: Memories of the Present in Kinshasa's New Wave Cinema (2008–2018)', *Francofonia*, 76 (2019), special issue 'Les enjeux de la mémoire dans la littérature et les arts contemporains de la République démocratique du Congo', ed. by Éloïse Brezault, 117–35.
68. Here I allude to Bhakti Shringarpure, 'Africa and the Digital Savior Complex', *Journal of African Cultural Studies*, 32.2 (2020), 178–94.
69. Andreas Malm, *How to Blow up a Pipeline: Learning to Fight in a World on Fire* (London: Verso Books, 2021).
70. In 2018, for instance, the average Canadian polluted 517 times more CO_2 than the average Congolese. Source: The World Bank.
71. Breaking the fourth wall is the temporary suspension of the convention in which an imagined wall (i.e. the screen in the cinematic arts) separates the audience from the (illusory) world presented by the film.
72. Catherine Roach, *Mother/nature: Popular Culture and Environmental Ethics* (Bloomington, IN: Indiana University Press, 2003).
73. The year 2021 saw the visit of American Special Forces, not only to fight the invisible and fabricated ISIS-DAESH, while the UN Group of Experts report rejected that any ties exist in Congo between rebels called ADF and ISIS, but also to 'evaluate the park rangers of the Virunga and Garamba national parks', *Note aux médias*, Ambassade des Etats-Unis Kinshasa, 13 August 2021.
74. Catherine Windey, 'Abstracting Congolese Forests: Mappings, Representational Narratives, and the Production of the Plantation Space under REDD+'(Antwerp: IOB Discussion Paper, 2020), https://www.uantwerpen.be/en/research-groups/iob/publications/discussion-papers/dp-2020/dp-202001 [accessed 04 August 2022].
75. See also: Miriam Tola's section 'The Trouble with Mother Earth' in her chapter 'Planetary Lovers: On Annie Sprinkle and Beth Stephens's *Water Makes Us Wet*', in Simon Ferdinand, Irene Villaescusa-Illán, and Esther Peeren (eds.), *Other Globes: Past and Peripheral Imaginations of Globalization*, Palgrave Studies in Globalization, Culture and Society (Springer: Palgrave Macmillan, 2019), pp. 231–48.
76. Fran Haddock, 'Stories from the Frontline – Episode 3: Fossil Fuel Free Virunga', in *Curious Earth*, July 2021, Stories from the Frontline – Episode 3: Fossil Fuel Free Virunga – Curious Earth | Environment & Climate Change [accessed 20 January 2022].
77. I put Anthropocene in quotation marks, since the use of 'Anthropos' (as a universal category) conceals the difference *within* this 'humanity', both in terms of responsibility as in regard to victimhood.
78. Shoko Yoneyama, 'Miyazaki Hayao's Animism and the Anthropocene', *Theory Culture & Society*, (2021), 1–16.
79. *Anima* = breath, soul, to give life (Webster).
80. Naomi Klein, *This Changes Everything: Capitalism vs. the Climate* (New York: Simon & Shuster, 2015), p. 176.
81. Ibid.
82. The title points towards the necessity of understanding the anthropocene from the perspective of Congo. See: De Groof, 'CONGOCENE…'.
83. Anselm Franke, *Animism* (Berlin: Sternberg Press, 2010), p. 120.
84. Edward Burnett Tylor, *Primitive Culture* (London: Murray, 1871).

Tracking the Potholes of Colonial History

Sinzo Aanza's *Généalogie d'une banalité* and Fiston Mwanza Mujila's *Tram 83*

Pierre-Philippe Fraiture

I needed a literature ascribing another form to words, another arrangement, a literature whose words are objects, for example, or sounds, surfaces and volumes. (Sinzo Aanza)[1]

This book is like a jazz piece. What is left after listening to a song? Nothing, or sometimes just a few notes, some words. (Fiston Mwanza Mujila)[2]

In this chapter, I will reflect on two Congolese novels, *Tram 83* (2014)[3] by Fiston Mwanza Mujila and *Généalogie d'une banalité* (2015) by Sinzo Aanza[4] and examine some of the factors underpinning the development of the Congo since 1885. These texts belong to a growing body of works – including literature,[5] films,[6] exhibitions, and installations[7] – on (post)colonial extractivism. They are part of a 'super-tanker literature, a cargo-plane literature, a pipeline literature that tells the way the story of extraction [is] taking place on a global scale'.[8] Alongside and often in collaboration with other Congolese artists and intellectuals from the DRC and the diaspora, Mujila and Aanza have engaged with the intermedial possibilities of the 'archival turn', a process characterised by a 'move from archive-as-source to archive-as-subject'.[9] In a context where performance and interpretation overlap,[10] the reading of colonial and African objects (in Tervuren) and their traces (in the DRC) is 'an agentive act' and one 'squarely focused on what we know and *how* we know it'. Here, the '[f]ocus on the politics of knowledge is a methodological commitment to how history's exclusions are secured and made'.[11]

While arguing that these two authors actively participate in this epistemic interrogation, my main objective here will be to establish how and why these two novels memorialise Belgian colonialism in Congo and Katanga, in particular. Mujila's novel takes place in a nameless 'City-State' and focuses on Tram 83, a bar but also a nightclub-cum-brothel where locals and international visitors from Africa, the West, and China listen to jazz, pay for sex, and strike questionable deals to appropriate the region's precious mineral resources. Although not explicitly based in Lubumbashi – indeed, there is no clear-cut reference to the Katangese city in this text – this novel unfolds in an urban space strongly reminiscent of Lubumbashi and Mbuji-Mayi. Sinzo Aanza's novel, on the other hand, is set in Elisabethville/Lubumbashi and can be read as an attempt to loosely chronicle the development of this mining centre since its creation in the wake of reconnaissance expeditions carried out by Congo Free State (CFS) agents such as Charles Lemaire at the turn of the century.[12]

The genesis of this city is linked to the rise of Belgian colonial capitalism in Katanga and the discovery of significant copper deposits in this part of the world.[13] The colonisers did not initiate copper extraction – a long mining tradition already existed before their arrival[14] ('Shaba', the other toponym for Katanga, means 'copper' in Swahili[15]) – but they streamlined its exploitation and submitted it to *modern* processes.[16] Élisabethville, which was first called Élisabethmine,[17] was established after the creation of the Union Minière du Haut-Katanga (UMHK), a company that until, the independence in 1960, held a monopoly over Katangese mineral deposits. This copper 'rush' became one of the defining moments of European expansion in Congo. From the outset, this enterprise had a definite international dimension. Of course, it was controlled from Brussels, but at the same time, it was built on an intricate network of agents from Europe and beyond who would set out to work towards the establishment of globalised operations. The CFS had also been a venture, which while reliant on Leopold II, had been predicated on a *multinational* logic. Indeed, the king of the Belgians – a CEO of sorts – would from the beginning appoint non-Belgian collaborators, as famously exemplified by H. M. Stanley's crucial role in the development of the CFS and the creation in the early 1890s of the notorious Anglo-Belgian India Rubber Company.[18]

While located in the Belgian Congo, Elisabethville would, from the moment of its creation onwards, rely on an international workforce – from the West, Asia, *and* Africa – and serve, as argued by Mujila and Aanza, the global objectives of the UMHK and its Congolese successor, the Gécamines. The original map of the city bears witness to this spatial regimentation and to the fact that the initial development of Elisabethville was conducted like 'a real estate operation rather than a genuine act of creating a pleasing urban landscape through planning and design'.[19] Indeed, the emergence of this city, and particularly its orthogonal configuration, reflects the objectives of 'efficiency, control and hygiene'[20] that had been pursued elsewhere in southern Africa – notably in Johannesburg – to domesticate the space, manage the available resources, and segregate White staff from African workers.[21]

Mujila and Aanza conduct an in-depth exploration of the constraints from which Elisabethville emerged and reflect on the way twenty-first century Lubumbashi relates to its colonial past and the strategies adopted by the Belgians to racialise space and time. Here the past is a *present past*, for its traces are everywhere to be seen. Via these texts, they suggest that it is impossible to position Lubumbashi *away* from Elisabethville. This lack of epistemic agency is reflected in the fragmentary structure of their novels and a self-reflective tendency to ponder the possibilities of this genre.

The development of *Généalogie* relies on an intricate narrative structure and one of its pivotal characters (and narrators), the 'master', who is also known as 'Kafka'. However, these narrators' stories of daily survival are mediated – in fact broadcast and hence doctored and censored – through a radio programme entitled 'Généalogie d'une banalité' [Genealogy of a Banality] and aired on *the* national channel (*la chaîne nationale*) based in Kinshasa. This unusual format – the novel or the radio novel? – offers the basis for an exploration of the precarious status of Lubumbashi – or Elisabethville as it is referred to here – within the *national* Congolese grand narrative. Indeed, the text of the novel does not seem to possess much credibility nor autonomy, not only because it is read out by a national celebrity with little attachment to Katanga but also because its progression is periodically interrupted and curtailed by irreverent radio hosts for whom the Katangese, albeit qualified as 'our fellow citizens', are also abjectly defined as those who treat the 'State' as 'their latrines' (*Généalogie*, p. 190). Through this process of scatological disqualification, the radio hosts intimate that these citizens' non-adherence to the national pact betrays on their part a lack of rationality and an inability to embrace the Congolese 'révolution de la modernité', a phrase used throughout the book.[22] In the narrators' eyes, however, the State appears as an entity whose agents – and the mining multinationals with whom they collude – have 'the power and the capacity to dictate who may live and who must die'.[23] Indeed, in their accounts, these narrators reflect on the difficulty to live in the destitute 'Bronx' district of Lubumbashi and to withstand the necropolitical effects of sovereignty, to refer to the well-known concept developed by Achille Mbembe, in the wake of other landmark studies on totalitarianism and state terror by Foucault, Giorgio Agamben, and Hannah Arendt. This aspect of the novel is best conveyed by the recurring use of the word *biologie*, employed to designate the Bronx inhabitants and to describe the bodily and biological functionality of a life – *zoe* [bare life] rather than *bios*[24] – reduced to sex, procreation, and survival. The novel, then, exposes the limits of Congolese biopower and explores its necropolitical negativity in a semi-colonial city, that is, in a space where 'sovereignty means the capacity to define who matters and who does not, who is *disposable* and who is not'.[25]

Tram 83 also explores the necropolitical slippages of sovereignty under the City-State's dictator. Unlike *Généalogies*, however, it relies on one single third-person narrator. This said, the novel is anything but naturalistic in its treatment of Congolese *reality*. It is underpinned by a recognisable plot, which, if stripped to the bone, can be summarised as follows: Lucien, a Congolese writer in search of a writing project, has moved from the 'Back-Country' to the City-State where he becomes a regular customer of Tram 83, reconnects with his old friend Requiem, gets conned into taking part in illegal activities involving the raiding of a copper mine, and becomes acquainted with a Swiss publisher who, while offering him a lucrative book contract, also attempts to control his creativity. Like *Généalogie*, *Tram 83* probes the limits of literature, its heuristic power, ability to render the truth, and translate lived experience, for beyond this schematic synopsis, this text captures the randomness of human encounters and the cacophony of verbal communication. *Tram 83* is a dissonant and deliberately disjointed narrative, which, again like *Généalogie*, obliquely testifies to the cultural and environmental ravages wrought by neocolonialism and Sino-Western capitalism in 'the age of global mobility', an era, as suggested by Mbembe, in which it is increasingly difficult to identify who decides on who may live and who must die:

> The claim to ultimate or final authority in a particular political space is not easily made. Instead, a patchwork of overlapping and incomplete rights to rule emerges, inextricably superimposed and tangled, in which different de facto juridical instances are geographically interwoven and plural allegiances, asymmetrical suzerainties, and enclaves abound.[26]

The City-State presents itself as a dystopian political construct that, while bearing striking resemblance to Lubumbashi (where Mujila was born) and the DRC, is led by the incongruously named 'dissident-General', a dictator whose oxymoronic title appears to conflate the memory of Lumumba, the dissident of sorts assassinated in Katanga, and that of Mobutu. This City-State is also an unregulated free-trade zone – a modern CFS – where sex, minerals, and cultural objects are exchanged, trafficked, misappropriated, and consumed.[27] In this perhaps not-so-fictional state where everything is subjected to the rules of market commodification, jazz, the music played and performed in Tram 83, is 'a mere product like any other'.[28]

The two novels, as will be explored now, are awash with hangovers from the colonial period, and while they obviously testify to the enduring effects of this past, they are also useful markers to measure how cultural agency and political emancipation are examined by these authors. In the following sections, I examine the way in which Mujila and Aanza explore former colonial sites of memory and their legacies. First, the *cordon sanitaire* and its lasting significance for twenty-first century Lubumbashi; then the focus will shift to Henry Morton Stanley and his Congolese railway project; in the following section, I shall explore (post)colonial extractivism and concentrate, in particular, on Congolese *creuseurs* [artisan ore diggers]; in the final part of this chapter, I ascertain how the analysis of these sites also constitutes a self-reflective attempt to define literature and its connections to other media.

Cordoned Off

Maureen Vanderstraeten is the first narrator of *Généalogie*. As a second-generation Katanga-born Belgian, she registers the toponymic transformation brought about by decolonisation: 'The first thing that changed were the names of the avenues' (*Généalogie*, p. 13). This reflection is utterly political because Maureen is presented as an African who cannot claim an African ancestry:

> This land [Katanga] is a slope of my heart. The other side is confused. There was a time when the childhood memories of my parents achieved cadastral work on the surface of my heart. They spoke with candour and nostalgia of their cavalcades in Ghent or in Lorraine [...]. They were unaware that the veins carry from the outside only the air of the land on which we cry, we love, [...], we die, we move and we live in a different way. (*Généalogie*, pp. 13–14)

Maureen measures here the limits of ethnicity as a reliable criterion to map out one's identity, and she wonders whether one is really defined by one's genealogy. She does not provide any straightforward answer but suggests that her Belgian parents' memories did not achieve their 'cadastral' objectives and that they were unsuccessful in their attempt to assign her to this elusive Belgian-ness. Her take on Africanity – she is a White African, and she feels it in her 'heart' and 'veins' – does not meet the approval of the radio host who immediately decides to edit out 'a few short sections' from Maureen's account because of her 'malicious reading of the history of our dear nation' (*Généalogie*, p. 14). All the narrators – Maureen, the Bronx inhabitants, and the so-called 'unknown author' – are forced to operate within the constraints of the host's identity politics as their own narratives are also disavowed – 'erased'[29] – when it is felt that they fail to comply with the official version of Congolese history advocated by this *national* channel. Thus, the novel examines the role of the media in publicising a simplified and overly ethnicised and racialised approach to the Congolese nation. By focusing on the potentially harmful instrumentalisation of the radio, Aanza reminds his readers (via his narrators) of the role played by this medium in disseminating ethnic hatred. Incidentally, Aanza's own native city, Goma, became the scene of a humanitarian crisis in the wake of the 1994 Rwandan genocide against the Tutsi,[30] a conflict notoriously triggered by hateful rumours spread by Radio-Télévision Libre des Mille Collines.[31]

Généalogie's narrators revisit some of the colonial sites responsible for cementing racial segregation during the colonial era. The city's major instrument of spatial control and disease containment, the so-called *cordon sanitaire*, a buffer zone used to separate and protect the European city from the 'squalor [*insalubrité*] of the African city' (*Généalogie*, p. 31),[32] is mentioned at various points in the novel to measure the extent to which the Lushois have been able to reclaim their city since 'independence' and 'during the disorders institutionalised by the tedious democratic transition' (*Généalogie*, p. 31). The status of this zone is vague. Indeed, it presents itself as a stretch of wasteland – *terrain vague* in French – which, while signifying the achievements of European modernity, also inscribes, in the very fabric of the cityscape, the purported developmental gap between the colonisers and the colonised. Thus, this vague terrain has the effect of spatialising time, as it drives a wedge between a *modern* present and the Congolese past.[33]

In *Généalogie*, Maureen contends that this zone has retained its separating power in the twenty-first century. Although the Bronx, the fictional district in which the novel unfolds, has sprawled on what used to be the *cordon sanitaire*, it is still regarded as a 'vacant space awaiting to be developed by the city council' (*Généalogie*, p. 31). It is legally vacant and yet occupied by real people, and the text explores this paradox. Its occupants – all the narrators-characters bar Maureen – are the unofficial dwellers of an unchartered city that has been forgotten – and could be erased – by Elisabethville's official custodians and *sovereigns*. The criteria presiding over the city's demographic distribution are no longer exclusively based on the colour bar. However, the text shows that a new and perhaps more insidious criteriology has developed. In this new logic, one can become Black *or* White regardless of one's skin colour. In his narrative, the unknown author registers Kafka's puzzlement when faced with this unexpected racial metamorphosis:

> There were also blacks and métis and they were so sophisticated that it was easy to believe that they had stopped being black. They were no different from whites and were so remote from the Bronx inhabitants that the master felt humiliated by their mere presence in front of him. (*Généalogie*, p. 155)

This process of transformation is predicated on economic success (or lack thereof), and by the same token, the unknown author mentions the example of 'whites who have become black after falling into homelessness' (p. 208). Money, rather than race only, is the discriminating marker between the Bronx dwellers and those living beyond what used to be the *cordon sanitaire*. Interestingly, the narrator intimates that these shifts from Black to White skins, precisely because they reflect changes in economic status, are not comparable to what is described in 'Peau noire [sic] masques blancs' (*Généalogie*, p. 156). By parenthesis, this point is perhaps a little overstated, for Fanon also argues that the efforts deployed by Martinicans to comply with the linguistic and societal norms of the French ruling elite are motivated by an ambition to elevate themselves culturally, socially, *and* economically. Fanon's analysis is useful to measure the relationship between the Bronx inhabitants and the rest of city. This relationship is not equal and is marked by the hierarchy that had once characterised colonial cities. For affluent Black and White visitors, a trip to the Bronx is a journey back in time and an opportunity to deny its dwellers of their coevalness. What is more, it reignites, in the twenty-first century, the ocular-centric regime that had been adopted to *know* the colonised as a 'being-for-others' [*pour autrui*][34] and regard their culture as a spectacle to be consumed. In the eyes of these visitors, the Bronx becomes a mere sociological phenomenon and a body of searchable data that they take upon themselves to archive and decipher with the help of the novel's central protagonist, Kafka, who reluctantly assumes the role of local informant: 'How many children do the Bronx women have? Does he know what the average is? Are there many males of working age?' (*Généalogie*, p. 156) Kafka is critical of the pseudo-ethnographic logic presiding over the visitors' surveyance (and surveillance). Their gaze generates the 'crushing objecthood' examined by Fanon in *Peau noire*[35] and demonstrates that the conditions engendered by the creation of the UMHK have provided the basis for the 'apartheid', which 'endured' and 'became a culture' (*Généalogie*, p. 171).

Tracking Time and Space

Tram 83 is also saturated with colonial figures used here to convey the idea that the Congo is trapped in a dystopian temporality characterised by obsessive repetitions and an inability to envisage the future. Indeed, the novel is set in an endless present marked by the frequent return of one symptomatic question posed by anonymous characters: 'Do you have the time?' This question remains unanswered throughout the narrative, which ends with the very words that had been used to introduce it. In the following extract, the focus is on the City-State's 'Northern Station':

> [An] unfinished metal structure, gutted by artillery, train tracks, and locomotives that called to mind the railroad built by Stanley, cassava fields, cut-rate hotels, greasy spoons, bordellos, Pentecostal churches, bakeries, and noise engineered by men of all generations and nationalities combined (*Tram 83*, pp. 1 and 220).

This short passage is programmatic, for it enumerates what the novel will examine (and has examined): an unfinished city that was never meant to last and which mushroomed to satisfy the commercial priorities of mining conglomerates such as the UMHK and meet the basic nutritional, sexual, and spiritual needs of their workforce. This sentence provides thus a bleak insight into what the city has experienced, since its foundation but also what the war-torn City-State is facing now under its new dictator.

The reference to Stanley and his railway project also reinforces the temporal discussion at the heart of *Tram 83*. Towards the end of the nineteenth century, the railway became one of the most significant tools to promote colonial modernity and accelerate the industrialisation of the CFS. Stanley, as is well known, was a staunch advocate of the railroad between Matadi and Léopoldville,[36] an eight-year project that was eventually completed at great human cost in 1898.[37] The introduction of the railway in the Congo served concrete commercial goals. However, the train, as a symbol, was also employed in colonial propaganda to spatialise time and consolidate the idea that remote corners of the Congolese hinterland, because they were deemed less developed, were of *another* time. The constant references to Stanley and his unfinished Northern Station in *Tram 83* is a reminder of the crude symbolism and discursive arsenal on which the imperial conquest had relied. For those who championed colonialism, Stanley, the rock breaker – *Bula Matari* in Kikongo – became a *modern* hero who advanced the cause of progress and technology by defeating African nature, which in Belgium and beyond was 'regarded as a "bad" timekeeper compared to the time provided by the railways'.[38] The frequent allusions to Stanley in *Tram 83* help Mujila's readers to remember their modern present in the same way as Tshibumba Kanda Matulu's paintings were executed to remember a Congolese present, which started with the Portuguese evangelisation in late fifteenth century and was still unfolding under Mobutu.[39] With this long present in mind, it is interesting to point out that the nickname Bula Matari (or Bula Matadi) was given to Stanley not so much to celebrate his bravery and ingenuity, as to signify his brutality for the Ba-Kongo believed that he was the reincarnation of the notorious Dom Francisco Bullamatari who, in the sixteenth century, had terrorised his fellow Africans[40] while fomenting an anti-Christian movement.[41] In everyday parlance, the expression *Bula Matari* was used by the colonised to designate all Whites and by extension the colonial administration and their ability to ruthlessly suppress all resistance.[42] Stanley, then, albeit a concrete historical reference, is also used in *Tram 83* as a synecdoche to remember the enduring presence of colonial violence. In the following quote, a police inspector, upon releasing Lucien after his failed raid of a copper mine, casts an eye on his immediate surroundings:

> The chief of police stood watching the prisoners, their wrists handcuffed, stuffed into the vans like sacks of gravel. Like on platform 17, the station that is essentially an unfinished metal structure, gutted by artillery, train tracks, and locomotives that call to mind the railroad built by Stanley. (*Tram 83*, p. 149)

In a novel intended to progress like a piece of music,[43] and, in fact, whose themes have been partly musicalised in collaboration with jazz musicians,[44] this reference to Stanley acts as the chorus of an unfinished composition. This violent scene and the environment in which it is taking place 'call to mind' – 'ramènent à la mémoire'[45] [bring back to memory] in the French original – Stanley's own violation of the Congolese landscape and propensity to treat the Congolese workforce like expendable resources and 'sacks of gravel'. As often in this novel, culture is shown to be caught in an analogous system of exchange in which aesthetic concerns remain secondary. Jazz, for example, is presented as a delocalised product and employed by the Tram 83 customers like 'a Bourdieusian marker of cultural achievement and sophistication [that] cannot simply be assumed to enable resistance and revolution'.[46] Classical music plays a similar role. Interestingly, the police station is also known as the 'Vienna Conservatoire' where the chief of police *conserves* the memory of canonical figures such as Bach, Mozart, Dmitri Shostakovich, and Sergei Rachmaninov to seduce the most cultured offenders and attempt to obtain bribes from them. Culture, then, is a mere currency and a means by which the characters of this novel mobilise the past to survive in the present.

The City-State is a *modern* enterprise, and it was undertaken as part of a new societal project that, while severing the links with the African precolonial past, would set out to promote the 'now' and facilitate the advent of a progressive future. This rejection of the past in the name of progress and change is one of the most distinctive features of imperial discourses. In his wide-reaching reflection on European modernity, Reinhart Koselleck convincingly demonstrated that the gradual secularisation of Europe in the eighteenth century was accompanied by a new relationship between past, present, and future. Hitherto, the past – the 'field of experience' – had constituted the only reference to manage the present and plan the future. In this pre-modern (and circular) temporality, past, present, and future were interdependent and mirrored one another, as the present and the future were merely expected to repeat this past. With modernity, this dialectic was transformed, and the past became the backwards region of human experience. Henceforth, political, technological, and cultural energy would be consciously mobilised to plan the future, *drive* progress, and open a new 'horizon of expectation'.[47]

In a context where colonialism and progress were coterminous, mining cities like Lubumbashi were presented as the concrete manifestations of this progressive mindset. In a 1954 promotional brochure, the UMHK informed its future European employees that 'the Belgian Congo is a colony, i.e. a country where backward populations were and are still in need of the European tutelage to progressively have access to the democratic organisation of our political institutions'.[48] Although shocking now, the opinion expressed in this short quote was still deep-rooted in the 1950s. Like most of the representatives of the famous colonial 'trinity' – State-Church-Capital – the anonymous author of this brochure is of the view that it is incumbent on the colonisers to drag the Congolese out of their backwardness and facilitate their entry into a *modern* temporality. It is suggested that this new Western time will harness the present and put measures in place to plan the future and bring about human progress (in the form of democracy). Interestingly, this linear time in which the Congolese is regarded as a *not yet* to be perfected was reliant on the missionaries' ability to turn the African UMHK miners into docile bodies and dependable employees who would patiently endure their worldly plight and wait for the advent of the Kingdom of Heaven.

In Mujila's City-State, time is marked by its indeterminacy: 'time had lost all purpose, we were in 2069 or 1735 or 926 or the Paleolithic era' (*Tram 83*, p. 187). From a spatial perspective, however, the novel is over-determined and replete with long enumerations of objects, historical figures, and references to music and literature. If the city can be inventoried, it seems that time, as it is deployed in this narrative, has lost its ability to invent a future and has been stripped of its utopian finality. In this sense, the City-State cannot escape a type of spatiotemporal double bind: it continues to inhabit the colonial field of experience – and the objective constraints of this past – but also replicates the colonisers' tendency to renege on their promise to democratise the Congolese horizon of expectation. *Tram 83* is trapped in a temporal loop and keeps returning where the official history of the Congo began when the Belgians set out to excavate mineral resources:

In the beginning was the stone, and the stone prompted ownership, and ownership a rush, and the rush brought an influx of men of diverse appearance who built railroads through the rock, forged a life of palm wine, and devised a system, a mixture of mining and trading. (*Tram 83*, p. 1)

On the Banality of Potholes

Généalogie is also steeped in temporal issues and offers an excavation of Katangese history to address the long-term effect of the DRC's 'geological scandal' (*Généalogie*, p. 74). The title of the novel – *and* the title of the radio programme in which the book is embedded – is rich in historical and epistemological resonance. At first sight, 'Genealogy' and 'banality' do not naturally sit next to one another. 'Genealogy' reflects the characters' attempts to trace the origins of Elisabethville, identify the legacies of Belgian paternalism and the different filiations generated by the city's transformation into Lubumbashi. 'Banality', on the other hand, indicates that the grand project announced by the word 'genealogy' will not be fed by the epic achievements of conventional heroes but by stories of survival experienced in the underbelly of the Katangese city. 'Mining' and 'trading' are also the key components of the genealogical quest informing a novel chronicling the Bronx *creuseurs*' desperate efforts to dig their way out of poverty.

The *creuseurs* are the Congolese artisan ore diggers. Since the collapse of the Gécamines in the early 1990s, artisanal mining has exponentially developed, and it is now estimated that approximately two hundred thousand men are engaged in this activity in Katanga alone.[49] The *creuseurs*, like Stanley in *Tram 83*, help us to remember Katanga's modern present. This present is a present past, for it encompasses colonial violence and the exploitative measures taken by colonial companies to appropriate Congolese mineral resources; but it also points to the neoliberal order established by the Congolese state at the beginning of this millennium and to a context in which lucrative deals are struck between multinationals and the State at the *creuseurs*' expense.[50] Interestingly, however, the focus on this activity in *Généalogie* also contributes to our understanding of precolonial times since *creusage* was practised well before the European occupation started.[51]

Aanza's focus on artisanal mining aptly fuses the political, the mythological, and the literary while exploring the dialectic between the precolonial past and the future. In the novel, *creusage* is managed by Kafka, the Bronx schoolmaster. This activity is carried out against the State and in a space, the former *cordon sanitaire*, constantly threatened by expropriation. Eventually, the network of galleries dug by the Bronx dwellers collapses and kills several miners. So, in addition to being used as a ploy to expose the (Congolese) state's rapacious nature and historic failure to redistribute the national wealth, this catastrophe (based on a real-life event) is also a strategy to draw the readers' attention to the hazards (environmental and otherwise) associated with unregulated mineral extraction in the DRC.

Beyond these concrete references, however, mining is also a metaphor for rethinking national myths, Congolese identity, the significance of the faith in daily life, and the role of fiction therein. *Creusage*, then, allows to write the Congo anew and question the main ideas and images that have facilitated its invention. Whether in his work as installation artist[52] and playwright,[53] Sinzo Aanza, who is a former seminarist,[54] has frequently explored the importance of Christianity and biblical ideas in the making of modern Congo. In an interview, he said that the 'kingdom of heaven', as a notion, has been one of the key utopian tenets to 'manage [*gérer*] the population' since colonial times.[55] He also argues here that in a country where there is virtually no book and literary culture, the 'strongest convictions' are to be found 'within Churches' and 'in the practice of the faith'.[56] Now, if we look back at the history of modern Congo, it is true that some of the most intriguing developments in Congolese intellectual life have stemmed from attempts on parts of local prophets to appropriate – or indigenise – biblical contents and messages.[57] That said, *Généalogie* bears witness to a context in which religious education is challenged by other epistemologies, by the legacies of the (spatiotemporal) colonial order but also by what Aanza calls 'pre-colonial spiritualities' in the same interview. The polyphonic structure of this novel demonstrates Sinzo Aanza's ambition to move the literary debate away from issues of evangelisation and thus dispute the cultural centrality of Congo's most significant publishing house, Médiaspaul. Aanza suggests that for this Catholic publisher, literary discussions exclusively revolve around texts dealing with the Church's evangelistic activity.[58]

Creusage is also an instrument to ponder the effects of diglossia in contemporary DRC and measure the entanglements and the rivalry between French and African languages. The 'unknown writer' reflects on a school system where French is the compulsory language and where pupils are caned for 'speaking Swahili, Tshiluba or Lingala during class' (*Généalogie*, p. 96). At various points, the status of francophone Congolese literature is explored in its local and diasporic guises. The 'unknown writer' takes stock of the gap between elite and popular literature, between Mudimbe's 'narrative and introspective webs' and the 'literary clutters' produced by novelists like Zamenga Batukezanga and other writers published by Médiaspaul (p. 96). With regards to this literary discussion, it is probably not superfluous to point out again that the main character of this novel is called Kafka and that, like the famous germanophone Czech writer, Aanza deterritorialises a major language to produce a 'minor' literature, as argued by Elara Bertho in a compelling article in which Sinzo's novel is shown to display the rhizomatic qualities explored by Deleuze and Guattari in their famous essay on Kafka.[59] Indeed, the intricate network of galleries excavated by the Bronx *creuseurs* under their own streets and houses mirrors the equally complex array of narrative voices deployed in this novel. *Creusage* is therefore a vehicle to mine *and* undermine the literary possibilities offered by the main linguistic medium – French – used in this text. In this regard, it is interesting to point out that the radio hosts are presented as the defenders of 'Molière's language' (*Généalogie*, p. 73) and that their normative and didactic position is an opportunity to engage with the alternative linguistic models adopted by the Bronx narrators: their frequent use of untranslated Swahili phrases, their tributes to Sony Labou Tansi's lexis – 'mocheté' [ugliness], 'hernie' [hernia], and 'honte' [shame] – and their tendency to represent the Bronx and *creusage* in a syntactically broken French. This latter feature is to be found in the passages narrated by the 'Cheminot' [railway worker], one of Kafka's most loyal co-*creuseurs*. The Cheminot's narrative interventions also reflect the way in which Kafka's poetry is perceived by Maureen on the other side of the *cordon sanitaire*: it is, in her own words, an example of 'littérature dans les ordures' [trash literature] (p. 16). While obviously deviating from the canon, this type of literary expression, assembled from (post)colonial scraps and leftovers, is evocative of the *creuseurs*' mucky digging. This poetry is also motivated by a visceral urge to survive and, intriguingly, Kafka's own poetry is compared to 'urine' gushing out of a 'sensitive biology' after 'being held back for too long' (p. 27). Elsewhere in the novel, defecation is used as a metaphor to signify the scrappy and grotesquely unsystematic tactics adopted by the Bronx dwellers to express their dissent. According to Katlijn, an art curator, Kafka is 'a bit of a cracked pot' (p. 17). Indeed, it can be argued that his presence in the text disrupts the State's attempt to implement the rational homogenisation of the Congolese nation, loosely described here as the 'révolution de la modernité'. At a Katangese level, he challenges the city's orthogonal (colonial) configuration by inviting the Bronx dwellers to look into the holes (see Bambi Ceuppens's chapter in this volume) wrought by (post)colonial regimes: 'The hole has become a local master trope, a conceptual figure, to express the dismal quality of urban life in the postcolonial city. In the minds of many, the city has quite literally become "hollowed land"'. And in Congolese cities, 'living in the postcolonial hole also means surviving on the meagre livelihoods provided by artisanal mining holes'.[60] In this sense, *Généalogie* falls into the novelistic subgenre designated by Patrice Nganang as the 'detritus novel'[61] in which the 'African city' emerges as a 'mad horse',[62] and where African novelists engage in a process of 'literary reconstruction', compose stories that become 'history' precisely because 'history has abandoned [them]' and 'ruined [their] city'.[63] Nganang adds that in this subgenre, novelists tend to 'uncover the city in its speciality and *banality*'.[64]

Mining Literature's Meaning

Tram 83 also explores the trivialisation (*banalisation* in French) of exploitation and violence. Like in *Généalogie*, this examination of a Congolese dystopian present past (and future) is accompanied by a meta-discursive focus on literature. The novel is studded with references to the difficult context in which diasporic francophone writers from sub-Saharan Africa operate to get published and be read. *Généalogie*, as suggested by Sinzo Aanza, was initially meant to be what the published novel reproduces and mimics, that is, a radio programme aired in the DRC.[65] If this simulacrum of orality greatly contributes to the novel's stylistic distinctiveness, it is important to remember that Aanza's original choice of format was a pragmatic decision. Indeed, as argued by Aanza himself, it was motivated by the fact that, in a country where the 'word "writer" [...] does not mean anything',[66] oral literature is likely to garner more attention. In *Tram 83*, Lucien experiences a similar predicament. As a budding novelist, he lives in a state of dependency and is aware that his potential rise to prominence will depend on his ability to join culturally relevant networks and abide by their rules. Thus, the novel traces his struggle to position himself to advance his career, market his own cultural capital and attain recognition within the Francophone literary field. Lucien finds himself torn between France, the City-State, their respective (reading) audiences – i.e. the 'capricious expectations' of non-African readers[67] – and cultural intermediaries. He is unable to respond to the demands of his friend and agent of sorts who has been promoting his work in France but is still awaiting the completion of a 'stage-tale' that would launch Lucien's career and pave the way for his literary consecration at 'the Festival des Francophonies en Limousin, the Tarmac and other Paris theaters [...]' (*Tram 83*, p. 43). In addition to constituting an impressive list of transnational connections to further publicise Lucien's work beyond France, this friend reminds him of the global nature of his literary *mission*:

> Lucien, what are you up to! All the blacks the world over are waiting desperately for you to complete this text. Chop-chop with your stage-tale, Lucien! The diaspora has run out of patience. Lucien. We blacks of France are waiting for your work to redeem us. (p. 142)

Tram 83 is a provocative novel in which parody and excess are relied on to articulate serious arguments. This quote seems to suggest that African literature is forever tethered to the liberation of the Black race and that its aesthetic pursuit remains subordinated to emancipatory goals. This redeeming logic, in turn, has shaped the expectations of publishers and readers of African literature and contributed to the emergence of a culture in which the marketability of African authors is measured against their ability to perform their Africanity and regurgitate exotic clichés for the benefit of Western readers.[68] Lucien's book project offers a commentary on this literary context whereby African writers are expected to play the role of redeemers. In his first encounter with Malingeau, the director of Joy Train Publications [Éditions Trains de Bonheur], the Swiss publisher interested in his work, Lucien endorses this historic mission assigned to African literature:

> I think [...] that literature deserves pride of place in the shaping of history. It is by way of history that I can reestablish the truth. I intend to piece together the memory of a country that exists only on paper. To fantasize about the City-State and the Back-Country with a view of exploring collective memory. (48)

Mujila's novel (like Lucien's stage tale) does all these things at the same time: while alluding to some of the figures responsible for the *invention* of modern Congo (e.g. Stanley), it also brings to the fore a present that, against the backdrop of globalisation, is fantasising about a better future. Lucien adds that this representation will also be accompanied by a focus on the Congolese underbelly: its 'baby-chicks' [underaged prostitutes], 'diggers [*creuseurs*] and famished students' (48). Malengeau does not approve of this Afro-pessimistic agenda. He remarks that he is 'concerned for the future of African literature' and that instead of focusing on 'squalor' and 'violence', African writers would be well advised to engage with the more joyous aspects of life: 'beautiful girls, good looking men, Brazza beer, good music' (p. 48).

Throughout the narrative, Malingeau continues to comment on the progress of Lucien's book and at various points he attempts to take control of its development. His mentorship is reminiscent of the constraining conditions under which 'African classics' have been published since the colonial period.[69] At a Congolese level, Malingeau's interventionist stance is a reminder that the publication and distribution of literature have remained contingent on extra-literary criteria. Under Mobutu, state-controlled publishers like the Éditions Lokole would insist on political compliance, and Médiaspaul only supports religiously correct authors.[70]

Lucien's antagonistic relationship with Malingeau, then, is also a means to explore the transnational effects of a type of literary capitalism that Pascale Casanova called 'the Greenwich meridian of literature', that is, an arbitrarily defined set of criteria that 'makes it possible to estimate the relative aesthetic distance from the center of the world of letters of all those who belong to it'.[71] Casanova adds that this meridian has temporal implications for it is applied to determine 'the present of literary creation, which is to say modernity'.[72] In his unequal dialogue with Malingeau, Lucien realises that his own literary production and, indeed, 'the future of African literature' (*Tram 83*, p. 48) is measured against this elusive centre. Although imaginary, this meridian is also real, and Lucien is aware that his own literary coevalness – and hence livelihood as a writer – depends on his ability or willingness to adhere to its principles.

With this common criterion in mind, Lucien, in another heated encounter with Malingeau, shows that his stage-tale 'takes place in a station. The play is divided into platforms. There are ten platforms, so ten tableaux' (*Tram 83*, p. 176). This synopsis is, however, deceptive and does not reflect Mujila's (and Lucien's) own literary projects. Indeed, this reassuringly ordered structure presents itself as a parody of linear fictions produced to entertain the readers of the aptly named Joy Train Publications. This appellation – Éditions Trains de Bonheur – seems to suggest that Malingeau's future African literature will be subsumed under the *littérature de gare* category. In addition to beer and music, this easy and cheap type of literature favours exotic locations, sleazy characters, and carnal pleasures: 'Here we live, we fuck, we're happy. There needs to be fucking in African literature too!' (*Tram 83*, p. 48), suggests Malingeau. Although *Tram 83* incorporates these features, exoticism, sleaze, and sex are only means to an end, as they are primarily the marks of the present past in which the novel (and the eponymous bar) is embedded and trapped.

Lucien's ambition to contribute to the development of what he calls 'locomotive literature' (*Tram 83*, p. 157) bears witness to Mujila's use of the railway as a metaphor of colonial modernity. However, the locomotive is also a vehicle to question the sacrosanct status of written literature and explore its intermedial possibilities. *Tram 83* is saturated with references to literature, film, and music. This deployment serves two distinct purposes. First, it provides a commentary on the marketisation of culture in an Africa where humans, ideas, and things are ascribed strict exchange values. Second, it is also an instrument to challenge the centrality of the literary meridian and the perpetuation of a literature produced, distributed, and consumed via conventional channels. For Lucien, 'locomotive literature' offers the possibility of bypassing these channels. Trains, locomotives, railroads, stations, and their passengers feed Lucien's creativity: 'Locomotive literature or train literature or tram literature or rail literature or railroad literature or literature of the iron road, my writing displays similarities with the railroad' (*Tram 83*, p. 157). Interestingly, he falls for a female singer and musician who has developed an analogous relationship with trains. An intermedial project emerges from this encounter: 'I plan to read and perform my texts over recorded railroad sounds, your recorded sounds. It will be a question of finding a creative space, me and my texts, you and your voice' (*Tram 83*, p. 159).

This quest for a creative space where music and literature would meet to explore Congolese culture is at the heart of Mujila's artistic project, and one he has concretely pursued in *On boit Lumumba*. As discussed by Ramcy Kabuya, who is also a writer from Lubumbashi, Mujila was at the forefront of a cultural initiative, 'Libre Écrire' [Free Writing], which aimed to mix different artistic media and organise public events where literary texts would be performed by slammers and rappers.[73] In a country where there is a shortage of literature readers, Mujila – like Sinzo Aanza – has since the beginning of his career sought to perform literature away from the printed text. He has also reflected on the possible interfaces between literature, painting, and sculpture and has, among other intermedial experiments, exhibited and collaged fragments of his own printed work within *and* alongside art objects.[74] While creating synaesthetic resonances, this exercise in repurposing and transmutation is ultimately driven by a pragmatic ambition to bring down the printed text from its 'pedestal' and bypass the constraints of 'traditional publishing' and the networks on which it depends.[75]

Conclusion

By means of mining cities founded by the Belgians, the two texts analysed here revisit the enduring legacies of colonial figures, toponymy, and objects. The insistent and imperious presence of this past in the second decade of our millennium does little to reveal Congolese emancipation and agency. Contemporary extractivism has reconfigured segregation, violence, and exploitation and has been the vector of new forms of necropolitical sovereignty even though the 'hole', as this trope has been poeticised by Congolese artists and writers, is 'a point for meditating on the city's pitfalls while revealing its inherent possibilities'.[76] Contemporary extractivism has also engendered new planetary industrial networks, the proliferation of different breeds of commercial intermediaries-mercenaries, and the emergence of fresh alliances between West and East, North and South in which it has become increasingly difficult to identify those in charge of dictating who may live and who must die. Sinzo Aanza and Fiston Mwanza Mujila record the tremors of an industrial landscape marked – and scarred – by railway projects, the foundation of the UMHK, its subsequent nationalisation by Mobutu's Gécamines, its collapse at the end of the twentieth century, and the renaissance of *creusage*. With different means, the two novelists explore the local and global ramifications of a process that largely takes place *underground*. These two texts offer a captivating meta-analysis of the place and role of Congolese literature within the larger francophone postcolonial field.

Généalogie presents itself as an anti-novel. Its overall architecture is constantly compromised by the shifting terrain on which Elisabethville/Lubumbashi was built and continues to sprawl. The complex imbrication of narrative voices on which this text relies mirrors the equally elaborate cartography of a city originally conceived to master Katangese geology and the locals' *biology*. Like other great African novelists of the city – Eza Boto, Kossi Efoui, and Jean-Luc Raharimanana – Sinzo Aanza makes use of a fissured and dispersed diegesis to render contemporary urban chaos. *Tram 83*, Mujila's high tempo first novel, is as imbricated. *Généalogie*'s narrative imbrication can be explained spatially: the *creuseurs*' subsoil lies under the Bronx, a district located at the periphery of Elisabethville/Lubumbashi, which, in turn, has been marginalised by Kinshasa. Mujila's novel, for its part, focuses on a bar in a mining city, situated in a country resembling Congo-Zaire. However, unlike other fictional bars – in *L' Anté-Peuple, Les Crapauds-brousse*, or *Temps de chien* – Tram 83 is not the locus of political dissidence but a space where a globalised colonial *now* keeps returning. Finally, these two Congolese novels bear witness to their authors' temptation to escape the constrains of the printed text. This ambition to challenge the primacy of written literature – and its *archival* (patriarchal and hegemonic) status[77] – is a means to reopen the history of the DRC, a process that was to a large extend completed by dutiful scribes. Indeed, these two texts bring to mind the intermedial experiments conducted by Sammy Baloji and Patrick Mudekereza to reappropriate the Katangese history via archives held at the Tervuren museum.[78] For Aanza and Mujila, then, the printed text is in competition with other media. They perform a delicate balancing act: while writing novels, they also evade this genre and its strictures.[79] If it is a paradox, it is also a tour de force.

Notes

1. S. Aanza, 'Pertinences citoyennes', exhibition held in Paris in 2018. Cited by Nicolas Martin-Granel in 'D'une rive l'autre: questions de génétique et poétique', *Continents Manuscrits*, 15 (2020), special issue on 'Congo Global', ed. by Silvia Riva https://journals.openedition.org/coma/6277 [accessed 12 June 2021]. All translations are mine unless otherwise stated.
2. Fiston Mwanza Mujila On His Debut Novel | Verve Magazine [accessed 8 November 2021].
3. F. Mwanza Mujila, *Tram 83* (Paris: Éditions Métailié, 2014). I will use here the English translation: *Tram 83*, trans. Roland Glasser, foreword by Alain Mabanckou (London: Jacaranda Books, 2015). *Tram* for all subsequent references to this text.
4. S. Aanza *Généalogie d'une banalité* (La Roque d'Anthéron: Vents d'Ailleurs, 2015). *Généalogie* for all subsequent references to this text.
5. See In Koli Jean Bofane, *Congo Inc. Le Testament de Bismarck* (Arles: Actes Sud, 2014) and F. Mwanza Mujila, *La Danse du vilain* (Paris: Éditions Métailié, 2020).
6. See *Mémoire* (2006) and *Pungulume* (2016) by Sammy Baloji.
7. See Baloji's and Mudekereza's 'Congo Far West' (Royal Museum for Central Africa, 2008); 'Congo as Fiction' (Rietberg Museum, Zurich, 2020–21); 'Mabele Eleki Lola!', an exhibition by Freddy Tsimba (AfricaMuseum, 2021) curated by In Koli Jean Bofane.
8. Xavier Garnier, 'Writing the Subsoil in the Contemporary Congolese Novel', *Journal of World Literature*, 6 (2021), special issue 'Contemporary Congolese Literature as World Literature', ed. by Silvia Riva and Julien Jeusette, 133–47 (139).
9. Laura Ann Stoler, *Along the Archival Grain: Epistemic Anxieties and Colonial Common Sense* (Princeton University Press, 2009), p. 44.
10. Maëline Le Lay, Dominique Malaquais, and Nadine Siegert (eds.), *Archive (re)mix. Vues d'Afrique*, preface by Alain Ricard and Ulf Vierke (Rennes: Presses Universitaires de Rennes, 2015), pp. 32–33.
11. Stoler, *Along the Archival Grain*, p. 45. My emphasis.
12. See Maarten Couttenier and Sammy Baloji, 'The Charles Lemaire Expedition Revisited: Sammy Baloji as a Portraitist of Present Humans in Congo Far West', *African Arts*, 41.1 (Spring 2014), 66–81.
13. See Bogumil Jewsiewicki, Donatien Dibwe dia Mwembu & Rosario Giordano (eds.), *Lubumbashi 1910–2010. Mémoire d'une ville industrielle/Ukumbusho wa mukini wa komponi*, preface by V.Y. Mudimbe (Paris: L'Harmattan, 2010).
14. See Timothy Makori, 'Mobilizing the Past: Creuseurs, Precarity and the Colonizing Structure in the Congo Copperbelt', *Africa*, 87.4 (2017), 780–805.
15. Serge Olivier Songa-Songa Mwitwa and Marc Pabois (eds.), *Lubumbashi, capitale minière du Katanga, 1910-2010* (Lubumbashi: Association Halle de l'Étoile, 2008), p. 2.
16. See Robrecht Declercq, Duncan Money, and Hans Otto Frøland (eds), *Born with a Copper Spoon: a Global History of Copper, 1830-1980* (Vancouver: University of British Columbia Press, 2022).
17. Serge Olivier Songa-Songa Mwitwa and Marc Pabois, p. 3.
18. See Daniel Vangroenweghe, 'The "Leopold II" Concession System Exported to French Congo with as Example the Mpoko Company', *Revue Belge d'Histoire Contemporaine*, 36 (2006), 323–72 (325).
19. Johan Lagae, Sofie Boonen, and Donatien Dia Mwembu Dibwe, 'M(g)r. De Hemptin(n)e, I Presume? Transforming Local Memory Through Toponymy in Colonial/Post-Colonial Lubumbashi, DR Congo', in Liora Bigon (ed.), *Place Names in Africa: Colonial Urban Legacies, Entangled Histories* (Switzerland: Springer International Publishing, 2016), pp. 177–94 (180–81). On De Hemptinne, see: Eva Schalbroeck, 'Centre Stage and Behind the Scene with the "Lion of Katanga": Benedictine Jean-Félix de Hemptinne's Congolese Career, 1910–1958', 32.1/2 (2019), 105-147; on colonial and post-colonial art and architecture in Congolese cities, see: Ruth Sacks, 'Congo Style: From Belgian Art Nouveau to Zaïre's Authenticité', unpublished doctoral thesis, University of Witwatersrand, Johannesburg, 2017.
20. Ibid., p. 181.
21. Ibid., p. 184.
22. In Fact, a political slogan created by President Joseph Kabila, see https://www.jambonews.net/actualites/20130604-rdc-vous-avez-dit-revolution-de-la-modernite/ [accessed 7 January 2022].
23. See A. Mbembe, 'Necropolitics', *Public Culture*, 15 (2003), 11–40 (11).
24. Giorgio Agamben, *Homo Sacer: Sovereign Power and Bare Life*, translated by Daniel Heller-Roazen (Stanford Calif.: Stanford University Press, 1998), pp. 1–2.
25. Mbembe, 'Necropolitics', p. 27.
26. Ibid., p. 31.
27. It is also a place where the foundational tenets of modern capitalism are forever tested and repeated. See: Eli Jelly-Schapiro's analysis of *Tram 83* in 'Extractive Modernity at Large: The Contempo-

rary Novel of Primitive Accumulation', *Interventions: International Journal of Postcolonial Studies* (2021), DOI: 10.1080/1369801X.2021.2003221 [accessed 5 January 2022].
28. Pim Higginson, *Scoring Race: Jazz, Fiction, and Francophone Africa* (Woodbridge, Suffolk: James Currey; Rochester, New York: Boydell & Brewer, 2017), p. 155. Higginson focuses here on *Tram 83*.
29. Elara Bertho, 'Cacophonies de la mémoire et éblouissements impériaux (Sinzo Aanza, *Généalogie d'une banalité*), *Francofonia*, 76 (2019), special issue 'Les enjeux de la mémoire dans la littérature et les arts contemporains de la République démocratique du Congo' ed. by Éloïse Brezault, 83–97 (91).
30. See S. Aanza, 'Note d'intention pour *Plaidoirie pour vendre le Congo*', *Continents Manuscrits*, 15 (2020), special issue on 'Congo Global', ed. by Silvia Riva https://doi.org/10.4000/coma.6212 https://doi.org/10.4000/coma.6212 [accessed 12 June 2021].
31. See Linda Melvern, *A People Betrayed: the Role of the West in Rwanda's Genocide* (London: Zed Books, 2009), pp. 81–85.
32. See Lagae et al., in Bigon (ed.), pp. 179–80.
33. See V. Y. Mudimbe, *The Idea of Africa* (Bloomington and Indianapolis; James Currey: Indiana University Press; London, 1994), p. 135 for a discussion on this zone.
34. Frantz Fanon, *Peau noire, masques blancs* (Paris: Seuil, 1995 [1952]), p. 13.
35. Ibid., p. 88.
36. Charles Blanchart et. al, *Le Rail au Congo belge, 1890–1920*, vol I (Brussels: Charles Blanchart et Cie, 1993), pp. 102–03.
37. See Isidore Ndaywel è Nziem, *Histoire générale du Congo. De l'héritage ancien à la République Démocratique* (Paris; Brussels: Duculot, 1998), p. 327.
38. Giordano Nanni, *The Colonisation of Time: Ritual, Routine and Resistance in the British Empire* (Manchester: Manchester University Press, 2013), p. 60.
39. See Johannes Fabian, *Remembering the Present: Painting and Popular History in Zaire* (Berkeley: University of California Press, 1996).
40. See François Bontinck, 'Les deux Bula-Matadi', *Études Congolaises*, 12 (1969), 83–97.
41. Olivier de Bouveignes, *Les Anciens rois de Congo* (Namur: Grands Lac, 1948), p. 52.
42. On naming and Congolese resistance and agency, see Osumaka Likaka, *Naming Colonialism: History and Collective Memory in the Congo, 1870–1960* (Madison: University of Wisconsin Press, 2009)
43. As stated by the author in an interview reproduced by Pius Ngandu Nkashama in *Portraits d'écrivains. Visages d'histoire littéraire* (Paris: L'Harmattan, 2016), p. 227.
44. See the jazz album *On boit Lumumba* (SWR Jazzhaus, 2020) in which the music (composed by Lukas Kranzelbinder) is accompanied by words written and recited by Mujila himself.
45. Mujila (2014), p. 138.
46. Higginson, p. 156.
47. See Koselleck, *Futures Past: on the Semantics of Historical Time*, transl. with an Introduction by Keith Tribe (New York: Columbia University Press, 2004 [1983]).
48. *L'Union Minière et la vie au Katanga* (Brussels: Presses de M. Weissenbruch S.A, 1954), p. 45
49. Makori, p. 798.
50. Ibid., p. 794.
51. Ibid., p. 786.
52. See S. Aanza, 'Projet d'attentat contre l'image' (Wiels Contemporary Art Centre, Brussels, 2017).
53. See S. Aanza, *Que ta volonté soit Kin* (Kinshasa: Éditions Nzoi, 2018).
54. S. Aanza, 'Note d'intention pour *Plaidoirie pour vendre le Congo*'.
55. see Sinzo Aanza / L'Officiel Art – YouTube [accessed 12 June 2021]
56. Ibid.
57. See Wyatt MacGaffey, *Kongo Political Culture: The Conceptual Challenge of the Particular* (Bloomington: Indiana University Press, 2000); Martial Sinda, *Le Messianisme congolais et ses incidences politiques*; Gondola, *Matswa vivant*. See also: Pieter De Coene, Margot Luyckfasseel and Gillian Mathys 'Voices from Exile: The Mpadist Mission des Noirs in Oshwe's Prison Camps in the Belgian Congo (1940–1960)' (2022) *International Journal of African Historical Studies*, 55.1 (2022), 89–114.
58. Céline Gahungu's interview of Aanza: 'Débords – Sinzo Aanza, *Continents Manuscrits*, 10 (2018), 1–6 (2–3) coma-1154 (1) DOI: 10.4000/coma.1154 [accessed 7 July 2021].
59. See Bertho, pp. 83–84 and 94 in which she refers to Gilles Deleuze and Félix Guattari's *Kafka. Pour une littérature mineure* (Paris: Minuit, 1975).
60. Filip De Boeck and Sammy Baloji, 'Positing the Polis: Topography as a Way to De-centre Urban Thinking', *Urbanisation*, 2.2 (2017), 1–13 (9).
61. Patrice Nganang, *Manifeste d'une nouvelle littérature africaine. Pour une écriture préemptive* (Paris: Éditions Homnisphères, 2007), pp. 259–82.
62. Ibid., p. 264.
63. Ibid., p. 266.
64. Ibid., p. 271, my emphasis.
65. Gahungu, p. 3.
66. Ibid., p. 2.
67. Kate Tidmarsh, 'Trains, traumatismes et transnationalisme dans les écrits de Fiston Mwanza Mujila', *Francofonia*, 76 (2019), special issue 'Les enjeux de la mémoire dans la littérature et les arts

contemporains de la République démocratique du Congo' ed. by Éloïse Brezault, 51–66 (52).
68. On this issue, see Graham Huggan, *The Postcolonial Exotic: Marketing the Margins* (London; New York: Routledge, 2001), p. 25.
69. Claire Ducournau, *La Fabrique des classiques africains. Écrivains d'Afrique subsaharienne francophone* (Paris: CNRS Éditions, 2017), p. 12.
70. Ramcy Kabuya, 'Écritures urbaines lushoises', *Études Littéraires Africaines*, 27 (2009), 63–73 (67).
71. P. Casanova, *The World Republic of Letters*, trans. by M. B. DeBevoise (Cambridge, Mass; London: Harvard University Press, 2007), p. 88.
72. Ibid.
73. Ramcy Kabuya, p. 69.
74. Ibid.
75. Ibid.
76. Filip De Boeck, 'Congoville-Putuville': Mirroring Models and Beyond in the (Post) Colonial World', in Pieter Boons, and Sandrine Collard (eds.), *Contemporay Artists Tracing Colonial Tracks: Congoville* (Leuven: Leuven University Press, 2021), pp. 64–81 (p. 79).
77. Jacques Derrida, *Mal d'archive* (Paris: Galilée, 1995), pp. 11–12.
78. See Johan Lagae and Sabine Cornélis (eds.), *Congo Far West. Sammy Baloji et Patrick Mudekereza en résidence au Musée Royal de l'Afrique centrale. Arts, sciences et collections* (Milan: Silvana Editoriale; Tervuren: Musée royal de l'Afrique centrale, 2011).
79. And the limits of the genre as *form*. See: Alexander Fyfe, 'Infrastructure and the Valences of the Literary in Fiston Mwanza Mujila's *Tram 83*, *Critique: Studies in Contemporary Fiction* (2021), https://doi.org/10.1080/00111619.2021.1875975 [accessed 7 January 2022].

Bibliography

'19 11 16 Return of the Congolese', YouTube <https://www.youtube.com/watch?v=Dp4jBhQIzX0> [accessed 18 December 2020]
Aanza, Sinzo, *Généalogie d'une banalité* (La Roque d'Anthéron: Vents d'Ailleurs, 2015).
——, *Que ta volonté soit Kin* (Kinshasa: Éditions Nzoi, 2018).
'A Baptist Mission Scandal. II', *John Bull*, 23 December 1911.
Abble, Albert [et al.], *Des Prêtres noirs s'interrogent*, Preface by Msgr. Lefebvre; published under the aegis of Présence Africaine (Paris: Éditions du Cerf, 1957).
Action Zoo Humain <https://www.actionzoohumain.be/nl> [accessed 14 July 2020].
Adekunle, Julius O., *Culture and Customs of Rwanda* (Westport, CT: Greenwood Press, 2007).
Adi, Hakim, 'Bandele Omoniyi: A Neglected Nigerian Nationalist', *African Affairs*, 90 (1991), 581–605.
Aldrich, Robert, 'Colonial museums in a postcolonial Europe', *African and Black Diaspora: An International Journal*, 2.2 (2009), 137–56.
Allard, Claude, Coralie Snyers, Isabelle Van der Borght, and Viviane Van Liempt, *Construire l'Histoire. Tome 4: Un monde en mutation (de 1919 à nos jours)* (Namur: Didier-Hatier, 2008).
Anckaer, Jan, *Small Power Diplomacy and Commerce: Belgium and the Ottoman Empire during the reign of Leopold I (1831–1865)* (Istanbul: The Isis Press, 2013).
Andersen, Frits, *The Dark Continent? Images of Africa in European Narratives about the Congo*, trans. by William Frost and Martin Skovhus (Aarhus: Aarhus University Press, 2016).
Anderson, Benedict, *Imagined Communities: Reflections on the Origins and Spread of Nationalism*, rev. ed. (London: Verso, 2006).
Ansiaux, Robert R., 'Early Belgian Colonial Efforts: The Long and Fateful Shadow of Leopold I' (doctoral thesis, University of Texas at Arlington, 2007) https://rc.library.uta.edu/uta-ir/handle/10106/382.
Anstey, Roger, *Britain and the Congo in the Nineteenth Century* (London: Longmans, Green and Co, 1982).
Apthorp, Shirley, 'Black "Human Zoo" Fury Greets Berlin Art Show', *Bloomberg News*, 3 October 2012 <http://www.businessweek.com/news/2012-10-03/black-human-zoo-fury-greets-berlin-art-show> [accessed 18 July 2014].
Archdiocèse de Bukavu, 'Coordination Diocésaine et Provinciale des Écoles Conventionnées Catholiques,' <http://www.archidiocesebukavu.com/diocese/commissions-diocesaines/coordination-diocesaine-et-provinciale-des-ecoles-conventionnees-catholiques/> [accessed 10 February 2021]
Arendt, Hannah, *Eichmann in Jerusalem: A Report on the Banality of evil* (New York: Penguin Books, 1979 [1963]).
Arens, Sarah, 'Memory in Crisis: Commemoration, Visual Cultures and (Mis)representation in Postcolonial Belgium', *Modern Languages Open* 1 (2020): n.p. <http://doi.org/10.3828/mlo.v0i0.328>
Arnaut, Karel, 'The Human Zoo as (Bad) Intercultural Performance', in *Exhibitions: the Invention of the Savage*, ed. by Pascal Blanchard, Gilles Boetsch, and Nanette J. Snoep (Paris: Musée du Quai Branly; Arles: Actes Sud, 2011), pp. 345–63.
Assmann, Aleida, 'Transformations of the Modern Time Regime', in *Breaking Up Time: Negotiating the Borders Between Present, Past, and Future*, ed. by Berber Bevernage and Chris Lorenz (Göttingen: Vandenhoeck & Ruprecht, 2013), pp. 39–56.
——, *Is Time Out of Joint?: On the Rise and Fall of the Modern Time Regime* (Ithaca, NY: Cornell University Press, 2020).
Austin, J. L., *How to Do Things with Words* (Oxford: Clarendon Press, 1962).
Badi-Banga Ne-Mwine, *Contribution à l'étude historique de l'art plastique zaïrois moderne. Fin XVe siècle? – 1975* (Kinshasa: Editions Malayika, 1977)
Bailey, Brett, 'Performing So the Spirit May Speak', *South African Theatre Journal*, A12.1/2 (1998), 191–202.
——, *The Plays of Miracle and Wonder – Ipi Zombi?, iMumbo Jumbo, The Prophet* (Cape Town: Double Story, 2003).

Baker, Mona, 'Reframing Conflict in Translation', *Social Semiotics*, 17. 2 (2007), 1470–219.
Balandier, Georges, *Afrique ambiguë* (Paris: Seuil, 1957).
Baloji, Sammy, *Mémoire/Kolwezi* (Brussels: Africalia & Stichting Kunstboek, 2014).
———, 'About *Congo Art Works*', in *Congo Art Works: Popular Painting*, ed. by Bambi Ceuppens and Sammy Baloji (Brussels: Éditions Racine/Royal Museum for Central Africa, 2016), pp. 63–86.
———, Lotte Arndt, Asger Taiaksev, Sandrine Colard, Yasmine van Pee, and Patricia van Schuylenbergh, *Hunting & Collecting* (Ostend: Kunstmuseum aan Zee, 2016).
Bangstad, Sindre and Bjørn Enge Bertelsen, 'Heart of darkness reinvented? A tale of ex-soldiers in the Democratic Republic of Congo', *Anthropology Today*, 26.1 (2010), 8–12.
Barber, Karin, 'African-Language Literature and Postcolonial Criticism', *Research in African Literatures*, 26.4 (1995), 3–30. <http://www.jstor.org./stable/3820224 accessed06/06/2015>
Barlet, Oliver, 'Representing the *Itsembabwoko*', *Black Camera, an International Film Journal*, 4.1 (2012), 234–51.
BBC. 'Exhibit B: Is Controversial Art Show Racist?', 24 September 2014 <http://www.bbc.co.uk/news/entertainment-arts-29344483> [accessed 24 September 2014]
Bellinck, Thomas and An van Dienderen, 'That's My Life Jacket! Speculative Documentary as a Counter Strategy to Documentary Taxidermy', *Critical Arts* (2019), 1–15.
Bellon, Michaël, 'KFDA012: Brett Bailey Takes to the Courtroom', *Agenda magazine*, 3 May 2012, KFDA012: Brett Bailey takes to the courtroom | BRUZZ> [accessed 18 July 2014 and 2 September 2021]
Bemba, Sylvain, 'La phratrie des écrivains congolais', *Notre Librairie*, 'Littérature congolaise', 92–93 (1988), 13–15.
Bentrovato, Denise and Karel Van Nieuwenhuyse, 'Confronting "dark" colonial pasts: a historical analysis of practices of representation in Belgian and Congolese schools, 1945–2015', *Paedagogica Historica*, 56.3 (2020), 293–320.
Bertho, Elara, 'Cacophonies de la mémoire et éblouissements impériaux (Sinzo Aanza, *Généalogie d'une banalité*), *Francofonia*, 76 (2019), special issue 'Les enjeux de la mémoire dans la littérature et les arts contemporains de la République démocratique du Congo', ed. by Éloïse Brezault, 83–97.
Bevernage, Berber and Chris Lorenz (eds.), *Breaking Up Time: Negotiating the Borders Between Present, Past, and Future* (Göttingen: Vandenhoeck & Ruprecht, 2013).
———,Eva Willems, Eline Mestdagh, Bruno De Wever, and Romain Landmeters, 'Commission Congo: la peur paralysante de l'historien', *Le Soir*, 24 August 2020 <https://plus.lesoir.be/320703/article/2020-08-24/commission-congo-la-peur-paralysante-de-lhistorien>
Bhambra, Gurminder K. and John Holmwood, *Colonialism and Modern Social Theory* (Cambridge; Medford, MA: Polity, 2021).
Biaya, T. K., 'La culture urbaine dans les arts populaires d'Afrique: Analyse de l'ambiance zaïroise', *Canadian Journal of African Studies / Revue Canadienne des Études Africaines*, 30.3 (1996), 345–70.
Biebuyck, Daniel, 'Répartitions et droits du pangolin chez les Balega', *Extrait de Zaire*, 9 (1953), 899–924.
Bigirimana, Raphaël, 'Le Chef de l'Etat s'associe aux fidèles de l'église du Rocher de Buye dans la prière dominicale', RTNB, 3 May 2020 <http://www.RTNB.bi/fr/art.php?idapi=4/1/131> [accessed 03 March 2021]
Bisschop, Alisson, 'L'Histoire coloniale de la Belgique exposée à Venise: Luc Tuymans et la série Mwana Kitoko (Beautiful White Man)', *Histoire de l'Art*, 80.1 (2017), 141–52.
Blachère, Jean-Claude, 'Sony Labou Tansi – La Ville et demie', *Francofonía*, 8 (1999), 121–36.
'Black History Month North Wales' <http://www.bhmnw.com/index.asp?pageid=580958> [accessed 18 December 2020]
'Black Lives Matter: Bristol's Colston Protest Police "Didn't Lack Courage"', BBC, 10 June 2020 <https://www.bbc.co.uk/news/uk-england-bristol-52993995> [accessed 5 September 2020]
Blanchard, Pascal, et al. (eds). *Human Zoos: Science and Spectacle in the Age of Colonial Empires* (Liverpool: Liverpool University Press, 2008).
——— and Maarten Couttenier, 'Les Zoos humains', *Nouvelles Études Francophones*, 32.1 (2017), 109–15.
Blanchart, Charles et. al, *Le Rail au Congo belge, 1890–1920*, vol I (Brussels: Charles Blanchart et Cie, 1993).
Boast, Robin, 'Neocolonial Collaboration: Museum as Contact Zone Revisited', *Museum Anthropology*, 34.1, 56–70.
Bobineau Julien, 'The Historical Taboo: Colonial Discourses and Postcolonial Identities in Belgium', *Werkwinkel: Journal of Low Countries and South African Studies*, 12.1 (2017), 107–23.
———, *Koloniale Diskurse im Vergleich. Die Repräsentation von Patrice Lumumba in der kongolesischen Lyrik and im Belgischen Drama* (Berlin: Lit Verlag, 2019).
Bofane, In Koli Jean, *Congo Inc. Le testament de Bismarck* (Arles: Actes Sud, 2014).
———, with Pascal Blanchard, Henry Bunjoko, and Bogumil Jewsiewicki, *Freddy Tsimba: Mabele Eleki Lola! La Terre Plus Belle Que Le Paradis!* (Brussels: Kate'Art Éditions, 2020).
———, *Nation cannibale* (Arles: Actes Sud, 2022).

Boffey, Daniel, 'Reappearance of Statue's Missing Hand Reignites Colonial Row', *The Guardian*, 22 February 2019 <https://www.theguardian.com/world/2019/feb/22/statue-missing-hand-colonial-belgium-leopold-congo> [accessed 21 August 2020]

Bogers, Koen and Patrick Wymeersch, *De Kongo in de Vlaamse fiktie- en reisverhalen* (Brussels: CEDAF/ASDOC., 1987).

Bokamba, Eyamba G., 'Arguments for Multilingual Policies in Public Domains', in *Linguistic Identity in Postcolonial Multilingual Spaces*, ed. by Eric A. Anchimbe (New Castle: Cambridge Scholars Publishing, 2007), pp. 27–65.

Bolen, Francis, *Histoire authentique, anecdotique, folklorique et critique du cinéma belge depuis ses plus lointaines origines* (Brussels: Memo & Codec, 1978).

Bolle, Jacques, *Les Seigneurs de la forêt* (Paris: Arthaud, 1958).

Bomgbose, Ayo, *Language, and the Nation: The Language Question in Sub-Saharan Africa* (Edinburgh: Edinburgh University Press, 1991).

Bont, Raf de, 'A World Laboratory: Framing the Albert National Park', *Environmental History*, 22 (3) (2017), 404–32.

Bontinck, François, 'Les deux Bula-Matadi', *Études Congolaises*, 12 (1969), 83–97.

Boons, Pieter and Sandrine Collard (eds.), *Contemporay Artists Tracing Colonial Tracks: Congoville/Hedendaagse Kunstenaars Bewandelen Koloniale Sporen* (Leuven: Leuven University Press, 2021).

Booth, General [William], *In Darkest England and the Way Out* (London: Salvation Army 1890).

Bostoen, Koen and Inge Brinkman (eds.), *The Kongo Kingdom: The Origins, Dynamics and Cosmopolitan Culture of an African Polity* (Cambridge: Cambridge University Press, 2018).

Bouffioux, Michel, 'Guido Gryseels, directeur du Musée de l'Afrique centrale: « C'est le moment du débat »' <http://www.lusingatabwa.com/2018/03/guido-gryseels-directeur-du-musee-de-l-afrique-centrale-c-est-le-moment-du-debat.html> [accessed 06 May 2019]

Bouveignes, Olivier de, *Les Anciens rois de Congo* (Namur: Grands Lac, 1948).

Bouwer, Karen, *Gender and Decolonization in the Congo: the Legacy of Patrice Lumumba* (New York: Palgrave Macmillan, 2010).

Boyle, Patrick M., 'School Wars: Church, State, and the Death of the Congo', *The Journal of Modern African Studies*, 33.3 (1995), 451–68.

Braeckman, Colette, *Rwanda, histoire d'un génocide, 1994* (Paris: Fayard, 1994).

———, *Terreur africaine. Burundi, Rwanda, Zaïre: les racines de la violence* (Paris: Fayard, 1996).

———, 'The Rwandan Genocide of the 1990s', in *A Historical Companion to Postcolonial Literatures – Continental Europe and its Empires*, ed. by Prem Poddar, Rajeev S. Patke, and Lars Jensen (Edinburgh: Edinburgh University Press, 2008), pp. 49–51.

———, *Lumumba, un crime d'État. Une lecture critique de la Commission parlementaire belge* (Brussels: Les Éditions Aden, 2009).

———, *L'homme qui répare les femmes: Le combat du Docteur Mukwege* (Waterloo: La Renaissance du livre, 2016).

———, 'Burundi: quelques «miracles» qui méritent une explication…', *Le Soir*, 13 May 2020 <https://plus.lesoir.be/300616/article/2020-05-13/burundi-quelques-miracles-qui-meritent-une-explication?referer=%2Farchives%2Frecherche%3Fdatefilter%3Dlastyear%26sort%3Ddate%2Bdesc%26start%3D10%26word%3Dnkurunziza> [accessed 03 March 2021]

———, 'Burundi: une élection contestée, mais un vainqueur qui n'est pas le pire', *Le Soir*, 25 May 2020 <https://plus.lesoir.be/302952/article/2020-05-25/burundi-une-election-contestee-mais-un-vainqueur-qui-nest-pas-le-pire?referer=%2Farchives%2Frecherche%3Fdatefilter%3Dlastyear%26sort%3Ddate%2Bdesc%26start%3D0%26word%3Dnkurunziza> [accessed 03 March 2021]

———, 'Bruxelles, capitale du Congo de grand-père? Le parlement régional veut décoloniser l'espace public', *Le Soir*, 29 May 2020 <https://plus.lesoir.be/303946/article/2020-05-29/bruxelles-capitale-du-congo-de-grand-pere-le-parlement-regional-veut-decoloniser?referer=%2Farchives%2Frecherche%3Fdatefilter%3Dlastyear%26sort%3Ddate%2Bdesc%26start%3D50%26word%3Dburundi> [accessed 03 March 2021]

———, 'Burundi: le Covid-19 décapite la classe dirigeante et plonge le pays dans l'angoisse', 12 June 2020 <https://plus.lesoir.be/306777/article/2020-06-12/burundi-le-covid-19-decapite-la-classe-dirigeante-et-plonge-le-pays-dans?referer=%2Farchives%2Frecherche%3Fdatefilter%3Dlastyear%26sort%3Ddate%2Bdesc%26start%3D0%26word%3Dnkurunziza> [accessed 03 March 2021]

———, 'Une association rwandaise dénonce déjà le groupe d'experts sur la décolonisation', Le Soir, 9 August 2020 <https://plus.lesoir.be/318060/article/2020-08-09/une-association-rwandaise-denonce-deja-le-groupe-dexperts-sur-la-decolonisation>

Bragard, Véronique, '"Indépendance!": The Belgo-Congolese Dispute in the Tervuren Museum', *Human Architecture: Journal of the Sociology of Self-Knowledge*, 9.4 (2011), 93–104.

——, 'Melancholia and Memorial Work: Representing the Congolese Past in Comics', in *Postcolonial Comics: Text, Event, Identities*, ed. by Binita Mehta and Pia Mukherji (New York: Routledge, 2015), pp. 92–110.

—— and Christophe Dony, 'Congostrip: la bande dessinée congolaise', *La Revue Nouvelle* (July–August 2010), 92–98.

Brain, Alan, *The Rumba Kings* (Shift Visual Lab, 2021).

Brezault, Éloïse, *Johnny chien méchant d'Emmanuel Dongola* (Paris: ACEL-Infolio, 2012).

Bridet, Guillaume, 'Introduction', in *Passeurs, alliés et transfuges à l'époque coloniale*, ed. by Guillaume Bridet (Paris: Kailash Éditions, 2019), pp. 9–45.

Brinker Virginie, *La Transmission littéraire et cinématographique du génocide des Tutsi au Rwanda* (Paris: Classiques Garnier, 2014).

Broqueville, Huguette de, *Uraho? Es-tu toujours vivant* (Grâce-Hollogne: Éditions Mols, 1997).

Bruner, Jerome, 'The Narrative Construction of Reality', *Critical Inquiry*, 18 (1991), 1–21.

Budagwa, Assumani, *Noirs, Blancs, métis: la Belgique et la ségrégation des métis du Congo Belge et du Ruanda-Urundi. 1908–1960*, preface by Colette Braeckman (Céroux-Mousty: Budagwa éditeur, 2014).

'Building Bridges', Croeso I Gymru, BBC Wales <http://www.bbc.co.uk/wales/audiovideo/sites/yourvideo/pages/norbertx_mbumputu_01.shtml> [accessed 18 December 2020]

Burgraff, Eric, '(Dé)colonisation: les référentiels d'histoire sont déjà réécrits, mais pas encore enseignés, *Le Soir* 10 June 2020 <https://plus.lesoir.be/306401/article/2020-06-10/decolonisation-les-referentiels-dhistoire-sont-deja-reecrits-mais-pas-encore?>

Burroughs, Robert, 'The Redeemed Life of Lena Clark, Christian Missionary and Humanitarian in the Congo Free State', *Cultural and Social History* (forthcoming).

——, 'The Racialisation of Gratitude in Victorian Culture', *Journal of Victorian Culture*, 25.4 (2020), 477–91.

'Burundi: 15 Years On, No Justice for Gatumba Massacre', 13 August 2019 <https://www.hrw.org/news/2019/08/13/burundi-15-years-no-justice-gatumba-massacre#> [accessed 03 March 2021]

Bustin, Edouard, *Lunda under Belgian Rule: The Politics of Ethnicity* (Cambridge, MA: Harvard University Press, 1975).

Byanafashe, Déo and Paul Rutayisire (eds.), *Histoire du Rwanda des origines à la fin du XXème siècle* (Huye: Université Nationale du Rwanda, 2011).

Cadiou, Yves, 'La structure du mot en kinyarwanda', in *Le Kinyarwanda, études linguistiques*, ed. by Francis Jouannet (Paris: SELAF, 1983), pp. 181–95.

'Carte blanche: Le dialogue sur les trésors coloniaux doit l'emporter sur le paternalisme', *Le Soir*, 17 October 2018 <https://www.lesoir.be/185112/article/2018-10-17/carte-blanche-le-dialogue-sur-les-tresors-coloniaux-doit-lemporter-sur-le> [accessed 05 May 2019]

Casanova, Pascale, *The World Republic of Letters*, trans. by M. B. DeBevoise (Cambridge, MA: Harvard University Press, 2007).

Castryck, Geert, 'Whose History is History? Singularities and Dualities of the Public Debate on Belgian Colonialism', in *Europe and the World in European Historiography*, ed. by Csaba Lévai (Pisa: Pisa University Press, 2006), pp. 71–88.

——, 'Whose History Is History? Singularities and Dualities of the Public Debate on Belgian Colonialism', in *Being a Historian. Opportunities and Responsibilities: Past and Present*, ed. by Sven Mörsdorf (Pisa: Cliohres.net, 2010), pp. 1–18.

Cazenave, Odile, 'Writing the Child, Youth and Violence into the Novel from sub-Saharan Africa: the Impact of Age and Gender', *Research in African Literatures* 36.2 (2005), 59–71.

Ceremonie teruggave stoffelijke resten Lumumba – Cérémonie de restitution de la dépouille de Lumumba – YouTube [accessed 22 June 2022]

Césaire, Aimé, *Discours sur le colonialisme* (Paris: Présence Africaine, 2004 [1955]).

——, *Une Saison au Congo* (Paris: Éditions du Seuil, 1966).

——, *Discourse on Colonialism*, trans. by Joan Pinkham (New York: Monthly Review Press, 1972).

Cettou, Maryline, 'Jardins d'hiver et de papier: de quelques lectures et (ré)écritures fin de siècle', *A contrario*, 11 (2009), 99–117.

Ceuppens, Bambi, 'From Colonial Subjects/Objects to Citizens: The Royal Museum for Central Africa as Contact-Zone', in *Advancing Museum Practices*, ed. by Francesca Lanz and Elena Montanari (Turin: Umberto Allemandi & C., 2014), pp. 83–99.

——, and Sammy Baloji (eds.), *Congo Art Works: Popular Painting* (Brussels: Éditions Racine; Royal Museum for Central Africa, 2016).

———, Vincent Viaene, and David Van Reybroeck (eds.), *Congo in België: koloniale Cultuur in de metropool* (Leuven: Leuven University Press).
Chenu, Bruno, *Théologies chrétiennes des tiers mondes, latino-américaine, noire américaine, noire sud-africaine, africaine, asiatique* (Paris: Éditions du centurion, 1987).
Chigudu, Simukai, 'Rhodes Must Fall in Oxford: A Critical Testimony', *Critical African Studies*, 12.3 (2020), 302–12.
Chikha, Chokri Ben, *De Waarheidscommissie/The Truth Commission*, unpublished, 2013.
Chong, Denis and James Druckman, 'Framing Theory', *Annual Review of Political Science*, 10 (2007), 103–26.
Chrétien, Jean-Pierre, 'Le passé colonial: le devoir d'histoire', *Politique africaine*, 98.2 (2005), 141–48.
——— and Marcel Kabanda, *Rwanda, racisme et génocide: l'idéologie hamitique* (Paris: Belin, 2016).
Clark, Phyllis, 'Passionate Engagements: A Reading of Sony Labou Tansi's Private Ancestral Shrine', *Research in African Literatures*, 31.3 (2000), 39–68 http://www.jstor.com/stable/3820872 [accessed 10 June 2020]
Clement, Piet, 'Rural Development in the Belgian Congo: The Late-colonial "Indigenous Peasantry" Programme and its Implementation in the Equateur District (1950s)', *Bulletin des Séances de l'Académie Royale des Sciences d'Outre-mer*, 60.2 (2014), 251–86.
Clifford, James, 'Museums as Contact Zones', in *Routes: Travel and Translation in the Late Twentieth Century*, ed. by James Clifford (Cambridge, MA: Harvard University Press, 1997).
Cole, Teju, 'The White Saviour Industrial Complex' <https://www.theatlantic.com/international/archive/2012/03/the-white-savior-industrial-complex/254843/> [accessed 5 January 2021]
Commémoration des Congolais morts à Tervuren, en marge de l'ouverture de l'AfricaMuseum – Le Soir [accessed 7 December 2021]
Comptes rendus de la Semaine Agricole 1947: Yangambi, Congo (Brussels: Institut national pour l'étude agronomique du Congo belge, 1947).
Congo as Fiction: Art Worlds between Past and Present, CONGO AS FICTION – Museum RietbergC'C [accessed on 3 December 2021]
Conquergood, Dwight, 'Performance Studies – Interventions and Radical Research', *The Drama Review* 46.2 (2002), 145–56.
Conrad, Joseph, *Heart of Darkness*, ed. by Robert Kimbrough, 3rd edn (London: W. W. Norton, 1988).
Conteh-Morgan, John, *Theatre and Drama in Francophone Africa: A Critical Introduction* (Cambridge: Cambridge University Press, 1994).
Conway, Martin, *The Sorrows of Belgium: Liberation and Political Reconstruction, 1944–1947* (Oxford: Oxford University Press, 2012).
Cookey, S. J. S., *Britain and the Congo Question, 1885–1913* (London: Longmans, 1968).
Cooper, Frederick, *Africa since 1940: The Past of the Present* (Cambridge: Cambridge University Press, 2002).
Cornélus, Henri, *Kufa* (Brussels: Renaissance du Livre, 1954).
Cornet, Joseph-Aurélien, Rémi de Cnodder, Ivan Dierickx, and Wim Toebosch (eds.), *60 ans de peinture au Zaïre* (Brussels: Éditions d'Arts Associés, 1989).
Coupez, André, *Grammaire rwanda simplifiée: méthode rwanda à l'usage des Européens* (Usumbura: Éditions du service de l'information, 1961).
Couttenier, Maarten, *Congo tentoongesteld: een geschiedenis van de Belgische antropologie en het museum van Tervuren (1882–1925)* (Leuven: Acco, 2005).
——— and Sammy Baloji, 'The Charles Lemaire Expedition Revisited: Sammy Baloji as a Portraitist of Present Humans in Congo Far West', *African Arts*, 41.1 (Spring 2014), 66–81.
Craig, Jill, 'Relations Between Burundi, Rwanda Deteriorating', *VOA*, 14 October 2015 <https://www.voanews.com/africa/relations-between-burundi-rwanda-deteriorating> [accessed 03 March 2021]
Crichton, Michael, *Congo* (London: Arrow Books Ltd., 1980).
Cros, Marie-France, 'Comment la situation au Burundi, un des trois pays les plus pauvres du monde, s'est encore aggravée depuis 2015', *La Libre Belgique*, 20 May 2020 <https://www.lalibre.be/international/afrique/comment-la-situation-au-burundi-un-des-trois-pays-les-plus-pauvres-du-monde-s-est-encore-aggravee-depuis-2015-5ec3ffbad8ad581c5400d923> [accessed 03 March 2021]
———, 'Burundi: pourquoi le nouveau président n'amènera que peu de changements?', *La Libre Belgique*, 18 June 2020 <https://www.lalibre.be/international/afrique/burundi-pourquoi-le-nouveau-president-n-amenera-que-peu-de-changements-5eeb74ca7b50a66a598c7db9> [accessed 03 March 2021]
Cruyen, Alphonse, 'Le problème des enfants mulâtres au Congo', in *Congrès international pour l'Étude des Problèmes résultant du Mélange des Races (11–12 octobre 1935)* (Brussels, Belgium), pp. 29–44.
Daley, Patricia, *Gender and Genocide in Burundi: The Search for Spaces of Peace in the Great Lakes Region* (Oxford: James Currey, 2007).

―――― and Rowan Popplewell, 'The Appeal of Third Termism and Militarism in Burundi', *Review of African Political Economy*, 43.150 (2016), 648–57.

Dallaire, Roméo, *Shake Hands with the Devil: The Failure of Humanity in Rwanda* (Toronto: Random House Canada, 2002).

Dan, Bernard, *Le Garçon du Rwanda* (La Tour d'Aigues: L'Aube, 2014).

Dauge-Roth, Alexandre, *Writing and Filming the Genocide of the Tutsis in Rwanda: Disremembering and remembering traumatic history* (Lanham: Lexington, 2010).

Davies, William, 'Destination Unknown', *London Review of Books*, 9 June 2022, 15–18.

Dawkins, H. C., 'INEAC in the "Forêt Dense", Impressions of some High-Forest Research in the Congo', *Empire Forestry Review*, 34.1 (1955), 55–60.

Debels, Thierry, *Kroongeheimen: Waarheid en leugens over het Belgisch koningshuis* (Manteau: Antwerpen, 2013).

De Boeck, Filip, 'The Apocalyptic Interlude: Revealing Death in Kinshasa', *African Studies Review*, 48.2 (2005), 11–32 <http://doi.org/10.1353/arw.2005.0051>

――――, '"Poverty" and the Politics of Syncopation: Urban Examples from Kinshasa (DR Congo)', *Current Anthropology*, 56.11 (2015), 146–58.

――――, '"Congoville-Putuville": Mirroring Models and Beyond in the (Post) Colonial World', in *Contemporay Artists Tracing Colonial Tracks: Congoville*, ed. by Pieter Boons and Sandrine Collard (Leuven: Leuven University Press, 2021), pp. 64–81.

――――, '"Illuminating the Hole": Kinshasa's Makeovers Between Dream and Reality' [n.d.], https://humanitiesfutures.org/papers/illuminating-the-hole-kinshasas-makeovers-between-dream-and-reality [accessed 6 January 2022]

――――and Marie-Françoise Plissart, *Kinshasa: Tales from the Invisible City* (Leuven: Leuven University Press, 2014 [2004]).

――――, Koen Van Synghel, and Vincent Lombume Kalimasi, *De gesproken stad: gesprekken over Kinshasa* (Kessel-Lo: Literarte, 2005).

―――― and Sammy Baloji, *Suturing the City: Living Together in Congo's Urban Worlds* (London: Autograph ABP, 2016).

―――― and Sammy Baloji, 'Positing the Polis: Topography as a Way to De-centre Urban Thinking', *Urbanisation*, 2.2 (2017), 1–13.

Declercq, Robrecht, Duncan Money, and Hans Otto Frøland (eds), *Born with a Copper Spoon: a Global History of Copper, 1830-1980* (Vancouver: University of British Columbia Press, 2022).

De Clercq, August (Mgr), *La Grammaire de la langue des bena Lulua* (Brussels: Polleunis et Centerick, Imprimeries, 1897).

De Coene, Pieter, Margot Luyckfasseel and Gillian Mathys 'Voices from Exile: The Mpadist Mission des Noirs in Oshwe's Prison Camps in the Belgian Congo (1940–1960)' (2022) *International Journal of African Historical Studies*, 55.1 (2022), 89-114.

De Groof, Matthias, 'CONGOCENE. Congolese Cinema in / on / against the Anthropocene', in *Rethinking the Past for a New Future of Conviviality: Opposing Colonialism, Anti-Semitism, Turbo-Nationalism*, ed. by Marina Gržinić and Sophie Uitz (Cambridge: Cambridge Scholars Publishing. 2019), pp. 87–109.

――――, 'Review: Kapita', *Ultradogme*, 13 May 2021 < https://ultradogme.com/2021/05/13/kapita/> [accessed 17 May 2021]

―――― (ed.), *Lumumba in the Arts* (Leuven: Leuven University Press, 2020).

――――and Alessandro Jedlowski, 'Congolese Cinema Today: Memories of the Present in Kinshasa's New Wave Cinema (2008–2018)', *Francofonia*, 76 (2019), special issue 'Les enjeux de la mémoire dans la littérature et les arts contemporains de la République démocratique du Congo', ed. by Éloïse Brezault, 117–35.

De Herdt, Tom and Kristof Titeca, 'Governance with Empty Pockets: The Education Sector in the Democratic Republic of the Congo', *Development and Change*, 47.3 (2016), 472–49.

Deleuze, Gilles and Félix Guattari, *Kafka. Pour une littérature mineure* (Paris: Minuit, 1975).

Delmas, Léon, *Généalogie de la noblesse (les Batutsi) du Ruanda* (Kabgayi: Vicariat Apostolique du Ruanda, 1950).

Delvaux, Béatrice, 'Colonisation du Congo: enfin ce geste si nécessaire, qui grandit le Roi et son pays', *Le Soir*, 30 June 2020.

Demart, Sarah, 'Histoire orale à Matonge (Bruxelles): un miroir postcolonial', *Revue Européenne des Migrations Internationales*, 29.1 (2013), 133–55 <https://doi.org/10.4000/remi.6323>

――――, 'Congolese Migration to Belgium and Postcolonial Perspectives', *African Diaspora*, 6.1 (2013), 1–20.

——, 'Resisting Extraction Politics: Afro-Belgian Claims, Women's Activism, and the Royal Museum for Central Africa', in *Across Anthropology: Troubling Colonial Legacies, Museums, and the Curatorial*, ed. by Margareta von Oswald and Jonas Tinius (Leuven: Leuven University Press, 2020), pp. 143–72.

——,Marie Godin, Adam Ilke, and Bruno Schoumaker, *Des Citoyens aux racines africaines. Un portrait des Belgo-Congolais, Belgo-Rwandais et Belgo-Burundais* (Brussels: Fondation Roi Baudouin, 2017).

De Meulder, Bruno, *De Kampen Van Kongo: Arbeid, Kapitaal, en Rasveredeling in de Koloniale Planning* (Amsterdam: Meulenhoff; Antwerp: Kritak, 1996).

Demissie, Fassil, *Postcolonial African Cities: Imperial Legacies and Postcolonial Predicament* (London: Routledge, 2013).

De Mul, Sarah, 'The Congo as Topos of Dystopic Transgression in Fin-de-Siècle Literature', *Tydskrif vir Letterkunde*, 46.1 (2009), 95–108.

De Nys-Ketels, Simon, Johan Lagae, Kristien Geenen, Luce Beeckmans, and Trésor Lumfuankenda Bungiena, 'Spacial Governmentality and Everyday Hospital Life in Colonial and Postcolonial DR-Congo', in *Neocolonialism and Built Heritage: Echoes of Empire in Africa, Asia, and Europe*, ed. by Daniel E. Coslett (London: Routledge, 2020), pp. 147–67.

'Der Anti-Disney', *Der Spiegel*, 24 March 1959, pp. 60–62.

De Roo, Bas, 'L'État indépendant du Congo, une machine à piller au service d'un Léopold II impitoyable?', *Le Congo Colonial: une histoire en questions*, ed. by Idesbald Goddeeris, Amandine Lauro, and Guy Vanthemsche (Brussels: Renaissance du Livre, 2020), pp. 33–49.

Derrida, Jacques, *Mal d'archive* (Paris: Galilée, 1995).

——, 'Archive Fever in South Africa', in *Refiguring the Archive*, ed. by Carolyn Hamilton et al. (Cape Town: David Philip Publishers; Dordrecht: Kluwer Academic Publishers, 2002), pp. 38–80.

Descola, Philippe, *L'Écologie des autres: l'anthropologie et la question de la nature* (Versailles: Quæ, 2011).

——, *Par-delà nature et culture* (Paris: Gallimard, 2015).

——, *Une écologie des relations* (Paris: CNRS, 2019).

—— and Pierre Charbonnier, *La Composition des mondes: entretiens avec Pierre Charbonnier* (Paris: Flammarion, 2014).

Deslaurier, Christine, 'Rwagasore for ever? Des usages contemporains d'un héros consensuel au Burundi', *Vingtième Siècle. Revue d'histoire*, 118.2 (2013), 15–30.

De Waarheidscommissie, Aktion Zoo Humain website, 2013 <https://www.actionzoohumain.be/nl/productie/de-waarheidscommissie> [accessed 22 January 2021]

De Wildeman, Emile, *Les Plantes tropicales de grande culture* (Brussels: Maison d'édition Alfred Castaigne, 1908).

De Witte, Ludo, *De moord op Lumumba* (Kessel-Lo: Van Halewyck, 1999).

——, *The Assassination of Lumumba*, trans. by Ann Wright and Renée Fenby (London: Verso, 2001).

——, *Moord in Burundi: België en de liquidatie van premier Louis Rwagasore* (Antwerp: EPO, 2021).

Diagne, Souleymane Bachir, 'Quand traduire est un acte de décolonisation' < https://www.youtube.com/watch?v=t0EZmfne_fY>[accessed 15 September 2021]

—— and Jean-Loup Amselle, *En quête d'Afrique(s). Universalisme et pensée décoloniale* (Paris: Albin Michel, 2018).

Diop, Cheikh Anta, *Nations nègres et culture: De l'antiquité nègre égyptienne aux problèmes culturels de l'Afrique noire d'aujourd'hui* (Paris: Présence africaine, 1955).

Djungu-Simba, Charles K., 'La figure de Patrice Lumumba dans les lettres du Congo-Zaïre: quelques observations', in *Patrice Lumumba entre Dieu et diable: Un héros africain dans ses images*, ed. by Pierre Halen and János Riesz (Paris: L'Harmattan, 1997), pp. 81–94.

Dongola, Emmanuel, *Johnny chien méchant* (Paris: Serpent à Plumes, 2003).

Donovan, Stephen, 'Congo Utopia', *English Studies in Africa*, 59.1 (2016), 63–75.

—— (ed.), *English Studies in Africa*, special issue titled 'Europe Made in Africa: The Congo Free State in Literature and Culture, 1885–1920', 59.1 (2016), 1–86.

Douglas, Mary, *Purity and Danger: An Analysis of Concepts of Pollution and Taboo* (London: Routledge, 1966).

Draper, Christopher, and John Lawson-Reay, *Scandal at Congo House: William Hughes and the African Institute, Colwyn Bay* (Llanwrst: Gwasg Carreg Gwelch, 2012).

Driver, Felix, *Geography Militant: Cultures of Exploration and Empire* (Oxford: Blackwell, 2001).

Drouère, Mélanie, 'An Interview with Faustin Linyekula', 2019 <https://www.theatregaronne.com/dossier/congo> [accessed 14 January 2022]

Drum, Henri, *Luéji ya Kondé* (Brussels: Éditions de Belgique, 1932).

Dubuisson, Martine, 'Une Commission parlementaire sur le passé colonial belge dès la rentrée', *Le Soir*, 18 June 2020 <https://www.lesoir.be/art/d-20200617-GGMA5C?referer=%2Farchives%2Frecherche%3F-

datefilter%3Dlastyear%26sort%3Ddate%2Bdesc%26start%3D40%26word%3Dburund> [accessed 3 February 2021]

Duchesne, Albert, *A la recherche d'une Colonie belge: Le Consul Blondeel en Abyssinie (1840-1842) - Contribution à l'Histoire précoloniale de la Belgique* (Brussels: Institut Royal Colonial Belge, 1953).

Ducournau, Claire, *La Fabrique des classiques africains. Écrivains d'Afrique subsaharienne francophone* (Paris: CNRS Éditions, 2017).

Duggan, Jo-Anne, 'From memory to archive', editorial of *Archival Platform*, 26 July 2011 <www.apc.uct.ac.za/apc/projects/archival_platform/memory-archive > [accessed 18 August 2011]

Duncan, Geo, *Blancs et Noirs* (Rixensart: Éditions de Belgique, 1949).

Dunn, Kevin, *Imagining the Congo: The International Relations of Identity* (New York: Palgrave Macmillan, 2003).

Durmarque, Didier, 'Le Nazisme est-il un humanisme?' *Philosophie de la Shoah*, 2014 <http://didier.durmarque.com/2014/07/le-nazisme-est-il-un-humanisme/> [accessed 14 November 2021]

Eaton, David, 'Diagnosing the Crisis in the Republic of Congo', *Africa: Journal of the International African Institute*, 76.1 (2006) <https://www.jstor.org/stable/40026156> [accessed 28 October 2018], 44–69.

'Ecrire pour le Rwanda', *Intersections*, 2 (2014).

Eco, Umberto, *The Open Work*, trans. Anna Cancogni (Cambridge, Mass., Harvard University Press, 1989).

Eisenstein, Sergei, *Eisenstein on Disney*, ed. by Jay Leyda, trans. by Alan Y. Upchurch (Calcutta: Seagull Books, 1986).

'Élections présidentielles au Burundi: le candidat du pouvoir élu', 25 May 2020 <https://plus.lesoir.be/302888/article/2020-05-25/elections-presidentielles-au-burundi-le-candidat-du-pouvoir-elu?referer=%2Farchives%2Frecherche%3Fdatefilter%3Dlastyear%26sort%3Ddate%2Bdesc%26start%3D0%26word%3Dnkurunziza%22> [accessed 03 March 2021]

Elias, Nicole M., Sean McCandless, and Rashmi Chordiya, 'Administrative Decision-Making Amid Competing Public Sector Values: Confederate Statue Removal in Baltimore, Maryland', *Journal of Public Affairs Education*, 25.3 (2019), 412–22.

Entman, Robert, 'Framing: Towards clarification of a Fractured Paradigm', *Journal of Communication*, 43.4 (1993), 51–58.

Enwezor, Okwui, 'Between Localism and Worldliness', *Art Journal* 57.4 (1998), 29–36.

——— and Chika Okeke-Agulu, 'Situating Contemporary African Art: Introduction', in *Contemporary African Art since 1980*, ed. by Okwui Enwezor and Chika Okeke-Agulu (Bologna: Damiani, 2009), pp. 8–17.

Ernst, Jean-Luc, 'La Compagnie des Chemins de Fer du Congo Supérieur aux Grands Lacs Africains ou CFL: Aperçu Historique', https://www.stanleyville.be/cfl.html [accessed 14 May 2021]

Esmeralda, Maria and Philippe De Gryse, *Mijn vader, Leopold III* (Tielt: Lannoo, 2001).

Etambala, Mathieu Zana Aziza, 'Congolese Children at the Congo House in Colwyn Bay (North Wales, Great-Britain), at the End of the 19th Century', *Afrika Focus*, 3.3–4 (1987), 237–85.

———, *Des écoliers congolais en Belgique 1888–1900: Une page d'histoire oubliée* (Paris: Éditions L'Harmattan, 2011)

———, *Congo veroverd, bezet, gekoloniseerd 1876–1914* (Gorredijk: Sterck & De Vreese, 2020).

Evans, Neil and Ivor Wynne Jones, 'Wales and Africa: William Hughes and the Congo Institute', in *A Tolerant Nation? Revisiting Ethnic Diversity in a Devolved Wales*, ed. by Charlotte Williams, Neil Evans, and Paul O'Leary, revised edition (Cardiff: University of Wales Press, 2015), pp. 106–27.

Ewans, Martin, *European Atrocity, African Catastrophe: Leopold II, the Congo Free State and its Aftermath* (London: Routledge, 2002).

———, Belgium and the Colonial Experience', *Journal of Contemporary European Studies*, 11.2 (2003), 167–80.

'Exhibits A, B, and C' <https://www.thirdworldbunfight.co.za/productions/exhibit-a-b-and-c.htmln> [accessed 10 August 2020]

Expansion Belge/Belgische Expansie 1831–1865 (Brussels: Académie Royale des Sciences d'Outre-Mer/Koninklijke Academie voor Overzeese Wetenschappen, 1965).

Fabian, Johannes, *Time and the Other: How Anthropology Makes its Object* (New York: Columbia University Press, 1983).

———, *Language and Colonial Power: The Appropriation of Swahili in the Former Belgian Congo 1880–1938*, foreword by Edward Said (Berkeley; Los Angeles; Oxford: University of California Press, 1986).

———, *Remembering the Present: Painting and Popular History in Zaire* (Berkeley: University of California Press, 1996).

———, 'On Recognizing Things: The "Ethnic Artefact" and the "Ethnographic Object"', *L'Homme*, 70 (2004), 47–60.

——, 'What is African Popular Art Doing in a Museum?', keynote speech at symposium 'Popular Imagination: Fiction with a Message', Amsterdam: Tropenmuseum, 22 September 2011.
Faïk-Nzuji, Clémentine M., *La Fiancée à vendre et treize autres nouvelles* (Saint-Maur-des-Fossés: Sépia/RFI/ACCT, 1993).
——, *Tu le leur diras. Le récit véridique d'une famille congolaise au cœur de l'histoire de son pays, 1890-2000* (Braine-l'Alleud: Alice Éditions, 2005).
Falisse, Jean-Benoît and Hugues Nkengurutse, 'From FM Radio Stations to Internet 2.0 Overnight: Information, Participation and Social Media in Post-Failed Coup Burundi', in *Social Media and Politics in Africa: Democracy, Censorship and Security*, ed. by Maggie Dwyer and Thomas Molony (London: Zed, 2019), pp. 171-94.
Fanon, Frantz, *Peau noire, masques blancs* (Paris: Seuil, 1995 [1952]).
——, *Black Skin, White Masks*, trans. by Charles Lam Markmann (London: Pluto Press, 1986).
——, *Les Damnés de la terre*, introduction by Gérard Chaliand, preface by Jean-Paul Sartre (Paris: Gallimard, 1991 [1961]).
——, *Les Damnés de la terre* (Paris: La Découverte, 2002 [1961]).
Farrant, Leda, *Tippu Tip and the East African Slave Trade* (London: Hamish Hamilton, 1975).
Fay, Jennifer, *Inhospitable World: Cinema in the Time of the Anthropocene* (Oxford: Oxford University Press, 2018).
Faye, Gaël, *Petit pays* (Paris: Éditions Grasset, 2016).
——, *Small Country*, trans. by Sarah Ardizzone (London: Hogarth, 2016).
Ferdinand, Malcom, *Une écologie décoloniale: penser l'écologie depuis le monde caribéen* (Paris: Éditions du Seuil, 2019).
Fleishman, Mark, 'Physical Images in the South African Theatre', *South African Theatre Journal*, 11.1/2 (1997), 199-214.
Flockemann, Miki, 'Facing the Stranger in the Mirror: Staged complicities in Recent South African Performances', *South African Theatre Journal*, 25.2 (2011), 129-41.
Fontenaille-N'Diaye, Elise, *Blue Book* (Paris: Calman-Lévy, 2015).
Forsyth, Alison and Chris Megson (eds.), *Get Real: Documentary Theatre Past and Present* (Basingstoke; New York: Palgrave Macmillan, 2009).
Fortin, Elizabeth, 'Reforming Land Rights: The World Bank and the Globalization of Agriculture', *Social & Legal Studies*, 14.2 (2005), 147-77.
Foucault, Michel, *Surveiller et punir: naissance de la prison* (Paris: Gallimard, 1975).
Fraiture, Pierre-Philippe, *Le Congo belge et son récit à la veille des indépendances. Sous l'empire du royaume* (Paris: Éditions L'Harmattan, 2003).
——, *La Mesure de l'autre. Afrique subsaharienne et roman ethnographique de Belgique et de France (1918-1940)* (Paris: Éditions Honoré Champion, 2007).
——, 'Modernity and the Belgian Congo', *Tydskrif vir Letterkunde*, 46.1 (2009), 43-57.
——, *VY Mudimbe: Undisciplined Africanism* (Liverpool: Liverpool University Press, 2013).
——, *Past Imperfect. Time and African Decolonization, 1945-1960* (Liverpool: Liverpool University Press, 2021).
Frank, Sybille and Mirjana Ristic, 'Urban Fallism', *City: Analysis of Urban Change, Theory, Action*, 24.3/4 (2020), 552-64.
Franke, Anselm, *Animism* (Berlin: Sternberg Press, 2010).
Frère, Marie-Soleil, 'Silencing the Voice of the Voiceless: The Destruction of the Independent Broadcasting Sector in Burundi', *African Journalism Studies*, 37.1 (2016), 137-46.
Fruchon-Toussaint, Catherine, 'Petit pays n'est absolument pas mon histoire', interview with Gaël Faye, RFI, 8 September 2016, https://www.rfi.fr/fr/culture/20160908-gael-faye-petit-pays-absolument-pas-histoire [accessed 8 August 2020]
Fryer, Peter, *Staying Power: The History of Black People in Britain* (London: Pluto Press, 1984).
Fyfe, Alexander, 'Infrastructure and the Valences of the Literary in Fiston Mwanza Mujila's *Tram 83*, *Critique: Studies in Contemporary Fiction* (2021), https://doi.org/10.1080/00111619.2021.1875975 [accessed 7 January 2022].
Gahigi, Gérard, *Kagame: Le fond d'une vie et le cheminement d'une pensée de l'homme libre et serein* (Butare: unpublished, 1976).
Gahungu, Céline, 'Le Kongo de Sony Labou Tansi', *Continents manuscrits*, 4 (2015) <http://doi.org/10.4000/coma.523>
——, 'Poétique du paysage dans *L'Anté-peuple* et *La Vie et demie* de Sony Labou Tansi', *Études littéraires africaines*, 39 (2015), 79-89 <https://doi.org/10.7202/1033133ar>

———, *Sony Labou Tansi: naissance d'un écrivain* (Paris: CNRS Éditions, 2019).
———, 'Débords – Sinzo Aanza, *Continents Manuscrits*, 10 (2018), 1–6.
Gann, Lewis and Peter Duignan, *The Rulers of Belgian Africa, 1884–1914* (Princeton: Princeton University Press, 1979).
Garnier, Xavier, 'Les littératures en langues africaines ou l'inconscient des théories postcoloniales', *Neohelicon*, 35.2 (2008), 87–99.
———, *The Swahili Novel: Challenging the Idea of 'Minor Literature'*, trans. by Rémi Tchokothe and Armand and Frances Kennett (Woodbridge, Suffolk: Boydell & Brewer; James Currey, 2013).
———, 'Writing the Subsoil in the Contemporary Congolese Novel', *Journal of World Literature*, 6 (2021), special issue 'Contemporary Congolese Literature as World Literature', ed. by Silvia Riva and Julien Jeusette, 133–47.
Garrone, Maria, Hannah Pieters, and Johan Swinnen, 'From Pralines to Multinationals: The Economic History of Belgian Chocolate', in *The Economics of Chocolate*, ed. by Mara P. Squicciarini and Johan Swinnen (Oxford: Oxford University Press, 2016), pp. 88–115.
Gasana, Anastase and Nkiko, Munyarugerero, 'Alexis Kagame et la problématique du langage: le cas des langues bantu', in *Alexis Kagame, L'homme et son œuvre*, ed. by Joseph Nsengimana (Kigali: Ministère de l'enseignement supérieur et de la recherche scientifique, 1987), pp. 143–48.
Gatwa, Tharcisse, *The Churches and Ethnic Ideology in the Rwandan Crises 1900–1994* (Milton Keynes: Regnum Books, 2005).
Gerits, Frank, '"Défendre l'œuvre que nous réalisons en Afrique": Belgian Public Diplomacy and the Global Cold War (1945-1966)', *Dutch Crossing: Journal of Low Countries Studies* ('The Cold War in the Benelux (1945-1991): Current Trends, New Perspectives'), 40.1 (2016), 68-80.
Frederick Cooper, *Africa since 1940: The Past of the Present* (Cambridge: Cambridge University Press, 2002), pp. 159–60.
Gevers, Marie, *Des Mille Collines aux Neuf Volcans (Ruanda)*, preface by Valentin-Yves Mudimbe (Brussels: AML Éditions, 2002).
Gewald, Jan-Bart, 'More than Red Rubber and Figures Alone: A Critical Appraisal of the Memory of the Congo Exhibition at the Royal Museum for Central Africa, Tervuren, Belgium', *The International Journal of African Historical Studies*, 39.3 (2006), 471–86.
'"Ghent, 1913–2013", the century of Progress' <http://1913-2013.gent.be/en/ghent-wants-have-largest-worldfair> [accessed 22 July 2014]
Giddens, Anthony, *The Consequences of Modernity* (Cambridge: Polity Press, 1990).
Gillet, Florence, 'Congo rêvé? Congo détruit... Les anciens coloniaux belges aux prises avec une société en repentir. Enquête sur la face émergée d'une mémoire', *Cahiers d'histoire du temps présent*, 19 (2008), 79–133.
Gishoma, Chantal, 'Une facette méconnue d'Alexis Kagame: un poète auto-traducteur', *Etudes littéraires Africaines* ('La question de la poésie en Afrique aujourd'hui'), 24 (2007), 42–47.
Gissibl, Bernhard, *The Nature of German Imperialism: Conservation and the Politics of Wildlife in Colonial East Africa* (New York: Berghahn Books, 2016).
Glissant, Édouard, *Le Discours antillais* (Paris: Seuil, 1981).
G. M. B., 'The Agricultural Development of the Belgian Congo', *The World Today*, 6.8 (1950), 348–54.
Goddeeris, Idesbald and Sindani E. Kiangu, 'Congomania in Academia: Recent Historical Research on the Belgian Colonial Past', *BMGN-LCHR*, 126.4 (2011), 54–74.
———, 'Postcolonial Belgium: The Memory of the Congo', *Interventions: International Journal of Postcolonial Studies*, 17.3 (2015), 434–51.
———, 'Colonial Streets and Statues: Postcolonial Belgium in the Public Space', *Postcolonial Studies*, 18.4 (2015), 397–409.
Godfroid, Marcel-Sylvain, *Le Bureau des reptiles* (Neufchâteau: Weyrich, 2013).
Gondola, Charles Didier, *Villes miroirs: migrations et identités urbaines à Kinshasa et Brazzaville, 1930–1970* (Paris: L'Harmattan, 1996).
———, *The History of Congo* (Westport: Greenwood Press, 2003).
———, *Tropical Cowboys: Westerns, Violence, and Masculinity in Kinshasa* (Bloomington: Indiana University Press, 2016).
———, *Matswa vivant: anticolonialisme et citoyenneté en Afrique-Équatoriale française* (Paris: Éditions de la Sorbonne) <https://doi.org/10.4000/books.psorbonne.82720>
Goris, Gie, 'Congolees kunstenaar neemt KVS over' *Mo**, 22 April 2008, <https://www.mo.be/artikel/congolees-kunstenaar-neemt-kvs-over> [accessed 6 January 2022]
Gossiaux, Axel Mudahemuka C., 'L'éducation permanente en lutte contre le racisme et la colonialité en Belgique francophone?', Étude, *FUCID* (2020), 1–32.

Green, Jeffrey, *Black Edwardians: Black Edwardians: Black People in Britain 1901–1914* (London: Routledge, 1998).

——, 'Edwardian Britain's Forest Pygmies', *History Today*, 45.8 (1995) <https://www.historytoday.com/archive/edwardian-britains-forest-pygmies> [accessed 18 December 2020]

Grosfoguel, Ramón, 'Decolonizing Post-Colonial Studies and Paradigms of Political-Economy: Transmodernity, Decolonial Thinking, and Global Coloniality', *Transmodernity: Journal of Peripheral Cultural Production of the Luso-Hispanic World*, 1.1 (2011) <https://doi.org/10.5070/T411000004>

Groupe de recherche Achac – Colonisation, immigration, post-colonialisme, 'Zoos Humains – Exhibitions. L'invention du sauvage', 2011 <https://www.achac.com/zoos-humains/exhibition-linvention-du-sauvage-2/> [accessed 07 January 2021]

Gryseels, Guido, 'Towards the Renewal and the Renovation of the Royal Museum for Central Africa', Paper Presented at the Africa-Atlanta 2014 Conference <https://leading-edge.iac.gatech.edu/aaproceedings/towards-the-renewal-and-the-renovation-of-the-royal-museum-for-central-africa/> [accessed 20 April 2021]

——, Gabrielle Landry, and Koeki Claessens, 'Integrating the Past: Transformation and Renovation of the Royal Museum for Central Africa, Tervuren, Belgium', *European Review*, 13.4 (2005), 637–47.

Guha, Ramachandra, 'Radical American Environmentalism and Wilderness Preservation: A Third World Critique', *Environmental Ethics*, 11.1 (1989), 71–83.

Guyer, Nanina and Michaela Oberhofer (eds.), *Congo as Fiction: Art Worlds Between Past and Present* (Zurich: Museum Rietberg; Verlag Sheidegger & Spiess, 2020).

Haddock, Fran, 'Stories from the Frontline – Episode 3: Fossil Fuel Free Virunga', *Curious Earth*, July 2021 <https://curious.earth/blog/stories-from-the-frontline-episode-3-fossil-fuel-free-virunga/> [accessed 20 January 2022]

Hadzelek, Aleksandra, 'Spain's "Pact of Silence" and the Removal of Franco's Statues', in *Past Law, Present Histories*, ed. by Diane Kirkby (Canberra: Australian National University E-Press, 2012), pp. 153–76.

Halen, Pierre, *Le Petit Belge avait vu grand. Une littérature coloniale* (Brussels: Éditions Labor, 1993).

——, 'Paysage exotique et paysage colonial', in *Le Paysage et ses grilles*, ed. by Françoise Chenet (Paris-Montréal: L'Harmattan, 1996), pp. 51–70.

——, 'De l'inusable imagerie du Cœur des ténèbres et de sa résurgence dans quelques représentations du génocide au Rwanda', in *Violences postcoloniales: Représentations littéraires et perceptions médiatiques*, ed. by Isaac Bazié and Hans-Jürgen Lüsebrink (Berlin: Lit Verlag, 2011), pp. 65–87.

—— and János Riesz (eds.), 'Images de l'Afrique et du Congo/Zaïre dans les lettres françaises de Belgique et alentour', *Textyles* [Hors Série, 1] (1993) <https://doi.org/10.4000/textyles.2184>

——and János Riesz (eds.), *Patrice Lumumba entre dieu et diable: un héros africain dans ses images* (Paris: L'Harmattan, 1997).

Hall, Stuart, 'Black Diaspora Artists in Britain: Three "Moments" in Postwar History', *History Workshop Journal*, 61.1 (2006), 1–24.

Harms, Robert, 'The World Abir Made: The Margina-Lopori Basin, 1885–1903', *African Economic History*, 12 (1983), 125–39.

Harrison, Olivia, *Transcolonial Maghreb: Imagining Palestine in the Era of Decolonization* (Stanford: Stanford University Press, 2015).

Harroy, Jean-Paul, *Rwanda: de la féodalité à la démocratie 1955–1962. Souvenirs d'un compagnon de la marche du Rwanda vers la démocratie et l'indépendance* (Brussels: Hayez, 1984).

——, 'Kagame Alexis', *Bulletin de l'ARSOM*, 28 (1982), 66–78.

Haskins, Victoria K. and Claire Lowrie (eds.), *Colonization and Domestic Service: Historical and Contemporary Perspectives* (New York: Routledge, 2015).

Hassett, Dónal, 'Acknowledging or Occluding "The System of Violence"? The Representation of Colonial Pasts and Presents in Belgium's AfricaMuseum', *Journal of Genocide Research*, 22.1 (2020), 26–45.

Hayman, Rachel, 'Abandoned Orphan, Wayward Child: the United Kingdom and Belgium in Rwanda since 1994', *Journal of Eastern African Studies*, 4.3 (2010), 341–60.

Hayner, Priscilla, 'Fifteen Truth Commissions – 1974 to 1994: A comparative study', *Human Rights Quarterly*, 16 (1994), 597–655.

——, 'Commissioning the Truth: further research questions', *Third World Quarterly*, 17.1 (1996), 19–29.

Headrick, Daniel R., 'Sleeping Sickness Epidemics and Colonial Responses in East and Central Africa, 1900–1940', *PLoS Neglected Tropical Diseases*, 8.4 (2014) <https://journals.plos.org/plosntds/article?id=10.1371/journal.pntd.0002772> [accessed 22 June 2021]

Hendriks, Thomas, 'Queer Complicity in the Belgian Congo: Autobiography and Racial Fetishism in Jef Geeraerts' (Post)Colonial Novels', *Research in African Literatures*, 45.1 (2014), 63–84.

Henriet, Benoît, '"Elusive Natives": Escaping Colonial Control in the Leverville Oil Palm Concession, Belgian Congo, 1923 –1941', *Canadian Journal of African Studies / Revue canadienne des études africaines*, 49.2 (2015), 339–61.

——, *Colonial Impotence: Virtue and Violence in a Congolese Concession (1911–1940)* (Berlin: De Gruyter, 2021).

Henry, Élise, 'Le *Mouvement géographique*, entre géographie et propagande coloniale', *Belgeo*, 1 (2008), 27–46.

Heremans, Roger, *Introduction à l'Histoire du Rwanda* (Kigali: Editions Rwandaises, 1973).

Herz, Manuel, Ingrid Schröder, and Hans Focketyn (eds.), *African Modernism: The Architecture of Independence: Ghana, Senegal, Côte d'Ivoire, Kenya, Zambia* (Zurich: Park Books, 2015).

Higginson, Pim, *Scoring Race: Jazz, Fiction, and Francophone Africa* (Woodbridge, Suffolk: James Currey; Rochester: Boydell & Brewer, 2017).

Hirtt, Nico, *Seront-ils des citoyens critiques? Enquête auprès des élèves de fin d'enseignement secondaire en Belgique francophone et flamande* (Brussels: Appel pour une école démocratique, 2008).

Hitchcott, Nicki, *Rwanda Genocide Stories: Fiction After 1994* (Liverpool: Liverpool University Press, 2017).

——, 'The (Un)believable Truth about Rwanda', *Australian Journal of French Studies*, 56.2 (2019), 199–215.

Hochshild, Adam, *King Leopold's Ghost: a Story of Greed, Terror and Heroism in Colonial Africa* (Boston: Houghton Mifflin, 1998).

Holdsworth, Nadine, *Theatre & Nation* (Basingstoke; New York: Palgrave Macmillan, 2010).

Hoyet, Marie-José, 'Quelques images de Patrice Lumumba dans la littérature du monde noir d'expression française. Un panorama', in *Patrice Lumumba entre Dieu et diable: Un héros africain dans ses images*, ed. by Pierre Halen and János Riesz (Paris: L'Harmattan, 1997), pp. 49–80.

Hron, Madelaine, 'Itsembabwoko "à la française"? – Rwanda, Fiction and the Franco-African Imaginary', *Forum for Modern Language Studies*, 45.2 (2009), 162–75.

Hubo, Bettina, 'Over de wereldwijde crisis en de creuseurs in Kolwezi', 2012, <https://www.bruzz.be/culture/expo/over-de-wereldwijde-crisis-en-de-creuseurs-kolwezi-2012-05-18> [accessed 6 January 2022]

Huggan, Graham, *The Postcolonial Exotic: Marketing the Margins* (London; New York: Routledge, 2001).

[Hughes, William], *Report of the Congo House Training Institute for African Children, Colwyn Bay, North Wales* (Colwyn Bay: H. W. Powlson, 1890).

Hughes, William, *Report of the Congo House Training Institute for African Students, Colwyn Bay, North Wales* (Colwyn Bay: H. W. Powlson, 1891).

——, *Dark Africa and the Way Out; or, A Scheme for Civilizing and Evangelizing the Dark Continent* (London: Sampson Low, Marston, 1892).

——, *Report of the Congo House Training Institute for African Students, Colwyn Bay, N Wales* (Colwyn Bay: Rev R. E. Jones and Bros [1893]).

——, *Annual Report of the British and African Incorporated Association, Otherwise Known as the African Training Institute, Colwyn Bay, North Wales* (Colwyn Bay: African Training Institute, 1909).

——, *Third Visit of the Rev. W. Hughes, Colwyn Bay, to the West Coast of Africa [...]* (Wrexham: Hughes and Son, 1917).

Hurel, Eugène, *Grammaire Kinyarwanda* (Kabgayi: Editions Morales, 1951)

Hutchison, Yvette, *South African Performance and Archives of Memory* (Manchester: Manchester University Press, 2013).

Hunt, Nancy Rose, 'Tintin and the Interruptions of Congolese Comics', in *Images and Empires: Visuality in Colonial and Postcolonial Africa*, ed. by Paul S. Landau and Deborah D. Kaspin (Berkley; Los Angeles; London: University of California Press, 2002), pp. 90–123.

——, 'An Acoustic Register: Rape and Repetition in Congo', in *Imperial Debris: On Ruins and Ruination*, ed. by Ann Laura Stoler (Durham, NC: Duke University Press, 2013), pp. 39–66.

——, 'Espace, temporalité et rêverie: écrire l'histoire des futurs au Congo belge', *Politique africaine*, 135.3 (2014), 115–36 <http://doi.org/10.3917/polaf.135.0115>

——, *A Nervous State: Violence, Remedies, and Reverie in Colonial Congo* (Durham, NC: Duke University Press, 2016).

Ingold, Tim, 'That's Enough about Ethnography!', *Journal of Ethnographic Theory*, 4.1 (2014), 383–95 <https://www.haujournal.org/index.php/hau/article/view/hau4.1.021>

International Crisis Group, 'Soutenir la population burundaise face à la crise économique', Report 264, 31 August 2018 <https://www.crisisgroup.org/fr/africa/central-africa/burundi/264-soutenir-la-population-burundaise-face-la-crise-economique> [accessed 21 June 2021]

Irakoze, David, 'Burundi-élections: la police burundaise menace d'une répression similaire à celle de 2015', *SOS Médias Burundi*, 13 May 2020 <https://www.SOSmediasburundi.org/2020/05/13/burundi-elections-la-police-burundaise-menace-dune-repression-similaire-a-celle-de-2015/> [accessed 3 March 2021]

——, 'Disparition de Nkurunziza: "il part sans que la vérité sur ses crimes soit connue"' (HRW), *SOS Médias*, 10 June 2020 <https://www.SOSmediasburundi.org/2020/06/10/mort-de-nkurunziza-il-part-sans-que-la-verite-sur-ses-crimes-soit-connue-selon-hrw/> [accessed 3 March 2021]

Irambona, Eric, 'Burundi-élections: Agathon Rwasa demande aux Imbonerakure de changer de comportement', *SOS Médias*, 15 May 2020 <https://www.SOSmediasburundi.org/2020/05/15/burundi-elections-agathon-rwasa-demande-aux-imbonerakure-de-changer-de-comportement/> [accessed 3 March 2021]

J. B., 'Bruxelles est la première ville rwandaise hors d'Afrique'. *La Libre.be*, 16 September 2010 <https://www.lalibre.be/regions/bruxelles/bruxelles-est-la-premiere-ville-rwandaise-hors-d-afrique-51b8c435e4b0d-e6db9bd7437> [accessed 22 July 2020]

Jelly-Schapiro, Eli, 'Extractive Modernity at Large: The Contemporary Novel of Primitive Accumulation', *Interventions: International Journal of Postcolonial Studies* (2021), DOI: 10.1080/1369801X.2021.2003221 [accessed 5 January 2022].

Jeurissen, Lissia, *Quand le métis s'appelait mulâtre. Société, droit et pouvoir coloniaux face à la descendance des couples Eurafricains dans l'ancien Congo Belge* (Louvain-La-Neuve: Academia Bruylant, 2003).

Jewsiewicki, Bogumil, 'The Great Depression and the Making of the Colonial Economic System in the Belgian Congo', *African Economic History*, 4 (1977), 153–76.

———, 'Political Consciousness among Peasants in the Belgian Congo', *Review of African Political Economy*, 7–19 (1980), 23–32 <http://doi.org/10.1080/0356248008703438>

——, 'Corps interdits: la représentation christique de Lumumba comme rédempteur du peuple zaïrois', *Cahiers d'Études africaines*, 36.141/142 (1996), 113–42 <www.jstor.org/stable/4392672> [accessed 12 August 2020]

——, 'Popular Painting in Contemporary Katanga: Painters, Audiences, Buyers, and Sociopolitical Contexts', in *A Congo Chronicle: Lumumba in Urban Art*, ed. by Bogumil Jewsiewicki (New York: The Museum for African Art, 1999), pp. 13–27.

——, 'Popular Memories of Patrice Lumumba, in *A Congo Chronicle: Lumumba in Urban Art*, ed. by Bogumil Jewsiewicki (New York: The Museum for African Art, 1999), pp. 59–69.

——, 'This is not a Collection', in *Congo Art Works: Popular Painting*, ed. by Bambi Ceuppens and Sammy Baloji (Brussels: Éditions Racine; Royal Museum for Central Africa, 2016), pp. 19–48.

——, 'Leaving Ruins: Explorations of Present Pasts by Sammy Baloji, Freddy Tsimba and Steve Bandoma', *African Arts*, 49.1 (2016), 6–25.

——, Donatien Dibwe dia Mwembu, and Rosario Giordano (eds.), *Lubumbashi 1910–2010. Mémoire d'une ville industrielle/Ukumbusho wa mukini wa komponi*, preface by V. Y. Mudimbe (Paris: L'Harmattan, 2010).

Joris, Lieve, *Terug naar Kongo* (Leuven: Kritak; Amsterdam: Meulenhoff, 1987).

——, *Het uur van de rebellen* (Amsterdam: Augustus, 2006).

——, *Back to Congo*, trans. by Stacey Knecht (London: Macmillan, 1992).

——, *The Rebel's Hour*, trans. by Liz Waters (London: Atlantic, 2008).

Jules-Rosette, Benedetta, 'Aesthetics and Market Demand: The Structure of the Tourist Art Market in Three African Settings', *African Studies Review*, 29.1 (1986), 41–59.

Kabamba, Maguy, *La Dette coloniale* (Montréal: Humanitas, 1994).

Kabasele Lumbala, François, *Alliances avec le Christ en Afrique. Inculturation des rites religieux au Zaïre* (Athens: Editions historiques S. D. Basilopoulos, 1987).

——, *Ndi muluba* (Louvain-la-Neuve: Éditions Panubula, 2004).

——, 'L'inculturation comme antidote à la violence en Afrique', *Revue des sciences religieuses*, 85.3 (2011), 427–46 <https://journals.openedition.org/rsr/1752>

Kabuya, Ramcy, 'Écritures urbaines lushoises', *Études Littéraires Africaines*, 27 (2009), 63–73.

Kadiebwe Muzembe Nyunyu, *Tshibula tshia mujangi* (Kananga: Ciam-Kasayi, 1998).

Kadima-Nzuji, Mukala, *La Littérature zaïroise de langue française (1945–1960)* (Paris: ACCT; Karthala, 1984).

Kagame, Alexis, *Inganji Kalinga*, vol I (Kabgayi: Éditions Royales, 1943).

——, *Isoko y'amajyambere*, vols I–III (Kabgayi: Éditions Morales, 1949–51).

——, *Le Code des institutions politiques du Rwanda pré-colonial* (Brussels: Institut Royal Colonial Belge, 1952).

——, *Les Organisations socio-familiales de l'Ancien Rwanda* (Brussels: Académie royale des Sciences Coloniales, 1954).

——, *Inganji Kalinga*, vol II (Kabgayi: Editions Royales, 1959).

——, *La langue du Rwanda et du Burundi expliquée aux autochtones* (Kabgayi: Editions Morales, 1960).

——, *Histoire des Armées bovines de l'Ancien Rwanda* (Brussels: Institut royal colonial Belge, 1961).

——, *Les Milices du Rwanda précolonial* (Brussels: Institut royal colonial Belge, 1963).

——, *Le Colonialisme face à la doctrine missionnaire à l'heure de Vatican II* (Butare: unpublished, 1964).

——, *Umulirimbyi wa Nyili-Ibiremwa* (Butare: unpublished, 1966).

——, 'Conscience chrétienne et conscience africaine', *Revue diocésaine: Foi et Culture*, 26 (1969), 23–45.

———, *Un Aperçu panoramique de la culture rwandaise* (Butare, unpublished, 1971).
———, *Réponse au pamphlet boomerang de M. André Coupez* (Butare, unpublished, 1972).
———, 'Une forme de christianisation de notre culture régionale' in *Revue diocésaine: Foi et Culture*, 47 (1977), 37–54.
Kalamo, Michael B. and Hugo Duchesne, *Fossil Free Virunga*, 350.org and MNKF Productions (350.org; MNKF Productions, 2021).
Kalanda, Mabika, *Tabalayi bana betu* (Léopoldville: Concordia, 1963).
Kalulambi Pongo, Martin, *Être luba au XXe siècle. Identité chrétienne et ethnicité au Congo Kinshasa* (Paris: Karthala, 1997).
Kamba, Jean, 'Kinshasa contemporain: Les arts visuels. 1ère partie' (2014) <http://jeankamba.centerblog.net/1-kinshasa-contemporain-un-article-de-jean-kamba> [accessed 6 January 2022]
———, 'Kinshasa: Decolonising Arts Education I. Towards an Open Approach or a Dead Letter?' (2016) <https://www.contemporaryand.com/magazines/towards-an-open-approach-or-a-dead-letter/> [accessed 6 January 2022]
Kamikazi, Joelle, 'Mort de P. Nkurunziza: son épouse se confie lors d'une prière', *SOS Médias*, 13 June 2020 <https://www.SOSmediasburundi.org/2020/06/13/mort-de-p-nkurunziza-son-epouse-se-confie-lors-dune-priere/> [accessed 03 March 2021]
Kaneza, Eloge Willy, 'Le Président Nkurunziza a été emporté par le virus covid-19 (sources concordantes)', *SOS Médias*, 12 June 2020 <https://www.SOSmediasburundi.org/2020/06/12/le-president-nkurunziza-a-ete-emporte-par-le-virus-covid-19-sources-concordantes/> [accessed 03 March 2021]
Karangwa, Camille, *Le Chapelet et la machette: sur les traces du génocide rwandais* (Pretoria: Éditions du jour, 2003).
Karangwa, Jean de Dieu, 'L'Abbé Alexis Kagame: un érudit engagé', *Congo-Meuse* ('Figures et paradoxes de l'Histoire au Burundi, au Congo et au Rwanda', ed. by Marc Quaghebeur), 2 (2002), 401–33.
Kasanda, Albert, 'Les figures de l'autre. Prismes et gestion de la différence en Afrique', in *Dialogue interculturel. Cheminer ensemble vers un autre monde possible*, ed. by Albert Kasanda (Paris: L'Harmattan, 2013), pp. 197–243.
Kasereka Kavwahireri, 'L'authenticité comme cadre de pensée et d'écriture au Congo-Kinshasa entre 1970 et 1982', in *Images, mémoires et savoirs: Une histoire en partage avec Bogumil Koss Jewsiewicki*, ed. by Isidore Ndaywel è Nziem and Elisabeth Mudimbe-Boyi (Paris: Karthala, 2009), pp. 625–48.
Kassim, Sumaya, 'The Museum Will Not Be Decolonised', *Media Diversified*, 15 November 2017 <https://mediadiversified.org/2017/11/15/the-museum-will-not-be-decolonised/> [accessed 04 May 2019]
Katahwa, Nestor Ngoy, *Initiation des Jeunes Hemba: Tradition et Modernité* (Kinshasa: Facultés Catholiques de Kinshasa, 2009).
Kayimahe, Vénuste, *La Chanson de l'aube* (Toulouse: Izuba, 2014).
Kennedy, Jean, *New Currents, Ancient Rivers: Contemporary African Artists in a Generation of Change* (Washington, DC: Smithsonian Institute Press, 1992).
Kenny, Gale and Tisa Wenger, 'Church, State, and "Native Liberty" in the Belgian Congo,' *Comparative Studies in Society and History*, 62.1 (2020), 156–85 <doi: 10.1017/S0010417519000446>
Kent, John, 'Lumumba and the 1960 Congo Crisis: Cold War and the Neo-Colonialism of Belgian Decolonization', in *The Ends of European Colonial Empires: Cases and Comparisons*, ed. by Miguel Bandeira Jerónimo and António Costa Pinto (London: Palgrave Macmillan, 2015), pp. 218–42.
Keza, Leila, 'Burundi-Élections: Le Ministre de la Communication Exige la Radiation de Certains Journalistes de la Synergie des Médias', *SOS Médias*, 16 May 2020 <https://www.SOSmediasburundi.org/2020/05/16/burundi-elections-le-ministre-de-la-communication-exige-la-radiation-de-certains-journalistes-de-la-synergie-des-medias/> [accessed 3 March 2021]
———, 'Gitega: plusieurs réfugiés Banyamulenge expulsés de la ville de Gitega', *SOS Médias*, 9 October 2020 <https://www.SOSmediasburundi.org/2020/10/09/gitega-plusieurs-refugies-banyamulenge-expulses-de-la-ville-de-gitega/> [accessed 3 March 2021]
Kiesel, Véronique, Kinshasa applaudit la volonté belge de rendre au Congo des objets traditionnels volés – Le Soir, 25 November 2021 [accessed 25 November 2021]
Kihl, Lorraine, 'Belgique: un niveau de discrimination à l'embauche similaire aux Etats-Unis pour les afrodescendants', *Le Soir*, 15 June 2020 <https://plus.lesoir.be/307408/article/2020-06-15/belgique-un-niveau-de-discrimination-lembauche-similaire-aux-etats-unis-pour-les?referer=%2Farchives%2Frecherche%3Fdatefilter%3Dlastyear%26sort%3Ddate%2Bdesc%26start%3D40%26word%3Dburundi> [accessed 03 March 2021]
Kimani, Peter, *Dance of the Jakaranda* (New York: Akashic Books, 2017).

King, Hazel, 'Cooperation in Contextualization: Two Visionaries of the African Church: Mojọla Agbebi and William Hughes of the African Institute, Colwyn Bay', *Journal of Religion in Africa*, 16.1 (1986), 2–21.

——, 'Mojola Agbebi: African Church Leader', in *Under the Imperial Carpet: Essays in Black History 1780–1950*, ed. by Rainer Lotz and Ian Pegg (Crawley: Rabbit Press, 1986), pp. 84–108.

King, Helen, 'What is it About the Pangolin?', *Wondersandmarvels*, 2015 <www.wondersandmarvels.com/2015/07/what-is-it-about-the-pangolin.html> [accessed 14 November 2021]

'King of the Jungle Films', *The Daily Herald*, 11 December 1959.

Kingsolver, Barbara, *The Poisonwood Bible* (New York: Harper Flamingo, 1998).

Kisangani, Emizet François and Scott F. Bobb, *Historical Dictionary of the Democratic Republic of the Congo* (Lanham: Scarecrow Press, 1999).

Klein, Naomi, *This Changes Everything: Capitalism vs. the Climate* (New York: Simon & Schuster, 2015).

Knighton, Ben, 'The Determination of Religion in Africa', *African Affairs*, 109, 435, (2010), 325–35.

Koch, Dirk-Jan, *The Congo codes* (Amsterdam: Prometheus-Bert Bakker, 2014).

Koselleck, Reinhart, *Futures Past: on the Semantics of Historical Time*, trans. by and with an introduction by Keith Tribe (New York: Columbia University Press, 2004 [1983]).

Kounda, Ghizlane, 'La Belgique présente sa politique de restitution des œuvres: « Une approche systémique qui permet d'éviter de restituer au cas par cas »', *RTBF Info*, 7 July 2021 <https://www.rtbf.be/info/monde/detail_la-belgique-presente-sa-politique-de-restitution-des-uvres-une-approche-systemique-qui-permet-d-eviter-de-restituer-au-cas-par-cas?id=10798431> [accessed on 08 July 2021]

Kourouma, Ahmadou, *Allah n'est pas obligé* (Paris: Seuil, 2000).

Krueger, Anton, *Experiments in Freedom: Explorations of Identity in New South African Drama* (Newcastle upon Tyne: Cambridge Scholars Publishing, 2010).

——, 'Gazing at Exhibit A: Interview with Brett Bailey', *Liminalities: A Journal of Performance Studies*, 9.1 (2013), 1–13.

Kutumbagana Kangafu, *Discours sur l'authenticité: Essai sur la problématique idéologique du 'recours à l'authenticité'* (Kinshasa: Presses africaines, 1973).

'La Belgique restitue la dent de Patrice Lumumba à sa famille, Alexander De Croo présente des excuses', https://www.lesoir.be/449534/article/2022-06-20/ [accessed on 21 June 2022].

Lacaze, Julie, 'Le pangolin d'Afrique est le mammifère le plus braconné du monde', *National Geographic*, 9 (2017) <www.nationalgeographic.fr/animaux/le-pangolin-dafrique-est-le-mammifere-le-plus-braconne-du-monde> [accessed 14 November 2021]

Lacger, Louis de, *Le Ruanda ancien*, vol I; *le Ruanda moderne*, vol II (Namur: Grands lacs, 1939).

'La Fondation Roi Baudouin a récolté 15 millions d'euros pour 1.100 acteurs de terrain: "Avec ces soutiens, des besoins urgents ont pu rapidement être satisfaits"', 5 June 2020, https://www.lalibre.be/belgique/societe/la-fondation-roi-baudouin-a-recolte-15-millions-d-euros-pour-1-100-acteurs-de-terrain-avec-ces-soutiens-des-besoins-urgents-ont-pu-rapidement-etre-satisfaits-5edaocc5d8ad58250fa92560 [accessed 03 March 2021]

La Fontaine, Jean Sybil, *City Politics: A Study of Leopoldville, 1962–63* (Cambridge: Cambridge University Press, 1970).

Lagae, Johan, 'Modern Living in the Congo: the 1958 Colonial Housing Exhibit and Postwar Domestic Practices in the Belgian Colony', *The Journal of Architecture*, 9.4 (2004), 477–94 <https://doi.org/10.1080/1360236042000320332>

——, 'Kinshasa. Tales of the Tangible City', *ABE Journal*, 3 (2013) <http://journals.openedition.org/abe/378> [accessed 7 January 2021]

——, Sofie Boonen, and Donatien Dia Mwembu Dibwe, 'M(g)r. De Hemptin(n)e, I Presume? Transforming Local Memory Through Toponymy in Colonial/Post-Colonial Lubumbashi, DR Congo', in *Place Names in Africa: Colonial Urban Legacies, Entangled Histories*, ed. by Liora Bigon (Switzerland: Springer International Publishing, 2016), pp. 177–94.

—— and Jakob Sabakinu Kivilu, 'Infrastructure, paysages urbains et architecture: témoins du «développement» ou instruments de « mise en valeur »?', in *Le Congo colonial: une histoire en questions*, ed. by Idesbald Goddeeris, Amandine Lauro, and Guy Vanthemsche (Waterloo: Renaissance du Livre, 2020), pp. 183–95.

Lame, Danielle de, '(Im)possible Belgian Mourning for Rwanda', *African Studies Review*, 48.2 (2005), 33–43.

Landmeters, Romain, 'L'histoire de la colonisation belge à l'école: décentrement, distanciation, déconstruction', *BePax*, 22 December 2017, 1–4 <https://bepax.org/publications/l-histoire-de-la-colonisation-belge-a-l-ecole-decentrement-distanciation-deconstruction.html>

Langan, Mark, *Neo-Colonialism and the Poverty of 'Development' in Africa* (London: Palgrave, 2018).

Lannoy, Didier de, Mabiala Seda Diangwala, and Bongeli Yeikelo Ya Ato (eds.), 'Tango Ya Ba Noko, "le temps des oncles": recueil de témoignages zaïrois', in *Les Cahiers du CEDAF/ASDOC-Studies*, 5-6 (1986).

Larlham, Daniel, 'Brett Bailey and Third World Bunfight – *Journeys into the South African Psyche*', *Theater*, 39.1 (2009), 7–17.
Laye, Camara, *L'Enfant noir* (Paris: Plon, 1953).
Lebel, Aline, 'Le récit d'enfance au prisme du génocide et de la violence politique: le motif du du "retour" vers la terre d'enfance chez Gaël Faye et Scholastique Mukasonga', *Revue Critique de Fixxion Française Contemporaine*, 17 (2018), 100–16.
Lebrun, Jean, 'Leplae (Edmond)', in *Biographie Nationale*, 1967–1968, book 34, vol. 565–71.
Lederer, André, 'La colonie belge au Guatemala', *Collectanea Maritima*, 6 (1968), 243–59.
Ledien, Stéphane, 'Entre médiation, tiraillement et éclatement, la crise identitaire de l'écrivain-narrateur d'autobiographie intellectuelle', *Itinéraires. Littérature, textes, cultures*, 2020-3 (2021) <http://journals.openedition.org/itineraires/8859> [accessed on 13 December 2021]
Le Lay, Maëline, *'La Parole construit le pays': théâtre, langues et didactisme au Katanga (République Démocratique du Congo)* (Paris: Honoré Champion, 2014).
Le Lay, Maëline, Dominique Malaquais, and Nadine Siegert (eds.), *Archive (re)mix. Vues d'Afrique*, preface by Alain Ricard and Ulf Vierke (Rennes: Presses Universitaires de Rennes, 2015).
Lemarchand, René, *Political Awakening in the Congo: the Politics of Fragmentation* (Berkeley; Los Angeles: University of California Press, 1964).
——, *Burundi: Ethnic Conflict and Genocide* (Washington, DC: Woodrow Wilson Center Press; Cambridge; New York: Cambridge University Press, 1996).
——, *The Dynamics of Violence in Central Africa* (Philadelphia: University of Pennsylvania Press, 2009).
'Le musée des civilisations noires: une vision d'avenir, Interview de Hamady Bocoum', *Présence Africaine*, 197.1 (2018), 183–94.
Lepape, Pierre, 'La pensée de la plate-bande', *Traverses*, 5–6 (1976), 28–36.
Leplae, Edmond, *Documents relatifs à l'agriculture du Congo Belge: L'agriculture coloniale dans la discussion du budget du Congo Belge pour 1914; Le programme colonial agricole de l'institut Solvay* (Leuven: F. Ceutrick, 1914), n.p.
——, 'Les cultures obligatoires dans les pays d'agriculture arriérée', *Bulletin agricole du Congo Belge*, 4 (1929), 458.
Leroy, Jean, *Les Funérailles de Monsieur Lumumba*, preface by Antoine Tshitungu Kongolo (Cuesmes: Éditions du Cerisier, 2007).
Lester, Alan, 'Time to Throw Out the Balance Sheet Approach', *Snapshots of Empire: University of Sussex*, 26 January 2016 <https://blogs.sussex.ac.uk/snapshotsofempire/2016/01/26/time-to-throw-out-the-balance-sheet/> (accessed 18 December 2020).
'Les Trois discours du 30 juin 1960', *Mbakamosika*, 1 June 2010 <http://www.mbokamosika.com/article-les-trois-discours-du-30-juin-1960-51503127.html> [accessed 29 July 2020]
Lévy, Bertrand, *Hermann Hesse, une géographie existentielle* (Paris: José Corti, 1992).
Lewis, Chloé, 'The Making and Re-Making of the "Rape Capital of the World": On Colonial Durabilities and the Politics of Sexual Violence Statistics in DRC', *Critical African Studies*, (2021), 1–18.
Likaka, Osumaka, 'Rural Protest: The Mbole against Belgian Rule, 1897–1959', *The International Journal of African Historical Studies*, 27.3 (1994), 589–617.
——, *Rural Society and Cotton in Colonial Zaire* (Madison: The University of Wisconsin Press, 1997).
——, 'Colonialisme et clichés sociaux au Congo Belge', *Africa: Rivista trimestrale di studi e documentazione dell'Istituto italiano per l'Africa e l'Oriente*, 52.1 (1997), 1–27.
——, *Naming Colonialism: History and Collective Memory in the Congo, 1870–1960* (Madison: University of Wisconsin Press, 2009).
Limond-Mertes, Arnaud, 'Tervuren rénové, une lecture critique', *Ensemble!*, 99 (2019), 63–72.
Limond-Mertes, Arnaud, 'Un espace de démonstration du "génie du colonialisme": Interview avec Elikia M'Bokolo', *Ensemble!*, 99 (2019), 49–55.
Linden, Ian, *Christianisme et pouvoir au Rwanda (1900–1990)* (Paris: Karthala, 1999).
Lippens, G. C. V. O., 'The Belgian Congo', *African Affairs*, XXXVIII.CLIII (1939), 419–26 <https://doi.org/10.1093/oxfordjournals.afraf.a101237>
Lismond-Mertes, Arnaud, '"Comprenez notre déception": Interview avec Billy Kalonji', *Ensemble!*, 99 (2019), 37–38.
——, '"Nous connaissons un succès spéctaculaire": Interview avec Guido Gryseels', *Ensemble!*, 99 (2019), 24–31.
——, '"Une renovation ratée": Interview avec Gratia Pungu', *Ensemble!*, 99 (2019), 32–36.
Loffman, Reuben, 'In the Shadow of the Tree Sultans: African Elites and the Shaping of Early Colonial Politics on the Katangan Frontier', *The Journal of Eastern African Studies*, 5.3 (2011), 535–52.
——, 'An Obscured Revolution? USAID, the North Shaba Project, and the Zaïrian Administration, 1976–1986', *Canadian Journal of African Studies*, 48.3 (2014), 425–44.

——, Interview with Abbot Molisho Jérôme, unpublished, 31 July 2015.
——, *Church, State, and Colonialism in Southeastern Congo, 1890–1962* (Basingstoke: Palgrave Macmillan, 2019).
——, Interviews (mobile telephone) with Juvenal Paipo, unpublished, 5 February 2021; 21 May 2021
Lomami-Tshibamba, Paul, *Ngando*, preface by Gaston-Denys Périer (Brussels: Éditions Georges A. Deny, 1949).
——, 'Témoignage de Lomami Tshibamba recueilli par Emongo Lomomba', *Les Cahiers du CEDAF/AS-DOC-Studies*, 5–6 (1986), 49–69.
Lonetree, Amy, 'Museums as Sites of Decolonization; Truth Telling in National and Tribal Museums', in *Contesting Knowledge: Museums and Indigenous Perspectives*, ed. by Susan Sleeper-Smith (London: University of Nebraska Press, 2009), pp. 322–38.
Longman, Timothy, 'Church Politics, and Genocide in Rwanda', *Journal of Religion in Africa*, 31.2 (2001), 163–86.
——, 'Identity Cards, Ethnic Self-Perception, and Genocide in Rwanda', in *Documenting Individual Identity: The Development of State Practices in the Modern World*, ed. by Jane Caplan and John Torpey (Princeton; Oxford: Princeton University Press, 2001), pp. 345–57.
——, *Christianity and Genocide in Rwanda* (Cambridge: Cambridge University Press, 2010).
Loupias, Paulin, 'Tradition et légende des Batutsi sur la création du monde et leur établissement au Ruanda', *Anthropos*, 3.1 (1908), 1–13.
Loutfi, Martine, *Littérature et colonialisme: l'expansion coloniale vue dans la littérature romanesque française (1871–1914)* (Paris; La Haye: Mouton, 1971).
Lowes, Sara and Eduardo Montero, 'Concessions, Violence, and Indirect Rule: Evidence from the Congo Free State', *National Bureau of Economic Research – Working Paper 27893* <https://www.nber.org/papers/w27893>
Lumumba-Kasongo, Tukumbi, 'Land Reforms in the Democratic Republic of Congo (DRC): A Study of the Political Economy of Underdevelopment and Nation-State Building', in *Land Reforms and Natural Resource Conflicts in Africa: New Development Paradigms in the Era of Global Liberalization*, ed. by Tukumbi Lumumba-Kasongo (New York: Routledge, 2015), pp. 150–79.
Luntumbue, Toma Muteba, 'Finding Means to Cannibalise the Anthropological Museum', in *Across Anthropology: Troubling Colonial Legacies, Museums, and the Curatorial*, ed. by Margareta von Oswald and Jonas Tinius (Leuven: Leuven University Press, 2020), pp. 174–85.
Lyamukuru, Félicité, *L'Ouragan a frappé Nyundo* (Mons: Éditions du Cerisier, 2018).
Lyons, Maryinez, *The Colonial Disease: A Social History of Sleeping Sickness in Northern Zaire, 1900–1940* (Cambridge: Cambridge University Press, 1992).
Maalu-Bungi, Crispin, *Mwakulu wa ciluba, leelu ne makelela* (Sudburry: Editions Glopro, 2004).
——, 'Quand la pratique lexicographique se modernise en RD Congo. Note sur *Nkongamyaku Ciluba-Mfwalansa*, dictionnaire bilingue de NgoSemzara Kabuta', *Lexikos* 21 (2011), 320–36.
——, *L'inconnue de l'histoire. La littérature créative en langues congolaises* (Paris: Présence Africaine, forthcoming).
MacCabe, Colin, 'Realism and the Cinema: Notes on Some Brechtian Theses', *Screen*, 15 (1974), 7–27.
MacGaffey, Wyatt, 'Education, Religion, and Social Structure in Zaire', *Anthropology and Education Quarterly*, 13.3 (1982), 238–50.
——, *Kongo Political Culture: The Conceptual Challenge of the Particular* (Bloomington: Indiana University Press, 2000).
Makengo, Nelson, *Théâtre Urbain* (Pantin: Sudu Connexion, 2017).
Makolo Musuasua, Bertin, *Kanyi kalambo* (Kananga: Éditions de l'ISP, 1979).
Makori, Timothy, 'Mobilizing the Past: *Creuseurs*, Precarity and the Colonizing Structure in the Congo Copperbelt', *Africa*, 87.4 (2017), 780–805.
Malaquais, Dominique, 'Postcolonial Dilemma: Parts I–III', *Ellipses: Journal of Creative Research* (2016) <www.ellipses.org.za/project/postcolonial-dilemma-parts-i-iii/> [accessed 16 May 2021]
——, 'Sans pathos. Des Kongo Astronauts, de Lamyne M', *Critique Editions de Minuit* (2020), 513–25 <https://halshs.archives-ouvertes.fr/halshs-03100460/document> [accessed 6 January 2022]
Malm, Andreas, *How to Blow up a Pipeline: Learning to Fight in a World on Fire* (London: Verso Books, 2021).
Malu, Flavien Nkay, *La Mission Chrétienne à l'Épreuve de la Tradition Ancestrale – (Congo Belge, 1891–1933)* (Paris: Éditions Karthala, 2007).
Mamdani, Mahmood, *When Victims Become Killers: Colonialism, Nativism, and the Genocide in Rwanda* (Princeton: Princeton University Press, 2001).
Mandin, Jérémy, 'INTERACT Research Report: An Overview of Integration Policies in Belgium'. Co-financed by the European Union, 2014 <https://cadmus.eui.eu/bitstream/handle/1814/33133/INTERACT-RR-2014%20-%2020.pdf?sequence=1> [accessed 24 August 2020]

Markowitz, Marvin, *Cross and Sword: The Political Role of Missionaries in the Belgian Congo, 1908–1960* (Stanford: Hoover Institute, 1973).

Marshall, Alex, 'Belgium's Africa Museum Had a Racist Image. Can It Change That?', *New York Times*, 4 December 2018 <https://www.nytimes.com/2018/12/08/arts/design/africa-museum-belgium.html> [accessed 15 April 2020]

Martens, Renzo, *Episode III – Enjoy Poverty* (Imagine Film Distribution, 2009.)

Martin, Carol, *Dramaturgy of the Real on the World Stage* (Basingstoke; New York: Palgrave Macmillan, 2010).

Martin-Granel, Nicolas, 'Congo concept', in *Littératures africaines et territoires*, ed. by Christiane Albert, Marie-Rose Abomo-Maurin, Xavier Garnier, and Gisèle Prignitz (Paris: Karthala, 2011), pp. 177–91.

———, 'Sony Labou Tansi, afflux des écrits et flux de l'écriture', *Continents manuscrits*, 1 (2018) <https://doi.org/10.4000/coma.260>

———, '"Le Fleuve commence ici", choix de textes', *Continents manuscrits*, 11 (2018) <http://doi.org/10.4000/coma/2890>

———, 'D'une rive l'autre: questions de génétique et poétique', *Continents manuscrits*, 15 (2020) <http://doi.org/10.4000/coma.6277>

Masolo, Dismas A., *African Philosophy in Search of Identity* (Bloomington: Indiana University Press; Edinburgh: Edinburgh University Press, 1994).

Mathys, Gillian, 'Bringing History Back in: Past, Present, and Conflict in Rwanda and the Eastern Republic of Congo', *Journal of African History*, 58-3 (2017), 465–87.

———, 'Colonial continuities: Tensions and opportunities' <https://africasacountry.com/2019/04/renovating-the-africamuseum> [accessed on 5 May 2021]

———, 'Questioning Territories and Identities in the Precolonial (Nineteenth-Century) Lake Kivu Region', *Africa: The Journal of the International African Institute*, 91-3 (2021), 493–515.

Maunick, Édouard, 'Sony Labou Tansi, l'homme qui dit tous les hommes', *Demain l'Afrique*, 40 (1979), 81–84.

Mbembe, Achille, 'Necropolitics', trans. by Libby Meintjes, *Public Culture*, 15.1 (2003), 11–40.

———, *Sortir de la grande nuit. Essai sur l'Afrique décolonisée* (Paris: La Découverte, 2010).

———, 'La vérité est que l'Europe nous a pris des choses qu'elle ne pourra jamais restituer', *Le Monde*, 1 December 2018.

———, 'À propos de la restitution des artefacts africains conservés dans les musées d'Occident', *Analyse Opinion Critique*, 5 October 2018 <https://aoc.media/analyse/2018/10/05/a-propos-de-restitution-artefacts-africains-conserves-musees-doccident/> [accessed 5 May 2019]

———, *Necropolitics,* trans. by S. Corcoran (Durham, NC: Duke University Press, 2019).

Mbula Paluku, André, 'L'enseignement des et en langues nationales au Zaïre. Bilan d'une expérience', *Revue Tranel*, 26 (1996), 15–32.

Mbu-Mputu, Norbert X. et al, *Bamonimambo (the Witnesses): Rediscovering Congo and British Isles Common History* ([Newport]: South People's Projects, 2015).

McCall, Vikki and Gray, Clive, 'Museums and the "new museology": theory, practice and organisational change', *Museum Management and Curator*ship, 29.1 (2014), 19–35.

McDermott, David, *From Enslavement to Environmentalism Politics on the South African Frontier* (Seattle: University of Washington Press; Weather Press, 2006).

McLeod, John, *Beginning Postcolonialism* (Manchester: Manchester University Press, 2000).

Meeuwis, Michael, 'Bilingual Inequality: Linguistic Rights and Disenfranchisement in Late Belgian Colonization', *Journal of Pragmatics*, 43 (2011), 1279–87.

Melvern, Linda, *A People Betrayed: the Role of the West in Rwanda's Genocide* (London: Zed Books, 2009).

Mensah, Ishmael, 'The Roots Tourism Experience of Diaspora Africans: A Focus on the Cape Coast and Elmina Castles', *Journal of Heritage Tourism*, 10.3 (2015), 213–32.

Mertens, Charlotte, 'Sexual Violence in the Congo Free State: Archival Traces and Present Reconfigurations', *The Australian Review of African Studies*, 37.1 (2016), 6–20.

Michel, Johann, 'Esclavage et réparations. Construction d'un problème public', *Politique Africaine*, 146 (2017), 143–64.

Michel, Louis, 'Quand la Belgique présentait ses excuses au peuple rwandais', *Libération*, 12 September 2011 <https://www.liberation.fr/planete/2011/09/12/quand-la-belgique-presentait-ses-excuses-au-peuple-rwandais_760468/>

Mignolo, Walter D. 'DELINKING: The rhetoric of modernity, the logic of coloniality and the grammar of decoloniality', *Cultural Studies*, 21.2–3 (2007), 449–514.

Ministère des Affaires Étrangères, Bruxelles (AAB) and Archives Africaines et de la Main-d'œuvre (AIMO), 'Rapport Général de l'Administration (RGA)', 1929.

Ministère des Colonies, *Plan Décennal pour le Développement économique et social du Ruanda-Urundi* (Brussels: Éditions De Vissher, 1951).

'Minutes of a Meeting of the Bay of Colwyn Town Council [...] on Monday 17th October 2016' <https://www.colwyn-tc.gov.uk/wp-content/uploads/2016/12/MIN-Council-17.10.16.pdf> [accessed 18 December 2020]

Mistrati, Miki and U Roberto Romano, 'The Dark Side of Chocolate – Child Trafficking & Slavery', YouTube, 2012 <https://www.youtube.com/watch?v=7Vfbv6hNeng> [accessed 25 August 2020]

Modest, Wayne, 'Decolonizing Museums in Practice Part 3', *American Anthropologist* <https://www.americananthropologist.org/podcast/decolonizing-museums-in-practice-part-3> [accessed on 30 June 2021]

Monaville, Pedro, *Students of the World: Global 1968 and Decolonization in the Congo* (Durham, NC: Duke University Press, 2022).

Monénembo, Tierno, *L'Aîné des orphelins* (Paris: Seuil, 2000).

Morel, E. D., *King Leopold's Rule in Africa* (London: Heinemann, 1904).

Morton, David, *Age of Concrete: Housing and the Shape of Aspiration in the Capital of Mozambique* (Athens, OH: Ohio University Press, 2019).

Mpoma, Anne Wetsi, 'Quand le temple dédié à la colonisation belge fait peau neuve', https://docs.wixstatic.com/ugd/3d95e3_86cdb150e1844154bc756110001487f6.pdf, [accessed 04 May 2019]

Mpoyi, Lazare, *Histoire wa Baluba* (Mbuji-Mayi: Institut Saint Jean-Baptiste de la Salle, 1966)

Mputubwele Makim, M., 'The Zairian Language Policy and Its Effects on the Literature in National Languages', *Journal of Black Studies*, 34. 2 (2003), 272–92.

Mudimbe, V. Y., *L'Écart* (Paris: Présence Africaine, 1979).

——, *L'Odeur du père: essai sur des limites de la science et de la vie en Afrique noire* (Paris: Présence africaine, 1982).

——, *The Invention of Africa: Gnosis, Philosophy, and the Order of Knowledge* (Bloomington and Indianapolis: Indiana University Press; London: James Currey, 1988).

——, *Shaba Deux. Les Carnets de Mère Marie Gertrude* (Paris: Présence Africaine, 1989).

——, *Parables and Fables: Exegesis, Textuality and Politics in Central Africa* (Madison: University of Wisconsin Press, 1991).

——, *The Rift*, trans. by Marjolijn de Jager (Minneapolis; London: University of Minnesota Press, 1993).

——, *Les Corps glorieux des mots et des êtres: esquisse d'un jardin africain à la bénédictine* (Paris: Présence Africaine; Montreal: Humanitas, 1994).

——, *The Idea of Africa* (Bloomington and Indianapolis: Indiana University Press; James Currey: London, 1994).

——, *Tales of Faith: Religion as Political Performance in Central Africa* (London; Atlantic Highlands: Athlone Press, 2016 [1997]).

Mujila, Fiston Mwanza, *Tram 83* (Paris: Éditions Métailié, 2014).

——, *Tram 83*, trans. by Roland Glasser, foreword by Alain Mabanckou (London: Jacaranda Books, 2015).

——, *La Danse du vilain* (Paris: Éditions Métailié, 2020).

Mukagasana, Yolande, with Patrick May, *La Mort ne veut pas de moi* (Paris: Fixot, 1997).

Mukasonga, Scholastique, *Notre-Dame du Nil* (Paris: Gallimard, 2012).

Mukumba, Pacifique, 'Escroquerie humanitaire du 21ème siècle. Les pygmées Baka du Cameroun exposés dans un parc animalier en Belgique', *Dossier. KMMA* (2002), 1–12.

Mureithi, Hezbon, 'THIS BELGIAN BRUTE', 10 March 2020, @HezMureithi <https://twitter.com/HezMureithi/status/1237411467118477312> [accessed 10 August 2020]

Musée des Civilisations Noires, *Rapport de la conférence de préfiguration, 28–31 July 2016* (Dakar: MCN, 2016).

Nabutanyi, Edgar, 'Archives of Troubled Childhoods in Contemporary African Fiction' (unpublished doctoral thesis, Stellenbosch University, 2013).

Nadaï, Alain, '*Degré zéro*. Portée et limites de la théorie de l'artialisation dans la perspective d'une politique du paysage', *Cahiers de géographie du Québec*, 51–144 (2007), 333–43.

Nahimana, Ferdinand, 'La conception de l'Histoire du Rwanda d'après Alexis Kagame', in *Alexis Kagame: L'homme et son œuvre*, ed. by Joseph Nsengimana (Kigali: Education, science et culture, 1987), pp. 255–71.

Nanni, Giordano, *The Colonisation of Time: Ritual, Routine and Resistance in the British Empire* (Manchester: Manchester University Press, 2013).

Nayigiziki, Saverio, *Mes Transes à trente ans. Escapade ruandaise*, introduced and ed. by Jean-Paul Kwizera (Metz: Centre Écritures, 2009).

——, *Mes transes à trente ans: histoire vécue mêlée de roman. I. De mal en pis. II. De pis en mieux* (Astrida: Groupe scolaire, 1955).

——, *Escapade ruandaise: journal d'un clerc en sa trentième année*, preface by J.-M. Jadot (Brussels: G.-A. Deny, [1950]).

Ndaywel è Nziem, Isidore 'The political system of the Luba and Lunda: its emergence and expansion', in *General History of Africa, V: Africa from the Sixteenth to the Eighteenth Century*, ed. by Bethwell A. Ogot (London: Heinemann International; Berkeley: University of California Press; Paris: UNESCO, 1992), pp. 290–99.

——, *Histoire générale du Congo. De l'héritage ancien à la République Démocratique* (Paris; Brussels: Duculot, 1998).

Ndikung, Bonaventure Soh Bejeng, 'Where Do We Go from Here: For They Shall Be Heard', *Freize*, 199 (2018) <https://www.frieze.com/article/where-do-we-go-here-they-shall-be-heard> [accessed 03 June 2021]

Ndimurwimo, L. A. and M. L. M. Mbao, 'Rethinking Violence, Reconciliation and Reconstruction in Burundi', *Potchefstroom Elektroniese Regsblad*, 18.4 (2015), 847–900 <https://doi.org/10.4314/pelj.v18i4.04>

Ndlovu-Gatsheni, Sabelo J., *Epistemic Freedom in Africa: Deprovincialization and Decolonization* (New York: Routledge, 2018).

Ndwaniye, Joseph, *La Promesse faite à ma sœur* (2006; Communauté française de Belgique, 2018).

——, *Le Muzugu mangeur d'hommes* (Brussels: Aden, 2012).

——, 'Le Rêve' <http://www.fureurdelire.cfwb.be/index.php?eID=tx_nawsecuredl&u=0&file=fileadmin/sites/fdl/upload/fdl_super_editor/fdl_editor/documents/publications/Plaquettes_2013/9951_Reve_Ndwaniye.pdf&hash=9c8dc53f5f5fead49672f14cf7117552ec2029b5> [accessed 23 July 2020]

——, *Plus fort que la hyène* (Ciboure: La Cheminante, 2018).

Nelson, Robert H., 'Environmental colonialism, "Saving" Africa from Africans'', *The Independent Review*, 8.1. (2003), 65–86.

Neumann, Roderick, *Imposing Wilderness in Africa* (Berkeley: University of California Press, 2008).

'New Law in DRC to finally protect Indigenous Peoples Land Rights', *International Land Coalition* <https://africa.landcoalition.org/en/newsroom/new-law-drc-finally-protect-indigenous-peoples-land-rights>

Ngal, Georges, *Giambatista Viko ou le viol du discours africain* (Lubumbashi: Alpha-Omega, 1975).

——, *L'Errance* (Yaoundé: CLÉ, 1979).

Ngandu Nkashama, Pius, *Le pacte de sang* (Paris: L'Harmattan, 1984).

——, *Bidi ntuilu, bidi mpelelu* (Lubumbashi: Editions Impala, 1998).

——, *Sémantique et morphologie du verbe en Ciluba. Etude de ku-twa et kw-ela* (Paris: L'Harmattan, 1999).

——, 'Les "enfants-soldats" et les guerres coloniales: A travers le premier roman africain, *Etudes littéraires*, 35.1 (2003), 29–40.

——, *Portraits d'écrivains. Visages d'histoire littéraire* (Paris: L'Harmattan, 2016).

Ngongo, Enika, 'Un autre front. Les officiers, soldats et porteurs des troupes coloniales belges lors de la bataille de Tabora', *Guerres Mondiales et Conflits Contemporains*, 272 (2018), 21–34.

——, 'The Forgotten African Soldiers and Porters of the Belgian Colonial Forces in the First World War', *Journal of Belgian History*, XLVIII, 1–2 (2018), 14–33.

Ngorwanubusa, Juvénal, *La Littérature de langue française au Burundi*, preface by Marc Quaghebeur (Brussels: Archives & Musée de la Littérature, 2013).

——, *Le Regard étranger: L'image du Burundi dans les littératures belge et française* (Oxford: Peter Lang 2014).

——, 'Kagame et la problématique du langage', in *Alexis Kagame, L'homme et son œuvre*, ed. by Joseph Nsengimana (Kigali: Education, science et culture, 1987), pp. 122–42.

Ngoye, Achille-Flor, *Kin-la-joie, Kin-la-folie* (Paris: L'Harmattan, 1993).

Ngũgĩ wa Thiong'o, *Decolonising the Mind: The Politics of Language in African Literature* (Nairobi; Kampala; Dar es Salaam; Kigali: James Currey, 1986).

Nkombe, Oleko, 'Méthode et point de départ en Philosophie africaine: Authenticité et libération', *La philosophie africaine. Actes de la 1ère Semaine Philosophique de Kinshasa*, 1 (1977), 69–87.

Nkusi, Laurent, 'Le Kinyarwanda peut-il devenir un instrument de communication scientifique Moderne' (Butare: unpublished, 1980).

Nlandu, Thierry, 'Kinshasa: Beyond Chaos', in *Under Siege: Four African Cities, Freetown, Johannesburg, Kinshasa, Lagos*, ed. by Okwui Enwezor (Ostfildern-Ruit: Hatje Cantz, 2002), pp. 185–99.

Norridge, Zoe, *Perceiving Pain in African Literature* (Basingstoke: Palgrave Macmillan, 2012).

Ntumwa, Jean, 'Elections 2020: ces prières du CNDD-FDD qui s'attaquent aux occidentaux et au Rwanda', *SOS Médias*, 1 May 2020 <https://www.SOSmediasburundi.org/2020/05/01/elections-2020-ces-prieres-du-cndd-fdd-qui-sattaquent-aux-occidentaux-et-au-rwanda/> [accessed 3 March 2021]

——, 'Gitega: le CNDD-FDD et Pierre Nkurunziza (guide suprême) défient la covid-19', *SOS Médias*, 29 May 2020 <https://www.SOSmediasburundi.org/2020/05/29/gitega-le-cndd-fdd-et-pierre-nkurunziza-guide-supreme-defient-la-covid-19/> [accessed 3 March 2021]

——, 'Cent premiers jours du gouvernement Ndayishimiye: un bilan controversé', *SOS Médias*, 18 September 2020 <https://www.SOSmediasburundi.org/2020/09/29/cent-premiers-jours-du-gouvernement-ndayishimiye-un-bilan-controverse/> [accessed 3 March 2021]

——, 'Burambi: des familles Tutsis de plus en plus ciblées par des Imbonerakure', *SOS Médias*, 18 September 2020 <https://www.SOSmediasburundi.org/2020/09/18/burambi-des-familles-tutsis-de-plus-en-plus-ciblees-par-des-imbonerakure/> [accessed 3 March 2021]

——, 'Makamba-Rumonge: les décisions de la CNTB divisent', *SOS Médias*, 10 November 2020 <https://www.SOSmediasburundi.org/2020/11/10/burundi-makamba-rumonge-les-decisions-de-la-cntb-divisent/> [accessed 3 March 2021]

——, 'CNC vs Médias: une rencontre prometteuse', SOS Médias, 1 February 2021 <https://www.sosmediasburundi.org/2021/02/01/cnc-vs-medias-une-rencontre-prometteuse/> [accessed 3 March 2021]

Ntwari, Adam, 'Fête du travail: Nkurunziza défend son bilan et énumère les boucs émissaires', *SOS Médias*, 1 May 2020 <https://www.SOSmediasburundi.org/2020/05/01/fete-du-travail-nkurunziza-defend-son-bilan-et-enumere-les-boucs-emissaires/> [accessed 3 March 2021]

Nugent, Gabriella, *Colonial Legacies: Contemporary Lens-Based Art and the Democratic Republic of Congo* (Leuven: Leuven University Press, 2021).

Nutall, Sarah, 'Literature and the Archive: the Biography of Texts', in *Refiguring the Archive*, ed. by Carolyn Hamilton et al. (Dordrecht; Boston; London: Kluwer Academic Publishers, 2002), pp. 283–300.

Nzongola-Ntalaja, Georges, *From Zaire to the Democratic Republic of the Congo*, 2nd edn (Uppsala: The Nordic Africa Institute, 1999).

——, *The Congo from Leopold to Kabila: A People's History* (London: Zed Books, 2002).

Oberhofer, Michaela and Nanina Guyer, 'Introduction: Fictions and Art Worlds of the Congo Between Past and Present', in *Congo as Fiction: Art Worlds Between Past and Present*, ed. by Nanina Guyer and Michaela Oberhofer (Zurich: Museum Rietberg; Verlag Sheidegger & Spiess, 2020), pp. 10–29.

'Observatoire des stéréotypes', https://www.cec-ong.org/observatoire-des-stereotypes/, [accessed 22 September 2021]

O'Dubhghaill, Sean, 'Mapping the Rwandan Diaspora in Belgium', International Organization for Migration, 2019 <https://publications.iom.int/books/mapping-rwandan-diaspora-belgium>

Ogier-Fares, Marie-Odile, 'L'enfant, voix de la terreur et de la beauté, une figure énonciative de la réconciliation dans *Petit Pays* et *En attendant Bojangles*', *Revue Critique de Fixxion Française Contemporaine*, 17 (2018), 17–25

Okowa, Phoebe, 'The Pitfalls of Unilateral Legislation in International Law: Lessons from Conflict Minerals Legislation', *International and Comparative Law Quarterly*, 69 (2020), 685–717.

Olsson, Göran Hugo, *Concerning Violence*, 2014 <http://dogwoof.com/films/concerning-violence> [accessed 12 May 2014]

Omasombo, Jean Tshonda, 'Lumumba. Drame sans fin et deuil inachevé de la colonisation', *Cahiers d'Études Africaines*, 173–74 (2004), 221–61.

Orban, J.-P., *Toutes les îles de l'océan* (Paris: Mercure de France, 2014).

'Organisons un débat mature et intégral sur le Congo et favorisons un menu de démarches positives', 19 June 2020 <https://www.lalibre.be/debats/opinions/organisons-un-debat-mature-et-integral-sur-le-congo-et-favorisons-un-menu-de-demarches-positives-5eec71a27b50a66a598c7e91> [accessed 3 March 2021]

Orjuela, Camilla, 'Remembering Genocide in the Diaspora: Place and Materiality in the Commemoration of Atrocities in Rwanda and Sri Lanka', *International Journal of Heritage Studies* (2019) <https://doi.org/10.1080/13527258.2019.1644529> [accessed 22 July 2020]

Ouali, Nouria, 'Muséologie et colonialité du pouvoir L'exemple de la « participation » des diasporas africaines au processus de rénovation du Musée royal de l'Afrique centrale de Tervuren', *Migrations Société*, 182.4 (2020), 77–95.

Pagès, Albert, *Un royaume hamite au centre de l'Afrique* (Brussels: Marcel-Hayez, 1933).

Parent, Sabrina, Véronique Bragard, and Maurice Amuri Mpala-Lutebele, 'Entre évitement et ressassement: le spectre colonial belge dans les productions littéraires, artistiques et culturelles', *Revue Belge de Philologie et d'Histoire*, 97 (2019), 677–88.

Pavlakis, Dean, *British Humanitarianism and the Congo Reform Movement* (Farnham: Ashgate, 2015).

Peers, Laura and Alison K. Brown, 'Introduction', in *Museums and Sources Communities*, ed. by L. Peers and A. K. Brown (London: Routledge, 2003).

Peghini, Julie, 'Représenter Kinshasa', *Critique*, 5/6/7 (2020), 563–74.

Peltier, Elian, 'Torn from Parents in the Belgian Congo, Women seek Reparations' *New York Times*, 3 November 2021 < https://www.nytimes.com/2021/11/03/world/europe/belgium-congo-kidnapping.html#:~:text=The%20women%20%E2%80%94%20Monique%20Bintu%20Bingi,the%2019th%20century%20to%20Congo%27s> [accessed 3 November 2021]

Peterson, Scott, *Me Against My Brother: At War in Somalia, Sudan, and Rwanda* (New York: Routledge, 2000).

Piketty, Thomas, *A Brief History of Equality*, trans. by Steven Rendall (Cambridge, MA: The Belknap Press of Harvard University Press, 2022).

Pigeaud, Fanny and Ndongo Samba Sylla, *L'Arme invisible de la Francafrique: une histoire du franc CFA* (Paris: La Découverte, 2018).
Planche, Stéphanie, 'Le "Roi colonisateur" à l'école: portrait ambivalent d'un (anti)héros', in *Léopold II: Entre génie et gêne. Politique étrangère et colonisation*, ed. by Vincent Dujardin et al. (Brussels: Racine, 2009), pp. 269–84.
Plasman, Pierre-Luc, *Léopold II, potentat congolais. L'Action royale face à la violence coloniale*, preface by Michel Dumoulin (Brussels: Racine, 2017).
Poncelet, Marc, *L'Invention des sciences coloniales belges* (Paris: Karthala, 2008).
Ponselet, Gaëlle, 'Belgium's colonial past: ten experts to set the scene', *Justiceinfo.Net*, 24 July 2020 <https://www.justiceinfo.net/en/truth-commissions/44974-belgium-colonial-past-ten-experts-to-set-the-scene.html> [accessed 6 January 2021]
Pontzeele, Sophie, 'Le Schème de la « Guerre Ethnique » dans la Médiatisation des Crises Africaines: Burundi 1972 et Rwanda 1994', *Les Cahiers du Journalisme*, 18.1 (2008), 166–82.
Pourtier, Roland, 'Transports et Développement au Zaïre,' *Afrique Contemporaine*, 29.153 (1990), 3–26.
Pratt, Mary Louise, 'Arts of the Contact Zone', *Profession* (1991), 33–40.
———, *Imperial Eyes: Travel Writing and Transculturation* (London: Routledge, 1992).
Prunier, Gérard, *The Rwanda Crisis: History of a Genocide* (New York: Columbia University Press, 1995).
Pungu, Gratia, 'Mémoire, stéréotypes et diaspora. Introduction', *Politique: revue belge d'analyse et du débat*, no. 65 (June 2010) <https://www.revuepolitique.be/le-congo-dans-nos-tetes-memoire/>
———, 'N'est pas post-colonial qui veut… La postcolonie, une alternative muséale utopique' <https://6274c06d-5149-4618-88b2-ac2fdc6ef62d.filesusr.com/ugd/3d95e3_e5ff44323157448283e04058bc9cf6ee.pdf> [accessed 04 May 2021]
Purdeková, Andrea, '#StopThisMovie and the Pitfalls of Mass Atrocity Prevention: Framing of Violence and Anticipation of Escalation in Burundi's Crisis (2015–2017)', *Genocide Studies and Prevention: An International Journal*, 13.2 (2019), 22–37.
Pype, Katrien, 'Political Billboards as Contact Zones: Reflections on Urban Space, the Visual and Political Affect in Kabila's Kinshasa', in *Photography in Africa. Ethnographic Pespectives*, ed. by Richard Vokes (Suffolk: Boydel & Brewer and James Currey: 2012), pp. 187–204.
Quaghebeur, Marc and Émile Van Balberghe (eds.), with Nadine Fettweis and Annick Vilain, *Papier blanc, encre noire. Cent ans de culture francophone en Afrique centrale (Zaïre, Rwanda et Burundi)*, 2 vols (Brussels: Éditions Labor, 1992).
———, 'Des textes sous le boisseau', in *Papier blanc, encre noire. Cent ans de culture francophone en Afrique centrale (Zaïre, Rwanda et Burundi)*, ed. by Marc Quaghebeur and Émile Van Balberghe, with Nadine Fettweis and Annick Vilain, 2 vols (Brussels: Éditions Labor, 1992), pp. vii–xciv.
Quijano, Aníbal, 'Coloniality of Power, Eurocentrism, and Latin America', *Nepantla*, 1 (2000), 533–80.
Qureshi, Sadiah, *Peoples on Parade: Exhibitions, Empire, and Anthropology in Nineteenth-Century Britain* (Chicago: University of Chicago Press, 2011).
Raffoule, Alexandre, 'The Politics of Association: Power-Sharing and the Depoliticization of Ethnicity in Post-War Burundi', *Ethnopolitics*, 19.1 (2020), 1–18.
Reychler, Luc and Jean Migabo Kalere (eds.), *RD Congo: pays de l'avenir. Construisons ensemble une paix durable pour un Meilleur destin. Livre ouvert*, 87 (Leuven: KU Leuven Centre of Peace Research and Strategic Studies, 2010).
'RD Congo: 5 femmes métisses déboutées par un tribunal belge après avoir porté plainte pour crime contre l'humanité', *Le Soir*, 8 December 2021, <https://www.lesoir.be/411290/article/2021-12-08/rd-congo-5-femmes-metisses-deboutees-par-un-tribunal-belge-apres-avoir-porte> [accessed 8 December 2021]
Renaut, Alain, 'Le crime contre l'humanité, le droit humanitaire et la Shoah', *Philosophie*, 67 (2000), 19–32.
Renders, Luc and Jeroen Dewulf (eds.), *The Congo in Flemish Literature: an Anthology of Flemish Prose on the Congo, 1870s–1990s* (Leuven: Leuven University Press, 2020).
'Repression and Genocidal Dynamics in Burundi', 15 November 2016 <https://www.fidh.org/en/region/Africa/burundi/repression-and-genocidal-dynamics-in-burundi> [accessed 3 March 2021]
Restitution Belgium, 'Ethical Principles for the Management and Restitution of Colonial Collections in Belgium', Restitution Belgium, 2018 <https://restitutionbelgium.be/en/report> [accessed 07 July 2021]
Ricard, Alain, *The Languages & Literatures of Africa* (Oxford: James Currey, 2004).
Ricœur, Paul, *Oneself as Another*, trans. by Kathleen Blamey (Chicago: University of Chicago Press, 1992).
Rittner, Carol, John. K. Roth and Wendy Whitworth (eds.), *Genocide in Rwanda: Complicity of the Churches?* (St. Paul: Paragon, 2004).
Riva, Silvia, *Nouvelle histoire de la littérature du Congo-Kinshasa*, prefaces by V.Y. Mudimbe and Marc Quahgebeur, trans. Collin Fort (Paris: L'Harmattan, 2000).

——, 'Congolese Literature as Part of Planetary Literature', *Journal of World Literature*, 6 (2021), special issue 'Contemporary Congolese Literature as World Literature', ed. by Silvia Riva and Julien Jeusette, 216–44.
Roach, Catherine, *Mother/nature: Popular Culture and Environmental Ethics* (Bloomington: Indiana University Press, 2003).
Robbins, Bruce, *The Beneficiary* (Durham, NC: Duke University Press, 2017).
Robert, Mireille-Tsheusi, 'Lettre ouverte au musée colonial du congo à Tervuren. Comment osez-vous ?!', <https://6274c06d-5149-4618-88b2-ac2fdc6ef62d.filesusr.com/ugd/3d95e3_61db-44196fa84233852196b4aa4552c5.pdf> [accessed on 04 June 2021]
——, '« Restitutions » postcoloniales: de quoi parle-t-on ? Entretien avec Martin Vander Elst' <https://docs.wixstatic.com/ugd/3d95e3_d6100c6979f9470193d222cee21f3d78.pdf> [accessed 12 July 2021]
Roberts, Allen F., 'History, Ethnicity, and Change in the "Christian Kingdom" of Southeastern Zaire', in *The Creation of Tribalism in Southern Africa*, ed. by Leroy Vail (Berkeley: University of California Press, 1991), pp. 193–214.
Roger, Alain, *Court traité du paysage* (Paris: Gallimard, 1997).
Roger, Aurélie, 'D'une mémoire coloniale à une mémoire du colonial. La reconversion chaotique du Musée Royal de l'Afrique Centrale, ancien musée du Congo Belge', *Cadernos de Estudos Africanos*, 9.10 (2006), 43–75.
Roisin, Jacques, *Dans la nuit la plus noire se cache l'humanité. Récits de justes du Rwanda* (Brussels: Les Impressions Nouvelles, 2017).
Rosoux, Valérie, 'The Two Faces of Belgium in the Congo: Perpetrator and Rescuer', *European Review of International Studies*, 1.3 (2014), 16–38 (19–20).
—— and Laurence van Ypersele, 'The Belgian National Past: Between Commemoration and Silence', *Memory Studies*, 5.1 (2011), 45–57.
Ross, Max, 'Interpreting the New Museology', *Museum and Society*, 2.2 (2004), 84–103.
Royal Museum for Central Africa, 'Dossier de Presse, Ouverture de l'AfricaMuseum,' 8 December 2018 <https://press.africamuseum.be/sites/default/files/media/Persdossier-FR%20web.pdf> [accessed 23 April 2020]
Rothberg, Michael, *Multidirectional Memory: Remembering the Holocaust in the Age of Decolonization* (Stanford: Stanford University Press, 2009).
——, *The Implicated Subject: Beyond Victims and Perpetrators* (Stanford: Stanford University Press, 2019).
RTNB, 'Le Burundi célèbre la journée internationale du travail et des travailleurs', RTNB, 1 May 2020 <http://www.*RTNB*.bi/fr/art.php?idapi=4/1/128> [accessed 3 March 2021]
——, 'Décès inopiné du Président de la République Pierre Nkurunziza', 10 June 2020 <https://*RTNB*.bi/fr/art.php?idapi=4/1/205> [accessed 3 March 2021]
——, 'Investiture du nouveau Président de la République: Gén Maj Evariste Ndayishimiye prend les rênes du pouvoir', 18 June 2020 <http://www.*RTNB*.bi/fr/art.php?idapi=4/1/213> [accessed 3 March 2021]
——, 'Gitega/Prière d'action de grâce: le Chef de l'Etat livre un message de consolation', 25 June 2020 <http://www.*RTNB*.bi/fr/art.php?idapi=4/1/231> [accessed 3 March 2021]
Rubbers, Benjamin, 'Mining Towns, Enclaves, and Spaces: A Genealogy of Worker Camps in the Congolese Copperbelt', *Geoforum*, 98 (2019), 88–96.
—— (ed.), *Inside Mining Capitalism: the Micropolitics of Work on the Congolese and Zambian Copperbelts* (Rochester: Boydell & Brewer; James Currey, 2021).
—— and Emma Lochery, 'Labour Regimes: a Comparative History', in *Inside Mining Capitalism: the Micropolitics of Work on the Congolese and Zambian Copperbelts*, ed. by B. Rubbers (Rochester, NY: Boydell & Brewer; James Currey, 2021), pp. 27–54.
Ruff, Véronique, Florence Caulier, and Audrey Elbaum, *Sophie, l'enfant cachée* (Brussels: CCLJ, 2013).
Rugero, Roland, *Baho!* (Paris: Vents d'ailleurs, 2012).
Rutayisire, Paul, *La Christianisation du Rwanda (1900–1945). Méthode missionnaire et politique selon Mgr Léon Classe* (Freiburg: Editions universitaires, 1987).
——, 'Le Tutsi étranger dans le pays de ses aïeux', *Les idéologies, Evangile et Société*, 4 (1996), 42–56.
Rutembesa, Faustin, 'Le génocide perpétré contre les Tutsi, Avril-Juillet 1994', in *Histoire du Rwanda, des origines à la fin du 20ème siècle*, ed. by Déo Byanafashe and Paul Rutayisire (Huye: Université nationale du Rwanda, 2011), pp. 518–77.
Ruti, Antoine, *Le Fils de Mikeno* (Lubumbashi: Éditions Impala, 1997).
Rwayitare, Uwindekwe P. and Florence Caullier, *D'Ici et d'ailleurs. Témoignages des survivants du genocide des Tutsi du Rwanda vivant en Belgique* (Brussels: Muyira asbl, 2016).
Ryckmans, Pierre, *Dominer pour servir* (Brussels: Librairie Albert Dewit, 1931).
——, *Barabara* (Brussels: Larcier, 1947).

Sabaratnam, Meera, *Decolonising Intervention: International Statebuilding in Mozambique* (London: Rowman & Littlefield, 2017).
Sacks, Ruth, 'Congo Style: From Belgian Art Nouveau to Zaïre's Authenticité', unpublished doctoral thesis, University of Witwatersrand, Johannesburg, 2017.
Said, Edward, *Culture and Imperialism* (London: Vintage, 1994).
Salter, Tom, 'Rumba: From Congo to Capetown' (unpublished PhD thesis, University of Edinburgh, 2007).
Sarr, Felwine and Savoy, Bénédicte, 'The Restitution of African Cultural Heritage: Towards a New Relational Ethics', Report for President Macron (Paris: November 2018).
Sassen, Robyn, 'Bailey rocks Grahamstown divide', CUE ON LINE, 2009 <http://www.thirdworldbunfight.co.za/files/PRESS_from_National_Arts_Festival.pdf> [accessed 7 August 2020]
Saur, Léon, 'La frontière ethnique comme outil de conquête du pouvoir: le cas du Parmehutu', *Journal of Eastern African Studies*, 3.2 (2009), 303–16.
Savage, Mike, *The Return of Inequality: Social Change and the Weight of the Past* (Cambridge, MA: Harvard University Press, 2021).
Schalbroeck, Eva, 'Centre Stage and Behind the Scene with the "Lion of Katanga": Benedictine Jean-Félix de Hemptinne's Congolese Career, 1910-1958', 32.1/2 (2019), 105-147.
Scheitler, Marcel, *Histoire de l'Eglise catholique du Kasayi* (Kananga: Éditions de l'Archidiocèse, 1991).
Schildkrout, Enid and Curtis A. Keim, *African Reflections: Art from Northeastern Zaire* (Seattle: University of Washington Press; London; New York: American Museum of Natural History, 1990).
Seibert, Julia, 'Travail forcé', in *Le Congo Colonial: Une histoire en questions*, ed. by Idesbald Goddeeris, Amandine Lauro, and Guy Vanthemsche (Waterloo: Renaissance du Livre, 2020), pp. 141–54.
Sémal, J., 'Camille DONIS', *Bulletin des Séances – Académie Royale des Sciences d'Outre-Mer/Mededelingen der Zittingen – Koninklijke Academie voor Overzeese Wetenschappen – Jaarboek – 1990 – Annuaire*, 36.1 (1990), 57-60.
Sembène, Ousmane, *Les Bouts de bois de Dieu* (Paris: Pocket, 1960).
Sénat de Belgique '1-611/7: Commission d'enquête parlementaire concernant les événements du Rwanda, rapport au nom de la commission d'enquête par MM. Mahoux et Verfhofstadt', 6 December 1997 <https://www.senate.be/www/?MIval=/publications/viewPubDoc&TID=16778570&LANG=fr> [accessed 24 July 2020]
Senghor, Léopold Sédar, 'Ce que le noir apporte', in *L'Homme de couleur*, ed. by Jean Verdier et al. (Paris: Plon, 1939), pp. 292-314.
Shringarpure, Bhakti, 'Africa and the Digital Savior Complex', *Journal of African Cultural Studies*, 32.2 (2020), 178-94.
Sieg, Katrin, 'Towards a Civic Contract of Performance: Pitfalls of Decolonizing the Exhibitionary Complex at Brett Bailey's Exhibit B', *Theatre Research International*, 40.3 (2015), 250–71.
Silverman, Debora L. 'Diasporas of Art: History, the Tervuren Royal Museum for Central Africa, and the Politics of Memory in Belgium, 1885–2014', *The Journal of Modern History*, 87.3 (2015), 615–67.
Sinda, Martial, *Le Messianisme congolais et ses incidences politiques: kimbanguisme, matsouanisme, autres mouvements* (Paris: Payot, 1972).
Smet, A. J., *Bibliographie de la philosophie africaine/bibliografie van de afrikaanse [sic] wijsbegeerte*, https://sites.uclouvain.be/sisp/sites/philafr/M.html [accessed 8 June 2022].
Sojcher, Frédéric, *La Kermesse héroïque du cinéma belge* (Paris: Harmattan, 1999).
Somers, Margaret and Gloria Gibson, 'Reclaiming the Epistemological "Other": Narrative and the Social Constitution of Identity', in *Social Theory and the Politics of Identity*, ed. by Craig Calhoun (Oxford: Blackwell, 1994), pp. 37–99.
Songa-Songa Mwitwa, Serge Olivier, and Marc Pabois (eds.), *Lubumbashi, capitale minière du Katanga, 1910–2010* (Lubumbashi: Association Halle de l'Étoile, 2008).
Sony, Labou Tansi [Sony Tendra], *Marie Samar*, 1970, Limoges, Bibliothèque francophone multimédia (BFM), Fonds Sony Labou Tansi (FSLT), SLT 68.
——, [Marcel Sony], *Le Bombardé*, 1971, Limoges, BFM, FSLT, SLT 60.
——, *L'État honteux* (Paris: Éditions du Seuil, 1981).
——, 'Je soussigné cardiaque' [interview], *Le Journal de Chaillot*, 25 (1985), 39, Limoges, BFM, FSLT, SLT 150 A.5.
——, 'Kinshasa ne sera jamais', in *L'Autre monde: écrits inédits*, ed. by Nicolas Martin-Granel (Paris: Éditions Revue noire, 1997), pp. 21–23.
——, [Untitled], in *L'Autre monde: écrits inédits*, ed. by Nicolas Martin-Granel (Paris: Éditions Revue noire, 1997), pp. 54–58.

——, 'Sony Labou Tansi à Lomé, le 15 février 1988', in *Travaux et documents no.65*, ed. by Didier Morin (Bordeaux: Centre d'étude d'Afrique noire, 2000) <http://www.lam.sciencespobordeaux.fr/sites/lam/files/td65.pdf> [accessed 1 August 2020]
——, *Paroles inédites*, ed. by Bernard Magnier (Montreuil-sous-Bois: Éditions théâtrales, 2005).
——, 'Le Sexe de Matonge', *Politique africaine*, 100.4 (2005 [1984]), 118–22 <http://doi.org/10.3917/polaf.100.0118>
——, *Cercueil de luxe/La Peau cassée*, ed. by Bernard Magnier (Montreuil-sous-Bois: Éditions théâtrales, 2006).
——, 'Donner du souffle au temps et polariser l'espace', in *Encre, sueur, salive et sang: textes critiques*, ed. by Greta Rodriguez-Antoniotti (Paris: Éditions du Seuil, 2015), pp. 65–71.
——, 'Je soussigné cardiaque', Limoges, BFM, FSLT, SLT 22.
——, [Untitled manuscript], Limoges, BFM, SLT, SLT 36.
SOS Médias, 'Burundi-elections: un orage se prépare selon Human Rights Watch', 15 May 2020 <https://www.SOSmediasburundi.org/2020/05/15/burundi-elections-un-orage-se-prepare-selon-human-rights-watch/> [accessed 3 March 2021]
Sousa Santos, Boaventura de, *Epistemologies of the South: Justice Against Epistemicide* (London: Routledge, 2014).
Sowry, Nathan, 'Silence, Accessibility, and Reading Against the Grain: Examining Voices of the Marginalized in the India Office Records', *InterActions: UCLA Journal of Education and Information Studies*, 8.2 (2012) <http://dx.doi.org/10.5070/D482011848>
Spence, Mark David, *Dispossessing the Wilderness: Indian Removal and the Making of the National Parks* (Oxford: Oxford University Press, 1999).
Spivak, Gayatri Chakravorty, 'Can the subaltern speak?', in *Marxism and the interpretation of culture*, ed. by Cary Nelson and Lawrence Grossberg (Urbana: University of Illinois Press, 1988), pp. 271–313.
Stanard, Matthew G., '"Bilan du monde pour un monde plus déshumanisé": The 1958 Brussels World's Fair and Belgian Perceptions of the Congo', *European History Quarterly*, 35.2 (2005), 267–98.
——, *Selling the Congo: A History of European Pro-Empire Propaganda and the Making of Belgian Imperialism* (London: University of Nebraska Press, 2011).
——, *The Leopard, the Lion and the Cock: Colonial Memories and Monuments in Belgium* (Leuven: Leuven University Press, 2019).
Stenger, Friedrich, *White Fathers in Colonial Central Africa: a Critical Examination of V.Y. Mudimbe's Theories on Missionary Discourse in Africa* (Münster; Hamburg; London: LIT Verlag, 2001).
Stengers, Jean, *Congo, mythes et réalités. 100 ans d'histoire* (Paris; Louvain-la-Neuve: Éditions Duculot, 1989).
Stewart, Gary, *Rumba on the River: A History of the Popular Music of the Two Congos* (London: Verso, 2003).
Stoler, Laura Ann, *Along the Archival Grain: Epistemic Anxieties and Colonial Common Sense* (Princeton: Princeton University Press, 2009).
——, 'Introduction: "The Rot Remains": From Ruins to Ruination,' in *Imperial Debris: On Ruins and Ruination*, ed. by Ann Laura Stoler (Durham, NC: Duke University Press, 2013), pp. 1–35.
Strother, Zoë S., *The Invention of Masks: Agency and History in the Art of the Central Pende* (Chicago; London: The University of Chicago Press, 1988).
——, 'From Performative Utterances to Performative Objects: Pende Theories of Speech, Blood Sacrifice, and Power Objects', *Anthropology and Aesthetics*, 37 (2000), 49–71.
——, *Humor and Violence: Seeing Europeans in Central African Art* (Bloomington: Indiana University Press, 2016).
Suzuki, Sarah, 'Kingelez "visionnaire"', in *Bodys Isek Kingelez*, ed. by Sarah Suzuki (New York: MoMA; Brussels: Mercator, 2018), pp. 9–30.
Szombati-Fabian, Ilona and Johannes Fabian, 'Folk Art from an Anthropological Perspective', *Studies in the Anthropology of Visual Communication*, 3.1 (1976), 1–21.
Taffin, Dominique (ed.), *Du Musée colonial au musée des Cultures du monde* (Paris: Maisonneuve et Larose, 2000).
Taylor, Diana, *The Archive and the Repertoire: Performing Cultural Memory in the Americas* (Durham, NC: Duke University Press, 2007).
Tchicaya U Tam'si, *Le Bal de N'dinga*, online audio recording, Radio France internationale, 31 August 2018 <https://www.rfi.fr/fr/emission/20180902-tchicaya-tamsi-congo-bal-ndinga-ca-va-le-monde-rfi> [accessed 25 February 2021]
Teapot, Mel, 'Petit pays: l'histoire d'un paradis perdu', *L'Envolée Culturelle*, 9 May 2017 <http://www.lenvoleeculturelle.fr/petit-pays-lhistoire-dun-paradis-perdu/> [accessed 23 July 2020]

Tempels, Placide Tempels, *La Philosophie bantoue*, trans. by A. Rubbens, preface by Aloune Diop (Paris: Présence africaine, 1949).

'The Contemporary Art Market Report in 2019' https://www.artprice.com/artprice-reports/the-contemporary-art-market-report-2019/african-artists-breaking-through [last accessed 6 January 2022]

The Remarkable Reverend William Hughes and the African Institute (Llangefni: Crefft Media, [2018]).

'The Truth Commission', 7 and 8 December 2018, Belgian Senate, Brussels <https://www.africamuseum.be/en/news/waarheidscommissie> [accessed 14 August 2020]

Third World Bunfight, 'Exhibit B' <http://thirdworldbunfight.co.za/exhibit-b/>

Thomas, Dominic, *Nation-Building, Propaganda, and Literature in Francophone Africa* (Bloomington: Indiana University Press, 2002).

——, 'From the Grotesque to the Fantastic: Sony Labou Tansi's *Qui a mangé Madame d'Avoine Bergotha ?*', in *New Francophone African and Caribbean Theatres*, ed. by John Conteh-Morgan, with Dominic Thomas (Bloomington: Indiana University Press, 2010), pp. 131–40.

Thompson, Linda, 'Africa Museum Renovation allows Critical View of Colonial Past', *The Bulletin*, 6 December 2018 <http://www.flanderstoday.eu/africa-museum-renovation-allows-critical-view-colonial-past> [accessed 10 August 2020]

Thompson, Matt, 'Modernity, Anxiety, and the Development of a Popular Railway Landscape Aesthetic, 1809–1879', in *Trains, Literature, and Culture: Reading/Writing the Rails*, ed. by Steven D. Spalding and Benjamin Fraser (New York: Lexington Books: 2012), pp. 119–56.

Thotse, Mahunele, 'Contesting Names and Statues: Battles Over Louis Trichardt/Makhando "City-Text" in Limpopo Province, South Africa', *Kronos*, 36.1 (2010), 173–83.

Titeca, Kristof and Tom De Herdt, 'Real Governance Beyond the "Failed State": Negotiating Education in the Democratic Republic of the Congo', *African Affairs*, 110, 439, (2011), 213–31.

Tödt, Daniel, *The Lumumba Generation: African Bourgeoisie and Colonial Distinction in the Belgian Congo*, trans. by Alex Skinner (Berlin; Boston: De Gruyter, 2021).

Tola, Miriam, 'Planetary Lovers: On Annie Sprinkle and Beth Stephens's *Water Makes Us Wet*', in *Other Globes: Past and Peripheral Imaginations of Globalization, Palgrave Studies in Globalization, Culture and Society*, ed. by Simon Ferdinand, Irene Villaescusa-Illán, and Esther Peeren (Springer: Palgrave Macmillan, 2019), pp. 231–48.

Tombu, Chantal (ed.). *Papiers de société: Kura Shomali, Raymond Tsham et Steve Bandoma* (Neufchâteau: Weyrich Edition, 2020).

'Town Council Welcomes Congolese Delegation', Bay of Colwyn: Town Council <https://www.colwyn-tc.gov.uk/town-council-welcomes-congolese-delegation/ https://www.dailypost.co.uk/news/local-news/bangor-universitys-historic-congo-link-11569154> [accessed 18 December 2020]

Trapido, Joe, *Breaking Rocks: Music, Ideology and Economic Collapse from Paris to Kinshasa* (New York; Oxford: Berghahn Books, 2020).

Trefon, Theodore, 'Introduction: Réforme et Désillusions', in *Réforme au Congo (RDC): Attentes et Désillusions*, ed. by Theodore Trefon (Paris: L'Harmattan, 2009), pp. 15–34.

Trouillot, Michel-Rolph, *Silencing the Past: Power and the Production of History* (Boston: Beacon, 1995).

Tsang, Michael, 'Decolonial? Postcolonial? What does it mean to "decolonise ourselves"?', 2021 <https://blogs.ncl.ac.uk/decolonisesml/2021/01/21/decolonial-postcolonial-what-does-it-mean-to-decolonise-ourselves/> [accessed 12 July 2021]

Tshisungu wa Tshisungu, José, *La Littérature congolaise écrite en ciluba. Histoire politique et recomposition culturelle* (Ontario: Editions Glopro, 2006).

Tshitungu Kongolo, Antoine (ed.), *Aux pays du fleuve et des grands lacs. Chocs et rencontres des cultures (de 1885 à nos jours)*, preface by Marc Quaghebeur (Brussels: AML Editions, 2000);

——, 'La mémoire du Congo: les manqués d'une expo', *La Libre Belqique*, 27 April 2005.

——, 'Belgique: une mémoire coloniale sélective', *Politique: revue belge d'analyse et du débat*, 65 (June 2010) <https://www.revuepolitique.be/belgique-une-memoire-coloniale-selective/>

Turner, Margaret A., *Housing in Zaire: How the System Works and How People Cope* (Madison: University of Wisconsin Press, 1985).

Turner, Thomas and Crawford Young, *The Rise and Decline of the Zairian State* (Madison: University of Wisconsin Press, 1985).

Tylor, Edward Burnett, *Primitive Culture* (London: Murray, 1871).

L'Union Minière et la vie au Katanga (Brussels: Presses de M. Weissenbruch S.A, 1954).

United Nations OHCHR, 'UN experts challenge Belgium to confront its colonial past', 11 February 2019 <https://www.ohchr.org/en/NewsEvents/Pages/DisplayNews.aspx?NewsID=24155&LangID=E>[accessed 04 August 2022].

Vallet, Cédric, 'Musée de Tervuren: Décolonisation Impossible?' *Médor*, 10 December 2018 <https://medor.coop/fr/articles/reportage-musee-tervuren-Congo-MRAC-colonialisme/> [accessed 04 May 2019]

Van Acker, Frank, 'Where did all the land go? Enclosure and Social Struggle in Kivu (D.R. Congo)', *Review of African Political Economy*, 32.103 (2005), 79–98.

Van Beurden, Sarah, '"Un Panorama de nos valeurs africaines": Belgisch Congo op Expo 58', in *Congo in België: koloniale Cultuur in de metropool*, ed. by Bambi Ceuppens, Vincent Viaene, and David Van Reybroeck (Leuven: Leuven University Press, 2009), pp. 299–311.

——, 'The Art of (Re)Possession: Heritage and The Cultural Politics of Congo's Decolonization', *The Journal of African History*, 56.1 (2015), 143–64.

——, *Authentically African: Arts and the Transnational Politics of Congolese Culture* (Athens, OH: Ohio University Press, 2015).

——, 'Museum renovation and the politics of collection and possession' <https://africasacountry.com/2019/04/renovating-the-africamuseum> [accessed on 3 May 2021]

Vandeginste, Stef, 'Ethnic Quotas and Foreign NGOs in Burundi: Shrinking Civic Space Framed as Affirmative Action', *Africa Spectrum*, 54.3 (2019), 181–200.

Van Den Avenne, Cécile, *De la bouche même des indigènes. Echanges linguistiques en Afrique coloniale* (Paris: Vendémiaire, collection Empire, 2017).

Van den Braembussche, Antoon, 'The Silenced Past. On the Nature of Historical Taboos', in *Świat historii. Prace z metodologii historii i historii historiografi i dedykowane Jerzemu Topolskiemu z okazji siedemdziesięciolecia urodzin*, ed. by Wojciecha Wrzoska and Jerzy Topolski (The world of history: works on the methodology of history and history of historiography dedicated to Jerzy Topolski on the occasion of his 70th birthday) (Poznań: Inst. Historii UAM, 1998), pp. 97–111.

——, 'The Silence of Belgium: Taboo and Trauma in Belgian Memory', *Yale French Studies*, 102 (2002), 34–52.

Van Der Poel, Ieme, *Congo-Océan: un chemin de fer colonial controversé* (Paris: L'Harmattan, 2006).

Van Goethem, Herman, 'Foreword by Herman Van Goethem, Rector University of Antwerp', in *Contemporay Artists Tracing Colonial Tracks: Congoville/Hedendaagse Kunstenaars Bewandelen Koloniale Sporen*, ed. by Pieter Boons and Sandrine Collard (Leuven: Leuven University Press, 2021), pp. 8–10.

Vangroenweghe, Daniel, 'The "Leopold II" Concession System Exported to French Congo with as Example the Mpoko Company', *Revue Belge d'Histoire Contemporaine*, 36 (2006), 323–72.

Vanhee, Hein, 'On Shared Heritage and Its (False) Promises', *African Arts* 49.3 (2016), 1–7.

Van Hooste, Emma, 'Metis in the Belgian Congo: an Archival Research on the Racial Categorisation and Colonial Treatment of Metis' (unpublished MA thesis, Ghent University, 2020).

Van Huis, Iris, 'Contesting Cultural Heritage: Decolonizing the Tropenmuseum as an Intervention in the Dutch/European Memory Complex', in *Dissonant Heritages and Memories in Contemporary Europe*, ed. by Tuuli Lähdesmäki, Luisa Passerini, Sigrid Kaasik-Krogerus, and Iris van Huis (London: Palgrave Macmillan, 2019), pp. 215–48.

Van Hove, Johnny, *Congoism: Congo Discourses in the United States from 1800 to the Present* (Bielefeld: transcript Verlag, 2017).

Van Melkebeke, Sven, 'Science as the Handmaiden of Coerced Labor: The Implementation of Cotton Cultivation Schemes in the Eastern Congo Uele Region, 1920–1960', in *Coercive Geographies: Historicizing Mobility, Labor and Confinement*, ed. by Johan Heinsen, Martin Bak Jørgensen, and Martin Ottovay Jørgensen (Leiden: Brill, 2020), 169–91.

Van Nieuwenhuyse, Karel, 'Increasing Criticism and Perspectivism: Belgian-Congolese (Post)Colonial History in Belgian Secondary History Education Curricula and Textbooks (1990–Present)', *Yearbook of the International Society of History Didactics*, 36 (2014), 183–204.

—— and Kaat Wils, 'Remembrance Education Between History Teaching and Citizenship Education', *Citizenship Teaching & Learning*, 7.2 (2012), 157–71.

Van Reybrouck, David, 'My Only True Country is My Body', 2006 <http://www.kabako.org/txt-entretiens/my-body.html> [accessed 6 January 2022]

——, *Missie* (Brussels: Koninklijke Vlaamse Schouwburg, 2007).

——, *Congo: the Epic History of a People*, trans. by Sam Garrett (London: Fourth Estate, 2014).

Van Schuylenbergh, Patricia, 'Entre science et spectacle: « Les seigneurs de la forêt », le film initié par Léopold III', *Museum Dynasticum*, 2 (2002), 17–23.

Vansina, Jan, *L'évolution du royaume Rwanda des origines à 1900* (Brussels: ARSOM, 1962).

———, *Antecedents to Modern Rwanda: The Nyiginya Kingdom*, trans. by Jan Vansina (Madison: University of Wisconsin Press, 2004).

———, *Being Colonized: The Kuba Experience in Rural Congo, 1880–1960* (Madison: University of Wisconsin Press, 2010).

Vanthemsche, Guy, *Belgium and the Congo, 1885–1980*, trans. by Alice Cameron and Stephen Windross (Cambridge: Cambridge University Press, 2012).

Van Zandijcke, Aimé, *Pages d'histoire du Kasayi* (Namur: Grands Lacs, 1953).

———, *Les Baluba dans la tourmente* (Kananga: Éditions de l'Archidiocèse, 1989).

Vargas Llosa, Mario, *El sueño del celta* (Buenos Aires: Alfaguara, 2010).

———, *The Dream of the Celt*, trans. by Edith Grossman (London: Faber & Faber, 2013).

Vellut, Jean-Luc, 'La Violence armée dans l'État Indépendant du Congo: Ténèbres et Clartés dans l'histoire d'un État conquérant', *Cultures et Développement*, 16.3/4 (1984), 671–707.

———, 'Ressources scientifiques, culturelles et humaines de l'africanisme en Belgique. Perspectives sur un patrimoine d'outre-mer et sa mise en valeur', *Cahiers africains*, 9–11 (1994), pp. 115–44.

——— et al., *La naissance de la peinture contemporaine en Afrique Centrale, 1930 – 1970* (Tervuren: Royal Museum for Central Africa, 1992).

Verbeeck, Georgi, 'Legacies of an Imperial Past in a Small Nation. Patterns of Postcolonialism in Belgium', *European Politics and Society* <10.1080/23745118.2019.1645422> [accessed 15 July 2020]

Verbergt, Bruno, 'Transitioning the Museum: Managing Decolonization at the Royal Museum for Central Africa (2000–2020)', *Journal of Cultural Management and Cultural Policy*, 2 (2020), 141–69.

Verhaegen, Benoît, *Rébellions au Congo*, 2 vols (Brussels: CRISP, 1966).

———, 'La colonisation et la décolonisation dans les manuels d'histoire en Belgique', in *Papier blanc, encre noire. Cent ans de culture francophone en Afrique centrale (Zaïre, Rwanda et Burundi)*, ed. by Marc Quaghebeur and Émile Van Balberghe, with Nadine Fettweis and Annick Vilain, 2 vols (Brussels: Éditions Labor, 1992), pp. 333–79.

Verreet, Adolf, *Het zwarte leven van Mabumba* (Leuven: Davidsfonds, 1935).

Verstraete, Frederik 'A virtual Reconstruction of the 1913 Fair at STAM – Ghent city museum', A virtual reconstruction of the 1913 World Fair at STAM – Ghent city museum | MWF2014: Museums and the Web Florence 2014 [accessed 13 January 2022]

Vick, Brian, 'Greek Origins and Organic Metaphors: Ideals of Cultural Autonomy in Neohumanist Germany from Winckelmann to Curtius', *Journal of the History of Ideas*, 63.3 (2002), 483–500.

Vidal, Claudine, *Sociologie des passions* (Paris: Karthala, 1991).

Villers, Gauthier de, 'Confusion politique au Congo-Kinshasa', *Canadian Journal of African Studies/Revue Canadienne des Études Africaines*, 'Special Issue: French-Speaking Central Africa: Political Dynamics of Identities and Representations' 33.2/3 (1999), 432–47 (434).

Vincent, Johan J., Paul Geens, André Vandenbunder, Rudolf De Muynck, and Anton Wilsens, *Naslagwerk over De Vlaamse Film: ('Het Leentj')* (Brussels: C.I.A.M., 1986).

Vittor, Amy Y., Gabriel Zorello Laporta, and Maria Anice Mureb Sallum, 'How deforestation helps deadly viruses jump from animals to humans', *The Conversation*, 2020 <theconversation.com/how-deforestation-helps-deadly-viruses-jump-from-animals-to-humans-139645> [accessed 14 November 2021]

Vlachos, Nathanael M., 'Brett Bailey's Traveling Human Zoo: Fragmentations of Whiteness Across Borders', in Unsettling Whiteness, ed. by Lucy Michael and Samantha Schulz (Leiden: Brill, 2014), pp. 59–67 <https://doi.org/10.1163/9781848882829_007>

Vlassenroot, Koen and Chris Huggins, 'Land, Migration and Conflict in Eastern D.R. Congo', in *From the Ground up: Land Rights, Conflict and Peace in Sub-Saharan Africa*, ed. by Chris Huggins and Jenny Clover (Pretoria: Institute for Security Studies, 2004), pp. 115–94.

Vuillard, Éric, *Congo* (Arles: Actes Sud, 2012).

Wa Karega, Joseph Jyoni, 'Le Rwanda sous la 1ère et 2ème République', in *Histoire du Rwanda des origines à la fin du XXème siècle*, ed. by Déo Byanafashe and Paul Rutayisire (Huye: Université nationale du Rwanda, 2011), pp. 422–516.

Walcott, Derek, *Collected Poems 1948–1984* (New York: Noonday Press, 1986).

Walschap, Gerard, *Oproer in Congo* (Amsterdam: Elsevier, 1953).

Walsh, John, 'Coming of Age with an AK-47: Ahmadou Kourouma's Allah n'est pas obligé', *Research in African Literatures* 39.1 (2008), 185–97.

Wauters, Alphonse-Jules, *Bibliographie du Congo 1880–1895. Catalogue méthodique de 3.800 ouvrages, brochures, notices et cartes relatifs à l'histoire, à la géographie et à la colonisation du Congo* (Brussels: Administration du Mouvement Géographique, 1895).

Weizman, Eyal and Sheik Fazal, *The Conflict Shoreline: Colonialism as Climate Change* (Göttingen: Steidl, 2015).

Werbner, Pnina, 'Rich Man Poor Man: or a Community of Suffering: Heroic Motifs in Manchester Pakistani Life Histories', *Oral History* 8.1 (1980), 43–48.

Wesseling, Henri, *Le partage de l'Afrique* (Paris: Denoël, 1996).

White, Bob, 'L'incroyable machine d'authenticité: l'animation politique et l'usage public de la culture dans le Zaïre de Mobutu', *Anthropologie et sociétés*, 30.2 (2006), 43–63 <https://www.erudit.org/fr/revues/as/2006-v30-n2-as1445/014113ar/> [accessed 10 May 2022]

——, *Rumba Rules: The Politics of Dance Music in Mobutu's Zaïre* (Durham, NC: Duke University Press, 2008).

Williams, Charlotte, *Sugar and Slate* (Ceredigion: Planet, 2002).

Williams, Denis, *The Third Temptation* (Leeds: Peepal Tree Press, 2010 [1968]).

Williamson Sinalo, Caroline, 'Narrating African Conflict News: An Intercultural Analysis of Burundi's 2015 Coup', *Journalism* (2020), 1–16.

——, Pierre Claver Irakoze and Angela Veale, 'Disclosure of Genocide Experiences in Rwandan Families: Private and Public Sources of Information and Child Outcomes', *Peace and Conflict: Journal of Peace Psychology*, Advance online publication (2020) <https://doi.org/10.1037/pac0000521>

Windey, Catherine, 'Abstracting Congolese Forests: Mappings, Representational Narratives, and the Production of the Plantation Space under REDD+', https://www.uantwerpen.be/en/research-groups/iob/publications/discussion-papers/dp-2020/dp-202001 [accessed 04 August 2022].

Wiot, Valériane, *Joseph Ndwaniye, La Promesse à ma sœur. Carnet pédagogique* (Brussels: Espace Nord/Fédération Wallonie-Bruxelles, 2019).

Wirth, Charlotte, 'Belgiens schweres koloniales Erbe', *Reporter*, 4 January 2019 <https://www.reporter.lu/neues-museum-fehlende-debatte-belgiens-schweres-koloniales-erbe/> [accessed 21 July 2020]

Witte, Els, Jan Craeybeckx and Alain Meynen, *Political History of Belgium: From 1830 Onwards* (Brussels: ASP, 2009).

Yates, Barbara A., 'Educating Congolese Abroad: An Historical Note on African Elites', *The International Journal of African Historical Studies*, 14.1 (1981), 34–64.

——, 'The Origins of Language Policy in Zaire', *The Journal of Modern African Studies*, 18.2 (1981), 257–79.

Yoneyama, Shoko, 'Miyazaki Hayao's Animism and the Anthropocene', *Theory Culture & Society* (2021), 1–16.

'Young Africans Explore Congo Roots', BBC Local: South East Wales <http://news.bbc.co.uk/local/southeastwales/hi/people_and_places/arts_and_culture/newsid_8234000/8234119.stm> [accessed 18 December 2020].

Young, Jason C., 'Environmental Colonialism, Digital Indigeneity, and the Politicization of Resilience, *Environment and Planning E: Nature and Space*, 4.2 (2019), 230–51.

Young, Robert J. C., 'Neocolonial Times', *The Oxford Literary Review*, 13.1 (1991), 2–3.

About the authors

Sarah Arens is a British Academy postdoctoral fellow (2019–2023) at the University of Liverpool with a project entitled 'Constructing a Geopolitics of Nationhood: The Belgian Scientific and Cultural Colonial Project (1830–1958)', which investigates the role of natural sciences and their exhibition through museums and world fairs as a pathway to better understanding the ideologies that fuelled Belgian colonialism and the resistance against it. She is also an assistant professor in French and the editor of the *Bulletin of Francophone Postcolonial Studies*.

Robert Burroughs is professor and head of English at Leeds Beckett University. His books include *Travel Writing and Atrocities* (2011), *The Suppression of the Atlantic Slave Trade* (2015), and *African Testimony in the Movement for Congo Reform* (2018). A previous recipient of funding from the Arts and Humanities Research Council, the Leverhulme Trust (Early Career Fellowship), and the Netherlands Organisation for Scientific Research, he is currently a Leverhulme Trust Research Fellow.

Bambi Ceuppens holds a PhD in social anthropology from the University of St Andrews in Scotland. She is a senior researcher and curator of contemporary African Art at the Royal Museum for Central Africa and a lecturer at KASK – School of Arts (Ghent) and Sint Lucas School of Arts (Antwerp). She has curated the exhibition *Indépendance! Congolese Stories about Congolese independence* (RMCA, 2010 - 2011) and co-curated the exhibition Congo Art Works: Popular Painting with Sammy Baloji (Centre for Fine Arts, Brussels, 2016); Congo Art Works: Popular Painting with Sammy Baloji and Valentin Diaconov (Garage Museum of Contemporary Art, Moscow, 2017); Congo Stars with Sammy Baloji, Gunther Holler-Schuster, Fiston Mwanza Mujila & Barbara Steiner (Kunsthaus Graz, Austria, 2018 - 2019; Kunsthalle Tübingen, Germany, 2019). Her research focuses on authochtony, Belgian-Congolese colonial history and cultural heritage, Congolese art and culture, Congolese in Belgium, decoloniality and representations of Africa(ns).

Matthias De Groof is a professor in film studies and visual cultures at the University of Antwerp, and a Marie Skłodowska-Curie Postdoctoral Fellow at the University of Amsterdam. He is interested in aesthetics as politics of forms and practices that contribute to the restoration of broken world views, while he also studies failing processes of decolonisation. He has held fellowship appointments at New York University's Tisch School of the Arts as a Fulbright scholar, at the Helsinki Collegium for Advanced Studies with Kone Foundation, at the University of Bayreuth's Africa Multiple Cluster of Excellence and at the Waseda University in Tokyo. His works include an edited book on *Lumumba in the Arts* (Leuven University Press, 2022), which reached a list of the top 100 'books to escape the news' (LitHub) and the films *Under The White Mask* (2020), *Palimpsest of the Africa Museum* (2019), *Lobi Kuna* (2018), *Diorama* (2018), and *Jerusalem, the Adulterous Wife* (2008), among others.

Pierre-Philippe Fraiture is professor of French studies at the University of Warwick, where he teaches postcolonial literatures. He is a member of the European Research Council-funded project Philosophy and Genres: Creating a Textual Basis for African Philosophy. His most recent publications include *Past Imperfect: Time and African Decolonization, 1945–1960* (Liverpool University Press, 2021), *The Mudimbe Reader* (Virginia University Press, ed. with Daniel Orrells, 2016), and *VY Mudimbe: Undisciplined Africanism* (Liverpool University Press, 2013). He is currently working on the notion of extractivism in Congolese art and literature.

Catherine Gilbert is currently a New Castle University Academic Track Fellow in the School of Modern Languages at Newcastle University, having recently completed a two-year Marie Skłodowska-Curie Individual Fellowship at Ghent University, Belgium (2018–2020). Her project, 'Genocide Commemoration in the Rwandan Diaspora', investigates the impact of place and displacement on commemorative practices within diasporic communities. More broadly, her research interests span postcolonial African literatures and cultures, with a particular focus on cultural memory, trauma and narrative. Her first monograph, *From Surviving to Living: Voice, Trauma and Witness in Rwandan Women's Writing* (Presses universitaires de la Méditerranée, 2018), received the SAGE *Memory Studies* Journal and Memory Studies Association Outstanding First Book Award in 2019. She has recently co-edited, with Kate McLoughlin and Niall Munro, the volume *On Commemoration: Global Reflections upon Remembering War* (Peter Lang, 2020).

Chantal Gishoma is a postdoctoral fellow at the University of Bayreuth in the European Research Council-funded project Philosophy and Genres: Creating a Textual Basis for African Philosophy. She is a researcher in African literature, specialising in Rwandan language and literature. Her thesis, defended at the Sorbonne nouvelle-Institut National des Langues et Civilisations Orientales, as well as her various publications, focus on the poetic work of the Rwandan poet and philosophers, Alexis Kagame, translation in literature, and radio theatre.

Hannah Grayson is a lecturer in French and francophone studies at the University of Stirling. Her research focuses on so-called crisis and its aftermath in 'French-language' African literature, and her current book project on Tierno Monénembo investigates his fictional depictions of *débrouillardise*. She has worked extensively on the testimonies of people who lived through the Genocide against the Tutsi in Rwanda. She was recently awarded British Academy funding for a project on decolonising discourses of resilience in the Arts and Humanities.

Dónal Hassett is lecturer in French at University College Cork. He holds a doctorate in history from the European University Institute in Florence. His first book, *Mobilizing Memory: The Great War and the Language of Politics in Colonial Algeria, 1918–1939*, was published by Oxford University Press in 2019. He was recently awarded an Irish Research Council New Foundations Research Grant for a project on the decolonisation of Irish public heritage.

Sky Herington holds a bachelor's degree in French and philosophy from the University of Oxford and an MA in comparative literature from the École Normale Supérieure of Lyon. She is a PhD candidate at the University of Warwick, where she teaches postcolonial literature. Her thesis (submitted in September 2022) focuses on embodiment and performances of power in Sony Labou Tansi's plays. She was awarded the Theatre and Performance Research Association Postgraduate Essay Prize (2020).

Nicki Hitchcott is professor of French at the University of St Andrews. She is a specialist in postcolonial literatures in French, particularly African fiction. From 2015 to 2018, Nicki led the AHRC-funded project, 'Rwandan Stories of Change' in partnership with NGO the Aegis Trust and the Genocide Archive of Rwanda. Her most recent publications include three books on Rwanda: a monograph, *Rwanda Genocide Stories: Fiction Since 1994* (Liverpool University Press, 2015) and two co-edited volumes, *Rwanda Since 1994: Stories of Change* (Liverpool University Press, 2019) and *After the Genocide in Rwanda: Stories of Violence, Change and Reconciliation* (I. B. Tauris, 2019).

Yvette Hutchison is a professor in Theatre and Performance Studies in SCAPVC, University of Warwick. Her research focuses on anglophone African theatre, history and narratives of memory, and how intercultural performance practices are challenged by ongoing postcolonial issues. She is associate editor of the *South African Theatre Journal* and the *African Theatre* series. Her Leverhulme project Performing Memory: Theatricalising identity in contemporary South Africa in 2012 culminated in her monograph *South African Performance and Archives of Memory* (Manchester University Press, 2013). From 2015 to 2017 she had AHRC funding to develop mobile app technology to create a virtual network of African women creative practitioners and other interested parties, resulting in the African Womens' Playwright Network (AWPN.org). Her latest publications include the co-edited *African Theatre: Contemporary Dance* (James Currey, 2018) and *Contemporary Plays by African Women* (Methuen, 2019).

Albert Kasanda is a research fellow of the Centre of Global Studies in the Institute of Philosophy at the Czech Academy of Sciences and member of the European Research Council-funded project Philosophy and Genres: Creating a Textual Basis for African Philosophy. He focuses on African social and political philosophy. In 2018, he published a monograph with Routledge, entitled *Contemporary African Social and Political Philosophy: Trends, Debates, and Challenges*. The book was subsequently translated into Czech. His earlier publications include *John Rawls: Les bases philosophiques du libéralisme politique* (L'Harmattan, 2005) and an edited volume entitled *Pour une pensée africaine émancipatrice. Points de vue du Sud* (L'Harmattan, 2004).

Maëline Le Lay specialises in African literatures. Her current research focuses on performing arts and literature of the Great Lakes Region (DRC, Rwanda, and Burundi). She also investigates the colonial history of theatre and literature written and performed in the former Belgian, British and French empires. She is a researcher at the CNRS (French National Centre for Scientific Research), affiliated at the THALIM research centre (Paris Sorbonne nouvelle). She was affiliated at IFRA-Nairobi (French Institute for Research in Africa) in 2018-2021.

Reuben Loffman teaches history at Queen Mary University of London and his research has largely focused on missionaries in the DR Congo. His first book, *Church, State, and Colonialism in Southeastern Congo, 1890–1962* (Palgrave, 2019), explored the relationship between Belgian administrators and the Catholic Church from the vantage point of a local case study, that of Kongolo.

The book argues that Church-state relations did not run seamlessly as Crawford Young (1965) suggested but, instead, the two institutions were competitive collaborators. His next project explores the turbulent relationship between the United States and the Congo in the colonial period and primarily through the lens of American Protestant missionaries, such as the Baptists, Methodists, and Presbyterians.

Caroline Williamson Sinalo is lecturer in world languages at University College Cork and author of *Rwanda after Genocide: Gender, Identity and Posttraumatic Growth* (Cambridge University Press, 2018) and co-author of *Transmitting Memories in Rwanda: From a Survivor Parent to the next Generation* (Brill, 2022). Williamson Sinalo's research focuses on conflict and violence in Africa's Great Lakes region, and has been supported by the AHRC, the Aegis Trust, the Irish Research Council, the Government of Ireland, and Enterprise Ireland.

Index

Aanza, Sinzo 23, 24, 33, 359-361, 363, 364, 369-372, 375, 376
Action Zoo Humain 125, 131, 132, 134
Adou Elenga 328
AfricaMuseum 76
Afro-descendants 82, 83, 95
Afrofuturistic 351
Afrophone literature 156-158, 161
Agbebi, Mojola 116
Agence France Presse 172
agency 294, 300, 303, 308
agriculture 31, 212-219, 221-223, 225, 226
agronomy 214-216, 219
alienation 306
alternative worlds 320
ambiance 326
American Baptist Missionary Union 108
amnesia 85, 86, 121, 124, 125, 137
Angali 24
Anglo-Belgian India Rubber Company (Abir) 104, 360
Angola 317
animals 342, 343, 345, 346
animism 337, 344, 346, 354, 355
anthropology 47, 50, 51, 53
Antwerp 171, 222
apocalyptic time 261
architecture 189-192, 195, 196, 201, 202, 206, 261-263, 265, 266
archives 19, 20, 23, 24, 27, 28, 30, 31, 121, 122, 124-127, 129, 130, 132, 133, 135, 138, 359, 365, 376, 379
art
    academic 320, 321, 323-325, 332
    classical 317, 319, 328, 332
    contemporary 316, 317, 319, 321, 324, 325, 327-332
    precolonial 320, 321, 323, 327, 328, 331
    urban 318, 321-325, 327, 331, 332
Arusha Peace Agreement (2000) 167, 169
Assmann, Aleida 18, 28
Association Internationale Africaine 14
Astrida 276, 280, 287
Atomium 25, 342
atrocities 104, 105, 125, 315, 329
authenticity 15, 16, 22, 32, 147, 153, 154, 212, 258, 320, 321, 323, 324
Bach, Johann Sebastian 367

Bagaza, Jean-Baptiste 11
Bailey, Brett 30, 125-130, 132, 133
    Exhibit A/B 127-130
Baloji, Sammy 12, 23, 24, 316, 317, 325, 329, 331
Balufu Bakupa Kanyinda 327, 330
Bandoma, Steve 24, 324, 325, 331
Baptist Missionary Society 108
Barly Baruti 330
Barret, Renaud 319
Baudouin (king) 256, 257, 322, 324, 339
Bayazi 202
Behr, Edward 316
belatedness 214, 215, 220, 222-224
Belgium
    apology by government of 82, 84, 92
    armed forces of 256
    Belgian colonialism 12-16, 20, 28, 29, 31, 32, 51, 122, 124, 127, 145, 146, 149, 160, 168, 169, 193, 201, 212, 215, 216, 218, 220, 223, 231, 232, 236, 247, 253, 254, 256, 261, 266, 267, 280, 302, 303, 315, 319, 331, 359, 366, 368
    citizenship education in 82, 91, 93, 95
    debates surrounding monarchy 15, 85
    federalisation in 19, 81, 85
    foreign aid from 174, 178, 179, 212
    government apologies from 27
    interest of population in colonial history 14, 16, 17, 44, 52, 56, 83, 211, 223
    linguistic communities in 15, 19-21, 30, 81, 85, 86, 91, 93
    media in 167, 168, 170-172, 175, 176, 178, 179, 181-183
    official apologies by 171
    politics of memory in 25, 82-86, 88, 91, 92, 170, 171
    popular support for empire 342
    public interest in colonial history 125
    racism in 21, 25, 171, 177, 182
    settlers from 256
    status as a colonial power 31, 105, 124, 215, 220, 223, 224, 226
    teaching of colonial history in 15, 30, 46, 55, 81, 82, 84, 86, 87, 91, 93, 96
Ben Chikha, Chokri 30
Bentrovato, Denise 83
Berlin Act (1884-1885) 143
Berlin Conference 13

Bertho, Elara 371
Bible 150, 159, 168
Biebuck, Daniel 343
Black Lives Matter 25, 81, 82, 125, 171, 182, 189
Blyden, E.W. 116
Boast, Robin 49
Bobineau, Julien 122, 131
Bobo, Fiona 24
Bodys Isek Kingelez 317, 326, 327
Boisdeffre, Pierre de 69, 70
Booth, William 107
Botalatala, Emmanuel 328
botany 215-217, 219
Boto, Eza (Mongo Beti) 376
Braeckman, Colette 12, 69, 172, 175, 176, 180
Bragard, Véronique 95
Brazzaville 253, 254, 264, 266
Brett Bailey
    Exhibit A/B 128
Broqueville, Huguette de 29, 65, 69-73, 77-80
Bruner, Jerome 173, 181
Brussels 16, 17, 25, 26, 43, 56, 64, 66-68, 73, 75, 76,
    78, 88, 89, 92-94, 171, 216, 262, 264, 265, 327, 329
    1958 World Fair in 216, 223
Bucumi-Nkurunziza, Denise 173
Bujumbura 301, 302, 304
Bula-Matari/Bula-Matadi 17, 366, 367
Bullamatari, Dom Francisco 367
Bumbu, Laurent 324
Burundi 11, 12, 15, 22, 26, 28, 29, 31, 32, 64, 121, 234,
    235, 273, 283, 287, 293-296, 298, 301, 302, 304,
    305, 309
    1993 presidential elections in 296, 304, 305
    2015 crisis in 169, 174
    2020 presidential elections in 31, 167, 174
    as recipient of foreign aid 174, 176, 178, 179, 182
    Belgian colonial administration of 13, 20, 168
    civil war in 169, 175, 293, 295, 303, 306, 307
    colonial construction of racial identities in
        168-170, 182, 302, 305
    ethnic based violence in 15, 169, 171, 182, 298,
        304
    ethnicization of social identity in 169-171, 175,
        296
    historiography of 51, 52
    independence of 11, 296, 304
    relations with Rwanda 175, 176, 304, 306
    traces of colonial past in 168, 295, 302, 303, 309
Butare 248-250, 276
Büttner, Carl Gotthilf 147
Buyoya, Pierre 169
Callewaert, Emilio 202
Canada 159
capitalism 104, 192, 211, 212, 220, 221, 332, 344, 352,
    360, 362, 374
Casanova, Pascale 374
Casement, Roger 104, 315
Castryck, Geert 85, 87, 123

Catholic Church 70, 72, 168, 169, 177, 201, 203, 205,
    232, 238, 244, 247, 276, 285
causal emplotment 173, 176, 177, 179, 180
Cellule Démocratie ou Barbarie 88, 90, 93
Centre Communautaire Laïc Juif (CCLJ) 93
Centre d'Étude et de Documentation Africaines
    (CEDAF)/Afrika Studie- en Documentatiecen-
    trum (ASDOC) 17
Centre Pluridisciplinaire pour la Transmission de la
    Mémoire (CPTM) 91, 94
Certeau, Michel de 281
Césaire, Aimé 48, 144
Ceuppens, Bambi 28, 32, 47
Chakrabarty, Dipesh 220
Cheri Benga 322
Cheri Cherin 322, 325
Cheri Samba 32, 317, 322
Chikha, Chokri Ben 125, 131, 132, 137
    The Truth Commission (2013) 125, 131-137
childhood 293-295, 297-301, 303, 304, 307, 308
chocolate 124, 125
Chrétien, Jean-Pierre 248
Christian proselytism 24, 146, 150-152, 159, 160, 232,
    241, 244, 245
churches 284-286
Ciluba 30, 143, 146, 147, 149-151, 153-161
cinema 316-318, 327, 330, 331, 337, 339-346, 348,
    350-352, 354
    eco-cinema 339, 347, 348, 350, 352
Cité Miroir 91
cities 360-362, 364, 365, 368, 375
    city space 23, 32, 254, 261, 263, 265, 266, 318,
        326, 327, 364
    urban planning 12, 262, 263, 326, 360, 366,
        371, 372
    urban space 190
    'ville' versus 'cité' 262
Clark, Frank Teva 110, 115
Classe, Léon 238, 239, 242, 245, 247
clichés 213, 214, 220, 223-226, 243
CNDD-FDD party (Burundi) 167, 169, 175, 177,
    180, 182
CNL party (Burundi) 167
cobalt 347
co-curation 49, 53
coded language 322
coevalness 365, 374
Cold War 15
Collectif Memoires Coloniales et Luttes contre les
    Discriminations (CMCLD) 124
Collège Liberman 204
colonial garden 263
colonial history 129, 321, 331
colonialism 63-77, 79, 80, 212-214, 217, 220-222,
    225, 226
coloniality 189-191, 195, 197, 199, 200, 203, 205, 207
colonial library 14, 27, 28
Colonial University (Antwerp) 14

Colonie belge (painting) 323, 324
commemoration 83, 91, 94
Compagnie du Congo pour le Commerce et l'Industrie (CCCI) 14
COMRAF 46, 53, 54, 58
Congo 147
    Belgian colonial administration of 13, 17, 22, 46, 52, 85, 149, 190, 192, 319, 320, 323, 325, 327-330, 366
    Belgian Congo 11-13, 16, 26-28, 122, 211-218, 220-223, 226-229, 243, 254, 280, 302, 320, 323, 340, 342, 360, 368
    Belgian settlers in 20
    civil war in 257
    Congo Free State 11-14, 16, 30, 82, 83, 85, 103, 105, 106, 108, 111, 116, 117, 122, 144, 145, 148, 149, 171, 211, 212, 214, 215, 217, 218, 220, 226, 315, 323, 329, 360, 362, 366
    Democratic Republic of the Congo 11-13, 23-27, 31, 33, 55, 114, 124, 143, 157, 158, 171, 178, 182, 189-191, 199, 203, 206, 207, 211, 212, 225, 253, 254, 261, 272, 288, 302, 306, 315-317, 320, 322, 324, 339, 359, 362, 369, 370, 372, 376
    diaspora in Belgium 82
    diaspora of 156-158, 359, 370, 372
    ethnic based conflict in 22
    ethnic based violence in 152
    historiography of 23, 25, 51, 52, 260, 319, 329, 332, 363, 368
    independence of 11, 15, 21, 47, 55, 86, 124, 151, 255, 256, 258-260, 263, 265, 280, 322
    Lower Congo 104, 109, 202
    Ministry of Hydrocarbons of 348
    Republic of the Congo (1960-71) 22, 204, 253, 317
    traces of colonial past in 23, 26, 321, 324, 329-331, 368, 369, 375
    Upper Congo 103, 104
    Zaire 15, 17, 22, 23, 55, 153, 321, 376
    Zaïre 197, 203
Congo Commission 96
Congo Crisis 256, 261, 323
Congo House 30, 106-108, 110-112, 114-117
Congo International Film Festival (Goma) 350
Congoism 32, 315-317, 319, 332
Congo reform movement 104, 105, 117
Congo River 255, 266, 267
Congo wars 325, 331
Conrad, Joseph 315
Conseil de la Transmission de la Mémoire 93
contact zone 45-47, 49, 52, 54, 57, 213, 217, 221, 222, 225
control 211, 212, 214-216, 224, 226
Coopération par l'Éducation et la Culture (CEC) 16
copper 360, 362, 367
cordon sanitaire 33, 281, 363-365, 369, 371
Coupez, André 234, 235

Courtens, Alfred 123
Covid-19 31, 167, 171, 177-181, 343
creativity 318, 332
creusage, creuseurs 33, 363, 369-371, 373, 376
Crichton, Michael 315
crossings 274, 288, 289, 302, 303, 308
Crowther, Samuel Ajayi 108
Dan, Bernard 29, 65, 73-75, 77, 80
Daniel Shongo 324
De Boeck, Filip 12, 23, 318
De Boe, Gerard 340
decolonisation 95, 211, 212, 224, 225, 255, 264
De Croo, Alexander 27
De Lame, Danielle 87
Deleuze, Gilles 371
Demaeseneer, Rony 66
Demissie, Fassil 191, 196
Democratic Republic of the Congo 72
Derrida, Jacques 122
Descola, Philippe 337, 344, 346
Désir, Caroline 97
De Stoeten Ostendenoare ('the bold Ostenders') 124
De Wildeman, Emile Auguste 216-219, 221-223
De Witte, Ludo 83
Dewulf, Jeroen 20
Dhanis, Francis 14
Dianga, Kennedy 325
Dieudo Hamadi 317
diglossia 233, 370
Diop, Cheikh Anta 156
disease 177, 364
Disney 339, 345
distance 293, 294, 303-305, 307-309
Djilatendo 201
Drion du Chapois, Ferdinand 69
Duggan, Jo-Anne 122
dystopia 362, 365, 372
echolocation 138
écoles-chapelles 202
ecology 337, 341, 344, 345, 347, 348, 350, 352, 355
Eco, Umberto 322
Éditions Lokole 373
education 146, 147, 149-152, 154, 158, 159, 168, 233, 234, 236, 240, 242, 245, 247
Efoui, Kossi 376
Eisenstein, Sergei 354
Ekete, Eddy 325, 328
Elmina 201
embodied practice/knowledge/performance 124, 130, 132, 135-138
enfants métis 26, 27
escape 307, 308
escapism 320, 326, 328, 331
Espace Nord 66, 78, 88-89
ethnographic displays 45-47, 49-52, 54, 56, 57
European Commission 347
European Union 174, 175, 347
exhibitions 122, 128, 131-134, 263, 315, 342

exploitation 212, 215, 216, 218-220, 222
Extinction Rebellion 352
extractivism 14, 23, 33, 343-348, 350, 354, 359, 363, 370, 375
Fabian, Johannes 12, 125, 135
Faïk-Nzuji, Clémentine 11, 23
Falone Mambu 329
Fanon, Frantz 18, 145, 148, 151, 156, 259, 365
Faye, Gaël 32, 92, 293-300, 302, 303, 305-309
    Petit Pays 293, 295, 297-299, 303, 308
Fédération Wallonie-Bruxelles (FWB) 84, 88, 93
Felly Pepe Manuaku 317
Ferdinand, Malcom 337, 341, 345, 352
Flanders 20, 26, 83, 124, 125, 131, 134, 137
    Flemish language 134, 136, 150
    Flemish nationalism 20
Floyd, George 171, 182, 189
Fondation Auschwitz 94
Forminière 14
framing theory 168, 170, 172, 173, 175, 182
France 64, 74, 75, 92, 103, 159, 235, 254, 267, 295, 309
    French colonialism 127, 148, 267
Francis, Ernestina 110
Francophonie 372
Franklin, John Lionel 111
Frantzen, Tom 76
FRODEBU party (Burundi) 169, 296, 305
Fulu Muziki 328
future 18, 19, 32, 255, 257, 259-261, 263-266, 328, 329, 365, 367-369, 372-374
Gabon 317
gardens 276, 281-284
Garnier, Xavier 158
gaze 51, 275-278
Gécamines 360, 369, 376
Ge'ez 146
Genocide against the Tutsi 63-70, 72-77
Germany 13, 168, 213, 232, 235
    German colonialism 13, 127, 280, 302
    Nazi Germany 339
Gevers, Marie 276, 277
Ghent 30, 131-133, 135, 137, 171
Giddens, Anthony 212, 220
Gitarama 306
globalisation 143, 147, 160, 161, 212, 217, 218, 220, 221
Goddeeris, Idesbald 29, 64, 83, 86
Godefroid, Marcel-Sylvain 21
Goma 316, 322, 337, 350, 352, 364
Gondola, Didier 12
Great Britain 30, 103-112, 114-117, 214, 215, 222-224, 284
    British colonialism 287
Great Lakes Region 32, 273, 277, 279, 282, 284, 288, 289, 339
Green Saviourism 348
Gryseels, Guido 43, 50, 51, 55, 56, 58, 125
Guattari, Félix 371
Habyarimana, Juvénal 11

Halen, Pierre 69, 70, 73, 79, 80
Hamitic hypothesis 31, 168, 171, 177, 182, 233, 240, 279, 302
hangars 202
Harrison, Colonel James J. 105
Harroy, Jean Paul 233, 239, 241
Hayman, Rachel 72
Hazoumé, Romuald 23
Heremans, Roger 239
hermeneutic composability 173, 181
Heusch, Luc de 12
hierarchy of cultures and languages 233, 234, 236
Himmelheber, Hans 23, 24
Himmler, Heinrich 340
historiography 220, 223, 226
history textbooks 83-86, 92
Hochschild, Adam 20, 21, 83, 105, 144
holes 371, 375
Holocaust education 82, 90
Hôpital Mama Yemo 190
Hron, Madelaine 65
Hughes, Rev. William 106-117
humanitarianism 103-106, 111, 116, 117, 177
human zoos 25, 128, 130, 131, 137, 342
Hunt, Nancy Rose 12
Hurel, Eugène 234, 238
Ibuka Mémoire et Justice (Belgique) 30, 93, 94
idealization 321, 326, 327
ideology 213, 214, 216, 217, 220-222, 225
Imbonerakure 167, 175, 176, 180, 181
implication 81, 293-295, 299-301, 303, 308
injustice 293-296, 299, 302, 303, 308
In Koli Jean Bofane 23, 24
innocence 293-295, 297-299, 306
Institut des Jeunes Noirs (Malta) 108
Institut Mwamba 203, 204, 206
Institut national pour l'étude agronomique du Congo belge (INEAC) 215, 222
Institut St.-Louis de Gonzague (Flanders) 108
intermediality 359, 374-376
Iviart Izamba 325
Jambo asbl 64, 96
jazz 317, 319, 359, 360, 362, 367, 378
Jewsiewicki, Bogumil 12, 322
Joris, Lieve 21
Junior Mvunzi 329
Kabamba, Maguy 23
Kabanda, Marcel 248
Kabasele, François 30, 143, 150, 156-161
Kabgayi 232
Kabila, Joseph 11
Kabila, Laurent-Désiré 11, 325, 329
Kafka, Franz 371
Kagame, Alexis 31, 184, 231-242, 244-247
    Inganji Kalinga 237, 249
    poetry of 232, 237, 241, 244-246
    Umulirimbyi wa Nyili-Ibiremwa 244, 245
Kagame, Paul 11, 84, 175

Kalanda, Mabika 153, 156, 160, 161
Kalulambi Pongo, Martin 151
Kamuanga Ilunga, Eddy 317, 325
Kapita (film by Katondolo) 348
Kapolowe 280, 281
Karangwa, Camille 22
Karisimbi, Mount 273, 274
Kasai 15, 22, 25, 156
Kasa-Vubu, Joseph 151, 329
Kasereka Kavwahireri 323
Kassim, Sumaya 53
Katanga 22, 192, 202, 207, 280, 330, 331, 359-363, 369
    secession of 15, 32, 257, 258, 261
Kayembe Kilobo 330
Kiangu, Sindani 83
Kigali 63, 280, 306
Kikongo 30, 149
Kimbangu, Simon 329
Kimpa Vita 331
Kinkasa 107-110, 113, 115
Kinshasa 16, 17, 190, 191, 254, 255, 257, 258, 261-267, 317, 318, 320-322, 324-328, 330, 361, 376
    Kin la belle 326
    Kin la poubelle 326
    Leopoldville 25, 32, 254, 256, 261, 366
Kinyarwanda 31, 181, 233-237, 244-246, 306
Kiri Katembo 32
Kivu, Lake 273, 278, 279, 289
Kongo 13, 17
Kongo Astronauts 328, 348
Kongo, kingdom of 317
Kongolo 31, 190-196, 198-204, 206, 207, 209
Kongolo, Antoine Tshitungu 83
Konono 317
Koselleck, Reinhart 13
Kuba 13, 25
Kura Shomali 325
Kuyangiko Balu, Hilaire 24
labour 192, 195, 197, 206, 212-214, 217-220, 225
La Libre Belgique 31, 167, 171, 172, 176-181
Lame, Danielle de 63, 69, 70, 76, 78, 79
Landmeters, Romain 82, 84
land reform 211, 213
landscape 32, 271, 273-284, 286, 287, 289, 290
language policy 143, 147, 148, 151, 152, 154, 160
Lauro, Amandine 29
League of Nations 11, 13
Lega 342-344, 347
Lemaire, Charles 360
Lemarchand, René 67, 68, 76, 79
Leopold I 214, 215
Leopold II 13, 15, 30, 46, 52, 64, 82, 85, 103-107, 116, 122-125, 128, 132, 143-145, 149, 171, 192, 212, 256, 257, 315, 360
Leopold III 32, 337, 339-341, 344
Leplae, Edmond 31, 214, 216-220, 222, 223, 225
Leroy, Jean 21
Le Soir 31, 167, 171, 172, 176-181

Leuven 171
Librism 324
Likaka, Osumaka 213, 214, 217, 224-226
Lingala 30, 149, 370
Linyekula, Faustin 317, 325, 329, 331
lithium 347
Littérature de gare 374
Liverpool School of Tropical Medicine 105
Logiest, Guy 68, 239, 241
Lomami Tshibamba, Paul 17
Lombume Kalimasi, Vincent 318
Lonetree, Amy 49
Longman, Timothy 70, 79, 80
Loutfi, Martine 17
Luba 13, 22, 30
Lubaki, Albert 317, 322
Lubaki, Antoinette 317, 322
Lubitsch, Ernest 330
Lubondo, Gosette 32, 325, 327
Lubumbashi 154, 191, 360-363, 368, 369, 375, 376
    Élisabethville 360, 361, 369, 376
Lubunda 202, 203
Luluabourg 145
Lumumba-Kasongo, Tukumbi 211, 212, 217
Lumumba, Patrice 11, 12, 15, 23, 26, 27, 32, 124, 257, 260, 261, 324, 329, 330, 362
Lunda 13
Maalu-Bungi, Crispin 146, 154, 157
Machini (film by Tétshim & Mukunday) 348, 354
Madya, Benoît 324
Maene, Maisha 32
Magema, Michèle 23, 24
Mahoux, Philippe 63
Makengo, Nelson 317, 327, 331
Makiadi Luambo, Franco 322
Mamdani, Mahmood 68, 72, 76, 79, 238, 240, 303, 308
Mampuya, Francis 324, 325
Manda Tchebwa 318
Martens, Renzo 316
Masters of the Congo Jungle, The (film) 337, 339, 340, 342-345, 348, 352, 354, 355
Mathilde of Belgium 27
matricide 341, 348, 352
Mbembe, Achille 48, 55, 227, 361, 362
M'Bokolo, Elikia 51
Mbuji-Mayi 360
Mbula Paluku, André 154
Mbu-Mputu, Norbert X. 114, 115
Médiaspaul 370, 373
Mega Mingiedi 325, 327
memory 16, 46, 121, 122, 124, 125, 130, 135, 138, 276-278, 281, 288, 294, 297, 308, 311, 362, 363, 367, 373
Miano, Léonora 332
Michel, Louis 84
Michel, Thierry 12
minerals 360, 362, 368-370
mining 346, 348, 350, 360, 361, 366, 368-371, 375

Index   421

Ministry of the Colonies (Belgium) 214, 217, 219
minority languages 234, 236
missionaries 103, 104, 106-112, 115, 116, 145, 146, 149-151, 159, 189, 193, 201-203, 206, 232, 234, 236-238, 240, 245-247, 280, 368
missions 280, 283-286, 289
Mitterrand, François 75
MNEMA asbl 91, 94
Mobutu Sese Seko 11, 14, 15, 19, 22, 23, 26, 32, 55, 147, 153, 155, 190, 197, 203, 207, 212, 253, 254, 258, 260, 261, 307, 318, 320-326, 328-332, 362, 366, 373, 376
modernisation 211, 212, 214, 216, 218-220
modernity 13, 18, 19, 23, 30, 31, 212, 216, 220, 223, 225, 232, 234, 361, 364, 366-368, 371, 374
Molière (Jean-Baptiste Poquelin) 371
Monénembo, Tierno 294, 298, 305
Monsengo Shula 24, 327, 328
monuments 28, 30, 122-124
Moonens, Laurent 320
Morel, E.D. 104
Morford, Joseph 110
Mother Nature (film by Maisha Maene) 337, 348, 350, 352, 354, 355
Mouvement Populaire de la Musique (Kinshasa) 326
Mozart, Wolfgang Amadeus 367
Mpala 280, 281
Mpala-Lutebele, Maurice Amuri 95
Mpane, Aimé 24, 326, 330, 332
Mudimbe, V.Y. 11, 12, 14, 18, 19, 22, 27, 32, 257, 272, 273, 275-278, 280-284, 289, 370
Mujila, Fiston Mwanza 23, 24, 33, 359-363, 366, 368, 373-376
Mukagasana, Yolande 22
Mukasonga, Scholastique 294, 297, 305
Mukunday, Frank 328, 330
Mulélé, Pierre 11
museum curatorship 12, 16, 23, 24, 26, 29, 46, 47, 49, 53, 54
Museum of Black Civilisations 44
music 11, 12, 16, 32, 33
Mutara III Rudahigwa (king) 232, 237, 239, 245
Muteba Luntumbe, Toma 46
Mutombo, Freddy 325
Muyira Arts et Mémoire asbl 89, 90
MuZee 316
Mwami 279, 280, 285, 286
Mwanga, Paul 318
Nada Tshibwabwa 329
Naigiziki, Saverio 32
Nairobi 283
narrative perspective 293-296, 298, 299, 304, 305, 308, 330
narrative theory 168, 172, 173, 179, 181
naturalism 344, 346, 352, 354, 355
natural resources 317, 319, 330, 332
nature 337, 339-341, 344-347, 352, 354, 355

Nayigiziki, Saverio 273, 274, 278, 279, 284, 285, 287-289
Nazism 340
Ndadaye, Melchior 305, 306
Ndala, Blaise 25, 26
Ndayishimiye, Évariste 167, 171, 179-183
Ndaywel è Nziem, Isidore 12
Ndele, Sarah 329
Ndi Umunyarwanda programme 243
Ndwaniye, Joseph 29, 65-67, 69, 71, 77-80, 88, 89
Négritude 246
neocolonialism 15, 22, 23, 31, 32, 58, 221, 253, 255, 258-260, 266
Netherlands 174, 224
New Museology 44-47, 49, 51-54, 56, 57
Ngal, Georges 22
Nganang, Patrice 371, 372
Ngandu Nkashama, Pius 155-158, 161
Ngongo Ramazani Primary School 204, 206
Ngoye, Achille 23
Ngũgĩ wa Thiong'o 148, 153, 155, 156
Nkanza 107-110, 113, 115
Nkundakozera, Anastase 64
Nkurunziza, Pierre 167, 171, 173-181
Nkusi, Laurent 248
nomads and nomadism 289
Nsengimana, Joseph 248, 249
Nyanga 342, 344, 347
Nyanza 278, 285, 286
Nyunzu 199
ontology 344, 346, 355
oral culture 322
orality 146, 151, 372
oral literature 232, 233, 237, 293, 372
Orjuela, Camilla 64, 76, 78, 80
Ostend 30, 123, 124
Paipo, Juvenal 198
Palais d'Egmont 27
Pan-Africanism 30, 106, 111, 114, 116, 117
pangolin 342, 343, 346, 347, 351, 355, 356
Papa Wendo 11
Parent, Sabrina 95
Parmhutu 15
past 11, 12, 14, 15, 17-19, 21, 23-27, 29, 30, 32, 361, 362, 364, 367-369, 375
peacekeepers 81
performance installations 125, 127, 129
performativity 321, 322, 331, 332
Philippe I (king) 27, 124, 171
Picasso, Pablo 317
Planche, Stéphanie 85
Pogge, Paul 146, 147, 154, 160
Pollack, Sydney 74
Portugal 222
  Portuguese colonialism 256
positionality 122, 131, 134, 136, 293, 294, 296, 299-301, 304, 305, 307, 308
postcoloniality 319, 322, 330-332

poverty 316, 318, 319
Pratt, Mary-Louise 213, 216
Précy Numbi 329, 330
present (time) 19, 21, 27, 31, 32, 364-368, 373, 374
  present past 19, 23, 25, 27, 28, 361, 369, 372, 374
progress 12, 18, 19, 31, 33, 366-368
prophetism 260
prophets 370
Prunier, Gérard 68, 75, 79
Pume Bylex 326, 327
Pungu, Gratia 53, 84
Rachmaninov, Sergei 367
radio 361, 363, 364, 369, 371, 372
Radio Bonesha 172
Radio Congo belge 320
Radio-Télévision Libre des Mille Collines (RTLM) 364
Radio Télévision Nationale du Burundi 31, 167, 171-181
Raharimanana, Jean-Luc 376
railways 13, 31, 33, 256, 287, 327, 363, 366, 371, 374, 375
  CFL workers' camp 195-201, 204, 206, 207
  Compagnie des Chemins de Fer du Congo Supérieur aux Grands Lacs Africans (CFL) 193, 195, 197, 199, 200, 202
  Compagnie du Chemin de fer du Bas-Congo au Katanga (BCK) 14
  Société Nationale des Chemins de Fer du Congo (SNCC) 197
  Société Nationale des Chemins de Fer Zaïrois (SNCZ) 197
Raubwirtschaft 13
RCN Justice & Démocratie 30, 94
reappropriation 282
Red Rubber scandal 12, 25, 105
Reisdorff, Ivan 70
Renders, Luc 20
resistance 213, 214, 216, 224, 226
restitution 44, 50, 55, 56, 58
restorative justice (Gacaca) 244
Rhodes, Cecil 189
Rhodesia 222
Rhodes Must Fall 36
Rietberg Museum (Zurich) 23
ritual objects 321, 322
roads 276, 279, 280, 286-288
Robert, Mireille-Tsheusi 55
Roelens, Victor 202, 205
Rose-Hunt, Nancy 191
Rosoux, Valérie 85
Rothberg, Michael 97, 293, 294, 296, 299-302
Royal Colonial Institute 14
Royal Museum for Central Africa (RMCA) 12, 14, 25, 26, 43-47, 49-58, 60, 81, 88, 125, 162, 234, 321, 322, 359, 376
  AfricaMuseum 23, 97, 98, 125
  Museum of the Belgian Congo 26

Royal Museums of Fine Arts (Brussels) 332
Ruanda-Urundi 11, 13, 17, 20, 27, 31, 32, 39, 64, 68, 70, 81, 83, 213, 241, 243, 302, 303
ruination 31, 200, 204-207
rumba 16, 32, 265, 317-322
rural areas 214, 216, 224, 225
Rutayisire, Paul 248-250
Ruti, Antoine 32, 272-275, 277, 278, 281, 283, 286-289
Rwagasore, Louis (prince) 11, 304
Rwanda 11, 12, 15, 19, 22, 26, 28, 29, 31, 121, 175, 182, 272, 273, 276-281, 285, 295, 296, 298, 303, 305, 306, 309
  1994 genocide against the Tutsi 12, 16, 19, 21, 22, 26, 29, 30, 32, 87, 90, 92, 170, 212, 231, 238, 240, 244, 293-296, 300, 301, 303-305, 307, 364
  Belgian colonial administration of 13, 20, 81, 90, 92, 231-234, 240, 247, 280
  civic education in 242, 243
  civil war in 294, 296, 297, 303, 307
  colonial construction of racial identities in 13, 213, 233, 235, 238, 240, 302
  diaspora in Belgium 81, 83, 87, 90, 94, 96
  ethnic based violence in 243, 244
  ethnicisation of social identity in 15
  German colonial administration of 232
  historiography of 31, 51, 52, 81, 83, 84, 87, 237, 239-242
  in Belgian school curriculum 82, 84, 87, 90, 92, 93, 95
  independence of 11, 15
  legal institutions in 244
  militias in 242, 243
  monarchy in 232, 237, 242, 245
  postcolonial 231, 234, 240-244, 247
  refugees from 295, 302
  relations with Burundi 306
  traces of colonial past in 302, 303
  traditional schools in (Itorero) 242, 243
Rwandan Patriotic Front (RPF) 70, 72, 73, 80
Rwasa, Agathon 167, 171, 174-176, 182
Said, Edward 17, 20, 227
Sambu,Yves 24
Sarr-Savoy Report 44
Savage, Mike 19
Schäfer, Ernst 340
science 212, 214, 215, 217-220, 224, 226
segregation 262-264, 266, 281, 360, 364, 375
selective appropriation 173, 176
Sembène, Ousmane 286
Service Photographique 191
Shongo, David 24
Shostakovich, Dmitri 367
Sinzo Aanza 319, 332
Société Générale de Belgique 14
Sola 202, 204
SOS Médias Burundi 31, 167, 171, 172, 174-181, 183

South Africa 126, 127, 132, 133, 137, 345
space 125, 254, 255, 262-265, 267, 271, 272, 274, 276, 278, 280-284, 289, 342
spatialisation of time 364, 366, 368, 376
Special Committee for Katanga (CSK) 192
Spelman Seminary (Atlanta) 108
Spiritans 192, 202, 203
Stanard, Matthew 25, 28, 83, 86, 122, 223, 231
Stanley, Henry Morton 14, 33, 103, 107, 360, 363, 366, 367, 369, 373
Stanleyville, siege of 316
statues 124
stereotypes 16, 28, 31, 32, 213, 214, 217, 220, 222, 223, 225, 226, 316, 321
Stoler, Ann Laura 31, 121, 190, 191, 199, 200, 206, 207
Storck, Henri 340
Stromae 92
Strother, Zoë 319
Swahili 30, 146, 149, 360, 370
Table ronde, Conference 27
Tanganyika Territory 287
Tansi, Sony Labou 11, 26, 32, 253-255, 258-267, 371
 Le Bombardé 254, 257-264, 266
 'Le Sexe de Matonge' 254, 255, 263-267
 Marie Samar 254, 255, 257, 259-262, 264, 266
Tanzania 345
Taylor, Diana 130
temporality 12, 19, 25, 254, 260, 261, 265, 266, 365, 366, 368, 369, 374
Territorial Administrator 200, 201
Territorial Bureau 199-201
Tétshim 328, 330
theatre 131-133, 137, 254, 259, 264, 323
Thys, Albert 14
Tippu Tip 145
Tobe, Géraldine 332
Total 348
transcolonialism 221, 222, 224
trash literature 371
Travélé, Moussa 235
travel narratives 273, 277, 278, 282
Tropenmuseum 58
Trouillot, Michel-Rolph 43
Truth and Reconciliation Commission (South Africa) 26, 132
Tshibumba Kanda Matulu 11, 23, 323, 330
Tshiluba 370
Tshindele, Pathy 24, 325
Tshisekedi, Félix 82, 171
Tshisungu wa Tshisungu, José 146, 147, 150, 157, 159
Tshyela Ntendu 317, 322
Tsimba, Freddy 23, 24, 325, 328, 331, 332
Tulizo, Pamela 316
Tutsiphobia 182
Twa 342, 344, 347
Uganda 273, 277, 287, 288
Union Minière du Haut-Katanga (UMHK) 14, 360, 365, 366, 368, 375

United Nations 68, 323
United States 103, 111, 159, 174, 175, 207, 345
urban fallism 189
Usumbura 283
Uwase, Laure 64
Uwiligiyimana, Agathe 63
Van Hove, Johnny 315
Van Impe, Abbot 108
Van Nieuwenhuyse, Karel 83, 86, 91
Van Reybrouck, David 12, 21, 28
Vansina, Jan 12, 22, 201, 239
Vanthemsche, Guy 29
Van Ypersele, Laurence 85
Vargas Llosa, Mario 21
vehicles 295, 304-308
Vellut, Jean-Luc 192
Venezuela 340
Verbeeck, Georgi 73, 76, 80
Verbergt, Bruno 47
Verhofstadt, Guy 63, 76, 84, 92
Versailles Treaty 13, 302
Viaene, Vincent 28
Vidal, Claudine 248, 249
villas 262, 301
violence 11, 19, 29, 30, 32, 81, 82, 85, 91, 104-106, 110, 114, 121, 124, 126, 127, 129-132, 148, 157, 169-171, 181, 182, 191, 201, 211, 213, 217, 218, 221, 225, 226, 243, 293-300, 302-308, 315, 320, 331, 332, 372, 373, 375
 colonial 47, 49, 51, 52, 54, 57, 105, 128, 200, 319, 367, 369
 cultural 235
 epistemological 11, 14, 235
Virunga 32, 339, 342, 345, 346, 348, 350, 352
visual arts 16, 33
Vitshois Mwilambwe Mwendo 324, 325
Von Wissmann, Hermann Wilhelm 146, 147, 154, 160
Vuillard, Éric 21
Walcott, Derek 190, 318
Wales 103, 106, 107, 109, 110, 112-114, 116
 Colwyn Bay 30, 106, 107, 109-111, 114-116
Wallenda, Marc 320
Wallonia 15, 26, 94
Wauters, Alphonse-Jules 14
Wayland Seminary (Washington) 108
Welles, Orson 340
Western charity 221, 222
Western time 368
West, Richard 333
Wetsi Mpoma, Anne 53
White Fathers 67, 69, 70, 72, 108, 192, 195, 202, 204, 205, 234, 238, 239
Wildeman, Emile de 31
Wilde, Oscar 332
Williams, Charlotte 112-114
Williams, Denis 112
Wils, Kaat 91

Wiot, Valériane 88, 89
witness/bearing witness 134
Wolf, Heinrich Ludwig 147
Womex (World Music Expo) 317
World Bank 176
World Fair in Ghent (1913) 30, 131, 133
World Fair/Universal Exhibition in Brussels (1958) 25, 340, 342

Yates, Barbara 148, 149, 151
Yoka Lye Mudaba, André 318
Yole!Africa 32, 316, 337, 350
Young, Robert J.C. 221
Zairianisation 15, 197, 268
Zamenga Batukezanga 370
Zana Aziza Etambala, Mathieu 12

CPSIA information can be obtained
at www.ICGtesting.com
Printed in the USA
LVHW020051060523
746226LV00004B/233